This Heritage

The Story of Lutheran Beginnings in the
Lower Shenandoah Valley and of
Grace Church, Winchester

by

WILLIAM EDWARD EISENBERG

Expanded Edition
Heritage and History Editorial Committee
Dorothy A. Boyd-Rush, Editor

Published by
Lot's Wife Publishing
Staunton, Virginia
2003

Copyright © 2003 Grace Evangelical Lutheran Church

All rights reserved. No part of this book may be reproduced, stored in a retrieval system, or transmitted, in any form or by any means, electronic, mechanical, photocopying, recording, or otherwise, without the written permission of Grace Evangelical Lutheran Church.

This book is set in Palatino type. Layout by Nancy T. Sorrells.

Lot's Wife Publishing
P.O. Box 1844
Staunton, VA 24402

Library of Congress Catalog Card Number 2003096614
ISBN: 0-9719370-7-9 (cloth)

Dedication to Expanded Edition

With love and appreciation for her devotion to Grace Evangelical Lutheran Church, this volume is dedicated to Evva May Miller, Archivist.

Foreword to the Expanded Edition

This Heritage by William Edward Eisenberg, a classic volume published in 1954 documenting the story of Lutheran beginnings in the Lower Shenandoah Valley and the first 200 years of Grace Evangelical Lutheran Church, has been reprinted here in its entirety. Only minor changes in style, punctuation and spelling have been made.

The *Heritage for the Future* document adopted by the congregation in 1991 fostered the establishment of the Heritage and History Task Group. Initiated by a letter from Judge Robert Woltz, the task group took on the project of updating Dr. Eisenberg's scholarly work for publication during the church's 250th Anniversary year of 2003. An Editorial Committee was established in 1999, and a contract with Lot's Wife Publishing Company of Staunton, Virginia, was signed. Dorothy A. Boyd-Rush, a Lot's Wife partner and Professor of History at James Madison University, began working intensely with the Editorial Committee in January 2001.

Members of the Editorial Committee took on the dual tasks of proof reading the computer-generated copy of Dr. Eisenberg's work and composing the text to tell of the events that have occurred in the last 50 years. A wealth of material was available, and great care has been taken to be both accurate and inclusive. The committee is indebted to many in the congregation and community for assistance with the expanded edition.

Archivist Evva May Miller capably organized all available church records, photographs, news clippings, Council minutes, issues of *Tidings* and Sunday bulletins. This greatly facilitated the work of the Editorial Committee as they searched for contemporary material. A line above and a line below the new text, which is given in reduced font, indicate new material in existing chapters. Names of members holding office after 1954 are, of course, new to this volume. Information is included as of December 31, 2002.

Letters and lengthy quotations have been offered in reduced fonts in the expanded edition. The text of the first three constitutions has been greatly reduced to save space. Summaries are given of the subsequent three constitutions. Complete versions of all constitutions are available on file in the congregation's archives.

As a result of the primary decision to retain the complete text of the earlier edition, the reader may encounter cultural biases of a previous time. Miss Gettie's diary is sprinkled with local phrases that we have attempted to explain with end-of-page notes. The section on African-American members is reprinted as originally written in the 1950s. As stated in Chapter XI, all persons believing in Jesus Christ, regardless of background, are welcome to worship with us and become members of Grace Evangelical Lutheran Church.

The passage of time has brought new material to light, and, when added to the early chapters, it is so noted at the bottom of the page. Time has obscured the original location of several works cited in 1954, and notations have been made to that effect. End-of-chapter notes provided by Dr. Eisenberg have been rewritten in current literary style to accommodate researchers we hope will use this expanded edition to gain deeper knowledge of the roots of the Lutheran Church in America and the development of the northern Shenandoah Valley.

James H. Utt composed the end of the Eisenberg years

in Chapter VI and the greater part of Chapter VII, "The Processional Continues." Sally Coates composed the section on James H. Utt. Charles W. Bailey contributed to Chapter XII, "A Heritage for the Future." Mary Froehlich added new information to Chapter IX, "Buildings and Properties," summarized many activities in the latter part of Chapter X, "Order, Officers, and Organizations" and summarized the new information in Chapter XI regarding the Godfrey Miller Home. Anne Olinger and Lenore Eavis were careful proofreaders who provided insight and direction to the writing. Nancy Braswell assisted the committee with research on the constitutions and missionaries. Kudos to our many occasional proofreaders!

An every name index for the narrative portion of the text and Appendix B, the Streit Diary, will aid in understanding the faithful who have sustained the congregation we know as Grace. Appendix A, the Stoever records, is widely indexed in other publications and has not been indexed in this volume. Those serving as officers of the congregation in Chapter X are listed chronologically, and their names are not included in the every name index. Names of members in Appendix C are listed in alphabetical order and are not in the every name index.

The Editorial Committee wishes to credit the following for providing new photographs for the expanded edition:

Photography by Westervelt: James H. Utt, Paul G. Gunsten, Mark E. Fitzsimmons, Jeffrey D. May, Martha M. Sims, J. Kenly Carr, Trustees 1987, Sanctuary 2003, Confirmation 2002, Office Staff 2002 and Editorial Committee 2002
Alan Lehman: Sanctuary 1994, Congregation Council 2002
Winchester-Frederick County Historical Society: C. Worthington Lowe, Sesquicentennial Celebration

Muhlenberg College: Henry Muhlenberg, Peter Muhlenberg
Halford (Red) Baker: Parsonage at 126 N. Cameron Street

Dr. Eisenberg wrote, "Out of the story of the past the congregation renewed its strength." The expanded edition of *This Heritage* features a congregation firmly rooted in Winchester, Virginia, with a continued strong commitment to serving the surrounding community spiritually and socially in the years to come.

Editorial Committee
October 2003

Editorial Committee, (seated, left to right) Mary Miller Froehlich (Chair), Robert K. Woltz, Evva May Miller; (standing, left to right) James H. Utt, Dorothy A. Boyd-Rush, Anne Olinger, Charles Bailey, Lenore Eavis. Not pictured: Sally Coates.

Dedication to First Edition

Dorotheae,
uxori meae carissimae

Grace Evangelical Lutheran Church

Preface to First Edition

The placing of the bronze tablet on the ruins of the old church in 1938 and the celebration four years later of the centennial of the present church building proved to be wonderful stimuli in arousing interest in the history of the Lutheran congregation at Winchester.

A Committee on History had been appointed of which Dr. A.D. Henkel, Miss Katie Miller, Mrs. J. George Baetjer, Eugene B. Cooper and Miss Mary Katherine Aulick were the members. This committee engaged the services of Mr. W.W. Glass, local historian, to prepare a manuscript. Because Mr. Glass's manuscript was almost wholly confined to the Minutes of the Church Council begun in 1813, it was not a complete story of the congregation. It was never published. And the committee suffered the loss of Miss Katie Miller, whose death occurred in the spring of 1944.

Not long after the present writer came to Winchester the History Committee approached him on the subject of writing the congregation's story. He agreed to undertake the assignment, and at the time pointed ahead to 1953, when the bicentennial would be observed, as an appropriate occasion for compiling the history. And so it was agreed. And the writer began to dig and to delve and to accumulate one by one the required materials. Meanwhile Dr. A.D. Henkel, a most enthusiastic member of the committee, died in May 1947.

The author is indebted to many for valued assistance, and he wishes here to acknowledge their help.

For material in the body of the manuscript his thanks are due:

To Dr. Theodore G. Tappert and Dr. John W. Doberstein for permission to use their unpublished manuscript for Volume III of the *Journals of Henry Melchior Muhlenberg*, and to Dr. Tappert for letters from the archives at Krauth Memorial Library, Philadelphia, as well as for various helpful suggestions;

To Dr. Abdel Ross Wentz for his appreciated criticism and advice;

To Mr. W.W. Glass for the generous use of his great fund of local history;

To Mrs. Henry H. Bagger and the Rev. Theodore K. Finck for permission to use the translation of Christian Streit's Diary made by their father, the late Rev. William J. Finck, D.D.;

To Mr. Garland R. Quarles, Miss Virginia Henkel, Mrs. J. George Baetjer, Miss Ethel Snapp, Rev. Roy C. Helfenstein, Mrs. Clarence E. Krumbholz, Dr. Charles J. Smith and Messrs. Klaus Wust and Robert S. Bell for source materials or information leading thereto;

And to Mr. C. Vernon Eddy, librarian, and the staff of the Handley Public Library; to Miss Margaret J. Hort and others on the staff of the Krauth Memorial Library; to the Historical Society of Pennsylvania and the Virginia State Library; to Lee N. Whitacre, Clerk of the Frederick County Circuit Court, and to Peyton J. Marshall and Mrs. Corinne B. Riley, Clerk and Deputy Clerk, respectively, of the Winchester Corporation Court; – for assistance in the use of books and records.

For pictures and photographs used as illustrations:

To Professor Paul A.W. Wallace, the Misses Laura, Margaret, Portia and Julia Baker, Mrs. J. George Baetjer, Mrs. Clark M. Smith, Mrs. Harry A. Schmidt, Mrs. John W. Riley,

Mrs. J.A. Richard, Mrs. Walter H. Bosserman, Robert S. Bell, Mrs. J. Luther Jones, Miss Virginia Henkel, Mr. and Mrs. Howard K. Grove, Mr. and Mrs. E.B. Cooper, Miss Nannie O. Cooper, Miss Mary Katherine Aulick, Charles W. Fries, Mrs. Ben F. Davis, Mrs. Ward Thresh, R. Thornton Bryarly, Richard E. Rush and John W. Jones.

I desire also to express my appreciation to Mrs. John G. Fosbrink and Mr. Robert K. Woltz for criticism of the manuscript; to Mrs. S. Vincent Miller [Evva May Miller], church office secretary, for her invaluable aid in typing the manuscript; and to Mrs. Baetjer, Miss Aulick and Mr. Cooper, the remaining members of the History Committee, for their unfailing interest, encouragement and cooperation.

William Edward Eisenberg
Winchester, Virginia
February 24, 1954

Contents

Chapter

I.	From Rhine to Shenandoah	1
II.	First Settler, First Shepherd	7
III.	Perils in the Wilderness	22
IV.	Altars of Faith and Freedom	36
V.	The Enduring Work of Christian Streit	75
VI.	Pastors in Processional, 1812-1967	115
VII.	The Processional Continues, 1968-2002	268
VIII.	That Un-Civil War	342
IX.	Buildings and Properties	366
X.	Order, Officers, Organizations	420
XI.	The Larger Vision	483
XII.	A Heritage for the Future	519

Appendices

A.	The Stoever Records	527
B.	Diary of Christian Streit	533
C.	Membership Lists	577

Index..........593

Chapter I
From Rhine to Shenandoah

This is a story of courage and adventure. It tells of wilderness conquest, of pioneer hardships and dangers, of the call and the spirit of liberty, of the frontiersman's part in the winning of national independence.

It is a story of environmental adjustment to new ways within a new land, to the exigencies of wartime invasion by friend and by foe, to victories won, defeats encountered and the entering of doors of opportunity.

It is a story of solid stability that gives strength and character to a community and that holds persistently to its course amidst the fluctuations of the passing years.

But above all else, this is a story of faith. It tells of humble men and women who treasured the religion of their fathers and transplanted it from the Rhineland hills of Germany to the Shenandoah Valley of Virginia when settlers first came in to possess the land. This story recounts the record of the hopes and fears and failures and accomplishments over the past two centuries of the Evangelical Lutheran Church of Winchester, now known as Grace Evangelical Lutheran Church; and it endeavors to show something of the meaning of this congregation to the surrounding community, and to the church at large.

For our starting point we must cross the North Atlantic to Rotterdam, Holland, and go back to the summer of the year 1709. From the valley of the Rhine and its tributaries, the Main and the Neckar, Germans, Swiss and French Huguenots were on the move. The English colonies of North America were their ultimate goal. The favorable attitude of the British government toward the settlement in America of Central Europeans of Protestant faith caused thousands of men and women to leave their homes. The liberal advertising of British colonial agents was beginning to produce results. Because so many of these people came from the Rhenish, or Lower, Palatinate, they were all, without discrimination, called "Palatines."[1]

Besides inducements from abroad, there were reasons at home for this exodus. Hardly had the region recovered from the devastation of the Thirty Years War, which closed in 1648, than the armies of Louis XIV of France under Marshall Turenne in 1674 laid it waste again, and Marshall Villars in the War of the Spanish Succession repeated the destruction in 1707. In addition there was the cruel fact that the winter of 1708-1709 had been bitterly cold. Wine froze into solid blocks, and birds on the wing fell dead from cold. The rapid Rhine was covered with ice, and coastal waters were frozen sufficiently solid to bear heavily loaded carts. Fruit trees and vineyards were killed. About half the emigrants, it is estimated, were vinedressers and husbandmen whose means of livelihood had been wiped out. Other contributing factors were the desires to get away from the strain of religious bickering, to escape high taxes and to obtain possession of land and homes.

Among the Palatine families that sought passage to America and that were destined to plant the Lutheran Church in the Valley of Virginia were those of Hans Jost Heydt, Christian Streit and John Conrad Weiser. They had left their native towns and villages and journeyed down the Rhine to Rotterdam, where they awaited transportation to London on ships made empty by the embarkation on the continent of the troops of the Duke of Marlborough. Records kept by Dutch authorities show that in the fifth party of emigrants, which embarked July 3 to July 10, and which sailed for London July 15, 1709, were "Joost Heyt & vrouw" and one child[2] and "Kristiaan Streit & vrouw" and five children. In the sixth party, which embarked for London July 27 and sailed July 28, were "Johan Koenraet Weiser & vrouw" and eight children.

These three families, among several thousand others that could qualify, had accepted the bounty of good Queen Anne of England for free keep and passage to the colony of New York. In return they were to labor in the ill-starred tar-making venture sponsored by the British government.

Five to six months were spent at Blackheath, London, and at the end of the year the America-bound redemptioners were loaded into ten vessels. In them they remained until April, when the flotilla finally set sail under convoy. After an appallingly frightful voyage, during which typhus ravaged the passengers with unchecked fury, the speedier vessels reached the mouth of the Hudson some two months later, while the slower ones required four months. The new arrivals were placed at once in quarantine by the terrified authorities of New York.

With the coming of fall many Palatines settled in seven villages on either bank of the Hudson ninety miles more or less from its mouth. Today Germantown remains to mark four settlements located on the east side, while West Camp, Evesport and Smith's Landing mark the three settlements on the opposite bank. The making of tar and other supplies for the British Navy proved a dismal failure, since the right species of pine for such purposes did not grow in sufficient quantity in the immediate area. Government subsistence came to an end September 12, 1712. This latter fact, coupled with a general dissatisfaction over treatment from authorities, caused many to move from their places of original settlement. Some went to the Schoharie Valley along the Mohawk River, some to Rhinebeck and to New York City, others to Hackensack in New Jersey and still others into Pennsylvania. Their failure to make a successful go of things and their difficulties with the colonial authorities contributed in turning the interest of subsequent eighteenth-century German immigrants away from the colony of New York toward the more extensively advertised colony of Pennsylvania. Hereafter, until the Revolution itself, Philadelphia was to be the chief port of entry to America for Germans seeking new homes.

John Conrad Weiser was among the Palatines who settled at Schoharie.[3] Through his friendship with a Mohawk Indian chief named Quaynant, his sixteen-year-old son, Conrad,[a] was permitted to live among the Mohawks for a winter, learning their ways and their language, and laying the foundation for a future career as Indian agent and interpreter for the colony of Pennsylvania, a position which so largely was responsible for Iroquois Confederacy support of the English colonies in the French and Indian War.

Let us, however, keep to the main trail of our story. Conrad, son of John Conrad Weiser, married Anna Eva Feck[b]

---

[a] He was born November 2, 1696, in Grossaspach to Johann Conrad Weiser and his first wife, Anna Magdalena Uebele. For information on the family of Conrad Weiser consult: Frederick Weiser, editor, *The Weiser Family: A Genealogy of the Family of John Conrad Weiser the Elder* (Mechanicsburg, Pa.: The John Conrad Weiser Family Association, 1960), especially the first chapter.

[b] While the date of her birth remains in doubt despite considerable research, she was the daughter of Johann Peter Faeg/Feg/Feck and his wife, Anna Maria Risch, originally from Idar in the Rhineland-Pfalz. Today Idar is often rendered as Idar-Oberstein. For additional information on the family of Conrad Weiser consult: Weiser, *The Weiser*

in 1720. A third child and second daughter named Anna Maria was born to them at Schoharie in 1727. Then the family moved to Tulpehocken in Pennsylvania in 1729, there to abide. In 1745 Anna Maria Weiser married Henry Melchior Muhlenberg, Lutheran minister who had arrived from Germany in 1742. Their first child, born October 1, 1746, was a boy to whom the name John Peter Gabriel was given. It is this great-grandson of John Conrad Weiser with whom our story is concerned in the 1770s.

Christian Streit, who had come originally from Switzerland,[c] took his wife and children, now increased to eight in number, to the region of Hackensack, New Jersey, prior to 1717.[4] In due time his son Leonhard[d] settled in the valley of the Raritan near Bedminster, where a son was born. The boy was named Christian after his grandfather. Grandson Christian looms large in the picture of our story. In 1785, after many intertwining experiences with Peter Muhlenberg, as well as with Peter's father and brothers, he came to Winchester to become the first Lutheran pastor in residence within the town, and in the Shenandoah Valley he remained until his death in 1812.

It is with Hans Jost Heydt, better known in Virginia annals as Joist Hite, that the local setting of our story actually

---

Family, especially 6-7; and, Henry Z. Jones, *The Palatine Families of New York: A Study of the German Immigrants Who Arrived in Colonial New York in 1710* (Universal City, Ca.: p.p., 1985) I, 220-222.

[c] He was baptized March 24, 1672, at Kirberg, located to the north of Wiesbaden, Germany. He was the son of Johann Leonhardt Streit and his wife, Anna Maria. Jones, *Palatine Families*, II, 1011.

[d] The son of Christian Streit and his third wife, Maria Ursula, Johann Leonhardt was born July 28, 1720, in Remobuch and baptized in Hackensack. Jones, *Palatine Families*, II, 1014.

begins.[5] In the spring of 1732 he brought sixteen families into a newly acquired grant of land in what is now Frederick County, and in so doing became the historically accredited first settler of the Valley of Virginia – though the claims of Adam Miller to have preceded Hite by several years now have wide acceptance. It was largely within the framework of the Hite relationship itself, as well as among the families brought into the Valley in 1732, that the Lutheran Church had its beginnings west of the Blue Ridge Mountains. The basis for this contention will be detailed in the ensuing chapter.

Endnotes – Chapter I

[1] In large part, this chapter is derived from W.A. Knittle's *Early Eighteenth-Century Palatine Emigration*, Philadelphia: Dorance & Co., 1936.
[2] Knittle, *Palatine Emigration*, 266.
[3] See *Conrad Weiser, 1696-1760, Friend of Colonist and Mohawk* by Paul A.W. Wallace, Philadelphia: University of Pennsylvania Press, 1945.
[4] See portions of "Zion, St. Paul and Other Early Lutheran Churches in Central New Jersey" by John C. Honeyman, New Germantown, N.J.: *Proceedings of the New Jersey Historical Society*, serialized, 1924-1927.
[5] See article by W.S. Laidley on "Joist Hite, Pioneer of Shenandoah Valley, 1732" in *West Virginia Historical Magazine Quarterly*, III, no. 2 (April 1903): 103.

Chapter II
First Settler, First Shepherd

For a hundred years after the settlement at Jamestown, Tidewater Virginia lived in blissful ignorance of the Shenandoah Valley. That the Potomac pierced the Blue Ridge, instead of rising in this range as does the Rappahannock, was not known until 1709. A few years later when Alexander Spotswood led his expedition to the banks of the Shenandoah, he was amazed to find that stream flowing north; and he concluded that it must empty into Lake Erie.[1]

No accurate conception existed in regard to the country west of the mountains. The extent of the multiple ranges of the Alleghenies was quite unknown. On the other hand it was well known that the same mountains to the westward were fraught with incipient dangers from unfriendly Indians, whose allies, the French, had already staked their claims to the heart of the continent and planted settlements and forts along the eastern tributaries of the great Father of Waters.

From the standpoint of Eastern Virginia, the country to the west of the Blue Ridge was abandoned to the Indians. At Albany in 1722 a treaty was made between the English colonies and the Indians of the Iroquois Confederacy. Pertaining to Virginia, the Indians agreed not to cross the Potomac east of the mountains and not to cross the mountains themselves, while southern tribes tributary to the northern Indians were neither to cross the Potomac to the north nor the mountains to the west. Thus the Shenandoah Valley became a thoroughfare for roving Indian hunting parties and Indian war parties moving north or south, and the inaccurate tradition arose that it was an uninhabited hunting ground and battlefield. This was not the case, however, for members of the Shawnee tribe lived within the Valley and in close proximity to the site of Winchester.

With the emerging pioneer spirit to push ever westward, quite obviously the Valley could not remain unsettled many years longer.

In the summer of 1730 there appeared at Williamsburg two men with the vision and desire to open the Valley to pioneer settlement. They petitioned Governor William Gooch and the Council of State for tracts of land on the west side of the mountains. These men were John Van Meter and Isaac Van Meter, believed to be father and son. John had lived along the Hudson near Esopus (Kingston) for a number of years. His petition declared that he and his eleven children, together with other relations and friends living in the government of New York, desired to remove to the Valley and settle there.[2] Isaac's petition declared him to be from West Jersey and that "he and divers other German families are desirous of settling themselves on the West side of the Great Mountains in this colony." It declared further that the petitioner had been "to view the lands in these parts and has discovered a place where further such settlement may conveniently be made."[3]

The petitions brought results. John was granted 10,000 acres for himself and family, and an additional 20,000 for twenty families to be brought in, provided settlement were made within two years. Isaac likewise was granted 10,000 acres to be settled within two years by his own and nine other families. These apparently were the first official grants issued for land beyond the mountains. But instead of leading new settlers immediately into the Valley, John and Isaac Van Meter for reasons unknown sold the rights to their 40,000 acres and postponed coming to Virginia.

This is the point where Joist Hite[a] steps upon the Virginia scene. But before he arrives let us pick up a few additional facts about him and the general setting.

It has been shown already that Hite, his wife and one child – a daughter, Mary – were with the Palatines arriving in New York during the summer of 1710. A native of Strasbourg,[b] he had married Anna Maria DuBois,[c] a member of a Huguenot family that had been forced to flee from France. A sister of Anna Maria had gone to Holland where she married a Dutchman by the name of Jan Van Meteren. Prior to 1700 this couple came to the former Dutch colony of New York and lived in the vicinity of Kingston. It was natural, therefore, that the Hites should make their home in the same Hudson River community upon their first opportunity.

---

[a] His first name is also often rendered as "Jost" or "Justus."

[b] The son of Johannes Heydt and his wife, Anna Magdalena, of Bonfeld in the Kraichgau region of Württemberg, he was born on the 5th of December 1685 and baptized as "Hans Justus." Henry Z. Jones, *The Palatine Families of New York: A Study of the German Immigrants Who Arrived in Colonial New York in 1710* (Universal City, Ca.: p.p., 1985), I, 353.

[c] Recent research has established that her name was Anna Maria Merckle. The Bonfeld church registers reveal considerable new information on the family. They are available on microfilm from the Public Record Office, London: T1/119: 6-10, 19-26, 58-65, 68-72 and 79-82. Henry Z. Jones, Ralph Connor and Klaus Wust, *German Origins of Jost Hite: Virginia Pioneer, 1685-1761* (Edinburg, Va.: Shenandoah History Publishers, 1979), 12. The latter source records that on the 11th of November 1704 at Bonfeld "Johan Justus Heyd, linenweaver and son of Johannis Heyd - butcher and civic councilor here - married to Anna Maria, daughter of Abraham Mercklin - citizen here." The surname variations include: "Merckle," "Mercklin" and "Merkel."

For about five years Joist and Anna Maria remained at Kingston where their daughters Elizabeth and Magdalena were born. Coming south into Pennsylvania they stayed for a time at the Pastorius colony of Germantown. Soon Joist acquired land along the Skippack, the Perkiomen and the Schuylkill. In 1720 he built a mill at the mouth of Perkiomen Creek and a dwelling, which property in later years became the country home of Samuel Pennypacker, governor of the state.

Because this area of the Pennsylvania frontier was subjected to Indian encroachments, a petition dated May 10, 1720, was sent to Governor Patrick Gordon begging protection.[4] It was signed by seventy-seven of "ye Back Inhabitors about Falkners Swamp and New Coshahopin." The name "Yost Hyt" appears among the signers, but contrary to frequent assertion, in a second petition for the same protection signed by seventy-four persons in 1728 his name does not appear.

Now it so happens that Falkner's Swamp, in Montgomery County, Pennsylvania, is the location of New Hanover Lutheran Church, claiming to be the oldest Lutheran congregation of German origin in the country. Its somewhat obscure beginnings go back into the 1690's. Its first resident pastor, Daniel Falckner, gave his name to the locality. It was this congregation which joined with the congregations at Philadelphia and Trappe to form the United Congregations, and it was the resulting single parish, which issued the call that brought Henry Melchior Muhlenberg to America.

No records prior to the year 1740 have been preserved at New Hanover Church. The two lists of petitions referred to above, however, furnish us with additional names of interest to our story. There is the name of Christian

Neyschwanger,[d] whose widow became the second Mrs. Joist Hite. There are the names of Anthony Henkel and Gerhardt Henkel, father and son, from whom Paul Henkel was descended, as well as the name of John George Dieter, who came into the Valley of Virginia with the early arrivals.

Another very important angle of interest centers in John Casper Stoever, Jr., who with his father arrived from Germany in 1728.[5] Curiously in signing their oaths of allegiance, they signed after their names "missionary" and "student of theology," though neither was ordained. The son had been educated for the ministry at home. His purpose in coming to America was to seek out scattered German Lutherans and minister to them, a purpose he began to carry out while still aboard ship. He, therefore, was the "missionary" and not the "student of theology." The father, a widower, had been a teacher and organist and had determined also to study theology. Soon after his arrival in Philadelphia he went to North Carolina where he took a second wife. Things did not turn out pleasantly in his new home,[e] so he wandered north into Virginia. In 1732 we find him among the Lutherans of Madison County, where he made his home and to which he later brought his family from North Carolina. Thus he became the first pastor of the oldest Lutheran congregation in the Old Dominion.

The two Stoevers arrived in America at a time when there

---

[d] The surname is usually rendered as "Neuschwanger" or "Nicewanger."

[e] Stoever's stormy marriage to his second wife, Maria Magdalena, is best summarized in Vernon Stiver and Patricia R. Donaldson, *Stöver-Stoever-Staver-Stiver: An Account of the Ancestry and Descendants of Johann Caspar Stoever of Pennsylvania*, (Saline, Mich., 1992), 22-27. Her surname may have been Pool or Poole.

were only half a dozen Lutheran pastors on the entire scene. Two were ministering to the Dutch Lutherans of the Hudson Valley in New York; there was one aged German pastor in New Jersey; and there were three pastors among the descendants of Sweden's colony on the Delaware planted a century before. But in Pennsylvania, there was not one ordained minister of the Lutheran Church to be found.

John Casper Stoever, Jr., had the eyes to see a tremendous need. His youth, his energy, his training and his life's purpose could not be thwarted, either by the lack of ordination or the lack of a call to minister in a specific field, under the urgent circumstances that confronted him. Beholding the spiritual destitution of a whole generation of his fellow countrymen, and remembering that in cases of necessity laymen were permitted to administer baptism, he yielded to the entreaties of the people to make use of his life's preparation, and he proceeded to officiate as a minister.

His residence was first at Trappe in Montgomery County and then at New Holland in Lancaster County. His work began within the several congregations already organized. This included New Hanover, but it could not be confined to any one community. All the German Lutherans between the Delaware and the Susquehanna became his flock. And as many of them passed his home in their wagons moving westward to take up new farmlands along new streams in new valleys, he bade them Godspeed and promised to visit them with the Word of Life.

For more than four years Stoever had to wait until the opportunity for ordination came. Then in the spring of 1733 both he and his father were ordained by John Christian Schulz at Trappe. This took place in the barn where services were held, as the congregation had no church building; and young Stoever was married on the same day.[f] Mr. Schulz was a regularly ordained minister who had come to Pennsylvania the preceding year. It was he who organized the Philadelphia, Falkner's Swamp and Trappe congregations into one parish and then persuaded them to send him back to Germany to solicit funds for churches and schoolhouses and to secure additional pastors. Alas for him and his congregations, this venture became a personal enterprise, and from it he never returned. Before leaving the country, however, he sought out the younger Stoever and requested him to take charge of his three churches. At the same time arrangements were made for the ordination of father and son, an event that occurred April 8.

The elder Stoever, having come from Virginia for the express purpose of being ordained, returned at once to his field of work. Here he remained until he, too, went to Europe in 1734 on a collecting trip on behalf of his congregation. From this undertaking he, likewise, was not to come back to America, but for an altogether different reason. On his return trip early in 1738 he died at sea.

The son, however, impelled anew by his ordination, felt a greater call to duty than ever. He at once broadened the scope of his itinerant missionary operations. Remembering his promise to those who had migrated from their homes in Eastern Pennsylvania, he went in search of them to refresh their souls with the things of the spirit.

Did the fact that the father had plans to go to Europe

---

[f] His bride was Maria Catharina Merckel, born May 14, 1715, in Lambsheim, the daughter of Christian Merckel. The ordination and the marriage actually occurred on April 8, 1733. Stiver and Donaldson, *Descendants of Johann Caspar Stoever*, 51.

determine the time of the son's first visit to Virginia? Did Casper, Jr., visit at his father's home east of the Blue Ridge Mountains? And did he minister in his father's parish during the latter's absence? It is possible that the correct answer to each question is an affirmative, but no corroborating evidence has been found.

This, however, is clear: that Stoever followed his land-prospecting friends to their new locations. From his home at Earltown (the present New Holland) he made systematic journeys year after year in many directions, preaching, marrying, baptizing, administering the Lord's Supper, setting up church records in many embryonic congregations, and all the while keeping a systematic journal of his ministerial acts. One itinerary, at least nine times repeated with minor variations, took him west and south: to Wright's Ferry on the Susquehanna, to the settlements on Kreutz and Codorus Creeks (York), to newly established homesteads on the Conewago (Hanover), still farther to those on the Monocacy (Frederick, Maryland), on again south of the Potomac into the Shenandoah Valley to the Opequon, to the Shenandoah (North Fork) and to "Moessennutten" (in Page Valley).

Precisely here our attention centers again on Joist Hite. In 1730 he sold his mill and farmlands and the following summer purchased from John and Isaac Van Meter their interests in the grants of 40,000 acres in the Shenandoah Valley received the preceding year. In this enterprise Hite was assisted by Robert McKay, a Quaker, Robert Green and William Duff. They obtained an additional grant of 100,000 acres from the Virginia Council in October 1731, on terms that one hundred families must be settled within two years. The time limit, however, for making these settlements was subsequently extended to Christmas 1735.

Hence it was that in the spring of 1732 a wagon caravan of sixteen families and such household effects as could be hauled moved from the Perkiomen along the road into Lancaster County. Crossing the Susquehanna at Wright's Ferry it followed the trail leading through the future cities of York, Hanover and Frederick, and coming to the Potomac, forded the stream at Pack Horse Ford and thus entered the Valley of the Shenandoah. Arriving at a place where the great Indian trail through the Valley crossed Opequon Creek, they called a halt to their tiresome journey and set about the task of dividing the land and building their homes. Rough pioneer cabins first were constructed. Then in a year or two houses and barns of stone began to appear, sturdy symbols of their stout-hearted builders.

Joist Hite built his home a few miles south of the future site of Winchester, where the present community of Bartonsville now stands. He erected two stone houses, one on either side of the road. The one to the east is supposed to have been built as a kind of fort in case of needed protection from the Indians. Its ruined walls are but a few yards removed from "Springdale," the mansion built by Joist's son, John, in 1753.

Hite and his party came into Virginia before any county government had been set up west of the Shenandoah River. This stream served as the western boundary for Spotsylvania County. It was not until August 1734 that Orange County was formed. Joist Hite became a justice of the peace, and James Wood, a young man from Eastern Virginia who had been elected county surveyor, bewitched by the charms of the Valley, took root in its limestone soil and so remained.

Altogether Hite and McKay brought in forty-nine families on the original grant purchased from the Van Meters. On their second and larger grant they were not so successful. They were able to procure but fifty-four families when the time limit expired.

Two factors are said to have been of prime importance in the settlement of the Shenandoah Valley. One was the desire of men like the Van Meters, Hite and McKay to speculate in lands. The other was the policy of the colonial authorities to encourage settlement beyond the mountains in order that a new line of defense against Indian attack might be established. On one hand the motive was economic: to get possession of good, rich lands well watered by streams, where wealth could be acquired, permanent homesteads erected, families reared, and life enjoyed; while on the other hand it was an expedient, long range, protective measure for the safety of "old" Virginia in any trouble that might eventuate with the French and Indians.

The settlement of the Valley cannot be said, therefore, to have been a missionary enterprise. But this is not to say that those who were bold enough to dwell on this frontier were without religious faith or church background. They brought their religious heritage with them, stowed away in their minds and hearts and bound in the large Bibles they treasured. Soon the English Quakers had their Hopewell Meeting (1734), the Scotch-Irish Presbyterians their congregation at Kernstown (1736) and the German Reformed theirs (1740). And the German Lutherans? Their organized congregation was slowest in evolving, unless perchance, records no longer known or in existence hide the fact of a possible union organization with the Reformed.

A word may be said at this juncture on the Lutheran concept of the church. Organization is not to be considered an absolute essential of the church, desirable as it may be. Wherever the Word of God is preached and the Sacraments of Baptism and the Lord's Supper are administered, there the church is to be found. By its own definition, therefore, when by word and sacrament the Gospel is proclaimed, there the church exists. Organization, important as it is, is secondary.

Thus the spring of 1734 marks the beginning in the Valley of Virginia of the Lutheran Church, for it was then that John Casper Stoever, Jr., first ministered on the Opequon and the Shenandoah.

Stoever's journal, diligently kept, provides us with precious information.[6] Here we find from the dates and places of baptisms and marriages he performed the names of the settlements he visited and the time of his visits. Moreover, in recording baptisms, he not only set down the child's name and birth date, but also the father's name and the names of sponsors or godparents. Thus, in the original German spelling, he has preserved the names of many of the Valley's earliest settlers, names that persist after more than two hundred years.

The journal lets us know that it was in April 1734 when the first visit occurred, and it tells of repeated visits to the Valley each year for eight additional years. Three locations are mentioned: "Moesennutten," Opequon and Shenandoah. The first refers to the settlement on Massanutten Creek in Page County west of Luray, where Adam Müller[g] led in a group of German Lutherans; the second to the Hite settlement on Opequon Creek, and the third to the settlement on the North Fork of the Shenandoah where Strasburg is located.

Throughout the nine years of Stoever's visits the record

---

[g] The surname is often rendered as "Müller" or "Mueller" and later became "Miller." See Appendix A, May 1, 1739.

gives seven baptisms performed at Massanutten, twenty-nine at Shenandoah, and fifty-five at Opequon. There is also the record of three marriages at Shenandoah and four at "Opecken." An interesting notation made in connection with two of the Opequon marriages is that they were performed in the presence of Lord Fairfax – on May 3, 1736, when Fairfax made his first trip to America. In the succeeding pages, however, we shall be concerned with the Opequon entries only.

Judged by the number of baptisms the Opequon field proved to be the most promising.[h] Joist Hite, like a true patriarch of old, surrounded by his four married daughters and their families and his five sons, John, Jacob, Isaac, Abraham and Joseph, unmarried as yet, was the chief reason. Altogether Pastor Stoever baptized sixteen of Hite's grandchildren.

Putting the imagination to work for a little while, let us reconstruct a scene that in all probability took place at *Grosspapa* Heydt's home.

> The date is May 16, 1735. True to his promise, Pastor Stoever had come to visit his former members and friends the year before, and when he left he assured them that he would return again the following spring. Now he is coming to them a second time. The word has gone out to all within the general vicinity, to come to Joist Hite's, because the *Pfarrer* will be there.
>
> At the appointed time they arrive and Pastor Stoever conducts for them a service that gladdens their hearts. They sing a hymn unaccompanied and from memory. The minister reads from the scriptures. He expounds the Word and prays. He gives to each the Bread and the Wine of the Holy Supper and souls are uplifted to God in gratitude and praise. At the close of the service children are brought forward for Holy Baptism. This takes some little time, for there are fourteen to be baptized.

---

[h] It is also the place where Stoever's sister, Anna Elisabetha Catharina, lived with her husband, Johannes Koontz, who was born in 1706 in Niederndorf in the Nassau-Siegen region of Württemberg.

There is Mary Hite with her husband, George Bowman, and their two boys and infant girl, John George, John Jacob and Elizabeth. Grandpa Joist is sponsor for George and Uncle Jake Christman for Jacob, and Aunt Lizzie Fromman for her namesake. Jacob Christman and Magdalena Hite, his wife, likewise present their two children, Abraham and Sara. Uncle John Hite is sponsor for little Abe and Aunt Mary Bowman for Sara. Next comes Paul Fromman and Elizabeth Hite with two-and-a-half year old Sara and seven-month-old John Paul. Auntie Sue Wiseman[i] sponsors Sara, and good friend Lewis Stephens, John Paul. Little month-old Anna Christine is brought forward by her parents, Abraham and Susanna Hite Wiseman, and her sponsors are Uncle John Hite and Miss Anna Christine Stephens,[j] for whom she is named. Peter Stephens has his friend Henry Krauss serve as sponsor for his son, John Henry, and Jacob Sickles has three sponsors for his boy, Zacharias: Joist and Anna Maria Hite and Abraham Wiseman. Mary Bowman again serves as sponsor, this time for Rebecca, eighteen-month-old daughter of John Colvert. John Snapp's Anna Catharine has Anna Maria Glaize as her godmother, and Elizabeth Hartzenbuehler godmothered John Philip Glaize's Mary Barbara. Finally, John Ulrich Bucher has Joist Hite, Susie Wiseman and Barbara Snapp as sponsors for his three-month-old baby girl, Rosina. And while this last baptism is taking place, Grandmother Anna Maria quietly withdraws from the little assembly and retires to the kitchen where she is joined by her daughters Mary and Elizabeth and by Mary Christina Stephens,[k] who assist her in making ready the bountiful feast anticipated and awaited by all.

Similar stories could be constructed for May 2, 1736, June 5, 1737, June 4, 1738, April 29, 1739 and April 29, 1740. All told, Pastor Stoever baptized five children of George and Mary Hite Bowman, five children of Jacob and Magdalena Hite Christman, four children of Paul and Elizabeth Hite Fromman, and Anna Christiana, daughter of John Hite and his wife Sara. These were all the grandchildren of Hans Joist

---

[i] The surname appears as "Weissman" in Stoever's register.
[j] Her name appears as "Anna Christina Stephanin" in Stoever's register.
[k] Likely Anna Christiana is intended.

This Heritage

and Anna Maria DuBois[1] Heydt. When on April 29, 1739, John's little daughter, who had been born on the previous Christmas day, was baptized, her grandmother, for whom she was named, was sponsor, together with Grandpa Joist. Anna Maria's death, therefore, did not occur in 1738 as is commonly stated.

From these records, also, we learn the names of other early pioneer families. By 1736 the families of Rudolph Mauck, William Crisp, Jacob Dellinger, Carl Ehrhart, had arrived and John Linville was on the scene to take Anna Christina Stephens for his wife and to move on farther southwest up the Valley. By 1737 we read of the families of John George Dieter, who like Hite had lived at Falkner's Swamp, of Christian Blanck, of Theobold Gerlach, of James McKnees, all on the Opequon. By the next year the Nicewangers and Brumbacks had arrived, for Casper Stoever married John Jacob Nicewanger and Mary Gertrude Brumback at "Opaken" on June 5, 1738. On April 30, 1739, he married Peter Mauck and Juliana Rhinehart. By this year Lawrence and Thomas Snapp were here, and Valentine Windle and Anna Elizabeth Stickley, and Henry Jones, and Maria Neyschwanger (Nicewanger). Had Christian Neyschwanger, Maria's husband, died before she left Falkner's Swamp? Or had he died after coming into the Valley? We cannot tell. We only know that Anna Maria Hite had died, and in 1741[m] Joist married Maria Magdalena, the "Widow Neyschwanger." Their marriage contract is a quaint

---

[1] Anna Maria Merckle.
[m] Frederick County, Virginia, Deed Book 1, 16: recorded September 3, 1745, and dated November 16, 1741. For additional information on the family and the marriage see Cecil O'Dell, *Pioneers of Old Frederick County, Virginia* (Marceline, Mo.: Walsworth Publishing Company, 1995).

piece of business. Joist made his will April 25, 1758. His date of death and place of burial have been cleverly hidden by time. His will was probated in 1761.

Whether Joist Hite became embittered on account of the lawsuit with Lord Fairfax over title to his lands, we do not know.[7] He did not live to learn the eventual outcome. Knowledge of his vindication, no doubt, would have been immensely pleasing to him.

So, too, of the church in his house. From those early ministering visits of Missionary Stoever, the Lutheran Church took root. It has brought forth its fruit in patience, and its fruit has remained.

Endnotes – Chapter II

[1] For the settlement of the Shenandoah Valley and the coming of Joist Hite to Virginia, see *West Virginia Historical Magazine Quarterly*, II, no. 2, (April 1902); and, III, no. 1 (January 1903) and no. 2 (April 1903).
[2] *Virginia Magazine of History and Biography*, XIII, 115.
[3] Ibid., XIII, 118.
[4] A facsimile of this petition is found in *A History of the Lutheran Church in New Hanover, Montgomery County, Pennsylvania* by John Jacob Kline (New Hanover, Pa.: The Congregation, 1910), 242.
[5] A.R. Wentz, *History of the Evangelical Church of Frederick, Maryland, 1738-1938* (Harrisburg, Pa.: Evangelical Press, 1938), 32-35. See also *John Casper Stoever, Colonial Pastor and Founder of Churches*, by R.L. Winters (Norristown, Pa.: Pennsylvania German Society, 1948).
[6] See Appendix A for a list of baptisms performed by Stoever in the Shenandoah Valley.
[7] This famous lawsuit, Hite vs. Fairfax, was argued in Virginia courts from 1749-1786. It was the case on which John Marshall made his reputation as a lawyer.

Chapter III
Perils in the Wilderness

There is a tradition, which says that the first two houses built within the bounds of Winchester were along Town Run near the point where Loudoun Street crosses it. These two houses were built by two Germans, according to the story. Just who the owners were, however, has not been handed down. This was before county government had been set up in the Valley.

In 1738 laws were passed establishing Frederick and Augusta counties out of the huge territory of Orange County lying west of the Blue Ridge Mountains. Because neither county was to be organized until there was a larger population, Frederick did not come into existence until November 1743, and Augusta until December 1745.

Frederick County found itself to be the westward extension of the Northern Neck of Virginia, a fact that made it a part of the 5,000,000-acre domain of Thomas, Lord Fairfax, Baron of Cameron. Thereby hangs an interesting tale of Virginia history.[1]

To go back to the year 1649, Charles I of England was beheaded January 30. Charles II carried on his father's cause, was defeated by his opponents under Oliver Cromwell in 1651, escaped with his life by hiding in the dense branches of the "Royal Oak" at Boscobel, and fled to the continent. His succession to the throne in England did not occur until 1661, but in the colony of Virginia he was acknowledged king by Act of Assembly passed October 10, 1649. This loyalty on the part of the Virginians led to the title "Old Dominion" being accorded to their colony.

To reward seven supporters of his father, Charles II executed to them a grant of land lying between the Rappahannock and Potomac rivers. The Blue Ridge, believed to be the source of both rivers, was considered the western boundary. This grant, first made in 1649 and renewed in 1663, came to be known as "the Northern Neck of Virginia," and was of the same nature as those made to William Penn and Lord Baltimore, but with this difference: it did not create a new colony.

A thorn in the side of the Virginia Colonial Government, efforts to have the grant annulled proved fruitless, nor could it be acquired by purchase from the patentees. By 1710, ownership of the tract was vested five-sixths in Lady Catherine Culpeper, wife of Thomas, 5th Lord Fairfax, and one-sixth in Lady Margaret Culpeper, by whose will her interest passed to her grandson, Thomas, 6th Lord Fairfax.

As far as the actual land in Virginia was concerned, there was little activity in connection with this grant until 1728. Then adventurers began to seek out the lands west of the mountains and to build their pioneer homes in the lower Shenandoah Valley. The question of the true boundaries of the grant, therefore, became a vital one.

Thus, until the Revolution changed things, the Northern Neck was a domain unto itself, distinct from the rest of Virginia. True, its proprietors had no political power, but they owned the land and gave title to all land not previously devised.

When Thomas, Lord Fairfax, the lone proprietor, at last learned that the Potomac cut deep into the western mountains, that his holdings included far more land than at first imagined, and that already settlers were encroaching upon his territorial claims, he determined it was high time to go to

Virginia to investigate for himself. He came, therefore, to America and into the Valley in 1736, only to return soon to England for a redefining of his boundaries. When he came a second time to Virginia, he came to stay – and with a determination to set up a baronial system of his own on Shenandoah Valley soil.

Some eleven miles southeast of Winchester, Fairfax established his home at Greenway Court in 1748. There on a 10,000-acre estate to which women were expressly forbidden access, he lived a life that resembled a cross between that of a monastery and a hunting lodge. Of those who purchased land from him he demanded, in addition to the cost, a quitrent of two shillings annually for each fifty acres. What is more, he held that all persons who had bought land from Joist Hite were squatters, and demanded of them quitrents as of the year 1745, the year where his title to the area had been clarified.

Thus began the legal tussle between Hite and Fairfax.[2] The Baron of Cameron soon found that he had a worthy opponent in the tough "old German Baron," as Hite was called. Since those conditioning experiences of the voyage to America and the years along the Hudson, Hite had drunk deep of the air of freedom he had enjoyed in Pennsylvania, and it was with the assurance of a similar liberty that he had led his pioneer caravan into the Valley. Not for a moment would he submit to any cloud on the title of land he sold to friends and neighbors. Because he would not yield to the claims of Fairfax, he brought suit in 1749. This famous case was drawn out in court for nearly four decades. At last in 1786 the verdict was issued in favor of Hite's contention, but only after both opponents were dead and gone. But again, was there not something of that leaven of the freedom that is America already at work when Joist Hite stood his ground against this lone representative of British nobility resident in colonial Virginia?

James Wood, the county surveyor, being a native of Winchester, England, was somewhat more impressed with the station in life and the claims of Lord Fairfax. He, too, ran into difficulties with him, but he trimmed his sails to suit the breeze. In 1744 he desired to set aside a small tract of his land — thirteen acres in all — for the use of the newly established county of Frederick. With tact and diplomacy he declared that his title was incomplete, and paid Fairfax his quitrents.

Here we have the beginnings of Winchester, known at first as Fredericktown. As founder of the town, James Wood laid out his thirteen acres in twenty-six half-acre lots, with two streets thirty-three feet wide running through them. A delay in getting the charter seems to have been due to Wood's inability to get complete title to his holdings. At the same time Fairfax caught a glimpse of the same vision of opportunity and added to Wood's twenty-six lots fifty-four more of his own. When the town was chartered in 1752 it included a total of 80 lots.[3]

To each house lot there was attached an out lot of three to five acres for garden or pasture. Houses had to be built within two years of purchase. Squared, dove-tailed logs could be used, the minimum dimensions being sixteen by twenty feet. But no buildings could be erected on the outlots, though these lots could be fenced in. Unfenced outlots became the village commons.

Such a policy tended to dwarf the town. James Wood remedied the matter in 1758 by adding an addition of one hundred six acres on the west side. This was known as "Wood's Addition." Fairfax countered with the "Fairfax Addition" in 1759, by adding one hundred seventy-three lots on the east side.

But old Fredericktown could boast an even more illustrious citizen than her founder or his titled associate from Greenway Court. A new star was on the horizon, dwelling in her very midst. The third and most famous personality connected with her early days was none other than the man destined to become the Father of His Country.

George Washington came into the Valley in 1748 as surveyor for Lord Fairfax. As a boy of sixteen his native abilities already began to assert themselves and to attract attention. The young surveyor here received his schooling both in frontier life and the ways of Indian warfare, and here he entered upon his political career. Providentially, he was preparing himself for larger and more important work. Soon he was placed in charge of the northernmost defense district of the Virginia frontier to protect it against hostile Indian attack.

For thirty years there had been peace on the frontier. So many families had pushed beyond the Shenandoah Valley proper to settle between the successive chains of ridges to the west, that Hampshire County had been formed in 1753. But there were unmistakable signs of unrest and nervous tension among the Indians, who watched with smoldering fury the relentless westward march of the colonists. The French, with the help of their Indian allies, were moving into Virginia claimed lands, and in 1754, the small band of Shawnees at Shawnee Spring, summoned by their tribesmen on the Scioto, disappeared quietly overnight in their removal to Ohio country.

Let it be remembered, then, that it was at Winchester Washington enlisted nine of his companions for that perilous winter trip to Ft. LeBoeuf, when he carried Governor Dinwiddie's message to the French Commander, and that it was to Winchester, some six months later, the prisoners taken at Great Meadows were brought and released. Here, too, came General Edward Braddock on his way to Ft. Cumberland and subsequent disaster; here Washington built Ft. Loudoun in 1756-1757 in defense of the town and lower valley; and it was from Winchester the following year that the Virginia contingent set out for the successful conquest of Ft. Duquesne.[4]

Thus Winchester in a very real sense became a French and Indian War town, serving as a base of military operations for repeated campaigns of the conflict. This fact is reflected in street names: Braddock, Loudoun, Amherst and Wolfe Streets being named for British military leaders, and Boscawen for the admiral who brought Braddock's troops to Alexandria and Wolfe's troops to Quebec.

The defeat of Braddock in 1755 was the green light to the Indians to kill and burn and plunder along the entire western frontier. Their raids throughout four successive seasons brought the loss of an estimated 3000 settlers, either killed or captured, together with the destruction of hundreds of pioneer homes and barns. Settlers who had penetrated the Valley's western mountain wall fled in terror to Winchester for safety. It is said that the whole of Hampshire County was thus deserted; while many residents of Frederick, both town and county, left for safer territory east of the Blue Ridge. The government at Williamsburg, at last awakened to the urgency of the situation, authorized the building of Ft. Loudoun, but grudgingly at best. The effectiveness of Washington's defense of the frontier was critically hampered by insufficient supplies of men and materials of war, occasioned largely by the unsympathetic and frivolous attitude of the governor of the colony.

This threat of destruction was repeated in 1763 with the conspiracy of Pontiac. Citizens of the area again lived in fear of lurking death. At this time also there were many who fled their homes in search of security. Among them was Carl Friedrich Wildbahn, at first the schoolmaster, then the licensed minister of the Lutheran congregation at Winchester. The throes of the French and Indian War thus provide the setting for the birth of the Lutheran Church.

No record has been preserved of the congregation's date of organization, it must be stated with much regret. The time of the formal beginning, in consequence of this undiscovered fact, must be left to conjecture. Such evidence as has been handed down, however, clearly shows the congregation to have come into existence in the period bounded by the years 1759 and 1762. The patent from Lord Fairfax to the original church property requires first consideration, after which the *Journal of Henry Melchior Muhlenberg* will throw additional light on the problem.

The Fairfax patent is quoted in full, as follows:

> The Right Honourable Thomas Lord Fairfax, Baron of Cameron in that part of Great Britain called Scotland, Proprietor of the Northern Neck of Virginia; to all to whom this present writing shall come sends Greeting. Whereas David Dederick, Jacob Sibert, Christopher Lambert and George Michael Lovinger of Frederick County having set forth to my Office in behalf of the people called Lutherans that Lotts No. (84) & (85) in the addition to the Town of Winchester in the said County, are conveniently situated for erecting & building a Meetinghouse for the use of the said Congregation, Know yee that for the causes aforesaid, for and in consideration of the annual rents & Covenants hereinafter reserved & expressed, I have given granted & confirmed & by these presents for me my Heirs & Assigns Do give grant & confirm unto the said David Dederick, Jacob Sibert, Christopher Lambert and George Michael Lovinger as Trustees appointed by the said Congregation the said recited Lotts for the use aforesaid and for no other purpose whatsoever, as bounded by a

Survey & Platt of the said addition made by Mr. John Bayliss as follows — on the Southw'd side by Water Street, on the Westw'd end by East Lane, on the Northw'd side by Phillpott Lane, & on the Eastw'd end by the Eastw'd line of the said addition — To have & to hold the said recited Lotts N. (84) & (85) Together with all and singular the appurtenances thereunto belonging To them the said David Dederick, Jacob Sibert, Christopher Lambert & George Michael Lovinger and their Successors forever, they the said David Dederick, Jacob Sibert, Christopher Lambert & George Michael Lovinger & their Successors appointed Trustees as aforesaid Yielding & paying to me my Heirs & Assigns, or to my certain Attorney or Attornies Agent or Agents or to the certain Attorney or Attornies of my Heirs or Assigns Proprietors of the said Northern Neck, yearly & every year on the feast day of St. Michael the Archangel the fee rent or sum of ten shillings sterling money for the said Lotts of Land — Provided, that if the said David Dederick, Jacob Sibert, Christopher Lambert & George Michael Lovinger & their Successors shall not pay the said reserved annual rent as aforesaid, so that the same or any part thereof shall be behind or unpaid by the space of thirty days next after the same shall become due if Legally Demanded, that then it shall & may be Lawfull for me my Heirs or Assigns Proprietors as aforesaid my or their certain Attorney or Attornies, Agent or Agents into the above granted Premises to reenter & hold the same so as if this grant had never passed. Given under my hand & Seal, Dated the fifteenth Day of May in the twenty sixth year of his Majesty King George the second's Reign A. D. 1753.

        Fairfax
David Dederick & c their Deed for
 Lotts N. (84) & (85) in Winchester for the
 use of the Church of Lutherans
  Ex. & W. Tho. Bry. Martin.

At first glance it may be asked, what more definite date is desired than the one given in the patent — May 15, 1753? Is not this the date traditionally observed by the congregation as the date of its beginning? But on second glance, the language concerning the location of the two lots specifically declares the "addition to the town of Winchester." This most emphatically means the Fairfax Addition of 1759, as indeed the lots are still located there in the very same place after almost two hundred years. Quite naturally the question then arises, how does one account for the 1753 date? The answer is that Lord Fairfax issued numerous patents as of May 15, 1753. These same patents often refer to surveys that did not occur until some five or six years later. It is not known why the above date was selected.

Henry Melchior Muhlenberg

Hence, it must be remembered that the date on a Fairfax patent is not to be considered the date on which the transaction itself took place, and in such a way must the patent date of the Lutheran Church property be explained.

Assuming that the patent was issued as soon as the Fairfax Addition had been annexed to the town, it may be argued that the organized congregation already existed in 1759. But there is no evidence to show that the patent was issued that year. Another lead must be followed.

The invaluable *Journal of Henry Melchior Muhlenberg* helps clarify the situation.[5] Under July 1, 1762, Muhlenberg writes: "A recently founded poor congregation in Winchester, in the province of Virginia, consisting of Evangelicals from Germany and some young people whose parents live among us, was given permission, in response to its urgent pleading, to collect contributions in our United Congregations toward the building of a church."[6]

It will readily be observed that the problem here centers in the precise meaning of "recently founded." Does the writer mean a few months or a few years? Who can say? No definite evidence pertaining to this point has been found. Our conclusion is that from such evidence as has been produced, the date of the Fairfax Addition, 1759, becomes the far boundary in point of time, and the 1762 convention of the Ministerium of Pennsylvania the near boundary. The date of the organization of the Lutheran Church at Winchester lies somewhere between the two.

It is from the Muhlenberg journal that much other important information is learned. From the start the congregation conducted a German school, employing a schoolmaster, Carl Friedrich Wildbahn. We learn facts about Wildbahn's life: that he was licensed by the Ministerium to serve in Winchester, and that he left the community in 1763 because of the Indian peril. Let us look at Muhlenberg's own account of it. We find it in his entry for November 5, 1768, when he reviews the status of Wildbahn for the Ministerium.

> The said catechist (Wildbahn) came to America with the soldiers some thirteen years ago (1755). He says that he was born in Saxony, he writes a neat hand, can sing excellently since he was perhaps a chorister, understands some

Latin, can read Greek, has a special gift for catechization, and is extraordinarily eloquent. He secured a release from the army because, as he says, he was ruptured while dragging a cannon, worked for a while in the printing shop in Philadelphia in the late Mr. Handschue's time (a Lutheran pastor), with whom as a fellow countryman, he became intimate, and went across the Susquehanna to the English and German charity school which had been established at that time. After the free schools had closed, he betook himself farther inland and began to conduct German school, read sermons on Sundays, and catechized the youth. He was called still farther to a district of Virginia by the German inhabitants of the city of Winchester. There he preached on Sundays and also baptized children in emergencies, because there was no ordained German preacher in that whole region, and because the people were unwilling to join the English Church although, according to the laws of that province, they had to pay annual tribute to the English preacher of the Established Church.

In 1762, immediately after the synodical meeting in Philadelphia (held June 27-29) when the members of the Reverend Ministerium and the delegates of the United Congregations had already dispersed and were returning to their homes, the above mentioned catechist, Wildbahn, arrived from Virginia with two delegates. They brought petitions from their congregations, and even a recommendation from the English government authorities, which gave a favorable description of the said catechist's teaching, life, and conversation, and urgently requested the Ministerium to examine and ordain this man. Since my brethren had imposed the office of president upon me, I had to act accordingly, summoned a committee made up of as many members of the Reverend Ministerium as were still on hand — His Reverence Dr. Wrangel, Pastor Handschue, and Pastor Hartwich — and, having laid the document before them, asked for their opinion. The said brethren gave mature consideration to the matter, examined the catechist, and gave me their opinion in writing, namely, that he passed his examination satisfactorily, and that, as president, I might authorize him to perform ministerial acts in the said congregations *usque ad ulteriorem probationem*. I gave him a written certificate in English according to the directions received, and dismissed him and the deputies with a hearty admonition.[7]

The journal for July 5, 1762, declares the visitors from Virginia arrived that day;[8] while the entry for July 8 says that Wildbahn brought the certificate from the examining pastors with their statement of approval, as a result of which Muhlenberg issued the license in English giving him the right to administer the sacraments at Winchester until further examination at the next meeting of the Synod.[9]

Continuing the account from the November 5, 1768, entry, Muhlenberg goes on to say:

> Since these new congregations had now been received into our Union, our congregations, although they were themselves still poor, were obliged to contribute some mites toward the building of their new church in Winchester. But scarcely a year or so elapsed when the savage tribes attacked the regions about Winchester, murdering and burning, and the said catechist left the district and moved with his small family to Canewage [Conowago, in the vicinity of Hanover] on the border of Pennsylvania, where he assumed charge of some congregations and preached and catechized in them.[10]

Muhlenberg's information about this first schoolmaster and catechist of the congregation, who served also as the first minister, unordained but licensed to perform pastoral acts, is all that we know concerning his early ministry at Winchester. His name has not been handed down in the annals of the church with the cherished memory of a first pastor. Is it because he fled in the face of danger and left his flock shepherdless? Or, is it because there was no resident pastor to succeed him until Streit arrived in 1785, whose subsequent ministry quite overshadowed the memory of the dim and early days until their record was forgotten completely? Whatever the reason, the fact remains that Wildbahn's name during the course of the intervening years became so disassociated with the Lutheran Church of Winchester that men like Charles Porterfield Krauth and David McConaughy Gilbert scarcely link him to the congregation. After a long probationary period, Wildbahn was ordained by the Pennsylvania Ministerium. He served several parishes with fidelity and his death in 1804 was lamented by the Synod.

When October 1763 arrived, Wildbahn was already living at Conowago. From Winchester no delegate could be sent to the meeting of the Ministerium at Philadelphia because of the Indian troubles. Instead, a written excuse was forwarded. The following summer conditions were no better. Muhlenberg reported under date of June 14: "Today we received the sad news from our frontier and from Virginia that the hostile Indians have horribly massacred many settlers and carried others away as prisoners into the wilderness."[11]

In times of common peril men of common faith, background and interest draw more closely together. So it was with the German Lutherans at Winchester during the French and Indian War. They banded themselves together into a congregation and comforted their souls in the establishing of their faith.

Endnotes – Chapter III

[1] See sketches by W.W. Glass on "The Northern Neck of Virginia" appearing in "Our Local Historical Series," *The Winchester Evening Star*, beginning July 24, 1949.

[2] A photostatic transcript of this case is found at Handley Public Library [now Handley Regional Library], Winchester, Virginia.

[3] T.K. Cartmell, *Shenandoah Valley Pioneers and Their Descendants: A History of Frederick County, Virginia, from its Formation in 1738 to 1908* (Winchester, Va.: Eddy Press Corporation, 1909), chapter XXVII..

[4] Frederic Morton, *The Story of Winchester in Virginia* (Strasburg, Va.: Shenandoah Publishing House, 1925), chapters V and VI.

[5] *The Journals of Henry Melchior Muhlenberg*, 3 volumes, translated by Theodore G. Tappert and John W. Doberstein (Philadelphia: Muhlenberg Press, 1942-1958). Hereafter cited as *JHMM*. [The third volume appeared in print after the publication of Dr. Eisenberg's work.]

[6] *JHMM*, I, 533.

[7] *JHMM*, II, 366 and subsequent pages. See also *Documentary History of the Evangelical Lutheran Ministerium of Pennsylvania and Adjacent States, Proceeding of the Annual Conventions from 1748 to1821* (Philadelphia: Board of Publication of the General Council of the Evangelical Lutheran Church in North America, 1898), 92 and subsequent pages.

[8] *JHMM*, I, 535.

[9] Ibid., 536.

[10] Ibid., 367.

[11] *JHMM*, II, 88.

Chapter IV
Altars of Faith and Freedom

Wildbahn's work at Winchester was not without fruit. The year following his departure the Lutherans laid the cornerstone of their original house of worship. The edifice they planned was to be no log structure of the frontier, but a building of native gray limestone, with sturdy foundations and walls, simple yet commodious, to meet the demands and the tests of time.

The site which had been obtained was at the top of a little hill, a slight eminence on the eastern edge of the village, for Winchester nestles, as it were, in the center of a shallow bowl completely encircled by low-lying hills. Immediately to the north, separated by a narrow strip of ground intended to be the eastward projection of Philpot Lane, lay the two lots belonging to the German Reformed Church, the Fairfax patent to which is identical to the one issued the Lutherans excepting names of trustees, lot numbers and boundaries. Here members of the Reformed congregation built a log church in 1758, it is claimed, which structure endured for nearly ninety years; but with the passing of a second century its exact location has been forgotten completely.

If the year 1758 is the correct date for the building of the Reformed Church, then in all probability the Lutherans constructed their school house on the southwest corner of their lot about the same time. Common language, continental European background and intermarriage made the Lutheran and Reformed groups a social unit in the community. Those old German forefathers were thrifty and practical, if they were anything. There would have been no logic in building two log churches, side by side, nor two school houses on adjoining lots. Is it not reasonable to assume that one group agreed to hasten the building of its church, while the other hastened to erect the building of its school, in order that both church building and school building might be available to both groups?

Certainly Wildbahn had to have a place to teach. And so did Master Antony, who followed him. But where? It is this writer's guess that the Lutherans put up their school house immediately upon organization as a congregation in order that German school might be conducted for the children of both Lutheran and Reformed families, and that this was the school house standing there when Christian Streit came in 1785. The Lutherans then turned their attention to the building of their church.

Judged by the time it took to rear the walls and complete the building, and making due allowance for the exceptional times, the digging of the foundation and the laying of the foundation stones must have been a matter of years instead of months. Wildbahn, leader of the congregation when it was received into membership of the Ministerium, appealed for financial assistance from Pennsylvania congregations. In this matter, we may assume, the two lay delegates who accompanied him from Winchester did not keep silent. And Muhlenberg tells us also of the family connection between certain members of his own parish and certain young people at Winchester. The appeal, therefore, was not likely to go unheeded. Nor did it. The New Hanover congregation responded by receiving an offering, further cementing the ties first established when Joist Hite and other of his co-settlers came from that community to the Shenandoah Valley.

Muhlenberg in his journal for December 15, 1762,[1] tells the incident: how on that day a Dr. Martins from Providence (Trappe, Pennsylvania) visited him in Philadelphia, and when the doctor made his departure, he took with him the New Hanover collection "to be given to Mr. Schrack for the Winchester Church." The amount of the gift is not stated. Here is an early evidence of interest and responsibility in the church's wider home mission enterprise that is deserving of notice. Mention of Mr. Schrack's name gives a possible clue to the origin of Nicolaus Schrack, one of the founders of the Winchester congregation.

By April 1764, the work on the foundation had proceeded sufficiently well to hold the cornerstone laying on the 16th day of the month. That day was Monday of Holy Week. The Rev. Johann Caspar Kirchner, ordained minister who had served congregations in York County, Pennsylvania, and Baltimore, Maryland, officiated at the ceremony. Fortunately for future generations he was a man who believed the building of a church on the American frontier an event of sufficient importance to be recorded for posterity. With correct judgment he sensed the significance of the occasion, and with an insight compounded alike of prophecy and history, a document in Latin was prepared to be placed within the cornerstone. What is more, he had the foresight to turn over a duplicate copy of this paper to officers of the congregation. The contents of this document, spanning the years and linking the past with the present, are a continuing source of inspiration to the congregation and a priceless treasure.

Reverently now, read those cherished lines.

> In the name of God, the Father, Son, and Holy Ghost. Amen.
> The foundations of this Temple, by the Grace of God, were

laid in the year of Christ 1764, on the sixteenth day of April.

The hearers and founders of this Temple are all and each members of the Evangelical Lutheran Church, at this time residing in this city of Winchester, to wit:

Thomas Schmidt	Christoph Altrith	Christian Neuberger
Nicolaus Schrack	Tobias Otto	Georg Schumacher
Christoph Heusckel	Eberhard Doring	Michael Roger
David Dieterick	Andreas Friedly	Michael Warnig
Christoph Wetzel	Christoph Heintz	Christoph Lambert
Peter Helfenstein	Imanuel Buger	Samuel Wendel
Georg Michael Laubinger	Dewald Hiegel	Michael Glueck
Jacob Trautwein	Julius Spickert	Henrick Becker
Joh. Sigmond Haenli	Balthasar Poh	Jacob Siebert
Johannes Laemly	Jacob Koppenhaber	Jacob Braun
Johannes Lentz	Henrich Weller	Stephen Traenckel

At that time bore rule George III, King of Great Britain, our most clement master, and his officers and governors in Virginia, Francis Fauquier in Williamsburg, there presiding with highest authority, and Thomas Fairfax, chief magistrate of this whole district, at that time residing not far from this city, who has given to us gratuitously and of good will two lots of ground, embracing one acre, for sacred uses.

This Temple has been consecrated to the Triune God and to the Evangelical Lutheran Religion alone, all sects whatever name they may bear, and all others, who either dissent from or do not fully assent to our Evangelical Lutheran Religion, being forever excluded.

As a permanent record of which to our posterity this paper is here placed and has been deposited for everlasting remembrance in this cornerstone.

Drawn up in Winchester April 16th, MDCCLXIIII.
Johann Caspar Kirchner, at that time Minister
of
the Evangelical Lutheran Church.
Scribe, Ludwig Adamus.
Antony, School Master in this city.

Now look at the foregoing document a second time and note four things. First, the words of consecration: "In the name of God the Father, the Son and the Holy Ghost...the foundations were laid.... This Temple has been consecrated to the Triune God and to the Evangelical Lutheran Religion alone." These words are words of deepest conviction rather than narrow sectarianism. Permit Charles Porterfield Krauth to dwell upon them for a moment in a passage from a celebrated sermon preached in 1854:

> To the blessed three, the Undivided One, they reared this house. It was hallowed by the doctrine to whose preservation and extension it was consecrated. Their view of freedom of conscience was not that of the indifference which mingles and confounds truth and error. "It is consecrated," says that same old document, "to our Evangelical Religion only, to the exclusion forever of sects, whatever name they may bear, and of all dissenting from, or not truly assenting to, our Evangelical Lutheran Religion." They did not simply say, "we consecrate it to religion," (though that would have been enough if none were in error as to what religion is) for even the Pagan calls his dark superstition religion; not simply "to the Christian Religion," for the Mormon calls his beastly materialism the Christian religion; but they used that definite term which placed their meaning beyond question, just as they found it necessary amid the "gods many and lords many," to say not simply "to God," but to "the one God, the Father, the Son, and the Holy Ghost." Knowing that their religion was no novelty, they placed the house beyond the invasion of error by consecrating it to the faith they confessed, and that alone. And when they said "our Evangelical Lutheran faith," what did they mean? They meant to confess the supremacy of God alone over the conscience, the divine authority of the Bible in every question of faith and life, the great doctrines of human corruption and loss, of the repairing and healing of our stricken nature in Jesus Christ, the regenerating power of the Holy Ghost, salvation by grace, justification by faith, which works holiness by love, the uncontaminated sacraments, unbroken in their essential elements, untouched at their heart by the worm of unbelief. To these great doctrines, old as Christianity and enduring as eternity, to these precious doctrines which after the lapse of

Altars of Faith and Freedom

nearly a hundred years are still preached to their descendants, and still show their saving power in many of their hearts, our fathers hallowed this church.²

Notice in the second place the dating and terms of conveyance. The dating follows the Biblical pattern set by St. Luke in recording the start of John the Baptist's ministry. The reigning king, the colonial governor and the district chief magistrate are mentioned in turn. Here, too, we find the evidence of Lord Fairfax's generosity. Contrary to the language of the patent which speaks of "annual rents and covenants" and an annual "sum of ten shillings sterling money" to be paid on the feast day of St. Michael, the cornerstone document declares emphatically that Fairfax gave the site "gratuitously and of good will" "for sacred uses." In view of the unreality of the patent's date, and here again the unreality of its terms of conveyance, one is driven to the conclusion more than ever that its language is but the stock phraseology of a set form that must be explained away in the light of conditioning facts.

The names of the officiating minister, scribe and schoolmaster are the third point of emphasis to be noted.

Johann Caspar Kirchner, "at that time minister of the Evangelical Lutheran Church," had received ordination in Germany. On coming to America he served several small congregations in York County, Pennsylvania. A nucleus of Lutherans in Baltimore obtained his services as their minister in 1758. From his Pennsylvania home he journeyed every sixth week to the Maryland city to preach and administer the sacraments, and in this visiting ministry he continued five years. In 1762, the first church building of Zion Lutheran congregation was built, but the year following Kirchner accepted a call too far removed from Baltimore to allow him to serve the congregation further. After two more years, however, he heeded a renewed call to Baltimore, moved to that place and became the first resident pastor of Zion Lutheran Church. He died in 1773. He never became a member of the Ministerium of Pennsylvania.

During the two years Kirchner was absent from Baltimore he continued to minister to congregations in York County, Pennsylvania. He corresponded occasionally with H.M. Muhlenberg, though the two apparently were never on close terms. The Muhlenberg journal for October 14, 1763, tells us that Kirchner resided on the "frontier between Pennsylvania and Maryland."[3]

In view of the scarcity of pastors it was not exceptional for ministers to roam far afield, leaving their regular parishes to serve vacant congregations temporarily. So it was, apparently, that Johann Caspar Kirchner came to Winchester in April 1764, to officiate at the cornerstone laying. The fact that he signed after his name "minister of the Evangelical Lutheran Church" shows that he did not consider himself pastor at Winchester, but simply an ordained minister, since the phrase was used by itinerant Lutheran preachers when they were out of the bounds of their own parishes. The laying of the cornerstone takes on added significance in the light of the fact that it marks the first occasion when a duly ordained pastor of the Lutheran Church ministered to the congregation.

Nothing further has come to light concerning the Scribe, Ludwig Adam, and so, too, must it be said in regard to Schoolmaster Antony. This latter gentleman is recorded in the printed copy of the cornerstone document appearing in Dr. Gilbert's well-known *Praises of the Lord in the Story of Our Fathers* as "Antony Ludi." Professor T.G. Tappert has made the suggestion that, since the Latin for schoolmaster is *ludi magister*, a part of his title had been mistaken for his surname. In consulting the copy of the document made from the duplicate that had been entrusted to church officers for safe keeping and written into the minute book of the Church Council, it was found that the *Ludi* had been written after Antony, then erased until it was barely discernible. The erasure seems clear evidence that the above suggestion is correct. Mr. Antony then was "Schoolmaster in this city," as the record specifically declares.

The fourth item from the cornerstone document for special consideration concerns the founding fathers. The names of thirty-three heads of families are given "all and each members of the Evangelical Lutheran Church, at this time residing in this city of Winchester." As we list them, we shall put in parentheses certain variant Americanized spellings of the names, then give such information as we have about them.

1. Thomas Schmidt (Smith) – served on Church Council, 1771.
2. Nicolaus Schrack – from Montgomery County, Pennsylvania.
3. Christoph Heusckel (Heiskel) – served on Church Council, 1771.
4. David Dieterick (Detrick) – one of the original trustees.
5. Christoph Wetzel (Whetzel) – preserved the Cornerstone Document in papers handed down to his daughter Nancy, at whose death (c. 1850) Dr. Krauth discovered the duplicate copy. Wetzel was an original lot owner in Winchester, 1752.
6. Peter Helfenstein (Helvestine) – born June 17, 1724, at Cologne, Germany, the son of a Lutheran minister; he studied surveying at the University of Bonn, where he graduated; with his brother Philip he came to America in 1743. According to family tradition the father wanted his sons to become

ministers. When they decided to come to America, they promised him to evangelize the Indians. According to another tradition, Peter, after coming to Winchester, helped George Washington with his surveying. He became Major of the Eighth Virginia Regiment during the Revolution, serving under Col. Peter Muhlenberg. He contributed of his own means to help raise this regiment. He served on the Church Council, 1771.[4]

7. Georg Michael Laubinger (Lovinger) – one of the original trustees. Served on Church Council, 1771.

8. Henrick Becker (Henry Baker) – the father of a long line of honorable descendants, many of whom have been outstanding leaders of the community and church. Served on Church Council, 1786.

9. Jacob Siebert (Seibert) – one of the original trustees. His name unfortunately was omitted from the list of founders on the bronze marker erected in 1938.

10. Jacob Braun (Brown).

11. Stephen Traenckel (Trinkle) – the name was misprinted Fraenckel in Dr. Gilbert's *Story of Our Fathers* and the misprint was carried over to the bronze marker of 1938.

12. Christoph Altrith (Aldrich, Eldridge).

13. Tobias Otto – one of the original lot owners of Winchester, 1752.

14. Eberhard Doring (Dearing).

15. Andreas Friedly (Fridley) – physician and surgeon to colonial troops under Washington during the French and Indian War. An original lot owner of the town, he lived at the southeast corner of the intersection of Piccadilly and Kent Streets.

16. Christoph Heintz.

17. Imanuel Buger (Bucher) – many persons by this name are still found in Frederick County.

18. Dewald Hiegel.
19. Jacob Trautwein (Troutwine) – a surgeon in the Revolutionary War. He lived at the southeast corner of Cameron and Clifford Streets.
20. Joh. Sigmond Haenli (Henley).
21. Johannes Laemly (Lemley) – many by this name reside in Frederick County today.
22. Johannes Lentz (Lantz) – a well-known Shenandoah County name.
23. Christian Neuberger (Newberger) – this name has been placed last on the list on the bronze marker.
24. Georg Schumacher (Shumaker) – a printer's error in Dr. Gilbert's *Story of Our Fathers* omitted the preceding surname, Neuberger, together with the given name, Georg, and produced "Christian Schumacher" instead. This error was carried to the bronze marker.
25. Michael Roger.
26. Michael Warnig.
27. Christoph Lambert – one of the original trustees.
28. Samuel Wendel (Windle) – a well-known Valley name.
29. Michael Glueck (Glick).
30. Julius Spickert
31. Balthasar Poh (Po, Poe) – the name is spelled Po on the copy of the cornerstone document. Streit's Diary spells the name Poh, which undoubtedly was the original form.
32. Jacob Koppenhaber (Copenhaver) – the father of numerous descendants in the community.
33. Henrich Weller – a well-known Valley name.

These thirty-three founders of the German Lutheran Congregation, with their wives and children, banded themselves together in the building of a spiritual home in the new land to which they had come from afar. Obscure and unknown, without the advantage of privilege or position, or means or wealth, they had come to America to create by patient toil a new homeland for themselves and their children. Because the fear of God was in their hearts they were not afraid of danger. Least of all were they afraid of work. When they laid the cornerstone of their temple in 1764, they laid an enduring foundation stone in the essential character of the America that was about to be born. They, together with other similar groups on the frontier of that day, gave of the faith which they possessed to the very soul of the young nation. Let us call upon Dr. Krauth again to bear witness to the kind of men they were.

> Many of them were good and wise men. They had their faults, but happy will it be for us if posterity shall not see that our faults are more serious than theirs. Happy shall we be if we leave to those that follow us as much as our fathers left to us. They were Germans, not ashamed of their origin. We do not claim that our fathers were men of noble blood; it is noble enough, however, to make strong arms, rational brains, and stout hearts. Theirs was the majesty of unpretending self-reliance, the stern independence which the resolve to toil promises, and the toil itself secures. Their motto was: "By working, the workman is made." Some derided their broken English, but they could not often deride them for broken promises. Some who never knew the value of a dollar because they never made one, despised the economy, which refused to squander what severe labor had won. Men laughed at the rough scales in which, whether an idea looked like silver or brass, our fathers persisted in weighing it. They kept the even tenor of their way. Clinging perhaps more tenaciously to their language and usages because they felt that they were the subjects of an indirect persecution, on they moved soberly and calmly, building up fortunes and demolishing English in their own fashion. Time, the great test of all things, has shown that they were wise men. While families

of other national stocks have vanished in their posterity, our fathers have grown stronger in theirs. That surely is not wise that tends to annihilation; and when we see the names of the deriders passing away, and those of the derided abiding, we are forced to ask, if we admit the claim of the former to have had more knowledge, was there not more wisdom shown by the latter – if the one had more intelligence, had not the other more good sense? I for one am quite satisfied with my patent of nobility furnished by the appearance of two ancestral names in the old Latin record of 1764, and shall be satisfied to leave to my children a name as truly honorable.[5]

For the next twenty years, i.e., from 1765 to 1785, our story becomes fragmentary. As means afforded, the building of the church went on, though never to the point of completion, and it does not seem to have been used by the congregation in an unfinished condition. Events of another character, we shall learn, were to commandeer the structure for their own purposes. The records for this twenty-year period are so meager and so disconnected that the continuity of the narrative cannot be preserved.

It was a period when itinerant pastors served numerous little flocks in widely separated areas. The number of Lutheran immigrants coming to America in the mid-eighteenth century far outstripped in proportion the number of pastors available to care for their spiritual needs. At the time of the congregation's founding it is said there were but sixteen ordained Lutheran pastors in the colonies. Demands from so many sources forced those few men, who were trying conscientiously to meet the most pressing needs, to spread out their fields of operation to include larger and broader parishes. The result, unfortunately, was that more work was undertaken than a man could do thoroughly and well, and his ministry became travel-worn, thin and ineffectual. It was a period, furthermore, of political unrest, revolution and war, an upheaval effecting every stratum of society, especially that of the grass-roots frontier. In the cause of independence, the Valley of Virginia made a magnificent contribution in which the Lutheran Church of Winchester had a record that maketh not ashamed.

The facts that are clear in the picture are these: visiting pastors include C.F. Wildbahn, John Christopher Hartwick, John Peter Gabriel Muhlenberg and Henry Moeller; the rearing of the church's walls and roof and steeple were accomplished; and many from the congregation took up arms in the Revolutionary War.

The chief problem was to obtain a pastor. Henry Melchior Muhlenberg, presiding officer of the only Lutheran Church organization existing in the country, was fully aware of, and highly sensitive to, the pleading of shepherdless flocks. But he would not yield to popular demands to lower the standards of the ministry, when frequently he was besieged by remote church councils demanding that this brother or that be licensed or ordained. Let him tell in his own language something about the problem he faced.

> It is exceedingly difficult to say yes or no in such circumstances. Ordained preachers live far away and are hardly able to visit such remote groups. The people would like to cling to the religion and practice of their ancestors. A number of preachers who were ordained and then dismissed on account of depravity in Germany wander about in America and serve in such forsaken congregations until their sinful life becomes too manifest that they must clear out in bad odor. Many others set themselves up as preachers and exercise the office without any ordination or examination whatsoever, if they have some gift of speech. If these people who live far away have nothing at all, they and their children either relapse into paganism or are dispersed among all kinds of peculiar sects. This raises the question, What is the best thing to do, or which is the least among many evils?[6]

The case of Carl Friedrich Wildbahn is an interesting case at point. As has already been shown, in 1762 he was given a license permitting him to perform ministerial acts at Winchester. When he settled the next year at Conowago and took charge of congregations there, his congregations approached the Ministerium again in his behalf, and the Ministerium placed him under the supervision of the Rev. Mr. Hornell, pastor at Yorktown (York, Pennsylvania), and stipulated that he might preach and catechize, and in cases of necessity, baptize; but the administration of the Holy Communion was to be performed by the ordained pastor from York. Soon afterwards, however, Hornell and the Ministerium parted company for it was revealed that he had committed a crime in Europe. Thus Wildbahn was left alone.[7] H.M. Muhlenberg writes:

> This was followed year after year by the receipt of two different petitions from the same congregations. Some pleaded longingly for the final examination and ordination of the catechist; others petitioned that this request be not granted. In his own letters the catechist asked the Reverend Ministerium to summon him to appear in order that he might reply to his accusers. But it was not expedient, for one is unwilling to put oneself between contending parties. The complainants presented a variety of charges against him, mostly concerning his former life. Now he was reported to have said that he had stabbed a man, now he was reported to have spoken disparagingly of religion, etc., and when his friends asked people who were reported to have said such things, they would not admit it, etc.[8]

Wildbahn, meanwhile, led an honorable and sober life. His ability to catechize and preach won him additional support from each new congregation he took under his care. He cherished the sincere desire to become an ordained minister and member of the Ministerium.

When the 1769 convention of the Ministerium was held

June 25-27 at Philadelphia, Wildbahn came with petitions and testimonials from his congregations in Pennsylvania, Maryland and Virginia. At the time he was serving St. James' Church and St. John's Church, both in York County, Pennsylvania; Silver Run, Great Pfeiff Creek, Thomas Creek and Owens Creek congregations in Frederick County, Maryland; Antiben Creek, Hagerstown and Sharpsburg congregations, also in Maryland; and "Shepherdstown and Winchestertown in Virginia" – a nice parish of eleven congregations in three colonies and more than one hundred miles from end to end. Happy to say, Wildbahn was at last received into full membership of the Ministerium, in which he served faithfully the rest of his days.[9]

Nothing further is known about Wildbahn's second Winchester pastorate, when it began or when it ended. That he made periodic visits for several years seems more than probable. Dr. D.M. Gilbert is the authority for saying that in the fall of 1776 Wildbahn once more visited the churches in this region, stopping at Winchester to minister to the congregation's needs and encourage the people to remain steadfast in their faith.[10]

There can be little doubt that John Christopher Hartwick, eccentric bachelor, itinerant preacher forever on the move, member of the Ministerium, resident of the colony of New York, visited the Winchester Lutherans on several occasions, preaching for them as long as he was in their midst and performing whatever pastoral acts might be needed, though specific proof regarding the exact time of his visits has not been found. Dr. A.R. Wentz credits him with visiting Wildbahn at Winchester in the latter part of June 1762, and initiating the idea that Wildbahn and two laymen go to Philadelphia to the meeting of the Ministerium with petitions to license the young catechist. The same author says Hartwick came again into Virginia in the summer of 1769, while from other sources it is claimed he was at Winchester in 1768 and 1770.¹¹ It was Hartwick's custom wherever he ministered to enter his acts in a bold handwriting in the official record book of the congregation. Such a record would give the kind of evidence we are looking for, but, alas, the records that exist at Winchester do not begin until 1813.

One bit of evidence has come to light which seems to indicate that J.C. Hartwick was in the vicinity in May 1775. It comes from the journal of Philip V. Fithian, itinerant Presbyterian minister, who journeyed through the Valley at the time. On May 26 Fithian was at Stephensburg (Stephens City) and he wrote as follows: "Dined with an old, starched, Dutch Lutheran Clergyman – He wished me much success in my Work – He professes to be a Scholar, & has attempted to institute a small academy in this County."¹²

Fithian's pen-portrait certainly resembles Hartwick, if anybody. Hartwick at the time was 61 years of age. He had planned for years before his death in 1796 to establish a seminary. By his will, Hartwick Seminary in New York State was founded.¹³ Fithian doubtless misunderstood the intended location of the school.

The known peculiarities and eccentricities of Lord Fairfax and Pastor Hartwick made kindred spirits of the two. Thus from the archives of Zion Lutheran Church, Baltimore, comes this interesting note, as a result of Hartwick's temporary ministering in that congregation.

> Especially to be mentioned is a preacher who had served in the Army of the late war as chaplain under General Amherst. He was a man of very good attainments, and obviously of exemplary conduct. This preacher, by the name of Hartweg, remained with us for a short while and preached to everybody's satisfaction. However, he loved a roaming

> manner of life and did not care to stay long with one congregation. He said plainly that he was willing to stay as long as he should see that he was of use, but did not want to be bound by a contract and remain anywhere against his will and conviction. Several times he came hither, remaining some weeks and even months, but mostly went to Virginia, where he was well esteemed by Lord Fairfax, and lived there.[14]

From evidence such as the foregoing, it is not at all unlikely that J.C. Hartwick ministered to the Lutherans in the lower Shenandoah Valley on numerous occasions.

Another man whose name is associated by Dr. Gilbert with the congregation is Henry Moeller. He was a young catechist, not yet licensed, at the start of a long ministerial career that was to cover fifty-four years. In the spring of 1775 he journeyed from Pennsylvania to visit the scattered Lutherans of northern Virginia. Winchester was a stop on his itinerary, but it is not known how long he tarried. Arriving in Madison County, the congregation there extended him a call, which he was inclined to accept. When he returned to Pennsylvania for licensure, it is said his betrothed refused to come to Virginia to live; whereupon, he accepted another call to Reading, Pennsylvania. His connection with the Winchester church would seem to have been very brief and slight.

The foregoing bits of information, inadequate for the full telling of the story that one might wish, serve nevertheless to emphasize the serious difficulty confronted by the congregation in those early years in obtaining the regular services of an ordained pastor.

What is more besides, Peter Mischler[a] lived in Winchester. Self-seeking, self-assertive, he had already caused trouble in several Pennsylvania congregations, where first, being welcomed hospitably, he prayed with the soul-hun-

---

[a] Johann Peter Mischler was born in Gersweiler, Germany, in 1732. He eventually settled in Pendleton County, Virginia [now West Virginia].

gry people, only to prey upon them as opportunity afforded.

Mischler was well known – too well known in fact – to Lutheran authorities. In 1769 he applied for reception into the Ministerium of Pennsylvania. He presented letters of recommendations after a fashion from partisans in several congregations, who demanded his reception in almost threatening language. Examined by the Ministerium, he testified that he had never been educated for the ministry and only partly trained for the tailoring trade, which he had followed until he had been urged to serve as a preacher. Then he had received unauthorized ordination at the hands of another minister. Needless to say, he was never received into the Synod, though suggestion was made at the time that he use his talents in more remote and more destitute regions.[15]

Unfortunately, Mischler came into the Shenandoah Valley. Jacob Franck,[b] pastor at Madison from 1775-1778, ran across evidence of his baneful maneuvering. Writing under date of September 30, 1776, he tells how he was visited on that day

> ...by several men from Pikkel [Peaked] Mountain in Augusta County who... reported that great discord had arisen in their congregations on account of a preacher named Mischler, and they declared that it was to be feared that he might ruin the whole congregation. I promised, God willing, to preach there on

---

[b] The Rev. Jacob Franck became the pastor of the German (now Hebron) Lutheran Church late in 1775. Although Franck was pastor there for less than three years, the church was energized by his presence. The number of baptisms increased dramatically, which is one reason that so many families long associated with the Hebron area seem to be making an appearance for the first time during the latter part of the 1770's. While Franck was obviously popular with the congregation and other Lutherans in the region, he abruptly left the ministry in 1778 and returned to Philadelphia and resumed his profession as a silversmith, taking his wife Barbara and small son, Jacob, with him.

October 9 and to do what I could to restore peace. This man Mischler lives in Winchester, and he is the drunken tailor who caused disturbance in Pennsylvania earlier.[16]

Did this "so-called preacher" worm his way into the congregation at Winchester? In view of no records to cover the period, silence is the only answer. Mischler in all probability lived in the community for a number of years. His name is found on a tax list for the year 1788.[17]

There was still another side to the problem of obtaining a pastor. Virginia had an established church. The laws were made to favor the Established Church. All other religious groups were dissenters who had to bear certain penalties on that account. True, the overwhelming majority of the early settlers of the Shenandoah Valley, as dissenters, enjoyed a fuller measure of religious freedom than their brethren to the east of the Blue Ridge, but it was a distasteful thing to them to be discriminated against, with the full consent of the law, because of their religion.

Consider this phase of the problem as it affected the Lutheran congregation in Madison County. John Casper Stoever, Sr., had been instrumental in collecting sufficient funds in Europe for the erection of a church and its endowment, but on the homeward trip had died at sea. He was followed by George Samuel Klug, from 1739 to 1764 pastor of the congregation. John Schwarbach took up the work in 1765 as a catechist and was ordained for this field the next year.[18] The officers of the congregation addressed a letter to the Ministerium on September 1, 1768, saying in part as follows:

> The efforts of Mr. Schwarbach, being not without fruit, please us very much, and we again thank the Honorable Consistorium for sending this active man among us. But our means prevent us from providing a proper salary for him, since

we must also contribute to the support of the English county preacher, who, however, is of no benefit to us. The English preacher officiates at marriages, but our Mr. Schwarbach dare not.... If through your aid and counsel we could be freed from the English parish levy, and our German preacher be permitted to marry the Germans, we would be greatly helped. But without your advice we will do nothing in this matter.[19]

In commenting on the above communication on the floor of the Synod, H.M. Muhlenberg further elucidated on the subject:

In Virginia, the Episcopal Church is established on a firm basis, and whatever dissents from it, be it called what it may, is bound by law to contribute annually to the established preachers, and the preachers also have the exclusive right to marry. Even if dissenting parties be married by dissenting preachers, it is not legal and they can escape with no less fees to the established county preacher, and must receive a certificate of marriage from him. If a dissenting preacher is on good terms with the English country rector or pastor, or lives in some style, he may do *some* things under indulgence. The late Rev. Mr. Klug is said to have been much liked by the established clergy, ... But because he had not kept within proper bounds in regard to adiaphora, and went to extremes, he had difficulties with his congregation, though not with the Established brethren. Although none of them advised him to go to the Mother and be regularly ordained, yet the Gordian Knot would thus have been cut at one stroke. But his health was too feeble to undertake such a journey and hardship. He had his son educated in an English academy and study theology. The son also several years ago travelled to England, and has returned with regular orders...Our German Lutherans in that place can scarcely be freed from the county parish tax in any other way by anyone, but by some German adventurer accepting a call from the congregation, then upon this call, travelling to the Mother (Church), signing her articles and canons, and being regularly ordained. This will bring exemption from double taxes.[20]

This keen analysis by the top leader of the Lutheran Church reveals the trend of his thinking at the time. Furthermore, H.M.

Muhlenberg's associations with the Anglicans of Philadelphia were on close and very intimate terms. He was welcomed in their circles and asked to participate in special church functions, while he in turn invited his friends, Dr. William Smith, provost of the Academy, and the Rev. Richard Peters and the Rev. Jacob Duchee, rectors of the English Church, to share in noteworthy occasions of the Lutherans. As a matter of fact the numerous German Lutherans of Pennsylvania, recognizing these close bonds between the leaders of the two communions, as well as the marked similarities in liturgy and practice, often referred to the Anglican Church as the English Lutheran Church. There can be little doubt that Muhlenberg talked over the problems of the shepherdless Lutherans of the Valley of Virginia with these good Philadelphia Anglican friends of his.

What is more, was not King George himself, although the legal head of the English Church, a member of the Lutheran House of Hanover, and did he not maintain a Lutheran chaplain at the Court of St. James? And was not this chaplain, Dr. Ziegenhagen, Muhlenberg's dear friend of bygone school days? He undoubtedly had received Episcopal ordination in order that he might perform his duties legally and enjoy the benefits of his office. To put it in the apt words of Dr. Gilbert: "The fathers argued, some of them, I doubt not, 'If a Lutheran minister, to meet the legal requirements of the case, may properly be re-ordained in London, in order that he may serve as chaplain the Lutheran King of England, why may not young Muhlenberg go over and serve the Episcopal authority in order that he may minister fully, and without risk of prosecution or persecution, to the many Lutheran Germans in the Valley of the Shenandoah'."[21]

Thus, from the standpoint of the Lutherans in general and of Henry Melchior Muhlenberg in particular, the ordination of

Peter Muhlenberg by the Bishop of London and his coming to the Valley of Virginia in 1772 as the first resident Lutheran pastor west of the Blue Ridge, constituted an honest attempt to solve this knotty two-fold problem, first, by providing a pastor to an area where one was so sorely needed, and in the second place, a pastor who met the full requirements of Virginia law.

Because the Lutherans of Winchester were included in the huge parish served by Peter Muhlenberg, and because James Wood, Jr., son of the founder of the town, took an active part in inducing the famous personality to come to Virginia, fuller details are of interest.

Members of the Church of England, few in numbers in the Valley in comparison to the German Reformed, Mennonites and Lutherans who made up the bulk of the population, especially in that part of Frederick County which, in 1772, became Dunmore County, were eager to obtain a rector for the newly established parish of Beckford. Being of the Established Church they felt the responsibility which their legal position imposed upon them, together with that wider Christian responsibility to provide a minister and services of worship for the general population that were as sheep without a shepherd. But the practical side of the question was a very real one. Where was an Anglican minister to be found who could also preach in German? Or, if a minister be obtained who knew no German, would not a ripe opportunity be missed in the prosecution of the Church's work? The situation soon resolved itself into the search for a German pastor with acceptable ordination, who could also preach in English.

In the spring of 1771, James Wood, Jr., had to make a business trip to New York. En route he stopped in Philadelphia where, among other things, he talked church matters over with the Rev. Richard Peters and conferred also with the Rev. Mr.

Muhlenberg about the possibility of his son, Peter, coming to Virginia. Proceeding to New York, he wrote Father Muhlenberg a letter on the same subject, and, under date of May 4, he wrote a second letter,[22] this one to Peter Muhlenberg, as follows:

> Revd Sir—
> I have been requested by the Vestry of a Vacant Parish in Virginia, to use my Endeavours to find a Person of an unexceptionable Character, either Ordained or Desirous of Obtaining Ordination in the Clergy of the Church of England; who is capable of Preaching both in the English and German Languages. The Living as established by the Laws of the Land with Perquisites, is of the Value of Two Hundred and Fifty Pounds Pennsylvania Currency, with a Parsonage House and a Farm of at least two Hundred Acres of Extreme Good Land, with every other convenient Out House belonging to the same, which will render it Very Convenient for a Gentlemans Seat, and having just now received a Character and Information of You from Mr: John Vanorden, of (New) Brunswich, I am Very Inclinable to Believe you would fully Answer the Expectations of the People of that Parish; the Gentleman of whom I have had information Does not know whether You are ordained by the Bishop of London or not. How ever be that as it will, if You can come well recommended to the Vestry, they will recommend you in Such a manner as to make Your Ordination certain. If You should think these proposals worth your Acceptance, I shall be glad You would write me an Answer, to be left in Philadelphia at the Sign of the Cross Keys, where I shall stay a few Days on my Return home, when, if I find You are Inclinable to accept of this Living, You may expect to hear further from me, Directed to the Care of the Gentleman, of whom I have been favoured with the Information, which I have received
>
> I am
tho' unacquainted
Revd Sir
Y: ob: Serv:
James Wood.
>
> Newyork 4th May 1771
> P.S. If you should determine to go to London I make no Doubt of the Vestry Advancing a Sufficient Sum to Defray the Expenses.

Peter Muhlenberg was interested. Within a month he came to Virginia to make personal investigation. Dr. Richard Peters wrote a letter and had him deliver it to Col. Hugh Mercer, "At or near Winchester." This letter,[23] given herewith in full, illuminates matters further:

To Colonel and Doctor Hugh Mercer Esquire
    at or near Winchester

                              Philadelphia 11 June 1771.
Dr Sir

    It is a long time since I have had the Pleasure of your Letters. They formerly gave me the highest Pleasure, as they were always Testimonies of a sincere and honest public and friendly Spirit; an Opportunity now offers of reviving the dead Ashes of a smother'd Flame. And I cheerfully embrace it. It is to sollicit Your Assistance to the Bearer Mr: Muylenberg, the Worthy Son of a very Worthy Father, who is among my first and most intimate Friends and Brethren. The thing You can assist this Young Man in, is fully expressed in a Letter, wrote to his Father by Justice Wood from Newyork, some necessary Business called Him from Winchester to Newyork, and in his Way he called on Mr: Muylenberg, who has the Care of the Lutheran Church in this City. Inclosed you have a Copy of Mr: Woods Letter, which will give you a full and proper Knowledge of the Rise and Situation of this young man's Affair. Be pleased to acquaint the Vestry and Mr. Wood, that the Academy of this City have a very great Attachment to the Reverend Mr: Muylenberg the Father, and that Dr. Smith, myself and Mr: Duchee will gladly write Letters to the Society, or Bishops and Arch Bishops in favour of this young and promising Divine, who is of an amiable Disposition and has gained great Esteem amongst both the Lutherans and English. These letters we shall write jointly as soon as we shall be favour'd with a perusal of the proceedings of the Vestry. I am, I suppose well known to several of them either in Person or character, and therefore take the Liberty thro' Your Goodness, to recommend this young Man to them as one, who will answer all their purposes as to both the Churches – that is to say German and English and thro' the divine Blessing may prove of general Benefit, to the Interest of vital and Scriptural Religion without Superstition.

I have sent You one of the Sermons, which I preached at the Opening of the Lutheran Church, for Yourself, and some for the Vestry, which you will give as You think proper. It will shew the constant Union and Harmony, which has subsisted between the Lutherans and Episcopal Church of England. I mean by sending You these Sermons, to strengthen and encrease our Love for one another. The Matter of the Sermon is perhaps too Spiritual for the Generality of Christians, but the Introduction conveys a clear and true Idea of our old and present Inter Community. I pray God may have you in his immediate and favourable Protection and bless you in all Your personal Undertakings, and make You and your Connections perfectly happy, I am
                    Dear Sir,
            Your very affectionate
                humble Servant
                      Richard Peters

Colonel and Doctor Hugh
    Mercer Esquire

                            a Ticket inclosed:
As Colonel Mercer may be absent or at too great a distance to be personally applied to by young Mr: Muylenberg, Mr: Peters has desired he would read the Letter which is not sealed and shew to Mr: Wood, and keep this Memorandum always in the Letter — that, when Colonel Mercer receives the Letter, he may receive this Memorandum with it.
                                    R. Peters.
11 June 1771.

The oldest of eleven children, John Peter Gabriel Muhlenberg was born at Trappe, Pennsylvania, October 1, 1746. He inherited much in disposition and taste from his maternal grandfather, Conrad Weiser, the celebrated Indian agent of the government of Pennsylvania. He grew up, so to speak, with a gun and a fishing rod in his hands. He learned more from nature and from people whom he met than he did from the books he studied as a boy.

When sixteen years of age Peter was sent to Halle, Germany, to attend his father's alma mater, the University of Halle.

With him went his two younger brothers, Frederick Augustus and Henry Ernest. Peter would have none of institutional life, however. After a month he was apprenticed to a grocer-druggist in the city of Lübeck for a period of six years, but three years of such tedium proved more than enough for him. He took French leave and joined a British regiment that was being recruited in Germany and was soon to sail for America for garrison duty. In the few months that he served in the British army—from August 1766 to January 1767—he learned much of value for later years. Upon his arrival home in Philadelphia on January 15, 1767, he was given an honorable discharge.[24]

Following this European escapade Peter settled down to the study of theology. His father's friend and colleague among the Swedish Lutherans of Philadelphia, Provost Charles Magnus Wrangel, pastor of Gloria Dei Lutheran Church (Old Swedes), took him into his home and taught him the fundamentals of Lutheran theology, practical and theoretical. Soon Peter was allowed to preach in outlying congregations. On Good Friday, 1768, he was permitted to preach in St. Michael's Church, Philadelphia, of which his father was pastor.

The name of Peter Muhlenberg first appears on the roll of the Pennsylvania Ministerium in 1769. He had been licensed to serve the three congregations at Bedminster, New Germantown, and Greenwich in New Jersey, but as yet had not been ordained to the office of the ministry. He came to the annual meeting of the Synod with delegates from his churches. Together with one other candidate for ordination he was examined by a duly appointed committee, but neither candidate was ordained. Peter continued his ministry without change of status.

His two brothers returned from Halle in 1770 after seven

years of study there. When the Ministerium met in Reading, Pennsylvania, in October, both brothers were ordained, but Peter continued to be unordained. He had remained in Philadelphia to look after the congregations, as he was then assistant to his father. No satisfactory explanation has ever been handed down as to the reason for this course of action.

Peter pondered his call to Virginia for months, not that there were any imponderable theological obstacles in the way. Had not his father steadily maintained that there were no doctrinal blockades between the two churches? Ordination by the Church of England would be no renunciation of his personal Lutheran convictions, but it would give him the additional right to minister in a full capacity legally in the Colony of Virginia.

Accordingly, Peter left Philadelphia March 2, 1772, arrived at Dover, England, April 10, and was ordained by the Bishop of London in King's Chapel on April 25. He was back in Philadelphia in July and at Woodstock in September 1772.[25]

Thus we have a distinct and singular circumstance in the ecclesiastical history of the Valley of Virginia. Here was a minister doubly equipped for a dual service. By his ordination he was acceptable alike to the Lutherans as to members of the Church of England, and by his knowledge of German and English he could minister to two linguistic groups. He had fulfilled, furthermore, the legal requirements demanded by Virginia authorities.

Ordination in London did not affect his membership in the Ministerium of Pennsylvania. He was commissioned to investigate the condition of the Lutheran congregation in Madison County, shortly after arriving in the Valley. The bulk of his four-year pastorate was connected with the Lutheran side of his call.[26] He preached in vacant churches and school houses over a wide area of Shenandoah and Frederick counties.

When the decision was made to accept command of the Eighth Virginia Regiment and to enter the Revolutionary War as a soldier rather than as chaplain, he withdrew from the ministry. His right to serve as a priest of the

John Peter Gabriel Muhlenberg

Church of England was automatically severed the moment he rebelled against the mother country. While he demitted the office of the ministry of the Lutheran Church and never took it up again, he remained an active and loyal layman of the Lutheran Church, serving the Ministerium of Pennsylvania in various needful ways, and, with the transition from the German to the English language, becoming a charter member of St. John's Lutheran Church in Philadelphia, an English language congregation.

General Muhlenberg died on his 61st birthday, October 1, 1807, and was buried beside his father in the churchyard at Augustus Lutheran Church, Trappe, Pennsylvania, near which he had been born.

Not long before he died he wrote to his fellow church members in Philadelphia: "Brethren, we have been born, baptized and brought up in the Evangelical Lutheran Church.... We wish nothing more than that we and our children and our children's children and all our posterity may remain faithful to this doctrine."[27]

Coincident with Muhlenberg's arrival in Virginia a marked spurt in building activities took place on the unfinished church at Winchester. Additional funds for the purpose were gathered, and men legally certified to solicit and collect subscriptions. Such facts seem to point to a new spirit, a new leadership and a new will to press on with the work. Is it not interesting to conjecture that the credit belongs to Peter Muhlenberg's energetic ministry in the Valley? One can but wish such theorizing were beyond the shadow of a doubt.

A few facts about the church building have been preserved. Both Dr. Krauth and Dr. Gilbert state with assurance that the walls were completed and roofed over in 1772. They base their assertion on findings contained in two more papers discovered by Dr. Krauth in the effects of Miss Nancy Whetzel. One, dated June 5, 1771, granted authority to Christopher Whetzel to collect certain sums of money subscribed by Hon. William Nelson of Yorktown, Virginia, William Byrd, III, of Westover, and George William Fairfax, Esq., "for building a Lutheran Church," to which the signatures of Peter Helfenstein, Jacob Bucher, Thomas Schmidt, Christopher Heiskel, Lewis Hoff and George Laubinger, elders of the congregation, were added. The other bore the date July 27, 1772, and was also signed by the elders, who authorized John Haenli and George Wetzel to "collect funds from the public for completing the Lutheran Church." This second paper, we are told, had annexed to it "a certificate of the

County Clerk, with the county seal attached, testifying to the appointment of John Haenli and George Wetzel as collectors of funds for the purpose above named; and also the certificate of five Justices of the Peace testifying to the same, as well as to the good character of the collectors."[28]

This information becomes the more entertaining in that it reveals the extent of the appeal for funds into eastern Virginia and shows that at least three well-to-do, public spirited members of the Established Church responded with gifts.

Another bit of testimony on the status of the church building in 1775 comes from the Fithian journal already mentioned. Coming south from Martinsburg, as Fithian approached Winchester he noticed the high spire of a church. It was the most striking object on the horizon, so he made note of it and of the hamlet at its feet. "It is a smart Village," he wrote May 22, "near half a mile in length and several Streets broad and pretty full – The situation is low and disagreeable – There is on a pleasant Hill North-East from the Town at a Small Distance, a large stone Dutch-Lutheran Church, with a tall Steeple – In the Town is an English Church – North of the Town are the Ruins of an old Fort wasted and crumbled down by Time."[29]

This is interesting testimony indeed. For it lets us know that when the walls were erected and the church put under roof, the first steeple also was built. This fact has been lost sight of, for Dr. Krauth implies that the steeple erected under Christian Streit's leadership was the original spire to the building. What Philip Fithian saw and reported seems to be conclusive proof that an earlier spire existed.

A new breeze was blowing o'er the land. Men were weary of paying taxes, taxes in the levying of which they had no say – stamp taxes, tea taxes, church taxes. Especially on the frontier where they breathed a cleaner, freer air, the spirit of freedom rose high into the heights. And no frontier in America was more zealously aroused than the Shenandoah Valley. The whole region echoed and re-echoed with a clarion shout: liberty or death![30]

What wonder, when George Washington, trained and matured in the Valley, took the lead; or when men like Daniel Morgan, Adam Stephen, Andrew Lewis, Peter Muhlenberg, Horatio Gates and Charles Lee – all residents of the Valley who became generals in the Continental Army, rallied their men from the Potomac to the Roanoke and led them off to war. Along with Washington, Morgan and Stephen and Lewis had won their spurs in the Indian wars, a type of warfare that proved so deadly to British regulars.

And so, too, had a number of members from the Lutheran congregation. Just how many there were and who they were, no one will ever be able to say, though the names of some have not been lost. Andreas Friedly, one of the founders, served as a doctor to Washington's troops, and Christopher Fry was a non-commissioned officer in Colonel Byrd's regiment in 1756. Peter Helfenstein, another founder, commanded a company under Colonel Adam Stephen in the Dunmore War. Among his men were Peter Lauck and John Grim. John Schultz also fought in the Dunmore War, while Conrad Kremer and John Cooke are listed among those who fought the Indians. Each of these eight names is found in existing church records. The name of another veteran, John Kiger, in all probability a member of the congregation, cannot, however, be substantiated as such. How many more names have been lost by translation into English equivalents, or by euphonic spelling, until their original German is no longer recognizable, can never be said.

The countryside was aroused to a fever pitch of excitement in the summer of 1775 with the departure of Daniel Morgan's Riflemen for Boston. On June 15, General Washington had taken command of the Continental Army. Morgan had been commissioned a captain, ordered to raise a company and proceed to the aid of the commander-in-chief. On July 14 he and his company of ninety-six sharpshooters set out on the famous "bee-line march," arriving at Boston August 7 without the loss of a man. Subsequently, the Morgan company joined in the expedition against Quebec. As a part of the American Army led by Benedict Arnold through the Maine wilderness, it engaged in the attack on the city, an engagement in which a belated juncture with General Montgomery's army first brought a partial success. The first American soldier to scale the walls of Quebec was Charles Porterfield, Frederick County native and 1st Sergeant of Morgan's Company. Montgomery was killed in the attack, Arnold wounded and Morgan, after taking command and winning a temporary triumph, was forced to surrender.

Only sixty-five of the ninety-six Morgan men are known to posterity. The names of six appear in the records of the Lutheran Church: Adam Heiskell, Adam Kurtz, John Schultz, Charles Grim, Peter Lauck and Simon Lauck; while the names of George Heiskell and Frederick Kurtz, believed to be members of the congregation also, do not appear. Another comrade, Jacob Sperry (Spirey) is believed to have been a member of the Reformed congregation. Adam Heiskell was wounded in the assault on Quebec; and Simon Lauck, Frederick Kurtz and George Heiskell escaped capture and eventually returned to Winchester. The other five, Adam Kurtz, Peter Lauck, Sperry, Schultz and Grim, together with Adam Heiskell, were captured and held prisoner for months.

The leader of the Lutherans in the Lower Valley, Pastor Peter Muhlenberg, could not keep silent in the cause of liberty. Nor could he refrain himself, having had a taste of military life, from taking an active part in the contest at arms. There was a time for all things. There was a time to fight. For Peter Muhlenberg that time had come. So it was he cast off his ministerial robe and donned the uniform of Colonel of the Eighth Virginia Regiment.

Peter expressed his inner feelings privately in correspondence to his brother Frederick. He wrote:

> I am a Clergyman it is true but I am a member of Society as well as the poorest Layman, & my Liberty is as dear to me as to any Man, shall I then sit still & enjoy myself at Home when the best Blood of the Continent is spilling? Heaven forbid it .... I am called by my country in its defence — the cause is just and noble — were I a Bishop, even a Lutheran one I should obey without Hesitation, and so far I am from thinking that I act wrong, I am convinced it is my Duty so to do & Duty I owe to God and my country.[31]

It is most unfortunate that no full roster of Muhlenberg's regiment has been saved. Abraham Bowman, grandson of Joist Hite, was appointed Lt. Colonel, Peter Helfenstein, elder in the Winchester Church, Major, and Christian Streit, friend and colleague in the Lutheran ministry, Chaplain. But the rank and file has not been preserved. Here, we feel sure, would be found the names of many more men from the congregation.

The famous sermon for which Muhlenberg is remembered was preached at Woodstock in January 1776. On January 12 he had received his commission as Colonel at Williamsburg. January 21 is the date the sermon is believed to have been delivered. Immediately thereafter recruiting for the "German Regiment" was well under way. Dr. Gilbert has recorded a local tradition, which he considered well founded, to the effect that the famous sermon was preached in a number of the congregations served by the "Fighting Parson," who used it as a rallying cry to enlist men for his regiment. If this be true, then we can well imagine that the congregation in Winchester heard it, too, and that many of the members were moved to action.[32]

Additional members, all of whose names are found in the records, who are known to have served in the Continental forces, were: Henry Baker, as a procurement agent for the commissary department; George Jacob Trautwein, a founder of the church, as surgeon; Philip Helfenstein, lieutenant of militia; Henry William Baker, John Grim and Conrad Kremer. Ensign Peter Heiskell and John Kiger, both veterans of the Revolution, are said to have been members, though there is no documentary evidence.

Another member of the congregation who came to Winchester in 1787 is known to have been a soldier of the conflict, though he fought in the British forces. He was Carl Christopher Edman Aulich. He came from the vicinity of Breslau in Lower Silesia, Germany, and arrived in New York in October, 1780, with his regiment of German troops, better known in American history as Hessians. Remaining with his regiment until April 1783, he went to Baltimore, married Margaret Sloots and four years later settled down in Winchester.

When the Revolution was over, and the uncertain years under the Articles of Confederation past, and life under the Constitution took on its settled way, and men began to live with the memories of unforgettable wartime experiences, those stout hearts from Winchester who had shared the march to, the assault upon, and the captivity of the city of Quebec were drawn together in an informal group. They called themselves The Dutch Mess, a name that had been conferred on their little clique in army days. By their camaraderie and oft repeated tales, they left behind a tradition, which the years have not erased. One by one they fell by the wayside, and with the exception of Adam Heiskell, all were buried in the adjoining Reformed and Lutheran cemeteries. Shortly after the death of the last survivor, John Schultz, a tribute appeared in *The Winchester Virginian* for September 27, 1843, to these men of the Revolution. They won a fitting place in the affections of the community. So too should their place in the annals of the congregation never be forgotten.

> In Memory of the Dutch Mess
>
> The last of the riflemen are gone: – the brave and hardy gallants of this Valley that waded to Canada and stormed Quebec, are all gone – gone too are Morgan's sharp shooters of Saratoga. For a long time two, that shared his captivity in Canada, were seen in this village, wasting away to shadows of their youth, celebrating with enthusiasm the night of their battle, as the year rolled round,—Peter Lauck and John Schultz. But they have answered the roll call of death and have joined their leader; the hardy Lauck wondering that Schultz, the feeblest of the band, whom he had so often carried through the snows of Canada, should outlive him.
>
> There is interest round the last of such a corps. Come step across to that old wooden church over South, – pass by that curiously wrought slab from England...a little to the westward on a white marble upright slab – is the short memorial of one of the six of Morgan's company known during the campaign as the Dutch Mess,[33] — all of whom lived to a great age; and five slept here: — Kurtz and Sperry — a few feet from this grave.
>
> In Memory of John Schultz,
> who departed this life 5th day of November, 1840,
> In the 87th year of his age.

A little to the east lies the other comrade, Grim, who some years since joined the corps in the grave – without a monument. There is no inscription for Peter Lauck, he lies a little farther on – in the rear of the stone church with the steeple, in sight of his residence on that beautiful hill out south, near that tablet that says the man that sleeps beneath was from Mannheim in Germany, more than a century ago – the man that disdained to set a private table for Louis Philippe in the little Village of Winchester, because as he said – none but gentlemen ever stopped at his house, or eat at his table; and turned him from his door for making the request.[34] The sixth one, Heiskell, sleeps in Romney.

What happened to the original spire? In another ten years it had disappeared entirely. The church was but an empty shell without doors or windows when Christian Streit took over in 1785.

Tradition has it that the building was used repeatedly as a barracks during the years of the Revolution. Fires were built within the unfinished edifice, the traces of which upon the blackened walls were plainly discernible on Streit's arrival. All this ties in with the fact that Winchester was the center for the entire surrounding area for recruiting and enlistment. Soldiers about to set off for war must have been quartered in the church before their departure. In this way, no doubt, the building suffered abuse, the ground timbers of the steeple being damaged and weakened to the point where it became necessary to remove the entire spire. It is sad to relate but true that churches in the zones of conflict in eastern Pennsylvania frequently suffered as great damage from American occupation as from British. From want of other specific evidence to the contrary, such seems to have been the case at Winchester, where no British invasion occurred.

Following the destruction of the stone church by fire in 1854, persons to whom the old building was dear sought to preserve the memory of its appearance by sketching its ruins and reconstructing its lines. One drawing that has been found is of the roofless ruins, when north wall, south wall and west wall were still standing also. Another clearly is an attempt to reconstruct the building from fond recollection, but all conspicuous external details have been remembered. Both drawings are at pains to show one thing: in the north wall, above the top level of the balcony windows, there is a circular stone not far below the apex of the triangle made with the roof. This stone, according to the sketches, bore the date 1779.

However one interprets the foregoing date, these facts stand incontrovertible: the foundations were laid when the French and Indian War brought terror to the frontier. The walls were finally completed, the steeple built and the roof put on when the Revolutionary War was raging. Surely the foundations were laid by the grace of God; and by the same sustaining grace of God the walls and spire were reared.

Endnotes – Chapter IV

[1] *The Journals of Henry Melchoir Muhlenberg,* 3 volumes, translated by Theodore G. Tappert and John W. Doberstein (Philadelphia: Muhlenberg Press, 1942-1948) I, 578. Hereafter cited as *JHMM.*

[2] From *A Discourse Suggested by the Burning of the Old Lutheran Church, on the Night of September 27th, 1854, Delivered in the Evangelical Lutheran Church, Winchester, Virginia, the nineteenth Sunday after Trinity, 1854,* by Charles Porterfield Krauth (Winchester, Va.: Printed at the Republican Office, 1855), 9.

[3] *JHMM,* I, 683.

[4] From family records in the possession of the Rev. Roy C. Helfenstein, Richmond, Virginia.

[5] Krauth, *Burning of the Old Lutheran Church,* 11.

[6] *JHMM,* I, 533.

[7] *JHMM,* II, 367.

[8] Ibid., II, 367-368.

[9] Ibid., II, 410.

[10] D.M. Gilbert, *The Praises of the Lord in the Story of Our Fathers: A Historical Discourse* (New Market, Va.: Henkel & Co., 1877).

[11] A.R. Wentz, *History of the Evangelical Church of Frederick, Maryland, 1738-1938* (Harrisburg, Pa.: The Congregation, 1910), 159.

[12] *Philip Vickers Fithian: Journal, 1775-1776*, edited by R.G. Albion and Leonidas Dodson (Princeton, N.J.: Princeton University Press, 1934), 16.

[13] H.H. Heins, *Throughout All the Years: The Bicentennial Story of Hartwick in America, 1746-1946* (Oneonta, N.Y.: Trustees of Hartwick College, 1946).

[14] Zion Lutheran Church Archives, Baltimore, Maryland, 10.

[15] *Documentary History of the Evangelical Lutheran Ministerium of Pennsylvania and Adjacent States, Proceeding of the Annual Conventions from 1748 to 1821* (Philadelphia: Board of Publication of the General Council of the Evangelical Lutheran Church in North America, 1898), 112, 114-115.

[16] From "Journal of Jacob Franck," Archives of Krauth Memorial Library, Lutheran Theological Seminary, Philadelphia, Pennsylvania. [Cited in 1954 by Eisenberg, this journal cannot at this time be located within the holdings of the archives. It also does not appear to have ever been published. Its whereabouts is unknown.]

[17] Frederic Morton, *The Story of Winchester in Virginia* (Strasburg, Va.: Shenandoah Publishing House, 1925), 268.

[18] W.P. Huddle, *History of the Hebron Lutheran Church, Madison County, Virginia, from 1717 to 1907* (New Market, Va.: Henkel & Co., 1908).

[19] *Documentary History*, 101.

[20] Ibid., 102.

[21] D.M. Gilbert, *Muhlenberg's Ministry in Virginia: A Chapter of Colonial, Luthero-Episcopal History: An Address Delivered at the Laying of the Corner-Stone of Emanuel Evangelical Lutheran Church,Woodstock, Virginia, Friday, August 8th, 1884* (Gettysburg, Pa.: J.E. Wible, 1884).

[22] Archives, Krauth Memorial Library.

[23] Ibid.

[24] Paul A.W. Wallace, *The Muhlenbergs of Pennsylvania* (Philadelphia: University of Pennsylvania Press, 1950), especially chapter VIII.

[25] Ibid., 80-82.

[26] Four organized congregations of Lutherans existed in Dunmore (Shenandoah) County when Peter Muhlenberg was pastor there: Strasburg, New Market, Woodstock and Pine Church, located west of Mt. Jackson. The county today has 27 Lutheran congregations with 3,000 communicants. The Episcopal Church has two congregations

in the county: Emmanuel Church, in Woodstock, with 49 communicants, and St. Andrews Church, in Mt. Jackson, with 27 communicants. These figures are for the year 1952.

[27] C.W. Cassell, W.J. Finck, and Elon O. Henkel, *History of the Lutheran Church in Virginia and East Tennessee* (Strasburg, Va.: for the Lutheran Synod of Virginia, Shenandoah Publishing Company, 1930), 48.

[28] Both documents were copied into the minutes of the Church Council, September 1, 1851.

[29] Albion and Dodson, *Philip Vickers Fithian Journal*, 13.

[30] Freeman H. Hart, *The Valley of Virginia in the American Revolution, 1763-1789* (Chapel Hill, N.C.: University of North Carolina Press, 1942).

[31] Wallace, *The Muhlenbergs of Pennsylvania*, 120-121.

[32] Gilbert, *Muhlenberg's Ministry in Virginia*, note, 20.

[33] The Dutch Mess consisted of Adam Heiskel, Charles Grim, Jacob Sperry, Peter Lauck and John Schultz, all of Winchester.

[34] The reference is to Philip Bush, a Winchester tavern keeper. See: *What I Know About Winchester, Recollections of William Greenway Russell, 1800-1891,* reprinted from *The Winchester News* by the Winchester-Frederick County Historical Society, edited by G.R. Quarles and L.N. Barton (Staunton, Va.: The McClure Publishing Co., 1953), 104.

Chapter V
The Enduring Work of Christian Streit

It was a twenty-five year wait for the Lutherans of Winchester before an ordained pastor came to settle down in their midst and dwell among them. It was one of those providential waitings, when men seem so impatient, and God seems to be so slow. But in His own way and wisdom He was preparing for them better things than they could have hoped or dreamed.

The coming of Christian Streit in the summer of 1785 brought the dawning of a new day. Grandson of the Palatine immigrant who had landed on the shores of the Hudson seventy-five years earlier, he had been born and educated in this country, he was at home in both the German and English languages, he had espoused the cause of American independence, he had already served congregations in New Jersey, Pennsylvania, South Carolina and Pennsylvania again, and he was in the prime of life at thirty-six years of age. He was, furthermore, a protégé of Henry Melchoir Muhlenberg, whose journals have preserved many vital facts concerning him, and a lifelong friend of the three Muhlenberg brothers, Peter, Frederick and Henry Ernest. His Lutheranism was part and parcel of the Muhlenberg tradition.

The Streit home in the Raritan Valley of New Jersey is believed to have been located in Bridgewater Township of Somerset County. Christian Streit, the pioneer,[a] had come with his family to this new location from the vicinity of Hackensack about 1735.

---

[a] Johann Christian Streit was born March 24, 1672, in Kirberg, Germany. For a discussion of the Streit family, see: Henry Z. Jones, *The Palatine Families of New York*, (Universal City, Ca.: H.Z. Jones, 1985), 1011-1014.

A son, John Leonard, had been born to him and his wife, Anna Ursula,[b] at Ramapo [Remerbach] July 28, 1720.[1] The boy was baptized less than a month later, on August 21, by Dominie Justus Falckner, who faithfully ministered to Lutherans of the Hudson Valley and northern New Jersey. A brother of Daniel Falckner who had given his name to Falkner's Swamp, Pennsylvania, Justus had the distinction of being the first Lutheran clergyman ordained to the ministry in America. A German by birth, he was ordained by Swedish Lutherans in Gloria Dei Church, Philadelphia, November 24, 1703, in order that he might serve the Dutch Lutherans of the Colony of New York. The coming of the Palatines added alike to his opportunities and responsibilities. He made it his business to follow up those who settled in Jersey and to care for their spiritual needs.[2]

In due time John Leonard Streit married, and his son, Christian, about whom this narrative is greatly concerned, was born at the family place in Somerset County, June 7, 1749.

The family were members of St. Paul's Lutheran Church, also called Pluckemin Church, but no longer in existence, located near Bedminster.[3] Leonard Streit was a member of the Church Council. There was difficulty in the congregation during the summer of 1753, so he drove his farm wagon to the Muhlenberg home in Pennsylvania and brought Henry Melchoir back with him. On this occasion, we may well believe, four-year-old Christian had the first glimpse of the famous personality who was to have so large an influence on the course of his life. This was the beginning of a warm friendship between the Streits and Muhlenbergs, and subsequently the Streit home shared its hospitality on numerous occasions with the visiting pastor from Pennsylvania.

---

[b] She was his third wife. Jones, *Palatine Families*, 1014.

With the magnetism of such an influence to encourage him, it is not surprising that young Streit should go to Philadelphia to study at the Academy and College. From this institution, which was to become the University of Pennsylvania, he graduated with distinction in the class of 1768. Three years later he was made a Master of Arts by the same school. Did Muhlenberg assist him to meet the financial obligations of his education? This question cannot be answered with a positive affirmative, but the following entry from Muhlenberg's journal for April 23, 1770, would seem to indicate it: "Paid to the Rev. Richard Peters, in the presence of his servant, £2 current, which I had subscribed in behalf of Christain Streit."[4] The above-mentioned Church of England rector was intimately associated with Dr. William Smith, rector of the Academy, who also had received Anglican orders.

Christian Streit

Muhlenberg, furthermore, arranged with his friend and colleague, Charles Mangus Wrangel, the Swedish pastor, to take Streit into his home for theological training. This was at the time that Peter Muhlenberg was likewise preparing for the ministry, and Dr. Wrangel gave to Christian the assignment of tutoring Peter in Latin and Greek.[5] There was a third student also, Daniel Kuhn, son of a Lancaster, Pennsylvania, physician. The three students were soon given opportunity to deliver "memorized catechetical discourses" in nearby congregations, preaching in the English language.

When the Synod met at New Hanover Church in November 1768, joining in the dedication of a new church building, for the sake of the English people present both Streit and Kuhn made short addresses. Christian "spoke briefly, edifyingly and concisely on Exodus 20:24: 'In all places where I record my name I will come unto thee and I will bless thee'."[6] And the next June, when Zion Church, Philadelphia, was dedicated, Kuhn, Streit and Peter Muhlenberg marched in procession and, together with other pastors, shared in the special prayers of the occasion.[7]

Soon these ministerial candidates were licensed for work in specific fields. From 1769-1770 Christian Streit and Peter Muhlenberg served alternately in the three congregations of Greenwich, Easton and Wilhelms (or Lower Saccona) Township on both sides of the Delaware in the vicinity of Easton, Pennsylvania.[8]

October 25, 1770, Streit was ordained by the Ministerium in session at Reading.[9] At the same time Frederick Augustus Muhlenberg, the future first Speaker of the United States House of Representatives, and his brother Henry Ernest Muhlenberg, future Lancaster pastor, first president of Franklin and Marshall College, and famous botanist, both of whom had recently returned from Europe, and John George Young were also set apart for the office of the ministry. Streit continued to serve the congregations in and around Easton. In 1772 we read that "certain small English congregations" in that area petitioned to be included in his ministrations.[10] When on March 20, 1776, he conferred with Henry Melchoir Muhlenberg about an army chaplaincy in Virginia, he was then pastor of four congregations – Easton, Greenwich, Wilhelms Township and Trucken Land [Dryland].[11]

That Christian Streit was a "natural" selection by Peter Muhlenberg for the chaplaincy of the Eighth Virginia [German] Regiment now seems fairly obvious. He would not leave his parish, however, until arrangements for its care had been completed. At the time he consulted his spiritual father he seemed disposed to accept, provided his four congregations would release him and another preacher be put in his place. But it was not until July 19 that he wrote Henry M. Muhlenberg making official announcement of his acceptance and requesting care for his churches.[12]

Old Father Muhlenberg at his home at Trappe began to write letters for Christian to deliver. There was one to his son Peter with his regiment in the deep south; another to his son-in-law Francis Swaine, with Peter in the army; a third to Hannah, his daughter-in-law, Peter's wife, at Woodstock; and a fourth to his daughter Maria, Mrs. Swaine, who was staying with Hannah. Christian finally arrived on August 23 and departed for Virginia the same day. Because he had no pass, and since it was a critical matter to travel under the existing conditions, in addition to the letters, he carried also the following lines:

> Whereas Bearer of these the Rev^d Mr. Christian Stright has received and accepted a call to be chaplain for the 8th Regiment of Regulars of the State of Virginia, and on his Journey to move there; these are therefore to certify that the said Revd Gentle man is a regularly ordained Minister of the Gospel, sound in Protestant Principles and sober in life, desirous and virtuous to promote the Glory of God and Wellfare of the State, and therefore recommended to all Friends and Wellwishers of Religion and State:
> per Heinrich Muhlenberg
> Senior Minister and President of the
> German Lutheran Ministry in
> the State of Pennsylvania
> Philadelphia, August 23, 1776.[13]

The next we hear of Christian Streit is on April 19, 1777. Accompanied by Adjutant and Mrs. Swaine he arrived from Virginia at the Muhlenberg house at Trappe. The question at once arises: where had he been in the meantime?

The military records in the files of the War Department give but little help. They reveal that Streit received his appointment as Chaplain of the Eighth Virginia on August 1, 1776, and that his name appears for the last time on a muster roll for July 1777, dated August 5.[14] Apart from defining his period of service, they tell nothing else. The story has to be assembled from other sources.

Let us then look next at the record of the Eighth Virginia Regiment. For two months Col. Peter Muhlenberg drilled the recruits he had enlisted. On March 21, 1776, they left the Valley, uniformed with hunting shirts and leggings, for Suffolk. Here the regiment remained until British forces threatened Charleston, South Carolina, and having been summoned to defend that city by General Charles Lee, it arrived June 23, in time for the sharp action against Fort Moultrie on July 28.

General Lee selected the Eighth Virginia for reasons he himself noted: "It was the strength and good condition of the regiment that induced me to order it out of its own province in preference to any other." Lee considered it the most complete regiment to be found, as well as "the best armed, clothed, and equipped for immediate service." Its arrival at Charleston, he said, "made us very strong." At the attack on Fort Moultrie, on Sullivan's Island, it was sent to reinforce Colonel Thompson's, which was trying to prevent the enemy from getting onto the island behind Fort Moultrie and thus attacking from the rear. A brilliant defense repulsed the British with vigor, and Lee reported officially: "I know not which corps I have the greatest reason to be pleased with, Muhlenberg's Virginians or the North Carolina Troops; they are both equally alert, zealous, and spirited."[15]

This success and reputation the Eighth Virginia had won at Fort Moultrie were followed, alas, by misfortunes. The regiment was ordered to Savannah with an expedition intended to destroy an enemy outpost on the St. Mary's River and to overawe the restless Indians of Florida. Neither objective was attained. Two months at Savannah in the middle of summer, without suitable equipment or adequate medical supplies, was an experience the hardy constitutions of the Valley men could not withstand. They fell prey to swamp fever. The health and morale of officers and men suffered sadly. Many were buried in unmarked Georgia graves. Others deserted. The regiment disintegrated. Peter Helfenstein made it home by the hardest and died a year or more after from the effects. Peter Muhlenberg contracted a disease of the liver which troubled him the rest of his days and finally caused his death.

By December 20, 1776, Peter Muhlenberg was back in Virginia. He was now instructed to bring his decimated regiment up to full strength and to send each company, as ranks were filled, on to Washington's camp at Morristown, New Jersey.[16] Promoted to the rank of brigadier general on February 21, 1777, he remained in Virginia long enough to restore order to the Virginia Line, reporting in April to General Washington. April 13 the First, Fifth, Ninth and Thirteenth Virginia Regiments were assigned to his brigade, to which the Eighth was added later. His instructions were to make ready at once to take the field. In pursuance of his orders he returned to Virginia.[17]

Quite naturally one wonders where and when Chaplain Streit caught up with his regiment. Did he go on to South Carolina and Georgia in the late summer of '76? We regret that these questions cannot be answered, though one is tempted to think that he went in search of his regiment until he found it.

This we know, however. April 20, 1777, the *Journal* records: "Magister Streit preached in Augustus Church [Trappe] on Romans 8:18, 'For I reckon that the sufferings of this present time are not worthy,' etc. I acted as cantor and played the organ. The rest of the day we spent in conversation and intermittent singing of edifying hymns."

Since General Muhlenberg's Brigade was in training at Morristown, not far from Bedminster, we may readily assume that the chaplain of the Eighth Virginia was a frequent visitor at his nearby home. Had he, on August 24, been a part of the grand parade of the American Army as it passed through Philadelphia? Muhlenberg's brigade had been chosen by Washington as the vanguard of this notable procession. Or had he been at Brandywine on September 11, attending the wounded and burying the dead? Here again we do not know. We hear nothing further from him until four days after Brandywine. A heavy rainstorm had visited Trappe that evening. "Late at night," the *Journal* reports, "the Chaplain, Magister Streit, arrived, bringing to a total of eighteen the souls who spent the night in this building." While the entry for September 21 states: "Yesterday Magister Streit took leave of us and rode to the Army." October 7, Streit and "his brother from the camp" visited at Trappe, on which occasion Christian told of his plans to go to Charleston, South Carolina, and on October 9 the two brothers called again. When news of the surrender of Burgoyne [October 14] became known, Christian came to Trappe on the twentieth from New Hanover to see if the British had left Philadelphia, and three days later he stopped by for various communications to friends in the south as he began his journey.

There was a letter for Pastor Jacob Franck of old Hebron

Church, Madison; memoranda for the congregations at Savannah and Ebenezer, Georgia; a letter for John Adam Treutlen, the governor of Georgia; a note for David Zubly and his sister, Madam Baart, near Savannah, concerning 39 dollars worth of medicine that Muhlenberg had furnished them; and a letter for a Mr. Kaltheisen in Charleston, in which Mrs. Muhlenberg had enclosed twenty-seven dollars for some linen.

To the letter for the governor of Georgia, Muhlenberg appended the following postscript:

> Bearer of these is the Rev^d Mr. Christian Streit, who has served as Minister several years in some of our United Luth. Congregations, and the last time as Chaplain in the 9th Reg. of Virg. and being desired to officiate in the german congregation at Charlestown, he intends to move there, and this gave me opportunity to commit unto him this Letter, being of humble Opinion it might not be amiss, if he should step over from Charlestown to Savanna and Eben Ezer in order to visit our Flocks, in case they should be quite destitute of a Lutheran Minister. If he should come there, I would humbly recommend him to Your Excellency's protection, as long as he behaveth accordingly as he has done here.[18]

It will be observed that Muhlenberg speaks of Streit as chaplain of the 9th Virginia Regiment. As no record has been found connecting Streit with this regiment, it is presumed that Muhlenberg was in error. It should be noted also that Streit's removal to Charleston was without an official call from the congregation there. If he had gone to Carolina to join his regiment, he no doubt made personal contacts with the church, or, Peter Muhlenberg could have put in a word for him and brought an invitation to him. Howe'er it was, the congregation soon after his arrival requested him to become their minister, and he accepted. This he reported to Father Muhlenberg in a letter of January 9, 1778.[19]

The Charleston church was in a state of transition from German to English. The members were eager for Streit's services because he could preach in English.

The next we hear of Christian is May 30. Frederick Muhlenberg visited his parents that day and turned over to them 66 dollars that Streit had sent to him by his brother to be forwarded. Thirty-nine dollars was in payment of the medicines, while the balance was a refund to Mrs. Muhlenberg of the money for the linen unobtainable in Charleston.[20]

Muhlenberg received a second letter June 15, which was dated March 27.[21] Streit had just retuned from Ebenezer where he had stayed a fortnight, preached seven times in Ebenezer and Goshen, administered Holy Communion to 150 at Ebenezer and 40 at Goshen and reported on the state of affairs ecclesiastical in general, though no mention of Governor Treutlen is made.

Another letter reached Muhlenberg November 17, 1779. It has been preserved and is given here in full because of its general interest.[22] It tells of the war in the south, of Mr. Treutlen's adversities, of the state of religion, and mentions various friends and acquaintances. Meanwhile Savannah had been captured in December 1778.

Charlestown Sept. 27th, 1779

Rev[d] and dear Sir! I received your two letters, the one with the Letters for Eben Ezer a short Space of time after one another, about the latter End of April and the Beginning of May. The Letters to Georgia, I could not safely transmit, till about ten Days ago, when our People had retaken Ebenezer from the Enemy. And the sad Disorders there and here during the last Summer have prevented me both from obtaining good Intelligence concerning the State of that Congregation and from writing to you sooner. I will give such as I have received, but can not yet say any thing certain as to their present Situation since we have again got in Possession of the Place. Mr: Treutlen late Governor of Georgia, having been obliged to fly from the Enemy into this State, with the Loss of Abundance of his Furniture, Negroes, Stock, etc: came to Charlestown some-time before the Incursion of the Enemy into this State in order to get a House for his Family, informed me, that Mr: Triebner,[23] since the British Troops came to Savannah, had got Possession of the Church again in the Town, had taken upon him the Right of absolving the most of the Members from their Allegiance to the United States, and brought them to Colonel Campbell to swear to the King; but that he had been afterwards turned out of the Church again, by its being converted into a Hospital, and on Account of some little Impertinencies he had offer'd to some of the Officers. I was also informed by a Prisoner taken with some others by the Heroic Sergeant Jasper, who has done many Exploits here, at Ebenezer Mill, that that worthy pious Lady Mrs Rabenhorst[24] was departed this Life. She is gone to a Place of everlasting Peace and Rest, where no British Soldiers will come to disturb her felicities ———— , This is all I can at present inform you concerning Ebenezer, only that they have never given any Call to Mr: Daser,[25] which you was desirous to know about in your last Letter, ———— Concerning the Congregation which I attend, I can say but little, only that the Members seem to be as yet well enough satisfied with their present Pastor, and are generally well united, I believe they are pretty unanimously attached to me, but I perceive a very remarkable Coldness and Indifference in them as to religious Matters. Their Minds and Words, Actions and Labors are so much employed in this grievous War, that they become neglectful of the Word and Worship of God. They have so much to do with fighting, that they think but little of praying. It seems to me, that Neglect of Religion and Corruption of Morals have encreased, in Proportion to the Chastisements we have met with from a Sin hating God. Here we may apply the Passages of Scripture Jerem: 5, 3 etc. Isa: 1, 5. which I believe is the Case in a great many more Places on the Continent besides Charlestown. But the Mercies of God are as little regarded by us as his Corrections, in this Place in Particular. He has displayed his Mercy even in the Midst of his Indignation. He permitted the cruel Foe to ravage thro' a Space of 100 Miles in this State, and even to approach within Sight of this Town, and to the Praise of his gracious Providence, they were obliged to return again without ever making an Attempt upon the City.

This Heritage

> We were however again brought to a very dangerous and Alarmming Situation by the Enemies being determin'd, as soon as they could obtain Reinforcement to make an other Tryal, and unless God Almighty had sent the French Fleet to prevent them, I verily believe they would have effected their Designs, for we are exceeding weak, altho' we have about 1500 Men, yet in the greatest Danger, we can scarcely collect one third of them—You expressed your affectionate Regard in your Letter towards several worthy Members of my Congregation and was desirous to hear of them: Mr: Kaltheisen has been gone from here with Commodore Gillo to France for upwards of a twelve Month. Mr: Kimmel has been very unfortunate in having his House burn'd down last Winter. Mr: and Mrs Werly are very well and desire to be remembered to you. My Spouse and I, and a little Son, with whom we have lately been blessed, are very well. And we unite our affectionate Regard to you and Mrs Muhlenberg, Miss Sally etc. etc;
> I am your most obedient humble Servant
> Christian Streight.

The war in the south continued to go badly for the American cause. General Lincoln, in charge of the defense of Charleston, was forced to surrender the place in May 1780. Though living in a captive city, Streit managed to get a letter through to Mr. Muhlenberg, who received it January 11, 1781. He tells of his difficult straits, how virulent fever had raged in the city the fall preceding, and how he would like to get away, but cannot. To which Muhlenberg makes the significant comment, "The inhabitants are being chastened with scorpions."[26]

By the summer of 1782 Streit had left Charleston and come north to Pennsylvania, where we find him as pastor of New Hanover Church.[c] The British had released him in an exchange

---

[c] Since the publication of *This Heritage* in 1954, several additional items concerning the Streit family have come to light. One is that the Winchester congregation approached Christian Streit to become pastor as early as 1782 when he returned north from a pastorate in Charleston, South Carolina. Church Bulletin, Grace Evangelical Lutheran Church, July 23, 1961.

of prisoners, it is said, for they continued to hold the city until December. Mrs. Streit and the little son, John Melchoir, were both ill when they arrived at Falkner's Swamp. Maria Muhlenberg Swaine was then living there, so she took them into her home and cared for them. The boy died a few weeks later, and his mother, whose maiden name was Anna Margaret Christina Elizabeth Hoff, was buried August 20 at the age of 22 years, 6 months and 2 weeks.[27] Streit remarried the following February. On the nineteenth he was united in marriage to Miss Salome Graef of Philadelphia.

The deprivations of war in a fever-ridden coastal city apparently left their effects upon Streit also. Throughout the summer he complained of delirium and in October and November Muhlenberg mentions his illness several times. The patient resorted to an old army remedy displeasing to his faithful friend and adviser. With a fatherly concern, and true to his calling, Muhlenberg tells us that on July 28 "I sent an admonitory letter to Magister Streit because I had heard to my sorrow that his deliriums were caused by heavy drinking." That Streit took no offense is evidenced by visits to the Trappe on August 14 and again on August 16 as he journeyed to and from Philadelphia.[28]

The New Hanover parish comprised four congregations. New Hanover itself was the principal church and the other three were outparishes. In writing to Dr. Wrangel, who had returned to Sweden, and wanted up-to-date information on the German Lutheran churches for a history he was preparing, Henry Muhlenberg informed his friend about the state of the church in Pennsylvania and how it had fared during the Revolution. He went to considerable length and detail, and so we find the following interesting paragraph in reference to Streit.

> [October 22-23, 1784.] I was obliged to serve the vacant congregation in New Hanover, from Providence [Trappe] for a couple of years, despite the great burden and my weakness until, after the war, your former pupil, Mr. Christian Streit, came to us with his sick wife from the purgatory of South Carolina, relieved me, and has up to this time continued to serve the congregation in New Hanover, the Oley Hills, near Molatton and New Store in the German and English languages.

By this time a new breeze was blowing from the south. The congregations at Winchester, Strasburg and Woodstock had sent urgent petitions to the meeting of the Ministerium in June at Lancaster asking for a minister. "They are numerous and well able to support a preacher," the minutes recorded, "and it is to be desired that they may be cared for, because then many surrounding districts, which are full of neglected Lutherans, may find some help and refuge."[29] Whether Streit, who was in attendance, was approached on the matter, or not, we cannot say.

At New Hanover, however, things were not going too well. Streit was becoming dissatisfied. The congregations were not providing for his physical support according to their promise. He talked matters over with Father Muhlenberg on September 28, on a visit with his wife to Trappe, and again in early October when both Mr. and Mrs. Muhlenberg repaid with a visit to New Hanover. In November General Peter reported to his father that Matthias Zehring, to whom he had sold his Woodstock home a year previous, had stopped by to say that on his journey from Virginia he had passed Pastor Streit on his way to Virginia on a prospecting trip.[30] Before the year was out the call to Winchester had been issued and received.

Father Muhlenberg did not lend much encouragement to his young colleague. He himself had declined to go to Virginia in 1777. The year before, he had left his Philadelphia home for a safe place in the country, only to find himself but a stone's throw from Valley Forge in the very midst of military operations and in the no man's land between contending armies. Under such circumstances Peter offered to take his parents to his Woodstock residence where they would be far removed from the theatre of war, but they declined. When, therefore, on April 12, 1785, Muhlenberg tells us that Christian came to see him to confer about his projected transfer to Winchester, that he had advised him to postpone his answer until the next ministerial conference in June, by which time "perhaps divine providence will make things clearer than they are now," we cannot help but conclude that Muhlenberg was not heartily in favor of the move, and that Streit was still undecided. No indication is given as to what effect, if any, the meeting of Synod of May had upon the decision.[d]

What matters most is that Divine Providence did make things clear to Christian Streit. He arrived in Winchester Monday, July 19, 1785, and immediately entered upon the work of the parish.

The new pastor came to a congregation sorely in need of leadership. The church building, never finished and badly damaged during the Revolution by the abuse of occupying troops, was in a sad state of repair and unused by the congregation, necessitating the holding of services in the adjacent

---

[d] A sister of Christian Streit became the wife of the Reverend John George Young, Lutheran pastor at Hagerstown, Maryland, during the 1780s and 1790s. When she moved to Maryland with her husband, her father, Leonhard Streit, moved with them from his New Jersey home. The fact, therefore, that Christian Streit had a father and a sister living in Hagerstown was an added reason that he should give favorable consideration to the call that came to him in 1785 from Winchester. Church Bulletin, Grace Evangelical Lutheran Church, July 23, 1961.

Reformed log church. The school house, however, seems to have been in usable condition and was the place of occasional meetings also.

Streit began keeping a diary the day he arrived in Winchester [See Appendix B]. He kept it fairly systematically for over three years, until November 28, 1788, to be exact. As a valuable source of information, it chiefly records pastoral acts with an occasional extra item thrown in. During the period of time that it covers, it accounts for (according to Dr. Gilbert's tabulation) 386 sermons, 429 baptisms, 163 confirmations, 157 marriages and 43 funerals. Twenty-five administrations of the Lord's Supper are reported. There are also the names of church officers elected and several lists of communicants.[31]

The diary gives a clear picture of the extent of the parish as it then existed. Winchester, Newtown (Stephens City), Steinkirche (Stone Chapel, Clarke County) and Stovertown (Strasburg) were the original congregations served. Winchester as the principal congregation had more frequent services than the others, which were the outparishes. One Sunday a month both a morning and an afternoon service would be held at Winchester, one in German, the other in English. Another Sunday the morning service would be held at Newtown and the afternoon service at Stovertown. These services were usually in German. Occasionally they were followed immediately by English services. A third Sunday would call for services at Winchester in the morning and Steinkirche in the afternoon, and a fourth Sunday would schedule a morning service either at Newtown or Steinkirche with the afternoon service at Winchester. Winchester then had four services a month while Steinkirche and Newtown each had two, and Stovertown one. Stovertown, however, had the services of Simon Harr, schoolmaster and catechist, who likewise conducted worship.

Gradually the congregations at Pine Hills (southeast of Stephens City near Nineveh) and Old Furnace (St. John's Church, Mt. Williams) were added to the circuit as regular preaching points, while on fifth Sundays perhaps, or on special invitation, Streit preached at the Trap Hill Meeting House near Battletown (Berryville), at Captain Slater's home (believed to be in the western part of Frederick County), at Mr. Horn's and Mr. Millschlagel's on the Cacapon River, at deMauz's (probably duMas, northwest of Gerrardstown), at Warm Springs (the present Green Spring near White Hall) and at the "Methodist Meeting near Hart's." He made three trips to Madison County for communion services, visited Pine Church in Shenandoah County, Peaked Mountain and Rader's in Rockingham, in addition to three journeys to Philadelphia, one to Lancaster and one to Hagerstown and Funkstown. In the years covered by the diary, Streit preached at Winchester 156 times; 58 at Steinkirche; 52 at Newtown; 26 at Strasburg; 28 at Old Furnace; 26 at Pine Hills; 6 at Cacapon; 4 at Warm Springs; and 30 at various places in Virginia, Maryland and Pennsylvania.

William Streit accompanied his brother's family to Winchester where he soon became the teacher of the German school. That his conduct of the school was the subject of criticism by some, the diary specifically states, and Christian loyally came to his defense. When on October 25, 1785, William married Rosannah Smith, his brother performed the ceremony. The following year Christian baptized Brother Will's child, and two years later he baptized William's second son, named William, whose father, the diary reports, had died but a few weeks before. Subsequently, Christian performed the ceremony for his sister-in-law when she took a second husband and married Casper Seever.

Christian himself conducted a Latin school, begun September 7, 1785, with three pupils while his brother ran the German school. A few weeks later a fourth pupil, Mr. May's son, enrolled. This venture seems to have been in competition with the previously established Grammar school which a little later was to become the Winchester Academy, for on June 6, 1786, Streit tells how he made a proposal to the Trustees of the Grammar School, which was taken as a "high affront," and a "great noise" resulted. "I was not a little exposed by my enemies," which fact made him the more watchful and zealous. How long this Latin school continued to operate we do not know. Streit was later associated with the Rev. William Hill, Presbyterian minister, in conducting a female seminary, and his daughter, Evelina Streit, likewise conducted school in the 1830s.

Another phase of Streit's teaching, which was of especial importance to the Lutheran Church in Virginia, was the theological preparation and assistance he gave first to Paul Henkel and then to William Carpenter from Madison County. This latter young man was taken into the Streit home to live while he applied himself to the queen of the sciences. In a day before any theological seminary had been established by the Lutherans, this was the accepted practice, similar to that in the legal profession before the establishment of law schools. That Streit was deemed a worthy teacher is attested to by the fact that in 1804 the Ministerium of Pennsylvania appointed him to be an approved and recognized "teacher for the instruction of young preachers."[32]

Soon after coming to Winchester Streit purchased a home that had been the property of General Daniel Morgan. Morgan in turn had bought of Philip Bush. Located on the west side of Cameron Street, the stone house and three adjacent parcels of land were conveyed to Streit February 5, 1787, for a consideration of 566 pounds.[33] Here the family resided. As it grew in numbers a stone addition was erected to provide needed accommodations.

Mrs. Streit, however, was not to enjoy her new home many months. A daughter, her third child, born December 16, died eleven days later, and the mother soon followed on January 6, 1788.[e] Her funeral two days later was conducted by Alexander Balmain, the Episcopal rector.[f] The grief of the bereaved husband is recorded in the diary. Salome's first child, a daughter, also had died in infancy, while Jacob her second, was an infant in arms when the move to Virginia was made.

Christian married again October 15, 1789. His friend, Mr. Balmain, officiated when he took Susannah Barr to be his third wife. To this union twelve children were born.

The first major project in the life of the Winchester congregation to engage Streit's attention was the restoration of the church to usability. He tells us how he called the members of the Council together less than two months after his arrival, how at that time (September 14) it was agreed that new shutters and doors should be made by "private persons, two or three joining together to make one door or window, to

---

[e] Leonard Streit's first visit to his son at New Hanover, Pennsylvania, was on the occasion of the funeral of Christian Streit's first wife. By coincidence, he made the long journey from Maryland and arrived on the day of his daughter-in-law's funeral. Church Bulletin, Grace Evangelical Church, July 23, 1961.

[f] A personal friend of Streit, Alexander Balmain had been born in Scotland in 1741 and served as a chaplain in the Revolutionary War. He was associated with the first Episcopal church in Winchester and was rector of Augusta and Frederick parishes. He died in Winchester in 1821.

*The Christian Streit Home
41-43 S. Cameron Street*

be done this fall that we might keep service in it." A scheme to obtain money was also decided upon, a plan abhorrent to sensitive souls, since the church has long since repudiated it as a means of raising funds, though at the time it was not uncommonly employed. A lottery was authorized by the Council and legal permission for it sought from the State Legislature.

The petition, here given in full, reveals among other things the near financial ruin that almost overwhelmed the colonies during the post-Revolutionary years prior to the adoption of the Constitution.[34]

To the Hon[ble] the Speaker and house of Delegates of the State of Virginia —
The Petition of the Minister and Elders of the German

Lutheran Church in the borough of Winchester, humbly representeth:

That your Petitioners previous to the commencement of the late War raised by Subscription a Sum of Money sufficient to erect the Walls and cover in a commodious Church for the purpose of divine Worship. — That the non-importation of materials, and the distresses naturally arising from a State of War, rendered it altogether impossible for them to raise the necessary Sums for compleating the Work, which has stood in an unfinished State to this day. — Your Petitioners beg leave further to represent to the Hon[ble] House, that their Society being small and all of them being devoted to the service of this Country, and steady adherents to the Liberty of it, were mostly great Sufferers by the depreciation of the Paper Currency, which with other Losses occasioned by the War renders them unable to finish their Church in such a manner as to answer the purpose of a decent place of worship – Your Petitioners impressed with the highest Opinion of the Zeal, in matters of Religion, which pervades the Hon[ble] House, are induced to pray that they may be indulged to raise a sum of money not exceeding five hundred pounds by Way of Lottery, to be applied to the religious purposes above mentioned. — Your Petitioners beg leave to offer to the Hon[ble] House, further reasons which may induce them to comply with this their humble Request; that they expect that the Contributions by Way of purchasing Tickets, will be made by People Zealous in the cause of Religion, and friends to their particular Church, and in a very great Measure by Members of the Lutheran Church in the neighbouring States. — Your Petitioners pray for the Consideration of the Hon[ble] House, and rely with confidence, that their Request will meet with a favorable and liberal determination. — And your Petitioners will ever pray &c.

Winchester Oct. 7, 1785   Christian Streit V.D.M.
　　　　　　　　　　　　　Lewis Hoff
　　　　　　　　　　　　　George Linn
　　　　　　　　　　　　　Michael Altrith
　　　　　　　　　　　　　George Kiger
　　　　　　　　　　　　　H.W. Baker

The foregoing petition was looked upon with favor by

the General Assembly, which passed the enabling legislation October 10, 1785.[35]

In due time the following information printed on handbills in both English and German placarded the town and countryside in general:

SCHEME
OF
A LOTTERY,

Authorized by an Act of Assembly, for raising a sum of money to be applied to the finishing of the German Lutheran Church, of the Borough of Winchester, in Virginia.

2000 Tickets at 3 Dollars each, is 6000 Dollars.

Prizes.		Dollars.		Dollars
1	of	500	is	500
1	— — — — — —	300	— — — — —	300
2	— — — — — —	100	— — — — —	200
3	— — — — — —	75	— — — — —	225
5	— — — — — —	30	— — — — —	150
10	— — — — — —	10	— — — — —	100
20	— — — — — —	8	— — — — —	160
540	— — — — — —	5	— — — — —	2700

Prizes 582		4335
Blanks 1418	For the Church	1665
2000		6000

A little more than 2 ½ Blanks to a Prize.

The following Gentlemen, are appointed Managers, who are under due obligations for the faithful discharge of their duty, *viz.*

Col. Charles M. Thruston	Mr. Philip Bush
Mr. Edward Smith	Mr. George Kiger
Maj. Thomas Massie	Mr. Henry Baker
Col. Joseph Holmes	Mr. Adam Heiskel
Col. James Gamul Dowdal	Mr. George Linn
Mr. John Peyton	Mr. Peter Lauck
Rev[d] Christian Streit	Mr. Frederick Hass
Mr. Lewis Hoff	

It is hoped the pious purpose of this Lottery, will be a sufficient recommendation, and the friends of Religion of all denominations, will cheerfully help to promote it by becoming adventurers.

The drawing of the Lottery, and a list of the fortunate members will be made known in proper time, and the prizes paid without any deduction, if demanded within twelve months, after the drawing is finished, otherwise they will be deemed a gratuity to the Church.

*   *   *   *   *   *   *   *

FREDERICK-TOWN; Printed by Matthias Bartgis.
   Subscriptions and Advertisements for the MARYLAND CHRONICLE, or the UNIVERSAL ADVERTISER, will be gratefully received by the Printer hereof.[36]

Thus items in Streit's Diary for May 4 and 5, 1786, became intelligible. Major Massie and Colonel Thruston each received lottery tickets, the former by coming for them, the latter by having them sent to him.

A second lottery was authorized in 1788, for which Henry Baker, Peter Lauck, Lewis Hoff, George Kiger and Conrad Kremer were managers. The congregation hoped to realize an additional $334, while the total value of prizes was $1,170.[37]

The expectations of the congregation seem to have been realized from the lotteries, judging from subsequent events. But their hope of obtaining further assistance from sister congregations of the Ministerium was doomed to disappointment. A letter was sent by the Church Council to the 1788 convention of Synod appealing for aid. The minutes of the meeting give the following answer:

"After mature deliberation it was resolved to give them the written reply that in the present hard times and in the great scarcity of money, the Ministerium desires to be spared from this proposition; especially since the Ministerium believes that the respective preachers have no right to give away public collections without consent of the elders and deacons. The Synod, however, recommends to each member to do the best for the congregation named, as far as possible, by private contributions."[38] It is inferred that this action by the Synod had a direct bearing on the initiation of the second lottery.

At this point we come to another spot in the story where tradition has served as guide for want of documentary evidence. It has to do with the steps in the final completion and dedication of the church. How extensive was the work that Streit spearheaded and superintended? When was the original steeple that Fithian saw and reported in 1775 replaced by a new one? And when was the edifice used for services of public worship?

Dr. Krauth is manifestly in error when he says that, "the spire was not erected as part of the original structure;" and at the same time he seems to be responsible for the tradition that a steeple was erected between 1789 and 1793. He informs us also that "in 1790 two bells of wonderful sweetness were cast in Bremen, expressly for this church, as the inscription on the one which still remains states. It was long the custom to ring them on Saturday evening to remind men of the approach of the day of rest. The larger one was unfortunately broken while tolling to announce a death. About 1795 the organ was placed in the church, where it remained until the summer of the present year." (1854)[39] And it is Dr. Krauth who says that when Christian Streit arrived the building had neither doors nor windows.

Dr. Gilbert, writing in 1877, adheres to the Krauth testimony, adding specifically that "the church was regularly occupied in 1789," and that "in 1793 the spire was erected."

The present writer, in trying to reconcile the verdicts of evidence and tradition, has come to the conclusion that the steeple seen in 1775 had become unsafe by decay, abuse and failure to maintain the property, as a result of which it had to be dismantled and a new one put in its place. Dr. Krauth is not in error about the fact of a steeple being built; it is his conclusion that it was the *original* steeple, which is at fault. The author also holds to the theory that the building was used for worship before 1789. Streit's diary entry for September 14, 1785, would indicate as much. While the interior structure apparently was not completed in its details and furnishings, (except the organ,) until 1789, the year it is said to have been occupied, it is unthinkable that the building would not have been used in an unfinished state. Streit himself is said to have been a mechanical genius of sorts who put his own skills to practical use in leading the way and assisting in the performance of the work. It is hard, therefore, to believe that four years elapsed before the congregation had its own place of worship.

No documentary evidence indicating a formal dedication of the building has been found. We must rely once more upon the tradition that 1793 is the date for this long awaited event. Let it be well remembered that the fathers of the congregation were most meticulous in their dealings with their fellowmen and with their God. They would not purchase what they could not pay for, and they would not go into debt to speed the completion of their church. And by the same reasoning they would not dedicate to the Glory of the Eternal something unfinished or on which a single dollar was owed. When the steeple had been replaced, when all work was completed and paid for, when money was in hand for the purchase of the bells and more still for the purchase of the organ then, and not before then, we may rest assured, the dedication took place. This, tradition says, was in 1793.

Meantime the congregation had widened its horizon. John David Young was supported as an associate pastor to Streit. He is not to be confused with John George Young, pastor at Hagerstown.[g]

David Young, a native German trained at Leipzig, came to America in 1789, obtained licensure from the Ministerium and began his ministry at Manheim, Pennsylvania. The next year he was in the Shenandoah Valley, serving the Martinsburg and Shepherdstown congregations and receiving part of his support from the Winchester church. In 1791 he was ordained.[40] Young's connection with the congregation has almost been forgotten entirely. The minutes of a Church Council meeting, December 7, 1857, tell the story.

Here we learn that "Jacob Baker read a translated copy (the original being in German in the possession of George W. Baker) of a subscription list, made in August 1790, for the support of Rev[ds] David Young and Christian Streit as ministers of the Lutheran congregation of Winchester, the whole amount being $138." Fortunately the paper was copied into the record and so preserves the names of sixty-two members with their financial subscriptions in support of the two pastors. It is given in full as follows:[41]

> We the undersigned promise hereby to pay quarterly to the overseers of the Lutheran Congregation in Winchester the several sums of money which each one shall write opposite to his name for the use and support of Mess[rs] David Young and Christian Streight, who promise on their side to attend to the congregation on all Sundays and festival days in the present year from the first of August 1790:
> Henry Baker (£3)   Charles Hoff (6s)
> Lewis Hoff (£2,8s)   Jacob Hoff (5s)

---

[g] John George Young was Streit's brother-in-law.

Peter Lauck (£2,10s)
Philip Hoover (£1,10s)
Adam Young (£1,5s)
Adam Heiskell (£1,10s)
Nicholas Mesmer (£1,4s)
H.W. Baker (£1)
Michael Altridge (£1)
Philip Bush (£1,10s)
John Cooke (£1,10s)
Martin Riley (£1)
Simon Lauck (£1,4s)
Christopher Wetzel (£1,4s)
John Grim (15s)
Conrad Long (6s)
Philip Arm (15s)
Jacob Rider (6s)
Conrad Kremer (£1)
Michael Copenhaver (6s)
George Kiger (12s)
John Riley (10s)
John Van Welden (5s)
Dedrick Gardner (6s)
Charles Aulick (10s)
P. Helfenstein (6s)
Adam Kiger (12s)
Catherine Rinker (6s)
John Goss (6s)
Michael Grove (6s)
Andrew Kiger (10s)

Charles Hetzell (3s)
Charles F. Heist (6s)
Catherine Brinker (£1)
Daniel Overaker (6s)
Rosina May (12s)
Barbara Lavinder (10s)
Jacob Kiger (15s)
Henry Fridley (6s)
Albrecht Eger (10s)
George M. Riley (6s)
John Shultz (10s)
Adam Kurtz (6s)
Abraham Lauch (6s)
Christopher Fry (10s)
Christopher Heiskell (10s)
John Sloat (6s)
Andrew Baker (6s)
John Bowman (5s)
George Linn (4s)
Isaac Sitler (6s)
P. Klipstine (6s)
F. Hoffman (6s)
John Hoff (4s)
P. Bower (15s)
John Conrad (12s)
Charles Grim (6s)
John Copenhaver (6s)
Philip Philips (3s)
Ernest Eltz (4s)

In all 41.8 – equal to $138.

The arrangement whereby David Young served as associate pastor continued for three, or possibly five, years. Young attended the 1793 synodical convention at Philadelphia, but Streit excused his absence with satisfactory reasons. Young is listed as pastor at Martinsburg, while his parish embraced the churches at Martinsburg, Shepherdstown, Winchester, Stephens City, Strasburg and Stone's Chapel. He reported that four German schools were in operation within the six congregations, and during the year 192 baptisms had been administered, 72 persons confirmed, communion given to 232 individuals and 18 funerals conducted.[41] Both Streit and Young were absent at the next two annual conventions, but by 1796 a change had occurred, which strangely enough has been completely forgotten at Winchester.

Before reporting what happened, however, it will be necessary to record an important event of the year 1793.

At the very beginning of the year, on the Feast of the Epiphany, the first special Conference of Lutheran pastors in Virginia was held. The Ministerium, anticipating the desire and need for district conference meetings, had for ten years past taken actions encouraging the same, but none had been held. The meeting at Winchester was the first of these specially authorized conferences. As such it became the third group of Lutheran pastors and congregations to organize in America, being antedated only by the Ministerium of Pennsylvania (1748) and the Ministerium of New York (1786). The date, therefore, is of peculiar significance to Lutherans in Virginia.

Let Dr. Gilbert's words recount the story of this first meeting:

> 1793, January 6th, 7th, the first Special Conference meeting of Lutheran ministers in Virginia was held at Winchester. The ministers present were Christian Streit, Winchester; John David Young, Martinsburg; Paul Henkel, New Market; and William Carpenter, Madison. The record opens thus: "We four ministers of the Evangelical Lutheran Church, living and serving congregations in the State of Virginia, being present in Winchester, on the sixth of January, 1793, began our Conference on this Epiphany Sunday by holding religious services."
>
> Rev. Paul Henkel preached in the morning from John 7:38, on 1. The nature; 2. The fruits of saving faith.

Rev. William Carpenter preached in the afternoon from Romans 8:2, on the contrast between the law of sin and death, and the law of the Spirit of life.

Monday, January 7th, the first business session was held. Christian Streit was elected president, and John David Young, secretary. Lay delegates were present from the church councils of Winchester, Martinsburg, Shepherdstown, Stone Chapel, Newtown, Strasburg, and Woodstock; but their names are not given.

The members of the convention resolved that a Conference meeting should be held annually on the first Sunday in October; that they would not separate themselves from the Ministerium of Pennsylvania, nor take any action that would come in conflict with its regulations; that lay delegates regularly chosen and presenting themselves properly accredited, regularly connected with the Synod, should be received into the Conference with the privilege of participating in all its business.... It was further resolved, that the Conference should always make "the devising of ways and means for the improvement of our young people and children in knowledge and piety a prominent aim;" and that "the proceedings of this Conference shall be made known to the congregations, and if approved by them they shall be laid before the Synod for examination and endorsement of these several resolutions."

The Conference was closed on Monday evening by a solemn and impressive public service in the church; Rev. John D. Young preached from the first Psalm, on "The blessedness of the man who walks in the way of faith and piety," after which the president expressed in a most feeling manner his thanks to his brethren and dismissed the congregation with the benediction.[42]

For twenty-five years this Special Conference continued to function. Its 1799 session was scheduled for Winchester, though no record of it has been preserved, and the 1808 convention was held there. Its last meeting was in 1818, and two years later it was absorbed in the newly formed Synod of Maryland and Virginia.

One of the consequences of the establishment of the Special Conference was the rearrangement of work on the part of several pastors. Paul Henkel moved to Staunton and ministered to congregations in Augusta County, and Christian Streit moved to Woodstock to serve the church there and other nearby groups. Carpenter continued to serve in Madison County, and Young at Martinsburg.

It is odd that this particular fact in Streit's life should have been so completely lost to view. Every sketch about him declares unequivocally that he served at Winchester continuously until his death. But consider the evidence.

Exhibit A comes from synodical convention minutes.[43] The 1796 convention lists Streit at Millerstown (Woodstock) and it makes special note of the fact that the Winchester congregation is vacant. Streit did not attend the conventions of 1797-1799. In 1800 he is still at Millerstown, but the minutes for 1803 list him back at Winchester.

Exhibit B comes from the record of marriages performed. Records at the Frederick County Court House show that Streit performed an average of forty-six weddings a year from 1786-1794.

In 1795 the number dropped to twenty-two, and the next year to one. Thereafter until 1812, the year of his death, the number is anywhere from six to nineteen annually. All told there are 636 weddings on record at Winchester which Streit performed.

Exhibit C comes from certain real estate transactions. On November 20, 1801, the property purchased from Daniel Morgan was conveyed to Henry St. George Tucker.[44] On June 30, 1820, the Streit heirs conveyed to Tucker a 60 acre parcel of land in Frederick County "which was sold by the said Christian Streit in his lifetime to the said Tucker at the price of 400 pounds, which price was settled in the price of a house and lot sold by the said

Tucker to him at 700 pounds, but no deed having been made by the said Streit."[45] On June 12, 1821, Tucker conveyed to Susan Streit, widow, the property on Cameron Street which Streit had purchased from Morgan.[46] These deeds indicate that Streit, sometime after 1801, exchanged the 60 acre farm with Tucker for the Cameron Street property which he sold to Tucker in 1801, but that he did not give Tucker a deed for the farm, nor did Tucker give him a deed for the Cameron Street property. A friendly suit on the part of the Streit heirs, and of Tucker, was necessary before legal title to both properties was obtained. The mutual respect and esteem between Christian Streit and Henry St. George Tucker is manifestly self-evident. The above clearly points to a change in residence on the part of the Streit family with a later return to the home that had been vacated.

Mrs. Susan Barr Streit
(Silhouette)

Exhibit D comes from an act authorizing a lottery at Woodstock in 1803. "Be it enacted by the General Assembly: That it shall and may be lawful for Christian Strite, William H. Dulany, Daniel Lee, Jacob Myers, Charles Masters, Philip

Spangler, John Altefoi, Henry Conrad, Jacob Ott, George Dellinger, Alexander Pollock and Jacob Dary, Gentlemen, Comissioners, or a majority of them, to raise by a lottery or lotteries, a sum not exceeding three thousand dollars, to be by them applied towards completing a church begun in the town of Woodstock and county of Shenandoah, by the Lutheran congregation. "This Act shall commence and be in force from and after the passing thereof." (Passed December 27, 1803).[47]

The four-fold cumulative evidence here produced seems to be conclusive that Streit moved to Woodstock about 1795; that he remained there until about 1803; that as pastor at Woodstock he was instrumental in building the second church edifice of that congregation; and that his ministry at Winchester was not a continuous, unbroken pastorate of twenty-seven years. Nothing has been found to throw light on the circumstances of his leaving or of his return. All that can be said is that this episode forms an interesting interlude between the opening and closing years spent in Winchester.

Christian Streit was a first-rate churchman zealous for the Church at Large. This, perhaps, has already been observed in his vision for the congregation to support an associate pastor, and his leadership in the formation of the Special Conference. We see it also in his loyalty to the Ministerium in which for forty-three years he took an active part. He was unable to make the long journey by horseback or by stage to Eastern Pennsylvania every year for the meeting of the Synod, though he managed to attend eight conventions while living in Virginia. In 1787 at Lancaster he witnessed the dedication of The German High School, later to become Franklin and Marshall College, of which his friend Henry E. Muhlenberg, pastor of Trinity Church and botanist with international reputation, was installed as first Principal and delivered the address of the day. At the same meeting of Synod he was confronted with a call to return to his former parish at New Hanover.[48]

The reports of pastoral acts that Streit submitted to the Synod from time to time reveal the extent of his activities and the numerical size of his parish. In 1803 he had 59 baptisms, 26 confirmations, 201 communicants, 15 funerals and 1 German school.

Synod met at Hagerstown in 1806 and Thomas Heist accompanied Pastor Streit from Winchester as lay delegate. The first printed financial reports occur in the minutes of this convention. The congregations at Strasburg and Stephens City were still a part of the parish, but Pennsbrook had taken the place of Stone Chapel. The contributions from the several congregations to the Synodical Treasury were as follows:

From Winchester	$15.12 ½
" Staufferstown	7.78
" Pennsbrook	3.38 ½
" Neustadt	3.43 ½
	$29.72 ½

Streit reported 69 baptisms, 8 confirmations, 119 communicants, 17 deaths and 1 German school.[49]

Ever on the move, Christian Streit is known to have visited the Peaked Mountain Church on May 27, 1804. He participated, along with the Reformed minister Johannes Braun (John Brown) in the dedication of the new union church at McGaheysville, in Rockingham County, Virginia. On this occasion Streit preached once in German and once in English. His text was from Psalms for the German sermon and from John for the English. The records of the church indicate that he confirmed 25 individuals and administered the sacrament to a total of 42. He again visited the Peaked Mountain Church on June 12, 1808. The same records indicate that 17 were confirmed and that as many as 43 individuals received the sacrament. Since the other confirmation and communion lists for the period at the Peaked Mountain Church do not indicate who officiated, it is merely probable that he visited at other times as well.[h]

---

[h] A photostatic copy of the unpaginated Peaked Mountain Register, written mainly in German script, is available at the Library of Vir-

In 1809 the last report to be submitted shows the parish to be made up of "1 congregation at Winchester, 1 in Neustadt, 1 in Stauferstadt and 1 on Biber Creek."[50]

March 10, 1812, Christian Streit entered into rest. His ministry was ended and his journey done. His loving friends and parishioners interred his body within the church under the square-brick pavement in front of the pulpit, while a great throng of people, sad of heart because of his death, but stronger and better because of his life among them, attended the scene.

The Winchester Gazette of Wednesday, March 18, 1812, carried the following story of Streit's death and funeral, together with a poetic tribute composed by Henry St. George Tucker.[51]

> Departed this Life on Tuesday night the 10th inst. the Rev. Christian Streit, Pastor of the Lutheran congregation in Winchester, after a severe illness of twelve days in the 63rd year of his age, leaving a disconsolate widow, with a large and promising family of children, to lament a loss irreparable. On Thursday at 11 o'clock, his remains were deposited

---

ginia (Accession numbers 23592 and 23591). The original has, unfortunately, disappeared. A selected portion of a partial translation done in the early twentieth century by William J. Hinke and Charles E. Kemper appeared in the *William and Mary Quarterly*, series 1, 13 (1904-1905), 247-256, and series 1, 14 (1905-1906), 9-19, 186-193. The arrangement of the published translation makes it difficult for those unfamiliar with German script to locate a specific record, even with the translation in hand. Another and more extensive typescript by William Perry Pence, who had earlier worked with Hinke and Kemper, is available at the Daughters of the American Revolution Library in Washington D.C. and at the Massanutten Regional Library in Harrisonburg, Virginia. However, the best English translation of material connected with the 1804 dedication of the Peaked Mountain Church is contained in yet another typescript drawn from the personal manuscript of P.C. Kaylor in 1934, 128-132. It too is at the Massanutten Regional Library.

in the tomb in the aisle fronting the pulpit in the Lutheran Church, attended by an unusually large concourse of people – His corpse was preceded by the Clergy of the place, and also by the young ladies of the Female Academy, of which, he, in connection with the Rev. Mr. Hill, had the charge.

Few deaths have occurred in this place, which excited more sensibility – Mr. Streit's character as a Christian was not only irreproachable, but highly exemplary – as a clergyman, ministerial and respectable – as a neighbor, charitable and benevolent, and throughout, that of an eminently honest man. In his death as well as in his life, he displayed the power of the religion of Christ – At an early period of his life he was called to serve his country as a Chaplain to the 3rd Va. Regiment – He was afterwards settled as a clergyman upon a very comfortable establishment in Charleston, South Carolina, where he was taken prisoner by the British. In the year 1785 he settled in Winchester, and acted as the minister of the Lutheran Church in this place with credit to himself and the society over which he presided, for nearly 27 years.

Christian Streit
(Silhouette)

The following is a tribute of respect to his memory by a friend of his in this place – It is written as if inscribed upon a tablet within the Lutheran Church, where his body now lies entombed.

> Within these walls, where late his warning voice
> Our pastor raised, that voice is heard no more.
> His meek and placid eye, his lips whence flowed
>   In accents gentle as the dew of heaven,
>   The mild, benignant doctrines of the cross,
> Are closed in death; and on his slender frame,
>   So oft in humble supplication bent
> Before the throne of God's most bounteous grace,
> Th' insatiate monster lays his icy hand.
> This consecrated house, within whose walls
> 'The pealing organ swells the note of praise,'
>   Is now his monument! The holy aisle
> No more his people crowd, no longer join
> With awful reverence the benignant prayer
> Poured from a father's fond and pious heart.
> To this sad spot they now repair, to view
>   The sad memorials of that father lost.
> Does hoary age or pensive youth approach
> To read these lines, upon his loved remains
>   To drop a tear of fond regret, and draw
> New lessons of instruction from his tomb?
> Speak, gentle spirit, from the silent grave,
> And let thy death, than any mortal tongue
> More eloquent, thy last, best percepts give.
> Bid them like thee pursue with steadfast course
>   The paths of virtue, and like thee acquire
>   The christian's best possession, a soul
> To peace attuned by meek-eyed gentleness
>   And humble resignation to his God!
> Tell them that then his terrors death shall lose,
>   And from the direst foe become the best
> Of friends: Tell them the everlasting gates
> Of heaven shall 'turn harmonious' to receive
>   Their souls, like thine, into the realms of bliss.

In 1876, almost sixty-five years after Streit's death, and twenty-two years after the burning of the Old Church, his remains were exhumed that they might be placed by the side of his kindred and that the exact spot of their sepulture might be known. The monument to his memory was erected thereafter.[i]

"One of the most unpretending and good men with whom a church has ever been blessed" was Charles Porterfield Krauth's estimate of Streit.[52] People remembered him for the lasting influence of his work as a teacher upon their lives, for the faithfulness of his ministry as a pastor, and for the quality of his life which spoke to them more eloquently than words. It is not strange that a small body of tradition should have been handed down concerning him.

One tradition deals with his love for music, his ability as an organist and his mechanical skill in constructing an organ for one of his congregations. The congregation at Strasburg has been associated with this story. Records there tell of the purchase of an organ in the 1790s at Baltimore. It is thought that after assembling the various parts, Streit put the whole together.

Another tradition says that Streit was educated at Princeton. This doubtless arose because of his New Jersey origin. No evidence is to be found, however, that he attended that institution.[j]

A third tradition declares he was ordained in 1769. This date is in error. He was licensed by the Ministerium

---

[i] Streit is buried in Mount Hebron Cemetery near the remains of the Old Church. It is a fitting final resting place.

[j] A complete list of all recipients of the A.B. degree is recorded in the manuscript minutes of the Board of Trustees. Those who attended but did not graduate is difficult to determine. The College of New Jersey, later Princeton University, either did not maintain matriculation registers or they did not survive. James McLachlan, *Princetonians, 1748-1768: A Biographical Dictionary* (Princeton, N.J.: Princeton University Press, 1976), xii.

that year, but his ordination occurred the following year, October 25, 1770.

And a fourth tradition makes of him the first native-born American Lutheran minister. This, too, is in error. John Abraham Lidenius, born in New Jersey and educated in Sweden, is entitled to first place, while Jacob van Buskirck, born of a Dutch family in New Jersey, was the first whose birth, education and ordination were American. Then there were the three Muhlenberg brothers, whose ministries began with Streit's. Instead, therefore, of being first, it may be said of Streit that he was numbered among the first half-dozen native-born Lutheran preachers in America.

When the news of Streit's death was reported to the Ministerium together with the news of the death of its president, Rev. Friedrich Schmidt, that circumspect body took the following action:

"That the members of this Ministerium wear mourning for thirty days in view of the decease of their dear and highly respected president, the Rev. Pastor Schmidt, of Philadelphia, and of the worthy Pastor Streit, of Winchester."[53]

After the death of Henry Melchoir Muhlenberg, October 7, 1787, Streit had preached a memorial sermon at Winchester, using for his text Psalm 73:24: "Thou shalt guide me with thy counsel, and afterward receive me to glory." He in turn, true shepherd that he was, had been the guide to many, who both here and in glory rise up to call him blessed.

Endnotes – Chapter V

[1] See serialized portions of "Zion, St. Paul and Other Early Lutheran Churches in Central New Jersey" by John C. Honeyman, New Germantown, N.J.: *Proceedings of the New Jersey Historical Society,* 1924-1927.

[2] Delber W. Clark, *The World of Justus Falckner* (Philadelphia: The Muhlenberg Press, 1946).

[3] *The Journals of Henry Melchoir Muhlenberg*, 3 volumes, translated by Theodore G. Tappert and John W. Doberstein (Philadelphia: Muhlenberg Press, 1942-1948) I, 358; and, II, 328. Hereafter cited as *JHMM*.
[4] *JHMM*, II, 432.
[5] Paul A.W. Wallace, *The Muhlenbergs of Pennsylvania* (Philadelphia: University of Pennsylvania Press, 1950), 72.
[6] *JHMM*, II, 365.
[7] *Documentary History of the Evangelical Lutheran Ministerium of Pennsylvania and Adjacent States, Proceeding of the Annual Conventions from 1748 to 1821* (Philadelphia: Board of Publication of the General Council of the Evangelical Lutheran Church in North America, 1898), 105 and 107.
[8] *JHMM*, II, 448.
[9] *Documentary History*, 126-27.
[10] *JHMM*, II, 515.
[11] Ibid., 718.
[12] Ibid., 725.
[13] Ibid., 736.
[14] W.J. Finck, *Lutheran Landmarks and Pioneers in America: A Series of Sketches of Colonial Times*, 4th edition (Philadelphia: United Lutheran Publication House,1913), 161.
[15] *Muhlenbergs of Pennsylvania*, 128-29.
[16] Ibid., 133.
[17] Ibid., 134.
[18] *JHMM*, [October 14, 1777], III, 85-86.
[19] *JMHH*, [April 3, 1778], III, 139-140.
[20] *JMHH*, [May 30, 1778], III, 158.
[21] *JMHH*, [June 15, 1778], III, 163-164.
[22] Archives, Krauth Memorial Library, Philadelphia, Pennsylvania.
[23] Christoph Friedrich Triebner, pastor at Ebenezer Church, Effingham, Georgia.
[24] Her husband, Christian Rabenhorst, had been pastor at Ebenezer Church also.
[25] Friedrich Daser, associate pastor of the Lutheran congregation, Charleston, South Carolina, the present St. John's Lutheran Church.
[26] *JHMM*, [January 11, 1781], III, 389-390.
[27] John Jacob Kline, *A History of the Lutheran Church in New Hanover, Montgomery County, Pennsylvania* (New Hanover, Pa.: The Congregation, 1910), 121-122 and 693.
[28] *JHMM*, [July 28, August 14, and August 16, 1783], III, 553 and 556-557.

[29] *Documentary History*, 192 and 194.
[30] *JHMM*, [December 29, September 28, October 3, and November 23, 1784], III, 640; 616; 617; and, 633.
[31] The Streit Dairy is included in this volume as Appendix B.
[32] *Documentary History*, 345.
[33] Frederick County Deed Book 21, 718
[34] Archives, Virginia State Library [now the Library of Virginia], Richmond, Va.
[35] William Walker Henning, *The Statutes at Large, Being a Collection of All the Laws of Virginia, 1619-1792*, volume 12, (Reprint, Charlottesville, Va.: University of Virginia Press, 1969), 228
[36] From original handbill in possession of Mrs. Mary Dosh Krumbholz.
[37] T.K. Cartmell, *Shenandoah Valley Pioneers and Their Descendants, A History of Frederick County, Virginia, from its Formation in 1738 to 1908* (Winchester, Va.: Eddy Press Corporation, 1909), 192; and, Frederic Morton, *The Story of Winchester in Virginia* (Strasburg, Va.: Shenandoah Publishing House, 1925), 211.
[38] *Documentary History*, 220.
[39] Charles Porterfield Krauth, *A Discourse Suggested by the Burning of the Old Lutheran Church, on the Night of September 27th, 1854, Delivered in the Evangelical Lutheran Church, Winchester, Virginia, the nineteenth Sunday after Trinity, 1854* (Winchester, Va.: Printed at the Republican Office, 1855), 7.
[40] *Documentary History*, 231 and 242.
[41] Ibid., 260 and 264.
[42] C.W. Cassell, W.J. Finck and Elon O. Henkel, *History of the Lutheran Church in Virginia and East Tennessee* (Strasburg, Va.: Lutheran Synod of Virginia, 1930), 82-83.
[43] *Documentary History*, 282, 284, 308 and 331.
[44] Winchester Deed Book 1, 235.
[45] Frederick County Deed Book 45, 48.
[46] Ibid., 52.
[47] Samuel Shepherd, *The Statutes at Large of Virginia...Being a Continuation of Hening, 1792-1807*, volume III (Reprint, New York: AMS Press, 1970), 29.
[48] *Documentary History*, 215 and 218.
[49] Ibid., 362 and 369.
[50] Ibid., 402.
[51] Henry St. George Tucker (1780-1848) soldier, lawyer, teacher, judge and member of Congress, 1815-1819.
[52] *Burning of the Old Lutheran Church*, 13-14.
[53] *Documentary History*, 437.

Chapter VI
Pastors in Processional, 1812-1967

It is the purpose of this chapter to permit the successors of Christian Streit to march by in processional, as it were. The highlights of their respective ministries will be reviewed, together with other pertinent or interesting facts of a biographical nature, both preceding and following their pastorates. The arrangement to be followed will be chronological. In succeeding chapters it will be topical.

ABRAHAM RECK, 1812-1827

Born January 2, 1791, at Littlestown, Pennsylvania, Abraham Reck had his ministry before him when he took up the work relinquished by Christian Streit in death. He received his theological training from the Rev. F.V. Melsheimer of Hanover, Pennsylvania, and in 1812, at the meeting of the Ministerium, as a ministerial applicant he was authorized to visit vacant congregations in New Virginia for three months with the understanding that he be permitted to accept a call should his services be wanted permanently. Thus we find him at Winchester before the end of the year.

One of Reck's first acts was to purchase a minute book for the Church Council. The Church order, or rules, by which the congregation had been governed was inscribed first in German, then in English translation, and these documents in turn were followed by an enlightening explanation, to wit:

> The above rules and regulations, which were adopted by the German Lutheran Congregation of Winchester in Vir-

ginia, is the only record of any regular proceedings of the congregation or Elders; as regular minutes of the proceedings of the Elders is deemed Essential for the well ordering of the conscins (conscience) of said Congregation. We the undersigned, have been regularly appointed Elders, agreeably to such rules as were adopted in the said congregation from time to time, Have concluded to commence Keeping Minutes of our proceedings, and we do hope, they will be continued. This congregation has been a German congregation but as the German Language is nearly extinct we are compelled to keep the proposed minutes in the English Language.

Philip Hoover   Thomas Heist
Peter Lauck   Lewis Hoff
Abraham Lauck   John Slagle, Elders.

    The transition from German to English, started at the very beginning of Streit's ministry twenty-seven years earlier, was now complete. No longer would the colloquial, though entirely unofficial, name of German Lutheran Church be applied to the congregation. For sixty-five more years the name would remain the same as it had been from the time of the laying of the cornerstone, simply The Evangelical Lutheran Church. Such minutes of congregational and Council meetings as the congregation possesses are all in the English language, and they begin January 1, 1813.[a]

    It must be remembered that the War of 1812, an unpopular conflict throughout the nation as a whole, but supported with enthusiasm in the southern states, was in the process of being fought. Winchester had been named as the recruiting station for several companies, and as a result a number of

---

[a] Grace Evangelical Church has within its archives a copy of a minute book that begins on January 24, 1814. It has been microfilmed in its entirety by the Library of Virginia: City of Winchester, Grace Evangelical Lutheran Church, Minute Book, vol. 1, 1814-1872.

men from the town saw service. Included among them were the following members of the Lutheran congregation: Frederick Aulick, Jacob Baker, Andrew Bush, Michael Copenhaver, Stewart Grant, Stephen Jenkins, Jacob Mesmer, John W. Miller, John Sloat, Augustus Streit and William Streit. No complete listing can be given in view of the fact that there is no official congregational roll for the period.

Abraham Reck

Reck entered upon his work with all the zeal and energy a young man can muster in his first parish. His people were pleased with him and so reported to the Ministerium. His own reports show something of his activities: from 52 baptisms in 1813 the number grew to 150 in 1819, his banner year, when he also performed 126 confirmations and reported 815 communicants in 5 congregations. No wonder the parish gave the Synod a second favorable testimonial regarding their preacher, for Winchester had become the largest Lutheran parish in the entire area. No wonder, too, that Winchester should have been chosen as the place for the organization of the new Synod of Maryland and Virginia.[1]

On October 11, 1820, eleven ministers and seven lay-delegates assembled in the Lutheran Church at 9 o'clock in the morning. Those in attendance at the two-day sessions were:

Rev. Daniel Kurtz, D.D., Baltimore Maryland
Rev. John Grob, Taneytown, Maryland

Rev. David F. Schaeffer, A.M., Frederick, Maryland
Rev. Martin Sackman, Loudoun County, Virginia
Rev. Abraham Reck, Winchester, Virginia
Rev. Benjamin Kurtz, Hagerstown, Maryland
Rev. Michael Meyerheffer,[b] Madison, Virginia
Rev. John Kehler, Middletown, Maryland
Rev. Michael Wachter, Frederick City, Maryland
Rev. Charles Philip Krauth, Shepherdstown, Virginia
Rev. Nicholas Schmucker, Woodstock, Virginia

Lay-Delegates

Frederick Loehr, Frederick, Maryland
John Baker, Winchester, Virginia
Abraham Reck, Taneytown, Maryland
George Shryock, Hagerstown, Maryland
Frederick Kiefer, Loudoun County, Virginia
Jacob Bishop, Shepherdstown, Virginia
Jacob Ott, Woodstock, Virginia

The Rev. Dr. Daniel Kurtz was appointed chairman, and Rev. David F. Schaeffer secretary.

The adoption of a constitution was the first important matter of business. John Baker was appointed to a committee of three pastors and three laymen to draft the same. When officers were elected, Dr. Kurtz was chosen president, Rev. David F. Schaeffer secretary, and Rev. Abraham Reck treasurer.

Another matter of importance determined at this same meeting was the request that each minister prepare materials for a Church Discipline. Here was the beginning of a work completed two years later by Dr. S.S. Schmucker which was to become the Formula of Government and Discipline of the General Synod, a document that proved distasteful to many

---

[b] The surname usually appears as "Meyerhoeffer."

in the Winchester church. The General Synod, founded October 22, 1820, at Hagerstown, by representatives of the Ministerium of Pennsylvania, New York, North Carolina, and Maryland and Virginia Synods, was the first general body to be organized by Lutherans in America.

In addition to the role played by Pastor Reck in sharing in the founding of the Synod of Maryland and Virginia, he proved himself influential in the cause of theological education. In 1818, Charles Philip Krauth, father of Charles Porterfield Krauth, came to Winchester from Frederick, Maryland, where he had been studying theology under David F. Schaeffer, to assist Pastor Reck in the work of the parish and to continue studying under his supervision. Krauth studied under Reck for one year. Again, when Reck's brother, John B. Reck, who lived with him at Winchester for a time, enrolled as a ministerial student under S.S. Schmucker at the latter's home at New Market, the Winchester congregation gave an offering of $13.34 for his support on May 15, 1825. Already a year earlier a society for aiding missionary and educational causes had been organized in the congregation, while Reck promoted a similar society on a synod-wide basis in 1828. When the Gettysburg Theological Seminary was established in 1826, S.S. Schmucker, chief founder, received valuable help from Abraham Reck, whose intimate friends, Benjamin Kurtz and Charles Philip Krauth, likewise played leading parts. Reck served as financial agent for this institution in Virginia, under authorization first of the General Synod, then of the Seminary Board of Directors; and when the cornerstone of the first building was laid in 1831, he delivered one of the addresses of the occasion. During his Middletown, Maryland, pastorate he was instrumental in sending into the ministry both David Bittle, founder of Roanoke College, and Ezra Keller, founder of Wittenberg College.

A keen interest in the home missionary work of the church likewise characterized Abraham Reck. He was appointed the traveling missionary of the Synod, and from his report a year later we glean interesting information. Leaving home October 9, 1822, he toured the counties of Hampshire, Hardy, Pendleton, Randolph, Harrison, Preston and Monongalia in Virginia; the counties of Green and Fayette in Pennsylvania; and the state of Maryland west of Cumberland. He spent some three months journeying from place to place and house to house, baptizing 13 children, preaching 85 sermons and riding 1,006 miles.[2]

Pastor Reck led his people into a fuller stewardship of their means. In a day when the benevolent causes of the Church were in the infant stages of organization, he encouraged the custom of receiving special offerings when Holy Communion was administered. This brought on opposition, resulting in the decision by the Council, February 5, 1823, "that all money collected on sacramental occasions, as well as others, shall remain in this place until all debts due by the church are paid." But Reck persisted, and in June the action was changed to permit one-half of the communion offerings to be given to the Synod.

A subscription in behalf of Reck's salary for the year 1816 amounted to $418.50. The custom was in vogue of dividing the town into wards and appointing collectors for each ward. As there was no parsonage the pastor lived in a house, which he rented from William Holliday. In 1822, however, the school house, used for some years as a home for the sexton, was renovated and converted into a parsonage. Here Reck lived until his departure from the town.

The same year extensive repairs were made to the church, including the rebuilding of the steeple and additions and repairs to the cemetery wall. Distasteful as it was to many, the church was in debt. John Miller and his brother Abraham made large advances for rebuilding the steeple, over and above the amount that could be borrowed on seven shares of Farmer's Bank Stock owned by the congregation, and Jacob Baker had to advance money on the cemetery wall, while Daniel Linn and Godfrey Miller, who had converted the school house into a parsonage, had not been paid for the money they had advanced. It became necessary to sell the bank stock to repay the loan secured by it. After two years had passed, we learn that John and Abraham Miller still were owed $237.95 and Jacob Baker $38.07. Abraham Lauck and Thomas Heist, accordingly, were appointed a committee "to wait on the citizens of this town, and well knowing that they have never called on them in vain, hope that they will be liberal in contributing their mite towards discharging the debts due by the Church."

Besides the indebtedness above-mentioned, which proved to be strike one against Reck's ministry, he had difficulty on occasion in maintaining order at the services of worship. He was a man full of great zeal and ardent enthusiasm in his preaching and personal work with individuals, but he seems to have approached the formal worship of the church with an utter informality conducive to disrespect for the house of God. It must be remembered that this was the period when the Lutheran Church in America was just beginning to feel thoroughly at home in its new environment. Having crossed the language barrier, it forsook for a time much of its own heritage in worship after the pattern of its stately liturgies and substituted the idiosyncrasies and vagaries of individualism.

Reck was an individualist who countenanced innovations and new measures, though he was respected wholeheartedly for the man that he was, and none cast aspersion at his character.

In the light of such observations, we must interpret the following question asked in a series of propositions submitted by Lewis Hoff to the Church Council, June 30, 1819: "Should not some regulations be adopted respecting the time and manner of conducting Divine Service in the Church and particularly as to the playing of the Organ?"

A week later the Council gave answer:

> That in the event of the choir of singers finding it necessary to practice any new church music, they be at liberty to do so with the organ, only having a regard to cease at least half an hour before the time appointed for public worship to commence; That the organ play, if found necessary, and thought proper, by the Organist, the first part of the meter, before the congregation sing; That the first and last hymns be none but easy tunes and such as the congregation can join in with – the second to be such a hymn and music as the Choir may feel disposed to sing, or introduce for the purpose of learning to the congregation; – No music by singing, or by the organ as the people are retiring after service, is to be introduced or practiced.

At the same time William Alexander Baker was invited to preside at the organ. Baker was a skilled musician and manufacturer of pianos. He, reputedly, favored new measures in the service and music of the church. In this he was opposed by many in the congregation who preferred the traditional heritage of the fathers. Apparently the two points of view clashed in vocal and instrumental expression in the services, to the distraction, dismay, amusement or chagrin of the assembled worshippers. To Mr. Baker the Council's rules governing organist and choir were objectionable and he could endure them no longer. According to family tradition he gave vent to his indignation on one occasion at a communion service by playing Yankee Doodle, which episode created a most inharmonious discord among the members. We learn something of the resulting confusion from a letter written by his father, Henry William Baker, to his brother Jacob, then in Baltimore.

> Winchester, April 24, 1821
>
> Son Jacob
>
> ...Last Sunday we had a high scene, the unauthorized lads set up their pipes (after the hireling had taken his seat) & before I could summon up resolution enow, your brother set up the organ pipes in full chime to some doxology & silenced me; after he was done I felt deeply mortified at the unexpected intrusion. A solemn silence ensued a few moments & I expected the (preacher) to begin his discourse, but my expectations were blasted, for by a wink of the eye to *Johnny* he & his clan set up the pipes again & I had no alternative but patiently submit till they finished their ditty, none of the other elders saying a word & if I had said anything about unbecoming conduct it would have been retorted back that I might be silent that your brother William was equally culpable; after service was over the *clan* remained in church nearly 2 hours, exercising under *Johnny* on the organ, opening the same with the key Camillus left to *Charlie*; next Sunday the same is to be acted over again, how it will end time will show, etc. etc.

The state of affairs being such, we can better understand the action of the Council, June 6, 1821: "Some general rules relative to conducting the public services of the Church agreeable to the custom of other Lutheran Churches and agreeable to the rules of the Pennsylvania Synod (Ministerium) having been discussed and adopted – the Consistory adjourned." And six months later Pastor Reck, John Miller and

Jacob Baker were appointed a committee to draw up and publish a code of rules designed to preserve and maintain good order.

This situation proved to be strike two against Abraham Reck's ministry. Strike three was his attempt to have the congregation adopt the Formula of Government and Discipline approved by the Synod of Maryland and Virginia and by the General Synod for congregations.

The Formula was discussed from time to time at meetings of the Council. By a vote of 7 to 1 the Council decided to submit it to the congregation for consideration at a meeting to be held July 9, 1824, and also instructed Pastor Reck "to write to one of the best informed members of the Synod in order to know what has been the custom in the Lutheran Churches in the United States heretofore, whether the females have been allowed the privilege to a vote in matters of importance or not." This action was taken June 2. Reck wrote to Rev. D.F. Schaeffer, the president of the Synod, read his answer to the Council June 18 and was instructed to read Schaeffer's letter and the constitution (whether the Formula is meant or the existing constitution of the congregation is not altogether clear) at the next time of preaching.

John Baker presided at the meeting July 9 and Jacob Baker was secretary. Let the minutes tell the story.

> After some debate upon the propriety of now adopting the Formula and some propositions to continue to be governed by the Old Constitution the meeting finally Resolved, that a committee be appointed to take into consideration and maturely weigh the effects of now adopting the Formula, or shall we continue to be governed by the Old Rules. The votes being called for upon the adoption of this resolution, it appeared there were 16 for and 12 against it. The chairman then

appointed the following persons a committee to carry the above resolution into effect: H.W. Baker, Conrad Kremer, Lewis Hoff, Abraham Lauck, & J.W. Miller & that they report accordingly. On motion, Resolved that this meeting be again convened at this place to receive the report of the committee so soon as it shall be prepared, notice of which will be given by the pastor of this congregation, and the meeting adjourned.

If and when the congregation reconvened, the minute book has nothing to say. But we know the outcome. The Formula was not adopted. Four years later the congregation had a brand new constitution of its own.

Because Abraham Reck and prominent members of the congregation could not see eye to eye on matters of debt, worship and church government, so that it became difficult to find men willing to serve on the Church Council, irreconcilable differences arose between them. This led to Reck's resignation in the summer of 1827. From Winchester he went to Middletown, Maryland, accepting a call that had been extended to him annually for seven successive years. Here he remained until 1836, when he removed to Indianapolis where he organized nine congregations in less than six years. He was at Cincinnati in 1841 establishing an English Lutheran congregation under many difficulties. His health declined, and after four years he went to Germantown, Ohio, then to Tarleton (1847-1851) and at last in retirement to Lancaster, Ohio, where he died May 18, 1869, from a throat affliction. It is said that the chapter of his sorrows was as wonderful as the chapter of his successes. He was an earnest, humble, godly man, who served his Lord with conscientious fidelity all his days.

LEWIS EICHELBERGER, 1828-1833

With the departure of Abraham Reck from Winchester, a Committee on Correspondence, whose business it was to obtain a new pastor, was appointed September 10, 1827. Lewis Hoff was chairman, Jacob Baker secretary, Daniel Linn, John W. Miller, William Grove and Joseph Slagle the other members. The congregation and the committee were guided most helpfully by Jacob Medtard, pastor at Martinsburg, whose spiritual ministrations during the interim of more than a year restored unity and harmony to the church. The committee went about its task with an intelligent dispatch that was most admirable.

Upon invitation of the committee Lewis Eichelberger, trained in theology at Gettysburg Seminary,[3] where he had been a member of the first class to enter the institution, came to Winchester and preached July 27, 1828. August 6, a congregational meeting was held which called him to the parish for one year at a salary of $400. He accepted September 8 and entered upon the field October 22.

Mr. Eichelberger was born in Frederick County, Maryland, August 25, 1803. Graduating from Dickinson College in 1826, he entered theological seminary and completed the two-year course. For him, too, Winchester became a first parish, and his coming to the congregation was a manifest satisfaction to his people. "And in connection with him," the Council minutes declare, October 27, "we hereby confess our sincere desire by all Scriptural and Christian means to promote the best interests and future welfare of said congregation." Here the minutes go on to say, "...and convinced that the present Constitution of our Church is little calculated to insure these advantages and aware that we should take up the subject of adopting a new Constitution with due deliberation and being apprised of the existence of a Committee of Correspondence, appointed by the members of this congregation, do therefore Resolve – That it is expedient to abolish the old and adopt a new Constitution, and that the Committee of Correspondence be invited to cooperate with us in framing a new system of Rules and Principles for the future government of the congregation to be submitted to the members of the Church for their adoption."

Obviously, no time was lost in getting the new preacher involved in past intricacies of the parish. Plunging into the stream, he swam with the current.

Lewis Eichelberger

A month later the members assembled at the lecture room of Dr. Hill, the Presbyterian minister, heard the first reading of the proposed new document, ordered three copies to be deposited with officers of the congregation – Lewis Hoff, Abraham Lauck and Jacob Baker – that individual members might examine them, designated Monday, December 8, as the day for voting upon its adoption and gave a special invitation to "females connected with the church" to attend the meeting.

When the appointed day arrived twenty-six gentlemen were present, but no mention is made of women in attendance. The new document, written by Jacob Baker in language fashioned after the Declaration of Independence, was adopted. It limited voting members to "all male members of good moral character." Before adjourning, the meeting elected elders and wardens and authorized that the organ be played under the superintendence of the Church Council.

Everything appeared to move along happily in the work of the congregation. The debt had been whittled down to about $90 by an arrangement whereby Daniel Linn and Godfrey Miller had been permitted to rent the parsonage, upon Reck's vacating it, and to apply the proceeds against their claims on the church. Further repairs were made to the church and cemetery fence, and a gravel walk was laid from the west end of the new Kent Street Presbyterian Church to the steps of the Lutheran Church. A monthly offering was pledged to the cause of missions, and the custom of receiving an offering each week to meet the incidental expenses of the congregation was begun. Miss Evelina Streit offered at a reasonable rent a room in her home in which to hold social and prayer meetings, which was duly accepted. The Masonic Fraternity was granted permission to hold a service in celebration of the festival of St. John the Baptist, and the Military of the Town obtained a similar permission to observe the Fourth of July. A register of pastoral acts was kept, something Mr. Eichelberger declared he never found on taking charge of the church. And the vexatious question of rules to govern the organ and choir, while causing some dissatisfaction, was handled with diplomacy, and Miss Mary Catherine Baker consented to be organist. A committee sent a letter to the dissatisfied and "politely but firmly, respectfully but candidly" stated the motives which impelled the passing of the measures that were taken.

Members of the Episcopal congregation, temporarily bereft of a place to worship, had been using the church, and through the secretary of their Vestry, Mr. Obed Waite, thanked the Council for the use of the building and the congregation for "their polite, friendly & accommodating conduct – such as shewed a catholic spirit worthy of an enlightened Christian community."

The Lutheran congregations in Virginia that had joined in the formation of the Synod of Maryland and Virginia had never been altogether happy with the results. Because its interests were concerned with developments north and west, rather than south, sentiment in Virginia soon crystallized into the conviction that a separate synod for Virginia was needed. In this whole question Lewis Eichelberger took a part. He was one of the eight pastors to meet at Woodstock, August 10-11, 1829, and thereby assisted in the founding of the present Lutheran Synod of Virginia.

Thus, when a year had gone by and a congregational meeting was held to consider the renewal of Eichelberger's call, the pastor seemed to have things pretty well under control. A call of unlimited tenure was extended to him. No fixed salary was promised him, however; he had only the assurance "that a subscription be annually circulated for his support and presented through the Council for his approval." Perhaps a subtle reasoning ruled in the minds of some members that, since the minister had married one of the flock, Miss Mary Ann, daughter of John Miller, prosperous merchant, papa would make up the difference anyway. It is not surprising, therefore, that the letter of acceptance should contain the following sentence: "Whatever may be the attachment of any congregation and pastor, and however mutually fond of each other – he, the pastor, must have a wherewithal to be fed & clothed, and should have something yearly laying up for a rainy day, else neither can expect their relation to be continued."

Forty-four male members, forming a constitutional quorum of two-thirds of all the qualified voters, had been present at the meeting. Their names recount an honored company from a by-gone day, names that should not be forgotten. Here they are in the order submitted by Jacob Baker and P.B. Streit, the secretaries: Henry W. Baker, John Miller, John Baker, Abraham Miller, Jacob Baker, John W. Miller, William A. Baker, Godfrey Miller, Henry Baker, Peter Miller, Henry F. Baker, William Miller, George W. Baker, Thomas Miller, Nathan C. Baker, Lewis Wolfe, Theophilus Conradt, Peter Lauck, John Heiskell, Joseph Slagle, Abraham Grove, John Crockwell, Jacob Mesmer, William H. Grove, John N. Crockwell, Abraham Lauck, Conrad Kremer, Thos. B. Campbell, John Schultz, John Sloat, William Washabaugh, Abraham Nulton, Jacob Kiger, George W. Grim, Lancelot Bell, Jacob Cooper, Stephen Jenkins, John Richardson, Stewart Grant, Philip B. Streit, Peter E. Sperry, Jacob Senseny, Charles F. Gelwick and George Aulick.

Here seems to be the proper place to insert a note on the Baker and Miller families. Both Henry Baker and Godfrey Miller had been pioneer settlers of Winchester; both had taken an active part in the Lutheran Church from the days of its infancy, Baker being one of the founders and Miller coming to Winchester a few years after its organization; both had prospered; and both had reared substantial families. Henry Baker was the father of six sons and a daughter, namely, Henry William, Isaac, John, Abraham, Joseph, Jacob and Elizabeth. Godfrey Miller had two daughters and seven sons: Anna Maria (Mrs. George Wolfe), Adam, John, Abraham, Rebecca (Mrs. Solomon Henkel), David, Godfrey, Samuel and Peter. The names of the majority of the children of these two men, and of the descendants of their children, recur constantly in the records of the church, and it is common knowledge that they were men and women staunch in character, dependable in their Christian obligations, and loyal to their church, as well as sturdy citizens of high standing in the community, who enjoyed the unfeigned respect of their fellow men.

We are indebted to Mr. W.W. Glass for the account of the following episode, which throws light upon our story at this juncture.

> At the period of the history of the church now under consideration, Henry William Baker and Abraham Miller were in a measure leaders of their respective clans. Both were eminently successful in their financial affairs, and both were equally fortunate in possessing the unqualified esteem of their fellow citizens. The two families enjoyed reciprocal relations of the most friendly nature.
>
> At this period of our history (exact date not now known), Abraham Miller, who lived in a frame dwelling on the east side of Loudoun Street (No. 24 South Loudoun), gave a *party* in his home to a considerable number of guests, among them several members of the Baker clan, including Mary Catherine Baker, the 23 year old daughter of Henry William Baker. Another of the guests was a Lutheran minister, then 35 years of age, viz: the Rev. Benjamin Kurtz, a native of Harrisburg, Pennsylvania.
>
> At the height of the festivities, Mr. Joseph Slagle, a prominent member of the Lutheran Church, and a friend of all concerned, joined Mr. Kurtz, and they both quietly left the house and went over to Dr. Abraham Miller's store which was north of, and adjacent to, the dwelling. Shortly thereafter Mary Catherine Baker quietly withdrew, and joined Mr. Slagle and Mr. Kurtz in the store.
>
> By previous arrangement made by Mr. Slagle, the Rev. William Hill, pastor of the Presbyterian Church, was on hand, and in short order performed the ceremony making the young couple husband and wife. Mr. Slagle and the contracting parties then returned to the entertainment, where Mr. Slagle presented the bride and groom to the astonished gathering. The members of the Baker clan there present immediately gave overt testimony to their disapprobation of the match, by tearing their hair, rolling on the floor, rolling over the ladies' bon-

nets which lay upon the beds, and staging a general rampage. The protesting parties assumed that the elopement had been planned, or at least sanctioned, by their host – Dr. Abraham Miller – and that the marriage ceremony had been performed by their pastor, the Rev. Lewis Eichelberger. Color was lent to this assumption by the fact that a short time prior thereto, the Rev. Lewis Eichelberger had led to the altar Mary Ann, the daughter of John Miller, and niece of Dr. Abraham Miller.

As a result of the uproar a number of the Baker clan discontinued their attendance upon the services in the church, and abandoned all intercourse with the Abraham Miller family. They were too *mad* to ask questions, and so the feud continued for a year or more, until it was learned that Dr. Abraham Miller was entirely innocent of any complicity in the episode, and that the Rev. Lewis Eichelberger was equally blameless. And so they all *made up*, the Bakers returned to their church; but it does not appear that the Rev. Benj. Kurtz was ever entirely forgiven. As shown by her tombstone in the old Lutheran cemetery Mary Catherine Kurtz died June 5, 1836, but the epitaph does not reveal the identity of her husband.

No reasonable explanation can now be given for the objection to the marriage, as the Rev. Benj. Kurtz had made an enviable record as a clergyman prior to the event here related. Biographical sketches in several church histories give him an unblemished character, and credit him with outstanding attainments. His picture published in several historical volumes reveals the assumption that *personal pulchritude* was not the quality that won his bride. He was, of course, impecunious, as were all clergymen of that period. The members of the early churches believed strongly in the graces of *humility and poverty* and took the position that if the Lord would keep their preachers *humble* they themselves would keep them *poor*.

The details of the above narrative were vouched for by Miss Mary Kurtz, a most estimable lady, who as a girl was present.

What has been related had harmful effects upon Lewis Eichelberger's ministry. The defection of all the Bakers save John and his family (the Henry Baker, carpenter, of the records was of another tribe) did the congregation no good. Jacob Baker, as secretary of the Council, resigned abruptly March 20, 1830. "Circumstances which it is unnecessary to detail, induce me to offer my resignation," he wrote. "No one can regret more than I do the necessity which urges me to this step."

No improvement could be noted in the affairs of the church by fall, when on November 26 a somewhat singular congregational meeting was held with a guest minister presiding. The visitor was none other than the Rev. Benj. Kurtz of Hagerstown, Maryland.

The minutes here need no elaboration.

> After several impressive views had been presented and the meeting seriously admonished and requested to aid in forwarding the prosperity, harmony, and brotherly love through forbearance the one towards the other, and the use of fervent prayer of all those who wished the building up of our beloved church and place her where she should stand, it was unanimously resolved
>
> 1st. That the present peculiar circumstances of the Lutheran Church in this place require more unanimity, interest and exertion among the members, more common love and forbearance, more of the true spirit of religion, of Christ, and of him whose name as Lutherans we bear, than has hitherto existed, and that without these things abounding in us richly, we need not look for our church to prosper....
>
> 2^{d}ly. That our coldness, indifference, and want of a proper spirit and regard for our church, and not the church itself, whose doctrine and practice as well as Name we mutually love, are the real and only cause why we seem neither to advance as a Church in strength or piety....
>
> 3^{d}ly. That we deeply regret that hitherto on repeated occasions, members have permitted little and unimportant causes to break in upon the peace and harmony of our Church, and more especially regret that at this time there are a goodly number of our people thus separated from us and the Church, notwithstanding the dear and great claims it has upon them...and as every such separation is painful to the Church, taking from it numerical force and strength, it becomes our

duty, by every proper means, to influence such to regard differently their Church and its claims, and to remain together as brethren should do....

4thly. That as members of our church are apparently separated from us, we hereby unanimously determine to use every proper exertion by persuasion, by intercession, and by the dear regard every Lutheran should have for the Church of his Fathers...again to bring them back...that for this end a special committee be appointed, consisting of John Baker, John Crockwell, John Hoff, John Miller, Daniel Linn and J.W. Miller, to wait personally in the name of the Congregation upon such and attend to the object of this resolution, and their success be recommended to us all, as a matter of earnest prayer & supplication with the great Head of the Church....

5thly. Resolved that the names of the Males and Females present be spread upon the record of the Church, to wit – The Rev. Lewis Eichelberger, John Baker, John Crockwell, John Miller, John Hoff, Abraham Grove, Jacob Mesmer, William Seemer, Daniel Linn, Thomas B. Campbell, John B. Campbell, Henry F. Baker, Joseph Slagle, Wm. H. Grove, Peter Miller, Michael Byars, John N. Crockwell, Solomon Dodd, Lewis A. Rosemiller, John W. Miller, Mrs. Peck, Mrs. Groves, Mrs. Slagle, Mrs. Kiger, Mrs. Miller, Mrs. Seemer, Mrs. Hampton, Mrs. Hoff, Mrs. M. Grove, Mrs. Conradt, Mrs. Miller, Mrs. Hoff, Mrs. S. Baker, Miss S. Wolfe, Miss P. Hoff, Miss R. Bell, Miss E. Linn, Miss S. Bile, Miss C. Wolfe, Miss M. Lauck, Miss Wolfe, Miss S. Hampton, Miss J. Kurtz, Miss R. Miller, Miss H. & S.A. Bowers, Miss Ball, and Miss Webber.

6thly. Resolved that the proceedings of this meeting be publicly read on the next Sabbath.

The approach to the problem was certainly a Christian and brotherly one, but it took time to produce beneficial results which Lewis Eichelberger was not to enjoy. He seems to have been confronted by an increasing financial problem. To augment his income he opened a school, the forerunner no doubt of his Angerona Seminary. As he did not occupy the parsonage, the building was rented and he was allowed $48 per annum from the rent. Because this figure did not represent the total income from rent, it became a bone of contention.

Eichelberger presented in installments his resignation to the Council during March and April 1833, requesting at the same time a "speedy settlement of all dues on the part of the congregation." He later billed the Council for items amounting to $18.47, besides parsonage rent due him, and laid claim to the full rentals from the parsonage. His note irked the councilmen and they said so in their minutes:

> Inasmuch as the note mentioned above contains certain insinuations of unfairness and absurdity in the course the Council had deemed proper to pursue—be it further resolved that the Council repel the insinuation of unfairness and absurdity directed against them, that a genuine and Christian forbearance admonishes them to attribute the dictation of that note, neither to motives of parsimony nor of a disposition to arraign the fairness and honesty of the Council, but to those of securing to himself his just rights.

With a background as stated, the Council's letter accepting the resignation is a gem.

> Winchester, April 1833.
>
> Rev^d and Resp^d Sir
>
> The Council of the Lutheran Church in this place received your communications of March last & of the present Inst., and has had them and their contents under consideration. Altho it be a source of deep regret, they cannot but concur with you in your opinions concerning the present condition of our church, and consider you perfectly justified in the course you have determined to pursue. Thy do so, however, not without such feelings as must necessarily be excited when about to separate from a Minister who has had the charge of their spiritual improvement & religious instruction for a space of more than four years.
>
> But they have come to the conclusion that it is not their duty, nor is it their work, to interfere with the wise dispensations of a Divine Providence, to do so, would in their opinions be an act of superarrogation.

Hence they are content in the Providence of God in removing you from our church. Permit them, Resp^d Sir, to unite their wishes with yours, that the vacancy about to be occasioned by your resignation will, under the favor of Heaven, be supplied by an ardent and zealous successor.

Suffer us in conclusion to say that we accept of your resignation, and do express our most cordial wishes for your personal prosperity and for your success as an Instrument in the hands of God in extending the Kingdom of Jesus Christ our Redeemer, The Light, The Truth, and The Way —

Rev^d and Resp^d Sir, Your Friends

J.W. Miller	Jno. Baker
William Seemer	John Hoff
Theoph. F. Conradt	W.H. Grove
	John Crockwell
	Peter Bell

While resigning from the Winchester congregation, Mr. Eichelberger continued to reside in the town and to serve the congregations in the country. In 1833 he established Angerona Seminary, a boarding and day school for girls, and conducted it until 1849. From May 1833 to April 1835 he edited and published at Winchester the monthly "Evangelical Lutheran Preacher and Pastoral Messenger, Being Sermons and Occasional Articles, Doctrinal and Practical, by Ministers of the Lutheran Church, with notes by the editor; All designed to Illustrate and Defend the Principles of Religion as Held and Taught by Lutherans." He likewise served for a time as editor and proprietor of a Winchester weekly newspaper, *The Virginian*. From 1849-1858 he was professor in the Lutheran Theological Seminary at Lexington, South Carolina. He received a D.D. degree from Princeton in 1853. His wife having died in 1837, he married two years later Penelope A. Hay. He was the father of six children. He died at Winchester September 16, 1859, and was buried in Mount Hebron Cemetery.

NICHOLAS WESTERMANN GOERTNER, 1834-1836

The pastorate of Nicholas W. Goertner began February 1, 1834, and ended June 1, 1836. It produced two events of considerable significance in the life of the congregation. The first was a rather drastic alteration to the interior of the church; the second the return of Jacob Baker and others of the Baker clan to active participation in the congregation's work and worship.

Goertner came to Winchester the end of December 1833 to preach a trial sermon, and he went away with a call in his pocket. A few days later he was notified that the congregation would pay him a salary of $360, and his letter of acceptance was written from Washington on January 6, 1834. He had been entertained in the home of John Baker, and a month later when he returned as pastor, he and Mrs. Goertner stayed at the John Bakers until they could find suitable living accommodations elsewhere. During their Winchester residence they did not live in the parsonage. The Council continued to rent that building and to apply the rental on the pastor's salary.

In accepting the call Goertner wrote: "I am aware, my friends, that in the present state of your congregation I shall have many difficulties to contend with which will require prudence, foresight, and decision that, perhaps, will exceed my ability. But I know that you will not leave me to contend singlehanded and alone, but that an efficient Council will be to my assistance."

The work started well. Before a month was up plans to alter the church's interior were under way. This included tearing out the south gallery and moving the organ to the north gallery, moving the pulpit from the east wall to the south wall, closing the doors in the west, north and east walls and opening two doors in the south wall where windows were. Two slips of pews were to be placed in the center, and a slip at each side. The renovation was estimated to cost $500. In April a committee was appointed to raise the money by subscription, and in August the work was authorized to be done. The following March the refinished edifice was offered to the Methodists for use during the sessions of their conference.

Nicholas Westermann Goertner

Goertner applied to the Council for a three-month leave of absence beginning in July 1835. His motive in so doing is not stated, but certain implications from the minutes point to the salary question. His request was granted, and in his absence the pulpit was supplied by the Rev. Henry Haverstick, a classmate of Lewis Eichelberger at Gettysburg Seminary, who had recently returned to the country from study in Germany. In view of the fact that there is a break in the Council minutes from July to January, the assumption is that Goertner remained away six months instead of three.

A congregational meeting in February 1836 voted unanimously to renew Goertner's call. He had been called for one year, but the subject of extending the call had not been attended to when his first twelve months expired. Lewis Eichelberger presided over this meeting. Because of his continued residence in Winchester, Mr. Eichelberger remained in harmonious fellowship with his late parish, frequently serving in various helpful capacities. Also at the above-mentioned meeting, Jacob Baker was chosen secretary. Once again he was elected to the Council, full evidence of his return to the fold.

Apparently Goertner waited to see what the subscription in behalf of his support would amount to before giving answer to his second call. The committee named to perform this duty had not completed its work by April 27. Three days later it reported, but the report, whatever it was, was not to the preacher's satisfaction. He resigned May 12, effective June 1, 1836.

Nicholas Westermann Goertner was born February 22, 1810, at Canajoharie, New York. A student at Hartwick Seminary and graduate of Union College (1831), he entered Gettysburg Seminary in 1832 and was ordained by the Maryland Synod in 1834. Winchester was his first parish. Upon his departure he served parishes at Rhinebeck, New York, and Lockport, New York. In 1848 he entered the ministry of the Presbyterian Church and was pastor of congregations at Palmyra, New York, Canandaigua, New York, New York City and Philadelphia, after which he became agent for the American Tract Society. From 1863-1880 he was pastor of the College Church at Clinton, New York, and for a time was professor in Hamilton College. Genesee College conferred upon him the D.D. degree in 1854. He died January 10, 1887.

THEOPHILUS STORK, 1837-1841

For sixteen months after Goertner's resignation the congregation was without a pastor. A committee on correspondence, consisting of Jacob Baker, Thomas B. Campbell, H.F. Baker and Lewis Eichelberger, had been appointed to fill the vacancy, but their work seems to have been taken over by the Council as a whole. During the summer of 1836 negotiations were carried on with Charles Martin, M.D., a student at Gettysburg Seminary, but nothing came of the matter.

Unfortunately the Council minutes during this period have a number of gaps. The continuity of the record is broken and desired details are missing. By spring, however, Lewis Eichelberger reported the name of another student at Gettysburg Seminary, Theophilus F. Stork, to whom approach was made. He was in Winchester September 23-24 and was authorized to give notice from the pulpit that a congregational meeting would be held Monday, October 9. At the same time the council appointed the church wardens a committee "to call upon the citizens of the town for the purpose of raising a salary for the Rev. Mr. Stork." Dr. D.M. Gilbert is authority for saying that Stork took charge of the church October 9, 1837, presumably the date on which he was called to the pastorate.

Son of a pioneer North Carolina pastor, Theophilus F. Stork was born near Salisbury in August 1814. A graduate of Gettysburg College (1835) and of Gettysburg Seminary (1837), he was another young pastor whose ministry began at Winchester. November 16, 1837, he married Miss Mary Jane Lynch, of Jefferson, Maryland. Their son, Charles Augustus Stork, born the following year at his maternal grandfather's home, was later to be the roommate of James A. Garfield at Williams College and to become head of Gettysburg Seminary.

Stork's four-year pastorate proved to be a popular one in the community as well as in the congregation, and he made for himself an enviable reputation both as preacher and pastor. It was under his leadership that the growing sentiment to move to a new location, held by many of the members, crystallized and came to action.

For a number of years the congregation had been toying with the idea of buying a more centrally located lot and building a lecture room. The prevailing notion seems at first to have been a desire to have a place for prayer meetings, evening services and occasional social gatherings. Evening services and prayer meetings in the church had been inaugurated by Abraham Reck. Miss Evelina Streit's offer in 1829 of a room in her home for "social and prayer meetings" was quickly accepted. Two years later Council appointed a committee to investigate the purchase of a lot and erection of a building. "Inexpedient at this time for want of funds" was the committee's report. By the end of 1832, a room was rented from the Messrs. Peter and William Sperry, and this seems to have been used until the present Boscawen Street property was acquired.

Theophilus Stork

Discerning minds could see, however, that more was involved than a mere lecture room. It was a question of new location for the church. It was no easy matter to embark upon a program which meant leaving the old church on the hill, an edifice that entrenched itself more securely in sentimental regard with the passing of every year.

When, therefore, a congregational meeting, held October 28, 1839, took action to buy the lot on Boscawen (Water) Street where the church now stands, its original decision was to purchase one-half of the lot only, or about fifty feet along Indian

Alley. The fifteen who voted in favor of this move, including Theophilus Stork and Lewis Eichelberger, thought simply in terms of the lecture hall, while the three who opposed it, Dr. Abraham Miller, Joseph Slagle and John Crockwell, thought otherwise. For the group it was a crucial decision to make, and for the future of the church it was imperative that the right decision be made.

The above action was questioned from the start by those who were thinking ahead of the rest. They got busy and had a second congregational meeting called for November 11. Jacob Baker, absent at the former meeting, spoke on the advantages of purchasing the whole lot. The decision of the preceding meeting was voted to be reconsidered, and new action was taken unanimously to buy the entire lot. Abraham Miller, Joseph Slagle, J.W. Miller, Jacob Baker and Pastor Stork were made the Collecting, Contracting and Building Committee, to which T.B. Campbell was added a year later, and they were given "full power to contract for the said lot of ground, and have said lot conveyed to them as the Trustees for the Lutheran Congregation, and to collect and receive all sums subscribed for and towards the accomplishment of the object heretofore expressed, and are further authorized and empowered to do all other acts in promoting the said object, and that full faith and credit should be given them as such."

Eleven hundred dollars was the price of the new lot, bought of George W. Baker and Emily Susan, his wife. The deed of conveyance was made January 29, 1840.

Mr. Stork was absent from Winchester for several months, following the decision to purchase the Water Street lot. During this time the church was supplied by the Rev. George Diehl. Then after another year Mr. Stork resigned somewhat abruptly. His resignation occurred August 17, 1841. It was tendered verbally at a Council meeting, followed by a letter. The Council did not anticipate such a turn in events, nor did it wish to. A letter was sent in reply, illustrative of the esteem for the pastor on the part of all. It follows.

> The members of the Church Council of the Lutheran Church in Winchester at a special meeting of said council convened for the purpose, have conferred together upon the subject of your resignation so unexpectedly communicated to the Council at its meeting on Monday evening last, and they deeply regret that they were not earlier apprized of your intended arrangements on this subject, affecting as they do so deeply the interest of the congregation, and appreciating as they can not fail to do, the relation you have sustained to the congregation and the extent of usefulness resulting from your services as its Pastor, and aware of the affectionate regard in which yourself personally and your labors as their minister are held, not only by the congregation, but by the whole community of Winchester, and believing that your separation from us at this particular crisis must materially, if not fatally affect the present flattering prospects of the congregation perhaps for years, and knowing also the unanimous wish of the congregation that your situation among them as far as the means of support are concerned, should be entirely comfortable and that difficulty need not be apprehended as concerns such increased support, the Council knowing fully the disposition of the congregation on this subject, the members of the Council and in behalf of the congregation they represent, earnestly desire that you will reconsider the subject of your removal from them, and again weigh more fully than they think you have done, the embarrassed situation in which your present separation from the congregation here will leave it, as well as the strong claims the congregation believes it has, growing out of a variety of circumstances with your past labors, upon your continuance with them. They propose this under a solemn impression of the great importance of the subject to the congregation, and in the earnest hope that upon such reconsideration you may yet feel it your sacred duty to continue as heretofore the pas-

toral relation you have sustained to it with so much success to its interests, and as they trust, with entire satisfaction to yourself personally.

The Council have, therefore, resolved to have no action upon the subject of your resignation addressed to them until they will thus have communicated with you more fully on the subject, hoping as they do, that under more matured views you may still take of it, your ultimate decision may lead you to continue with us.

Meantime, Stork had gone on to Philadelphia to become pastor for one year of St. Matthew's Lutheran Church. He wrote a reply to the foregoing letter, accepting the work at Winchester once more and promising to return in the spring, or at the end of his year. But when May 1842 arrived he wrote again asking to be released from his obligation to return, as matters of health were involved. To this request, the Council acquiesced graciously.

Mr. Stork continued to serve St. Matthew's, Philadelphia, until 1850, then for eight years he was pastor of St. Mark's Church in the same city. From 1858-1860 he was president of Newberry College in South Carolina. Returning north with the threat of war, he served St. Mark's Church, Baltimore, for five years and then St. Andrew's Church in Philadelphia, from 1865-1871. Dr. Stork was one of the founders of the former East Pennsylvania Synod. As a writer he edited several religious journals and was the author of eight books on New Testament and Luther themes. His wife died in 1846. For his second wife he married Miss Emma Baker. Besides his son Charles A., he had two other sons, William L. and Theophilus B. He died March 28, 1874, at Philadelphia.

JAMES ROBERTSON KEISER, 1841-1843

When it became known to the Council in October, 1841, that Theophilus Stork would return to his former parish the following year, an effort was made at once to obtain a supply minister to bridge the gap of the temporary vacancy. A letter was addressed October 23 to James R. Keiser, a graduate of Gettysburg College in 1838, whose theological preparation had been obtained both at Gettysburg Seminary and the seminary at Andover, Massachusetts. He was available, not having yet settled in a parish. After the exchange of several letters Mr. Keiser decided to come to Winchester as a stated supply. He began his work the last Sunday in the month of November. Upon the release of Mr. Stork from his engagement to return, the congregation elected Mr. Keiser pastor, July 18, 1842, and in this official capacity he served until February 1843. Mr. Keiser's relationship to the congregation, therefore, extended over a little more than fourteen months, of which time far more than eight months he was acting pastor only.

Regardless of the brevity of this ministry, the time when it occurred was most important in the life of the church. For the new building was erected and dedicated. As with the size of the lot, so too with the original idea of the building, a lecture room, modest in size and expense, was first planned. When, however, it was determined to buy a lot big enough for a church, that decision forced the expansion of the plans for what was to be built. The result was a plain brick structure, stiff and stolid, two stories high, without any of the adornments or refinements that set off a building at a glance as a church. The ground floor was used for lecture room and Sunday School, and the upper floor for the services of worship. It was no easy matter to wean the members away from their old stone house of prayer,

This Heritage

and it took time to make the new sanctuary a worthy successor to the old, where devout hearts would feel at home amidst their new surroundings.

The first use of the new building of which there is record occurred December 8, 1842, when a congregational meeting was held in "the Lecture Room of the New Church" to name a trustee to succeed Dr. Abraham Miller, deceased. Peter Miller was duly elected. The five trustees, John W. Miller, Jacob Baker, Joseph Slagle, Thomas B. Campbell and Peter Miller, were then unanimously elected trustees of the "old church property." They were already serving as trustees for the new. At the same meeting "on motion of Jacob Baker, it was resolved to commence a succession of prayer meetings in this house on this night week, to continue until the commencement of the meetings appointed for the consecration of the church."

James Robertson Keiser

Sunday, January 1, 1843, witnessed the services of dedication. The Rev. Frederick W. Conrad, then pastor at Waynesboro, Pennsylvania, was the preacher. The new property had been obtained at a total cost of $6,592.30, and of this amount $2,300 was owing to the Bank of the Valley. A month after the dedication the pastor presented his resignation and made his departure.

James Robertson Keiser was a native of Waynesboro, Virginia, born September 28, 1812. On leaving Winchester he served Lutheran parishes at New Germantown (Oldwick), New Jersey (1843-1849); Schoharie, New York (1849-1856); St. James, Gettysburg, Pennsylvania, (1858-1861); and Dixon, Illinois (1861-1864). From 1856-1858 he was agent for the American Tract Society. About 1864 he entered the ministry of the Presbyterian Church, served a congregation at Theresa, New York, and then was with the American Sunday School Union in New Jersey. In 1843 he married Miss Eliza Murphy. He died near Petersburg, Virginia, October 12, 1872.

JOSEPH FEWSMITH, JR., 1843-1848

A nine-month vacancy followed upon the heels of J.R. Keiser's pastorate. For a time Robert B. Wolfe, at the request of the congregation, carried on personal negotiations with the Rev. Mr. Conrad, without result. Then on June 3, 1843, a congregational meeting attended by thirty-nine voting males assembled. "The object of the meeting was explained to be the subject of adopting a speedy mode of supplying our pulpit with a useful & satisfactory pastor, and after various suggestions and much conversation, it was unanimously resolved that a direct call for that station should be extended to the Rev. J. FewSmith of Valatie, New York." So the minutes read.

The subsequent exchange of letters reveals a number of points of interest. The committee of correspondence, composed of Lewis Eichelberger, Jacob Baker, William Miller, John W. Miller and Thomas B. Campbell, wrote Mr. FewSmith June 6, informing him of the action, and that $500 was promised for his support. "We are also enabled to state," the letter went on to say, "that from two other congregations in the vicinity of Winchester, and heretofore served by the pastor of this congregation, an additional sum of $100, it is supposed, will be raised."

Since Mr. FewSmith was not at all acquainted with the congregation or with Winchester the letter further explained:

> The Lutheran congregation in Winchester is probably the largest in the place, during the last year a large addition has been made to the number of its members, and in many respects its interest and its prospects are encouraging. We believe that we only need the services of a pious and efficient minister, with the blessing of God, to make them greatly successful. We have recently erected a new and spacious house of worship in a more central and advantageous location than the old building, which is now completed, and will greatly add to the advantage of the congregation. Winchester is a pleasant and healthy residence, containing about 4,000 inhabitants, has a good market, and living by no means dear. We are a little over 100 miles from Baltimore, a railroad connecting the two places and travel only about eight hours between them.

Mr. FewSmith, in Philadelphia, replied to Mr. Eichelberger June 24:

> It is impossible for me at present to give any intimation as to the acceptance of the invitation of your church. My people at Valatie are very unwilling that our connection should be dissolved, and are making efforts to provide for my better support. Allow me to say that I was surprised that a church of the character which I have attributed to the one at Winchester, should offer so small a salary; and am doubtful as to its adequacy to maintain a man and wife comfortably.

Mr. FewSmith, having returned to his home at Valatie, wrote the entire committee July 21:

> At present the probability is that I shall accept your invitation.... If I should decide to become your pastor, I should not be able to be with you previous to about the first of October.... Please state

in your reply to this, what probability there is of your furnishing a suitable parsonage – also at what price good board and lodging, including washings, can be obtained, for myself, and also in case of my marriage, what arrangements could be made?

July 26 the committee responded:

Your favour of the 21st has... inspired increased confidence in the hope that you will still feel constrained to regard the strong solicitations of the church here, as a sufficient indication of Providence to determine you in favour of the call.... A suitable parsonage such as would be entirely comfortable and convenient may be had at about $100, boarding, including washing etc., at about $120, and for two (in case of your marriage) at about double that sum. Relative to the matter of support we are enabled to state that the amount of subscriptions on the presumption of your acceptance of the call has already been increased to over $550 and which the Council, after conferring with the congregation, at once engage to increase to $600, $100 over what was originally stated in our call."

From Brooklyn, August 15, Mr. FewSmith replied:

After painful & prayerful deliberation already too long protracted...I have reached the conclusion that it is my duty to accept.... I cannot now state definitely the time when you may expect me but I fear it will not be before the 1st of November.... It is proper to state that I expect to be married before settling among you.

The committee answered August 21:

It has been our increasing prayer that the Providence of God might lead you into our midst, and we believe that the great Head of the Church will bless the connection formed to the good of His cause, and your abundant usefulness amongst us.... You will of course inform us in due time by letter when we may expect you amongst us, though we cheerfully leave the time to be governed by the conveniency of your own arrangements, we still hope that you may be able to get to Winchester somewhat earlier than the time designated. As you advise us that you will be married before settling amongst us, if we knew the lady of your choice, we should solicit her intercession on our behalf for an abridgment of the time. We unite our congratulations in this particular and hope that your change in this important incident in life may prove all that you desire it.... Mr. Eichelberger will be able to furnish rooms convenient for your accommodation; you will be better able to make the necessary arrangements for procuring a house and preparing for occupying it, than to procure one immediately, and hence advise that these arrangements be left undetermined until after you arrive...With Mr. Eichelberger you will be furnished with every accommodation until they are made. The Committee agree with you that it would be useless to visit the congregation before you come on to take personally the charge of it....

The new minister, sight unseen, and his bride came to town about the first of November. His first sermon was delivered the first Sunday of the month, and a splendid ministry of four years and four months it turned out to be. The Council's first request of him was to select a pew for the use of his family in the new church.

A scholarly preacher, he soon won a following among his own people and his fellow citizens of the town. Prayer meetings were held each Wednesday and Saturday evening. He preached at the "Yeackley Congregation" once a month, presumably in addition to the other two rural congregations mentioned in the call. Through his vision the congregation purchased a 36-foot lot immediately west of the new church with future needs in mind. Plans were inaugurated to place a cupola on the church and to move the bell from the old building into it, as well as to dispose of the old organ and purchase a new one.

When the Diocese of Virginia met in Winchester, the church was offered to the Episcopalians, and when the Winchester presbytery met here, it was tendered to the Presbyterians. A request, however, from the Old School Baptists for use of the old church for an indefinite length of time was denied.

Joseph FewSmith, Jr.

Pastor FewSmith's handling of finances was especially vigorous and business like. He insisted that he be paid what had been promised him, and without undue delay, and that the congregation bear the cost of his house rent, $150 annually. In the same manner he tackled the problem of the church's debt. There is evidence that on one occasion some money for this purpose was raised by a fair, though the sum is not stated. His method of raising funds was direct giving for the specific need at hand. Thus, at a congregational meeting, January 12, 1846, held to deal with the question, he raised on the spot $934 from the twenty men and their families present. A similar procedure was followed even after he had submitted his resignation and it had been accepted. Fifteen hundred dollars was still owed on the new church, and the expense of operating the oil lamps had brought on a debt of $123 for coal oil. At a meeting of the Council, February 7, 1848, to which other members of the church had been invited, it was determined to liquidate the entire debt, and $1,230 was subscribed by those present. A committee appointed to visit absentees raised another $500 so that all bills were erased from the records and FewSmith could leave the congregation with its church building debt free.

Mr. FewSmith resigned January 17 in order to accept the call to the chair of Sacred Rhetoric and Pastoral Theology in the Theological Seminary at Auburn, New York, the resignation to be effective March 1. And the Council in accepting it did so with mingled sentiments of sorrow and gratification. "For while we feel sincere sorrow at the severance of a connexion which has been fruitful in much good and pleasure to us and those we represent, we feel gratified that the high qualities and acquirements which adorn your character are so appreciated by others as in the Providence of God to call you to a more extensive and liberal sphere of usefulness." This letter was signed by John Crockwell, Jacob Baker, Wm. H. Grove, Wm. Miller, Wm. Seemer and Thos. B. Campbell, Elders, and by Peter Miller, Robt. B. Wolfe, Caspar Nott, Ed. Hoffman, John S. Heist and Wm. B. Baker, Wardens.

In preaching a farewell sermon, February 27, 1848, Mr. FewSmith summarized his work as follows:

> During my ministry in Winchester there have been added to the church 31 persons. Of these 9 were received on profession, the remainder on certificate. I have baptized 26 children, have attended 32 funerals, of these not more than 11 were for members of the church. There have been contributed to the Bible and Tract Societies, Foreign and Domestic Missions, Education and other objects upwards of $800, or about $200 per annum, while during the same period the sum of $2,500 has been paid in liquidation of the church debt, and for repairs, and for interest and incidental expenses. The text of the sermon, Philippians 4:1, was: 'Therefore, my brethren, dearly beloved and longed for, my joy and crown, so stand fast in the Lord.'

Joseph FewSmith, Jr., was born in Philadelphia, January 7, 1816. He attended Yale College, where he graduated in 1840, and proceeded with the study of theology at Western Reserve College. In 1843 he was ordained to the ministry of the Lutheran Church at Rhinebeck, New York, while serving as pastor of the Lutheran congregation at Valatie. Before coming to Winchester he married Miss Emma C. Livingston, New York City, on October 31, 1843. He occupied the Bellamy and Edward Professorship of Sacred Rhetoric and Pastoral Theology at Auburn Seminary, 1848-1851, after which time he became pastor of the Second Presbyterian Church, Newark, New Jersey, where he continued to serve until his death, June 22, 1888. He was the recipient of the D.D. degree from Columbia College in 1855. He published a number of sermons, articles and tracts.

CHARLES PORTERFIELD KRAUTH, 1848-1855

Before Mr. FewSmith left Winchester, he saw to it that the congregation extended a call to a successor. On February 28, 1848, a neighboring pastor from Shepherdstown and Martinsburg was invited officially at a salary of $600 to take charge of the church. The Council notified him by letter the next day, declaring: "We take great pleasure, Dear Sir, in making this communication, and we trust that you will be led by divine Grace to comply with our invitation. The unanimity which has been manifested in the action of the congregation will not fail to have weight in your mind, as in some measure indicating the will of God." And when on March 9 the letter of acceptance was written, it stated: "The unanimity with which you assured me the choice was made, I regard with you as Providential in its character. . . .I trust that under the gracious smile of divine favour time will prove that the call and acceptance alike were directed by God." Time indeed proved that they were.

And so it was that the most distinguished pastor the Lutherans of Winchester ever had began his labors among them on April 9, 1848.

It was one of those natural and fitting situations that contributed to Charles Porterfield Krauth's acceptance of the call. Here his father, Charles Philip, had studied for a year under Abraham Reck, during which time, no doubt, he made the acquaintance of Miss Catharine Susan Heiskell, whom he later married. Their son was born to them on March 17, 1823, at Martinsburg, where the father ministered. Graduating from Gettysburg College at the age of sixteen, from Gettysburg Seminary at the age of eighteen, and being ordained a year later, Charles Porterfield Krauth served a mission congregation at Canton, Baltimore; then from 1842-1847 he was pastor of the Lombard Street Church in the same city, from which he went to his father's first parish at Shepherdstown and Martinsburg, where he himself had been born. In coming to Winchester he came to the parish his mother's people had helped establish. He had just passed his twenty-fifth birthday and came with a wife, the former Miss Susan Reynolds, whom he had married November 12, 1844. His ministry extended to October 1, 1855, and was memorable in a number of ways.

The new church was adorned and more fully completed with cupola and columns and frescoing and new lights and organ. Initial plans for these improvements were begun in December 1849, and a committee was named to procure subscriptions. This committee reported the end of January that $352.50 had been subscribed by 26 members, five of whom made their gifts on the condition that the requisite amount be raised and no church debt be created, and it was estimated that another $150 could be raised. Since, however, a larger sum would be needed, a different procedure would have to be followed. After further consideration of the whole project, it was then decided to add a new organ to the appeal for cupola, lights and painting and let the members subscribe to a "list naming each of the four improvements and request subscribers to state the amount they wish to contribute to each or any of them." By the end of February some $1,200 had been pledged, the work was authorized, and Jacob Baker, William Miller and Thomas B. Campbell constituted a committee to carry out the resolutions of the Council and empowered to borrow an amount necessary to meet the expenses until the subscriptions should be paid.

Charles Porterfield Krauth

These improvements were made during the summer and fall of 1850, and the church was reopened for worship on November 24. The cost of building the cupola and hanging the bell from the old church in it, of painting and fresco work, of lamps, tables, chairs and settees for the gallery, came to $1,965.99, of which $1,150 had to be borrowed, while the organ cost an even one thousand dollars, of which three hundred had to be borrowed. From the proceeds of a fair conducted by the ladies of the congregation, a contribution of $835 had been made toward the total cost, $400 of which went to the organ and the rest to the other improvements.

The second noteworthy accomplishment of the Krauth

The Church — 1850-1876

pastorate was the purchase of the parsonage on the northeast corner of Loudoun and Cecil Streets. It had been the property of George W. Seever, and Mr. and Mrs. Krauth were occupying it when it was bought. While there was talk of building a parsonage in June 1848, three more years were required for the movement to gain momentum. Regenerated interest in the matter occurred in April 1851, and soon the women were passing a subscription paper around and the men were doing likewise. As a partial result of the effort made by the ladies, over $1,000 was raised, payable in five annual installments, and about $750 was obtained by the committee on the gentlemen's list, payable in the same way. On May 15, Jacob Baker, of the parsonage committee, reported that a thorough examination of the Seever property had been made, that committee members "were well pleased with it in every particular, that they thought it best to secure it at once, and they had accordingly purchased it for the sum of $3,000." A bequest from John Hoff, who died about this time, provided another $750 for the parsonage.

    The illness and death of Mrs. Krauth added a somber note to her husband's ministry in Winchester. In September 1852, on account of her ill-health, the Council granted a leave of absence to Mr. Krauth. He and his wife went to the West Indies and spent the winter and did not return to Winchester until the end of June. Meanwhile Mr. Krauth supplied the pulpit of the Dutch Reformed congregation at St. Thomas, during the absence of its pastor, and Milton Valentine, fresh out of Gettysburg Seminary, took charge in Winchester. His services were most acceptable to the congregation and he was given a "handsome and valuable gift" by his admirers at their termination. The condition of Mrs. Krauth, temporarily improved by the change of climate, grew worse on her return home. She died November 18, 1853.

A fourth item to which special notice should be given was the meeting of the General Synod, which convened at Winchester, May 21, 1853. It was a sizable undertaking for the congregation since there were one hundred seventy-five delegates and official guests in attendance, and the Krauths were still away.

Varied and extensive preparations had to be made by the members of the Council. The committee to procure accommodations reported on May 16 that places had been provided for 131, 70 in the homes of families of the congregation, and that 15 or 20 more could be entertained, if necessary. Caspar Nott, Edward Hoffman and W.B. Baker were the committee. Jacob Baker, William Miller and Thomas B. Campbell were appointed a committee to distribute the delegates on their arrival, to be assisted by Messers. Nott, Hoffman and W.B. Baker, and Messrs. J. Baker, W. Miller and T.B. Campbell and Rev. Mr. Valentine were to receive the delegates at the church, while other members of the Council were to receive them at the cars and stage offices.

The Church Council at its meeting on June 6 directed the following very interesting minutes to be entered in the official record:

> The General Synod of the Evangelical Lutheran Church in the United States, convened in this place on Saturday, the 21st ult. The convention was regularly organized in the afternoon and the following officers elected:
> Rev. Dr. J. Bachman, President
> Rev Chas. A. Hay, Secretary
> J.D. Martin, Esq., Assistant Secretary
> P.S. Michler, Treasurer
> The Synod then adjourned until Monday morning at 9 o'clock.
> On Sabbath at 11 A.M. Revd S.S. Schmucker, D.D., preached the usual synodical Sermon from Acts 9:31.
> The Synod met again on Monday, and continued to hold

two sessions daily until Thursday evening, when it finally adjourned to convene at Dayton, Ohio, on the 14th day of June, 1855. Much business of interest to the Church and promotion of its welfare was transacted. The afternoon sessions were usually devoted to the business of the several benevolent Societies connected with the Synod. Anniversaries of these Societies were held at night. That of the Foreign Missionary Society was celebrated on Monday night. After a number of addresses, life-memberships and a collection were taken, together amounting to about $350.

The Home Missionary Society met on Tuesday night. Addresses were delivered, and then life-memberships were constituted and a collection was taken, both adding $1100 to the funds of the association.

On Wednesday night the Parent Education Society held its anniversary. The proceeds from life-memberships and the collection this night were about $580.

On Thursday night there was a meeting of the Historical Society, and after the usual address, Rev^d Dr. Bachman, President of the Synod, in its name, acknowledged the kind hospitality of the people of Winchester and dismissed the Convention.

There were in attendance at the Synod 102 regular delegates, clerical and lay, representing 20 District Synods. Besides these, there were about 75 visiting ministers and other strangers enjoying the hospitality of the congregation and community.

W.B. Baker, Secty.

The fifth event of importance, although a major calamity to the congregation and entire community, was the burning of the former house of worship, the old stone church upon the hill. This much-lamented tragedy took place the night of September 27, 1854. Let Mr. Krauth, an eyewitness of the event, tell in his vivid way what he saw.

> I confess when with hundreds of others I stood and gazed on the slow progress of the flames on the church, as though they were reluctant to execute their work, my first impression was that it might easily be saved. But when I reflected on the intense drouth, not of weeks but of months, which had

made that roof like tinder, remembered that the slow spreading of the flame upon it showed that the fire was burrowing in the dry moss and incipient decay on its surface, saw with what difficulty the fierce fire raging below it with residences all around was subdued owing to the great scarcity of water, I felt that it would not be easy, even at an early period, to extinguish the flames.... Many eyes that gazed upon it were in tears, as if an old friend was slowly dying. There it stood so meekly, offering its silent plea for preservation; the fire spreading, yet lingering, as if not unwilling that some hand should check it. First a single light tongue of flame seemed to play upon the edge of the roof, and then another, and another, creeping each toward each. At last high upon the spire began to blaze out a lone, lurid star of flame, like Mars upon the horizon of a sultry day, and then hearts began to tremble which up to that moment had not doubted that the Old Church might be saved. But the appointed hour had come. It had not come without a warning. Like an old man admonished by paralysis that the next blow will come from a hand which will lay him in the grave, our church had more than a year ago been touched by lightning stroke, which proved an omen of that fiery death which was now at hand. At last through doors and windows, as if infuriated at having been so long neglected, the flames surged like the surf of ocean through the cliffs it has worn into openings. Scarcely could flame justify itself as an image of wrath in a form more vivid than that which it now showed itself. It had leaped from point to point, exultant and panting. At first it had been like some serpent softly moving toward its prey, its head bent low, its scales trailing softly along the ground, its forked red tongue playing silently; now with towering crest, and gleaming eyes, and frightful hissings, it whirled its coils of fire around its victim. Portions of roof, rafters, and gallery fell, with a sound like thunder. The flame spread among the graves, through the dry grass with the parchings of an unexampled summer, it fiercely followed through all their windings the dead roots of the venerable trees which once stood before the Church, and spared not the sweetbriar which for years had breathed its fragrance by the door. The spire, which so long had pointed to heaven, lifted its finger to the last, like some brave old martyr unsubdued by the flames. Till the last iron ligament was sundered, it pointed with holy obstinacy up to God, and when everything else that flame could absorb had vanished, it stood, though in fragments, rooted amid massive stones, and towering to the skies.

The origin of the fire apparently was never determined, though by common consent it was regarded as the work of an incendiary hand. There was criticism too, of the fire companies for their failure to put out the flames, but Krauth wholly exonerated them from any such blame.

October 23, "The Burning of the Old Church" was taken as the theme for the pastor's sermon. It was a memorable discourse based upon the text from Isaiah 64:11 – "Our holy and beautiful house, where our fathers praised Thee, is burned up with fire." Already it has been the source of extensive quotation, for it rescued from oblivion many facts connected with the congregation's first hundred years of life. The pathos and sentiment and sympathetic understanding that it manifested, the glowing appreciation of the past from which lessons for the present were drawn with such deft precision, the lift of the vision upward, the poetry of expression, the craftsmanship of the workman, all combined to make of it an unforgettable message. Two days after its delivery, a group of citizens sent Mr. Krauth the following letter:

Winchester, Virginia, October 25, 1854.
Rev. C.P. Krauth:

Dear Sir – We desire to express the pleasure which we in common with a very large audience derived from the instructive and beautiful discourse delivered by you on Sunday last, and suggested by the burning of the venerable edifice to which every citizen of our town has been attached by strong ties from infancy.

We but express a general wish, when we ask that you would place in our hands a copy of your discourse for publication. It is the more proper that you should comply from the

This Heritage

fact that such an event deserves to be made memorable, and such a building, with so many hallowed associations clustering about it, should not perish without the perpetuation of its history in a form durable and worthy of the theme. We say no more than it merits, when we add that your discourse was eminently worthy of the subject.

We are, with high regard, your friends,

J.R. Tucker	William Miller
Jo. Tidball	Jacob Baker
H.J. Mesmer	Tho. B. Campbell
J.S. Carson	Robt. B. Holliday
T.A. Tidball	F.W.M. Holliday

The next day Krauth replied:

> Lutheran Parsonage, Winchester, Va.
> October 26, 1854.
>
> J.R. Tucker, Esq., and Others:
>
> Gentlemen – I am not less willing to commit to you the discourse you so kindly ask for publication, because I feel that your estimate of it is one of the heart and not of the judgment. I meant but to lay a garland on an altar, and I thank you that your reverence of the memories to which I meant to do homage, has given value to so inadequate an offering.
>
> I am truly and gratefully yours,
> Charles P. Krauth.

Thus the sermon came to be printed, and posterity rejoices that it has been preserved, for its message is vibrant and pertinent still. The concluding paragraphs are here given.

> It is gone – but its consecration shall be preserved to it – it shall be hallowed to God still. Its shattered walls wake new and not undevout thoughts. 'Where will you find shelter,' was said to Luther in a dark hour; 'if you are deserted by your last friend, where will you find shelter?' With his hand uplifted, he replied: 'Under the heavens.' And thus our church, hallowed to the pure faith he restored, stands not unsheltered. A fuller light of heaven now beams into it; its roof, which in covering feeble man also

veiled a part of the glory that cometh from above, is gone – open now to the heavens, it seems to say: 'Let the lightnings burst, let the storms of summer beat upon me and the snows of winter shroud me, I have done my work for God, and not without Him shall a single stone that gave shelter to his children or echo to his praise, not a single stone shall fall to the ground.'

Now the noontide sun lies full upon its heart, the firmament covers it above, the moon sheds her pale beams where they entered not before, the stars shine softly down upon it, and nightly the dews fall as though they wept that it is gone. Removed from temples for the limited worship of a single congregation, Nature by her stern and fiery hand has caught it back and claimed it for her own, a part of her universal temple:

'That dome of nobler span
That temple given
To faith, no bigot dares to ban,
Whose space is heaven.'

The significant events that have been mentioned thus far as marking C.P. Krauth's ministry all have been external things. But let it here be said with emphasis that there was growth and enrichment within the congregation in things spiritual as well as in things material. Scholar that the pastor was, and conscious of the true heritage in worship of the Lutheran tradition, it is not at all surprising that under his leadership the regular use of the liturgy of the church was followed at morning services. This came about, apparently, as the result of an action by the Council, January 6, 1851, wherein "the pastor was respectfully requested...to take into consideration the propriety of using the Liturgy in the Sabbath morning services in the Church"; but one may well imagine the patient hours of spade work and seed-sowing put in by him preliminary to this event. Here again the congregation hewed true to the line of its Muhlenberg heritage.

Growth in the practice of Christian stewardship of possessions was another manifestation of the congregation's inner spiritual development. The synodical treasury received an annual contribution, as did the Education Cause and the Missionary Cause. Assistance was given St. Paul's, a sister church in Washington City; a special offering was received for the Virginia Bible Society, another for the Church Extension Society and another for the Orphans' Home at Pittsburgh. The congregation's horizons were extending far beyond the limits of the Blue Ridge and the Alleghenies.

Still another phase of internal development may be seen in the expanding role played by the women of the congregation in the financial scheme of things. The Sewing Society with its annual fair raised hundreds of dollars to assist in paying off church indebtedness. The good ladies gave repeated demonstrations of their ability to raise funds, and while they had no vote in the affairs of the church, an increasing influence was exercised by them through the large and dependable gifts that always came from them when the need arose.

During Mr. Krauth's pastorate several other items of passing interest occurred.

The western half of the lot known as the Slagle lot on Water Street, purchased less than two years earlier, was sold to the Corporation of Winchester in 1848.

The application of the Sons of Temperance for use of the church on July 4, 1849, apparently was denied in the light of a resolution offered by the pastor, though never adopted by the Council, "that the use of this church will not be granted to any persons or society for any other purpose than that of preaching the Gospel of Christ."

The unoccupied schoolroom in the church basement was authorized to be rented.

A book for church records was bought at a cost of $5.50.

The Sunday evening service was held for a time at 4:30 P.M. and then at 6:30 P.M., though the hour soon returned to the more acceptable 8 o'clock.

The Rev. John Eichelberger, a son of the congregation, preached a special sermon November 14, 1852, upon the death of Daniel Webster.

In 1853 when the Methodist congregation was temporarily deprived of a place of worship, the Old Church was placed at their disposal and used by them.

The installation of gaslights was authorized in June 1855.

The use of the Lecture Room was granted to Mr. Kemmerer for one night in each week for the purpose of holding his "juvenile singing class therein." This in July 1855.

Early in 1855 Mr. Krauth made a visit to Pittsburgh where his friend, William A. Passavant, had founded an orphans home and the first Protestant hospital in America and was pastor of the First English Lutheran Church. He reported to the Church Council, March 5, concerning his trip, that he had received a call to the First Church, and that he was then inclined to the opinion not to accept. Was it because he had fallen in love with a Winchester girl that he was not at first interested in moving to Pittsburgh? Some two months later he married Miss Mary Virginia Baker, daughter of Jacob Baker.

By September, however, the decision to go to Pittsburgh was made. He resigned at a meeting of the Council held the third day of the month. The minute book tells the story:

> The Chairman here announced to the meeting that he had a few hours since received a communication from Pittsburgh, Pennsylvania, which had decided him to accept the pastoral charge, at an early day, of the Lutheran Church at that place. He spoke in feeling terms of the pain and regret

which a separation from his people here, with whom he had so long and pleasantly laboured, would cause him, yet believing that duty called him to sever these dear ties, he had after long and prayerful reflection, determined to accept the call to Pittsburgh, which had been recently renewed.

Requested to put his words into writing, the letter of resignation, written a week later, is given here in full.

Winchester, September 10th, 1855

To the Council of the Evangelical Lutheran Church
    Winchester, Va.
Dear Brethren:
    Under decided convictions of duty I have accepted a call to become pastor of the First English Evangelical Lutheran Church of Pa. This step renders necessary a sundering of the relation in which for the last seven years and a half I have stood to the church you represent. From the first of October I wish you to consider my place as vacated.

    With regrets too deep for utterance I take a step which severs ties so hallowed and dear. The happiest years of my life have been spent with you. I go, led as I believe, by Providence to enter on a wider field of usefulness, but no where do I hope to find truer sympathies or more cordial cooperation than you have given me. Not one act you have done, not one word you have spoken during all my connection with you, would I wish to forget. For all that you have done, for all that you have been to me, accept my heartfelt thanks and the assurance that you and my dear people hold a place in my affections and my grateful remembrance, of which no changes in life can deprive them and you. May He who has so richly blessed us, still smile on our beloved Church, preserve her concord and her spiritual life, and enable you to be in the future, as you have been in the past, faithful guardians of the sacred trust she confides to your hands.

    'The Lord bless you and keep you' is the prayer of
Your friend and brother in Christ,
C.P. Krauth

Subsequent to his departure from Winchester, Dr. Krauth

remained in Pittsburgh four years. In 1859 he became pastor of St. Mark's Church, Philadelphia. Later on he served St. Peter's and St. Stephen's mission churches in the same city. In 1861 he resigned from St. Mark's to devote his whole time to the editorship of *The Lutheran*, a church weekly which, under his guidance, became the principal champion in preserving to American Lutheranism its conservative heritage from the Reformation, a task for which he was preeminently fitted. When the Philadelphia Theological Seminary was founded, in 1864, he became professor of dogmatic theology, and at the installation of the first faculty he delivered the inaugural address, defining the theological position represented by that institution, and remaining a member of its faculty until his death. He was one of the founders of the General Council (1866), a general body of Lutherans that arose out of protest to practices within the General Synod, and was president of this body from 1870-1880. In 1868 he was appointed professor of mental and moral philosophy at the University of Pennsylvania; in 1873, vice-provost of the institution, and in 1880, to the chair of history in addition. His multitudinous duties soon broke his health, alas, and he died January 2, 1883.

Considered by many as the most brilliant scholar the Lutheran Church in America produced in the last century, Dr. Krauth was a prolific writer. His work in the field of liturgics resulted in the publication of the Church Book. He served as a member of the American Committee for Bible Revision; translated Tholuck's *Commentary on John* (1859); edited Fleming's *Vocabulary of Philosophy* (1860); and was the author of *Christian Liberty in Relation to the Usages of the Evangelical Lutheran Church* (1860), *The Augsburg Confession with Notes* (1868), *Historical Sketches of the Thirty Years' War* (1870), *The Conservative*

Reformation and Its Theology (1872), *Infant Baptism and Infant Salvation in the Calvinistic System* (1874), *Berkeley's Principles* (1874), *The Strength and Weakness of Idealism* (1874), *A Chronicle of the Augsburg Confession* (1878), a number of poems and sundry other articles for encyclopedias and reviews.

ABRAHAM ESSICK, 1856-1857

No sooner had C.P. Krauth left town than a candidate arrived to occupy the vacant pulpit. He had been recommended by Mr. Krauth, who invited him before departing. He was James Allen Brown, the pastor of St. Matthew's Church, Reading, Pennsylvania. Unfortunately for Mr. Brown, he was afflicted with whooping cough at the time. He himself records that "it was a sad, gloomy and suffering visit." The result was that although he came and saw, he did not conquer. For the congregation suddenly became interested in Joseph Augustus Seiss, then pastor at Baltimore, and although this gentleman did not reciprocate the interest, he diverted attention from Mr. Brown, whose temporary incapacity had prevented him from getting a wholly sympathetic hearing.

An approach was made, therefore, to a third possible candidate, James L. Schock, pastor in New York City. The committee on correspondence, consisting of William Miller, Robert B. Wolfe and W.B. Baker, kept writing to him for three months and finally had him visit Winchester and decline the call that was extended him. From this correspondence we learn that the congregation "is now more numerous, more united and prosperous, and more spiritual than it has ever been.... We number about 220 communing members and have a large and flourishing Sabbath School."

By March 1856, the above committee had had its attention directed toward the Rev. Abraham Essick, Springfield,

Ohio. He had been recommended by both Dr. Charles Philip Krauth of Gettysburg and by a Mr. Schultz of Zanesville, Ohio. Mr. Essick, on hearing from the committee, replied that he would be willing to visit Winchester. The committee in turn sent him money for travel. He preached April 6 and on April 9 was called to the pastorate at a salary of $800. He began his work May 1.

Mr. Essick was at the disadvantage of having to follow an illustrious predecessor, so that his ministry of nineteen months suffered somewhat by contrast. But while it was a brief ministry, the quality of the workmanship was good and sound. It is with the pastorate of Mr. Essick that congregational records of membership lists, baptisms, confirmations, marriages, funerals and communion attendance actually begin, that is, in so far as they have been preserved and handed down. Whatever became of the record book begun by Lewis Eichelberger is a dark mystery, and the new $5.50 book, purchased in C.P. Krauth's time, was bequeathed to posterity without a single entry, the present writer hates to record.

July 20, the Rev. John B. Davis, president of the Lutheran Synod of Virginia, assisted by the Rev. George Diehl, Rev. Charles Porterfield Krauth and Rev. Lewis Eichelberger, installed the new pastor to office. At the same service the Holy Communion was administered to "about 130" persons. The record preserves the names of 118 members of the congregation. Since it is the first official list of communicants that the church possesses after nearly a century of history as an organized body, it has been rearranged in alphabetical order and is given elsewhere in this volume.[c]

In the official entry of members of the congregation, Mr.

---

[c] See Appendix C.

This Heritage

Essick recorded a list of 209 names. During his pastorate 31 members were added, 16 of them by confirmation. He baptized 19 infants, married 8 couples and conducted 9 funerals.

It was customary to hold preparatory service on the Saturday morning preceding the administration of the Holy Communion on Sunday.

The pastor was instructed by the Council to preach an annual sermon on the Home Mission Cause and another on the Education Cause, at which times a special offering should be received to meet the annual pledge to Synod of $50 for each appeal.

The desire to have the pews of the church assigned to specific families was defeated at a congregational meeting by a vote of 18-15.

Abraham Essick

A committee of three men and three women was appointed on the first Sunday of each month by the pastor to serve as visitors from the congregation to the Sunday School.

Born near Quincy, Pennsylvania, November 14, 1822, Abraham Essick had been educated at Gettysburg College from which he graduated in 1847, the next two years being spent at Gettysburg Seminary. From 1848-1850 he served a parish at York, Pennsylvania, from 1850-1854 he was professor in Capital University, Columbus, Ohio, and for the two years prior to his coming to Winchester he was pastor at Springfield, Ohio. When he resigned, therefore, on October

19, 1857, with the desire that his resignation take effect "on or about the 25th of December," he did so to return to the field of teaching as principal of the Lutherville Female Seminary. Here he remained a year, after which he served pastorates at St. James Church, Gettysburg (1861-1864), Bedford, Pennsylvania, (1864-1866) and New Franklin, Ohio (1866-1870). Shortly thereafter he united with the ministry of the Presbyterian Church, moved to the far West and ministered there. He married Elizabeth R. Livingston, December 19, 1851, who died December 30, 1859. Sallie R. Smith became his second wife, January 28, 1862. He died December 31, 1904.

WILLIAM MILLER BAUM, 1858-1862

The last communion conducted by Abraham Essick before he relinquished his pastoral duties was held November 22, 1857. By special invitation of the Council, the Rev. Edwin Dorsey, M.D., Jefferson, Maryland, was present to preach and to assist. He so favorably impressed the congregation that, on December 9, a call was extended to him by the 51 voting members present, an unusually large representation. Dr. Dorsey declined, however, because he had accepted already a call to St. John's Church, Martinsburg.

The committee on correspondence, Mess[rs] W.B. Baker, R.B. Wolfe and William Miller, went into action and on January 25, 1858, reported a name recommended by Theophilus Stork. It was that of Rev. William M. Baum, of Barren Hill, Pennsylvania. A letter was sent him next day inviting him to occupy the pulpit at an early date and enclosing twenty dollars to meet the expenses of travel. Mr. Baum did not feel at liberty to decline such an invitation. He preached here February 14 and the call was issued February 18. A salary of $800 per annum was offered him, and moving expenses were to be met by the congregation.

The letter in which the call was transmitted also contained sentiments such as these: "Allow us to state that, should you, under a sense of duty, decide to accept this call, you may find comfort and encouragement in the prospect of living in a remarkably healthy and pleasant town." Ordinarily speaking, these words were and are altogether true. The committee on correspondence must not be criticized too severely for failing to foresee the nation's most extraordinary crisis in the years immediately ahead, and Winchester at the very center of it.

Mr. Baum wrote his letter of acceptance March 4 and was at work in his new field May 1. He got off to an excellent start; was installed June 13 by Rev. J.P. Smeltzer and Rev. William Rusmiselle, representing the Synod, and Theophilus Stork from Philadelphia; and on June 27, his first communion, he received sixteen new additions and administered the sacrament to one hundred forty-seven members.

The new pastor gave prompt attention to liquidating certain accumulated debts, to setting the current expenses of the congregation on a sounder footing, to repairing the parsonage, to ministering with material aid to the wants of needy families, to enlarging the sense of stewardship among the members; all moneys collected for missions and education henceforth were to be given to those causes, especially when more than the annual hundred dollar pledge was paid in.

Under Mr. Baum's leadership the church said "no" to two important matters. One was the proposed sale of its property to the Baptist congregation, the other, the proposed founding of a female seminary at Winchester by the Synod.

How the proposed sale of the church originated is not

clear. At a meeting of the Council, August 16, 1858, the matter was presented by William Miller, and Council went on record recommending the sale to the congregation "provided, with the amount thus received, a sufficient sum can be had by subscriptions to build a new church." William Miller, R.B. Wolfe and W.B. Baker were appointed a committee to confer with the Baptists. A month after, Mr. Baker reported the Baptists were not ready to negotiate.

Two years later, however, a proposition was submitted. The Baptist Church on October 4,1860, appointed W.S. Ryland, George W. Ward and Amos Pierce a committee and authorized them "to offer the sum of four thousand five hundred dollars ($4,500) for the Lutheran house of worship." The furnaces, chandeliers and church furniture were desired by the prospective purchasers, but they were not interested in the bell, organ or books; and the use of the building would be shared until the Lutherans could obtain a new house of worship. When formal presentation of the matter was made to the Council on December 5, the collective mind of the body had been made up, for, after a short discussion, "it was unanimously resolved that it is inexpedient to entertain the proposition submitted by the Baptist Church." And the secretary was requested to inform the Rev. Mr. Ryland of the action.

The second "no" was also made in the year 1860. The Lutheran Synod was considering the establishment of a woman's school in the Valley of Virginia. Winchester, Woodstock and New Market were viewed as potential sites. The Council was asked to give its opinion on the subject. It agreed that such an institution was desirable, but that Winchester was not the place for it, because the town had seminaries aplenty and local patronage that could be anticipated would be limited. The success of existing schools was not such as to justify the least expectation for an additional one. Furthermore, Council believed that any such venture should be run as a private enterprise. Let Synod pick the man to serve as principal, give him encouragement and endowment, have him visit with the several proposed localities, pick the site, "and at his own risk pecuniarily open the institution.... As almost everything in such an enterprise is dependent upon the adaptation of the principal for the position, the Synod ought not to run the risk of experimenting. Under bad administration a large fund would speedily disappear and involve the Synod in heavy pecuniary loss. We therefore recommend a private effort, under synodical endorsement, as the most promising." With war but one year away, it is probably fortunate that this viewpoint prevailed.

William Miller Baum

Random items of interest that occurred during Mr. Baum's pastorate included the following: Sunday morning prayer meetings were held at 9 A.M.; meetings of the Church Council were begun with the singing of hymns and the reading of scripture; the practice of assigning pews to families was again followed; use of the church was granted to the Young Men's Christian Association for its anniversary meeting in January 1859, upon condition that ministers only should have use of the pulpit; the infant department of the Sunday School was given permission to hold its sessions in the church; the organist, Miss Shephard, was paid a salary of fifty dollars a year; baskets were substituted for boxes in the collection of offerings; and the parsonage stable was rented and the proceeds given the pastor.

William Miller Baum was born January 25, 1825, at Earlville, Pennsylvania. Educated at Gettysburg, he graduated from the College in 1846 and from the Seminary in 1848. For four years he was pastor at Middletown, Pennsylvania, and then from 1852-1858 at Barren Hill, Pennsylvania. He married Maria Louisa Croll, May 8, 1851. Being a native Pennsylvanian and educated in that state, where he had lived all his life before coming to Winchester, his sympathies quite naturally lay north of the Mason and Dixon line, when the conflict between North and South broke out. Yet there is nothing in the records of the congregation to indicate personal or bitter feelings, either of the pastor or his people toward him. There seems to have existed a very genuine mutual esteem.

The firing on Fort Sumter occurred April 12, 1861, and The War was on. Virginia joined the seceding states May 17. Ten days later the Council met at the home of Jacob Baker with Pastor Baum, the chairman, presiding. The usual opening exercises were conducted by the chairman. Several minor matters were then attended to, after which it was resolved "that the Rev. W.M. Baum be granted a release from his pastoral duties until the 1st of August next. After singing and prayer the Council adjourned."

Following this action, Mr. Baum with his family returned to Pennsylvania. But before August 1st had arrived, the conflict had begun in dead earnest in Virginia. Bull Run was fought July 20. The possibility of Baum's return had vanished.

Recognizing the state of existing affairs, the congregation waited until the end of August, when a meeting was held and the secretary was instructed to "communicate, if possible, with Mr. Baum by letter, to state the condition of the congregation, and request that he will, at an early day, advise them what course he proposes to adopt." Accordingly, the following letter was addressed to him.

Winchester, August 31, 1861

Rev. W.M. Baum
  Dear Brother:
    At a meeting of the Lutheran congregation of this place held on Monday evening, the 28th inst., in accordance with a resolution of the Council adopted at its last monthly meeting, the secretary was instructed to communicate, if possible, with you by letter, and to make known frankly and plainly the unsettled condition of the congregation, and the evils growing out of it, and the urgent necessity of adopting measures to restore the regular services of the church as early as practicable.
    This action seems to be made necessary from the fact that the period of the release granted to you expired on the 1st inst., and that no communication has, in the mean time, been received from you, most probably because of the non-intercourse existing now and for some time past between the two sections of our country, and from the further fact, that the circumstances which induced you to leave them temporarily still exist in an enhanced degree, and will make it unpleasant for you to return to this place, as a field of labour, at least during the present unsettled and distressed condition of our national affairs.
    This congregation deeply deplore the necessity which has deprived them of your pastoral services during the past three months, and sensibly feel the want of the stated and regular means of Grace – so necessary to the well-being and spiritual growth of all congregations – and therefore ask that you will, at your earliest convenience, advise them what course you propose to adopt.
    Receive from me, individually, and through me, from those I represent, our united wishes for your future welfare and happiness, and our earnest hope that God will in His Providence soon restore our country and our church

>to a condition of peace and prosperity.
>On behalf of the congregation,
>Yours truly in Christian affection,
>W.B. Baker, Secty.

The foregoing letter was sent to Mr. Baum at Middletown, Pennsylvania, via Romney, and a duplicate copy also was sent via Harper's Ferry, while, a short time later, Mr. Baker wrote a private letter to Mr. Baum, which he entrusted to a Sister of Charity to be mailed at Frederick, Maryland, advising him that an official letter and duplicate had been sent as above stated.

The fall and winter months came and went, but no word came from Mr. Baum. There were those who wanted to declare the parish vacant and proceed with the election of a new pastor, but wiser heads forestalled such action.

At last in April 1862, the long awaited news arrived. Sent from Middletown the preceding September, the letter of resignation had taken seven months to reach Winchester.

Mr. Baum served the congregation most acceptably for three years and one month. He received 65 new members, 36 of them by confirmation, baptized 38 infants, performed 12 marriages and conducted 29 funerals. He subsequently served St. Paul's Church, York, Pennsylvania (1862-1874), and St. Matthew's Church, Philadelphia (1874-1902). He was a member of important boards of the General Synod and was president of that body in 1873. He was a trustee of various institutions and then president manager of the Pennsylvania Bible Society. The doctor of divinity degree was conferred upon him by Gettysburg College in 1867. He died February 6, 1902. Three sons of Pastor and Mrs. Baum became Lutheran ministers, John C., William M., Jr., and Frederick J. Baum. Of the three William M. Baum, Jr., was born at Winchester, June 30, 1858.

THOMAS WILLIAM DOSH, 1862-1871

A son of the Valley of Virginia, Thomas William Luther Dosh had been born at Strasburg, November 21, 1830. He, too, had been educated at the college and seminary at Gettysburg, graduating from the former in 1856, and from the latter two years later. The same year he was licensed by the Virginia Synod for missionary work in Western Virginia and ordained the following year. Founder of the English Lutheran Church at Wheeling, he was its pastor from 1859-1861.

With Western Virginia, and especially that portion of the state that bordered on the Ohio, strongly sympathetic to the Union cause, Mr. Dosh, with his Confederate leanings, found himself in the same kind of predicament as confronted Mr. Baum. The climate of the Ohio Valley was no more healthy for him in the spring of 1861 than had been the Shenandoah Valley for the minister at Winchester. Each determined, therefore, that it was best to return to friendly soil.

Less than a month after Mr. Baum had departed north, Mr. Dosh had been engaged to supply the pulpit on Sunday mornings and Wednesday evenings for the duration of the leave of absence. When fall came and still no word was received from Mr. Baum, other ministers that could be procured were invited to hold services. This arrangement went on until the end of January 1862, when Mr. Dosh was again invited to occupy the pulpit for three months. Before this period had expired Baum's resignation had been received, making the way clear to elect a successor. On May 21 the church extended a formal call to Mr. Dosh, who accepted May 24.

The story of certain phases of the congregation's wartime experiences will be detailed in another chapter. They form an integral part of Mr. Dosh's pastorate and must always be kept in mind as the background for the years of his Winchester ministry. In view of such adverse conditions of upheaval and havoc, the record is amazingly good and testifies to the pastor's fidelity and self-sacrifice. Here we shall consider the less dramatic and more routine developments.

Take church membership for example. During December 1862, the membership roll was revised by the Council. Prior to the revision the roll embraced 297 names. Of that number, 35 names were removed on account of death and 50 names because of removal from the community or transfer elsewhere. The minutes, which tell of this action, also state there were 18 others about whose whereabouts or membership there was doubt, and nine whose walk and conversation were "not regarded as being perfectly exemplary." The nine, whose names were penciled on the margin of the page, were won back; but if we assume that the 18 persons who could not be located were pruned from the list, then the total membership was reduced by 103 names, leaving a congregation of 194 persons. Taking Mr. Dosh's ten-year pastorate as a whole, the names of 129 new members were recorded, 99 children were baptized, 66 couples married and 61 funerals conducted.

In view of the following note appended to the record of communicants, however, the plain inference is that all pastoral acts have not been recorded.

> The foregoing record is only an approximation to absolute correctness, owing partly to the confusion of the war, in part to the neglect of many communicants to hand in their names at preparatory service, and in a good degree (underscored) to my want of promptness in making the entries...relying too much on my private records until they accumulated greatly on my hands. They however subserved their immediate purpose, and I hope will be found sufficiently correct for future reference. Thos. W. Dosh.

Consider next the matter of finances. Three kinds of currency, each with a different value, were in use: Virginia Bank notes, Confederate and U. S. money. At the opening of the war everybody took Confederate money patriotically. With the tide of fortune running against the South, Virginia Bank notes came to be preferred. Soon, however, "Northern money" alone proved acceptable in business transactions.

The Valley of Virginia has been for two centuries an important wheat producing area. It proved itself a breadbasket during both the Revolutionary and Civil Wars. The long-headed, hard-headed Church Council would convert the congregation's offerings, received in Confederate money, first into wheat, then sell the wheat in the new state of West Virginia for U.S. currency, or else exchange it for coal, thereby considerably increasing the value of their original Confederate dollars.

Thomas William Dosh

The cost of heating and lighting the church skyrocketed. In April 1862, coal was selling at $19 a ton. A year later it was unobtainable in Winchester, but it could be procured at Martinsburg for $6 a ton Northern funds. A written permit for the purchase of three tons for the use of the church was issued by Colonel McReynolds of the Union Army, and a wagoner, who contracted to haul it, went to Martinsburg armed with the permit, but the provost marshal in that town "positively refused to allow it to be brought away." It became necessary, then, to borrow two large, ten-plate, wood-burning stoves and to install them in the church.

As gas for lighting the church was no longer obtainable, oil lamps were purchased, but what service were they without coal oil? The special Committee on Oil reported one-half gallon obtained, October 3, 1864, though prior to that, in September, seven and one-half gallons had been found. An effort was made to buy candles at Wheeling and Baltimore.

Current expenses could not be met promptly. Bills remained unpaid for six or eight months or longer. Frequent special offerings had to be taken to keep heads above water. The treasurer reported his accounts in "mixed funds," in "Confederate funds" and in "Northern funds." It was hard to keep a sexton willing to accept his pay of $5 per month in Virginia Bank notes. With the consent of John I. Baker, organist, his salary was cut to $25 a year, though he gave up the position shortly thereafter. At the close of the war the $138.20 treasury balance in Virginia and other "uncurrent" funds went with the wind.

Mr. Dosh, a bachelor when he came to Winchester, did not live in the parsonage. Following receipt of Mr. Baum's resignation the Council took action to rent it. It would appear, however, that the dwelling was not rented until April 1864, with Mrs. G.W. Ward as occupant. Rent was fixed at $10 a month, Virginia Bank notes. The rent was given the pastor in addition to his salary. The following year it was rented to Dr. Lupton for $150 (Virginia bank notes), but the military would not permit Dr. Lupton to move into town from the country. It was then rented to Dr. W.A. Bradford for $125 in Northern funds.

Meantime on November 3, 1864, the minister married Miss Kate Baker Brown, daughter of Mr. and Mrs. Oliver M. Brown, and a member of the congregation. At a subsequent date the Doshes moved into the parsonage.

More frequently than not, Mr. Dosh's salary was in arrears. The unusual circumstances under which he began his work as supply minister, coupled with the economic disaster attendant upon the war and its aftermath, go far to explain the reason. No salary figure is stated in the record of his call. Apparently he accepted what the congregation could pay. In 1867 the sum of $965 was subscribed for his salary and current expenses combined, of which amount the pastor received less than $650. In 1868 one hundred thirty-four subscribers contributed $953.87, of which $700 went to salary, and in 1869 one hundred thirty-two members raised $833.63, salary being credited with $742.

To augment the income of the church, pews were rented to members desiring to pay for them, and to augment the income of the pastor, he and R.M. Baker were granted use of the lecture room for a schoolroom.

In the midst of such financial stringency, there was the temptation, too, to misappropriate funds. Council was guilty of this on one occasion. A sum of $51.60 had been collected during 1860-1861 for Foreign Missions. With the onslaught of hostilities the treasurer was ordered to retain the sum in his possession for future and more favorable disposition. This money had never been dispensed by 1868, so it was ordered to be added to the collections for benevolent objectives of the Synod. Before it was sent away, however, a reconsideration of this action resulted in placing the amount in the hungry current expense account.

And there was the case of Mr. Mullen. In 1866, Christ Lutheran Church, Cumberland, Maryland, (now St. Paul's) the Rev. A.J. Weddell, pastor, out of a spirit of fraternal love sent the Winchester Lutherans a gift of one hundred dollars. It had been delivered to S.M. Mullen, who at the time failed to hand it over to the church treasurer. When, after three years, on account of personal financial involvements, the money still remained unpaid, the Council asked for an accounting. Mr. Mullen acknowledged the debt and promised to pay, though he could not do so immediately. The matter was put off until January 1870, when an order and a note were given, the order being drawn on Mr. Dosh, presumably representing a claim against him for $30, and the note being for the amount of $70.

The Council cancelled the order on Mr. Dosh and referred the collection of the note to him. He in turn favored further lenience toward Mr. Mullen.

A special meeting was held April 21 at the request of Mr. Mullen in order that he might make a statement to the Council. At the same time he took exception to a communication he had lately received from Mr. Dosh. Statements were heard from Mr. Mullen and Mr. Dosh, and resolutions were adopted censuring the former for not living up to his promises, and the latter for the "mode adopted to communicate his views." Not until November 1871 did Mr. Mullen pay off the note. He was released from the payment of interest due.

While the church wrestled with the pinch of scarcity, it must not be assumed that it closed its eyes and ears and heart to wider needs. It continued to receive offerings for the Missionary and Education Causes of the Synod, not less than $20 per month for the above purposes being voted for the year 1870. Two years before, a grant from a special fund was given to Roanoke College. The poor of the congregation were cared for systematically. Charity boxes for voluntary contributions were installed in the church, and communion Sunday offerings were appropriated to the same purpose. The Virginia Synod was entertained in 1866, and the old General Synod South in 1870.

Ever sensitive to the spiritual development of his people, the pastor constantly endeavored to quicken their zeal for Christ and His Kingdom. Church Council meetings heard his fervent and conscientious pleas, as well as the assembled congregation at worship.

Besides money for operating expenses, pastor's salary and benevolent objectives, there was the persistent drag of repairs. Because the church was used repeatedly as a hospital, repairs that would not have had to be made under ordinary circumstances became urgent necessities. And they were more costly than ever. Blinds had to be refitted, pews refinished, new lights procured, the furnaces repaired, walls and woodwork both inside and out had to be repainted, the carpet renewed, a front fence erected, the lecture room renovated throughout and an ample supply of spittoons obtained. More than one thousand dollars had to be expended. In addition, the parsonage had to undergo its quota of improvements. Women's groups came into greater prominence and importance by raising practically all the funds required for the above items.

One thing became more obvious all the while: the income of the church would have to be increased. But how — in the face of decreasing subscriptions, both in number and amount? The propriety of adopting the weekly contribution system with the use of envelopes was proposed for trial in 1870. The Rev. J.I. Miller, pastor at Staunton, where this plan was already in use, addressed the congregation by request upon the subject. He did not convince his hearers to accept the new plan immediately, though they did decide to lift a basket collection at each Sunday morning service and to have a circular letter dealing with the financial situation and a pledge card printed and sent to all members, in hope of obtaining increased support. The amount needed for pastor's salary and current expenses was $1,200. Less than $1,000 was subscribed.

A year later, when subscriptions were gathered, a sentiment on the part of a small minority became outspoken in its desire for a change of pastor. This led to Mr. Dosh's resignation. He presented it November 8, 1871, to take effect January 1, 1872. It called forth from the Council "earnest words of regret and feeling," but it was accepted. The letter follows:

> Winchester, Va., Nov. 8th, 1871
> To the Council of the Evangelical
> Lutheran Congregation of Winchester, Va.
> Dear Brethren:
> Grace and Peace.
> The period has arrived in the history of our mutual fellowship and cooperation in the work of the Lord, when I feel constrained by a conviction of duty, to resign my position as Pastor of the congregation which you represent and I now respectfully ask your official consent to the dissolution, at the close of this year, of that relation endeared by so many joys and sorrows, labors and associations.
>
> I am moved to this request by an impartial regard for the interests of our Beloved Church here and elsewhere, as also by a persuasion of what is due myself and family. This determination has been reached through earnest enquiry and solicitude for more than a year past – and especially during the last few months – during which I have desired only to know the will of God as to what would be best for His Kingdom, in which He has been pleased to appoint me "an ambassador for Christ."
>
> In taking this step, allow me to assure you, my Brethren, of my deep Christian affection for you all, and for the congregation in which I have spent so many seasons of blessed fellowship and communion. I have never ceased to love you "in the bowels of Jesus Christ," and sincerely hope and pray that if there may have existed any other feeling on the part of yourselves or any of the congregation, it will now and forever pass away. And may we part on earth, as we hope to meet in heaven, united in this all-conquering love of our Di-

vine and Glorified Saviour. May God, our Father, cover you with His blessing, as a Council and as a congregation, that your souls may prosper, and your sanctuary "be as the Garden of the Lord, and gladness be found therein, thanksgiving and the voice of melody."

Very affectionately
Yours in the Lord,
T.W. Dosh

The tone of the letter from the Council, written in reply, was on an equally exalted strain.

Winchester, Va., Nov. 24, 1871

Rev. T.W. Dosh

Rev. and Dear Sir:

Your letter tendering your resignation of the pastoral charge of this congregation we represent has been received and considered, and it is with deep regret that we announce our acceptance.

When we remember that you came amongst us Providentially, as we believe, at a time when war had lost to us our Shepherd, and we knew not where to look for another, and that at the invitation of this Council you then cheerfully supplied our pulpit temporarily; that when you were soon after called by the congregation to its Pastoral charge, you promptly entered upon its duties and faithfully laboured in the work of the Master throughout the war and afterwards upon an inadequate salary; and that for several years past you have actively continued this labour of duty and love, in this congregation, in its Sabbath school, and in our church at large, we can look forward to your departure from our midst only with the deepest sadness – a sadness mitigated, however, by the confidence we feel that you leave us from a sense of duty to that cause, which is dearest to every Christian heart.

Though we are now called officially to sever ties which have bound us together through many years of trials and difficulties – ties too peculiarly tender and endearing to many of our congregation; yet we feel gratified that the high and Christian qualities which adorn your character, are so appreciated by others as, in the Providence of God, to call you to a more extensive and liberal field of usefulness.

Accept from us individually, and through us from those

we represent, our sincere and fervent wish that you may be eminently successful in your new field of labour, and that the choicest blessings of God may ever rest upon you and yours.

Yours with Christian love and esteem,

H. S. Baker	)		
	)	Albert Miller)	
Jacob Baker	)	)	
	)	J.A. Richardson)	
E. Hoffman	)	)	
	) Elders	S.S. House)	Deacons
C. Nott	)	)	
	)	V.H. Flinn)	
G.S. Miller	)	)	
	)	C.F. Eichelberger)	
W.B. Baker	)	)	

Upon leaving Winchester Mr. Dosh became pastor of St. John's Lutheran Church, Charleston, South Carolina (1872-1876), and of St. John's Church, Salisbury, North Carolina (1876-1877). Roanoke College conferred on him the D.D. degree in 1875. In the spring of 1877, he was elected President of Roanoke College and Professor of Moral and Intellectual Philosophy to succeed the late Dr. David F. Bittle, founder of the school. At that time the Lutheran Theological Southern Seminary was located at Salem in connection with the college. After serving one year as president, he accepted the call to become a professor in the seminary, where he taught until the Salem existence of the institution came to an end in 1884.

Dr. Dosh edited *The Lutheran Visitor* (1874-1878) and *The Lutheran Home* (1864-1886). Re-entering parish work in 1886 at Burkittsville, Maryland, he ministered there until his death, December 24, 1889. His body was brought to Winchester for interment. Dr. and Mrs. Dosh were the parents of two sons and five daughters. Mrs. Dosh, with her children at home, returned to Winchester to live following her husband's death.

DAVID MCCONAUGHY GILBERT, 1873-1887

For a year and three months following Mr. Dosh's tenure the pulpit remained vacant. Ministers of the town were invited to supply from time to time, as well as others from a distance, and Christ Episcopal Church kindly invited the Lutherans to worship with them when without services of their own.

Consideration was given first to Stephen Albion Repass, Salem, then to Harvey Washington McKnight, who was living at the time at Charles Town, and then to A.J. Weddell, who had removed from Cumberland to Norristown, Pennsylvania, and then to W.P. Ruthrauff, Akron, Ohio. Mr. Repass' name was presented to a congregational meeting, but no vote was taken. Mr. McKnight, after supplying for a number of services, permitted his name to be submitted as a candidate but withdrew it before action was taken. Mr. Weddell was called, visited Winchester and declined. Mr. Ruthrauff preached for the congregation and had his name brought before an official meeting, only to have no vote taken. It was difficult to unite the members on any one candidate.

By the end of 1872, D.M. Gilbert's name had been recommended. Mr. Gilbert at the time was pastor at Staunton, Virginia. On December 18, he was unanimously elected pastor at a salary "not less than one thousand dollars," with the expense of moving family and furniture also included.

The paragraphs, concluding the letter containing the call, throw light upon the situation that existed. They read:

> It is well known to you that we have been without a Pastor for nearly a year. During this long interval many ineffectual efforts have been made to secure perfect union of action in the selection of one, and now that this much desired result has been obtained, may we not hope that the call thus made will receive a favorable response from you.

We are aware that the congregation you are now so faithfully serving have many and strong claims upon you, and that they cannot easily be sundered, and we dare not press you to give us a prompt and definite reply, much as it is to be desired. We therefore leave this question to your own prayerful consideration and conviction of duty, trusting that in the Providence of God, you may be led after a reasonable time to accede to the wishes of ourselves and those we represent.

The letter was signed by W.B. Baker, C.F. Eichelberger and V.H. Flinn, M.D., the committee on correspondence. Mr. Gilbert acknowledged receipt of the call, December 26, from Berkeley Springs, West Virginia. One month later he wrote his acceptance from Staunton. He planned to begin his ministry April 1, 1873.

At the urgent suggestion of the Council, however, Mr. Gilbert came to Winchester in February to receive a class of new members and to administer the Holy Communion. This he did February 22-23. He baptized one infant and seven adults and administered the rite of confirmation to twenty-five others in a most auspicious prelude to the actual beginning of his pastorate six weeks later.

The parsonage was repaired and put in readiness to receive its new occupants. There was a nine-month-old son in the family, as well as an older brother, and the house at the foot of Potato Hill was to witness the arrival of two girls and three more boys during the course of the next ten years.

David McConaughy Gilbert was a native of Gettysburg, Pennsylvania, where he was born February 14, 1836, the son of David and Jane E. Brown Gilbert. Educated at the college and seminary of his hometown, he graduated in the classes of 1857 and 1859, respectively. His first pastorate was at Staunton, which he served on two separate occasions, 1859-1863, and 1871-1873, and between them came an eight-year ministry at Savannah,

Georgia, during which time (October 29, 1866) he married Miss Mary Rutledge Falligant. Winchester, therefore, was the fourth pastorate of Mr. Gilbert, who was a man of thirty-seven years when he entered upon this field. Under God, his ministry was richly blest, and fruitful and productive of much lasting good.

Mr. Gilbert's acceptance led the congregation to take a progressive step before he arrived as pastor. The members voted to give the weekly envelope system a tryout from April 1 to the end of the year. By this means regular offerings were received for pastor's salary, current expenses and the benevolences of Synod. The results obtained proved to be gratifyingly successful. It was voted to continue this systematic procedure throughout 1874, then again for 1875, after which the plan became the accepted *modus operandi*. Seven months after its use had been inaugurated, the minister's salary was increased to $100 a month and benevolence to Synod to $150 a year.

At the start of Mr. Gilbert's second year as pastor, the matter of church repairs began to get serious attention. It was at first estimated that $2,500 would be required. Council thought that amount to be a lot of money just for repairs. The idea of a new church, therefore, was broached. Solicitors were appointed to canvass the membership and to find out how much could be raised for repairs, on the one hand, and for a new building, on the other. Two tentative goals had been set: for repairs, $3,000; and, for a new church, $10,000. The solicitation produced subscriptions of $2,490 for the former and $6,795 for the latter. Those persons who had subscribed for the repair fund were then approached successfully and persuaded to give permission to have their pledges transferred to the new church account. An architect was consulted. Plans and specifications, if obtained, would cost $150, it was reported.

Members of the Council let this information mellow in their heads over winter. Meanwhile, both the idea to repair the building, as well as the one to erect an entirely new structure, underwent modification. The two were combined, so to speak, into one. Sentiment favored early action.

By April sketches were submitted of fronts of churches that had been prepared by Mr. Weber, a Baltimore architect. The general plan called for "a new and churchly front" and other alterations and improvements. The committee on church improvements, in whose hands responsibility for decision reposed, reported a month later that one of Mr. Weber's plans had been accepted, and as soon as the estimated cost was known, a new subscription would be solicited. In all of this evaluating of projected plans, the committee had received the invaluable technical advice and assistance of Mr. F.A. Ohrenschall, a member of the congregation, who was then placed upon the committee.

David McConaughy Gilbert

Architect Weber visited the church in June, examined the building, made the necessary measurements and began work on the specific plans. The amount of $4,400 was available in July. Recognizing its insufficiency, the committee was authorized to create a church debt, not to exceed $1,500. It may be said here, however, that $4,000 had to be borrowed from the bank, and additional indebtedness incurred, before the undertaking was completed. With these preliminaries out of the way, the actual work of tearing down and building up began in the fall of 1875.

Once more the Vestry of Christ Episcopal Church graciously offered the use of their sanctuary to the Lutherans for worship on alternate Sundays, and of their chapel on Sundays and weekdays for Sunday School and other services. And again the invitation and offer were accepted with appreciative thanks.

When December came, a temporary stove was fitted up in the lecture room, which auditorium was used for Council meetings and small group meetings throughout the winter. By the close of the year, 1876, the entire structure was finished and dedication plans were formulated.

The dedication took place January 14, 1877. Again the Rev. Frederick William Conrad, who had delivered the sermon at the dedication of the original building in 1843, was called upon to bring the message. Since 1862, Dr. Conrad had been the influential editor of *The Lutheran Observer*. His sermon was based upon the text, Ephesians 2:4-6.

It was upon the occasion of this dedication that the congregation was christened with a new name. By the grace of God the forefathers had been permitted to find new homes in a strange land; by His grace they had been preserved through the ravages of three destructive wars; and by His grace they had banded together into a congregation and built their houses of worship to His glory. What more appropriate name could be selected? Grace it was to be therefore, and Grace it was named – Grace Evangelical Lutheran Church.

The cost of the reconstructed edifice to the congregation, then numbering 240 communicants, was placed by Mr. Gilbert at $11,550. An indebtedness of $6,500 existed, but by systematic annual reductions it was wiped out in six years.

The committee on church improvements was composed of W.B. Baker, C.F. Eichelberger, F.A. Ohrenschall, Edward Hoffman, Henry Baetjer and Albert P. Miller. In making report of the detailed cost of operations, there was included the following paragraph:

> We would do violence to our feelings did we not here express our gratitude, and return our thanks, to the ladies of the Sewing and Mite Societies, not only for the large amount they have contributed to the building fund, but also for the prompt aid and encouragement rendered by them and by other ladies of the congregation in many other ways; and it is no exaggeration to say that the complete success of the enterprise was due in no small degree to the deep interest and hearty earnestness they manifested throughout the progress of the work. The two societies here mentioned had contributed $1,075.

The Council in glowing terms duly thanked the above-mentioned committee and continued it with power to devise plans for the reduction of the indebtedness, until the entire obligation should be liquidated.

Once the church debt had been paid off, the congregation took on a broader sense of responsibility and contributed more of its financial strength to the wider work of the Church at large. Not only was an increasing amount for the general work supported by the Synod channeled through that body, but special benevolent objectives were assumed. One of these was the Richmond Mission, now the First English Evangelical Lutheran Church of Virginia's capital city. Beginning in 1874 and continuing for nine years, gifts approximating $1,200 were sent to this sister congregation. When Charleston, South Carolina, was devastated by earthquake, and when the building of the Mt. Jackson Lutheran congregation was burned, special offerings were received and sent to the aid of stricken churches. Howard University, the Virginia Bible Society and the Richmond Aid Society likewise received special gifts. Two theological students at the Seminary at Salem were aided, and donations made to the Fund for Disabled Ministers.

Especially in the realm of Foreign Missions did Pastor Gilbert arouse and encourage a larger support. An annual contribution for work in India was started in 1877 and averaged more than one hundred dollars for the remaining ten years of the pastorate. Both the Infant Class of the Sunday School and the Sewing Society were led to pay the cost of educating a Hindu boy. And the Women's Home and Foreign Mission Society, begun in 1885, added enlightenment, zeal and further gifts to the missionary cause. By Mr. Gilbert's influence, a practice of giving extra aid to foreign missions was started, which has continued for three-quarters of a century.

Furthermore, the needy of the congregation were neither forgotten nor forsaken. The records reveal nine or ten individual cases to which financial assistance was given. For some the rent was paid. To others a small allowance for food was made. Still others had clothing provided them. It became necessary for the Alms Fund, financed by a quarterly collection, to be augmented by "a penny collection" each Sunday evening. Five dollars a month was received in this way.

Members of the Council assisted the pastor not only in the material needs of the church, but in moral and spiritual concerns as well. When one brother's "moral and Christian character" became a source of scandal and offense, a committee of three went to see him in an endeavor to have him rectify his personal problems. Another committee was sent to another brother, on whom drunkenness was locking its ball and chain, with the set purpose to reclaim him from his evil ways. A very strange paragraph from the minutes is to be found in connection with such matters. "After a long and interesting discussion as to the religious condition of the congregation, it was suggested to the Pastor, that should there be at any time, indications in the congregation of special interest on the subject of religion, that he should adopt such measures to encourage it, as he may think best." This, quite likely, must be interpreted in the light of a revivalist-type of religion that seems to have been held by some within the Council.

The parsonage at 320 S. Loudoun Street.

Mr. Gilbert's abilities and worth were recognized beyond Winchester, where he was held in high esteem by the entire citizenry. His influence on the Virginia Synod was noteworthy. For six years he served as treasurer of that body, and for six years he was its president. He received from Roanoke College the Doctor of Divinity degree in 1880.

But it was his interest in church history, resulting in a number of excellent sermons and addresses in this field, that won for him a well-deserved reputation. Among his historical writings were: "The Praises of the Lord in The Story of Our Fathers," delivered in Grace Church, May 13, 1877; "The Lutheran Church in Virginia, 1776-1876," delivered at the convention of the Synod at Strasburg in August 1876; and "Muhlenberg's Ministry in Virginia: a Chapter in Colonial Luthero-Episcopal Church History," given at the laying of the cornerstone of the new Emmanuel Lutheran Church, Woodstock, Friday, August 8, 1884. Twenty years later, Dr. Gilbert returned to Woodstock to attend the celebration of the seventy-fifth anniversary of the founding of the Synod of Virginia and to deliver still another major historical contribution: "The Virginia Synod's History: Its Influence on the Lutheran Church in America."

While pastor at Winchester, Dr. Gilbert's personality was felt throughout the entire southern Lutheran Church. He was a recognized leader of the old General Synod, South, and then of the former United Synod, South. The Lutheran Church in this country never split into factions North and South, as did a number of other ecclesiastical bodies a hundred years ago. Synods of the southern states had been members of the General Synod, organized in 1820. With the formation of the Confederacy, however, the bonds were forcibly sundered that held North and South together. For the sake of self-preservation, Southern Lutherans tried for a number of years to preserve the segment of their former general church body in what was called the General Synod, South. This in turn gave way to The United Synod of the South, in 1886. Dr. Gilbert was elected first president of the new body, serving in this capacity for one year prior to his removal from Winchester. He was a frequent delegate from the Virginia Synod to general conventions of the General Synod. The 1878 convention was entertained by Grace Church.

During Dr. Gilbert's pastorate the practice was begun of granting an annual month's vacation to the minister; it was customary for the offering at services to be received following the first hymn; the membership of the choir was enlarged to include young men and young women; Miss Hardesty, a soprano soloist, was paid $5 a month for her services; four young men, not members of the Council, were appointed ushers; permission was granted Mrs. C.F. Eichelberger and Miss Gettie Miller to occupy the front corner pews of the church with their singing class during service in March 1879; after the Christmas morning service there was the habit of holding a congregational meeting for the election of deacons; Week of Prayer services are first mentioned as being observed in 1883; the Sunday morning prayer meetings were enlivened by music and the singing of hymns; two dozen Books of Worship were obtained for the use of visitors.

Pastoral acts of Dr. Gilbert's ministry of more than fourteen years were as follows: 126 infant baptisms; 193 accessions by confirmation, transfer, etc.; 79 marriages; and 144 funerals.

It was but inevitable that a man of Dr. Gilbert's stature and standing should be sought by other congregations. In March 1887, a three-man committee from Zion Church, Harrisburg, Pennsylvania, came to Winchester to survey the scene. This visit caused anxiety in the hearts of many in Grace Church. The Council increased the pastor's salary to $1,500 and sent him a very fine letter, from which the following paragraphs are taken:

The Council regard it as a plain duty made incumbent upon them as the official representatives of the church, to see to it that you have an adequate and comfortable support for yourself and family.

Your ministry of 14 years in this congregation, under circumstances, at times, not especially favorable to success, has been marked by encouraging evidences of God's favor and blessing — by an increased interest on the part of our members in all departments of church work, especially in the Mission and benevolent operations of the church — and by an increase of the membership of the congregation and Sunday School relatively greater than the increase of the population of our town, and it can be stated with confidence that our church is now in a more united and spiritual condition than at any former period of its history.

The best interests of our congregation, of the Synod of Virginia, and of the United Synod, South, demand that all proper efforts be made to retain your services, influence and experience, which are in the opinion of the Council, invaluable to these several interests.

Dr. Gilbert wrote in reply:

I can at least assure you, that every doubt arising in my mind as to the course to be pursued...would be resolved in favor of remaining with the church in which I have reason to believe I have, under God's blessing, been fairly useful, and to the membership of which I am most warmly attached by many tender ties.

By September, however, Dr. Gilbert was no longer in doubt as to his course. His letter of resignation is here given.

Grace Church Parsonage
Winchester, Va., Sept. 26, 1887
To the Council of Grace Evangelical Lutheran Church
Winchester, Virginia
My dear Brethren:
After much anxious, prayerful consideration I have been reluctantly led to the conclusion that it is my duty to accept the

call recently extended to me by Zion Evangelical Lutheran Church at Harrisburg, Pa. I, therefore, hereby respectfully tender my resignation as pastor of Grace Church, to take effect upon the first day of December next, unless such arrangements may be found possible as will make an earlier date for the termination of my duties in the congregation desirable.

In pondering this step I have humbly endeavored to resist all influences save such as might have the approval of the great Head of the Church, and it is now taken with a sadness that is inexpressible, and yet with the earnest hope and prayer that it may, with God's blessing, result beneficially to all the interests to be affected by it.

I would be doing great violence to my feelings were I to close this communication without assuring you, and the congregation you represent, of my warm, heartfelt gratitude for the unfailing kindness shown me and mine during the years of my ministry among you. That God may abundantly reward you for it, my dear brethren, and command His richest blessings upon all who are in any way connected with Grace Church, is the fervent prayer of your friend and brother in Christ.

D.M. Gilbert

Council accepted the resignation "under deep feeling and a full realization of the great loss" about to be sustained, and responded with appropriate resolutions.

> Resolved, that this Council...in reluctantly accepting it [the resignation of Dr. Gilbert] desire to place on record their high appreciation of his Christian character, his meek dignity of deportment, and his eminent pulpit and administrative ability, as shown by the many prominent official positions he had for many years occupied in the Southern Lutheran Church; by the very marked increase in the annual contributions, in the Christian zeal and in the missionary spirit of our congregation, and by the exalted estimation in which he is held by our community generally.
>
> Resolved, that whilst we, and those we represent, feel unspeakably sad because of the speedy severance of the ties which have bound us together for so many years in Christian love and church work, yet we are gratified that his acquirements and ability are so appreciated by others, as under God's ordering, to

call him to a larger congregation and a wider field of usefulness; and we earnestly pray that the divine favor may ever follow his labors, and that the choicest blessings of God may rest upon him and his family.

Dr. Gilbert's Harrisburg pastorate extended from the time he left Winchester until his death, October 16, 1905. Here, also, the impact of his influence on his congregation and throughout the General Synod was notable. His zeal for the cause of foreign missions continued unabated.

LEWIS GODFREY MEINEKE MILLER, 1888-1895

Among the pastors of Grace Church, L.G.M. Miller stands unique. He was a fourth-generation member of the congregation. He was confirmed and married in the church. And his wife, a daughter of the congregation, numbered among her forebears one of its founders.

The son of John Samuel Miller, who was the son of John Miller, who was the son of the pioneer Gottfried Mueller, Lewis Godfrey Meineke Miller was born at Strasburg, April 15, 1848. His mother's maiden name was Jane Foster. His father operated a general store for a time at Strasburg, then moved back to Winchester, where the son received catechetical instruction and was confirmed by Pastor W.M. Baum, June 27, 1858. His college education was obtained at Kenyon and at Washington and Lee, and his theological training at the Philadelphia Seminary,[4] from which he graduated in the class of 1874. Ordained by the Pennsylvania Ministerium that year, his first pastorate was at North Wales, Pennsylvania, and from there, in 1875, he went to College Church, Salem, where he enjoyed a twelve-year ministry that terminated when he came to Winchester. Roanoke College awarded him the Doctor of Divinity degree in 1884. October 15,

1875, he married Miss Laura M. Campbell, daughter of Thomas B. Campbell and descendant of George Michael Laubinger, the ceremony being performed by Pastor Gilbert. Obviously, therefore, he was bred in the bone to the Winchester church.

Before Dr. Gilbert had moved to Harrisburg, William B. Baker, Charles F. Eichelberger and Oscar Barr had been appointed the committee on correspondence to seek a new minister. Mr. Miller, being well known to the congregation, was invited by letter from Mr. Eichelberger to come to Winchester at an early date to preach. His reply so impressed the members of the Council that then and there they decided to recommend his name for a vote. Accordingly, on December 28, 1887, a call was extended to him at a salary of $1,200. It was at this congregational meeting that, for the first time in the history of the church, the women members had a vote.

Lewis Godfrey Meineke Miller

It all came about in this way. At a Council meeting November 7, a document was presented, bearing the signature of twenty-one male members of the congregation, asking the council to inquire through a committee into the propriety of altering the constitution so as to give female members the right to vote at elections for pastor. A month later the committee – C.F. Eichelberger, G.F. Glaize and Hugh Green – reported that it could see "no just grounds for withholding this privilege from said female members," and it recommended that "all females who are in full communion with this church, who submit to its government and discipline regularly administered, and who contribute according to their ability and engagements to the pastor's support and all other necessary expenditures, shall be lawfully constituted electors of this church," and it was further recommended that Council bring the question before the next congregational meeting as the number one item of business.

When, therefore, the congregation met on December 28, it acted first upon the foregoing resolution, which "was adopted by an almost unanimous vote." Then followed the vote on Mr. Miller "in which most of the ladies present joined." Eight of them, however, declined to vote.

The committee on correspondence wrote the pastor-elect the next day, informing him of his call, and saying in part:

> We feel sure it will be as gratifying to you as it is to us, that yours was the only name brought before the meeting and that the utmost harmony and unanimity characterized all its proceedings. This, permit us to say, together with the associations of your early life, the high position this congregation holds in this Synod, and the many warm personal friends you have in and out of the church here, should have their proper influence upon your decision.

Mr. Miller replied from Salem on the 31st.

> I have duly received the call, forwarded by you, to become pastor of Grace Church in Winchester. I deeply esteem an expression of confidence such as this, coming from a congregation among whom I was reared, and a church whose memories are more sacred to me than any other. I thank you from the heart for the kindly sentiments toward myself contained in the letter, and unite my prayer with yours for divine guidance. I feel the solemnity of the decision which you have presented, and shall give the call that earnest consideration which it demands, and the more so from me, because of my relations to the congregation.

At the same time he expressed a desire to visit Winchester before making his decision.

A note in the record states that the projected visit was made January 15. The resignation from College Church was submitted January 24, and a letter was written the same night accepting Grace Church's call. March 15, 1888, witnessed the start of a new pastorate.

Besides the minister and his wife, the parsonage family included three daughters and one son. The congregation showed an immediate concern for their well-being and comfort by purchasing a new parsonage. The former South Loudoun Street property, bought during Dr. Krauth's time, was exchanged for a home on the east side of North Cameron (Market) Street near Piccadilly and, in addition, the church had to assume a $3,000 indebtedness resting on it. The contract for this deal was drawn up January 21 and ratified February 8, and the deed executed and recorded prior to April 9, the date the Council was so informed. Possession of the new property came to the church April 1. This was to be the parsonage for the next forty years and more.

Under L.G.M. Miller's leadership, Grace Church continued to prosper. The membership and the Sunday School grew numerically. The benevolent spirit of the congregation expanded. A challenging foreign mission program was started in which the congregation assumed support of its own missionary to Japan. A healthy congregational life prevailed.

Look at the membership. In seven years 232 accessions were received. The communing membership increased from 191 in 1888 to 274 in 1895. One hundred twenty-five infants were baptized. Funerals numbered 123, marriages 38. In the Sunday School the enrollment grew from 258 to 350, and average attendance from 149 to 206.

Take a glance at the expanding benevolence. Support for synodical objectives advanced from $220, an amount given for a number of years, to $470 in 1893. Home mission congregations at Augusta, Georgia, Knoxville, Tennessee, Buena Vista and Norfolk, Virginia, received substantial aid. When the Johnstown flood occurred, relief was sent to that community. A famine in Russia in 1892 brought forth a gift of $572 from the membership. Succor was sent to Louisiana flood victims in 1893 and to "western fire sufferers" during the next two years. The newly established Orphan's Home at Salem received a yearly appropriation. Nor were the poor of the church overlooked, the funeral expenses of several being borne by the alms fund.

The biggest and brightest achievement in this connection, however, was in behalf of the cause of Foreign Missions. The congregation was led to assume the support of its own missionary. The seed-sowing of Dr. Gilbert was to bear a fine harvest under the continued enthusiastic cultivation of Pastor Miller.

One version of how this all came about has been preserved in the following story, related by the late J. George Baetjer concerning his father, Henry Baetjer, for years a member of the Church Council and treasurer of the congregation.

> One of the members of the church, Mr. Henry Baetjer, had invested a little money in a glass sand mine some distance west of Winchester and must have told Dr. Miller of it on one of the pastor's visits to his store, where they were accustomed to have long and intimate conversations.
> Later on, when Dr. Miller had a thousand dollars which he wanted to invest, he went to Mr. Baetjer and asked him to invest it for him in the same mine. Mr. Baetjer advised his pastor against it, and refused to do it for him. But Dr. Miller was determined, and finally prevailed upon

Mr. Baetjer to make the investment for him.

In the course of time, the project failed and both men lost their money.

Now, Mr. Baetjer, being very conscientious, and feeling somewhat to blame that his friend and pastor had sustained the loss, went to Dr. Miller and offered him $1,000. Dr. Miller refused it, and said it was his own fault, and that he did not hold Mr. Baetjer in any way responsible for his loss. Mr. Baetjer, however, insisted, and Dr. Miller, seeing how much in earnest he was, and how badly he felt over the affair, consented to accept. But in so doing, he said he did not feel he could use it himself. Instead, he would give it for Christian mission work in Japan.

With the decision of the former United Synod of the South to establish a Lutheran mission field in Japan, two young men, both graduates of the class of 1890 at Roanoke College, were sent out two years later. One of these, Rufus Benton Peery, was supported by Grace Church at a salary of $750 a year. Missionary Peery's support began in 1892, upon his graduation from Gettysburg Seminary.

Already in our story two destructive fires have been mentioned – the loss of the treasured old church on the hill in 1854 and the loss of the school house-parsonage-tenant house in 1863. Two more fires, less extensive in their damage, fortunately, have occurred, also, the latter in 1902. It is concerning the fire of 1893, the congregation's third fire, that attention is here directed.

This conflagration, supposed to be of incendiary origin, broke out at 1:20 A.M. on Monday morning, April 10, in the loft of Haddox's ice house turned into a stable, and threatened great damage to nearby buildings. George Bushnell's drug store, Captain Van Fossen's store and C.A. Heller's dry goods store were set ablaze, as well as the church. Insurance to the amount of $1,154.77 was collected from the Royal Fire

Insurance Company, a settlement over which the Council was "perfectly satisfied." In addition to the repairs necessitated by the fire, the interior had to be repainted and a new carpet laid down.

The evening of the fire, Council appointed T.J. Cooper, H.K. Green and John G. Miller a committee to wait upon the City Council to urge the passage of an ordinance requiring all new buildings used as stables erected in the crowded central portion of the city to be constructed of brick or stone and to be covered with metal or slate, and John G. Miller and Oscar Barr were appointed to draft a resolution of thanks and gratitude to be presented to the several fire companies "for their heroic efforts in saving our church from total destruction; and also to express through the city papers the gratitude we feel to the public for their sympathies and assistance in saving the property of the church during the conflagration."

J.E. Cooper, George F. Glaize, Oscar Barr and H.K. Green composed the committee to repair the damages. A painting contractor named Staling, from Strasburg, was awarded the job of redecorating at $350, "exclusive of scaffold"; and pew holders were invited to carpet their own pews, the carpet being obtainable from the committee at cost. Then the council as a body was asked to decide on appropriate designs and colors, an impossible procedure. Because the council could not agree, the decision was delegated to Mr. Staling, and a committee of ladies was asked to select the carpet. The outcome of this ill-advised course was that carpet for the entire floor had to be purchased and paid for by the congregation as a whole; and because there was a "great want of taste displayed in frescoing the chancel," the ladies' committee on carpet was instructed to "examine the work done in the chancel and suggest

Church Interior — Easter 1897

what changes, if any, could be made," said changes to be paid for by private subscription already promised. Proposed changes, however, appear never to have been made.

Other incidental items of interest of Dr. Miller's ministry include: a small locked box was placed in the church vestibule for messages for the pastor; Mr. Beutel's singing class was granted permission to use the lecture room on Tuesday evenings; permission was given to "proper persons connected with this congregation" to use the organ for practice; a placard was posted in the narthex announcing that all seats in the church were free, and that strangers were cordially welcome; the sexton, Gabriel Festus by name, received $8 per month wages; a committee from the Council was appointed to receive at the church doors the names of communicants when the Lord's Supper was administered; the committee on pews reported slow progress in rearranging the seating habits of worshippers, and continued embarrassment in finding pews for some of the members; the committee on church improvement was instructed to look into "the advisability of cleaning up the lecture room so that pastor and people could kneel without soiling their apparel"; the Young People's Society presented the lecture room with a "beautiful lectern"; "a leak in gas at the pulpit"

– of all places – received necessary attention; movable hitching posts were placed in front of the church and beside it; and in 1891, water closet accommodations were built for the use of the Sunday School.

Dr. Miller presented his resignation to the Church Council March 4, 1895, in order to accept a call, which he had received from St. Mark's Church, Roanoke. Dr. Miller wrote:

> I feel deeply and shall ever continue to feel, your kind expressions of desire that I should still continue among you, and I assure you that I have not been unmindful of the reasons you have given why I should not go at this time. My heart clings to you, and the dear people you represent, and shall always do so, and it is with much pain that I contemplate this step; and were I to follow simply the inclinations of my heart, I would not lay this paper before you…. But though we now be separated for the time, I shall never cease to bear you upon my heart, and to call upon God for you, and rejoice that in Christ we are bound together in bonds that never can be broken, and shall look forward to that meeting which is clouded by no fear of parting forever.

The Council in due course adopted appropriate sentiments.

> In parting…we do so with no ordinary degree of sorrow, and out of the abundance of the heart we desire to bear testimony that his faithful and fearless proclamation of the truth from the pulpit, and among men on all occasions, his pastoral oversight of the membership, his tender sympathies and ministrations in the sick room, and in our hours of bereavement and spiritual depression, have enshrined him in the hearts of our people…. We can truthfully say that all our relations, as pastor and people, have been of the most harmonious character, and he leaves his work in a most prospered condition.

Leaving Winchester May 1, Dr. Miller served St. Mark's Roanoke, until 1903, when he became professor of exegesis in the Lutheran Theological Southern Seminary, in which position he continued for fifteen years. He died at Columbia, South Carolina, January 20, 1918, and was buried in Mount Hebron Cemetery, Winchester.

WILLIAM LEVIN SEABROOK, 1895-1901

With the hope of filling the vacancy as soon as possible after Dr. Miller should leave Winchester, the Council appointed a six-man committee on correspondence March 20, 1895. J.E. Cooper, C.F. Eichelberger, Henry Baetjer and G.G. Baker represented the Council, H.K. Green and J. Few Brown the congregation at large. At the end of a month they were in touch with W.L. Seabrook, at that time acting pastor of Zion Lutheran Church, Lebanon, Pennsylvania.

Mr. Seabrook accepted the invitation to preach on May 5. The next day Council voted to recommend his name to a congregational meeting that had been announced for May 8. At a well-attended session he was unanimously elected pastor on the first ballot at a salary of $1,200. Duly notified of this action, he replied and accepted May 11 and began his work June 1.

A native of Frederick, Maryland, William Levin Seabrook was born November 15, 1856. He was a student at Western Maryland College, St. John's College and Gettysburg College, graduating from the last named school in 1877. He studied law at the University of Maryland, where he took his LL.B degree in 1879, and followed the legal profession for nine years thereafter, until his decision to prepare for the ministry at Gettysburg Seminary, which he attended from 1888-1889. Going to Kansas, he was pastor first at Wichita (1889-1890), and then at Abilene (1890-1894), whereupon he returned to Pennsylvania and took up his temporary duties at Lebanon.

For six years and seven months Mr. Seabrook served Grace Church. Under his administration the congregation continued to advance and move forward in benevolent undertakings. The salary of Missionary Peery, who meanwhile had married, was increased to $1,050 per annum, and in addition, the Sunday School took on the support of a native Japanese pastor, Rev. Naomaru, for $135. Home missions in this country likewise received assistance. The Norfolk mission continued to be a special beneficiary. Then there were the Browntown and Timber Ridge Missions near at home and the Newport News and Atlanta Missions farther afield. A congregation at Jacksonville, Florida, was assisted in rebuilding its church. Western sufferers were relieved, and funds sent to famine-ridden India and to destitute Armenian Christians. And the poor were ministered unto, and the orphans remembered.

Pastoral acts recorded by Mr. Seabrook included 43 infant baptisms, 119 accessions by confirmation and transfer, 25 marriages and 61 funerals.

Twice during the pastorate the Virginia Synod held its annual convention at Winchester. August 17, 1897, it convened at Grace Church and again two years later. The 1899 session had been scheduled originally for Norfolk, but due to the outbreak of yellow fever in that city, the meeting place was hurriedly changed. For two years, 1900-1902, Pastor Seabrook served as president of the Synod.

Mr. and Mrs. Seabrook were the parents of two sons and a daughter. When they moved to Winchester, they occupied the parsonage on Market [Cameron] Street. It had undergone certain minor repairs before their arrival. The house, however, was none too well constructed, and as a home it was not comfortable. For three years the parsonage family put up with existing conditions until the Council was prevailed upon to make a personal inspection. This is what was found:

The roof leaked, the cellar walls admitted water, brickwork needed re-pointing, the chimneys recapping, window sash had to be repaired, doors straightened and mantels reset. No wonder the Seabrooks were pleased to move into a house owned by Jacob E. Baker on Piccadilly Street which the church rented at a cost of $240 a year. The parsonage in turn was rented at $15 a month. This arrangement of affairs continued until 1902.

William Levin Seabrook

The outstanding accomplishment of Pastor Seabrook's ministry was the enlarging of the church building. The congregation and the Sunday School had outgrown existing facilities. Accommodations were no longer adequate. The low-ceilinged lecture room, when crowded, was especially hard to ventilate. These things had been recognized for some years.

In 1898 consideration was given to a plan to erect an annex on the vacant ground to the west of the building. A Baltimore architect, J. Evans Sperry, prepared an initial sketch exploring the possibilities of this idea. There were those on the Council, however, who believed that a better plan would be to extend the church building to the north. Should this be done, additional land would have to be purchased in that direction.

W.V. Hodges, owner of the land adjacent the north line of the church property, would not talk business immediately. He would not at first set a price upon his ground. Meanwhile, Architect Sperry, who had been directed to increase the size of his plans, had come to the conclusion that it was inadvisable to make the alterations as proposed, as the lot in its existing proportions was not suitable both for church and Sunday School building. This cleared the atmosphere for the alternate proposition. It was left to simmer for two years.

In 1900 the building was in need of a new heating system. On April 20, Council appointed a committee to obtain estimates on the same, as well as to investigate the cost of minor alterations in the lecture room. The committee also was empowered to secure estimates on a larger program of renovation, involving the purchase of land and the reconstruction of the north end of the building, with new pews, new carpet and refrescoing thrown in for good measure.

To decide which course to pursue, the congregation met on May 30. With characteristic caution, the opinion was expressed that improvements should be made, but the Council was instructed to have two plans and two sets of estimates prepared exhibiting the relative cost of the lesser and greater improvements, the same to be submitted to the membership, whose subscriptions would be the votes that should determine which plan to follow.

Under date of June 14, Council sent the following circular letter to all members.

> To the Members of Grace Evangelical Lutheran Church, Winchester, Va.
>
> Pursuant to the instructions of a congregational meeting held May 30, 1900, the Council caused its committee to formulate the plans and approximate estimates of the cost of the proposed improvements of the church property.
>
> Two methods of improvements have been suggested. One method contemplates the improvement of the lecture room by lowering the floor three steps, enlarging the windows, putting in steam heat, and re-carpeting the church. The esti-

mated cost of this improvement is $2850.

The other, which is the plan approved and recommended by the Council, if the necessary funds can be provided, contemplates the enlargement of the building, and changes as follows: Extending the building back 20 feet, re-modeling the chancel and placing organ and choir loft at side of same, new pews and carpet, frescoing, improved lighting, new heating apparatus and system of ventilation in lecture room and auditorium, lowering the floor of the lecture room, enlarging and improving the same.

In order to make this improvement it will be necessary to purchase a portion of the lot in the rear of the church and change the course of the alley. The Council has an option on the lot, and the property owners adjacent to the alley and the City Council have consented to the proposed change.

The cost of these improvements, including the purchase of the lot will be about $7500.

Three professional architects have been consulted and they state most positively that from the proposed lowering of the floor no danger of dampness need be feared.

A committee will wait upon the members of the congregation to ascertain their preference of method of improvement and solicit their subscriptions.

The Council request you to consider carefully the proposed changes and state to the committee what subscription you will make in cash and what amount you will pledge monthly for three years.

By order of the Council
J.E. Cooper, Sec.

June 14, 1900

When the canvassers began their work, it became apparent that the proposed lowering of the lecture room floor did not meet with approval. This item, therefore, was soon abandoned in favor of a sloping floor. By August more than $4,500 had been subscribed for the "greater improvement" and wheels of action were set in motion. Responsibility for the project was placed in the hands of a building committee, composed of T.J. Cooper, chairman, J.L. Maphis, secretary and treasurer, J.K. Lewis, G.H. Heist, Henry Baetjer, E.M. Barr and H.K. Green. A portion of the Hodges lot was bought for $1,100, and the work was begun.

The congregation continued to use the building while the improvements were under way. To complete the work, an amount up to $4,500 had been authorized to be borrowed. Needed funds were obtained from Lewis F. Cooper at 5 percent.

Services of re-dedication were held throughout the whole of May 26, 1901. Dr. D.M. Gilbert was the preacher morning and evening, while Rev. J.W. Strickler and Rev. John E. Bushnell, D.D., delivered afternoon addresses. Pastor Seabrook and Rev. Taylor B. Yeakley participated also.

Church Interior after the 1901 Renovation

The cost of the improvements totaled $9,753. An indebtedness of $4,000 remained. With the increased valuation of the property, Council authorized the insurance policies to be changed so that a larger sum would be placed on church furnishings, especially the frescoing, organ, electric fixtures and steam heating.

Sidelights on the Seabrook pastorate may be gleaned from minor incidents. Beginning June 1, 1897, the pastor's salary was raised to $1,400, since he had reported that "his present salary was not sufficient to meet his expenses."

The bronze plate bearing the name of the church, the name of pastor, etc., on the front of the building was placed there in the summer of 1900.

By ballot of the congregation, October 21, 1900, 59 members voted for a Saturday morning preparatory service, 57 for Friday night, 15 for Sunday morning and 5 for various other times.

When the Council was confronted with the request of the representative of the Anti-Saloon League for use of the lecture room, Monday, December 31, 1900, to effect an organization of the League, it passed the buck to the pastor for decision.

Miss Kate Wolfe and the choir were requested to continue to conduct the music at all Lord's Day services during 1901, when the pipe organ was required, but for Sunday School and weeknight services other persons would be responsible.

Mr. Seabrook personally canvassed the congregation for funds for synodical benevolence during the late summer of 1901, and when he reported that all but $70 had been raised, members of the Council made up the balance.

It may here be stated that in earlier life, on account of an accident, Mr. Seabrook had lost his left hand. He wore an artificial hand, therefore, concealed by a glove.

In order to accept the call of the Lutheran Church of the Redeemer, Newberry, South Carolina, Mr. Seabrook resigned November 7, 1901, to take effect the end of the year. His letter to the Council stated in part:

> In all the years of my service, it is a source of great joy to me that the relations between pastor and council have always been cordial, sympathetic and fraternal. There has never been, on the part of the council, or any individual member thereof, any word or act, which could have wounded the feelings of the most sensitive man. Uniformly, every member of

the council has been courteous and kind. Between council and pastor there has never been an unpleasant disagreement. For all your kindness, I am deeply grateful.

And the council replied: "We desire to assure you that it is a matter of great gratification that all our relations during your pastorate have been of the character you describe in your letter; and that we have been enabled thus to illustrate the pleasantness of brethren dwelling together in the 'unity of the Spirit and the bond of peace.'

The resignation was accepted.

Mr. Seabrook departed to South Carolina January 1 and remained at Newberry five years. In 1907 he moved to Westminster, Maryland, where he became pastor of Trinity Lutheran Church, and at the same time, resumed the practice of law. In the legal profession he served as state's attorney for Carroll County and later as county attorney. He was also a United States referee in bankruptcy. But he never demitted the ministry, and until his death on January 23, 1931, he continued to serve Trinity Church. He was buried at Gettysburg, Pennsylvania.

GEORGE SPENER BOWERS, 1902-1918

Between the Seabrook and Bowers pastorates an eleven-month interval occurred. The tenants in the parsonage, the Misses Briggs, were asked to vacate in order that the building might be put in better condition before a new pastor should come. Extensive repairs were required and, in order to meet their cost, the Kent Street end of the lot was sold to F.A. Graichen and Carrie D. Graichen for $535.

A committee on correspondence had been appointed a few days after Mr. Seabrook's resignation was accepted. Oscar Barr, Henry Baetjer and J.E. Cooper were the council's representatives, while Camillus S. Baker, Henry Schneider and J. Few Brown represented the congregation.

By January 1902, the above committee recommended James A.B. Scherer, Charleston, South Carolina, for pastor, and the Council in turn voted to recommend the name to a congregational meeting to be held January 29. But the inclemency of the weather kept many members from attending, and no action was taken until February 9. Then, in addition to Mr. Scherer, Dr. L.G.M. Miller was nominated as a second candidate. After taking three ballots Mr. Scherer received a two-thirds majority necessary for election, whereupon a rising vote was taken and the call was made unanimous. Mr. Scherer, however, did not see fit to accept the call, and he so informed the committee from his St. Andrew's parsonage under date of February 25.

A second unsuccessful attempt was made in the direction of the Rev. August Pohlmann, Baltimore, former missionary to Africa. He occupied the pulpit May 10, pleased the congregation and was recommended by the Council to a congregational meeting on August 31. When the meeting was held, private sources declared that he would be unobtainable, and no action was taken.

The interim of which we are speaking is primarily important by reason of the fact that the congregation's fourth fire occurred on the morning of August 25. Again it was a building in the rear of the church – a livery stable owned by E.L. Henry on land of W.V. Hodges – that caught fire and set the building aflame. The blaze was discovered at 1:40 a.m. Chemical fire extinguishers soon had it under control, but not before the five windows on the north side of the edifice had been ruined, the window frames burned, the organ charred, the chancel frescoing blistered, and the whole sanctuary blackened by smoke. Insurance appraisers assessed the damage at $695. Ironically enough, the stable occupied the same spot as the former fire-trap that caused the trouble in 1893. It would seem that the city fathers had let go unheeded the effort of the Council to have a safer building code put into effect.

Following this unfortunate incident, an approach was made to Rev. George S. Bowers, for nine years pastor of St. Mark's Church, Hagerstown. A call was extended him, October 22, at a salary of $1,200. He accepted under date of October 27.

November 30, 1902, Mr. Bowers began his ministry in Grace Church. It was to continue for sixteen years and was to be rich in blessing in numerous ways.

George Spener Bowers

There was the stimulus of the Sesquicentennial Celebration of 1903 to get the new pastorate off to a fine start. Commemorative exercises took place August 25-28. They began with a thanksgiving service on Tuesday evening at which time L.G.M. Miller preached an appropriate sermon. The next night D.M. Gilbert delivered an historical address and W.L. Seabrook spoke on "Our Future in the Light of Our Past." On Thursday afternoon a scheduled service at the site of the first church had to be postponed on account of rain. It was held on Friday afternoon. Thursday night Missionary R.B. Peery, home from Japan, addressed the congregation on "The Lutheran Church Abroad," and on Friday night a reception honoring the Peerys and the former pastors was given at the parsonage by the Young People's Society. Dr. and Mrs. Peery and their children had been the special guests of the congregation for the week and were entertained by the Misses Wolfe on West Piccadilly Street.

Out of the story of the past the congregation renewed its strength.

Mr. Bowers, at the beginning of his ministry, had to contend with three vexatious problems connected with the church's physical equipment. The heating plant was the number one headache. Although newly installed during the renovation of 1901, it failed to measure up to guaranteed specifications. What was required of it was that at zero temperature outside it must heat the building to a comfortable seventy degrees with but five pounds of pressure. When the installing contractor failed to make good on his guarantee, Council sought the services of another and then another. After some five years and the installation of additional radiation and an electric pump for forced circulation, the heating system gave satisfactory service.

But the furnace pit was still a "plaguy" nuisance. Its walls let in water from without and, because of its low depth, whenever Town Run went on a rampage and overflowed the properties on Water Street, the furnace pit was converted into a veritable cistern. This condition was finally corrected by erecting a "sea wall" on the west and north sides of the church, which diverted flood waters from this vulnerable spot.

Then, too, the effects of the 1902 fire left their permanent marks upon the organ. It assumed the role of a pampered *prima donna* and became thoroughly temperamental. It had to be nursed along and given constant attention. Wisely did the Council earmark a bequest of $700 as the start of a fund for a new instrument.

This Heritage

Sesquicentennial Group Picture — August 28, 1903

Throughout Mr. Bowers' ministry, the congregation enjoyed a continuous growth. There was nothing spasmodic or flashy about it. Rather it proved to be steady and substantial, prepared to stand the tests of time. There was a quickening of spiritual life. Systematic attempts were made to win new members, especially other Lutheran residents of the community not members of Grace Church. A new emphasis was placed upon the season of Lent. *Tidings*, a four-page paper, was published monthly in the interest of the work. The official church paper, *The Lutheran Visitor*, went into one hundred homes.

Adult accessions of the pastorate numbered 342, infant baptisms 129, marriages 166 and funerals 272.

In the realm of finances a generous spirit flourished. Apportioned benevolence for the work of Synod was met in full. Institutions supported by the Synod – Roanoke College, Roanoke Women's College (later Elizabeth College, now extinct), the Southern Lutheran Theological Seminary, the Orphan's Home at Salem, the Lowman Home in South Carolina – were aided by regular or special gifts. Home missions at Newport News, Portsmouth and Birmingham, Alabama, were assisted materially. Emergency aid went to victims of the San Francisco earthquake and fire, to the starving Armenians, and to the wartime program for Soldiers and Sailors Welfare.

But the interest of the congregation was centered chiefly in supporting the mission in Japan, especially since L.S.G. Miller, son of Dr. L.G M. Miller, had become its missionary in the foreign field. His official send off occurred in Grace Church on the evening of November 10, 1907, an informal farewell service in which the members of the Presbyterian Church participated. At first Missionary Miller's support was $800 per annum. In 1910 it was increased to $1,200 a year, and later to $1,300.

When, in 1912, A.J. Stirewalt and C.W. Hepner were sent out also as missionaries to Japan, their farewell service was held in Grace Church on special invitation of the Council.

Moreover, the Sunday School supported several native Japanese evangelists. First there was Mr. Yamanouchi Naomaru, then Mr. Hatanaka, then Mr. D. Ronda. Missionary Miller would report to the church regularly by letter, as did the above gentlemen to the Sunday School. Interest was kept on a high level.

The congregation sent gifts in 1907, 1908 and 1911 totaling $5,256 for the erection of the Boys School at Kumamoto, as the result of an appeal made by Missionary Charles L. Brown in 1906, and after L.S.G. Miller, on his first furlough home in 1914, presented the need and opportunity afforded by the city of

Hakata, the Young People's Society, assisted by certain "old guard" from the general membership, responded by erecting a church building in that city at a cost of $4,000. Individual members also were influenced to leave bequests for work in Japan.

The local church, likewise, was remembered by devoted friends and members. A tablet in memory of Henry Streit Baker was given by his daughters in 1907 and placed within the church on the south wall.

The installation of a new organ had been anticipated since 1909 when the Nora C. Nott bequest was designated the "new organ fund." Not until January 1914, however, was any definite action taken. A committee was authorized to make investigations and obtain estimates. By the end of April, Chairman T.J. Cooper was authorized to close the contract with the Möller Organ Company, Hagerstown, Maryland, which firm installed the present pipe organ[d] – the congregation's third – during the month of August. Sunday, September 6, witnessed its first use.

The new organ cost $2,750 installed. The Young People's Society raised $1,200 for its purchase. This, together with the Nott fund and $150 received from the sale of the former organ, left $600 to be cared for by congregational subscription.

Next, the chime in the church tower was installed in 1917. A memorial to David Brevitt Glaize, son of Mr. and Mrs. David S. Glaize, it was made possible by the will of Mrs. Elizabeth Baker Glaize, the mother. This set of ten bells was purchased from the McShane Bell Company, Baltimore, at a cost of $5,000. Ready for initial use at the services of Easter Sunday, it was dedicated with appropriate ceremonies the next evening, and a special concert took place the day following. Mrs. Glaize

---

[d] This organ is now in the possession of Bethel Lutheran Church, Winchester, Virginia.

also provided means for the maintenance and ringing of the bells, as well as for the "Brevitt" window in the church tower.

Other improvements also were made the same summer. In order to conceal the stairway made necessary for access to the chime, a new south wall was constructed in the gallery on a line with the front faces of the tower, with the extension of the side cornices across this part of the gallery. At the same time the circular gallery window and the doors on either side were built, and the present hard wood floor was laid and the sanctuary refrescoed.

By April 1918, twelve new windows adorned the edifice. The will of Mrs. T.T. Wall left a sum of $2,500 to the church for this purpose. Wartime emergencies had delayed their arrival, and when they did come there was talk of not accepting them, but that notion soon passed by and they were installed, together with new lighting fixtures.

The parsonage, too, received needed improvements. In anticipation of the Sesquicentennial in 1903, a bathtub was purchased by the Mite Society, while the Council paid for the needed fittings and repairs, but it was not until 1909 that a sewer connection was authorized. A wing was added to the building in 1910 and a new heating plant also, which items cost $2,071.

Throughout the pastorate of Dr. Bowers the influence of the congregation was given in support of the Anti-Saloon League and the accompanying Prohibition Movement.

Duplex envelopes were introduced with the year 1912. The financial method known as the every member canvass seems to have been employed for the first time in December 1915.

At the special request of the Council, Mrs. W.A. Bell and her sisters, Misses Margaretta and Marianna Miller, assumed charge of the communion vessels in 1903, preparing the elements for administration on communion occasions. These ladies, with the permission of the Council in 1908, sent certain altar linens and communion vessels not needed by the congregation to the Japan mission.

In order that the apportionment to Synod might be paid in full in 1905, the sum of $700 was borrowed from trustee's funds.

The Ladies Mite Society donated a handsome pulpit Bible to the church in 1908.

Beginning in July 1911, the hour for Sunday School was changed from afternoon to 9:30 A.M. for the summer months.

The Young People's Society in 1918 was given permission to place a chest in the church in which to receive special gifts for a new carpet for the home church and for furnishings for the chapel in Hakata, Japan. This society also gave the Sunday School a piano.

Five chimneys not in use on the church building were removed in 1917.

The Four Hundredth Anniversary of the Reformation was celebrated December 2, 1917, with the Rev. J.S. Simon, D.D., Hagerstown, Maryland, delivering "a strong and acceptable address on Projecting the Reformation."

Not until the high cost of living brought on by World War I began to pinch was Dr. Bowers' salary raised from the original $1,200. Effective January 1, 1917, he received an increase of $300. Beginning June 1, 1918, the sexton was paid $15 a month.

With America's entry into war, again young men from the church were called to the colors. Those members who served the nation, 1917-1918, were:

G. Gibson Baker	William E. Harloe	J. Alan Maphis
G. Hubert Bowers	Alfred S. Henkel	J. Luther Maphis, Jr.
Melville D. Bowers	Roy Kohlhousen	Clark S. Pifer
William H. Brown	Carl P. Kremer	Joseph H. Roe
Eugene B. Cooper	J. Richardson Kremer	Glenn W. Ryan
V. Wayne Cooper	Paul Kremer	Carl F. Schmidt
Curtis G. Harloe	Hugh M. Lewis	Louis E. Snapp
		Leslie M. Snapp

The following men affiliated with the Sunday School also saw service:

Frank F. Beck	William H. Hillyard	E. Romie Lonas
Walter E. Beck	William Hottel	Claude H. Ryan

Two service flags were placed in church in August 1918, one in the sanctuary and the other in the lecture room. "They are to remind us," wrote Dr. Bowers in *Tidings*, "of the young men who have gone forth from our church and homes. May they also remind us of our duty to pray earnestly for these young men, that they may be kept from all evil and safely returned to their homes when the war is over."

The venom with which the war was being fought in America against everything of German origin or ancestry left its effect in Winchester. The Lutheran Church, despite its role in the struggle for independence, despite its contributions to community and state in the solid character of the rank and file of its members and despite its men in the service, was under suspicion. And so was faithful Pastor Bowers, even though both sons had answered their country's call. Because he refused to lose his head to the frenzy and hysteria and bitterness of the time, his patriotism was challenged, and it cut him to the quick.

He resigned, therefore, and on September 22, the congregation met to consider the matter. Lewis F. Cooper presented the following statement and resolutions:

Mr. Chairman and Members of Grace Evangelical Lutheran Congregation:

I feel constrained to say that I think we are facing one of the most unfortunate and critical conditions that has ever confronted our congregation.

I take it for granted that every member of the congregation not only desires to be fair in this matter, but wants to act and speak in a truly Christian manner, and that all that may be said and done will be prompted by a truly Christian desire to do justice to ourselves and no injustice to others, to the end that the cause of Christ and His blessed words, 'My peace I leave with you,' may be glorified and exalted in this His holy sanctuary.

Nearly sixteen years ago Dr. George S. Bowers answered the call of this congregation to become our pastor. We called him for the purpose and with the full expectation and assurance that he would preach to us Christ and Him crucified.

During all this time, in season and out of season, he has faithfully labored to serve us as only a truly consecrated, consistent man of God could serve his congregation. It can truly be said of him that every one of his sermons has been a pure Gospel sermon. In his deep, sympathetic nature, he has shared alike with us in our joys and sorrows. He has always held the banner of Christ up to us above all things, at all times and all places. He has proven himself a speaker of unusual ability. His private and public life and walk among us have been above reproach, exemplification of the highest Christian type and example of the meek and lowly Jesus. It can be truly said of him that no pastor of our congregation has ever labored more devotedly, faithfully, or more successfully in the up-building of our church and city in all the spiritual and moral things along the line of the teachings of Christ than he has done. In recognition of these facts I deem it proper to offer the following preambles and resolutions:

1st – Whereas – Our beloved pastor, Dr. Bowers, has felt constrained to tender his resignation to the congregation: and

2nd – Whereas – It appears that Dr. Bowers has been misrepresented and misjudged as to his patriotism and devotion to his country and its flag; and

3rd – Whereas – Dr. Bowers has had the Christian courage to proclaim his love and devotion to the banner of Christ to be paramount to everything else, which has probably been the cause of his being misrepresented and misjudged; and

4th – Whereas – Dr. Bowers' devotion and loyalty to his country and its flag has been proven by his faithful and lifelong adherence to them – therefore be it

Resolved 1st – That the members of Grace Evangelical Lutheran Church in congregational meeting assembled this Sabbath day, September 22nd, 1918, do hear with deep regret his proffered resignation.

Resolved 2nd – That we earnestly and sincerely request him to withdraw the same.

Resolved 3rd – That we express to him our high appreciation of his devotion and fidelity to his church and his country, and his earnest, consecrated efforts in the upbuilding of our church and its community in his administration to all our spiritual needs, and that we pledge anew our endeavor to follow his guidance as he continues to teach us from the Holy Scriptures and to lead us in the green pastures and by the still waters provided by our Lord and Savior Jesus Christ for all those who humbly seek to follow Him.

The foregoing resolutions were passed by a rising vote.

This effort to persuade Dr. Bowers to withdraw his resignation, however, went without success, even though a second meeting of the congregation, held November 3, requested him to reconsider. His pastorate terminated November 30, 1918, his last services being held November 24. The morning sermon was entitled "One Master – All Brethren," and his evening sermon "Commended to God."

George Spener Bowers was born at Jefferson, Maryland, August 3, 1858. He graduated from Gettysburg College in 1880 and from Gettysburg Seminary in 1882. For two years he was tutor at the Burkittsville Female Seminary, after which time he served parishes at Grafton, West Virginia (1884-1885), Upper Frankford, Pennsylvania (1885-1888), St. Luke's, York, Pennsylvania (1888-1893), St. Mark's, Hagerstown (1893-1902), Grace, Winchester (1902-1918), Incarnation, Baltimore (1918-1928), and St. Paul's, Mt. Winans, Maryland, supply

(1928-1945). Roanoke College conferred the D.D. degree upon him in 1908.

Dr. Bowers married Frances Annette Dorey, October 8, 1884. They were the parents of one daughter and two sons. Following retirement from the active ministry, they moved from Baltimore to Norfolk and made their home with their son Hubert. Mrs. Bowers died October 7, 1949, while Dr. Bowers died three weeks later on October 30. They are buried at Norfolk.

AUSTIN AUGUSTUS KELLY, 1919-1924

A three-man committee on correspondence, H.K. Green, T.J. Cooper and Dr. A.D. Henkel, got to work promptly on their next assignment. Through their invitation the Rev. A.A. Kelly, Philadelphia, came to Winchester and preached on January 5, 1919. He made "a very favorable impression on the congregation." Council voted to recommend his name at a salary of $2,000, and when the congregation met, on January 19, with one hundred sixty-six qualified electors present, one hundred nineteen voted for Mr. Kelly. Dr. Bowers' name also had been nominated, and he received forty-seven votes. Mr. Kelly, having received the necessary two-thirds majority, was declared elected, and the congregation was asked to make the call unanimous. When this vote was taken there was but one dissenting voice.

Mr. Kelly was duly notified, and his prompt reply is given herewith:

>Philadelphia, Penna.
>5145 Cedar Ave.
>January 23rd 1919.

To the Church Council and Members of
Grace Lutheran Church, Winchester, Virginia
Dearly Beloved:

Grace be unto you from God our Father and from our Lord and Savior Jesus Christ.

Having received the call to become your pastor which your official committee tendered me in the name of Grace Lutheran Church, Winchester, Virginia, I hereby, in the name of God accept the same and will start my ministry with you, the Lord permitting, on February eleventh, nineteen hundred nineteen.

May I ask that you pray God to make your and my relation a most pleasant one, and that through our services as pastor and people, many souls may be born for the Kingdom and God honored and glorified.

Wishing you all the blessings of God and the baptism of the Holy Spirit,

I am yours in Christ,

Austin A. Kelly

Mr. Kelly's Winchester ministry began just three months after the close of World War I. Likewise was it just three months after the organization of the United Lutheran Church in America, in process of formation at New York City, when the armistice was declared. And still a third fact to be remembered was that the severe epidemic of Spanish influenza was raging in America.

These happenings were to affect the life of the congregation. The Lutherans of America were called upon to send money and food and clothing to their brethren in the faith throughout the war-devastated lands. Benevolence moneys for the work of the church at large were to be channeled henceforth through the newly established general body. And largely because of the flu epidemic, the chalice, or common cup, at the administration of the Lord's Supper was to be abolished in favor of the individual glass.

The first communion services following Mr. Kelly's arrival,

the services of Easter 1919, witnessed this change. Communicants preferring the common cup were given the opportunity to receive the wine from the chalice. A few preferred it that way, but the great majority of members accepted the innovation with approval. The dissenters quickly acquiesced. Two methods of administration did not have to be repeated a second time.

Mr. Kelly entered upon his work with a fervor and zeal that captivated his audiences. After being two months on the field he received sixty-four persons into membership at the Easter services. Throughout his pastorate of five and one-half years he was continually adding new members to the life of the church, a talent in which he excelled. His accessions totaled 291 persons. Of these, 59 were by adult baptism, 49 by renewal, 60 by confirmation and 123 by letter of transfer. Infant baptisms during his tenure numbered 49, marriages 124 and funerals 31.

Possessed of jovial warmth and a sense of the common touch, Mr. Kelly had an especial appeal for the men of the congregation and community. By organizing the Men's Bible Class in 1919, he captured a source of strength and influence that the congregation had not known before and won for it a new potential power.

The growth of the church and of the Men's Bible Class in particular brought with it the problem of enlarged Sunday School facilities. The first move was to purchase the old fire engine house west of the church and to convert it into temporary quarters for the Men's Class. The cost of this property was $3,085 cash. By January 1920 a second move was considered, which was to buy the Baker property west of the fire hall. For this stone house and lot $10,000 was wanted, a price the Council considered too high at first. When it was bought two years later, however, the cost was $10,250.

Meanwhile, George Casper Fries offered a gift of $25,000 for the erection of a new Sunday School building to occupy the combined sites of the fire hall and Baker property not yet bought. This most generous offer was the stimulus needed to proceed. January 15, 1922, the congregation accepted Mr. Fries' offer and at the same meeting authorized purchase of the Baker house. The decision to erect the new building was made May 28, and Council was empowered to employ an architect and obtain plans.

Austin Augustus Kelly

The firm of Richter and Eiler, Reading, Pennsylvania, architects, was consulted, and A.A. Richter visited Winchester in June and was authorized to make initial drawings. In October a building committee was appointed, of which Lewis F. Cooper was chairman, and Harry A. Schmidt, Walter H. Bosserman, G. Casper Fries and Dr. J.A. Richard were members, and in December the committee was instructed to sign an agreement with the architect to get to work on detailed plans.

As the proposed building was expected to cost $60,000, ways and means for providing the remaining $35,000 needed had to be determined. The matter was entrusted to Lewis Cooper, Harry Schmidt and Dr. Richard, who submitted a report to the congregation, April 15, 1923, outlining what the members would be expected to do financially and calling for a reaffirmation of purpose about the whole program. Whereupon, the congregation "by a rising vote and without opposition voted unanimously that a new Sunday School chapel is needed." A canvass for subscriptions was ordered. Headed by Howard K. Grove, the canvassers obtained $21,583. This was enough for the "go" sign to be given, April 29.

The bid of E.R. Himelright to raze the fire hall and Baker house, accepted by Council, could not be carried out on account of the death of the bidder. This delayed matters, together with some desired changes in the architect's plans. The Baker house was rented until February 1924. A bid of $301 by L. Jackson for removing the two buildings was accepted in January.

Complete specifications and building plans had been received the previous August, but after advertising for and receiving construction bids, it was felt that the cost was too high. All bids accordingly were rejected and the plans scaled down further in price. New bids on new specifications had to be obtained, with the result that on March 24, 1924, the bid of

Church Interior — Easter 1920

the Titzel Construction Company, Harrisburg, Pennsylvania, for $55,776 was accepted. The agreement of contract was signed by the trustees April 7.

Work was begun without delay and by June the cornerstone was laid.

And then unexpectedly, out of the clear, at a Wednesday evening service, came Mr. Kelly's resignation. A congregational meeting held to consider the matter, July 16, asked him whether, under any circumstances, he would stay on as pastor. "He replied by saying that he desired the resignation to be accepted. He said he made his resignation for the benefit of the congregation, as well as himself, and should be disappointed if it were not accepted." Whereupon he was asked "whether he could reconsider the resignation. Mr. Kelly replied, saying that it would be to the best interests of the congregation to accept the resignation, and requested it to do so." After extended discussion the resignation was accepted. Mr. Kelly left Winchester in early August 1924.

Here are a few sidelights on the pastorate:

The alms fund was discontinued in 1919 with the understanding that the poor would be cared for out of the general current account.

There was complaint about water from spouting at the parsonage running into the cellar of the adjacent Baptist parsonage. Even a Baptist preacher, it would seem, does not want water in his cellar.

Mr. Kelly was the first pastor of the church to own an automobile. A garage was built at the parsonage during the summer of 1919 at a cost of $324; and, repairs to the Sunday School at an outlay of $672 were made the same summer.

A new church record book was begun, the communion records of the pastorate being entered, while other pastoral acts were recorded in the previous register. Unfortunately, there are no communion records from the Bowers pastorate.

The Maryland Synod, in session at Martinsburg in October 1920, by special invitation of the Church Council visited Winchester, the scene of its founding a century earlier, and was entertained for lunch at the Rouss Fire Hall, the meal being served by a caterer.

The Messenger, a weekly bulletin, was started in 1919.

The first apportionment for the United Lutheran Church amounted to $300 in 1919; in 1921 to $1,109.

Money was sent to sufferers in Poland, Armenia and China, to other European relief, and by the bequest of H.K. Green, $3,000 in addition went to the Japan Mission in 1920.

Mr. Kelly's salary was given a $500 raise in October 1919, a second $500 raise in April, 1920, and a $300 raise in April 1921.

The sexton's pay was increased to $30 a month; and, the choir director's to $25.

After deciding to erect the Sunday School building, it was felt necessary to dispense with gathering subscriptions for missionary work within the Sunday School until some future time.

In July 1923, the church steeple was struck by lightning, with minor damages resulting.

The Council looked askance at Sunday movies, May 1924, "as it desecrates the Lord's Day."

And there was talk of establishing a mission congregation in East Winchester.

Austin Augustus Kelly was born at Littlestown, Pennsylvania, June 3, 1870. Educated at the college and seminary at Gettysburg, he graduated from the former in 1893, and from the latter in 1896. He was pastor of parishes at Trindle Springs, Newville, Harrisburg and Waynesboro, Pennsylvania, before coming to Winchester, and afterwards he served churches at Norwood and York, Pennsylvania. He married Mary C. Bushman, September 9, 1896, and to them one son, George Benner, was born. Retiring from the active ministry after more than fifty years of service, Mr. Kelly now lives with his son in Tucson, Arizona.[e]

CHARLES ABRAM FREED, 1925-1929

It was a fortunate thing that the committee, entrusted with the responsibility of the Sunday School building, was composed of able men who were both willing workers and respected leaders within the congregation. For Mr. Kelly's sudden withdrawal in the midst of the building operations left matters in a bewildered state. And it was a full year before a new pastor would take the helm. The quality of lay leadership proved itself staunch and ready at the needful hour.

The Council appointed Dr. J.A. Richard in August 1924, to be its chairman for the duration of the vacancy. In September Dr. Richard, Clark M. Smith and W.H. Bosserman were requested to act as a committee to secure a pastor, and Lewis F. Cooper was added a month later as a fourth member.

The committee consulted the Superintendent of the Lutheran Synod of Virginia, the Rev. George H. Rhodes, who came to Winchester in November to advise with the group. He highly recommended the name of Dr. C.A. Freed, which had been referred to the committee previously, though no immediate approach was made to the Newberry, South Carolina, pastor.

---

[e] He died September 25, 1956, and was buried in Gettysburg, Pennsylvania. *Biographical Sketches of Lutheran Pastors in Virginia, 1820-1987* (Salem, Va.: Lutheran Church in America, 1992), 117.

Services were conducted by numerous supply ministers. Among them were Philip Hiram Ribold Mullen, Swissvale, Pennsylvania, Frederick John Baum, Poughkeepsie, New York, son of William Miller Baum [Pastor 1858-1862], and Luther Bowers Hafer, pastor at Taneytown, Maryland, 1911-1923, who had also studied law with W.L. Seabrook and had been admitted to the Maryland bar. Of these three, Mr. Hafer supplied on two occasions for a number of consecutive Sundays, first in October, and then the following March and April. Thus it was that he was serving as supply pastor when the Sunday School building was dedicated March 29, 1925, and that two weeks later, on Easter Sunday, he received twenty-two new members into the church.

Charles Abram Freed

By April 20, the committee to obtain a new pastor recommended the name of Charles A. Freed. Council in turn voted to recommend him to the congregation at a meeting to be held May 10.

When the meeting took place, Dr. Freed was not the only one to be nominated. So were Luther B. Hafer, Fred L. Baum and Philip H.R. Mullen. On the ballot Dr. Freed received 115 out of 172 votes. This being a required two-thirds majority, the congregation by rising vote made the call unanimous. The salary was "$3,000 and parsonage and $300 for incidentals including automobile." Dr. Freed accepted the call in due time and began his ministry July 1.

Born near Waynesboro, Virginia, August 23, 1868, Charles Abram Freed had grown up in Augusta County, attended Roanoke College, from which he graduated in 1890, and the Philadelphia Seminary, where he completed his theological course in 1893. For ten years he was pastor at Middlebrook, Virginia, and from 1903-1921 of Ebenezer Church, Columbia, South Carolina. Newberry College conferred on him the doctor of divinity degree in 1911. From 1913-1921 he served as chaplain of the South Carolina Senate, until he moved to Newberry to become pastor of the Church of the Redeemer where he remained until coming to Winchester. He had been president both of the Synod of Virginia and the Synod of South Carolina. Since 1908 he had been vice-president of the board of trustees of the Southern Theological Seminary. A leader in the affairs of the United Synod of the South, he had served on the Merger Committee that brought the United Lutheran Church into being. Since 1920 he had been a representative of the National Lutheran Council. Dr. Freed was a man of stature within the church.

Stepping into the picture at Grace Church at a time when the congregation had the heaviest debt in its history, the new minister found his work cut out for him. The situation was not easy. There was a tendency to let up a bit after the drama and clamor of construction had passed. Paying off the debt became a stern and sometimes grim struggle that was wearying to the soul.

And there was the temptation to go easy on benevolences, and to keep the money at home. The record, however, shows how successfully such temptation was met and overcome. The Young People's Society sent a gift of $1,000 to the Orphan's Home for a new building program. Lutheran World Service, Marion College, the Theological Seminary and Florida hurricane victims were aided. L.S.G. Miller's salary was continued at $1,300, though other extra foreign mission support was curtailed. Apportionment of $1,800 was paid regularly, and the money was borrowed, if need be, to meet the full amount. And the appeal for ministerial pensions, of which Charles W. Fries was treasurer, netted $2,265 and $1,100 in 1928 and 1929, respectively. And two or three thousand dollars was whittled away each year from the debt.

The record stands, and it is good. But each year a deficit was faced either in current expenses or in benevolences, and deficits are discouraging things. Dr. Freed's pastorate seems to have been without zest.

Practices that have become quite customary were introduced by Dr. Freed, as follows:

He was the first pastor to wear the ministerial robe;

Vestments were provided for the choir;

Early Easter morning service in the cemetery was inaugurated;

Family Night, when the congregation meets for informal dinner and the adoption of a budget for the succeeding year, was instituted; and,

The practice of administering Holy Communion on Thursday night of Holy Week was begun.

For sometime there had been talk of selling the parsonage. Such action seemed imminent before Dr. Freed's arrival. Some members of the Council favored such a move, but the majority ruled that the building should be patched up once more to serve its purpose for another five years.

The custom of assigning pews to families was still practiced in 1927.

A request to hold a demonstration of commercial prod-

Sunday School Building and Church

ucts in the Sunday School was refused by the Council, who unanimously agreed that the building would not be available for such abuses.

The sexton's salary was increased to $45 a month.

When the town council contemplated the opening of shoeshine stands and soda fountains on Sundays, Council went on record opposing such an ordinance.

In the absence of a pastor, members of the Council regularly conducted Wednesday evening prayer service.

Pastoral acts performed by Dr. Freed included 80 infant baptisms, 92 accessions of adults, 62 marriages and 41 funerals.

In April 1929, Dr. Freed made known the fact that he had received a call to the Church of the Ascension in Columbia, South Carolina. He announced to the Council that he had decided to decline. Several weeks later, however, on April 28, he presented his written resignation. A portion of his letter explains the situation. After he had declined the call

> ...in a few days a special delivery letter was received asking me to reconsider and urging the claims of the large opportunity which the presence of our Theological Seminary presents, in addition to the present opportunities of the congregation. Also every organization of the congregation wrote pledging loyal support. This renewed call I cannot see otherwise than to accept, and hereby with deep regret present my resignation as Pastor of Grace Church, which I trust the Council will graciously accept. The time of closing my work, I would ask to be about the middle of June, if that is agreeable. Furthermore, I tender my services to aid in securing my successor, if they are desired.

At the same meeting the Council accepted the resignation, and on May 15 the congregation ratified the action.

Before entering upon his ministry at the Church of the Ascension, Dr. Freed visited the Holy Land. In 1932, upon the retirement of Dr. A.G. Voigt as dean of the Southern Seminary, the trustees of that school of the prophets decided to elect a president to head the institution. Their choice fell upon Dr. Freed, in which office he served until his death, April 6, 1938, at Columbia. He was buried at St. James Lutheran Church, near Waynesboro, Virginia.

Dr. Freed married Miss Ada Grove in 1895. They were the parents of two sons and two daughters – Conrad, Janet, Elizabeth and Joe.

LUTHER ALEXANDER THOMAS, 1930-1936

A week following the submitting of Dr. Freed's resignation, a committee was appointed to obtain a new pastor. W.H. Bosserman, Dr. J.A. Richard, George Heist, Harry Schmidt and H.K. Grove were the members thereof. They had been given the names of several possible candidates, so they journeyed south with eyes and ears open. When they made report on May 19, 1929, they recommended Luther A. Thomas, Concord, North Carolina. Lewis F. Cooper, Fred Thwaite, Carl R. Ritter and Robert W. Schultz then went to Concord to hear Mr. Thomas preach, and they were unanimous in their approval of him.

The congregation met to take action on June 2. A unanimous rising vote was given and the call was issued at a salary of $3,300. Before giving decision, Dr. Thomas came to Winchester to look over the situation. Upon his return home he declined the call in early July.

Then followed six months of hearing supply preachers, including the writer, who appeared in town wearing a derby hat.

The pulpit committee, on January 5, decided to recommend that a new call be issued to Dr. Thomas. In this Council concurred unanimously the next day. Dr. Thomas was telephoned immediately and apprised of the situation. The congregation on January 12 then issued a second call to him. By March he was in Winchester on the field.

Luther Alexander Thomas, born at Salisbury, North Carolina, August 8, 1888, was graduated from Roanoke College in the class of 1911 and from the Southern Seminary of the Lutheran Church in 1914. He had served three parishes before coming to Winchester, namely, St. Stephen's, Lexington, South Carolina, St. Mark's Mooresville, North Carolina, and St. James', Concord, North Carolina. Under his guidance in his third parish a fine new church was built. Lenoir Rhyne College in 1929 conferred on him the D.D. degree.

Two things of primary importance were accomplished at the outset of Dr. Thomas' ministry at Grace Church. First there was a new (the present)[f] parsonage, and second, a new constitution for the congregation.

While the Cameron street parsonage seemed always to be in need of vital repairs and never to have been a very comfortable home, its location was such that with the passing of the years it became a valuable business site. Because it lacked so much as a house, there were those in the church who wanted to dispose of it years earlier. But others who saw its increasing value also saw reason to hold on to it.

In April 1930, the firm of Hansbrough and Carter made an offer of $20,000 for the property. Council thought this goodly nibble might lead to a bigger bite and countered with a $25,000 proposition, but this only served to frighten away

---

[f] Located at 605 S. Stewart Street, it housed the pastors from 1931 until 1970.

Luther Alexander Thomas

the prospective catch. Council then returned to the original offer and so recommended its acceptance to the congregation. Action was taken June 22. At the same meeting the Council was authorized to provide another parsonage.

With such a sum of money in hand it was reasoned that a lot could be purchased and a new home erected for $15,000, while the balance would make a nice contribution to the Sunday School debt. This seemed all the more probable when the Misses Margaretta and Marianna Miller came forward with the offer of a South Stewart Street lot for this purpose. Their most generous gift was gratefully accepted July 2.

Council then appointed H.A. Schmidt, L.F. Cooper, J.A. Richard, Fred Thwaite and W.H. Bosserman a parsonage building committee and left the matter in their hands.

The exact location of the lot had to be selected first. Because of the lay of the land, a committee majority chose the site immediately south of the Pierce property. Captain Cooper, however, presented a minority report in which he argued in favor of the site immediately north of the Sloat property. Council agreed with him, despite the larger amount that would be required to put the grounds in shape. Having won his point, Captain Cooper then obtained from the Misses Miller an additional frontage on Stewart Street, so that the lot came to have a 90 foot street frontage all told.

Plans for the house were adopted and work was begun without delay. It was completed in the spring of 1931 at a cost of $18,000. The Sunday School debt could not be reduced, therefore, by the sum originally anticipated.

The second important event of the Thomas pastorate was the adoption of a new constitution. This was the third governing document in the life of the church. The first, originally in German, weathered the transition to English and was in use until 1828. From that date until 1931 the instrument written by Jacob Baker had been in force, subject only to minor changes. For a number of years there was talk of adopting a new constitution, but for one reason or another, nothing came of such proposals.

Soon after Dr. Thomas arrived he was appointed by the Council to be chairman of a committee on a new constitution. Capt. L.F. Cooper, J. George Baetjer and Harry A. Schmidt served with him. The committee, after preliminary work covering some eighteen months, reported on what had been accomplished in September 1931. Council in turn reviewed each article item by item, proposing and executing a number of changes, until it approved the document as a whole and handed it on to the congregation for adoption. Meanwhile printed copies were obtained and sent to all families of the church. The congregation met on December 20, 1931, to take action, and when time for the official vote arrived, there was one unanimous voice of approval.

Under the new constitution the office of elder was dropped. Councilmen henceforth would be deacons only. The first election took place December 27, 1931. J. George Baetjer, Robert Schultz and S. Porter House were elected for a term of four years; Charles W. Fries, C.K. Over and Fred Thwaite for a term of three years; Robert L. Jones, Lewis F. Cooper and Carl R. Ritter for two years; and, J.P. Miller, Ben F. Davis and

Clark M. Smith for one year. At the same meeting Captain L.F. Cooper, Dr. A.D. Henkel and J. George Baetjer were re-elected trustees of the church.

It fell to the lot of Dr. Thomas to be pastor during the years of the great depression of the 1930s. While the Valley of Virginia continued to enjoy a relative prosperity in comparison with highly industrialized areas of the nation, the existing economic condition forced financial retrenchment in all avenues of life. And so the church was very materially affected.

The income of the congregation was insufficient to meet operating expenses and mounting monthly deficits became the rule. The budget had to be reduced. Support for Missionary Miller had to be cut to $1,100, then to $1,000 and then to $600. The pastor's salary was reduced to $2,700. Expenses of the choir were cut, and benevolent payments to Synod. And then there was interest of nearly $1,000 a year to be paid on indebtedness. Occasionally money had to be borrowed for current expenses as well as benevolences.

The effort to make ends meet sometimes produced within the Council an overly emphasized money consciousness that often grew suspicious or childish. There was a tightening of rules for spending for local charities. There was a desire to count all money before turning it over to the financial secretary. There was a demand for an annual audit of books. These things frequently set nerves on edge.

Dr. Thomas had 220 accessions to the membership roll and 63 infant baptisms during his six years and four months pastorate.

The Cameron Street parsonage was occupied by the Thomases when they arrived in Winchester. Upon completion of the Stewart Street parsonage they were its first residents. Dr. and Mrs. Thomas had two sons and a daughter, Luther A., Jr., Karl and Grace. During their stay in Winchester the family unfortunately was visited with considerable illness.

Called to Emmanuel Lutheran Church, Lincolnton, North Carolina, Dr. Thomas submitted his resignation May 10, 1936. Two weeks later it was accepted by the congregation to take effect July 15.

James A. Miller, C.M. Smith, S.G. Miller, R.F. Cline and Oscar Brown were appointed a pulpit committee by Dr. Thomas on June 2. The chairman, Dr. J.A. Miller, suggested engaging a student supply for a term of six weeks from the beginning of the vacancy, with the understanding that the engaged supply be not a candidate for permanent pastor. Council accepted this idea and agreed to pay $150 a month together with the free use of the parsonage to a supply pastor.

Following Dr. Thomas' removal to North Carolina, the congregation was host to the annual convention of the Women's Missionary Society of the Synod of Virginia. The president of the local society, Mrs. J. George Baetjer, assumed full responsibility as hostess for the convention.

Since leaving Winchester, Dr. Thomas has been pastor of three parishes, Emmanuel, Lincolnton, North Carolina, Holy Trinity, Miami, Florida, and Epiphany Church, Miami Beach, Florida, which he organized and serves at the present time. From 1947-1949 he was president of the Synod of Florida.[g]

---

[g] After retiring in 1957, Thomas returned to Lincolnton and was Pastor Emeritus of Emmanuel Lutheran Church. At the time of his death, June 16, 1978, he was the senior pastor of the North Carolina Synod having served for 64 years. Information on his later years appeared in Grace Evangelical Lutheran Church's publication, *Tidings*, November 19, 1978.

CHARLES WORTHINGTON LOWE, 1936-1938

Charles Worthington Lowe

Following a brief career at the College of William and Mary and his ordination by the Maryland Synod in 1936, Charles Worthington Lowe was called to Grace Lutheran Church in September of the same year. Those who heard him were impressed with his eloquence. He was formally installed as pastor the following June.[h] Differences over the management of the congregation and its finances subsequently led to dissolution of the pastoral relationship between Mr. Lowe and the Winchester congregation. Suspended as pastor in May of 1938, the Lutheran Synod of Virginia subsequently removed his pastoral authority and efforts made by Lowe to develop a separate Lutheran congregation in Winchester, the Lutheran Church of Our Saviour, came to naught after only a few years.[i] In 1942, following continuing questions about his draft status, he affiliated with the Ninth Street Christian Church in Washington, D.C.

CARL ADAMS HONEYCUTT, 1939-1943

There are events in life that are so close to the participants that they cannot be seen in their true perspective. There are incidents and happenings and episodes that so grip our feelings that one can do none other than see and think with the emotions rather than with impartial vision and reasoned judgment. Time is required to view such things in their right relationship. Time is essential to true perspective.

Congregations like individuals can experience such events. When emotionalism in any one of its forms assumes con-

---

[h] See *The Winchester Star*, September 8, 1936, and June 12, 1937.

[i] Lowe was deposed from the ministerial office by unanimous vote of the Convention of the Lutheran Synod of Virginia, in session at Roanoke, January 27, 1939. See the minutes of the 110th Annual Convention, p. 81.

trol, reason and will are overbalanced, and religion, depending on all three to maintain a steady equilibrium, takes on fantastic forms. So it was, alas, for a two-year period in the story of Grace Church, and the results were tragic.

Carl Honeycutt came to Winchester to salvage and restore and heal. Invited by the Council on the recommendation of the Rev. R. Homer Anderson, D.D., superintendent of the Synod, he came as a supply pastor for three months from mid-August to mid-November, 1938. His work was blessedly effective.

Carl Adams Honeycutt

Then followed various supply pastors, mainly men from the faculties of Gettysburg Seminary and Gettysburg College, whose wise and helpful temporary ministries brought further balm and benediction. On June 25, 1939, Mr. Honeycutt received the official call of the congregation to become pastor at a salary of $2,400. After visiting Winchester once more and interviewing the Council, he wired from his home at Marion, Virginia, on July 2: "By God's grace I accept the call to Grace Church, effective August 1."

For four years and three months Mr. Honeycutt served the congregation with marked ability and fidelity. During his pastorate the debt remaining on the Sunday School building was liquidated. This was accomplished in the fall of 1943 when the final amount was wiped from the books.

Two events of historic interest should be noted. The first was the placing of a bronze memorial tablet on the remaining east wall of the old church. For a number of years a descriptive marker had been contemplated. Dr. Alfred D. Henkel was the moving spirit in this project, and it was he who was largely responsible for the money involved in re-pointing the wall and in erecting the tablet. Unveiling of the marker took place on the afternoon of November 6, 1938. The principal address was delivered by Judge Philip Williams of Winchester. Dr. W.J. Finck, Lutheran pastor from New Market, Dr. S.L. Flickinger, of Centenary Reformed Church, Winchester, and Supply Pastor Honeycutt participated in the program also.

The second occasion was the celebration of the one hundredth anniversary of the present church building. Stimulating services were held October 28 to November 1, 1942. Former pastors, Luther A. Thomas and George S. Bowers, were present to speak on the evenings of October 28 and 29, respectively. The next night a fellowship dinner was held when addresses were made by General Secretary Edwin Moll, of the Board of Foreign Missions, Supt. R.H. Anderson and Mrs. J.G. Baetjer. Sunday morning, November 1, President Charles J. Smith, Roanoke College, preached, and in the evening Professor H.D. Hoover, Gettysburg Seminary, and the festivals of Reformation and Harvest Home or Ingathering were observed. A $1,200 offering was received. Cabinets made of wood taken from the timbers of the old church were placed in the rear of the sanctuary to house articles intimately associated with the congregation's past. Out of the best traditions of former years, members of the church were inspired to face demand and challenge with renewed resolution.

The outbreak of World War II and America's participation in the conflict in 1941 meant the entrance into the armed forces of many sons of the congregation. Seventy-two men were listed on the church's roster. They were:

W.H. Bosserman, Jr.	R. Kelly Estes	James A. Miller
James H. Bott, Jr.	Linwood Fultz	Paul H. Miller
Richard A. Buncutter	Richard K. Goode	S. Vincent Miller
Julian H. Buncutter	Hugh Green	William H. Miller
Alfred W. Bushong	John W. Greene	Charles F. Mort
Leroy F. Cahill	Winston C. Grim	Vernon C. McClintock
Ralph A. Cain	Howard K. Grove, Jr.	Fred P. Nelson, Jr.
Carl Campbell	Boyd J. Hamman	Charles O'Connor
John W. Carpenter	Claude M. Henkel, Jr.	Alfred A. Parlett
Richard M. Carpenter	Emerson D. Henkel	L.G. Polhamus, Jr.
L. Marshall Castleman	Wilbur H. Jenkins	Wilson Pugh
R. Fred Cline	Benny H. Jones, Jr.	William J. Ritchie
Charles A. Cochran	Forrest E. Jones	Joseph C. Ritter
E. Clinton Cochran	Jack E. Jones	M. Franklin Ritter
John C. Cochran, Jr.	John W. Jones	Oliver T. Ritter
Charles A. Coe, Jr.	Robert L. Jones, Jr.	Randolph Ritter
Norman E. Cooper, Jr.	James E. Keffer, Jr.	R. Brown Ritter
W. Douglas Cooper	Harry C. Kern	Paul Schneider
Frederick A. Crisman	Raymond W. Kern	Edwin T. Snider, Jr.
Richard Z. Crisman	Douglas A. Lake	George H. Snyder
Ben F. Davis, Jr.	Carl W. Lamp	Howard F. Stine
Frank M. Dick	Ralph E. Lamp	Eston H. Tevalt
Edwin B. Estes, Jr.	Robert H. Lamp	James W. Thrift
Melvin A. Estes	James D. Locke	W. Godfrey Zirkle

Three sons of the congregation lost their lives. Emerson D. Henkel was lost at sea when his merchant marine vessel was sunk. The plane of William H. Miller of the air force was destroyed over the North Sea. Major Ben F. Davis, Jr., after serving throughout the conflict on General MacArthur's staff in Australia, was lost at sea in the Pacific off Hawaii, while en route home.

While pastor at Winchester Mr. Honeycutt had accessions to the number of 132, 34 infant baptisms and 80 funerals. He began a new set of church records in a new parish register. Under his leadership generous responses were made to the annual appeal for Lutheran World Action and to the special appeal for Marion College. By the close of 1943, the congregation stood second highest in the Synod in payment for benevolence.

Remaining East Wall of Old Church

Radio broadcasting of the church service was done for the first time over Winchester Station WINC in January 1942.

In August 1942, the Church Council directed a letter of protest to the president of the City Council in regard to the Little Theatre giving a performance on Sunday.

A twilight Good Friday service, inaugurated by Mr. Honeycutt, met with a wide response.

A letter of resignation, written September 26, 1943, was submitted to the congregation October 10. Mr. Honeycutt had been called to Zion Lutheran Church, Sunbury, Pennsylvania. A resolution, presented to the same meeting earnestly invited him to withdraw his resignation and to continue as pastor, and 182 members voted in favor of his doing so, not being willing to have him go. A second congregational meeting, October 31, released him from his duties as pastor, since he had already accepted the call to Sunbury.

Carl Adams Honeycutt, born June 19, 1905, at Concord, North Carolina, was graduated from Mt. Pleasant (North Carolina) Collegiate Institute in 1928, from Roanoke College in 1930, and from the Lutheran Theological Southern Seminary in 1933. Before coming to Winchester he served parishes at Burke's Garden, and at Marion, in Southwest Virginia, and following his ministry in Sunbury he became pastor of Ebenezer Lutheran Church, Columbia, South Carolina. Roanoke College conferred on him the D.D. degree in 1947. Mrs. Honeycutt was the former Miss Mary Elizabeth Barre. They are the parents of two daughters, the elder, Mary Carolyn, having been born at Winchester.[j]

WILLIAM EDWARD EISENBERG, 1944-1967

A seven-month vacancy followed Mr. Honeycutt's removal to Pennsylvania. Professors from the institutions at Gettysburg, especially Drs. Harry F. Baughman, Harvey D. Hoover and William C. Waltemyer, ministered to the congregation most effectively. William Edward Eisenberg arrived to take up his duties, June 1, 1944. He had been invited to preach in Grace Church, Sunday morning, March 26, and on April 16 he had been called to the parish. Born at Staunton, Virginia, January 3, 1903,[k] he was educated in the public schools of his native town, at Roanoke College and at the Lutheran

---

[j] He served at Ebenezer Lutheran Church until 1963. From 1963-1971 he was pastor at Good Shepherd Church in Tampa, Florida. Following his retirement, he served as chaplain at Crafts-Barrow State Hospital, was the chairman of Lutheran Southern Seminary Board, and the co-director of the World Hunger Appeal of South Carolina. Pastor Honeycutt died February 27, 1983, in Columbia, South Carolina. *Biographical Sketches of Lutheran Pastors in Virginia, 1820-1987* (Salem, Va.: Lutheran Church in America, 1992), *102-103.*

[k] One of six children, he was a son of Carl Frederick William Eisenberg (1866-1936), who had been born in Willershausen, Germany, and Mary Ella Rodeffer (1870-1951) of Loudoun County, Virginia. Information on his family is derived from a letter written by Dr. Eisenberg in 1990 to Doris R. Ifert, Jefferson, Maryland. A copy is in the church archives.

Theological Seminary, Mt. Airy, Philadelphia, where he graduated in 1928. For two years thereafter he held graduate fellowships at the seminary and studied in the department of history at the University of Pennsylvania. From 1930-1939 he was pastor of Holy Trinity Church, Greenville, Pennsylvania, and from 1939-1944 he served College Church, Salem, during which pastorate he wrote *The First Hundred Years — Roanoke College 1842-1942*, commemorating the centennial of the institution. June 30, 1930, he married Dorothy Darlington Jones, of Philadelphia. They were the parents of two daughters, Dorothy Darlington and Mary Martha.

William Edward Eisenberg

A prisoner of war camp had been established at Winchester in 1945. From September until May of the following spring, the pastor of Grace Church conducted services each Sunday afternoon for Protestant prisoners. On December 25, by special permission, some fifty prisoners, guarded by a lone top sergeant, came to Grace Church through pouring rain for a special Christmas service with Holy Communion. Organist and sexton were the only other persons present at this service.

During the past nine years (1944-1952 inclusive) the Sunday School building and the church edifice have been renovated throughout. The church was re-dedicated at a special service held on the afternoon of Sunday, October 7, 1951, with the president of Gettysburg Seminary, Dr. Harry F. Baughman, preaching the

This Heritage

Chancel October 7, 1951

sermon. As of January 1, 1953, the membership numbered 811 baptized souls, 658 confirmed members and 462 communicants. There have been 198 baptisms, 52 being adult baptisms and a total of 304 adult accessions; $80,680 has been expended for benevolence, $81,419 for current expenditures and $28,307 for unusual expenditures, a grand total for nine years of $190,406.

From May 1950 to July 1951, the Rev. Philip Alexander Tammaru, a pastor of the Estonian Lutheran Church and a refugee from Nazism and Communism, lived in Winchester with his wife and son and served his "American apprenticeship" in Grace Church.

In observing 1953 as the congregation's bicentennial year, the Shenandoah Conference of the Synod of Virginia was entertained February 12. The Rev. Franklin Clark Fry, D.D., LL.D., president of the United Lutheran Church in America, was guest of honor and preacher at a commemorative service in the evening.

June 14, the Godfrey Miller Home was dedicated. The Rev. Clarence E. Krumbholz, D.D., Director of Welfare of the National Lutheran Council, delivered the address of the occasion. Owned, developed and controlled by Grace Church, this home for women was made possible by the will of Miss Margaretta Miller. The congregation accepted the trust, January 15, 1947. From that time until the official opening, June 1, 1953, the house and grounds were made ready for use through the generosity of members of the congregation. This undertaking marked a bold venture in faith for the third century of challenge for Grace Church.

September 29 to October 1, the congregation was host to the seventieth convention of the Women's Missionary Society of the Virginia Synod. An attendance of 403 delegates and visitors was recorded.

December 10, a Bicentennial Banquet was held, bringing to a conclusion the observance of the congregation's two hundredth anniversary. Dr. Carl A. Honeycutt was the banquet speaker, and greetings from the community were brought by State Senator Harry Flood Byrd, Jr. A huge birthday cake was cut on this occasion, and the whole affair proved to be a happy and enjoyable event.

Nineteen fifty-three was something of a "crowning year" for the congregation and Pastor Eisenberg's pastoral leadership. The goals that had been established by the Bicentennial Committee, which had been appointed by the Church Council in May of 1952 had certainly been accomplished and celebrated.

In addition to these accomplishments, 1953 proved to be a year of growing membership; hiring an organist on a permanent basis; renovating the kitchen in order to serve better the anniversary year plans; organizing a "couples club"; supporting Mr. and Mrs. James A. Scherer as missionaries to Japan; improving office equipment by purchasing an electric typewriter, mimeograph machine, and an addressograph; refurbishing the "social room"; lighting the outside bulletin board; updating the constitution and increasing the congregation's insurance coverage.

The year ended with the congregation authorizing the publication of Pastor Eisenberg's work, *This Heritage,* subtitled "The Story of Lutheran Beginnings in the Lower Shenandoah Valley and of Grace Lutheran Church, Winchester." It was not an easy task!

To publish a book in 1953 was no small accomplishment given the costs associated with printing a voluminous work of three hundred ninety-five pages. The congregation's finances were strained as every dollar had been stretched to cover the additional expenses of the anniversary year. Throughout the year there had been concerns expressed by members, and the Church Council had many discussions as to how the expenses of publication would be covered. On November 4, 1953, at a meeting of the congregation during a Wednesday Family Night dinner, the motion was made after considerable discussion that funds be allocated from resources held by the trustees of the congregation. It was agreed that this allocation would be recognized as a loan arrangement with the funds from the trustees to be repaid by the sale of the book.

At this point in the meeting, a member suggested the absence of a quorum necessary to conduct the business of the congregation. The count taken of those present found that seventy-nine confirmed, communing members eligible to vote was fourteen members short of the ninety-three members necessary for a quorum to conduct the congregation's business. It was then decided that a meeting of the congregation be held immediately following the regular church service on Sunday, November 8, 1953. At that meeting a motion was made to authorize the "appropriation of an amount necessary to underwrite the publishing of the Grace Church history, and that any monies received up to the amount needed from the Trustees Fund be replaced in the Trustees Fund as the histories are sold." The motion carried unanimously. The meeting was adjourned and the matter was settled to everyone's relief.

A pre-publication cost of $3.00 was set for those who wanted to order copies in advance. Four dollars was charged for each volume after publication. The long-awaited first copies of *This Heritage* were finally delivered on May 1, 1954, by the printer, Carr Publishing Company, Boyce, Virginia. Five hundred hard bound copies and two hundred copies not bound were printed. By June 7 three hundred copies had been sold. Council voted to give copies to all new members as long as the copies lasted. The Church Council offered Pastor Eisenberg an honorarium of $300 for his writing of the congregation's history. He refused to accept the honorarium but did accept a payment of $150 for expenses he personally incurred.

Records indicate that he began research on the history when he arrived in Winchester in 1944. However, he did most of his writing and editing during the bicentennial year. Pastor Eisenberg dedicated his work to his wife, Dorothy, and often referred to his efforts of research and writing as a "labor of love." Evva May Miller, parish secretary at the time, had the arduous task of taking handwritten drafts and typing each page. To this day *This Heritage* is considered a scholarly account of early Lutheran beginnings in America, which has been referenced by other scholars in works of church history.

In recognition of Pastor Eisenberg's historical scholarship, especially his earlier work of researching and writing of his first book, *The First Hundred Years – Roanoke College 1842-1942*, and in appreciation for his leadership throughout the Lutheran Church, Roanoke College, his alma mater, conferred upon him the honorary degree, Doctor of Divinity, at the graduation ceremonies of the college on Sunday, June 7, 1953. From that time on, he became affectionately known in his remaining years of ministry as "Doctor Eisenberg."

The remainder of the 1950s proved to be years of steady growth and positive changes in the life of the congregation.This was a welcome relief to a pastor and people who had struggled to regain strength and energies for mission and ministry following the negative impact of the schismatic years of the late 1930s and the necessary time and resources given to the recovery, healing, and very survival of the congregation in the early 1940s. The significant loss of members in the late 1930s and the limitation of available resources during a time of war combined to make recovery slow and difficult throughout the late 1940s and early 1950s.While these years had offered their challenges, by 1954 the pastor, entering his second decade of ministry with the congregation, and the people of Grace were ready to grow and change by building upon the hope and enthusiasm that the bicentennial year had helped to regain.

From 1955 to 1960 baptized membership grew from 873 to 991. During this same time general offerings to the regular budget increased from $16,453 to $25,997. Special giving increased especially in the support of foreign missionaries, capital improvement appeals from various institutions of the church and in response to various disasters throughout the world. Each year additional benevolent dollars were given, particularly for the Synod's "Home Missions Congregations" emphasis as new Lutheran congregations were being planted in record numbers across Virginia. The congregation also sponsored the Rudolf Kendziorra family as refugees from Germany.

By 1956 the Church Council hired its first full time janitor, or church sexton, and increased the pay of the parish secretary from sixty to seventy-five cents per hour. In 1958, as a result of a congregational self-study program entitled "The Sector Project", which emphasized development of consistent financial support through an annual pledge drive, 98 percent of the congregation's highest budget to date was pledged. The success of the program and the amount pledged, which exceeded over $6,000 the highest amount of pledges from any of the previous years, firmly established the annual stewardship drive and pledge system for generating consistent support for the growing congregation's future budgets.

Growth and changes were also evident in the worship services and educational ministry programs. Worship attendance increased and choirs – adult and youth – expanded in size and repertoire under the direction of Marian Pasquet. In 1955 the congregation approved a $12,500 contract for a major rebuilding of the organ and additional funds for renovations in the chancel area for accommodating the changes in the location of the organ console. The Church Council authorized the printing of additional worship bulletins. By 1958 the congregation's musical leadership along with the pastoral leadership of Pastor Eisenberg combined to make for an easy transition from the *Common Service Book* to the new *Service Book and Hymnal*, which became affectionately known as the "red book."

Sunday School classes, especially for children and youth, grew to such an extent during this time that students from the Lutheran Seminary at Gettysburg were hired to help teach classes and lead youth programs. At the January 12, 1956, annual meeting of the congregation it was noted that the numbers of children in all levels of the Sunday School program had taken sharp advances making it necessary to turn over the Sunday School auditorium for the primary department.

It was at this same annual meeting that a motion was made to begin the study of remodeling the Sunday School building. In addition to these concerns for future facilities needs, the need to study the possibility of hiring a full time religious education instructor or Director of Christian Education was also advocated by the pastor. Although the recommendation was tabled at this annual meeting, the idea was continuously before the Council during the years that followed.

As is the nature of the church when facing challenges from growth and change, it took time for many of the ideas and recommended changes to be implemented in the life of the congregation. The Sunday School building was finally renovated in 1961 and dedicated as the Parish School Building on Sunday, March 4, 1962. After several attempts to try and finance the position, write and rewrite a job description and search for the right person, in September 1963 the Church Council hired Martha Stine Cahill as the first full-time Director of Christian Education. Her duties were combined with those as the head teacher and superintendent for Grace Church Kindergarten, which had opened in September 1962 with an initial enrollment of thirteen students. And, although the congregation had amended the constitution to allow for the election of women to the council in 1958, it was not until the annual business meeting in 1962 that the first woman, Mary Katherine Aulick, was elected to the Church Council.

As the bicentennial year, 1953, had been the "crowning year" for the congregation, 1964 was something of the "crowning year" for the twenty-year tenure of dedicated ministry and service that Pastor Eisenberg had faithfully fulfilled at Grace. In those twenty years he had offered strong and consistent pastoral leadership in establishing the congregation's financial stability, expanding the educational programs, growing the membership and championing the congregation's commitment to causes and concerns beyond the local parish. These had not always been easy tasks and for some pastors the challenges would have been too much. But Pastor Eisenberg's strong sense of call, his scholarly command of details and his love of Grace persevered as the congregation moved confidently into what would be the more complex and difficult challenges to his style of pastoral ministry for the late 1960s. What is evident in the congregation's records of this year are the love and appreciation that pastor and congregation had for one another. The following letter, read at the June 1, 1964, meeting of the Church Council offers documentation of the congregation's sentiments for their pastor of twenty years:

> Dear Pastor Eisenberg:
> On the date of the twentieth anniversary of your pastorate here, we think it would be amiss not to express our feelings concerning it, and do so in written form as a momento [sic] of the occasion. Looking back over the past twenty years, though the incidents are, of course, too numerous to detail, some of them stand out in our minds perhaps more than others. We remember the rather unusual duty you performed in ministering to the religious and other needs of prisoners of war held at Winchester. Related to that we recall your taking the lead in sponsoring the family of one of those prisoners as immigrants to our

country and community, as well as your counsel and aid to others of our Faith who were displaced as a result of the upheavals of war and came to Winchester, including your assistance to Pastor Tammaru during his internship with us.

As a matter of statistics, while you have led this flock it has increased in size and responsiveness to the needs of the Church. The increased giving of the congregation during the twenty years has been startling and dramatic. But realizing that they are mere surface indications of matters of much deeper significance, we dwell no further on statistics.

One of the highlights of these twenty years has been the two hundredth anniversary of our congregation. We do not forget your strenuous efforts in preparing and executing in a most fitting and proper manner the celebration of this important milestone in the life of Grace Church. Most particularly in this respect we should not overlook your long and arduous labors, with no monetary recompense to yourself, in writing and publishing the history of the first two hundred years of the congregation, a document whose accuracy and worth, not only to the congregation but to this area, attests well to your scholarly inclinations, your ability as a historian and your love for this congregation and the Church in Virginia.

Your efforts and patience which contributed so materially to the renovation of the church interior and the organ cannot be overlooked. Nor certainly can the more recent completion and dedication of the Parish Education Building, the greatest undertaking with respect to the physical property of the congregation since the building of the present church structure itself, which accomplishment witnesses to the vitality of the congregation and its consciousness of the needs of future generations. Your guiding and helping hand was always present in these achievements.

We should not fail to mention that we have with some pride been willing to share your time and talents with the Church at large, recollecting your services as delegate to national conventions and as a member on synodical and national boards and on the boards of the Church's institutions of higher learning. We are pleased to have had a pastor whose interests and contributions have been more than merely parochial.

In this twenty years there are naturally too many incidents of service and devotion, both large and small, to recount and undoubtedly many are known only to a few or to yourself alone. In concluding this brief resume, however, we should by no means overlook your continued teaching and preaching, sound in doctrine, squarely based upon the Gospel and full of the Holy Spirit.

This communication of our sentiments would fall short did we not also mention with affection your wife and her willing and untiring labors at your side in so many phases of the life of the congregation. What we have said here must be said not only to you but in some measure to her as well.

"Well done, thou good and faithful servant" as shepherd of twenty years to this flock, and on this occasion we also extend our best wishes for your success, well-being and happiness in the years yet to come, and transmit these greetings to you through our Council.

Your Parishioners of Grace Church.

The "years yet to come" would be less than three. In those years the congregation became the beneficiary of numerous gifts and bequests. A new constitution reflecting the congregation's strong support of the newly formed Lutheran Church in America (LCA) and the Virginia Synod of the Lutheran Church in America was adopted. A Parish Benevolent Fund was established which provided monies to be given at the discretion of the pastor to members of the congregation in greatest need. Benevolence payments to the Synod and foreign missions support continued strong as funds were sent to support the building of Phebe Hospital in Liberia, Africa. Grace Church Kindergarten continued to grow. But Sunday Church School attendance began to drop at this time. The Weekday Church School conducted on Wednesday afternoons began having fewer participants. While total baptized membership grew modestly, current-operating offerings dropped between 1965 and 1967. In May 1967 the Church Council authorized the creation of a Core Committee for "the purpose of carrying out work in all phases of Church activity.... The responsibilities of such a committee to be the general servielance [sic] of Church activity, any new activity needed – to make recommendations and suggestions." It appears that the Core Committee was intended to aid the various standing committees in fulfilling their responsibilities, to recruit members of the congregation to serve more actively in various leadership capacities and to encourage better communication between leaders and the regular members of the congregation. The Core Committee continued to function until August 1968.

During these years Pastor Eisenberg proved once again his scholarly aptitude for researching and writing church history. Synod records indicate that as early as 1955 the Committee on History of the Virginia Synod, United Lutheran Church in America, had approached Pastor Eisenberg with the task of writing a definitive history of the Synod including a narrative of each congregation. While he agreed to research and attempt to write the story of Lutheran beginnings in Virginia, he flatly refused to write narratives of each congregation's history that the committee insisted be a part of any history of the Virginia Synod. Six years passed before the Committee on History, reconstituted with new members by this time, approached Pastor Eisenberg with the offer of "editorial assistants" who would research and write the narratives under his editorial supervision. He notes in the preface of the publication, "As the prospective date for the Lutheran Church in America merger was fast approaching it was hoped to start work as soon as possible, in order that the project thus initiated might win approval of the new church body. Succumbing to the pressure of such a challenge, the author yielded to the temptation in a moment of weakness and gave consent." In 1962 Pastor Eisenberg was asked to deliver an address on the "History and Development of the Lutheran Synod of Virginia, 1922-1962" at the annual convention of the Synod. The substance of his address became the framework for one of sixteen chapters in the final manuscript. In the words of the author, "work on production of the manuscript was given an impetus" with the request to deliver this address.

Pastor Eisenberg notes in the preface to his work that the manuscript was written in the parsonage study and "pieced together between the hours of 4:00 and 8:00 a.m." He also notes two major interruptions to his research and writing. The first being his attention to a sister who had a prolonged illness beginning in September 1962 and dying in December of that same year. This is indicative of his loving devotion to his sisters and his dedication to serving the role of younger sibling and only brother. The second prolonged interruption is indicative of his stature as a churchman and historical scholar throughout the church. From July to September of 1963, he served as a delegate from the Lutheran Church in America to the Lutheran World Federation Convention in Helsinki, Finland. During this time, he and Mrs. Eisenberg traveled extensively throughout Germany, visiting the Eisenberg family, doing research and traveling also throughout Switzerland, Scotland and the Scandinavian countries.

The Lutheran Church in Virginia, 1717–1962 was finally published in 1967 by the Trustees of the Virginia Synod (LCA). Fifteen hundred copies were printed by the J.P. Bell Company, Inc., in Lynchburg, Virginia. The sales price was set at $7.50. The Executive Committee of the Synod authorized that complimentary copies of the history be given to each pastor on the rolls of the Synod and that the colleges, seminaries, libraries of institutions of the church, archives of the church and offices of neighboring Synods receive copies as well. To this day, Pastor Eisenberg's most scholarly effort is considered a classic reference resource for any serious student of Lutheran church history in America.

On Sunday, August 13, 1967, Pastor William Edward Eisenberg submitted his letter of resignation effective October 10, 1967, at a special called meeting of the Church Council. Minutes of that meeting indicate that the Council took no action. The letter reads as follows:

Dear Brethren:

After serving Grace Church as pastor for more than twenty-three years, I feel that the time has come for me to relinquish the office. In accord with the provision of the congregation's constitution, I submit my resignation to you, the official board of the church, to take effect on October 10th, 1967. Since my tenure of office has been held under the call of the congregation, it is my purpose to read this letter to the congregation assembled for worship at today's 11 o'clock service.

Two primary considerations move me to make this decision. One has to do with my age, and the other with the length of my service, already extensive.

In January I shall enter the age bracket of permissive retirement. While it is my plan, dependent upon God's gifts of health and strength, to continue in the active work of the ministry of the Church, I have never had it in my heart to impose myself upon Grace Church until the time for retirement will have arrived, nor do I intend to do so. The duration of the years that I have served you already make my continued service impractical in the light of the congregation's best interest. In these increasingly complex times, I am well aware of the need for a younger and new leadership to pilot the congregation.

Let me hasten to say that the years of my ministry in Grace Church have been exceedingly happy years for me, for Mrs. Eisenberg, and for our two daughters as long as they were at home with us; and the same may be said for our years of residence in Winchester. It is not without reluctance, therefore, that this decision is made.

We shall always treasure the bonds which our long association has formed. From the depths of our hearts we thank you for your love and esteem and loyalty which have blessed the church and have enriched our sojourn in your midst immeasurably. The Quicksburg Parish in Shenandoah County has extended me a call to become pastor of its three congregations, St. Martin's, Mt. Zion, and St. Mark's. In accepting this call the challenge of the work of a rural parish will be undertaken. It is my purpose, God willing, to begin my ministry there on October 15th.

In the spirit and language of the Great Apostle, "I bow my knees unto the Father of our Lord Jesus Christ...that He would grant you...to be strengthened with might by His spirit...that Christ may dwell in your hearts by faith...unto Him be glory in the church throughout all the ages...Amen.

Faithfully yours,
Wm. E. Eisenberg

The response of the congregation is summed up best perhaps by a letter from the Church Council on behalf of the congregation presented to Pastor Eisenberg at the Council's September 5, 1967, meeting, at which it officially accepted the pastor's resignation:

Dear Pastor Eisenberg:

It is with a very deep sense of loss and sincere regret that the congregation of Grace Lutheran Church accepts your resignation as its pastor effective October 10, 1967.

We accept your decision to resign only because we acknowledge the fact of your twenty-three years and more of ministry in a parish that has not always been easy to serve and that all men have the right to look forward to retirement after long years of service. We truly hope the "bad moments" will be forgotten when remember the "good moments" while you were with us.

When we remember the renovation of our sanctuary, the establishment of the Godfrey Miller Home, the writing of our congregational history, our Weekday Church School, the renovation of our Parish Building and its subsequent use, the start of Grace Church Kindergarten, and the list goes on and on, we find our words of thanks becoming inadequate to express to you our appreciation of your unfailing faith and example to us, both as individuals and as a congregation. Your leadership has been and we are sure will continue to be a source of inspiration and strength.

We would be greatly remiss if we did not also express our heartfelt thanks and appreciation to Mrs. Eisenberg who has been untiring in her many and varied labors in the life and work of the congregation.

We take this means of expressing to you both our love

and esteem and we extend our very heartiest wishes for God's continued blessings of health and strength.
Sincerely,
John M. Ewing
Secretary of the Church Council and on behalf of the Council and Congregation of Grace Lutheran Church.

From the advantage of historical perspective, it is clear to this writer that Pastor Eisenberg's resignation not only marked the end of his call to serve Grace as pastor, it also marked an end to an era in the long history of Grace. While he had truly grown to love and cherish the Grace congregation in his twenty-three years of ministry, he came to acknowledge that his style of pastoral leadership would no longer serve well the church he had helped to reclaim its great heritage and build toward a hopeful future. In the best traditions of the ordained Lutheran ministry that he had been taught and which he honored wherever he served, and in true love and devotion to Grace, he did that which he knew was best for the Church he loved. He moved on and served faithfully for another four years the congregations of the Quicksburg Parish, 1967–1971.

In his twenty-three years at Grace he performed the following pastoral acts which were reported in the last issue he edited of *Tidings*, October 1967: Child baptisms – 391; children received by transfer into Grace – 264; total child accessions – 655. Adult baptisms – 97; confirmations – 263; adults received by transfer to Grace – 613; total adult accessions – 973. Total baptized accessions – 1,628. Funerals conducted – 345. Marriages performed – 4,787.

In that same issue of *Tidings* he wrote:

Pastor and Mrs. Eisenberg want all their friends at Grace Church to know that their years in Winchester have been most happy years, that they leave with reluctance in their hearts, and that they wish for Grace Church and all its people the best blessings that God in His wisdom knows how to bestow upon His people. After all we shall continue to live and labor in the same district, the same Synod, and the same great Kingdom where Christ our Lord is Ruler and Head. May we all endeavor to serve Him loyally and faithfully as long as He enables us.

The Rev. William Edward Eisenberg, D.D., retired from active parish ministry on May 16, 1971. He and his beloved wife, Dorothy, moved back to Winchester that same year – an indication of their love for the community where over half of his forty-one years of active ordained ministry had been achieved.

Following his retirement he continued to serve the church as a member of the Board of Trustees of Roanoke College until 1984. He also served as a faithful supply preacher up into his 90s for congregations throughout the northern valley area and even into the remote reaches of West Virginia where many small congregations welcomed his pastoral presence on Sunday mornings. Some Sundays he would travel as many as a hundred miles out from Winchester to preach in West Virginia congregations that would have no more than five worshippers in attendance. Such was his life-long dedication to the Office of Word and Sacrament.

His distinguished career as pastor and scholar included the following church-wide positions: United Lutheran Church in America Board of Education, 1941-1950 and 1952-1962, and the Lutheran Church in America Board of College Education and Church Vocations, 1962-1964. He served as a trustee of Thiel College, Greenville, Pennsylvania, 1932-1935, and instructor in Bible at Thiel College, 1934-1937. He was a member of the Virginia Synod (ULCA) Executive Council, 1942-1945, 1948-1952 and 1955-1959, and the Executive Board of the Virginia Synod (LCA), 1963-1969. He served as a trustee of the Lutheran Theological Southern Seminary, Columbia, South Carolina, 1943-1962, and president of that board from 1958-1961. He served on the board of two Lutheran Church related colleges in Virginia: Marion College, Marion, Virginia, 1944-1952 and 1963-1968, and Roanoke College, Salem, Virginia, 1959-1984. Locally, he was active in the ministerial association and served as president of the Godfrey Miller Home from 1948-1967.

After years of attending to Mrs. Eisenberg's failing health and with a gentleman's reluctance to give up his long walks on the streets of Winchester and long hours of working in his garden, Pastor and Mrs. Eisenberg moved to the National Lutheran Home for the Aged in Rockville, Maryland, in November 1995. Dorothy Darlington Jones Eisenberg died February 8, 1997. William Edward Eisenberg died January 13, 2000. Thus, they returned once more to Winchester and are buried together in the historic Lutheran cemetery section of Winchester's Mount Hebron Cemetery close to the east wall of the original church building which still stands to this day as a enduring witness to the faithful people of Grace and her beloved pastors.

Endnotes – Chapter VI

[1] For the organization of the Synod of Maryland and Virginia, consult A.R. Wentz's *History of the Evangelical Lutheran Synod of Maryland of the United Lutheran Church in America, 1820-1920* (Harrisburg, Pa.: The Evangelical Press, 1883), especially chapter III; and, Also, C.W. Cassell, W.J. Finck and Elon O. Henkel, *History of the Lutheran Church in Virginia and East Tennessee* (Strasburg, Va.: Lutheran Synod of Virginia, 1930), 97.

[2] Wentz, *History of the Maryland Synod*, 104.

[3] For alumni of Gettysburg Seminary, the writer is indebted to "The Alumni Record," the second half of A.R. Wentz's *History of the Gettysburg Theological Seminary of the General Synod of the Evangelical Lutheran Church in the United States and the United Lutheran Church in America, 1826-1926*, (Gettysburg, Pa.: Directors, Gettysburg Theological Seminary, 1927).

[4] For alumni of the Philadelphia (Mt. Airy) Seminary, the writer is indebted to the *Philadelphia Seminary Biographical Record, 1864-1923*, edited by Luther D. Reed.

Chapter VII
The Processional
Continues, 1968-2002

VIRGIL ALBERT MOYER, JR., 1968-1973

"Pastors in Processional" in the long history of Grace continued in 1968 with the call of the Rev. Virgil Albert Moyer, Jr., as the congregation's twenty-second pastor. The records of the congregation reveal that the processional continued in a swift and confident manner. Moyer was called as pastor at a congregational meeting on February 18, 1968, just over four months following the departure of his predecessor, Dr. William Edward Eisenberg, who had served the congregation for twenty-three years. Generally speaking, following such a long pastorate, many congregations the size of Grace and with its history take their time to find that new pastor who will best lead them as they face the necessary changes and new challenges that a transition in leadership inevitably brings. Such, however, was not the case with Grace. Before Eisenberg's last Sunday, the Church Council had already appointed a Pulpit Committee, conducted a meeting of the committee and Council with the President of the Virginia Synod, Dr. J. Luther Mauney, to review the unfamiliar process of calling a new pastor and solicited names of potential candidates among the membership. At the congregational meeting, the vote to extend the call was 202 in favor and 4 against. Following this casting of votes by written ballot, the chairman asked for a show of hands in favor of extending a unanimous call, and, without objection, the secretary of the congregation was instructed to cast a unanimous vote. In Moyer, the congregation was confident they had found the spiritual and pastoral leader needed for a new day in the life of Grace Church.

Virgil Albert Moyer, Jr., was born a son of the Shenandoah Valley in Waynesboro, Virginia, October 28, 1920, the son of Virgil Albert, Sr., and Ruth McCune Moyer. Baptized and confirmed at Grace Lutheran Church in Waynesboro, he could also be considered a son of the Virginia Synod. Following his theological education, he returned to Virginia to serve his entire ordained ministry in the territory of the Synod. A graduate of Roanoke College in 1943, he finished his theological studies in two years, graduating from Lutheran Theological Southern Seminary in Columbia, South Carolina, in 1945. The Virginia Synod of the United Lutheran Church in America (ULCA) ordained him in 1945 upon receiving his first call to serve as pastor of a young congregation, Ascension Lutheran Church, in Danville, Virginia. While in Danville he met and married Jacqueline Mildred Jones. In 1947 he returned to the Valley of his birth and served the Mt. Jackson Parish, composed of Bethel, Mt. Calvary and St. James congregations located in Shenandoah County. From 1950 to 1953 he served Christ Lutheran Church, Radford, in southwest Virginia. He returned to the Valley when he was called as pastor of St. Peter Lutheran Church, Shenandoah, 1953-1958.

Virgil Albert Moyer, Jr.

His pastoral skills and leadership abilities were acknowledged in 1959 when he was called by the Executive Council of the Virginia Synod to become the first full-time ordained assistant to the president of the Synod. This was a staff position created to give additional assistance to pastors and congregations across the Synod's territory and to help with the administrative demands of a Synod expanding its programs and adding new congregations. While serving in this position, Moyer came to know Grace, Winchester, and the congregation came to know him. This was made possible particularly when he was assigned to serve as worship leader and supply preacher on at least two Sundays at Grace during the pastoral vacancy following Eisenberg's departure. While no written record exists to confirm this conclusion, undoubtedly the Pulpit Committee was urged to approach Moyer to inquire of his openness to consider a call to Grace and a return to parish ministry.

Moyer accepted the call in person at the eleven o'clock service on Sunday, March 17, 1968. The following letter from Moyer was shared with the congregation:

> To the Members of Grace Evangelical Lutheran Church,
> 26 West Boscawen Street, Winchester, Virginia
> Peace to you and peace from God, our Father, and from

our Lord Jesus Christ: I have attempted to give prayerful consideration to your Call to become the Pastor of Grace Church. It has been my effort to seek the Will and Purpose of God for my life in regard to your Call. Believing my decision to be made under the guidance of God's Spirit, my response is to accept your Call in accordance with the conditions set forth in the Official Call, issued on February 18, 1968. In order to enable me to bring my present responsibilities to a satisfactory conclusion, the effective date of my acceptance will be July 16, 1968.

Following the service, a reception for the Moyers was held in the fellowship hall in order to give members of the congregation an opportunity to meet their new pastor, his wife and their adult son, Keith. In the week following the reception, Moyer sent a letter to the congregation asking that it be printed in the congregation's newsletter. What is significant about this letter is Moyer's observance of his own concern for returning to parish ministry and his request for the congregation's understanding and patience. Records indicate that he had raised this concern with the Pulpit Committee and Church Council before they recommended him to be called as the next pastor. That he would acknowledge his concerns to the congregation following the unanimous vote to extend the call to him reveals his keen awareness of the high expectations the congregation would have of him and his insight to the depth of the task of being the next pastor following a long pastorate marked by a leadership style very different from the one he would bring to a congregation ready to change. The letter says it well:

Dear Friends:

I want to take advantage of the opportunity provided by our church's newsletter to share with you some comments relative to the new relationship that is in the process of development. Some of these matters have been mentioned in other situations.

First, I am very appreciative of the confidence that you have shown in me in extending the Call to become your pastor. I have accepted your Call with the pledge that I will do my best to confirm and live up to that confidence.

Second, our family appreciates the very warm and friendly welcome that you have shared with us in all our contacts and visits. You have certainly made us feel "at home" in your midst in Winchester, and this makes the period between now and mid-July, when we will actually move to Winchester, seem all the longer.

Third, I will need – and do ask for – your understanding and help and patience as I begin my ministry with you. My present position has had little to do with the responsibilities of a parish pastor for over nine and one-half years, so it will doubtless take some time for these kinds of activities to become part and parcel of my life again.

Fourth, your continuing support of the life and work of Grace Church is needed now, in order that our witness and service might be carried on in our community, and outside it. Under the guidance of the Church Council and various committees, with Dr. L.S.G. Miller as the vice-pastor, and with able assistance provided by the members of the church staff in the persons of Mrs. Cahill, Mrs. Miller and Mrs. Pasquet, we should look for a full schedule of activities relating to the ministry that God has given us to fulfill here.

Finally, may we all pray and work to be more faithful in our discipleship in the weeks and years that are ahead of us as fellow workers with God.

       Cordially yours,
       V.A. Moyer, Jr., Pastor-elect

The Rev. Virgil Albert Moyer, Jr., was officially installed as pastor of Grace Evangelical Lutheran Church on Sunday, August 4, 1968, at the eleven a.m. service. The eight-thirty service was cancelled for that Sunday morning. Dr. J. Luther Mauney, President of the Virginia Synod (LCA), conducted the service of installation. During the service, President Mauney dedicated an altar service book in honor of Dr. L.S.G. Miller in appreciation for his faithful service as vice-pastor during the pastoral vacancy.

Though the process of calling Moyer had been swift and confident, it had not been absent of serious questions and long debates. Chief among the concerns questioned and debated was the salary that the Church Council recommended for the call of a new pastor. "Considerable discussion" is how the minutes of the November 9, 1967, Family Night congregational meeting describes the debate over the pastor's salary. The $7,500 that had been mentioned plus an auto allowance for a new pastor must have been something of a shock to a congregation that only recently had raised the pastor's salary into the $5,000 range. The debate concluded with the agreement to leave $5,900 in the proposed budget for 1968 with a $620 auto allowance also to be paid to the pastor. In the end, the congregation accepted its responsibility to provide compensation more in line with the times. The compensation package approved at the called congregational meeting on February 18, 1968, offered "a base salary of $8,000, a car allowance of $1000, a utilities allowance of $1,000, free use of the parsonage, pay moving expenses from Roanoke to Winchester, eight percent payment toward the Ministerial Pension and Death Benefit Plan of the LCA."

Minutes of the Church Council meetings during the vacancy indicate that another concern, which also received considerable attention, was that of the parsonage, both its state of repair and its future use. When the house was vacated in 1967 a very thorough study was done to refurbish the home for use by the next pastor. The heating system was replaced and the kitchen was remodeled. Members of the congregation organized to paint the interior before Pastor and Mrs. Moyer took up residence in July 1968.

The parsonage had long been a source of pride for the congregation and was considered one of the larger and nicer homes in Winchester. Located at 605 S. Stewart Street, it was within easy walking distance to the Winchester Memorial Hospital and the church. That a pastor and his family might want to live in their own home instead of a parsonage was a new concept being embraced by many pastors and congregations in the 1960s. Such was the desire of the Moyers, who had owned their own home in Roanoke while Moyer had served on the Synod staff. This presented a dilemma for both the congregation and the new pastor. Minutes of Church Council meetings indicate the Council's reluctance to either rent or sell the parsonage and provide a housing allowance prior to the new pastor's arrival. The minutes also indicate the Moyers' hope of owning a home at some point in the future. As a compromise, the Council approved at its March 4, 1968, meeting a provision for the pastor to exercise in the future the option of receiving a housing allowance in lieu of the free use of the parsonage. In November 1969, Moyer announced plans to purchase a lot and build a new home.

At a special called meeting of the congregation on Sunday, March 15, 1970, the Church Council was authorized to proceed with plans to sell the parsonage "at the best possible price." During the week of April 5, 1970, the Moyers moved to their new home on Oak Ridge Road. The parsonage was sold on April 13, 1970, to Peter D. Shoemaker, Jr., for $50,000. A formal closing on the contract was set for September 1, 1970. On June 21, 1970, the congregation voted 124 in favor and 1 against authorizing the trustees to finalize all details of the sale. As recommended by the Council and approved by the congregation, monies from the sale of the parsonage were placed in a special designated Parsonage Fund to be managed by the trustees and the interest from which the pastor's housing allowance was to be paid.

After his call but before his arrival, Moyer encouraged the congregation to invite the Virginia and Maryland Synods to hold jointly their 1970 conventions in Winchester in recognition of the 150th Anniversary of the founding of the Maryland and Virginia Synod at the Lutheran Church in Winchester on October 11 and 12, 1820. At the 149th annual convention of the Virginia Synod, convened at Resurrection Lutheran Church in Arlington, Virginia, on April 23, 1968, the delegates approved a resolution from the Executive Board: "That the invitation of Grace Lutheran Church to hold its [the Synod's] convention in Winchester be accepted and authorize the appointment of a Planning Committee to begin preparation for a worthy celebration of the 150th Anniversary of the Synod." At that same convention, Moyer was elected to the Executive Board of the Synod. For a congregation to host a synodical convention was a major task. That the Maryland Synod would also conduct its convention jointly only complicated an already complex task. But the congregation was up to the call, accepting the responsibilities placed on it by history, and fulfilled its responsibilities admirably with the experienced leadership of Moyer and his familiarity with the details of planning and conducting synodical conventions.

As the host congregation, Grace members and their new pastor gave considerable time to planning and making sure everything would go as smoothly as possible with the historic conventions. Meals, receptions and refreshments had to be planned and coordinated, along with the hundreds of tables and chairs that had to be set up and taken down at the many different venues between various joint events and separate business sessions of the Synods. John Handley High School and Shenandoah College auditoriums and cafeterias, as well as other congregations in the downtown area, were host to special addresses of guests from across the Church, as well as for historical presentations and special worship services. Grace was the hub of activity assisting with registration and overall coordination.

Moyer did his best to prepare the congregation for the historic occasion. In the February 1970 issue of *Tidings,* he wrote the following letter to the congregation:

This Heritage

Most anniversaries (except those that emphasize our aging!) are occasions for celebrating, and the one that our church will be hosting in May is no exception. As has been indicated previously, the 150th Anniversary of the formation of the Maryland-Virginia Lutheran Synod will be held in Winchester on May 10-11-12, 1970, and our church will be the center of many of the activities during this joint convention. Grace Church was the place where the Synod was formed in 1820.

One of the values of such an occasion for the host church is the chance to hear and become acquainted with the leaders of our church. We will surely have that opportunity multiplied for us. Dr. Robert J. Marshall, President of the Lutheran Church in America, will be present for the entire convention and will speak at the closing banquet on Tuesday, May 12. The Presidents of both Synods, Dr. J. Luther Mauney of Virginia and Dr. Paul M. Orso of Maryland, will be with us.

The Executive Secretaries of several of the boards and agencies are to be here: Dr. Donald L. Houser of American Missions, Dr. W. Kent Gilbert of Parish Education, Dr. Carl E. Thomas of Social Ministry, and Dr. C. Thomas Spritz, Jr., of the Lutheran Council in the U.S.A. These men will participate on Tuesday morning.

Mrs. Bernard Spong, President of the LCA Lutheran Church Women, will be luncheon speaker for the ladies on Tuesday. Dr. Edmund Steimle, well known as the Lutheran preacher for the *Protestant Hour* [radio broadcast], will be the preacher at the Communion Service on Monday night.

Another value to our congregation is the opportunity to assist in the many details of getting ready for, and helping carry through, the convention arrangements. One such opportunity for our ladies is noted elsewhere in *Tidings*. Other opportunities will be provided for other ladies and men as well.

I hope you will be present for as much of the celebration as you can and will respond to the requests for help when they are made. The total program will be shared with you when completed.

Your fellow worker with God, Pastor Moyer

Members of Grace did participate and respond. The ladies prepared and served food at two major receptions. Men and boys of Grace served as ushers for the many worship services at various locations and helped to move hundreds of tables and chairs. Overall, Grace proved to be an excellent host, and the City of Winchester provided ample accommodations and a good environment for the meeting of the two Synods.

The Virginia Synod expressed its appreciation by adopting the following resolution: "That we express our thanks to the members of Grace Lutheran Church for the extensive prior planning for this convention and for all the expressions of hospitality given abundantly to us all during the convention." Speaking on behalf of the Maryland Synod, President Paul Orso offered the following thanks and compliments: "I want to express to the members of Grace Lutheran Church our thanks for all the sacrifices and cooperation which they gave to the many-faceted responsibilities which they so willingly accepted. It was a real joy to be at Grace Church, to be in Winchester, and for us to have had a joint convention." Other expressions of appreciation and compliments for the hard work of Grace came from many others who attended.

Evidently, with all these Lutherans in Winchester, there was something of a heat wave that hit during the time of the convention. In his *Tidings* letter of appreciation to the congregation, Moyer notes:

> There were times when things did not go as well as we had hoped, but most of them were beyond our control. The hot weather was one such matter, and we appreciate those who responded with electric fans to help make the situation more bearable.
>
> Finally, to numerous other people who helped in numerous ways, we thank you for your assistance. Working together, you showed that Grace Church could undertake a sizeable task and do a fine job with it. I am sure we benefited from this undertaking.

During his five-year tenure, Moyer's leadership brought swift and confident changes to many areas of the congregation's mission and ministry:

- Appointed scripture lessons published for each Sunday were subscribed to and inserted in the bulletins.
- The idea and practice of lay communion assistants was introduced, and, after training, they were used in assisting the pastor in the distribution of the elements of Holy Communion.
- The process of "continuous communion" was initiated so that the blessing was offered after all had communed rather than after each "table."

- The constitution was amended to allow for youth representation on the Church Council, to provide for better administrative operation of the congregation at annual meetings and to set monthly meeting dates for the Council and a standardized agenda.
- Guidelines were established for wedding services and other uses of the congregation's facilities.
- The congregation's first pictorial directory was published.
- A "fellowship hour" was initiated following the 8:15 a.m. worship service and prior to the Sunday School hour.
- New Sunday Church School, Vacation Bible School and catechetical curricula were introduced. VBS was tried in the evening hours.
- First Communion, at a time other than after confirmation, was studied and moved to a time during the fifth grade year following instruction.

Moyer also brought needed attention and leadership to the congregation's financial and property concerns. The congregation began to experience stronger financial support following Moyer's arrival. Offerings were strong enough to insure the congregation's full payment of its apportioned benevolence. General fund balances were so positive that, in the fall of 1968, the congregation celebrated the "note burning" of the remaining indebtedness on the Parish School Building renovation [1961-1962]. Numerous gifts were received in the forms of bequests and special offerings. The Grace Lutheran Thanksgiving and Memorial Fund was established in 1969 to receive special gifts for causes above and beyond current expenses, debt reduction and benevolence. The number of pledges and the amounts pledged continued to rise each year. This generally healthy financial state of affairs helped to encourage the congregation's full participation in a number of LCA and Virginia Synod appeals for special causes. Special gifts of money and in-kind gifts of labor, supplies and materials were also given to Moyer's favorite synodical project, the outdoor camp at Caroline Furnace in the Fort Valley south of Winchester.

Moyer brought a "handy man" attitude and his own energy and gifts to the congregation that helped to address property matters from top to bottom. Loose and broken slate shingles on the steeple were repaired or replaced. Wooden support beams for the Brevitt Chime inside the spire were reinforced. After months of debate and studies by engineers and consultants, the congregation's facilities were finally air conditioned in 1970. Folding doors were added to the fellowship hall, providing much-needed room for expanding adult

Sunday Church School classes. The kindergarten and other children's groups purchased a portable stage for use in the fellowship hall. The uneven brick sidewalk in the front of the church was dug up and repaved with portions in brick and portions in concrete. In addition to an interoffice phone system, a new sound system for the sanctuary and fellowship hall was installed. A new office for the pastor was built and new office equipment was bought and constantly updated.

In 1971 Moyer requested that the Church Council study the need for an assistant pastor to help with the responsibilities of the pastoral office in the areas of visitation, counseling and work with youth. An Assistant Pastor Committee was appointed in December 1971, and, within three months, the committee had found a candidate. John Charles Morrill, II, began his duties as assistant pastor on Sunday, June 18, 1972. The account of Pastor Morrill's tenure is recorded later in this chapter.

Swift and surprising would be the terms that best describe Moyer's leaving Grace. For almost five years the congregation had experienced positive growth in all aspects of its life – membership, finances, property – along with expanded fellowship and educational programs for all ages. Moyer himself describes in detail the health of the congregation in his *Tidings* letter in January 1973, but he notes in the closing paragraph, "Yet this is not to say that we have *arrived*. Far from it. There are always more things we ought to do than we can actually accomplish. We will have the opportunity in 1973. We invite you to participate." Little did the congregation know they would be participating in the call process for the next senior pastor to lead Grace.

Moyer tendered his resignation at a special called meeting of the Church Council on Sunday, April 29, 1973. The following day, the Council sent a copy of the letter of resignation from Moyer to the congregation. It read as follows:

> By letter dated April 2, 1973, I received word of my appointment as a member of the Deployed Staff of the Division for Mission in North America of the Lutheran Church in America.
>
> I have given this appointment my prayerful consideration, as well as keeping in mind the call under which I am now serving as pastor of Grace Church. My decision is that I should accept this appointment.
>
> I am hereby submitting my resignation to you as pastor of Grace Church, so I can accept the staff appointment with the DMNA of the LCA. It is my request that the effective date for this resignation be May 31, 1973.

> In submitting my resignation, I want to express my sincere and deep appreciation to the members of Grace Church for the loyal support and the joyful partnership in the Gospel that have been evidenced to me and my family since we came here on July 15, 1968. Since we will continue to make our home in Winchester for some time into the future, I promise you my continuing support in the work of Grace Church.
> Yours in Christ!
> V.A. Moyer, Jr.

The Church Council called a special meeting of the congregation for Sunday, May 13, at 10:30 a.m. to deal with the pastor's resignation and specifically the impact it would have on the call of the new assistant pastor. The congregation was reminded that, under the terms of Pastor Morrill's call, it was necessary for him to submit his resignation at the same time. But, upon advice from President Mauney of the Virginia Synod, the congregation agreed to offer a temporary extension to Pastor Morrill's service. Council informed the congregation that a search for a new pastor would begin as soon as possible with the naming of a new Pulpit Committee. Minutes of the meeting also note the Council's request for "cooperation and support during this period when we are arranging for new pastoral leadership for our church. We would especially like to remind those of specific responsibilities in our church program to plan ahead and notify the church office and staff well in advance of needs that should be cared for."

Moyer served on the staff of the Division for Mission in North America of the LCA as regional mission consultant until he was elected President of the Virginia Synod on the third ballot at the Synod's annual convention in Richmond, Virginia, on Saturday, May 8, 1976. He was named Bishop of the Virginia Synod in 1981 and served in that capacity until his retirement on December 31, 1987. Moyer led the Synod through its transition from the Lutheran Church in America (LCA) to the new Evangelical Lutheran Church in America (ELCA), which came into existence in January 1988. In this transition he supported the creation of the Metropolitan Washington Synod and the West Virginia-Western Maryland Synod, which meant fewer congregations for the newly aligned Virginia Synod (ELCA). He was instrumental in keeping the Synod aligned with the more southern-oriented Region 9 of the ELCA.

JOHN CHARLES MORRILL, II, 1972-1973 (Assistant)

At the request of Pastor V.A. Moyer, Jr., the Church Council initiated a study of the need for an assistant pastor in 1971. It was noted that, while Pastor Eisenberg had pastors who assisted him during various times in his tenure as pastor, there had never been a formal call to a congregational-approved assistant pastor position. At the annual business meeting of the congregation on Sunday, October 24, 1971, the Church Council noted that an assistant pastor was needed for the following reasons: to assist with more visitations to inactive members, more visitations to prospective members, family counseling demands and the need for more trained leadership for youth programs. The report also noted that an assistant pastor would require an additional $12,000 to the proposed 1972 budget with $6,600 designated for base salary and $5,400 needed in other expenses. The congregation approved the position of an assistant pastor by a secret ballot vote of 107 in favor and 17 against. The Church Council appointed an Assistant Pastor Committee in December 1971.

After three months of interviews with candidates, the Assistant Pastor Committee recommended John Charles Morrill, II, to the Church Council for call by the congregation. Council voted unanimously to accept the recommendation and called a special meeting for Sunday, April 23, 1972. Recommended total remuneration was set at $9,600. The following is Morrill's letter of acceptance:

> Grace and Peace from God our Father and from the Lord Jesus Christ. I hereby formally accept your call to be your assistant pastor. I pledge to you my effort to preach and teach the Word of God and to perform all the duties of the Gospel Ministry.
>
> I want to thank you for your friendliness and warm welcome extended to me and my wife, Gail. I am looking forward to being with you and together working to spread the news that God is our strength in life and together to strengthen our faith in Him.
>
> Again, many thanks for extending to me a call to be your assistant pastor. I am looking forward to getting acquainted with all of you. The Lord be with you!
> Sincerely yours,
> John C. Morrill, II

Upon his graduation from the Lutheran Seminary at Philadelphia, Pastor Morrill began his pastoral duties at Grace on Sunday, June 18, 1972, when he was installed by Dr. J. Luther Mauney, President of the Virginia Synod, at the 11:00 a.m. service. A buffet luncheon

This Heritage

followed the celebrative service.

Pastor Morrill's tenure as assistant pastor was short-lived due to the "co-terminus" condition of his call. Upon the resignation of Pastor Moyer in April 1973, Pastor Morrill was also obligated to resign as assistant pastor effective May 31, 1973. However, the Church Council recommended at a called council meeting on April 29, 1973, that Pastor Morrill's term of service be extended beyond May 31 "until a call be developed to which he responds, but no longer than the beginning of the date of the next pastor of Grace Church." Pastor Morrill began serving as the congregation's first "interim pastor" on June 1, 1973. He served in that capacity until his resignation effective October 15, 1973, to accept the call to become the pastor of the Stephens City Parish, which consisted of Trinity Lutheran Church, Stephens City, located just five miles south of Winchester, and St. Paul Lutheran Church, located on the Cedar Creek Grade road in southwest Frederick County, Virginia.

John Charles Morrill, II

The following portion of his letter of resignation speaks to the significance of having served Grace, if even for a short period of time:

> I would like to say that it has been a meaningful experience for my wife, Gail, and I to be with you, the members of Grace Lutheran Church. This is the first parish that I have ever served as an ordained minister. I have made many friends at Grace and will miss seeing all of you. I want to thank all of you for your help and encouragement – it has meant a lot to me. I wish all of you nothing but the best in the future. I am confident in your continual mission to reach people for God and to enrich their lives. God Bless All of You!
> In His Peace,
> John C. Morrill, II

John Charles Morrill, II, was born October 21, 1946, in Brooklyn, New York, the son of John Charles and Alma Smolin Morrill. He graduated from Susquehanna University with a B.A. in 1968 and from the

Lutheran Seminary at Philadelphia with a M.Div. in 1972. He married Gail Frances Nielsen in 1971. They had two children, Christopher Ryan and Jason Alan. They divorced in 1991. He subsequently married Patricia Ryan in 1996.

Pastor Morrill served the Stephens City Parish from 1973 until 1976. He then served as pastor of the St. Paul/St. Luke Parish in Page County, Virginia (1977-1978) and St. Paul Lutheran Church, Roanoke, Virginia (1978-1987). He transferred to the Maryland Synod in September 1987. He served Messiah Lutheran Church, Sykesville, Maryland, 1987-1996. In 1997 he was called to St. John Evangelical Lutheran Church, Westminster, Maryland.

ROBERT WARREN KOONS, 1974-1982

The Rev. Dr. Robert Warren Koons was called as the twenty-third pastor of Grace at a special meeting of the congregation on Sunday, October 7, 1973. Once again the congregation wasted no time in seeking their next shepherd for the pastoral office. Following Pastor Moyer's resignation in May, a Pulpit Committee set to work interviewing pastors who would provide the leadership necessary to keep the congregation's momentum of growth and development going. Koons brought years of experienced parish ministry leadership and the reputation as a good preacher when he began his ministry at Grace on January 1, 1974.

Born July 11, 1917, in Altoona, Pennsylvania, to John Raymond and Kathryn Annabelle Herr Koons, Koons graduated from Gettysburg College (1943), Gettysburg Seminary (1946) and was ordained May 15, 1946, by the Central Pennsylvania Synod. Married to the former Grace Bowman in 1949, they had three children: Stephen, Philip and Ann. His first call was as assistant at St. John Lutheran Church, Hagerstown, Maryland. From 1950 to 1960 he served Zion Lutheran in Sunbury, Pennsylvania, followed by seven years at Christ Lutheran in Gettysburg. A call to serve Holy Trinity in Lynchburg brought him to Virginia in 1967.

Robert Warren Koons

Koons' leadership on the synodical level was extensive. He served

This Heritage

on the Executive Board of the Central Pennsylvania Synod from 1962 to 1967. He was a member of the Board of Trustees of Susquehanna University from 1957 to 1967. In recognition for his church leadership and service to Susquehanna, this Lutheran institution of higher education conferred on him the honorary degree, Doctor of Divinity, in 1958. In the Virginia Synod he served on the Board of the Lutheran Children's Home of the South (1970-1980) and as that board's president (1979-1980). He also served as the Dean of the Northern Valley Area of the Virginia Synod, a member of the Synod's Council for Parish Life and helped guide numerous synodical task groups and committees. He was elected to serve as a delegate to the 1976, 1978 and 1980 conventions of the Lutheran Church in America. Also on the national church level, he served as the secretary of the Board of College Education and Church Vocations of the LCA.

Koons wasted little time in responding to the call of Grace Church. Just three days following the issue of the call, the congregation received this letter of acceptance, dated October 10, 1973:

> To the Members of Grace Lutheran Church, Winchester, Virginia
> Dear Friends:
>
> It was delightful being with you at last Sunday evening's congregational meeting, and I have many good feelings as I write this letter accepting, as of January 1, 1974, the official call you have extended me to become your pastor.
>
> First and foremost, I have felt all along that our negotiations with each other were guided by the Holy Spirit, and deep within myself I believe this decision is in accord with His will. That gives me a strong sense of confidence, commitment and eagerness as I look forward to my work among you.
>
> Also, I'm feeling joyful because the associations I've had with members of Grace Church so far have been warm and genuine, leading me to expect that we can develop some really close relationships in the bonds of Christian love.
>
> Then, too, I'm excited to think of the many ways in which, as a staff team and entire congregation, we can help advance the mission of Jesus Christ within the Church, community and world.
>
> Until I am able to come among you, I'll often have you in my thoughts and prayers and will try to keep in touch by means of an occasional letter.
>
> Love, joy and peace be yours now and always, through Christ our Lord!
>
> Sincerely yours,
> Robert W. Koons, Pastor

Even with his years of experience, that "strong sense of confidence, commitment and eagerness..." would be needed as the new pastor and the congregation faced exciting yet difficult challenges in parish ministry during the remainder of the 1970s and the beginning of the 1980s.

First among those challenges would be introducing a new style of pastoral leadership for the congregation. Koons brought with him the idea of a "staff team" – members of the congregation's paid staff, ordained and lay – working together with lay leaders and members of the congregation in leading the standing committees and setting ministry goals. To inaugurate this new style of leadership and get quickly acquainted with the members, Koons called for a series of Pastor and People neighborhood meetings to be held in homes of members throughout the parish.

Over the course of two months, 18 neighborhood meetings were held with over 150 members attending. Koons noted in a letter to the congregation in the March 1974 issue of *Tidings*: "From my viewpoint, the Pastor and People neighborhood meetings have been delightful and exciting. I sincerely appreciate the cooperation of those who planned them, the hosts and hostesses and all who attended.... Throughout these evenings together we've learned to know each other better and have gathered valuable suggestions for our congregation's development and mission. Those ideas will be compiled, reviewed by the Church Council and referred to committees."

Minutes of the April 1974 meeting of the Council indicate that some 290 suggestions, classified according to committee responsibilities and possible implementation, were made at the neighborhood meetings. Suggestions ranged from considering one worship service at an earlier hour than eleven a.m. be tried the Sundays in the summer to having more fellowship and social events in order for members of the congregation to get to know one another better. The new pastor and staff team had their work cut out for them in the years ahead.

Koons also wanted to add to the staff team by calling a new "associated pastor." Within weeks of his installation, the Church Council appointed another Pulpit Committee to interview and recommend to the congregation a candidate to serve as an associate pastor. By the end of March, the committee was ready to recommend William C. Wood. On Sunday, April 21, 1974, Wood was extended the call to become the congregation's second partner in ordained ministry, and he was installed on June 20, 1974, exactly six months from the official installation service of Koons as senior pastor. For the first time in its history, Grace Church had two pastors installed in the same year. It is also interesting to note that this was not a new working relationship between the two new pastors of the congregation. Koons had served as supervising pastor for Wood as he fulfilled the seminary's requirement for an internship, which he had done the previous academic year, 1972-1973, at Koons' previous call, Holy Trinity Lutheran Church, Lynchburg, Virginia.

Upon the arrival of the new Associate Pastor and with the presence of Martha Cahill already on staff as Director of Christian Education, Koons was ready with them to initiate a new style of staff leadership which recognized each staff member's particular gifts and abilities for ministry. Within days of starting to work together, these three members of the staff team attended a workshop for multiple-staff congregations at Roanoke College. In a letter to the congregation in the July 7, 1974, issue of *Tidings*, the three staff members outlined the new working relationships among staff members and expressed "our aim to extend the concept of a team ministry throughout the total life of the congregation – Church Council, committees and other groups – so that we see ourselves as working together for the mission of the Church." Some events in the life of the congregation over the next seven years challenged the staff team idea that Koons wanted to implement for Grace.

One of those challenges came in the form of recruiting, training and supporting more members to serve in the congregation's organizational structure to help with expanding the educational and youth ministry programs and to deal with the increased demands of members in the church and the surrounding community with basic social needs. A new way of recruiting more members in leadership roles was introduced in the January 1975 issue of *Tidings*. After a listing of the various parish life committees and a description of each committee's responsibilities, members were asked to sign up on a form at the bottom of the page and turn in their responses as soon as possible. This would be the beginnings of what later became the practice of asking members to make pledges of time and talent along with their financial pledge. Minutes of the Church Council meetings and articles in *Tidings* indicate that recruitment and increased involvement of members in the organizational structure of the congregation continued to be a challenge to the staff team concept of leadership for the congregation.

Nineteen seventy-five was also the year of facing the financial challenges in the life of the congregation that had begun to demand the critical attention of the senior pastor and Church Council. Possibly reflecting a downturn in the national economy, regular giving had not met budgeted expenses for almost two years. Deficit spending had been covered by borrowing money from designated funds and endowment funds with the commitment of paying back the amounts borrowed when finances turned around. The Stewardship Committee noted that finances were not going to turn around, given the current level of offerings for minimal general expenditures. Offerings in the final months of 1974 and pledges for the 1975 budget were so insufficient that the Church Council had to recommend a reduction of $11,000 in projected budgeted expenses before the budget for 1975 was finally approved at the January annual report meeting. The extent of the congregation's financial crisis even raised questions of continuing to support financially the preschool program and the possibilities of cuts in staff salaries and ministry programs. Other evidence of the degree of the crisis was seen in the Church Council's concern for the congregation's taking on additional appeals for the greater church. Commitment to assigned goals for appeals of the LCA, the Virginia Synod and other institutions of the church such as Lutheran Theological Southern Seminary's Outreach Appeal were severely under-subscribed.

Upon advice from the Stewardship Committee, Koons and the Council invited a trained stewardship consultant from the Lutheran Layman's Movement for Stewardship (LLM) to meet with the Council at its February 1975 meeting. At that meeting, Chuck Bartlett from LLM offered an interpretation of the congregation's financial crisis and outlined a program that had proven to be helpful for congregations in attaining their potential for financial growth. Following the presentation, Council decided to recommend the program to the congregation.

The recommendation met with strong opposition in the congregation. One reason for the opposition was the projected cost of the services that LLM would provide. Of the $4,125 needed for the contract, the Siebert Foundation of Milwaukee announced that it would provide a $3,000 grant because of the foundation's commitment to helping "Lutheran programs and causes, including churches which are making major, special efforts to strengthen their life and mission." Before the vote on the recommendation, the Stewardship Committee began a series of occasional "Plain Talk" inserts in the congregation's newsletter. For the most part, these served to inform the members of the facts about the giving patterns in the congregation, admonish members to do better by changing long-held attitudes about giving and encourage support for the recommendation to hire someone to come in from the "outside." This, too, was new to the congregation and was another reason for the congregation's reluctance to change. The recommendation narrowly passed at a special meeting of the congregation on Sunday, June 22, 1975. The vote was 81 in favor and 70 against.

But the leadership held firm, and plans for the program moved ahead. Strong lay leaders stepped forward to give their support, and scores of members were recruited and trained to make every-member visits. Finally, the program for changing giving patterns and challenging long-held attitudes about church and finances was implemented in the latter part of October. The program was entitled "Growth in Grace" and was conducted over a five-week period of time. Even though there had been strong opposition voiced for such an effort, the vast majority of members responded positively to invitations for visits in their homes, where straight talk was offered by a team of trained visitors about the potential giving of every family unit in the congregation. "A Message from the Pastors" in the December 9, 1975, special issue of *Tidings* provided a good summary of the program's impact on the life of Grace:

> This special issue of *Tidings* is meant to prepare you for the congregational meeting this Sunday. It brings you a report on the recent Stewardship Development Program and the proposed budget for 1976.
>
> Briefly, the Stewardship Development Program in various ways was an encouraging success! It helped to develop a corps of good leaders and well-trained, experienced visitors. For a significant number of members, it resulted in considerable stretching and growing as responsible, committed Christian stewards of God's gifts and graces. Financially, it more than paid for itself by a 30-percent increase in a balanced budget for 1976. It has brought us around the corner of deficit spending so that we can move ahead toward an increasingly strengthened stewardship program throughout the coming years. More details about the benefits of our effort will be given in a later issue of *Tidings*.
>
> Words of thanks are also due to those hundreds of people who helped with making the survey, phoning, visiting and serving in many other tasks that were part of this team effort. We have reason to express our very special and hearty appreciation to LLM Director Charles Stief, Campaign Secretary Ann Hoffman, Parish Secretary Kim DeHaven, General Chairman Jerry Kerr, Advance Visits Chairman Gene Fisher,

General Visits Chairman Jim Diehl, Publicity Chairperson Henrietta Ritter, Proposal Chairman Charles Greeb, Audit Chairman David Drayer, Chief Hostess Mary Whitehill, Dinner Arrangements Chairpersons Jack and Jane Jenkins, Prayer Chairman Jim Brown. They were all willing, able and dedicated workers.

With this new beginning in stewardship which we have experienced as a congregation, may we now go from strength to strength in the service of Jesus Christ and His Kingdom!

Indeed, the congregation in the coming years experienced "strength to strength" in many areas of its life. Financially, the "Growth in Grace" stewardship program had a lasting impact. Deficit spending patterns were eliminated, and good stewardship practices were further developed and implemented. Pledges increased both in the number of pledges and in the amounts pledged. Record budgets for mission and ministry expenditures were adopted and balanced with realistic goals of anticipated giving. The congregation's history of strong financial support for benevolent causes, locally and throughout the greater church, was affirmed through its involvement with the newly developed Community-Congregation Action Program (C-CAP) and with positive responses to the LCA's Strength for Mission Appeal, the National Lutheran Home Appeal and the capital fund appeal for Caroline Furnace Lutheran Camp. The congregation also reaffirmed its financial support of the Virginia Synod and LCA by consistent payment of its fair share of apportioned benevolence.

The congregation adopted its first formal mission statement on Sunday, June 22, 1975, and in the years ahead experienced renewed strength as many of the suggestions from the Pastor and People neighborhood meetings which shaped the mission statement began to be implemented.

Mission Statement of 1975

GRACE LUTHERAN CHURCH is a body of people loved by God and called by the Holy Spirit to faith in Jesus Christ. That faith is nourished toward Christian maturity by Word and Sacrament. It is expressed by good works in partnership with any who serve God's will. The church is concerned for people's total well-being, their growth in every way and their development toward the fulfillment God intends. The mission of the church is to have its members individually and corporately live their faith in action every day. We do that by loving, forgiving, serving, caring for and sharing with all people in need within our own fellowship, in the surrounding community and everywhere.

The church is committed to strengthen and support, equip and direct its community. It brings others into it by using and blending talents of all in worship, fellowship, education, witnessing and service. United in baptism as diverse people who respect each other's uniqueness and importance, the church is a unifying influence in the world. It is continually open to the Holy Spirit's renewal for implementing its mission. The church offers the means of salvation and care for the whole creation.

"Strength to strength" was also shown in the area of worship and music under Koons' leadership. Holy Communion services were scheduled more often, and two Christmas Eve services were initiated. Children's sermons were introduced, and children were encouraged to come to the communion table with their families to receive a blessing. A 30-voice Celebration Choir for children was started. An outdoor worship service was conducted in the side yard of the Godfrey Miller Home. A special Labor Day worship service recognizing the daily ministry of the members of the congregation was held. At the service Koons wore a specially made chasuble with patches of cloth from members' homes forming a full-length cross on the white eucharistic vestment. More lay leaders were recruited and trained to serve as ushers, readers, communion assistants and liturgists. The corps of acolytes, crucifers and banner bearers was enlarged by including children in the fifth through the seventh grades. The use of new chancel appointments such as the processional cross, torches, processional Bible and a Paschal Candle was introduced, elevating the sense of formality in the congregation's worship services. New liturgies for services of the Word and Holy Communion were introduced with new contemporary musical settings and hymns used on Thursday evenings. Chancel dramas were produced and performed for midweek Lenten services. Bread and wine were made by members for use in Holy Communion services to further symbolize the reality that all aspects of the liturgical form of worship was the work of the people and not the performance of a few.

The Worship and Music Committee and staff team planned a series of special training sessions and rehearsal segments of worship services to introduce portions of new liturgies in an attempt to prepare the congregation for the new *Lutheran Book of Worship*, which was scheduled to be introduced to Lutheran congregations in 1978. These plans proved to be especially important due to the announcement of the retirement in December 1977 of Marian Pasquet, organist and choir director for twenty-five years. A special Thanksgiving reception was given by the congregation to honor her "faithful years of service and devotion" to the music program at Grace. She continued to serve past December, while a special search committee tried to find a worthy replacement. Her last Sunday as organist/choir director was Easter, March 26, 1978. On that same day, at a special meeting of the Church Council, Alice Cussen was hired as the new organist and choir director. Unfortunately, her tenure "on the bench" was interrupted by health problems, finally resulting in her resigning the position within a year. Once again the congregation searched for an organist and choir director who would be musically talented and strong enough to meet the rigors of leading the congregation and choirs through the liturgical changes that were coming with the use of the new worship resource. Fortunately for the congregation, Carol Black Westervelt, a member and former chair of the Worship and Music Committee, served capably in this capacity during this extended transitional time. Finally, in March 1979, the congregation was able to secure the services of the youthful and enthusiastically talented Steven Shaner, a Lutheran student attending Shenandoah College and Conservatory of Music.

The change from the popular *Service Book and Hymnal*, affectionately known as the "red book," was not readily accepted by all the members of the congregation. In an attempt to respond sensitively to those who resisted the changes, the Worship and Music Committee recommended a compromise which provided for occasional use of the more familiar "red book" as part of the motion to accept the new liturgies and hymns. With this compromise, minutes of the annual business meeting of the congregation on Sunday, December 10, 1978, indicate that the adoption of the new *Lutheran Book of Worship* passed, after long discussion, with 117 in favor and 33 against. The *Lutheran Book of Worship* was fully introduced with the congregation's competent use of two settings for Holy Communion and other liturgies of the Word throughout 1979.

"Strength to strength" in adapting to change was displayed in other areas of the congregation in these years of transition. At the November 12, 1978, meeting of the Church Council, Pastor Wood announced his intention to resign as associate pastor effective May 31, 1979. In his announcement, he indicated a career change by entering graduate study in the field of engineering at the University of Virginia. Wood had obviously discussed his plans for a career change with Koons. At the same meeting of the Council, Koons presented and Council approved a recommendation that the congregation participate as an internship church for third-year theological students who needed, as part of their theological training, practical experiences and supervision for one year. In the November 26, 1978, issue of *Tidings*, Koons noted the reasons for this recommended change from an associate pastor to a "student pastor."

> Another recommendation of the Council is "that application be made to the Lutheran Theological Seminary at Gettysburg, Pennsylvania, for an intern to serve Grace Lutheran Church preferably for a calendar year beginning July 1, 1979, or as close to that date as feasible."
>
> I also support this recommendation because (1) it will provide for continuity of staff assistance following Pastor Wood's leaving in June; (2) an internship has the double benefit of service to the congregation and a learning experience for the seminary student; (3) lay members will be challenged to fulfill their ministry more fully since the services of an intern will not equal those of an ordained pastor; (4) a variety of talents and insights can be offered by different students serving as interns during the succeeding years; (5) the cost is about $5,000 less than for an ordained pastor and is therefore more commensurate with our present financial stewardship.

The recommendation was approved by the congregation. For the remainder of his tenure as senior pastor, Koons served wisely as a supervising pastor, and the congregation rejoiced in the gifted interns who served as "vicars." In July 1979 the congregation welcomed Bill Hoffmeyer, the first of three interns who would experience the joys and challenges of parish ministry. Hoffmeyer worked primarily with the youth and assisted Koons in the usual duties of the pastoral office – preaching, teaching, visiting and attending meetings. Hoffmeyer was followed by the congregation's first female intern, Louise Mierzwa, during the academic year 1980-1981. Mierzwa proved to be popular with her warm personality and, like Hoffmeyer, proved to be competent in her assistance to Koons as a "student pastor." Sue Lang was welcomed as intern for the academic year 1981-1982. Lang's internship proved to be especially helpful to the congregation, while challenging to her, as 1982 brought significant and permanent changes to the staff team.

Nineteen seventy-eight was also a year for celebrating the strength of the congregation's history. Koons and other members of the congregation believed that time and resources of the congregation should be given to celebrating the congregation's 225th Anniversary. Plans were made to commission a pen-and-ink drawing of the church for reproduction on special bulletin covers and for producing commemorative plates and tiles which members could purchase as mementos of the anniversary year. A liturgical service used among eighteenth-century Lutheran congregations in the Shenandoah Valley was used on a special Sunday. One of the most popular events was the "Former Pastors Sunday," September 24, when four former pastors – Honeycutt, Eisenberg, Moyer and Morrill – returned to assist in leading the two morning worship services. Records indicate that over 500 were in attendance for the worship services, and the fellowship hall was filled to capacity for a special recognition dinner following the late morning service. The last of the anniversary commemorative services was held on All Saints Sunday, November 5. At these services members were given an opportunity to write their names on a document to be included with other important information of the congregation's history and 225th Anniversary year. All of these historic items were placed in a time capsule dedicated in memory of Paul H. Miller, to be opened on the occasion of the congregation's 300th Anniversary in the year 2078.

The strength of the congregation's outreach ministry was extended under Koons' pastoral leadership. A strong advocate for support of the church's wider ministries, Koons encouraged the congregation to expand its support of foreign missionaries. In addition to the historic support Grace had provided for missionaries in Japan since 1892, in 1979 Frederick and Dolores Wehrenberg were sponsored as Lutheran missionaries to Liberia, Africa, thus extending the outreach ministry of Grace to a second continent. Working with Lutheran Refugee and Immigration Services, the congregation sponsored and relocated three refugee groups – three Cambodian men, seven members of the Vietnamese Huynh family and the Boseks from Poland. The congregation adopted Duane Steele as a son of the congregation and assisted him as he sought to be the first person without sight to graduate from seminary and be ordained into the Office of Word and Sacrament. Following a tragic diving accident at the beach which broke his neck, Pastor Fred Ritter, a true son of the congregation, was supported in many ways during his long rehabilitation. The congregation led the efforts of the Virginia Synod and many of Ritter's friends to purchase a handicap accessible van. Strong financial support was also given to the LCA's World Hunger Appeal. The Parish Life and Ministry Development team recommended, and the congregation approved, setting aside a minimum of three percent of each year's operational budget exclusively for support of local benevolent causes. Koons encouraged the congregation to open its doors for regular use by community-based, non-profit human services organizations such as Alcoholics Anonymous.

"Strength to strength" was also experienced in the areas of Christian Education and Youth Ministry. Two new adult Sunday Church School classes were added, and the pastors led educational retreats for both youth and adult groups. Numerous weekday opportunities for small group Bible study and learning experiences were offered. Grace Lutheran Preschool expanded, and children's participation in Vacation Bible School grew. New standards for catechetical instruction were adopted, and more children were encouraged to participate in First Communion classes. A new committee structure was developed to better plan and implement youth events for both junior and senior high youth groups. The number of youth participating in Synod youth events expanded. Amendments were made to the congregation's constitution allowing for youth to more fully participate in the decision-making processes of the congregation, including youth representation on the Church Council.

The "strength" of the congregation's property was enhanced during Koons' tenure. Besides the day-to-day general maintenance and repairs necessary for such large facilities, at least three major property projects were accomplished. The exterior of the church sanctuary was sandblasted and restored to its original brick look in 1974. The east wall of the original church structure in Mount Hebron Cemetery was repointed in order to secure loose stones in the wall and reduce further deterioration. In 1980, 35 windows were covered with new, clear Lexon or Luxite materials in order to protect the beauty of the windows and provide for some insulation from loss of heat.

From the beginning, Koons' ministry and leadership style emphasized the importance of the "ministry of the laity." Within the life of the congregation, this meant renewed efforts to develop lay leadership and involvement of more members in all aspects of the congregation's organizational life and programs of ministry. To foster these efforts, Koons initiated weekly rather than monthly publication of the congregation's newsletter, *Tidings*. Copies of each year's annual reports of mission and ministry were printed and made available to members. Minutes of Council and standing committee meetings were posted as well as summarized in *Tidings*. Frequent questionnaires and surveys were used to seek opinions and help prepare the congregation to make major decisions. A congregational directory of members was printed along with helpful information about the operations and organizational structure of the church. "Listening Posts" and other informational sharing meetings were held for members to attend in order to channel ideas and develop lay ownership of new program initiatives in the life of the congregation. A Pastoral Relations Committee was formed to support and advise the pastors and provide members a group to turn to in order to offer constructive criticism. The masthead for the printing of the bulletins and *Tidings* began with this line, "The Members of Grace – The Ministers" followed by a listing of the staff. Known for his powerful and sometimes controversial sermons on social justice issues such as the nuclear arms race, Koons printed his sermons for distribution to members who requested them. In his sermons and in almost every annual report, he noted the importance of the daily ministry of God's people in their homes, their work and their relationships with both neighbor and stranger.

On Sunday, December 6, 1981, Koons informed the Church Council that he intended to retire in 1982. The following letter was sent to the members of Grace the next day:

Dear Members of Grace Church:

As 1981 draws to a close and we move on toward the new year, it means the approach of my 65th birthday in July. Although the Lutheran Church in America does not require a pastor's retirement at that age, I have chosen that option because I believe this is an appropriate time for Grace Church to have new leadership and because I want to devote more time to members of my family and to the part-time ministries, voluntary and otherwise, which retirement will make possible.

Accordingly, at last night's meeting of the Church Council I submitted my resignation as pastor of Grace Lutheran Church, effective July 1, 1982. The Council accepted the resignation and also granted me the month of June for vacation accumulated through 1981 and 1982. This means that I will conclude my work among you on May 31. Immediately after that, Grace and I will move to our home in Gettysburg, Pennsylvania.

While I am looking forward to the new opportunities which my leisure will afford, I find it painful to think about concluding my associations with the people of Grace Church whom I have loved and served since 1974. With many of you I have shared some of life's deepest sorrows and hurts; with others, some of its most fulfilling joys; with all of you, the spiritual bonds which our common faith in Jesus Christ has nurtured. In the past it has never been easy for me to sever such ties, and I am therefore asking your prayerful

This Heritage

support and understanding during these coming months.

I am also calling for your continued and sustained devotion to the Lord and His Church in the immediate future and throughout the years ahead. Our congregation is in a strong and wholesome condition, with many possibilities for increased growth and effectiveness as we move ahead in the pursuit of our mission. I have much confidence in the ministry of the laity that has developed so noticeably during these recent years.

At the same time, I caution you not to be anxious about the change of pastors which you now will be confronting but to pray for and trust the Holy Spirit's leading as you follow the procedures outlined by the Synod and supervised by our bishop. The first question to consider is not who the next pastor will be, but what the congregation wants to become and do during the years ahead. Then it will be possible to seek a person who seems suited to that task. The Parish Life and Ministry Development process in which we have been engaged was intentionally initiated by me for that purpose.

During these closing months my attention will be devoted more to personal ministries than to program development. I am hoping that the remainder of our time together will be rich in many blessings for us all. After my leaving, all of our capable and devoted staff will continue their important ministries; and our intern, Sue Lang, will serve until the end of August.

I am grateful for the privilege of having been among you as your pastor and friend and have high hopes for what our future years may hold. The Lord be with and bless you all!

In His name and love,
Robert W. Koons, Pastor

At the annual business meeting of the congregation on the following Sunday, December 13, 1981, Charles Greeb, vice-president of the congregation, read the following resolution to Pastor Koons:

We, the congregation of Grace Church, take this occasion to acknowledge, with deep feelings of regret, the announcement of your plans for retirement. It is too early to say "goodbye," but it is not too early for us to begin saying "thank-you." We do wish to acknowledge our gratitude to you and to your helpmate, Grace, for your many ministries among us. When the time for partings comes, you will be sorely missed by the many members with whom you have established close ties of mutual love and affection. We know that you are looking forward to the time when you can lay down the burdens and cares of the office, but we know, too, that you will always retain a deep sense of commitment to us. We ask that the Lord guide you, and us, as you go through the next few months of disengaging from the ministry to our congregation. May we be mutually supportive. We ask also that the Lord grant us as a congregation an effective transition so that that which is good in your ministry among us will be preserved and strengthened. May God's rich blessings be with you and Grace always.

The remainder of Koons' time at Grace Church was given to helping with the transitions in pastoral leadership that the congregation would face throughout 1982. The transition was more difficult than anticipated. First, Martha Cahill, Director of Christian Education since 1962, announced in early February her intention to retire effective May 15, 1982. Second, while Sue Lang's internship was scheduled to conclude in August, no one had anticipated Steven Shaner stepping down in that same month from his staff position as organist and choir director in order to pursue graduate work at Wittenberg University in Ohio. The Rev. Conrad Christianson, Pastor, Bethel Lutheran Church in Frederick County, was appointed vice-pastor of the congregation and helped in finalizing Lang's last three months of internship and advising the Church Council as it dealt with issues during the transition to new pastoral leadership. When the Council realized that the work of the Pulpit Committee and the acceptance of a call by the next pastor might extend through the remainder of the year, Pastor John C. Bellingham, retired Air Force Chaplain and well-known to the members of the congregation, was asked (and he accepted) to serve in the role of "interim pastor." The Worship and Music Committee was fortunate in securing the talented Dorothy L. Tillotson as Organist and Director of Music. Indeed, 1982 proved to be the year not just of one but many transitions in the leadership of the congregation.

WILLIAM COLLINS WOOD, II, 1974-1979 (Associate)

William Collins Wood, II, was called within two years of the arrival of the first assistant pastor. It was his second career, as he previously taught science in Burke County Public Schools in Morganton, North Carolina. This was also the second opportunity he would have to work with Pastor Robert W. Koons. For that reason,

Wood was Koons' first choice to serve with him as the second ordained pastor of the staff team that Koons envisioned for a new style of pastoral leadership for Grace. Hopes and expectations were no doubt high for both the ordained team and a congregation willing to move so quickly and confidently in its choices of pastoral leadership within one year.

Wood was extended the call to serve Grace through a unique arrangement of a special called meeting of the congregation on Sunday, April 21, 1974. Instead of a single meeting of the congregation, two sessions were held, one following each of the two morning worship services at which Wood himself was present and assisted with the reading of the appointed scriptures. The motion to extend the call to Wood and approve the $11,000 proposed compensation, which included salary, pensions, death benefit and all allowances, was placed before each session. Following the first service the vote was 62 in favor and 3 against. Following the second service the vote was 118 in favor and 2 against. Total vote of the two sessions was 180 in favor and 5 against.

Wood was born September 14, 1948, in Lakeland, Florida, the son of a Lutheran pastor, the Rev. William Collins Wood, Jr., and his wife, Margaret Lois Howell Wood. He married Linda Carol Mangum on December 27, 1969. He graduated in 1970 from a Lutheran college, Lenoir Rhyne, in Hickory, North Carolina. He graduated from the Lutheran Theological Southern Seminary, Columbia, South Carolina, in 1974. Wood was ordained by the North Carolina Synod of the LCA in 1974. Wood's letter of acceptance was printed in the May 12, 1974, issue of *Tidings*:

> Dear Brothers and Sisters in Christ:
> God works in fantastic ways, and it is my belief that He has been busy with us during the process leading to your extending an Official Call to me to become associate pastor at Grace Lutheran Church. It is then with the awareness of the presence and support of God that I accept your call to be your associate pastor, effective on or about June 20, 1974, and pending completion of seminary and ordination into the Lutheran Church in America. During this time of transition, my thoughts carry me back and forth between Columbia and Winchester, and I am warmed and excited as I think of you and the possibilities of ministry with you and with Pastor Koons. Ministry involves us all working together, discovering and carrying out God's vision and specific mission for us in our particular place

and time both as individuals and as a congregation.

As I enter the ordained ministry and anticipate our ministry together, I bring expectations for that ministry which I would like to share with you. I expect to rejoice and to suffer with those whom I serve. I look to share myself with others, and they with me and for us both to grow together. I hope for growth of individuals and of the congregation in the capacity for compassion, in handling our own resources, in discovering new potentials and using them. I expect to feel the presence and guidance and strength of the Lord in our ministry and our lives together. I expect to affirm others as they are being themselves and to be affirmed by them for being myself. I expect and hope from all concerned growth in caring, forgiving and accepting, as we are constantly cared for, forgiven, accepted and affirmed by God.

It is now with great joy that Linda and I look forward to our joining you in Winchester where we will work and live together in the awareness of the ever-present love, strength and guidance of our Lord, Father and Helper.

Yours in the Service of the Lord,
William Collins Wood, II

Wood was installed at one scheduled worship service at 11:00 a.m. on Sunday, June 23, 1974, by the Rev. Dr. J. Luther Mauney, President of the Virginia Synod, who preached the sermon and officiated at the installation.

Initially, traditional responsibilities between the two pastors (preaching, presiding at services of Holy Communion, teaching, visiting the sick, counseling and visiting prospective members, etc.) were shared equally. Assignments to committees and certain program and administrative tasks were also shared among the pastors and other members of the paid lay staff according to the abilities and interests of the members of the staff team. This was a new approach to pastoral leadership for the congregation, and it took some time and effort for Koons and Wood to work out their new working relationship with the rest of the staff and lay leaders of the congregation. Confusion about pastoral roles, questions about authority and decision-making and differences in viewpoints on the role of the pastors' working relationship with each other and other staff members finally prompted Koons in September 1975 to appoint, with approval by the Church Council, a special committee to address these issues.

Most of the issues were clarified by the work of this committee and the less authoritative style of both pastors in their leadership capacities were acknowledged. The new style of leadership through the staff team was affirmed, but particular areas of responsibilities were adjusted to fit better the congregation's expectations of all the staff members and particularly the role of the associate pastor. Wood addressed these expectations, their resolution, and their impact on his pastoral development in his annual report for 1975:

William Collins Wood, II

> During the past year there have been a number of significant changes in my growth and development as a pastor. Particularly important has been the latter half of 1975. It seems that it took about a year for me to feel that I belonged here at Grace and that I had something worthwhile to contribute to the congregational life. As the year progressed, I found myself assuming more pastoral responsibility, both in pastoral care and administrative duties. Part of the team ministry approach is that both pastors and the Director of Christian Education would share significant responsibilities within the congregation, with the duties and responsibilities being designated on the basis of talents, interest and congregational needs and desires. Therefore, I have not been solely a "helper"; I have been an integral part of the ministry team of our church, a role in which I am becoming increasing more comfortable.
>
> As has been stated in the past, one of my primary duties has been with the youth of our church. What may not be widely known is that, in extending a call to me, the Pulpit Committee and the Church Council decided not to recommend someone with a specialty in youth ministry, but rather someone, myself, who had broad interests and capabilities and who was admittedly not as strong in youth ministry as in other areas. Because this was not clearly conveyed, there developed a gap between the expectation of the youth and the congregation on one side and what I was able to deliver on the other. However, I am very

pleased to report that there have been significant improvements in my relationships with our young people and that the youth program of our church is improving, particularly under the direction of the Youth Educational Ministry Committee, which I initiated and continue to support....

For a period of about eight months after I arrived, I shared the responsibility of preaching about equally with the senior pastor. In response to expressed desires that he preach more often, we adapted the preaching so that I would preach about once a month. The change has provided extra time for me to use particularly in increased visitation, and it has, over a period of time, contributed toward my sermons being more in touch with the pulse of the congregation.

Wood continued to grow as a pastor and served the congregation well for the next four years. New adult Sunday Church School classes were started and, given his mathematical abilities, greater attention was given by the pastoral team to management of the congregation's finances. During his tenure as associate pastor, he and his wife, Linda, experienced the birth of their two daughters, Laura Kathryn and Patricia Ann.

Portions of a letter that Wood wrote to the congregation on November 20, 1978, conveyed the depth of his struggles with his sense of vocation.

> This letter comes at the end of the most difficult struggle that I have faced. Now I am relieved that the struggle is over, and I am looking excitedly and joyfully ahead. I have recently decided on a course of action that will over the next months take me out of parish ministry and in an entirely new career direction. However, as I write I am filled with much sadness. I am sad because this will mean leaving many people here that I care about very deeply, and I am sad because I am leaving one phase of my life in order to move into another...
>
> I have decided that the field I want further education in is a relatively new field of Systems Engineering. As I've explored it, that branch of engineering for me builds quite heavily on both my college studies in math and physics as well as my experiences with people, my values for Christian service, and my insights into team building and effective communication...If all goes as I expect it to, I'll begin graduate studies in June of next year in the School of Engineering and Applied Science of the

University of Virginia working on a Master of Engineering.

The next few months of ministry at Grace confirmed the validity of his decision, and he expressed appreciation for his years of ministry. Heartfelt thanks and gifts in support of his graduate study expenses were expressed to him and his family at a dinner given in his honor following his last worship service on Sunday, May 27, 1979.

Wood received his Master of Engineering in 1980 and went on to earn his Doctor of Philosophy in the same field of study in 1984 from the University of Virginia in Charlottesville. He has taught on the college level since earning his graduate degrees in engineering. Wood resigned from the roll of ordained clergy in 1982.

JOHN CHAMBERLAIN BELLINGHAM, 1982 (Interim)

The congregation was fortunate to have Pastor Jack Bellingham, a member of the congregation since 1976, capable of stepping into the role of interim pastor following the eight-year pastorate of Robert W. Koons. Although the congregation had called the next pastor, James H. Utt, in September, Utt indicated that he would not be able to begin his pastoral duties until January 1, 1983. Arrangements were made with Bishop V.A. Moyer, Jr., of the Virginia Synod, to have Bellingham appointed to the role of interim pastor. For the congregation this meant a continuity of worship leadership, particularly over the Advent and Christmas seasons, the availability of scheduled office hours and consistent pastoral care and visitation for members in need.

Having retired as a Chaplain in the United States Air Force with the rank of Major, Bellingham and his wife, Claire, moved to Winchester in 1976 and began a private counseling practice. Both became involved in many community-based, non-profit human services organizations. Bellingham served as the Executive Director of the Lord Fairfax Interchurch Council, an interdenominational ecumenical agency providing chaplain and pastoral counseling services to jails, institutions of higher education and other agencies throughout the northern Shenandoah Valley region. He co-founded the Northern Shenandoah Valley Men's Council. He served as president of the Board of Directors of the Shenandoah Area Agency on Aging. He was also a board member of The Shelter for Abused Women. He served as a trainer of volunteers for Concern Hotline and Blue Ridge Hospice. As an adjunct faculty member at Lord Fairfax Community College and Shenandoah University, he taught courses in human development, interpersonal relationships and stress management. He also served as a supply pastor for congregations without a pastor throughout the Shenandoah Valley and eastern West Virginia.

The Processional Continues

John Chamberlain Bellingham

John Chamberlain Bellingham was born on February 15, 1928, in Erie, Pennsylvania, the son of John David Bellingham and Mae Fors Bellingham. He graduated from Thiel College, Greenville, Pennsylvania, in 1949. Following graduation from the Lutheran Theological Seminary in Philadelphia, he was ordained upon being called as the mission pastor for Apostles Lutheran Church in Penn Station, Pennsylvania. He became an Air Force Chaplain in 1956. His tours of duty stationed him in New York, Great Britain, Florida, Louisiana and Labrador, Canada. His last tour of duty was in Illinois, where he and his wife attended Eastern Illinois University. Both earned their master's degrees in counseling and pursed additional studies on a doctoral level.

Bellingham married Claire Kay Austin on March 30, 1960, in Philadelphia, Pennsylvania. They raised three daughters – Virginia, Rebecca, Kristin – and a son, Jonathan. Following years of heart problems, Pastor Bellingham died at his home in Winchester on Sunday, May 13, 2001, and his memorial service was held at Grace. His ashes are inhumed in the Grace Lutheran Church Memorial Garden on the site of the original church of the congregation in Mount Hebron Cemetery, Winchester, Virginia.

Upon concluding his service as interim pastor in December 1982, he wrote the following as his report in the congregation's 1982 Annual Report booklet:

> My three months as Interim Pastor have been some of the most meaningful times of my ministry. It was not difficult to serve people who welcome you so graciously and respond so positively. To many of you I have already said that this time with you has filled a void that I didn't know I had. To visit with you in the hospital, to share in the life of your homes and to work together for the advancement of God's Kingdom on earth, to be a part of both sorrow and joy have touched me deeply.
>
> I can now place many faces with names that were only a

mystery before. Through discovering each other I have had my life touched by many new friends and deepened the understanding and enrichment with many others. Both of the Christmas Eve services are at the top of my memories of meaningful services and I thank you all for that. I thank the youth for their support in the worship services and Carolyn Mummert, who got them there. I thank the choirs for their beautiful anthems and dependability and Dorothy Tillotson, who got them there, for her difficult task of having to adjust and readjust to my whims. My thanks to Joan Bly, whose infinite patience and vast store of information made it possible for me to survive without being overwhelmed. Most of all, my thanks to the three- and four-year-olds for their Monday, Wednesday and Friday hugs. I think I'm going to miss that most of all.

One of the nicest things about it is I won't be leaving but will be surely changing the place where I sit. I'm looking forward to our continuing life together in Grace Lutheran Church.

Yours in Christ,
John C. Bellingham

Pastor Bellingham served Grace well in a time of transition from one pastor who retired at Grace from the parish ministry to another pastor who was coming with only six years of experience.

JAMES HOWARD UTT, 1983-Present

Within a week after receiving Pastor Koons' resignation, Church Council contacted Virginia Synod Bishop Moyer regarding the impending pastoral vacancy. Council minutes indicate that, during the next six months, Bishop Moyer met three times with members to provide guidance throughout the selection process. By February 21, 1982, Council established a pastoral selection committee headed by Roger Milburn. In accordance with procedures set by the Virginia Synod, a congregational profile was created, and questionnaires were sent to all confirmed members to determine the pastoral leadership needs of the congregation. By the end of April, the five most important characteristics and leadership expectations of a successor pastor were identified:

- Preacher to prepare and deliver sermons that proclaim the gospel effectively and that are relevant and appropriate to the needs of worshippers.

- Leader of Worship to plan and conduct effective worship services.
- Teacher of Youth to teach, work and relate well with high school and college age-persons.
- Minister in Crisis to support persons in the midst of crises such as bereavement, sickness, birth, trauma, success and other significant personal events.
- Counselor to assist persons facing problems or decisions through counseling sessions.

James Howard Utt

Bishop Moyer met with the selection committee on May 9 to provide input on specific candidates. Interviews of candidates took place during the summer. By September, the selection committee was confident that they had succeeded in locating a pastor who could effectively direct Grace Church in the years ahead. They found that person in 33-year-old James Howard Utt who, for six years, had been pastor of Ascension Lutheran Church, Danville, Virginia.

James Howard Utt, son of Eldon W. and Maxine Lyon Utt, was born June 29, 1949, in Radford, Virginia. He graduated from Hillsville High School in 1967, attended Wytheville Community College and earned his Bachelor of Science degree in secondary education from the University of Tennessee in 1972. He married Mary Susan Owen on August 26, 1972, in Chattanooga, Tennessee. That same year, he entered the Lutheran Theological Seminary in Columbia, South Carolina. He served his internship at St. Peter's Lutheran Church, Miami, Florida. He graduated *cum laude* from seminary in May 1976. On May 6, 1976, he was ordained by the Virginia Synod (LCA), and began serving as pastor of Ascension. A long-time ardent supporter of the Virginia Synod, Utt served as chairman for the Council of Ministry and was a member of the Synod Executive Board. He and Susan were the parents of Emily Reeve, age five, and Tyson James, age two, when they arrived in Winchester.

At a special called meeting of the congregation on September 19, 1982, the congregation, by written ballot, voted 189 in favor and 12 against to call Utt to become the twenty-fourth pastor of Grace. The

Official Call, including a compensation package of $33,603, was extended September 22 and was signed by Charles Greeb, Jr., Vice Chairman, and Eloise S. Joppa, Secretary of the Church Council. In a letter written and dated October 10, 1982, Utt accepted the call. He affirmed that he would begin his ministry in Winchester on January 1, 1983. His letter of acceptance was read to the congregation during the worship services on Sunday, October 17, 1982.

> Dear Brothers and Sisters In Christ,
>
> Peace and love to you from God our Father and our Lord Jesus Christ.
>
> On Sunday, September 19, 1982, you honored and challenged me by extending to me the call to become your pastor. It has been with much prayer for guidance from the Holy Spirit, discussions with my family and deep thought that I have anticipated this challenging and exciting call to become a partner with you in the ministry of Jesus Christ in your community of His great Kingdom. Now, it is with thanksgiving, joy and humble excitement that I accept your call.
>
> Upon completion of my remaining duties and responsibilities to the people of Ascension, Danville, I shall begin my ministry with you January 1, 1983. Susan, Emily, Tyson and I ask from each of you your prayers of love and support as we now enter into this transitional time of our lives, and we pledge you the same as we begin to take leave of our family and friends here and to anticipate our becoming a part of God's loving family gathered at Grace, Winchester.
>
> May God's Holy Spirit continue to guide us in the days ahead. With joyful anticipation to that time when we shall begin our partnership in Christ's ministry, I am
> Your servant in Christ,
> James H. Utt

At the November 14, 1982, Council meeting, members voted to approve a $45,000 loan to Utt for the purchase of a home at 319 W. Leicester Street. The procedure for authorizing a loan was put into place by Church Council eleven months prior to the request. In January 1982, in conjunction with the impending call of a pastor to serve the needs of the congregation, Church Council advised the trustees that, if so directed, they were to use non-restricted trust funds to secure a loan to the incoming pastor. The trustees were further advised that such a loan would bear interest at a reasonable rate, but in no event be less than the current bank passbook rate on savings.

In December, Church Council, at the request of Utt, approved a temporary change of schedule for Sunday worship services. As explained in *Tidings*, "Pastor Utt expressed a strong desire to serve the congregation in a unified setting, at least until Easter, to enable him and all of us to know one another better." Council made the change effective December 26. Under the new schedule, Sunday School began at 8:45 a.m. and one worship service was held at 10:00 a.m.

The installation service for Utt was held on January 23, 1983. It was a cold, icy, dismal day that was filled with inspiration and celebration as the new pastor and congregation committed themselves to Christ's ministry. Presiding minister for the occasion was Bishop V.A. Moyer, Jr., former pastor of the church. In honor of Utt's installation, the offering received at the service was given to the Lutheran Children's Home of the South, where Utt served as a member of the Board of Trustees.

In his first report to the congregation, Utt wrote, "If 1982 was a year of transition for Grace Lutheran Church (and indeed it was!), then I would like for 1983 to be our year of vision!" Paraphrasing a comment he read in a book entitled *Servant Leadership: A Journey Into the Nature of Legitimate Power and Greatness* by R.K. Greenleaf, Pastor Utt stated: "For something great to happen, there must be a great vision. Behind every great achievement is a dreamer of great visions. Much more than a dreamer is required to bring it to reality; but the vision must be there first. In 1983 I ask you to discover with me a great vision for our great church." So began Utt's "ministry of vision" that to this day continues to inspire and provide hope to members of the congregation, the community and the church-at-large.

By the end of Utt's first year, membership increased by 60 persons. The church's financial budget of $147,733 was fully funded. The Altar Guild and the Order of St. John were established. Utt revived the tradition of the Easter Sunrise Service by inviting the community and downtown churches to participate in the service held at the old stone wall landmark in Mount Hebron Cemetery. Two worship events of historical interest took place. Area Lutherans and Episcopalians joined together in a service of Holy Communion on November 20 at Christ Episcopal Church. This sharing of the Eucharist was in response to official action taken by the national bodies of the Lutheran and Episcopal churches that altered their relationships to each other. The second event marked the observance of Martin Luther's 500th birthday and included a service using Luther's German Chorale

Mass and the choir singing the Bach Cantata. Chairperson of the Worship and Music Committee, Vera K. Crawford, illuminated the "Year of Vision" by writing the following in her 1983 annual report to the congregation: "As the committee's work is summarized, we acknowledge the leadership of Pastor Utt, for he plans and executes the services. His messages are timely, inspirational and thought-provoking, and we thank him for sharing his experiences and wisdom with us." Dorothy Tillotson established a strong worship partnership with Utt and continually nurtured the adult and children's choirs

In the year that followed, Utt's personal goal of providing supervision to an intern became reality. Marcia Cox, a third-year student at the Lutheran Theological Seminary at Gettysburg, was afforded the opportunity to be involved in numerous aspects of Grace's parish ministry program. She led worship services, preached sermons, visited members, assisted in the administration of sacraments and attended many meetings. During her internship the tape ministry program for shut-ins was begun, and the Youth Sunday School classes sponsored a child in Africa. The congregation rallied to support Vicar Marcia when she underwent back surgery followed by six weeks of recuperation. In her farewell address to the congregation she wrote, "I thank all of you for being my professors as well as my parishioners. It has been a full year!"

Her "professors" were understandably proud when Vicar Marcia graduated from Lutheran Theological Seminary at Gettysburg in 1986 and was ordained on June 7, 1986, at St. Andrew's Roman Catholic Church in Roanoke, Virginia. She began her ordained ministry at Christ Lutheran, Fairfax, Virginia, and earned her Doctorate in Ministry from Wesley Theological Seminary in 1992. The Rev. Dr. Marcia Cox currently serves as pastor of Augustana Lutheran Church, Washington, D.C.

By December 1984, a full six months after the internship program was reinstated, a committee was appointed to study future staffing needs of the church. Six months later, the internship program was dissolved, and Assistant Pastor Paul G. Gunsten was called. A paid nursery attendant was also hired to provide consistent care for the children.

Upon the completion of Utt's fifth year of service to the Congregation, 279 new members had been added to the membership roster. During this same period of time, 189 members were removed from the rolls due to death, transfer to other congregations or inactivity. The budget increased from $147,733 in 1983 to $219,480 in 1987, an average of 5.8 percent per year. Church records indicate that the congregation was financially healthy and sound fiscal management was exercised. Major improvements to the facility included the addition of solid sound barrier walls in the choir room, remodeling of Eisenberg Hall, painting and application of silicon to the exterior of the building and replacement of slate shingles on the Education Building. A fire alarm system was procured, computers purchased and chairlifts were installed to make the facilities somewhat handicap accessible. A new telephone system was purchased to replace the one that was bought in 1968.

Adult Sunday Church School classes were restructured and renamed to allow for the better utilization of teachers, materials and church facilities. The sacrament of Holy Communion was offered every Sunday, and a new Communion process was implemented that provided for continuous flow. Volunteer receptionists were recruited and trained. The congregation continued to support local human service organizations as well as a hospital in Tanzania and foreign missionaries in Africa and Japan. It also sponsored the Souvannasoth family from Laos.

Special historic occasions that occurred during the mid-to-late 1980s included:

- Wilbur Kern's faithful 46-year service as carillonneur was recognized on January 15, 1984.
- The 70th Anniversary of the Dedication of the Brevitt Chime and the unveiling of a new plaque took place on October 25, 1987.
- An acceptable and architecturally correct bulletin board was installed on the outside of the church building and dedicated May 29, 1988, in honor of the Jeffcoat family.

During these early years, Utt's style of leadership served him well, and his vision for the congregation slowly gained acceptance. In the September 28, 1986, issue of *Tidings*, he declared:

> Dear Partners: I want evangelism – proclaiming the good news of Jesus Christ – to be at the center of everything we do in this congregation...To make evangelism the conscience agenda of this entire congregation — the members, the Church Council, the Pastors, the committees – that's the agenda of evangelism. I believe the time is right and the place is right! This is the right congregation, the right staff, you are the right people, and above all – we have the right message to share with a broken and hurting world.

In the 1988 Church Council report, Hunter Hollar, Vice President, wrote:

> Our annual retreat took place in February at Massanetta Springs, and, for the second year in a row, focused on our mission statement. Probably Council's most important action of the year occurred in April, when the mission statement presented by the Mission Statement Task Group was unanimously approved by Council for congregational action.

Thus, the congregation retired the mission statement adopted on June 22, 1975, and on May 8, 1988, accepted a new one that more accurately reflected the vision and growing mission of the congregation:

Mission Statement 1988

Grace Evangelical Lutheran Church as part of the body of Christ, **Lives** to celebrate and proclaim the gospel through word and sacrament; **Gathers** to provide for the needs of people through worship, education, fellowship and support; **Goes** to extend the gospel to the broader community through personal involvement and financial support; **Grows** in the stewardship of all God's gifts through the care of creation and the use of resources for ministry.

The mission statement was written to give direction to the future of the congregation. Additionally, Utt presented a report to the Council that called for the formation of a long-range planning task group. Church Council responded by appointing such a committee on November 13, 1988. Jerry Kerr, a trustee and life-long member of the congregation, was elected chairman of the committee. For two years, dedicated members of the Long-Range Planning Committee held meetings, surveyed the standing committees and the congregation-at-large, appointed task groups and wrote and revised goals and objectives. A report of the committee was published in the January 21, 1990, issue of *Tidings*:

> Dear Partners,
> At the last meeting of the Long-Range Planning Committee a significant amount of time was given to identifying those values that the committee felt would be most significant in developing preliminary long-range goals and objectives for our congregation in the coming years. I want to share those

values with you and encourage your reflection and discussion of these values with members of the committee and Church Council.

This congregation values most highly:
- The faithful proclamation of the Gospel of Jesus Christ and the celebration of the Holy Sacraments;
- The centrality of worship and music to our corporate expression;
- The caring for people inside and outside our congregation;
- The commitment to grow in membership and parish programs to meet the needs of people of *all* ages;
- The commitment to grow in stewardship of all of God's creations and resources for ministry;
- The commitment to a downtown parish location and ministry;
- The celebration of its history and traditions;
- The expansion of our educational programs;
- The making accessible our facilities to *all* people;
- The commitment to inclusiveness in all aspects of our corporate existence;
- The commitment to planning for the next ten years with immediate concern for goals and objectives to guide mission and ministry in the next three-to-five years;
- The commitment to liturgical worship practices with emphasis on good proclamation of the Word and leadership of worship;
- The commitment to benevolent support of the church-wide ministry and missionary efforts;
- The identity with the ELCA and the Virginia Synod and its leadership role within these expressions of the church;
- Lay leadership and all individuals who respond faithfully to the various calls of service to the church;
- Appropriate use of space and architectural beauty as expressions of God's created order;
- And, the importance of a competent parish staff.

Along with the mission statement, survey results, present statistics and projected trends, it will be these values that will give guidance and direction to the next step in long-range planning – the development of preliminary long-range goals and objectives.   Jerry Kerr, Chair, LRPC

Four major goals and twenty-one objectives were identified in an ensuing five-to-ten-year mission and ministry plan entitled *Heritage for the Future* and adopted by the congregation on January 20, 1991.

A common thread embodied in all four goals was soon realized – the need for additional and redesigned facilities. Thus, a Redesign and Remodeling (R&R) Task Group was appointed, and, with the outstanding leadership of Jim Diehl, and, after his death, Charles Woodruff, this task group worked tirelessly for over three years to coordinate all aspects of the remodeling process. Architects were hired, and a three-phase renovation project was envisioned.

Quite unexpectedly, in the spring of 1992, an opportunity arose that allowed the congregation to purchase an adjacent building located at 16 N. Braddock Street. Acquisition and renovation of the Noble's Travel World building, the former bus station, for nearly $500,000 provided immediate space for additional Sunday School classrooms and allowed expansion of the preschool. The June 13-20, 1993, issue of *Tidings* gave Pastor Utt's eloquent response, clearly from a historical perspective:

> Dear Partners,
>
> We followed faithfully in the great heritage that has been passed on to us in this congregation. By approving the recommendation to implement Phase 1 of our *Heritage for the Future* facility goals and objectives, we committed our initial resources to children and their Christian education. That's what the first Lutherans did in this community over 240 years ago. They built a school for their children before they started building their church.
>
> We have also upheld the long-held value of this congregation so well known in the community: We are not here just for ourselves; we are here to serve others. The renovated Children's Education Center will be a bold witness to our outreach to the community as new children's oriented programs will be explored, developed and implemented in the years ahead.

The cost of purchasing and renovating this additional building and the initial estimates for redesign and remodeling of the church facilities far exceeded what was anticipated. An attempt was made to cut major costs without compromising the integrity of the original plan. At a special called meeting held March 20, 1994, the congregation approved a limited Phase 2 of the redesign and remodeling renovation. The revised plans included expansion of the sanctuary by twelve feet for the creation of a sacristy, vesting room and new organ chamber, remodeling of the narthex, balcony, sanctuary, undercroft and chancel areas. It also included abatement of asbestos, repair of the valuable stained glass windows, refurbishing of the pews, construction of a new altar, pulpit and baptismal font as well as the addition of a much-needed elevator. The congregation also approved the purchase of a specially designed $240,000 Schantz organ that featured a movable console, twenty-eight ranks of pipes and two stops. To make way for the major facilities renovation program, the sanctuary was vacated at the conclusion of the services on Easter Sunday, April 3, 1994. Worship services were held in Eisenberg Hall until the congregation once more returned to the renovated sanctuary for Christmas Eve services, December 24, 1994.

Reverting back to the year 1990, Gunsten was called to serve a Roanoke church, and the congregation entered a transitional time that continued for eight months. In the May 6, 1990, issue of *Tidings*, Utt stated:

> Dear Partners,
>
> During this time in pastoral leadership, I want to reaffirm what have been and will continue to be the priorities which will receive my time and energy. **Word and Sacrament** – I will continue to give the time and effort necessary to prepare and write sermons, prepare for worship leadership, visit those who desire to be baptized and take Holy Communion to the homebound members of our congregation. **Pastoral Care and Counseling** – Continued visitation of those in need, the sick, the hospitalized and those with special needs will continue to receive my attention. **Visitation** – As best as I can, I will try to keep up a regular schedule of visitation of members, focusing first on those in need, prospective, new and other members who express a desire for me to visit. **Teaching** – Bible study, confirmation, SCS and other opportunities to help others grow in the faith will be a priority. **Parish Programming and Administration** – Support of the parish program, care for administrative details and working with volunteers to delegate responsibilities will also receive my time and energies. People and their needs are always first in parish ministry. Other things will be attended to as the limits of time and energy will allow. For your support, understanding and prayers, I express my heartfelt thanks.

In January 1991, Pastor Mark Fitzsimmons began the first of his five years of shared ministry with Utt. Church Council appointed a task group to develop specific plans for recognizing and celebrating the history, heritage and contributions of Grace Evangelical Lutheran Church. The primary efforts of this group were to initiate planning for the 250th Anniversary celebration in 2003, to develop a written record of the congregation from 1953 to the present and to plan an archives and appropriate repository for historical records. In December 1991, the congregation adopted a new Constitution and Bylaws that were required by the 1988 formation of the new Evangelical Lutheran Church in America (ELCA), a result of the unification of the nation's three largest Lutheran Church bodies. Other noteworthy changes that took place during the early-to-mid 1990s were the establishment of weekly Children's Worship Time, introduction of a contemporary worship liturgy *Now the Feast and Celebration*, the beginning of the Shepherding Ministry Program, the electrification and computerization of the Brevitt Chime and the purchase of Church Alley from the City of Winchester.

The baptized membership of Grace Evangelical Lutheran Church grew to a high of 1,173 and the average weekly worship attendance was over 300. Financial concerns constantly plagued congregational leaders. The signs first appeared when the 1991 proposed budget of $290,840 was cut to $257,658 because of the "general economic atmosphere" of the congregation. While in the throes of planning for the renovation program, the treasurer's report noted major cash flow problems and deficit spending. Designated funds were borrowed to pay current operating expenses. Despite a major stewardship emphasis in the spring of 1993, the financial crunch continued. Church records indicate that the Pastor, Stewardship Committee, Finance Committee, Evangelism Committee and the Congregation Council Executive Committee addressed the issue with pleas, "two-level" budgets and consideration of various creative financing methods. Phase 3 of the R&R, renovation of the Administration/Education (Ad/Ed) Building, was put on hold indefinitely. Finally, Chairperson of the Finance Committee, Wayne Carbaugh, submitted the following report: "The Finance Committee is happy to report that offering and gifts to the General Operating Fund and Heritage for the Future Fund were excellent in 1997. We ended 1997 with a General Fund surplus, and there was greater debt reduction giving than was budgeted for in 1997."

With the departure of Fitzsimmons in March 1996, Congregation Council made numerous staff adjustments. Retired Pastor

The Processional Continues

Rudolph Keyl faithfully served as part-time Pastoral Assistant on an as-needed basis, and Pastor Sherry M. Brumback was under contract for seven months. The lay parish staff greatly increased with the addition of a Parish Administrative Assistant, a Musical Assistant, an Educational and Youth Ministries Assistant and a Parish Nurse. A long search for another full-time pastor ended when Jeffrey Dennis May became Co-Pastor on June 1, 1998. About this same time, a new full-time sexton was hired.

Special historic occasions that took place during the last decade of the twentieth century were:

- Grace Lutheran Preschool celebrated its 30th year of operation in 1992.
- In January 1993, Nancy S. Braswell was elected the first lay president of the congregation.
- The 100th Anniversary of the establishment of the Japanese Lutheran Church was celebrated with commemorative programs in 1993.
- The remodeled Children's Education Center was dedicated on September 5, 1993.
- The 200th Anniversary of the completion of the first Lutheran church built in Winchester was observed with a worship service and a processional to the site of the original church where "living history" vignettes were performed. This took place on September 19, 1993.
- A Dedication and Celebration of the Redesigned and Remodeled Sanctuary was held on January 8, 1995.
- On January 22, 1995, a Community Worship Service in celebration of the remodeled sanctuary was held with representatives of the contractor, architect, subcontractors, local congregations and elected officials in attendance.
- Time capsules, old and new, were dedicated on November 19, 1995.
- The Archives Room was dedicated in a ceremony on October 27, 1997, and Evva May Miller was recognized as Archivist.

The new millennium brought forth adoption of a new long-range plan entitled *Growing in Grace*, purchase of the G&M Music Building for $289,000 and the dedication of a Memorial Garden at the site of the original church. Utt accepted an award on behalf of the congregation for extensive efforts made to preserve the historic church wall, a community landmark in Mount Hebron Cemetery.

In the year that followed, the congregation contracted with an architect to design plans for renovating the former G&M Building and the Ad/Ed Building, approved a corporate gift of $50,000 to the Godfrey Miller Home's building fund and approved a budget in excess of $500,000. Grace Place, a casual service with an alternative liturgy, was launched on Saturday, April 21, 2001. Its immediate success triggered a ten-percent increase in the average number of weekly worship participants. A surprise reception honoring Utt on the 25th Anniversary of his ordination was held in June. By year's end, May resigned, and the Call Committee began to search for a replacement.

The year 2002 proved to be one of a challenge with activities centered on the upcoming yearlong celebration of the congregation's 250th Anniversary. The 250th Anniversary Committee finalized details pertaining to the planned events; volunteers carefully stitched needlepoint designs for placement onto kneelers; and the Editorial Committee researched, wrote and edited copy for the expanded edition of *This Heritage*. Pastor Martha Miller Sims was installed as Co-Pastor, the preschool celebrated its 40th Anniversary and a community observance of the first anniversary of September 11, 2001, was held in the sanctuary.

The congregation proudly honored Dorothy Tillotson for her 20 years of outstanding music ministry at Grace Church. Tillotson helped the congregation grow in appreciation and practice of its great liturgical heritage, taking the members to even greater heights of worship and praise.

As a part of its May 2002 commencement exercises, Shenandoah University bestowed the prestigious Honorary Doctor of Divinity Degree upon Utt. A portion of the citation read:

> The Reverend Doctor James Howard Utt has made a career of expanding his parish beyond the local congregation without neglecting the welfare of those who called him to be their pastor.
>
> From the outset of his tenure in Winchester, he has shown an active interest in Shenandoah University, despite the fact that it is related to the United Methodist Church. Those who know him attribute this to his varied interests: people, education, music, literature and social causes, to name a few. Since 2001, he has been an honorary member of Shenandoah's Psi Chapter of Theta Alpha Kappa, the National Honor Society for Religious Studies.
>
> Besides his parish and his association with Shenandoah, Pastor Utt is active in the Winchester-Frederick County Ministerial Association and Coordinator of the Downtown Clergy

Fellowship. His interest in the social application of religion led him to become a founding member of the Board and first president of the Northern Shenandoah Valley Free Medical Clinic, a member of the Winchester Coalition for Racial Unity and clergy representative to the Northwestern Parish Nurse Coalition.

With high regard for his devotion to Grace Lutheran Church and appreciation for his overall ecumenical spirit, Shenandoah University honors James Howard Utt with the honorary degree, Doctor of Divinity.

In his acceptance speech, Utt remarked: "By honoring me you also honor Grace Evangelical Lutheran Church. This congregation has freed me to be a pastor to this community. This is a congregation that has been unselfish in sharing me, its staff and its resources and facilities for the greater good of this community."

Evidence that the congregation "gracefully" and unselfishly shared its talented senior pastor with the community is documented in the pages of numerous annals. He served on the Board of Directors of the Godfrey Miller Home, Kids Are Our Concern, *Shalom Et Benedictus* and the Widowed Persons Service. He served as Vice Pastor of Bethel Lutheran Church during its time of transition in 1995 and was honored to be Festival Prelate for the Coronation of the Apple Blossom Queen in 1988. He has also been active with the Chamber of Commerce's Community Health Service Committee. As "Dean" of the Downtown Clergy Fellowship, his peers value his wise counsel, organizational ability, love of Christ and church, his humor and deep commitment to ecumenism.

Utt's steadfast allegiance to the Virginia Synod of the ELCA has never swayed, as witnessed by the leadership he continues to provide in numerous committees and task forces. From 1988 to 1999, he was Dean of the Northern Valley Conference Council of the Virginia Synod.

But, for the members of Grace Evangelical Church, the bonds forged between pastor and laity are of another fiber. Time and time again, Utt's parishioners and others have felt his genuine passion for pastoral care and ministry manifested through the extraordinary way he extends compassion and understanding during times of need. His wisdom is applauded largely because of his scholarly ability to relate a life situation to a Biblical episode or theological statement. His meticulous attention to detail, especially in relation to church services, only serves to strengthen and enhance religious experiences for worshipers. Such are the ties that bind.

Additionally, as the "first lady" of Grace, Susan endears herself to the congregation with radiant warmth and understanding. Her cheerful disposition and sound values are an inspiration to all. And the children – what a joy it has been for parishioners to participate in the lives of Emily and Tyson as they progressed through childhood, adolescence and into adulthood. Such are the links that fasten.

In many and varied ways, the congregation of Grace has conveyed its respect and admiration to Utt. Gifts of time and treasure were granted him as he pursued his doctoral degree during the years of 1992 to 1996. A reception was held to honor him on the 20th Anniversary of his ordination and the awarding of his Doctor of Ministry Degree from McCormick Theological Seminary. In recognition of his need for personal and professional revitalization, a three-month sabbatical was approved for the summer of 1994. Some years later, when he and his wife traveled to Tanzania, the congregation helped to support the mission trip that had been a dream for ten years.

Likewise, the sense of genuine appreciation that Utt continues to share with the congregation for such courtesies is overwhelmingly evident year after year. While referencing his experience in seminary course work he wrote in *Tidings* on February 13, 1994, "Dear Partners, Your support, prayers and cooperation have and continue to be a source of strength in this arduous discipline. I am grateful for this investment in me and for further growth in our shared ministry in the years to come." In the 1994 annual report to the congregation, he penned:

> Transition means "the act of passing from place, condition or action to another; change." Nineteen hundred and ninety-four was that kind of a year for me bringing with it the requisite challenges, frustrations and joys. I experienced them all as we moved from sanctuary to fellowship hall back to remodeled sanctuary. I experienced them all as we were together then apart for sabbatical and then together again. I experienced them all as members moved and visitors came and relationships changed.
>
> In and through it all there were the faithful people of Grace helping the congregation with the challenges of change, supporting me and one another during the frustrations of change and joining in all the fun and excitement of the joy of change. For all of you, I give thanks to God for making 1994 the most significant year of personal and professional growth in the twelve years I have had the privilege of serving as a pastor of this congregation.

During the twenty years of ministry he has given to Grace, Utt performed the following pastoral acts: adult baptisms – 48; child baptisms – 321; confirmations – 185; persons received by transfer to Grace – 855; total baptized accessions 1,224; marriages performed – 163; funerals conducted - 286.

A portion of an article written by Utt in commemoration of Winchester's 250th birthday seems appropriate for the close of this written record of Utt's ministry. It personifies one man's respect for historical achievements and his "ministry of vision" that continues to stir the hearts and souls of not only this parish, but also the community and the church-at-large:

> With an ever-increasing appreciation for its past, growing confidence in its present and exciting hope for its future, this congregation's story will continue under the constant blessings of Almighty God as men and women, all baptized, some ordained, young and old, rich and poor will continue to be called, gathered, sanctified, enlightened and kept in the church by the Holy Spirit.

PAUL GERHARD GUNSTEN, 1985-1990 (Assistant/Associate)

Six years passed after the resignation of Bill Wood before Grace called its third partner in ordained ministry. During that time, four seminary interns served as "student pastors" – three under the supervision of Pastor Robert W. Koons and one under the supervision of Pastor James H. Utt. The positive experiences of the internships, along with the growth of the congregation and expansion of its ministry programs, raised questions of how best to meet the growing pastoral demands of the congregation and provide for a more consistent pastoral leadership and presence with the growing number of youth in the congregation.

Utt asked the Church Council to initiate a study of the future staffing needs of the congregation in the fall of 1984. Time was taken by a committee to study the congregation's past staffing arrangements, the effectiveness of the internship program for meeting demands of the pastoral office and how best to help the senior pastor with these demands. At the January 13, 1985, meeting of the Council, the report of the Staffing Study Committee was unanimously accepted calling for the congregation to take "the steps necessary to call an assistant pastor." The report noted the importance of the internship program for the church and reminded the congregation that it could re-enter the program at any time in the future. The report also affirmed Utt's concerns that the assistant pastor's job description be flexible enough in order that "the two pastors work out the best use of their talents for the sake of the common good of the congregation" and that "an assistant pastor should be recognized equally with the senior pastor as an ordained servant of the Lutheran Church in America." After appointing a Call Committee and holding meetings with Bishop V.A. Moyer, Jr., and his assistant, The Rev. Dwayne J. Westermann, names of potential candidates were shared with the committee, and interviews were conducted with each over the course of the next two months.

Paul Gerhard Gunsten, "Chip" as he would become affectionately known, was recommended by the Call Committee, and Church Council unanimously agreed to submit his name to the congregation to be called as the next assistant pastor. Gunsten was extended the call at a special meeting of the congregation on Sunday, April 28, 1985. The following is Gunsten's letter of acceptance:

> Dear Brothers and Sisters in Christ,
>
> I am greatly honored to have received the Letter of Call which you, the congregation of Grace Lutheran Church, have extended to me. Taking seriously the call to ordained ministry, I have prayerfully considered and discussed with Kris this opportunity and challenge. It is with reverence and joy that I accept this call as Assistant Pastor, looking to God's gracious presence and power of the Holy Spirit within this community of faith to guide me in the ministry of the Gospel of Jesus Christ.
>
> Having been greatly impressed with the mission and ministry of Grace Lutheran Church, I share your enthusiasm in hopes and dreams for the future. I marvel at the gifts and abilities within this congregation and am eager to support your ministry in the priesthood of all believers. Having high regard for the gifts and manner of ministry of Pastor Utt, I look forward to our partnership in the ministry of Word and Sacrament.
>
> Kris, Sarah, and I have enjoyed our visits to Winchester and have appreciated your hospitality and willingness to acquaint us with your community. We look forward to making our home in your midst and to have our family become a part of your family – the family of Grace Lutheran Church.
>
> May God's Spirit continue to direct and nurture us as we join hands and share together our call to become disciples of Christ Jesus.
>
> God's Peace be with you,
> Paul G. "Chip" Gunsten

Gunsten was born July 16, 1954, in Harrisonburg, Virginia, to Paul H. and Lucretia Colleen Post Gunsten. He grew up in the college towns of Bridgewater and Blacksburg, Virginia. He attended Muhlenberg Lutheran Church, Harrisonburg, Virginia, and after his family's move to Blacksburg he was active in the congregation of Luther Memorial Lutheran Church. He attended Caroline Furnace Lutheran Camp in the Fort Valley of Virginia throughout his school years. At six feet, eight inches tall, he was a basketball standout at Blacksburg High School. During the summers of his college years at Virginia Tech, he served on the staff of Caroline Furnace. After graduation from Virginia Tech in 1977, he was hired to serve on the staff of Koinonia Camp, a Lutheran residential camp in Highland Lake, New York. Building upon his years of experience as a summer staff member at Caroline Furnace and in recognition of his relational and teaching skills with youth, he was named director of Koinonia's environmental education program and summer youth camp. While serving in this capacity, he met Kristin Ruth Hanson, whom he married on September 1, 1979. Chip and Kris became parents to two girls, Sarah Colleen and Anna Kristin.

It was during this time at Koinonia that his gifts for pastoral ministry were affirmed, and he was encouraged to go to seminary. He graduated with a Master's in Divinity from Luther-Northwestern Theological Seminary on Pentecost Sunday, May 26, 1985. He was ordained by the Virginia Synod on May 31, 1985, at Hollins College, Roanoke, Virginia. Gunsten was installed at Grace Church at a special evening service of worship on Sunday, July 21, 1985. The Rev. Dwayne J. Westermann, Assistant to the Bishop of the Virginia Synod, served as the presiding minister and preacher.

Gunsten was known for his skills of working with the youth and being a youth leader. These skills certainly provided for the development of an exciting youth program at Grace that saw a dramatic increase in the involvement of teenagers in the life of the congregation. Gunsten became famous among the youth because of his willingness to take them on "high adventure" trips to the beach and even to New York City. In all of these experiences the youth had more than fun, they grew in faith and saw the greater world and the work of the church throughout all levels of society. He also helped plan and implement Children's Worship Time – a time set aside within the worship service to provide children a worship experience at an age-appropriate level.

Gunsten was effective in his leadership with the Christian Education program at Grace. He helped redefine adult education classes around interests such as social issues or Bible studies, rather than according to age or marital status. Gunsten helped initiate a new catechetical curriculum and took the pastoral lead in implementing a new required catechetical experience at a week-long learning event each summer at Caroline Furnace called Confirmation Camp. He was also instrumental in expanding the camp to include other pastors and congregations in the Virginia Synod. Gunsten aided in developing and implementing an evangelism emphasis that included training members of Grace to make visits to homes in their neighborhoods in Winchester. He planned and implemented a lay visitation training workshop for the pastors and congregations of the Northern Valley Area of the Virginia Synod.

Paul Gerhard Gunsten

Gunsten's leadership skills and work with youth were recognized within the community. He served on the boards of Parents Anonymous, Community and Law Enforcement Against Narcotics (CLEAN) and Grafton School's External Human Rights Committee. He was a group facilitator for the Handley High School Insight program. He was often called upon by other congregations in the community to help with planning youth events.

Gunsten was very active throughout the work of the Virginia Synod. He was a leader in the Synod's youth programs serving several times as a small group leader for Lost and Found and co-director and chaplain for Winter Celebration. He additionally served on several occasions as the co-director of Kairos, a week-long youth leadership development school at Roanoke College. He served on the program committee for Caroline Furnace Lutheran Camp.

During his tenure, Gunsten's title as Assistant Pastor was changed to Associate Pastor in recognition of his leadership skills and initiatives for beginning new ministries. This was particularly true in his work with the Mission Statement Task Group and helping initiate a long-range planning process. Adoption of the new mission statement on May 8, 1988, was a significant achievement during the partnership between Gunsten and Utt.

Gunsten announced his resignation to the Church Council at their annual retreat on the weekend of February 11, 1990, at the Northern Virginia 4-H Center just outside of Front Royal, Virginia. The congregation was informed by a letter printed in the March 11, 1990, issue of *Tidings*:

Dear Brothers and Sisters in Christ,

In a letter shared with members of Church Council in May 1985, I accepted your call to partnership in ministry at Grace Evangelical Lutheran Church and noted, "Having been greatly impressed with the mission and ministry of Grace Lutheran Church, I share your enthusiasm in hopes and dreams for the future. I marvel at the gifts and abilities within this congregation and am eager to support your ministry in the priesthood of all believers."

I feel just as strongly about this today as I did when I first joined this community over four years ago. Yet one must be open to the movement of the Holy Spirit, knowing that there may exist other ministry opportunities and challenges to which one may feel called. Therefore, it is with great and varied emotion that I wish to inform you that I have received and accepted a call to be pastor of St. Philip Evangelical Lutheran Church, Roanoke, Virginia, beginning May 1, 1990.

Kris, Sarah, Anna and I face this time of transition with both excitement and sadness. As much as we look forward to joining a new community of faith, we grieve this separation from good friends with whom we have been blessed to share our lives. As much as we look forward to the potential growth found in a new setting, we lament knowing that we will not participate in the fulfillment of hopes and dreams that are a part of the exciting mission of this congregation. As much as I look forward to the challenge of a new staffing configuration and building the sense of mutual ministry with a new part of the body of Christ, I will greatly miss the friendship and partnership that I have shared with Pastor Utt, Dot, Adair, Sherri and the members of Grace. I anticipate that my last Sunday of worship leadership would be April 22. I trust that this time prior to our move would provide opportunities to anticipate ministry needs and concerns and to allow Kris, Sarah, Anna and me to share our deep appreciation for the love, support and friendship that you have expressed to us as we have been a part of this family of faith.

Pastor Gunsten

Gunsten served St. Philip until the end of August 1999. During his years there, the congregation grew in membership and relocated to new facilities just north of Hollins College. Gunsten earned his Doctor of Ministry degree from the Lutheran School of Theology in 1998.

Recognizing his leadership skills and positive work with youth and congregations in the areas of education, evangelism and stewardship, Gunsten was asked by Bishop James F. Mauney to serve as one of three assistants to the Bishop's Office of the Virginia Synod. He began his service in that position on September 1, 1999.

MARK ELMER FITZSIMMONS, 1991-1996 (Associate)

The Rev. Mark E. Fitzsimmons was called as the fourth associate partner in ordained ministry at Grace at a special meeting of the congregation on Sunday, November 25, 1990. Following the vote, Carol Kerr, chairman of the Call Committee, telephoned Fitzsimmons to inform him of the congregation's actions. Fitzsimmons responded with his letter of acceptance addressed to Kerr.

> Dear Carol,
>
> Dana and I were overjoyed to receive your phone call regarding last Sunday's congregational meeting. After prayerful consideration of the potential match between Grace and myself, I confidently and joyfully accept the call to be your Associate Pastor, effective January 1,1991.
>
> Yes, the fact that the vote was unanimous is very exciting. I hope the congregation realizes that the feeling is mutual. My immediate response to this call is evidence of my excitement, optimism and enthusiasm regarding the people of Grace.
>
> I appreciated that the compensation and benefit package approved by the congregation generously covers the basic needs of my family and provides funding and time for continuing education. I pray that the fulfillment of my pastoral duties may prove equally as supportive, loving and generous.
>
> Please share this letter with the congregation on the first Sunday possible. Moreover, pass on to them our wishes for a blessed Advent, a Merry Christmas and a hopeful New Year. We cannot wait to become members of Grace. As a parishioner I look forward to growing, learning and serving together in such a loving community. As a Pastor, I look forward to

being a co-worker with Pastor Jim Utt, Dot Tillotson, and Sherri Lee.

In Christ,
Mark E. Fitzsimmons

Unlike the call of the previous assistant/associate pastors, Fitzsimmons was the first called to the position with previous parish ministry experience. This was intentional in searching for and recommending Fitzsimmons to the congregation. The congregation's growth in membership, the expanding ministry programs, the increasing demands of the pastoral office and plans for the future development of the congregation called for the next pastor to be a strong and experienced ordained partner who would continue to build on the positive contributions of the previous associate and contribute his own unique pastoral talents in partnership with the senior pastor, James H. Utt. The unanimous vote was confirmation that the Call Committee had found the right pastor. Fitzsimmons began his pastoral duties on January 1, 1991. The Rev. James H. Bangle, Pastor, Ebenezer Lutheran Church, Marion, Virginia, and Dean of the Highlands Conference of the Virginia Synod, installed him at a special evening service of Holy Communion on Sunday, February 3, 1991. Bangle had served as supervising pastor for Fitzsimmons' internship in southwest Virginia.

Mark Elmer Fitzsimmons was born to Elmer and Margaret Staehli Fitzsimmons in Cincinnati, Ohio, on February 29, 1960. Fitzsimmons graduated from the University of North Carolina at Chapel Hill in 1982. In preparation for his entrance into seminary, Fitzsimmons taught himself Greek in order to pass the Greek language proficiency exam necessary for earning the Master's of Divinity degree. The North Carolina Synod (LCA) ordained Fitzsimmons on May 30, 1986, after his graduation earlier in the month from the Lutheran Theological Southern Seminary, Columbia, South Carolina. His first call to parish ministry was to Bethany Lutheran Church, Boone, North Carolina, beginning in June 1986 and continuing through 1988. He arrived at Bethany as a bachelor, but left, married to Dana Gail Weaver, to accept a call to serve Christus Victor Lutheran Church in Chapel Hill, North Carolina, beginning January 1, 1989. Fitzsimmons had begun a master's degree in counseling at Appalachian State University in Boone and looked forward to continuing his graduate studies at his college alma mater while serving as pastor to the Chapel Hill congregation. Fitzsimmons resigned as pastor of Christus Victor in 1990. At the time of his call to Grace, he was officially listed on the clergy roster of the North Carolina Synod as a pastor on graduate study leave.

Fitzsimmons made notable contributions to the life of the congregation in a number of areas. He helped to introduce new liturgies for use at special services of Holy Communion and on festival days during the liturgical year. He was particularly helpful in introducing the congregation to a modern musical setting of Holy Communion entitled *Now the Feast and Celebration*. He was known for his excellent sermons delivered in his unique relaxed and humorous style of preaching. His worship leadership style and popular sermonizing helped to maintain solid attendance of the congregation during Utt's three-month sabbatical, when the congregation worshipped in Eisenberg Hall during the renovation of the sanctuary.

Mark Elmer Fitzsimmons

Fitzsimmons also contributed to the educational ministry of the congregation. He designed and taught numerous Sunday Church School classes which allowed for in-depth study of Biblical and theological topics. He helped rewrite and introduce a new catechetical curriculum and expanded the program to include more retreats and weekend learning events, instead of the normal after-school classes held throughout the year. With his guidance, the Christian Education Committee established a new set of practices for preparing younger children for their First Communion. He also developed a special stewardship emphasis program that brought changes to the congregation's process for seeking the pledged support of the members in areas of their time, talent and treasure.

The congregation experienced two major renovations of its facilities during Fitzsimmons' tenure. The first was the renovation of the newly purchased Noble's Travel World building located just to the back of the Ad/Ed Building. It was redesigned in order to be the congregation's Children's Education Center (CEC) that would provide new space for the expanding Grace Lutheran Preschool program and the congregation's growing Sunday Church School and Vacation Bible School education programs. The second was the redesign and remodeling of the sanctuary.

Fitzsimmons was active in Synod youth events and helped plan and implement the first Servant Camp for senior high youth of the Northern Valley Conference. He served as a vice-pastor to Trinity Lutheran

Church, Stephens City, Virginia, during its pastoral vacancy and assisted the Synod in a feasibility study for a mission congregation in Clarke County, Virginia.

Fitzsimmons announced his resignation to the congregation with the following letter, dated December 27, 1995:

> Dear Members of Grace:
>
> Last week I received a letter of call from the Lutheran Church of the Nativity in Arden, North Carolina. After time for prayer, reflection and discussion, I have decided to accept this call. Therefore, last night I submitted my resignation to the Congregation Council, effective February 14, 1996. My last Sunday at Grace will be February 11.
>
> Several factors have come together in this decision. First and foremost, the activity of the Holy Spirit is discernable in this call process. The matching of my gifts, needs, spiritual journeys and timing between Nativity and myself has been more than coincidental. Secondly, relocating closer to family has a strong appeal at this stage of life.
>
> My five years with you have been a time of joy and growth. I have particularly enjoyed working with the gifted lay leaders of the congregation and a wonderful staff. I give thanks especially for Jim Utt, who has been a blessing as a partner and mentor to me and a good pastor to my family. Dana, Kyle, Evan and I will leave Winchester with many fond memories of the people of Grace.
>
> Finally, I am excited for the possibilities which my resignation creates for Grace. The work of the Spirit is not just involved in my journey, but in yours as well. Even now God is no doubt at work to set up new and wonderful things at Grace. I will keep you in my prayers throughout the next year as you study staffing needs and participate in the call process.
>
> Please feel free to call or drop by in these weeks ahead as we conclude our time together. You will be missed.
>
> In Christ,
> Mark E. Fitzsimmons

Fitzsimmons and his wife, Dana, had two children while in Winchester, Kyle Weaver, born February 28, 1992, and Evan Weaver, born June 28, 1993.

His annual report for 1995 serves as a good summary of Fitzsimmons' years of ministry at Grace:

> I have enjoyed our five years of ministry together. Please do

not be anxious in the months ahead. Take the time to study the staffing needs of Grace and to set some goals for future growth. The demands for providing pastoral care, programming Christian Education and Youth Ministry and office hour accessibility are all legitimate needs competing for a finite amount of time. Needless to say, the past five years have been busy, but exciting. Grace has grown. I have grown. A final word of thanks goes to Pastor Utt, Dot Tillotson and Sherri Lee for their professionalism, dedication, wisdom and friendship. I shall miss all of you. I will continue to follow your adventures in *Tidings*. Please drop in if you find yourself in Asheville.

RUDOLF JOSEPH STEPHANUS KEYL, JR., 1994-Present
(Pastoral Associate)

Following the resignation of Fitzsimmons, senior Pastor James H. Utt again recommended to the Congregation Council that a task group be appointed to "study and recommend to the Council future staffing needs of the congregation." More than Fitzsimmons' resignation prompted the recommendation for the study. With the congregation's continuing growth in membership and ministry programs, Utt and members of the Council felt a more comprehensive study of future staffing needs was required, especially in light of the congregation's financial resources being diverted to servicing of indebtedness resulting from the 1994 renovation of sanctuary. Twelve members of the congregation were appointed to the Future Parish Staffing Task Group, which met for the first time on April 17, 1996. For the next six months, the task group reviewed past staffing configurations, conducted two surveys of the congregation to receive input from members as to their perceptions for the staff needed to serve the congregation and studied the demographics of the congregation and the surrounding community.

The task group's recommendations affirmed the congregation's need and desire to have two pastors serve in the Office of Word and Sacrament. It also affirmed the need for the congregation to move ahead with at least part-time assistance in the areas of educational and youth ministries and with assistance in the office operations and organizational administration of the parish. Given the financial realities of the congregation, a pastoral associate was suggested to help Utt while a search was conducted to find a part-time interim associate pastor, as recommended for the short term by the task group. Pastor Rudy Keyl, a retired Lutheran Church – Missouri Synod

The Processional Continues

Rudolf Joseph Stephanus Keyl, Jr.

(LC-MS) pastor, who, with his wife, Barbara, had become associated with Grace, agreed to assist with pastoral duties until such time that a second pastor was brought on staff. Pastor Keyl had already been involved with pastoral responsibilities, assisting Fitzsimmons during Utt's sabbatical in 1994 and responding to other invitations to perform pastoral acts throughout 1995. Keyl began offering pastoral assistance on March 1, 1996. He notes in his annual report to the congregation for 1996 that it was "good to be re-retired" in December.

Rudolf Joseph Stephanus Keyl, Jr., was ordained into the Holy Office of Word and Sacrament on July 24, 1955, at Trinity Lutheran Church, Delray Beach, Florida, by the Eastern District of the LC–MS. A fifth-generation "ordained son" of the LC-MS, Keyl graduated from Bloomfield College, New Jersey, in 1951. Upon graduating from Concordia Theological Seminary, Springfield, Illinois, in 1955, he received a call to serve St. John's Lutheran Church in Angola, New York. From 1959 to 1965 Keyl served as pastor of Grace Evangelical Lutheran Church in Vestal, New York. While serving Grace, he began a campus ministry for students attending the liberal arts campus of the State University of New York at Vestal. It was also at this parish that Keyl initiated a ministry to "brain-injured" children and their families. From late 1965 through 1972, he served as pastor of Faith Lutheran Church in Groton, Connecticut, a parish ministry defined by the dynamics of a military community in the "submarine capital" of the world that was heavily influenced by the political realities of the height of the "cold war" years. Keyl retired from parish ministry in 1993, after serving for twenty-one years as the senior pastor of Somerset Hills Lutheran Church in Basking Ridge, New Jersey.

Throughout his active years of parish ministry, Keyl advocated the importance of Christian discipleship formation through Christian education. Every congregation he served expanded its educational ministry programs and built additional facilities for classrooms. Keyl was also involved in serving the larger church through various positions of leadership with the LC-MS. He served as chairman of the New Jersey District Pastoral Conference and as first and second vice-president of the Board of Directors of the New Jersey District. He also served as chairman of the district's Social Ministry and Missions Committee.

Keyl was born June 14, 1930, in Patterson, New Jersey. His parents were the Rev. Rudolf Joseph Stephanus Keyl, Sr., and Ida Christina Emelia Dickhart Keyl. He married Barbara Anne Hoffmeier on June 26, 1955. They are the parents of three children: Stephen, Deborah and Timothy. They moved to Winchester in June 1993.

In 2001, Keyl applied to the Virginia Synod (ELCA) for acceptance onto the official retired roster of ordained clergy for that church body. Keyl's decision came after years of prayer and struggles over feeling increasingly insolated from and at theological odds with many of the official positions of the LC-MS, many prohibiting any relationship to congregations and functions of the ELCA. Keyl was accepted onto the official roster on September 16, 2001. His words best describe its significance to him and to the congregation he and his wife, Barbara, have grown to love:

> Dear Partners,
>
> It is with thankfulness and joy that I have been accepted as a clergy member in the ministerium of the Evangelical Lutheran Church in America – retired roster. As such, I also become a "full partner" with you at Grace. For it is in the role of being a servant that I can truly find my wholeness and identity in the ministry of Word and Sacrament. I will continue in that servant mode as I assist Pastors Utt and May and ultimately you in a pastoral role. I am still retired, but will find joy in teaching, preaching and serving when and where I am able in your midst. I have always felt a part of the ministry at Grace, but with this move my ministry among you is complete. Thank you for your prayers and your support. I especially want to thank Pastors Utt and May for their support and love for me as I moved from the Lutheran Church-Missouri Synod to the ELCA. I also promise to continue to pray for you and the partnership ministry we have together.
>
> Pastor Rudy Keyl

Keyl's pastoral presence has been a blessing to Grace as he continues to serve as a pastoral associate in the Holy Office of Word and Sacrament.

SHERRY MORRISON BRUMBACK, 1996-1997
(Interim Associate)

The Congregation Council hired Sherry Morrison Brumback on Sunday, November 14, 1996, to serve in a half-time position as interim associate pastor. Council approved the recommendation for this temporary pastoral staffing configuration because of the financial realities facing the congregation and also because it allowed for flexibility in exercising future staffing options and developments that had been recommended by the Future Parish Staffing Task Group. She began serving at Grace Church on December 1, 1996.

The daughter of Stanley and Barbara Morrison Morrison was born December 25, 1961, in Detroit, Michigan. She graduated from Wayne State University in 1987, and from the Lutheran Theological Seminary at Gettysburg, Pennsylvania, in May 1994. Upon receiving a call to serve as pastor at Holy Trinity Lutheran Church, Queens, New York, she was ordained June 18, 1994, by the Southeast Michigan Synod (ELCA). She served Holy Trinity from July 1994 through October 1996. On October 21, 1995, she married Philip Lee Brumback. Brumback was able to respond to the offer at Grace because of returning to Gettysburg with her husband to finish his senior year of studies at the Lutheran Theological Seminary.

Brumback's contract for services outlined the range of pastoral responsibilities that she would fulfill. This arrangement provided for assisting Pastor James H. Utt with the general pastoral duties of preaching, leading worship, teaching and visiting members at home and in times of special need. While Brumback chose to commute from Gettysburg, the arrangement of hours of service and the pastoral responsibilities she was given proved effective in her faithfully fulfilling the terms of her contract from December 1996 through June 1997.

The June 22-29, 1997, issue of *Tidings* offers a good summary of her time and service at Grace:

> Dear Partners,
>
> I can hardly believe it is already June! My seven months with you have passed quickly. I have long said that God provides, and this is most certainly true of my experience with you at Grace. God has provided me an opportunity to discover the benefits of serving as an associate partner in ministry. You, the congregation, have helped prepare me to say farewell from a positive ministry experience. God provided me with the ben-

This Heritage

efits of your wonderful music ministry and helped produce a better liturgist. Most importantly God provided me with an environment of trust and challenge.

I thank Sherri Lee (parish secretary) for her friendship. I thank Nancy Braswell (editor of *Tidings* and parish administrative assistant) for helping me look good in print as well as giving me her ear from time to time. I thank Teresa Lehman (educational and youth ministries assistant) for her energy and attention to detail in everything she does. I thank Pastor Utt for his partnership – for being a vehicle through whom God worked healing and growth in my life and ministry. Most especially I thank you – the people of Grace – for an awesome seven months of ministry in Winchester!

Sherry Morrison Brumback

I am interviewing in the Metro DC Synod at a church in Centreville, Virginia. I believe it is in God's plan that Lee and I will not be far away physically or spiritually. We continue to pray for you as you seek a full-time associate.

In Christian love,
Pastor Sherry Brumback

Brumback was called on Sunday, July 20, 1997, to serve as associate pastor of St. Andrew Lutheran Church, Centreville, Virginia.

Keyl's pastoral assistance and Brumback's interim service were not only helpful in meeting the pastoral demands of the congregation, but their leadership proved once again the importance of providing consistent full-time pastoral leadership – especially in the areas of pastoral care and theological guidance in educational and youth ministry programs. Before Brumback finished the terms of her contract, Utt requested that the Council conduct an evaluation of the part-time position. The evaluation and its results are summarized in the following letter, which Utt wrote to the congregation in the April 27-May 10, 1997, issue of *Tidings*:

Dear Partners,

At its April 13 meeting, the Congregation Council received an important report from the task group appointed by the Council to evaluate the part-time associate pastor's position. This was not an evaluation of Pastor Brumback, but an evaluation of the effectiveness of the part-time position. Members of the task group reviewed the part-time position description, asked for comments from the parish staff and met to discuss and recommend actions to the Congregation Council. It was the conclusion of the task group that the part-time position is some help to me, especially in sharing responsibilities on Sundays and in the areas of visiting and teaching. However, the nature of the position does not allow for consistency in leadership responsibilities (e.g., attending committee meetings, meeting with lay leaders to plan programs, providing trained theological leadership). A part-time position does not allow for consistent development of staff working relationships and pastoral care and follow-up. The part-time position also does not provide the necessary presence needed of a second pastor in the coverage of emergencies and members in crises, nor does it help with assistance with occasional services such as weddings and funerals.

From these conclusions, the task group recommended that the Congregation Council appoint a Call Committee to develop and recommend to the Council, with the approval of the congregation, the process for calling a full-time associate pastor as soon as possible. The Call Committee is being recruited as this is being written. The Call Committee will develop a call/job description for the full-time associate pastor's position; identify the needed qualities, gifts and skills expected in the full-time associate; and work with the Finance Committee to develop the proposal for financing the costs of a second full-time pastor.

I encourage your support of these conclusions and the subsequent recommendations that will be developed for action by the Council and the congregation before we proceed with the actual call process. The task group's report and the minutes of the Council are available for you to read and study. If you have any question or concerns, please do not hesitate to talk with members of the Council or me. Your prayers are needed.

Peace...+ Pastor Utt

The congregation approved the recommendations of the task group and amended the 1997 budget to include the necessary funds for proceeding with the call process and interviews for a full-time associate pastor with parish ministry experience. After meeting with Bishop Richard F. Bansemer of the Virginia Synod, the Call Committee identified and interviewed three candidates.

JEFFREY DENNIS MAY, 1998-2001 (Co-Pastor)

Jeffrey Dennis May was among the candidates to be interviewed in the summer of 1997. While the other candidates proved to be very strong, it was May's thirteen years of parish experience along with his musical leadership skills and reputation for working with youth that finally convinced the Call Committee and Utt to recommend him to the Congregation Council. However, once May was approached as the primary candidate to be recommended, the Call Committee and Utt were disappointed to learn of his hesitancy and finally his request to have his name removed from consideration. May noted that his reluctance was due to wanting to follow through on some tasks begun where he was currently serving, consideration of his wife's teaching position and support of the educational opportunities that their children were experiencing and would continue to have where they were living. By this time the other candidates had either withdrawn their names from consideration or had moved on in the call process with other congregations. The fall of 1997 proved to be a time of searching for other candidates without any luck or enthusiasm on the part of the Call Committee or Utt for those who expressed interest for consideration.

In January 1998, May contacted Utt with the news that he and his family had discussed their concerns over a move to a new parish ministry call and new community in which to live. If he (Utt), the Call Committee, and the Council were willing, May indicated he would offer his name for consideration once again. It took little time for the Call Committee to recommend and the Council to propose to the congregation that May be called as Co-Pastor to Grace. This term was used instead of Associate Pastor to denote that a new designation for an ordained partnership between two pastors could exist without the requirement of the "co-terminus" clause in the document that the Virginia Synod required of congregations being served by two pastors. The document, Principles and Guidelines for a Shared Ministry, not only outlined areas of responsibility for each pastor, but also set forth the conditions in the event of the resignation of the pastor with the most seniority. Without the "co-terminus" clause, May would not have to offer his resignation if Utt were to leave, therefore, leaving open the option of the Co-Pastor remaining as Pastor of the congregation. After negotiations over salary and benefits were concluded with May, the Council called a special meeting of the congregation on April 15, 1998, to consider calling May as the first Co-Pastor of Grace. The vote was 127 in favor and 2 against.

May was born September 29, 1954, in Bergton, Virginia, son of Dennis Grant and Mary Jane Turner May. He married Karla Kay Rosenow on May 14, 1978, and they became parents of Melissa Lynn and Nathan Blaine.

Jeffrey Dennis May

He graduated from James Madison University, Harrisonburg, Virginia, in 1979 with a Bachelor of Music Education degree. After graduation from the Lutheran Theological Seminary, Gettysburg, Pennsylvania, in May 1984, May was ordained by the Virginia Synod upon receipt of his first call to serve as pastor of Toms Brook Parish, Toms Brook, Virginia, 1984-1987. From 1987 to 1990 he served as pastor of St. James Lutheran Church, Fishersville, Virginia; 1990-1992, pastor of Christ The King Lutheran Church, Richmond, Virginia; 1993-1998, pastor of the Timberville Parish, Timberville, Virginia. May was also an instructor in religion at James Madison University and a music teacher for Shenandoah County Public Schools.

May's letter of acceptance was printed in the May 10-23, 1998, issue of *Tidings*:

Dear Partners,
   Grace to you and peace from God the Father and the Lord Jesus Christ! Having received the official call dated April 6, 1998, to become Co-Pastor of Grace, I have given much prayerful consideration to the call. I hereby accept that call and plan to begin my work with you on June 1, 1998.
   It is with great joy and anticipation that I await our partnership in the ministry of the Gospel of Jesus Christ. My prayers are with you in your ministry, and I encourage you

to strengthen each other as ministers of the Lord as you also await our work together in Christ. I request your prayers for my family and me as we enter the very difficult time of saying good-bye.

Thank you for this opportunity to share with you in the work of the Gospel. May the Lord richly bless us in his ministry.

In Christ!
Jeffrey D. May

During his three-and-one-half year tenure, May was instrumental in working with the Worship and Music Committee and Director of Music, Dorothy Tillotson, to introduce new liturgical settings of worship. *Holden Evening Prayer*, a modern version of the ancient evening prayer service, was introduced in Advent 1998 and has become a liturgical favorite for that season of the church year. With his musical background, May was able to recruit members with skills on various instruments to form ensembles to accompany the congregation in singing contemporary hymns blended with traditional liturgical settings of Holy Communion. Particularly inspiring were the Youth Sunday services that featured the youth in leadership roles, and many youth with musical talents accompanied praise songs at synodical youth events. It was primarily through his initiative and leadership that Grace Place was offered as an additional weekly worship service of Holy Communion with an alternative liturgical style on Saturday evenings.

May was instrumental in developing opportunities for more children to become involved in meaningful ways in the worship life of the congregation. With the help of a Project Leadership Team, May and others wrote a grant proposal seeking funds from the Lutheran Brotherhood Foundation through the ELCA's Initiative for a New Century Program. A $5,000 grant was awarded to help the congregation achieve three goals: 1 - educate children in the liturgical heritage, 2 - engage unchurched children in the liturgical experience through the use of music and 3 - expand the involvement of children in the overall worship experiences of the congregation. As a result of this initiative and the awarding of the grant, a new part-time staff position, Children's Worship and Music Ministries Assistant, was added to assist in implementing these goals. In the summer of 1999, Sharon Hetland was hired for this position to work with May and others on the staff to implement new worship experiences for children. One of the first efforts was the planning and implementing of a Vacation Bible School follow-up event that was particularly designed to reach unchurched children. "Christmas in August" involved over a hundred children and adult leaders. From this experience, the Liturgical Arts and Music Camp was developed and is offered each summer for children to explore even deeper the riches of the liturgical heritage of the church and its rich musical traditions. Children's Worship Time was re-evaluated and revised to incorporate a more focused emphasis on the experience of the Word proclaimed for them on an age-appropriate level. Children's Word Time became the new designation as children remained in the sanctuary for the reading of the scriptures and then processed with a children's banner to the Children's Word Time chapel for a brief encounter through story and music with the Word just heard. May helped to train more adults to be Children's Word Time leaders, and a new effort was initiated to reorganize the Order of St. John, the congregation's corps of older children and youth trained to serve as acolytes, crucifers and banner bearers.

May brought significant changes to the congregation's youth ministry and educational programs. Working with Teresa Lehman, Educational and Youth Ministries Assistant, the Youth Ministry Committee approved recommendations to gradually divide the one Grace Youth group into separate junior high and senior high groups. Youth ministry activities for both groups focused around three major emphases important to the faith development of youth: service, learning and fellowship. Youth helped with various outreach efforts of the congregation, participated in congregational and synodical learning events and enjoyed numerous fellowship events. In 1999 the Youth Room was expanded and newly furnished to provide a more inviting atmosphere. GELYROL (Grace Evangelical Lutheran Youth Room Open Lounge) began as a mid-week evening opportunity for youth to gather for fellowship, support and help with homework.

With May's emphasis on participation in Synod and church-wide youth events, more youth attended the Lost and Found weekend retreat for junior high youth and the Winter Celebration for senior high youth. During his time at Grace, the synodical youth leadership asked him to help develop a Synod-wide event for older children that has become known as Seventh Day – a two-day overnight experience for children in grades five and six. In the summer of 2000, twelve senior high youth and four adults from Grace attended the ELCA National Youth Gathering, held in St. Louis, Missouri.

May designed a new curriculum for catechetical instruction. Classes in addition to the Sunday Church School hour were moved to Saturday mornings instead of after school weekdays. May added participation in the Lost and Found Synod youth event as an important component in the catechetical process. Emphasis continued on participation in summer Confirmation Camp, and youth participation in service projects was also a part of a new confirmation covenant that May and Lehman developed. May was known for his acting abilities and was a big hit with the children in the Vacation Bible School openings. New adult Sunday Church School classes were offered, and, along with Utt, the congregation was introduced to the Bible study series *Alpha*.

During May's tenure the congregation adopted a new long-range plan. The name for the new plan, *Growing In Grace*, was suggested by May along with the logo to symbolize the plan's emphasis on growth. The G&M Music Building was purchased, and plans were made to expand the congregation's outreach ministries in the community as well as the educational and youth ministry programs of the congregation. Parish Nurses Lisa Zerull and Mary Sonafelt were added to the staff to assist Utt and May with the follow-up care of members and with visitation to members in special care living in nursing homes or needing assistance in their own homes. Various teams were appointed to implement objectives of the long-range plan. May particularly enjoyed working on the Architectural Review Team. He also served on the board of the Grace Lutheran Preschool.

May announced his resignation to the congregation by letter dated November 11, 2001:

> Dear Friends in Christ,
>
> Grace to you and peace from God our Father and the Lord Jesus Christ! I have received a call from the Synod Council of the Virginia Synod of the Evangelical Lutheran Church in America to serve as Mission Developer for a new ministry in Massaponax, Virginia. I have, after much prayerful consideration, accepted that call to serve as Mission Developer, effective January 1, 2002. Therefore, I hereby resign as pastor of Grace Evangelical Lutheran Church, Winchester, Virginia, effective December 31, 2001. My last Sunday with you will be December 30.
>
> Karla, Melissa, Nathan and I are certainly filled with mixed emotions at this decision. You have been much more than gracious and loving to us during these past three and one-half years. My experience here with you has been such a fulfilling one, and it is not without regret and anguish that I now feel called by the Holy Spirit to leave. Thank you, each of you, for the ministry that we have shared and will still share in the Church, the Body of

Christ. Your many acts of love and kindness will never be forgotten, and we will look back on our time here with you with great delight. We leave many friends who have been a source of joy for us.

My heart is also torn to know that I will not be able to work day-to-day with my wonderful friend and colleague, Pastor Utt. It continues to be joyful to share this ministry with him. Still, we continue to serve together as brothers in Christ, called to the ministry of Word and Sacrament. Thanks to him and the entire staff for a blessed partnership in the Gospel.

My prayers will remain with you and for you. I know that you now face an uncertain time, and I pray and certainly trust that God will guide and strengthen you as you enter the study and call process. Do not ever doubt that God's love and grace are with you! May God bless you and keep you in his grace and peace!

In Christ!
Jeffrey D. May, Pastor

MARTHA MILLER SIMS, 2002-Present (Co-Pastor)

After Jeffrey Dennis May's resignation and departure to develop a new mission congregation, Grace wasted little time in seeking the next Co-Pastor to keep the mission and ministry momentum going and growing for the congregation. Congregation Council appointed a Call Committee at its first meeting in January 2002. A meeting of the Council and members of the Call Committee, chaired by Gary Braswell, was held with Bishop James F. Mauney of the Virginia Synod on Sunday, February 10, 2002. At this meeting Bishop Mauney announced that the number of potential candidates for interview would be limited due to the overall shortage of seminary graduates available for the number of "first-call" congregations and also because of the high level of qualifications which the congregation was expecting of potential candidates. The Call Committee held its first meeting on February 13, 2002, to review the process for calling a new Co-Pastor, to make changes to the Leadership Profile that was used when May was called and to communicate ways of seeking input from members of the congregation. Members of the congregation were encouraged to suggest the names of prospective candidates.

"Mobility papers" – resumes of potential candidates – were, indeed, limited. as the Bishop had indicated. After review by Utt, the committee was fortunate to have at least two candidates to interview. Utt interviewed one other candidate, a second-career seminary graduate, but the candidate withdrew his name for consideration by the Call Committee. Of the two interviewed, one candidate was both known to the congregation and considered to be among the best possible candidates the Call Committee could hope to interview.

Martha Miller Sims had been one of the candidates interviewed four years earlier when May was called as the first Co-Pastor. At that time she was serving the Gravel Springs/St. John Lutheran Parish in Frederick County just a few miles southwest of Winchester. Sims withdrew her name following her first interview at Grace when she and the Call Committee raised common concerns and questions about moving from one call to another in such close proximity to each other. That she was open to a call and available for an interview four years later was recognized by the Call Committee and Utt as good timing on the part of the Holy Spirit.

Sims met or exceeded the qualifications that the Congregation Council and Call Committee had established in the Leadership Profile for Co-Pastor at Grace:

- Five-to-ten years of ordained parish ministry experience demonstrating a positive commitment to the mission and ministry of Jesus Christ and His Church in its various expressions: congregation, Synod, church-wide. She had served from 1994 to 1998 as pastor of the Gravel Springs/St. John Lutheran Parish. From 1998 to July 2002, she served in a special "shared call" position as the Associate Pastor at Muhlenberg Lutheran Church and Campus Pastor at James Madison University, Harrisonburg, Virginia. During this time she was active in various synodical youth events and assisted in worship leadership at Synod assemblies and other gatherings of pastors and lay leaders throughout the Synod.
- Ability to be a team member and work well within a multiple staff team ministry setting. Sims was familiar with the dynamics of team ministry as an associate pastor. She had also demonstrated to Utt her ability to work with other pastors and be a team member while serving at her first call. While there she became involved with a cooperative effort among pastors in the Synod to plan and implement a Confirmation Camp at Caroline Furnace Camp and Retreat Center. She also worked with Utt in planning and implementing a Northern Valley Conference Youth Servant Camp held at Hun-

Martha Miller Sims

gry Mother Camp, the Synod's camp and retreat center in southwest Virginia. She had experience working as a layperson on the staff of her home congregation in Tucson, Arizona.

• Proven leadership skills and ability to work with all ages, especially with children, youth and young adults. Sims was considered particularly gifted in this area, making special use of her musical talents and abilities to relate to all ages in various congregational and ministry settings.

• Commitment to continuing education and care of self and family. Sims was an outstanding student in seminary and described herself as a "disciplined reader." In her interviews she noted numerous continuing education events she participated in as part of her plans for continued personal and professional growth. On November 28, 1998, she married the Rev. George L. Sims and became stepmother to Kristen and David Sims.

• Willingness to live in the community. Because of concerns raised for the impact that commuting had on May in his last months of service at Grace, this qualification was added in order to communicate the congregation's expectation that the Co-Pastor live in the community. After accepting the call to serve Grace, Sims and her husband bought a house in Winchester.

Born November 25, 1957, to Carl and Marilee Miller in Mesa, Arizona, Sims graduated from the University of Arizona in 1988 with a Bachelor of Arts in Religious Studies. Following her graduation from Lutheran Theological Southern Seminary, she was ordained by Bishop Richard Bansemer of the Virginia Synod (ELCA) on June 26, 1994.

Martha Miller Sims was called as the first full-time woman pastor of Grace Evangelical Lutheran Church at a special meeting of the congregation on Holy Trinity Sunday, May 26, 2002. The written ballot vote was 171 in favor and 4 against. Sims' letter of acceptance was printed in the June 9-22, 2002, issue of *Tidings*:

Dear Partners,

On Holy Trinity Sunday, May 26, 2002, you honored me by extending to me the call to serve as Co-Pastor of the congregation. After prayerful consideration, and with great joy, I have made the decision to accept the call. I will conclude my responsibilities at Muhlenberg Lutheran Church on July 7, 2002, which will include two weeks of vacation, and I will begin ministry among you on Monday, July 8, 2002. I give thanks to God for you and pray for God's blessings as we begin this new ministry together.

Christ's peace,
Pastor Martha Miller Sims

Sims was installed as Co-Pastor at a special service of Holy Communion at Grace at 4 p.m. on Sunday, August 4, 2002. The Rev. Robert H. Jones, Pastor, Good Shepherd Lutheran Church, Front Royal, and Dean of the Northern Valley Conference, was the presiding minister. The Rev. George L. Sims, Executive Director of the Mission Office for Planned Giving, was selected by Sims to be the preacher for the occasion. In his sermon, Pastor George Sims gave to both Utt and Sims a shepherd's staff with the reminder that, in their partnership, the model of the Good Shepherd would serve them well as they seek to guide, prod and serve the people of Grace and the community of Winchester.

Sims's gratitude for the installation service and a sense of her hope for the coming years of ministry with Utt and the people of Grace were expressed well in her letter to the congregation in the August 18-31, 2002, issue of *Tidings*:

Dear Partners,

Now that I have been duly "put in my place" at the service of installation, I want to thank you all for welcoming George and me so hospitably. I especially want to thank the Call Committee for the many hours you served, for representing Grace so well and for being the first to make me feel welcome. I also want to say thank you to all those who made my installation service so special – the staff, Call Committee, the Choir, instrumentalists, lectors, acolytes, crucifer and the representatives of the various ministries of Grace. I feel honored to be serving as one of your pastors and to be a partner in the gospel with you

and with my friend, Pastor Utt. I look forward to the coming years of ministry together with joy.
Christ's peace,
Pastor Sims

As 2002 came to a close, both pastors, lay leaders, parish staff and members of the congregation recognized the phenomenal pastoral and lay leadership over the last 250 years and prepared to celebrate fully the heritage and history of Grace Evangelical Lutheran Church in 2003.

Chapter VIII
That Un-Civil War

It was Winchester's destiny during the war years of 1861-1865 to be the most frequently contested spot on the map of the whole country. Local historians do not agree on the number of times the town exchanged hands. The highest counters say the number is eighty-four, while the lowest maintain a mere sixty-eight. The latter figure is sufficient evidence to impress upon the reader that citizens of the community had their fill of the military, both gray and blue.

The census of 1860 reported 701 families in the place for a total of 4,403 persons. The white population numbered 3,040. Of the Negroes, 655 were freedmen and 708 were slaves. The sentiment of the Shenandoah Valley as a whole had never looked upon slavery with an enthusiastic or unanimous approval. It took John Brown's raid at Harpers Ferry to weld opinion into the defense of a system that was not deemed right in and of itself, but was an existing part of the life and economy of the whole area. The very persons who were antislavery in attitude often became even more opposed to the projected revolutionary overthrow of the evil.

So, too, was strong pro-union sympathy to be found. Sentiment favoring the preservation of the Union prevailed in this area throughout 1860. Delegates to the Virginia Convention of 1861 were Union men elected by majorities of better than five to one. But again, resort to arms turned the balance of influence to the side of secession, and Winchester was to become ardently Southern.

Both geography and the game of military science as it was then practiced conspired to make the Lower Valley of Virginia, with Winchester the focal center, the goal of martial operations. Nine roads converged on the town from all directions. But thirty miles south of the Potomac, but twenty-two miles south of the Baltimore and Ohio railroad connecting east and west, and but seventy miles west of Washington, it was highly strategic to control such an objective, while the surrounding countryside with its rich farms could easily support an army's demand for rations and provender. This helps to explain the fact that at least 112 engagements of the conflict were fought in this region and that five of them, the two battles of Kernstown and the three battles of Winchester, all rated as major engagements, were in the immediate locality of the town.

Winchester has had three forts to defend it. First there was Fort Loudoun, built by George Washington in French and Indian War days. Located on an eminence on the village's northern exposure, it gave to that particular vicinity the name Fort Hill. North Loudoun (Main) Street now runs through the old fortification and in its continuation becomes the Martinsburg Pike. Along this road, a mile more or less from the town, the soldiers of General Johnston hurriedly erected Fort Collyer[a] in 1861 around the residence of Isaac Stine. Two years later when General Milroy was in possession of the place, Star Fort was built on a hill two miles north, and lying to the west of Fort Collyer.

If, however, one travels in the opposite direction and goes south on Loudoun Street, the ground begins to rise after crossing Cork Street and one ascends a gently sloping hill. This is known locally as Potato Hill.

The winter of 1861-1862 Stonewall Jackson made Winchester his headquarters. The approach of General Banks' army forced

---

[a] The spelling became "Collier."

his evacuation March 11. The First Battle of Kernstown followed, March 23. Two months later, May 25, Jackson returned to win the First Battle of Winchester and to drive Banks out of the Valley. Federal forces under General White took the town again that summer, but yielded to the Confederates September 2. The men in gray in turn yielded December 2, to the men in blue, first to General Geary and then to General Milroy, who remained in possession until June 1863. June 13-15 occurred the Second Battle of Winchester, when Ewell drove out Milroy's forces. A year afterward, July 24, 1864, Generals Early and Crook engaged in the Second Battle of Kernstown, and on September 19, General Sheridan defeated Early in the Third Battle of Winchester, and took the town, which Federal forces held thereafter. Interspersed among these major engagements in addition were numerous cavalry raids and minor skirmishes in which possession of the town passed from one side to another.

With this acute state of war existing in the community for so long a period, and with such continuous excitement, terror and exasperation, one wonders how any semblance of normal family or church life could be pursued. Yet in spite of these abnormalities and dislocations and all the strain and stress of high tensions and aroused feelings, the life of home and congregation held to a more even tenor than may be first imagined. Because everyone had to grow accustomed to the making of emergency adjustments, deprivations and hardships were borne with remarkable equanimity.

Submitted as evidence are excerpts from the diary of Margaretta Miller.[b] Born January 22, 1850, she was the thirteen-year-old daughter of Mr. and Mrs. Godfrey Sperry Miller

---

[b] Her nickname was "Gettie" and she was an active member of the Winchester community until her death in 1938.

and lived with her parents and two sisters, Emma and Marianna (Nannie), in a big stone house on Main Street. From March 23, 1863, to September 19, 1863, she kept her journal faithfully,[c] setting down in her charming and naive way many household, church and community happenings. Her parents were active members of the Lutheran congregation, her father serving on the Church Council and directing the church choir, and she herself being a member of Rev. Mr. Dosh's catechetical class. Quite naturally she mirrors the sentiments of the circle in which she moved.

Monday, March 23, 1863
The 27 day of this month is fast and prayer day by Jeff Davis's appointment. It seems right hard that [they] cannot have church. If I was a preacher I would have church anyhow in spite of these hateful Yankees.

Tuesday, March 24
We cannot go out at night anymore. We have to come in at eight o'clock. The Yankees have guards out every night. I have been halted by the guards once or twice coming from Ginnie Sperry's. I was so scared I was afraid they would take me and put me in the guardhouse.

Wednesday, March 25
I wish our men would come and [drive] these Yankees out like they did old Banks.

Thursday, March 26
Emma and I have been sewing on our quilt this evening, and I only made one square.... Grandma has been down here and she brought us each a cake. It tasted very good. These times we never get many cakes and it is quite a treat to taste one. I wish we had some molasses to make some taffy. We used to have so much fun a pulling it. I think

---

[c] Today, her diary is a part of the Godfrey Miller Collection housed in the Archives of the Handley Regional Library, Winchester, Virginia. It consists of 24 leaves and was written in an accounting book that was used in the 1840s, probably in connection with the family mercantile business. The book measures 12 by 7 ¾ inches and the front and back covers are of a soft material. The spine is bound in leather, which is now much deteriorated, and the pages are in remarkably good condition.

these Yankees might let the citizens have some goods brought up, but they think they can starve us out. But we will manage to scrape up something if it is nothing but dry bread.

Saturday, March 28
Em went down to the provost to get a permit to get some potatoes, but he asked her if she was loyal. She told him that she was not and he would not give her a permit. He asked if her mother was loyal and why she did not come.

Sunday, March 29
I went to Church this morning and it was so very windy that I could hardly get along. Ginnie Gensle was there with her Yankee husband. She looked very nice. Had on a purple silk with flounces round the tail. Mr. Dosh examined us on the catechism. I did not answer any of the questions, but I knew some of them.

Tuesday, March 31
I want to try and Aprilfool Emma tomorrow. I hope I will have a chance. I do not know what I shall tell her.

Wednesday, April 1
Ginnie was over to invite us over to spend the evening and she told Em she must come over before Molly and me. Molly came over for me so we went over, and Ginnie and Emma had gone out and left a note for us, saying that we must excuse them as it was Aprilfool, that we must call again when they were at home.

Thursday, April 2
Some of the Yankees took Mr. Dosh's clothes, and I pity him so much for I don't expect he can get any more. He ought to make old Milroy pay for them or get him some more.

Friday, April 3
I think it is so mean in these Yankees to not let anyone go out in the country unless they guard them. They say they came to free us but I rather think they are putting us in bondage.

Sunday, April 5
Today is Easter Sunday. It is dreadful walking out this morning. When we got up the other side of the street was covered with snow. It had drifted off the houses and this side had not hardly any. We did not go to church this morning, nor Sunday School, as Ma and Pa had to go to church this evening. I think they ought to put it off until next Sunday. It does not seem like Sunday. It is because I have not been to church.

Wednesday, April 8
Em went out with Mary Harris and Mary would ask every Yankee

how long they could stay out, and one of them said, "as long as their noses." That was a very smart answer, but they are so hateful and mean that they would say anything.

Saturday, April 11
This morning Pa dug most of our little flower garden, and after he had dug I smoothed the beds over. It looks like a different garden. I planted my tube rose out today and hope it will bear this year so that I can put the flowers in the parlor. They are so pretty and white and look like waxwork and smell so sweetly. My violets are in bloom and they look so pretty right by the porch so that they scent the whole air. I want to get some lilies of the valley to plant with the violets so that they can be with each other as they are both such delicate looking flowers.

Sunday, April 12
Today is so changeable that I hardly know whether to call it pleasant or not. It looks like it was going to rain this evening. I wish it would give one good shower and not rain all the time. This morning I went to church and it was so crowded that I could hardly get a seat and some of the children had to sit on a little step around the pulpit.... Cousin Sid has gone to Baltimore and has not got back yet, so we had to have another teacher. I do not know her name, but I hope Cousin Sid will be back by next Sunday. I don't like to have a different teacher when I am used to one. I am always afraid I do not know my lessons. Mollie Russell went to Sunday School with us. The little infants did not sing as well as they generally do. They did not keep very good time.

Thursday, April 16
I went up to Cousin Lib's to see what the lesson was for this evening at class but she said they were not going to have any until warm weather so that we can have it in the church, because the Yankees have taken Mr. Baker's house. I hope they won't hurt anything. They have such a nice house.

Sunday, April 19
Emma and I went to church this morning and we had a right full church.

Friday, April 24
The Yankees have issued an order that every man that does not take the oath will have to shut up their stores. But that don't hurt them. They can shut them up, [just] so they don't make them take it anyhow. I hope that Pa won't take their nasty oath unless they make him.

Sunday, April 26
It is very pleasant out today. Emma and myself went to church this

morning, but I do not know what the text was. We did not go to Sunday School, we wanted to go to Uncle Jack's funeral. Mollie and Ginnie went with us. They say he was so wicked he died so sudden, that I don't expect he had time to repent.

Sunday, May 3
I did not go to church this morning. I had no dress to put on except my winter one and that was too warm, I would have most smothered. I brought Minnie around to take her to Sunday School. She behaved very well. Cousin Sid did not come to Sunday School. Cousin Lib said she was sick so we did not have any teacher and did not say any lessons. I did not know my lessons very well, anyhow.

Wednesday, May 6
It has been a very dull day. Mammy went down to Aunt Lottie's to wash so that we had to get dinner. We had nothing but rice and cream for dinner and that was very nice. If we can always get that I will be perfectly satisfied. If our confederacy is recognized we can get rice all the time. I don't think that I would ever get tired of it. Emma has got tired of it already, but we have not had very much of it here lately. I have been reading a novel, but I am almost ashamed to say it. I never can read history, if I read these novels. They are so interesting, but they are very injurious to the mind.

Thursday, May 7
I hope Sunday will be a pretty day. I expect it will. It is most always different from the other days in the week.... It is so dull. I wish we had some sugar and other things so that we could have company. Mr. Dosh was here this evening. He wanted to know whether we had a cow. If we had, I reckon he would stay to tea.

Friday, May 8
We have another rainy day. I can't go out much. My shoes are full of holes. Emma has to go every day after the milk. Aunt Kate and Aunt Annie came over here this evening to help Ma to sew. They made Emma a garabolera, Ma had made mine. They are black silk with little brass buttons on the shoulders and down the front. They are so pretty. I like them better than Ginnie Sperry's.

Saturday, May 9
Mr. Dosh has appointed Saturday for class. He has got some catechisms. We have to learn so many references in the Bible I don't believe I can learn them. He gives such long lessons.

Wednesday, May 13
Ma and Aunt Annie and Aunt Kate made our sacks – both of them – today. I am very well pleased with mine. It is plum colored silk. It is

just as pretty as black silk. It is such good quality. It was some Ma got out of Pa's store thirteen years ago. It is as old as I am nearly.

Thursday, May 14
It has been reported that Jackson was surrounded with thirty thousand men but I don't believe it. If he was he would fight his way through them.

Friday, May 15
Ma went up to Aunt Mary's to tea. She is much pleased with that Yankee lady up there. She says she is a real lady. I would like to see her. To see a Yankee lady is a rarity. I am very glad there is one. I have not seen one yet.

Mr. Dosh is sick and we can't have any class now. We had such a hard lesson, it took me the whole day to get it, but of course I did not sit steady to get it. We had fifty-six verses to learn. I think that is entirely too much for anybody to learn.

Sunday, May 17
We did not have any church this morning as Mr. Dosh is sick, but we had morning meeting and Sunday School. Not one of us went to church. Emma and I went to Sunday School and Miss Strother taught us. Cousin Sid has got the typhoid fever. So many persons have that. Mrs. Heironimus, I believe, has got it, and so has Goff Miller.

Monday, May 18
Poor Jackson, we heard, was shot by our own men. He got the pneumonia by putting so much cold water on his wound, it sounds almost as bad as if we were whipped to lose such a good and brave General as Jackson. But if we are going to gain our independence, we can do it without Jackson.

Tuesday, May 19
I hardly know what to write now, but we see nothing but blue Yankees. If they stay here much longer I expect persons will hate blue.

Wednesday, May 20
Next month will be June and the month after that on the 18th Nannie will be two years old. She is growing so large. She is so heavy that I can hardly carry her any. I am glad we have got her a nurse. She is a great help, although she lets her fall. Saturday she let her fall all the way down the front steps.

Thursday, May 21
The Yankees sent sixty women and children out of the lines. They passed by and stopped here at the door. They did not stay all night. Before they came, one of the Yankees came here and wanted to see Ma. He wanted to tell her that she must be prepared to take four families

but they did not stop but a little while. They did not get out of the wagon. In one of the wagons one of the ladies was talking to one of the Yankees and she talked so loud that we could hear all she said. She said that they took all their money but a hundred dollars. And she said there was a widow lady that had a great many children and one of them was a little baby two years [old], and they sent her to Camp Chaise and would not even let her take her baby with her, and then quartered their men in her house with her children, and not a person to take care of them. We went up to Aunt Mary's and took Nannie up to see that little Yankee girl.

Friday, May 22
We went to Mr. Bob Reed's funeral this evening. He was buried at six o'clock and he had just died this morning at nine o'clock but I believe mortification had set in and they could not keep him.

Monday, May 25
I am so dumb and stupid that I can't do one thing. I wish we had a nice school here so that we could learn something.

Sunday, May 31
Last night Mary stayed all night and this morning before we had got up Aunt Lottie came here and said Nannie Bushnell was dead. She said she died so hard they think that the fever went to her brain. We went to Sunday School and at six o'clock we went to little Nannie's funeral. There were so many little girls there and they sang "I Want to Be an Angel," and as soon as they begin to sing that, Nellie could not help crying, and I had to cry, too.

Monday, June 1
We fixed up the parlor this evening and I fixed some flowers in a dish. We have not very many flowers so that I cannot arrange them as nice as I would like to. The Council is going to meet here this evening.

Saturday, June 6
It is so hard to find anything to write. The times are so dull, and to look at the stores, it looks like Sunday. This morning the Yankees came around with a wagon and threw a pile of lime[d] at nearly every house in this neighborhood.

---

[d] As they were in control of the city, this should be regarded as an activity done in the interests of sanitation. They were, however, probably not motivated to do so in a "neat" manner. The next sentence in the diary further clarifies the action. It states: "It was so funny to look up [the] street and see most every [one] putting the lime along the gutters."

Sunday, June 7
Pa went to church but Emma and I stayed home. Mary stayed here to dinner, and after dinner I went up with her and stayed until five minutes of two and would have stayed longer if Mary had not told me I forgot I had to go to Sunday School. When we got there Sunday School was in and Mrs. Baker taught us. I hope Cousin Sid will be well enough to teach next Sunday. I don't like to have strange people to teach me.

Tuesday, June 9
I expect Pa is very tired. He has been working very hard all morning, nearly, and part of the evening. I feel tired, but I did not work near as much as Pa did.

Saturday, June 13
Last night there was great excitement and this morning the cavalry were running in and out and they brought in their wounded and sick and the sutlers[e] have been moving and they have been firing their cannons and making a great to do about it. I was so glad, I thought the rebels were coming in town. The Yankees shot one of their shells in a house and set it on fire. It belonged to the Lutheran congregation. I wish our men would see the smoke and make a rush in here and drive these wretches out. We did not go to class this evening. I did not get my lessons.

I have been to the door most all day looking at the Yankees. How scared they are! One of them came in on a horse. He was wounded in the hand. Oh, I am so glad that they got scared once. I don't believe our men are coming in. I expect I would have to cry for joy if they would. The Yankees are firing off their cannons now. I hope they will get tired of it after a while.

Sunday, June 14
This is a glorious day for us. Our men are coming. The Yankees have been firing their cannons all day, and we went up in the garret and looked out the trap door, and we could see the Yankees up by Mrs. Senseny's, and our men were in the woods back of there. Every now and then I could see one or two of our men come out of the woods and shoot. The Yankees have all gone up to the fort. Our men cannonaded the fort until they had to leave that and went down the Martinsburg road. I hope our men will catch old Milroy on his way. They say they have him surrounded. I

---

[e] They are often described as "camp followers," as individuals who "peddled" provisions to the soldiers. In reality, they could be described as "mobile merchants."

expect our men will come here tomorrow. It will be splendid to see the rebels again. We have not seen them for six months. It seems such a long time.

Monday, June 15
This morning we got up very early and that is something unusual for us, and before we could get dressed some of our men came in. They looked so sweet. It was good for sore eyes to see them. There came so many of them. [They] came after we were dressed. I had no idea there was so many of them. We heard that General Elliott was killed. I would rather it had been old Milroy, but I do not want any of them killed. I want them to go back to their homes and stay there, and never poke their noses in the south. We ought to have a high wall between us so that they could not come over.

Tuesday, June 16
Oh, we have so many prisoners. The court house yard and the fort is full of them.

Saturday, June 20
This morning we were getting our lessons when the prisoners came along, and the sutlers behind them, and next came the sight of the Yankee women. Some of them had bundles on their heads. They were the commonest looking things, and one of them said, as she was going past, "You hateful old secesh."[f]

It commenced raining after dinner and at three o'clock Emma went around to see if there was any class, and there was none, so we stayed home.

Thursday, June 25
It is so lonesome when it rains all day.

Saturday, June 27
Mr. Dosh has gone away so we can't have any class this evening. I hope the next lesson will be shorter than this one.

Monday, July 6
I did not go to church yesterday, but Ma and Emma went and I went to Sunday School.... I wish we could have a party. We have so much fun. Or a picknick. We have not had one for so long. Our Sunday School had one once and we had such a nice time. I think they had a swing.

Tuesday, July 7
There are so many wounded men in town and they are going past here all day with their arms and feet shot. It seems that all of them are shot in the arms and legs, poor things. I pity them so. I know they are not half taken care of. I wish the war would stop.

---

[f] A term of abuse derived from the word "secessionist."

Wednesday, July 8
I gave a soldier some bisquit last night. He said he hadn't eaten anything since last Tuesday, poor fellow. They seemed so tired. Ma has been feeding them. She took some soup around to the hospital for them.

Sunday, July 12
I did not go to church this morning and Ma did not go either, but Emma and Pa went. I went to Sunday School and Mrs. Baker taught us and I lost one of my mit-gloves and some preacher prayed and all the time he was shaking his [head] so hard that it was enough to give him the headache. Em says he preached in church this morning and I am glad I was not there to hear him. I don't see how anyone can listen to him.

Monday, July 13
Yesterday they brought in the Yankee prisoners and I think it must have taken them an hour to go through. I know they took so long that I got tired a looking at them. I don't think our men ought to take them prisoners. They ought to shoot every one of them. But they would do the same to ours, so that is not a very good plan. How I do wish this war was over. We would not know what to do with our silksᵍ if there were not any soldiers here. It would be so very lonesome and quiet.

Monday, July 20
Yesterday Emma and I went to church and a strange preacher preached. It was a splendid sermon. It interested me more than any sermon that I have heard for a long time. We did not go to Sunday School this evening.

Friday, July 24
Good [Baker] and Em and I went out and got some blackberries. After we had got our berries we filled our pockets and dresses with apples. They were so nice. We brought them home to make pies with. When we came home we found the town deserted. Our men had all gone. It looks so quiet not to see the soldiers. They have broken up I don't know how many guns and thrown them in the street, and Ma went down and got a ramrod. They are so nice to hang fish on. I hope the Yankees won't come in.

Sunday, July 26
We did not go to church this morning but we went to Sunday School. Cousin Em Miller taught us as Cousin Sid was not well enough to come. Her foot is very much swollen. I hope she will soon be well

---

ᵍ Given the context of the sentence, it is possible that the word "silks" is a misreading – the word might actually be "selfs." It is, however, also possible that "silks" refers to the clothing that was recently made of silk material, i.e., see the entries for the 8th and the 13th of May.

enough to teach us. It is not very pleasant to have so many teachers. I don't like it at all.

The Yankees made a raid in here. It makes me so mad to see them riding about, when just before our men were in here. But they did not get anything but those old broken guns in the street and of course they did not take them.

Wednesday, July 29
This evening Emma and I were ironing and Mammy was washing the dishes. She said that the Yankees were coming and we ran to the window and saw it was two of our men running. We looked up on Potato Hill and then we saw the Yankees flying down the hill after our men. I was so scared. I was afraid the Yankees would shoot them, they were within shooting distance of them. It is a wonder they did not shoot them. They shot an old man on the road because he said to them (in fun) "Stop boys, and give the rebels a chance." They say the man that shot him was drunk. I wish they would go and leave us. They would leave shoot us down as not. But never mind, they will get their reward hereafter.

Friday, July 31
We have been making fans for the hospital. We made them of pasteboard and Pa put handles to them. They are very nice and give right smart wind. We have the Yankees still with us. They are not so considerate as to leave us. I believe they come here just to tantalize the citizens. They had better be home tending to their business.

Saturday, August 1
I hope our men will come soon, but I expect they will let the Yankees stay all winter. It seems as if our men don't stay any time, and the Yankees stay so long. I wish we could go out to pick berries but the Yankees won't let us, and it is so hateful in them. When our men are here we can go any place we choose. I would like to pick some berries for the hospital. It would be a treat for them. We took our fans around to the hospital. I hope they will be of some use to them. I expect they will to them up in the third story. It must be very warm up there for them.

Monday, August 3
Yesterday we did not go to church. There was not any at our church. Mr. Dosh has not come home. I expect he is so much pleased that he don't want to come home.

Wednesday, August 5
I am so glad the Yankees have gone. It is such a relief to us. I hope they will stay away and let our men stay here all the time.

Thursday, August 6
It is so lonesome here now without any soldiers.

Friday, August 7
After supper we went around to the hospital to take some bouquets. We had three beautiful ones. One of our men wanted some milk and we went to Mrs. Reed's and got some very nice, it looked so rich. I am saving some tomatoes to take around. I hope I can get enough to [take] for a large mess. I expect they will taste good to them. I wish I had enough of things to take them some every day. I like to go very much when I have something good to take them.

Saturday, August 8
I wonder whether we are going to have class any more. I hope if we do he [Mr. Dosh] will give us an easier lesson next time. He is up to Staunton yet, I expect. I wish we could get a preacher that don't preach so long.

Tuesday, August 11
Ma is going to send Em and myself to Boarding School in Baltimore, if she can get us there. I hope she can't. We can't hear from home. Well, I wish the war would be over by school time. It would be splendid to go down there then. We will grow up to be dumb if we don't get to school very soon. I hardly know a thing about my lessons. I ought to be ashamed to say it. I wish Mrs. Eichelberger would take a select school.

Thursday, August 13
The Yankees made another raid in here, but did not disturb anything.

Monday, August 17
The Yankees made another raid in here this morning. They came in before we were up. I don't think they got any prisoners. I hope not. They did not stay very long. I am very glad they did not. I hate them to come to stay. They stay so long. They made some of our citizens bring the beds out of their hospital but they soon sneaked off. They ordered Uncle Charley to but he slipped into Mr. Hartman's and jumped over the fence.

Yesterday Em and myself went to Church and Mr. Webster Eichelberger preached. I got so tired listening to him. He is such a drone. Cousin Sid did not come to Sunday School so that Miss Mary Strother taught us. I don't like any person to teach us but Cousin Sid. I know her better than the others.

Tuesday, August 25
It has been raining very hard. The streets were covered with water down below the bridge. It was nearly up to the curbstones. We have not had a flood here for ever so long. I don't remember but one and then Ma was not home. The streets looked so pretty and clean after

the water had all gone. We have not had many rainbows this summer. I think they are so pretty. Next Tuesday we will have to go to school to Mrs. Eichelberger. I would rather go there than Boarding School these times, but don't know where we are going to get our books from. We have not any but small ones that won't do. I wish we could get some up from Baltimore. I am getting to be so dumb. So, if I don't make haste and learn very fast, I won't know anything but how to read novels, I am sorry to say.

Thursday, August 27

Ma and Miss Mary Brooke and Mrs. Denny are all going to Baltimore tomorrow morning.... Ma and Pa went out to Mrs. Baker's to see if they [the Bakers] wanted her [Ma] to bring them anything and they met three Yankees out on the road. They came to bring provisions for the hospital. They drew their revolvers at Pa and Ma and Mr. Dosh (he was out there and came in with them). I expect they thought they were rebels, and asked them where they were going.

Saturday, August 29

I wish it was next Saturday instead of this.... We have to start to school. I hate to go when Ma has gone away. I have not had hardly any time to write here lately. I do not know what we will do when we go to school. Ma had been away from home for a week, and as soon as she came home she went off to Baltimore. I wish I could think of a heap to write. It is so lonesome without Ma.

Monday, August 31

Emma and I did not go to church this morning but stayed home and got our Sunday School lesson. I am so glad that Cousin Sid is well. This evening Em and I went to Choir meeting with Pa. They have a very nice one and they sing very well too, a great deal better than the one we used to have. Sometimes they don't keep very good time, but they are just practicing and of course they have to make some mistakes or else there would be no need of practicing. Pa is their teacher and he says they do very well.

Tuesday, September 1

This morning we went to school. Luly Page came down after us. It is so hard to go to school when you have had holiday for so long a time. We did not go all last winter so we are that much behind the girls that went. I wish I had gone last winter, I would have known that much more.... Uncle Aleck is in town, but he is going out this evening. He heard the Yankees were not very far, so he thought he had better be going. It was well he did, for this [morning] two Yankees came in town. I expect some of the Union people told them the rebels were in town, for I saw one of them tear up on Fort Hill as fast as his horse could take him and after a while (it did not seem more than five minutes) all the cavalry came dashing in and one of them turned around and shot at a dog and afterward they went up the street.

Wednesday, September 2

I wish I could always write a heap at a time. Yesterday I had so much to say, but now I can hardly think of anything. It is so provoking to write, I don't like it very much. I wish I did, then maybe I would take more pains. I hope I will learn a heap at school. I need it very much. I am getting so old and don't know anything. I have forgotten most all I did learn at Mrs. Powell's. I like the first day at school. We don't have to get hardly any lessons, and then don't have to know them perfectly.

Thursday, September 3

We went to school again; I don't like the thought of going every morning for ever so long. I wish we could go every other day. It would be so much nicer. We would have the whole day to prepare our lessons. I think we would know them better.

Friday, September 4

Tomorrow evening we expect Ma home. I hope she will come. I am so afraid we will be disappointed that I don't know what to do.

Saturday, September 5

I hope Ma will come tonight, I would be so disappointed if she did not. This evening came, and then long after the time that the man generally comes, and Ma did not come. I was so disappointed that I had to cry a little. I could not help it. I did not know what kept her.

Sunday, September 6

This morning before I was up Ma came driving up in the carriage. I was so glad to see her that I did not know what to do.

Saturday, September 19

In the morning the Yankees came dashing in after about twelve of our men. Before our men got out of sight the Yankees came over Fort Hill. One of the Yankees was bringing one of our men in. He was a prisoner, and when they got out at the edge of town two Yankees were coming in front of them. But just before they got up to them, they turned around the corner and our man saw there was no Yankees near. He was walking beside the Yankee. He made a spring and grabbed the Yankee's pistol and they were fighting for it. The Yankee fell off his horse, and our man got the pistol and jumped on his horse and ____[h]

It must be remembered that the acute condition of war

---

[h] The extant entries of the diary end abruptly at this point.

that Gettie Miller describes began in the summer of 1861 and persisted until the fall of 1864. Then followed occupation of the town by Federal soldiers, not simply to the end of the conflict in 1865, but to the end of Reconstruction in 1870.

How did the church fare during those weary years? Look first at the church building. On four separate occasions it was commandeered for use by the military forces in control.

The first occupation took place in the summer of '61. Confederate troops under General Joseph E. Johnston had moved into Winchester from Harpers Ferry. Hundreds of raw recruits were getting their initial taste of army life. Twin epidemics of mumps and measles had broken out among them. Two out of every five men were sick. When on July 18 Johnston marched east to assist Beauregard at First Manassas, he left behind 1,700 of his men in improvised hospitals. The Lutheran Church was one of them. As soon as the sick recovered they rejoined the army. The temporary hospital lasted no more than a few weeks, but it disrupted the life of the congregation, and because of abuse to the property it brought on unnecessary damage.

The Church Council took note of the situation at a meeting on August 12 and appointed a special committee to have "the lecture-room cleaned and put in good order, the fences, pavement, etc. renewed, and the damages to the church property arising from its occupancy by the military legally assessed." A month later R.B. Wolfe made a full and satisfactory report of the progress of the work assigned to the committee.

The second occupation occurred in January '62. Scarcely had the needed repairs been completed than Confederate forces took the building again. The Council, on the 27th, authorized Benjamin Miller, William Miller, David Slagle, Edward Hoffman and William B. Baker to wait upon the Medical Director of the Army and respectfully request that the lecture room be vacated as soon as practicable. This request, seemingly, brought results, for by February 5 the room had been vacated and cleaned and was ready for use a few days later.

The church was occupied a third time in the late winter and spring of '63. It was when the Federals under Milroy held the town. On March 2, C.W. Price, David Slagle and C.F. Eichelberger were authorized to have the building cleaned and put in readiness for use by the first of April. When Council met on April 13, however, the committee reported that it deemed it inexpedient to put things in order at that time. Whereupon the committee was ordered to have the window blinds removed to a place of safety and to procure glass to repair the windows of church and lecture room. David Slagle later reported (July 6) that he had taken the blinds to his residence. Meantime the Second Battle of Winchester had taken place in mid-June. How long this particular occupancy lasted is not altogether clear. Apparently it continued throughout the summer until fall. From the testimony of Gettie Miller, the second-floor church sanctuary does not seem to have been appropriated for use.

When September came a new committee was named to put the lecture room in order. H.S. Baker took the place of C.W. Price. November 2, the committee reported that the windows had been repaired, and on November 30, that the benches had been mended and the room cleaned and ready for use.

The fourth occupation followed the Third Battle of Winchester. The record states it simply. "On the 20th of September our church and lecture room were occupied as a hospital by part of the wounded of the 19th Army Corps - most of the pews and benches having been previously removed."

This Heritage

The battle had been fought on Monday. The preceding Thursday there had taken place in the church a special memorial service by the entire community for Thomas Jonathan Jackson. The eulogy was delivered by the Rev. Dr. Lacy, Presbyterian minister and chaplain in the Confederate Army.

The use of the building by Sheridan's men continued until March 4, 1865, during which period no services could be held within it. For a time services were held in the homes of members. Mrs. Godfrey Miller was first to offer her residence as the place to hold the 4 P.M. Wednesday service, and other offers soon followed. One came from the Episcopal Church, which was not occupied. The vestry of Christ Church graciously offered their building for use on alternate Sunday mornings, beginning January 1. Council readily accepted this offer.

Anticipating the time when the church would be vacated by the Federal authorities, a committee to prepare it for occupancy had been appointed in January, consisting of R.B. Wolfe, Edward Hoffman, W.J. Slagle and W.B. Baker. The day the medical corps moved out this committee addressed a letter to Capt. Lee, A.A.G. of Maj. Gen. Sheridan, requesting the Government to furnish the congregation with materials — lumber, glass, paint, nails, etc.— necessary to repair the damages. Capt. Lee in turn promised to detail government workmen to repair all damages, but nothing came of this.

Material loss to the congregation came in another way. The original school house on the corner of the old church property was destroyed by shell and fire during the Second Battle, as Gettie Miller informs us. Later used as a parsonage, then rented out to various parties and used as a sexton's home, it had stood at the intersection of Boscawen (Water) and East Lane for more than a hundred years. No details of the structure of the building have been recorded. That it was of log construction to which weather boarding later had been applied, seems to be indicated by the completeness of the work of the devouring flames from the shell fire that struck it. Its razing opened up the cemetery to preying stock so that a new fence had to be built. The Mount Hebron Cemetery Company erected a temporary plank fence. Mr. Taylor, church sexton, was given permission to remove several burnt trees that stood near the old building.

No attempt is made to enumerate the losses that came to individual families within the congregation, either in members killed, homes damaged or destroyed, or businesses ruined. Suffice it to say that the able bodied manpower of the community was in the army, that it is recorded that 200 homes in, and within the immediate environs of Winchester, were demolished outright, and that 100 homes on Main Street were turned into stables or slaughter houses before peace arrived.

When the news of Appomattox reached Winchester there was general jubilation among the Union Soldiers. Bands played and cannons boomed all night. An illumination of the town was ordered for the following week. Some citizens failed to comply, but the celebration was carried forward, none the less. Suddenly all was quiet and the lights went out. The news of Lincoln's assassination brought somber forebodings. Observers noticed that the spirit of conciliation that had prevailed stiffened to one of retaliation.

It was Winchester's destiny, furthermore, to be a hospital town throughout the entire length of the struggle. The aggregate of casualties in the many engagements of the Lower Valley is estimated at 50,000, and many thousands of these were brought into the town for medical attention. After the battles of Antietam and Gettysburg additional casualties were brought to Winchester hospitals. It laid upon the entire community a tremendous responsibility.

York Hospital was the principal Confederate hospital of the community, located in the property of Miss Billings' School on South Market Street (the present Fairfax Inn).[i] Here Miss Mary E. Kurtz gave long and devoted hours of service in nursing the sick and wounded and in the general oversight of the institution of which she was matron, or head nurse. Likewise did she and other women of the town care for the wounded on the battlefield by day and by night.

Not only did Mary Kurtz play a leading role in ministering to the disabled and dying, but she also, when the war was over, was a founder of the Ladies' Memorial Association, the purpose of which was to care for the graves of the soldier dead. Because there were hundreds upon hundreds of scattered graves within a radius of twelve miles, ground for Stonewall Cemetery was purchased, and the bodies, collected from their places of original burial, were re-interred there. In 1879 a shaft was unveiled to Virginia soldiers. Mary Kurtz was credited with raising the major portion of the cost. Quite appropriately, therefore, did the honor of unveiling it fall to her.

Mary Kurtz was born July 30, 1821, at the corner of Braddock and Cork Streets. Her home, no longer standing, was adjacent to the building used by George Washington when he built Fort Loudoun. She was the daughter of Abraham Kurtz, and the family were members of the Lutheran Church. She lived her life and died May 8, 1905, in the house where she was born, and her funeral was conducted by the Rev. George S. Bowers.

---

[i] It is currently referred to simply as the Fairfax Building.

Credit should here be given to an enterprising group of ladies from the congregation who made a substantial contribution to the purchase of Stonewall Cemetery and the repair of the church. Mrs. Godfrey S. Miller seems to have been the prime mover in the idea that readily met the approval of the Church Council. Having family connections in the city of Baltimore and many friends within the congregation of the First Lutheran Church, arrangements were made through them to hold a fair in that city. Souvenirs were collected from all the neighboring battlefields. Musket balls and cannon balls, buttons and bayonets, all were gathered together and hauled to Baltimore. Solomon Henkel carved trinkets out of bones from Turner Ashby's favorite white cavalry horse. Curios, relics, and odds and ends of war mementos made up the numerous objects for display and sale.

This "Fair and Festival" was held Tuesday evening, February 27, 1866, at the Club House on Charles Street. Admission was twenty cents per adult and ten cents per child. Due to the invaluable assistance of the Rev. Dr. John McCron and the ladies of the First Church, the affair was a sell out and $3,005 was cleared. No wonder the Church Council should pass a preamble and resolution like the following:

> Inasmuch as it was deemed expedient and proper by us, as a Church Council, to encourage certain ladies of our congregation in their proposition to hold a Fair in the City of Baltimore, for the purpose of relieving us from some of the pecuniary embarrassments and disabilities entailed by the ravages of war, as well as to provide for the proper interment of the gallant dead among us, and
>
> Whereas, in the execution of this purpose, they received the most generous and essential assistance and cooperation of many noble-hearted friends in Baltimore, through whose energetic aid the effort was crowned with success, and without which it must have proved a failure,
>
> Therefore, Resolved That to Dr. J.N. McCron, and through

him to those in his congregation, who thus without ostentation in well doing, made themselves conspicuous objects of our highest admiration, and to any and all other friends, whose names cannot here be enumerated, who in like manner or in any degree, aided our ladies in this two-fold object, we do now cordially, sincerely, and with the most profound respect and Christian affection, tender our heartfelt and lasting gratitude, and fervently pray that the blessing of the Highest may rest and abide upon them, now and evermore.

A second set of resolutions thanked Mrs. G.S. Miller and those associated with her "for their zeal in behalf of the church and in the cause of humanity," and set official approval on the proposed division of proceeds, *viz*, "one half for the use of the Church, and the other half to be added to the soldiers' cemetery fund."

Among those who assisted in the undertaking and who went to Baltimore for the fair as recalled by Miss Gettie Miller in 1934, were: Mrs. Alcinda Baker, Sally Hoffman, Anna Miller, Mrs. Godfrey S. Miller, Gettie Miller, Mrs. Mullen, Charles Price and John Billy Schultz.

Any claim which the congregation had against the Government for damage to the church from its occupancy as a hospital in 1864-1865 met with no response until fifty years afterwards. At a Council meeting, February 1, 1909, the secretary reported the ancient history of the facts, and was instructed to draw up an itemized statement showing the exact cost of repairs. A formal claim of $1033.38 for repairs and $200 for occupancy was then submitted and placed in charge of Thomas S. Martin, U.S. Senator from Virginia, who introduced a bill in the Senate in support of the claim. Counsel in Washington was employed to look after the measure. The U. S. Court of Claims later allowed the sum of $810. This amount was certified to Congress for an appropriation and was finally approved in 1915. August 2, the secretary of the Council reported that this war claim against the United States Government had been paid, and that the sum of $729 had been deposited to the Trustees account in the Shenandoah Valley National Bank, legal counsel having been paid ten percent.

Both country and congregation had weathered the storm, praise the Lord. But say what you please, it was a most uncivil affair.

Chapter IX
Buildings and Properties

To this point in the story it has been necessary to give the main facts relating to the properties and buildings owned by the congregation. In connection with such things there are, to be sure, a great many other details of interest to many persons. It is the purpose of this chapter, therefore, to amplify this phase of the narrative by supplying additional information from the records.

The Lutheran Cemetery.

The grant of two half-acre lots by Lord Fairfax has already been related. They were located within the limits of the town on land that formed part of the Fairfax Addition. On the southwest corner of this property a school house was first erected, followed in 1764 by the laying of the cornerstone of the stone church. The ground surrounding the church, especially the ground to the north and to the east, became the congregation's burying ground. Here many early citizens of the community were laid to rest. As time went along a small addition was made to this original grant, as well as two smaller subtractions.

The addition, slightly more than a quarter of an acre, was obtained in 1825. It consisted of a strip of land, approximately sixty by one hundred ninety feet, adjoining the north side of the property, which originally had been intended for the eastward projection of Philpot Lane. Under the authority of a special act of the state legislature, this conveyance was made by the Corporation of Winchester to the trustees of the church for a consideration of $35. By this acquisition the cemeteries of the Lutheran and Reformed congregations became contiguous.

The first subtraction from the total area of the Lutheran property occurred about 1870 when the Winchester and Strasburg Railroad was constructed. It became necessary to sacrifice a narrow strip of ground along the East Lane side of the property to the railroad right of way. H.S. Baker, Godfrey S. Miller and Dr. William Miller were appointed a committee to assess the damages and to confer with the railroad company. Their verdict was set at "about $500, exclusive of removing and renewing the fence." The record does not state what amount of damages was collected.

In 1844 Mount Hebron Cemetery, lying to the east of the Lutheran burying ground, was dedicated, and at the close of the Civil War, Stonewall Cemetery, east of Mount Hebron, was set apart for Confederate dead. In time Mount Hebron became the principal cemetery of the whole community. Through the generosity of Charles B. Rouss, Winchester benefactor, the iron fence given to enclose Mount Hebron and Stonewall likewise included the Lutheran and Reformed cemeteries in one large enclosure. This matter was first proposed in 1891 and carried out that year. In April 1892, the church trustees received a bill for $205 as their proportionate share of the cost of the fence in excess of Mr. Rouss' gift. "Said bill, after discussion, was laid on the table for future action."

The combined mortuary chapel and caretaker's house at the main entrance to Mount Hebron was erected in 1902. The chapel stands upon a parcel of land (approximately 1800 square feet) deeded to the cemetery company by the trustees of the church.[a]

As now constituted, therefore, the Lutheran Cemetery comprises the original Fairfax lots, plus the one-quarter acre end of Philpot Lane, from which must be deducted the strip along East

---

[a] On November 1, 2001, the Reverend Dr. James H. Utt of Grace Lutheran Church conducted a ceremony of dedication following the chapel renovation.

Lane and the southeast corner along Boscawen Street.

In conveying the parcel of land at the cemetery entrance to the Mount Hebron officials, the church trustees insisted on the following provisions:

> 1. That the proposed mortuary chapel be erected within three years according to specified plans;
> 2. That the double gate and curb-way by which access was given to the Lutheran Cemetery be adjusted so as to give the same facilities in the future;
> 3. That the Mount Hebron Cemetery Company receive the grant of land as a full equivalent for any benefit accruing to the Lutheran Cemetery by the erection of the iron fence in 1891;
> 4. That the cost of this conveyance be borne by the Mount Hebron Company.

By October 1903, nothing had been done to fulfill the second provision. The trustees formally requested the cemetery officials to complete the contract. The officials replied by saying the matter would be given proper consideration. Nothing, however, was done by June, when the trustees wrote again insisting on the stipulated terms. Their insistence led the Mount Hebron officials to take action. Iron gates in their possession were given the trustees with permission to erect them in the line of the fence at least twenty feet from the chapel; but the right to construct a driveway across the pavement leading to Mount Hebron, while granted, contained the proviso that the existing grade was not to be changed or altered, and that the pavement must be kept in good repair; and should the trustees fail in keeping the pavement in repair, then it became the right and duty of the cemetery company to close the gates and forbid their use.

By November the trustees were willing to compromise the issue to the extent of paying the cost of erecting the gates.

Buildings and Properties

As for the right to close the gates to the Lutheran Cemetery, they declared:

> Inasmuch as the congregation we represent has for a great many years claimed and exercised the right of entrance into its cemetery from that [Water] street, we do not concede the right or privilege, asserted in the action of the Mount Hebron Cemetery Company, July 14th aforesaid, to close the proposed driveway or to forbid said entrance to the Cemetery of the Lutheran congregation in any event whatsoever. And whilst we desire to have the driveway satisfactory in appearance and durability to the Mount Hebron Cemetery Company, we claim final decision in the construction thereof.

The gates were installed at last in 1906. The cost was paid by a member of the Church Council. But no one has been found who can say with positive assurance that the gates were ever used thereafter.[b]

While dealing with the subject of the cemetery, mention should be made of the stone wall which partly enclosed it. The construction of this wall "from the north corner of the graveyard to the gate" was authorized in 1816. The "north corner" meant what would have been the southeast corner of East Lane and Philpot Lane. The gate was located on East Lane opposite the west door of the church. This work evidently was executed shortly after authorization.

Six years later action was taken to extend a stone wall "in front of the church, that a neat gate be placed opposite the front door, and that steps be made at the front door." In December 1822, Jacob Baker reported the completion of this work, and that "with the consent of the consistory, he has

---

[b] In recent years the gates have been used to admit maintenance vehicles into the cemetery.

had the wall extended quite up to the parsonage house." The wall thus extended along the East Lane side of the property, while a wooden fence enclosed the other sides. A wooden covering was placed on top of wall in 1824.

These improvements to the property, together with the purchase the next year of the Philpot Lane extension, led to a subscription of funds from the public, a fact which indicated the general use of the Lutheran Cemetery by Winchester citizens.

This list has been preserved with the accounting of the funds raised, and both are given herewith from the minutes of November 2, 1825.

> The enlargement of the Lutheran graveyard being rendered necessary, and a favorable opportunity being now presented to procure it from the Corporation of Winchester (*viz.*) the parcel of ground in front of the Church, an appeal is now made to the liberality of the citizens. Therefore we the Subscribers promise to pay to Daniel Linn the sums annexed to our names respectively, for the purpose of purchasing the ground aforesaid.

Name	Amount	Name	Amount
John Heiskel	2.00	George M. Adam	1.00
Isaac Hoff	1.00	F. McCormick	1.00
Henry M. Brent	1.00	M.B. Richards	1.00
Edward Smith	3.00	Andrew Nolen	1.00
John Brun [?]	1.00	Samuel L. Hesser	1.00
Peter Bell	1.00	James Paten	2.00
Bell & Byers	1.00	Judith Singleton	1.00
Matthias Schultz	1.00	John Copenhaver	1.00
Samuel Fry	1.00	Jacob Copenhaver	1.00
Geo. Heist	1.00	Isaac Kiger	1.00
Solomon P. Spangler	1.00	Jacob Everly	1.00
Wm. Jones	1.00	Daniel Hartman	2.00
Lewis Hoff	5.00	Ebon Melton	1.00
Ephraim Hawkins	1.00	John Fletcher	1.00
A.S. Baldwin	1.00	John B. Campbell	1.00
Stewart Grant	1.00	Thos. B. Campbell	1.00
E.H. Pendleton	2.00	Jacob Mathias	1.00
Joseph W. Ware	1.00	J. Newborough	1.00

Buildings and Properties

Geo. Aulick	1.00	Davenport Orrick	1.00
Province McCormick	1.00	A.S. Tidball	1.00
Daniel Taggert	1.00	Martin Brown	1.00
Jno. Anderson	1.00	Jacob Harmer	1.00
Wm. Roberts	1.00	Geo. Kreemer	1.00
Geo. Wm. Seevers	2.00	Jesse Myers	1.00
Andrew Kiger	1.00	Sam. C. Baker	1.00
Fred Aulick	1.00	Augustus Kiger	1.00
Geo. Schultz	1.00	Geo. Pelter	1.00
Joseph Sherrard	1.00	Danl. Brown	1.00
Robt. T. Baldwin	1.00	Phil. Sherer	1.00
Wm. M. Sperry	1.00	John Slote	1.00
Nathaniel Seevers	1.00	Jacob Slote	1.00
Peter E. Sperry	1.00	Geo. Barnhart	1.00
Joseph Comes	1.00	John Brown	1.00
Wm. Morris	1.00	Jacob Shearer	1.00
Josiah Massie	2.00	Wm. Seemer	1.00
Henry Slote	1.00	Julia Von Riesen	1.00
Stephen Jenkins	1.00	Geo. B. Graves	1.00
Geo. Wolfe	1.00	Jacob Sperry	.50
Fred Schultz	1.00	Thomas Marshall	1.00
Jacob Walls	1.00	Received for old gate	3.50
Robert Brannon	.70	Received from	
John Walls	2.00	Consistory	3.50
		Amount *in toto*	$100.20

Expenditures as balancing the above
To cash paid for the Lot of ground				$35.00
Do "	nails			1.80
Do "	plank			6.80
Do "	putting up a stone wall			13.00
Do "	covering	Do		6.25
Do "	nails			.27
Do "	painting	Do		2.50
Do "	plastering	Do		2.50
Do "	painting	Do		1.00
Do "	Sand	Do		1.00
Do "	Locust posts			1.00
Do	Do	Do		1.50
Do "	Sundry Persons plank			12.25
Do "	Lime			2.00
Do "	Negro William for labor			4.50
Do	Do	Do		.83

Do	Stephen Jenkins	.50
Do	Godfrey Miller's bill	3.18
Do "	plank	4.50
	in toto	$100.38
	balanced	100.20
		00.18

By the will of Matthias Schultz, the sum of $500 was devised to the church trustees for the upkeep of the cemetery. The money was to be invested and the interest so used. A poor investment seems to have been made, for in 1889, two years later, a note, considered of doubtful value, was being held for collection.

From 1865 to 1889 the custody of the cemetery was in charge of Dr. William S. Miller. Charles F. Eichelberger next assumed this duty and served until his death in 1895. Dr. Alfred D. Henkel followed in order, likewise serving until his death in 1947.

An arrangement now exists whereby the Lutheran Cemetery is cared for by the management of Mount Hebron Cemetery.

Church Council approved a new Lutheran Cemetery policy similar to the policy adopted by the adjacent Reformed Cemetery on November 5, 1962. Only immediate relatives of persons already interred would be buried there. For each new grave the sum of $100 would be paid to the trustees of Grace Lutheran Church. In 1971 the sale of lots was discontinued, and only those presently owning lots there would be interred. The most recent burials were for Dorothy and William Eisenberg. The amount paid to Mount Hebron for maintenance and mowing was raised from $150 to $300 per year. The cost for maintenance was increased to $500 per year in 1982. Mowing costs are extra.

Memorial Garden.
To provide a spiritually, theologically and ecologically appropriate space on the property of the congregation for the inhumation of ashes from cremation, Congregation Council ap-

proved creating a task group to implement and finalize details for a Memorial Garden in Mount Hebron Cemetery. Appointed to the task group in December 1997 were Pastor Utt, Trustees Ken Carr and Jerry Kerr, Roger Milburn, David Ray, Sally Coates, Lenore Eavis and Pastor Rudy Keyl. By February 1998 gifts totaling $8,000 had been received for the Memorial Garden Fund established by the trustees. On October 18, 1998, Congregation Council adopted policies and guidelines for the Grace Evangelical Lutheran Church Memorial Garden and authorized the purchase of a bronze memorial plaque to hold 250 names.

The Memorial Garden is located within the area where the original sanctuary stood. The existing wall marks the east boundary and the northeast and southeast corners. In-ground engraved granite markers were installed to designate the northwest and southwest corners. The large bronze plaque to hold names and dates was mounted on a specially made limestone base in the center of the original church area. A brochure was published to provide information regarding the scattering of ashes on this sacred ground as a part of a Christian service for any member or spouse or child of a Grace Evangelical Lutheran Church member.

The School House.

The first building owned by the congregation was a school building, believed to have been constructed of logs as early as 1759. The first positive reference to it is found in Streit's Diary, but the fact that the congregation had Carl F. Wildbahn as schoolmaster prior to 1762, and Master Antony in 1764, would certainly argue in favor of the building's early existence. The matter has been discussed elsewhere in this record.

First reference in the minutes is found under date of October 13, 1815. Peter Lauck and John Slagle were ordered "to have such repairs done to the school house as they may deem necessary." Gilbert Nokes, the sexton, was living in the school house at the time. He was dismissed as of April 1, 1816, and ordered to clean the house before his departure. The wages of a sexton, it must be remembered, were more than covered by the cost of lodging. Thus Nokes' successor as sexton and tenant of the school house, Benjamin Matson, paid to the treasurer of the congregation the sum of thirty dollars a year for the use of said building, while four years later James Foster, sexton and school house occupant, was required to pay twenty dollars a year rent.

In 1821 the question of a parsonage began to be agitated. Christian Streit had lived in his own house, and Abraham Reck had been renting from William Holliday. Efforts to have the other congregations of the parish join in providing a home for the pastor proved of no avail. If anything were to be done, the Winchester congregation would have to do it alone.

Initial plans called for the removal of the school house and the erection of a stone building on its site, "if practicable." But such plans were soon deemed quite impracticable, the design was abandoned, and it was decided "to repair the school house for the present accommodation of the pastor." Joseph Slagle, John Miller, Daniel Linn and John W. Miller were appointed to supervise the work.

The conversion of the school house into a parsonage became part of a general program of improvement for the congregation's property. As it turned out, expenditures exceeded expected costs. Daniel Linn and Godfrey Miller advanced the money needed to complete the renovation, which included a new addition on the west side and the erection of a stable near the house. Pastor Reck occupied this first parsonage for about five years. On his departure from Winchester, it was rented and the proceeds turned over to Messrs. Linn and Miller to repay their loan.

Because Lewis Eichelberger did not dwell in the parsonage, it continued to be rented. Abraham Grove, the sexton, lived in the east end, or old half of the house. Wages having risen, he received free rent, joint use of the stable, the use of half the ground for a garden, and six dollars half-yearly in cash. The west, or new, half of the house was rented to an unnamed second party for thirty dollars annually. Reuben Seals was the tenant in 1834.

The parsonage continued to be rented throughout the pastorate of N.W. Goertner; in fact it continued just to be rented, as no other pastor of the church occupied it. John T. Taylor, church sexton, occupied it for a number of years prior to its destruction. The building was set ablaze by gunfire during the Second Battle of Winchester, June 13, 1863, and so destroyed.

The Old Church.

From the night of the burning of the old church [1854], almost one hundred years have passed [1953]. The commonplace things about it have been forgotten almost completely. Which direction did the building face? And was the spire located on the north or south end of the structure? Because no authentic drawing or detailed description has been found to answer the questions of the curious, such information as exists is all the more appreciated in the light that it casts on the subject.

By the interested foresight of Dr. Gilbert the measurements of the building have been preserved.

> The foundation walls were 3 feet 6 inches in thickness, and those of the superstructure 2 feet 5 inches. The building was 52 feet 6 inches in length, 42 feet in width, and from the square of the foundation to the square of the superstructure, 23 feet 6 inches in height. From the floor to the ceiling the measurement was 19 feet 6 inches. The aisles were paved with square bricks.[1]

Here is information enough, added to the east wall still standing, as a starter for someone interested in the science and art of re-creating the past. Perhaps someday the spirit of the

Sketch of Old Church by Regina Sperry (date not known)

Williamsburg Restoration may invade Winchester and the old church of so many of the fathers of the community may be built up again to reveal its simple dignity and its common glory.

Something of the importance of the building may be had from the study made by R.E. Griffith, Sr., whose conclusion is that it was the largest public building in Virginia west of the Blue Ridge until 1840, when the present Frederick County Court House was erected.[2]

Buildings and Properties

And something of the building's character may be seen in the letter written from Winchester, April 20, 1799, by Mrs. Susanna Knox (nee Susanna Stuart Fitzhugh, the wife of an English gentleman who settled in Virginia at Boscobel) addressed to her daughters and containing the following interesting recital:[3]

> I was at the Dutch church last Sunday, a very handsome stone building about as large as our church. It has a fine steeple, is nicely finished off within, and looks more like a church than any I ever saw except Potomack (an Episcopal church in Stafford County). The minister preached in English that day, and all the pews were so crowded that many sat on benches in the aisles, from which I judge that the miscreant Tom Payne's *Age of Reason* has had no effect here. There is one of the finest organs in it I ever heard, so you may perceive I am quite in my element, fine society, charming music, excellent living, and no trouble about it.

The steeple was the church's most prominent outward feature, giving distinction and character to the solid, stone structure. It is well to remember, therefore, that in the sequence of the years the edifice had three steeples.

As has already been pointed out, the first steeple was the one seen by Rev. Mr. Fithian in 1775. How long it stood, no one seems to know. It was not there when Christian Streit arrived upon the scene ten years later. The second steeple was built between 1789 and 1793 and faithfully pointed heavenward for about thirty years. This brings us into the range of the congregation's records and we begin to tread on firmer ground.

The Renovation of 1822.

Attention to the steeple was given by the Council at a meeting on August 6, 1818. Foundation timbers were to be inspected, and if examination showed them to be in sound condition, then other repairs were to be made.

Inspection having been duly made, it was reported the following April that the timbers were found to be decayed and "insufficient to admit of being repaired." Steeple Number Two, therefore, was ordered to come down, and by the end of June it was reported as having been taken down.

Then followed a renovation of the church interior. John W. Miller and Jacob Baker superintended the repairs and alterations. In November 1820, they reported to the Council that they had proceeded with the most essential improvements to the extent of the funds available. Expenditures were made

> ...for finishing the large gallery – extending and altering the organ gallery – building a new pulpit and altering the side pews – breaking and finishing 4 windows at the 'Gavel' ends – Paints and painting, whitewashing, plastering – Trimming for the pulpit and organ gallery – Materials for the whole work and sundry small items – for which they have reference to the account handed to the committee appointed to investigate it – Three Hundred and Sixty Four dollars and Sixty Seven cents – which has been paid by a loan upon the credit of the Bank Stock of Three Hundred and Thirty dollars – and the residue of Thirty Four Dollars and Sixty seven cents by John Baker and of the Treasury.

In planning for these improvements, mention was made of a proposed "new alter." Nothing, apparently, was done about this item. But the specifications for the new pulpit demanded that it be "furnished with black curtains and cushions and is customary in other churches in other places besides Winchester." And the clergyman's pew was to be "curtained around with green bombazette, or other suitable stuff, supported with small iron bars, as is usually done."

Gallery windows were not a part of the original structure. The fact that four windows were broken through the north and south walls leads to the information that galleries were located at both ends; while a longer gallery ran along the east side of the building. This was the "large gallery" referred to in the first item of the foregoing report. Here seats were maintained for colored persons.

The organ gallery occupied the south wall. The pulpit, presumably on the same level as the gallery, was to the east with the communion table on the floor level beneath. In the aisle in front of the communion table was the burial place of Christian Streit. On April 4, 1821, Jacob Baker was ordered "to purchase a sufficient quantity of crimson marine to Trim the communion Table; also a sufficient quantity of Fringe to trim the curtains at the Organ Gallery."

The Old Church: Reconstructed and sketched by Alison D. Cooper, 1953.

At the time these repairs were made the west door, the door facing East Lane, was considered the front door to the building. From this door a path led out to the gate in the stone wall built along that street. There was a door also in the east wall, used primarily on funeral occasions.

It is the writer's conclusion that the steeple was on the north end of the structure and that its foundation was pierced by a doorway through the north wall. Sketches reveal a single door at one end, and the Philpot Lane addition to the cemetery is described as lying "in front of the church." On the basis of this conclusion the sketches submitted in this work show the north and west fronts, rather than the south and east, as the present entrance through Mount Hebron Cemetery and the approach from the east lead many to suspect.

On tearing down the second steeple, many timbers of which were badly decayed, the foundation timbers were found to be in a far better state of preservation than originally imagined. After a thorough re-examination they were deemed amply strong enough to bear the weight of a new steeple. Carpenters qualified for such work were obtained at $1.25 to $1.50 per day. The third steeple, therefore, was ordered to be built upon the foundation of the second, and a subscription for the same to be raised. A year elapsed from April 1821, when the above action was taken, until work was begun. This third and last steeple had been completed by December 1822. "Large advances" of money were made by John Miller for its construction.

The Renovation of 1834.

A second major renovation of the old church took place in 1834. The proposed changes to the interior have already been related under the pastorate of Nicholas W. Goertner. It would seem that the proposition there stated was never actually carried into execution. What that proposal called for would have made the south end the front of the building, with the pulpit immediately to right or left of the two and only doors. From the standpoint of worship this would have created a most impracticable arrangement.

The renovation of 1834, so far as the east wall of the

church was concerned, closed not only the door, but two of the windows as well; yet nothing is said in the proposed plan about closing windows.

Furthermore, it is this writer's contention that the existing sketches of the old church were made from memory after the conflagration had occurred, and as such they depict the church in the form in which it last stood. Granted that this be true, the proposal to make two doors in the south end certainly was never carried out. Instead, the single north door became the main entrance of the building, as indeed it had always been the front door from the standpoint of structure. Then, to move the pulpit to the south wall, the organ to the north gallery, and to install two slips of pews with a center and side aisles could have been carried out quite readily. Still, it must be admitted, the exact interior arrangement is not known.

A final item on the old church deals with the fire that destroyed it. A newspaper account,[4] taken from *The Winchester Virginian*, relates the following story:

> Winchester was visited, on Wednesday night last [September 27, 1854], by a fire which may well be termed serious, in that, though it caused comparatively little pecuniary loss, it deprived us of what money cannot restore, a relic of the past. The Old Lutheran Church, the most venerable building in the town, and forming, with its spire, the land mark of Winchester to generations of approaching travelers, is a ruin.
> The fire broke out, about an hour after dark, in the stable of Mr. Philip Young, on the short cross street called Baker Street [now Philpott Lane], in a neighborhood which has suffered from one or two previous fires or attempts. After destroying, with the stable, Mr. Y's horse, six hogs, and some provender, and also the stable of J.P. Riely, esq., it swept eastwardly before the wind, consuming the row of outbuildings to the end of the square. The sparks covered the roof of the church fifty yards distant, and it was soon on fire in a dozen places. The dryness of the old tim-

bers, and the great elevation and distance from water, baffled every effort of the firemen and citizens. It is, however, believed by many that the church could have been saved but for a difficulty arising between two of the fire companies. We will not doubt that the officers of the company supposed in fault, will succeed in vindicating themselves. On Saturday evening smarting under the censure of citizens, they determined to resign and surrender their engine to the Mayor; but, upon consultation, they yielded to the wishes of many citizens and are again reorganized. Hitherto our firemen have kept free from the disgraceful feuds of the city companies; and it is to be hoped they will continue to do so. The tall steeple, for so many years conspicuous by day, became for the first time a beacon at night. The light was visible throughout a circle bounded only by the mountains. It was noticed at Knoxville, Md., three miles beyond Harpers Ferry; and at Charlestown, twenty-two miles distant, it drew together quite a crowd in the upper part of a three-story building. The spire fell at a quarter past nine.

There is a tradition that says that while the old church burned music from the organ was distinctly heard. It is difficult to say how traditions of this character come into existence. Yet from the vivid depiction of the scene by Dr. Krauth, one can well imagine that in the infernal lapping and hissing and roaring of the flames, a kind of rhythmic sequence from the abyss is heard.

The fact of the matter is, the organ, said to have been the first in any church in the Valley of Virginia, had been sold the preceding spring for $50 to a German Lutheran congregation in Baltimore. The minutes for May 1854, report that the check for the same had been received from the Rev. E.C. Weyl and that the instrument itself had already been removed to that city.

On the other hand, the fact that the organ remained in the little used old church for some twelve years following the building of the new church, made it an object of investigation for night prowlers, who got into the old building on occasion, and whose curiosity and desire to hear the organ's tones – not to mention the relative harmlessness of their prank – caused them to make the organ peal forth at midnight hours to the haunting concern of any who might hear the sound.

Old Lutheran Church Wall.

Ruins of the old Lutheran Church east wall became a familiar landmark of the city after the fire in 1854. Concern was raised in 1971 regarding the status of the remaining wall. In 1978 Church Council directed the trustees to make repairs not to exceed $2,000 and an appeal for those funds was made to the congregation as a part of the 225th Anniversary celebration.

By 1998 deterioration of the old church wall had become substantial. The July 19 issue of *Tidings* carried a full report of a meeting called to assess the situation. Congregation Council referred repairs to the Church Property Committee. On October 11, 1998, a task group (later named the Old Lutheran Church Wall and Grace Cemetery Task Group) was appointed that included Gene Fisher, David Ray, Susan Short, Ken Carr, Polly Manuel, Robert Woltz, Jim Brown, Irv Henschen, Pastor Utt and Pastor May. Council also established an Old Church Wall and Cemetery Preservation Fund to be used and managed by the trustees. In the October 29, 1998, issue of *Tidings* Pastor Utt wrote:

> Our old Lutheran church wall that stands in our cemetery, which is within the confines of the larger Mount Hebron Cemetery, could fall at any time, according to engineers from Terra Tech, of Leesburg, Virginia, and engineers from Howard Shockey and Sons, of Winchester. The wall is unstable due to a number of factors over time—deterioration of mortar joints, unique forces of pressure (especially since it was not built to stand alone) and certainly the effects of weather since it was erected in 1764.
>
> We have been advised that a heavy rain, strong wind, or no apparent reason other than the forces already at play, especially on the lower end where most of the forces are concentrated, could cause the wall to fall. The situation requires immediate action because of safety, the need to protect the graves and grave markers around the wall, and the questions of responsibility for preserving this symbol of heritage for our church and its significance as a historical landmark for the Winchester community.

Warning signs were posted, the area surrounding the wall was roped off and Howard Shockey and Sons covered the cap of the wall with a temporary tarp. Members of the congregation stepped forward with significant monetary gifts to see that the wall—all or portions of it—and the surrounding graves and grave markers were preserved and maintained for generations to come. The recently established Memorial Garden Task Group continued to work within this situation to accomplish its goals.

On November 8 the task group reported that it needed a higher level of expertise. After various contractors, architects and engineers presented many very expensive solutions, the task group followed the recommendations of the Virginia Department of Historic Resources and Scott Brooks-Miller, the state architectural historian in-residence. The large pine tree at the south end of the wall was removed and a no-fee archaeological investigation of the wall's foundation was performed by the Office of Historic Preservation unearthing pieces of glass and charred wood. Howard Shockey and Sons was contracted to build a concrete abutment against the southeast corner of the wall for $11,844. John Robinson was contracted for $22,000 to do the masonry work where the cracks were filled, the joints were repointed with an approved mix of sand, lime and cement provided by the architect and the top of the wall was capped with concrete to shed water. Work was completed in 2000, and on May 10 Preservation of Historic Winchester, recognizing the congregation's efforts to stabilize the wall to preserve a community asset, presented Grace Church an award.

The Boscawen [Water] Street Site.

The purchase of the Boscawen Street site for a lecture room and new church has already been related under the pastorate of Theophilus Stork. This action was taken by the congregation November 11, 1839, while the deed of conveyance was made January 29, 1840. The following is quoted from the deed:

> Now this indenture witnesseth that in consideration of the premises & for the sum of Eleven hundred dollars paid to him or secured to be paid by the parties of the second part, at & before the sealing & delivery of these presents, they – the said George W. Baker and Emily Susan his Wife – have granted, bargained, sold & conveyed...to the said John W. Miller, Jacob Baker, Abraham Miller, Joseph Slagle & Thomas B. Campbell the lot of

ground…lying and being in the Corporation of Winchester, being the same lot of which the late Jonathan Robinson died seized and which was sold & conveyed to the said George W. Baker by Charles H. Clark, acting as Special Commissioner under a decree of the County Court of Frederick sitting in Chancery, the deed from whom to said Baker bears date the 27th day of November, 1838, and is of record in the Clerk's Office of the County aforesaid. The old lot is therein described as a certain part of Lot No. 6 in the addition made to the town of Winchester by James Wood, on the North side of Boscawen or Water Street, between Loudoun & Braddock, being that part of said lot of which Mary Powers died seized, bounded on the east by ____ alley, and on the west by Joseph Slagle, and running back to a Ten foot alley to be left open from Braddock Street to the alley first mentioned, together with all rights, privileges & appurtenances to the said property belonging.

On January 18, 1847, the congregation voted to purchase the vacant lot adjoining its property to the west. It had a 36-foot frontage on Boscawen Street and had been owned by Joseph Slagle. Mr. Slagle, it would appear, ran into financial difficulties and his property had to be sold. Robert B. Wolfe, trustee for the bank, conveyed the property by deed under date of November 21, 1846. Several members of the congregation had agreed to underwrite its purchase for the church, so Thomas B. Campbell reported to the Council on January 11, at which time the whole matter was ordered to be submitted to a meeting of the congregation to be held one week later. The price paid appears to have been $585, bond for the same being given. The deed was made out to John Hoff, William Miller and William B. Baker, trustees.

In the light of subsequent needs of the congregation, it was unfortunate that the vision that led to the purchase of this lot grew dim so soon. At a meeting November 4, 1848, action was taken selling 20 feet of the above property, commencing with the western line and running east. It was sold to the Corporation of Winchester for the sum of $500. This particular parcel of land became the site of the Union Fire Company and had to be bought a second time by the congregation.

To enlarge the church building to the north, it became necessary in 1900 to buy an irregularly shaped parcel of ground, 1,682 square feet in area. The price paid was $1,100. Certain real estate maneuvering was required before it could be bought.

At the time, Church Alley ran in a straight line from east to west from Indian Alley, or Fairfax Alley, as it was also called, to Braddock Street. Across this alley to the north was the property of W.V. Hodges. What the church actually needed was the alley itself, owned by the Corporation of Winchester, plus a small strip of Mr. Hodges' land. Mr. Hodges, furthermore, wanted to sell the whole of his lot along Indian Alley and Church Alley, rather than a fractional part, and the church was not interested in that kind of deal.

What happened was this. Hodges sold his lot to George Clarence Miller and the City of Winchester deeded the east end of Church Alley to him. Miller in turn sold the desired 1,682 square feet to the church trustees and the city changed the course of Church Alley to accommodate the enlarged edifice. The deed bears date of September 10, 1900.

As plans evolved to redesign the sanctuary in the early 1990s the city was again approached, and the property known as Church Alley was conveyed to Grace Lutheran Church for $9,970. The congregation approved the purchase on June 6, 1993.

Two further acquisitions of land were made to the present Boscawen Street property in order to erect the Sunday School building. The first was the Union Fire Company property purchased in 1919 for the sum of $3,085; the second, known as the

Baker property, was purchased from the heirs of Jacob E. Baker for $10,250 in 1922.

Early in 1992 the property known as Noble's Travel World (formerly the Greyhound bus station) at 16 N. Braddock Street was offered for sale at $387,000. The congregation approved the purchase on May 10, 1992. The facility was renovated in the summer of 1993 and dedicated as the Children's Education Center (CEC).

Even with fully remodeled facilities in the CEC the congregation realized a continuing need for space to accommodate Christian Education programming and community outreach activities. The congregation on June 11, 2000, approved the purchase of the G&M Music Building at 38 W. Boscawen Street for $289,000.

Evolution of the Present Church.

The purchase of the Boscawen Street property in 1839 led to the building three years later of what is now the original unit of the present edifice. That unit was plain and simple. When it was built the congregation had not fully made up its mind to leave the old church as a place of worship. Many still thought in terms of a lecture room, and as a matter of fact it was that type of building that was planned at first.

From a report submitted by the trustees to the congregation, September 18, 1845, we obtain the following information of interest:

> A condensed view of debts due and expenses incurred by the Trustees in the erection and finishing of the New Church –
>
> To wit: The undersigned, appointed Trustees on the 23rd of Nov. 1840, for the purpose of holding in trust and improving a lot at that time purchased by the Lutheran Congregation on Water Street, deem it proper to report for the information of the Congregation - That they have from time to time, since the above date, received from individuals and otherwise, to be applied to the payment of lot & improvements, the sum of $4,092.30; That they have received from the Bank of the Valley $2,500, money borrowed; making the total amt. received from all sources $6,592.30; and that they have paid for the congregation for the purchase of the Lot on

Water Street $1,104.50; for building church and improving the Lot $4,764.15; for interest on loan at the Bank $502.65; for insurance of church against fire $21; for reducing the Bank debt $200 - making in all a like sum of $6,592.30. It will be seen by the congregation there is yet due to the Bank of the Valley $2,300, being a part of the debt contracted in Bank by your Trustees and secured under the Trust as a loan upon the Church and Lot. Your committee would respectfully urge at this time the adoption of some plan more efficient than any heretofore pursued for the reduction of this debt. The committee refer the congregation to the accounts of the Treasurer Thos. B. Campbell's Books for the particulars of the above statement, all of which is

respectfully submitted by
Jacob Baker
J.W. Miller
Thomas B. Campbell
and Jos. Slagle.

The Renovation of 1850.

In 1850 portico and cupola were added to the building. The bell from the old church steeple was removed to the cupola. New lights were installed, the interior was frescoed, and a new organ purchased. The cost of these noteworthy improvements is detailed in the following report of the Improvement Committee, submitted March 3, 1851.

Amt. expended during the summer of 1850 in erecting a Cupola, refitting & procuring an Organ.

To Cash paid for Lumber	$224.93
" " " " Drayage	4.00
" " " " Oil Painting	110.00
" " " " Fresco Painting	211.80
" " " " Repairing Blinds	22.00
" " " " Carpenter's Work	523.87
" " " " Lamps, Tables & Chairs	275.95
" " " " Furnaces etc.	105.62
" " " " Brick & masonry	29.75
" " " " Tinning	46.44
" " " " Plastering	5.00
" " " " Baker & Brown	34.33
" " " " Spire etc.	11.00

"	"	"	"	Wm. Miller & Sons	336.30
"	"	"	"	Collection boxes	5.00
"	"	"	"	Settees for gallery	20.00
					$1965.99
"	"	"	"	Organ	1000.00
					$2965.99

CR.

By Amt. paid on subscriptions	$383.50
" sale of 2 stoves	19.00
" Proceeds of Ladies fair, $835,)	
of which $400 was directed to be)	
paid on Organ, as below)	435.00
notes discounted)	1128.49
	$1965.99
By Amt. from Organ sub.	281.50
" " " Ladies Fair	400.00
" " " Notes disct.	318.50
	1000.00
	$2965.99

Your committee have at this time in the Bank of the Valley two notes unpaid one for $1150 – on general improvement acct., the other for $300 on organ acct. All which is respectfully submitted
February 3, 1851   Wm. Miller   )
T.B. Campbell, Treasurer   Jacob Baker   ) Committee
                              T.B. Campbell)

Three thousand dollars worth of insurance was carried on the building, including the organ and furniture.

The lamps, discarded when new lights were procured, were given to Hebron Lutheran Church, Capon Lake. Necessity during the Civil War forced a return from gaslights to coal oil lamps. At war's close, fourteen coal oil lamps were given to the Strasburg congregation.

Outside shutters were added in 1853 and the sliding doors between the two basement rooms were installed.

In September 1855, the committee appointed to have gas lighting installed reported that $175 had been subscribed toward defraying the expense and that "the chandeliers would probably be in readiness by the time the gas works are started."

The ornamental iron fence, seen in the picture of the church with cupola and portico, was not erected until 1870. It was made and put up by the Snapp Foundry of Winchester at a cost of $500.

Sycamore trees, predecessors of the ones now standing in front of the church property, are reported there in 1871.

The Renovation of 1876.

The renovation of 1876 resulted in building the present church tower and steeple. It meant also adding to the height of the walls and placing a new ceiling and roof over the whole structure.

The report of the building committee is herewith submitted in full:

> The undersigned, who were appointed by you in February, 1875, as a Building Committee to make such alterations and improvements of, and additions to, the old Church as in their judgment were best adapted to give it a modern, architectural and attractive appearance, having completed the work assigned to them, now submit the following statement of the receipts of money subscribed and borrowed, of the principal items for which it was expended, and of the total cost of the improvements; as follows –

>   Receipts
> Amt. rec'd from the subscription list of 1875 $ 3186.00
>   "   "   "   "   Ladies Societies   1075.00
>   "   "   "   "   Will Try Society   30.00
>   " borrowed of the Shenandoah Valley N. Bk.   4000.00
>   " rec'd from cash subscriptions on Dedication Day 1466.86
>   "   "   "   monthly pledges   123.45
>   ─────────
> Total amount of money received by the Committee $9881.31

Expenditures

For the Architect's plans	$ 130.00
" " Bricks & brick work	2555.20
" " Granite work	379.50
" " Carpenter's work, exclusive of the spire	1760.70
" " Galvanized iron work	449.60
" " Tin roof and plank for it	435.00
" " Spire complete	1060.00
" " Lumber, exclusive of spire	499.13
" " Hardware, iron & iron work	234.20
" " Plasterers' work	522.17
" " Frescoing	250.00
" " Paints and painting	513.75
" " Stained glass windows & wire frames	517.94
" " Chandeliers & gas fixtures	307.52
" " Furnaces complete	200.00
" " Carpets & upholstering	267.50
" " Railroad freights	154.50
" " Repairing & tuning organ	127.65
" " Insurance (carpenter's risk)	46.00
" " Interest on loans	180.32
" " Labor & sundries	121.91
" " Pulpit Furniture	180.00
Total cost of the improvements	$10892.59

$1011.28 of this cost remains unpaid, which, with the debt of $4000 due to the Shenandoah Valley Nat. Bank, is provided for, in part, from the following sources, viz:

Amt. due on the Subscription list of 1875	$ 80.00
" " " cash subs. on Dedication Day	278.00
" " " monthly pledges	2043.75
" promised by sundry persons, but not in writing	100.00
" in the Treasurer's hand	73.28
Total amt.	$ 2575.03

The balance of the debt, $2436.25, the Committee have confident reason to believe will be further largely reduced during this and next year, through the energetic efforts of the Ladies Sewing Society, and of other friends.

We would do violence to our feelings did we not here express our gratitude, and return our thanks to the ladies of the Sewing and Mite

Societies, not only for the large amount they have contributed to the building fund, but also for the prompt aid and encouragement rendered by them and by other ladies of the congregation in many other ways; and it is no exaggeration to say that the *complete success* of the enterprise was due in no small degree to the deep interest and hearty earnestness they manifested throughout the progress of the work.

Respectfully reported,
W.B. Baker
C.F. Eichelberger
F.A. Ohrenschall   Committee
E. Hoffman
H. Baetjer
A.P. Miller

The Renovation of 1901.

The cost of the enlargement of the church and its renovation in 1901 were detailed in the final report of the committee appointed to superintend that operation. Here is the report:

To the Council:
Your Building Committee beg to submit the following report.

Receipts

By cash from Colored Church, old pulpit	$25.00
" " " Subscriptions	3,885.47
" " " Dedication Collection	187.53
" " " G.C. Miller, recording deed	2.25
" " " J.L. Maphis, old brick	.25
" " " Old Lumber, sold various parties	38.90
" " " Timber Ridge Church, on pews	25.00
" " " cr. For One Old Furnace	25.00
" " " Stone sold, J.W. Seabright	39.25
" " " Stone sold, J. Stephenson	1.95
" " " G.G. Baker, for Hymn Board	7.40
" " " L.F. Cooper, on loan	3650.00
Total	$7888.00

Expenditures

To cash paid Luther Stull, for excavating	$ 72.38
" " " J.W. Seabright & extra work	870.46
" " " McKim Diffenderfer, contract & extra labor	1647.72
" " " J.S. Solenberger & Co., heater etc	1266.33

" " "	F.H. Jackson, architect fee	159.95
" " "	D.M. Anderson & Co., wiring & part electric fixtures	553.00
" " "	W.G.&E.L.Co., running wire	16.00
" " "	Copenhaver & Grim, plastering	331.00
" " "	Chas. Emel, stucco work	71.66
" " "	Emmart & Quartley, frescoing	642.92
" " "	Quaker City Stained Glass Works	85.00
" " "	J.K. Lewis, painting	252.09
" " "	G.C. Snyder & Co., reredos etc.	167.98
" " "	J.C. Knipp & Bro., lectern	90.00
To cash paid Glaize & Bro., lumber		$ 237.24
" " "	Manitowoc Seating Works, on acct.	236.10
" " "	J.G. Wilson for rolling partition	129.00
" " "	Glass for lecture room	31.69
" " "	F.R. Snapp, columns lecture room	55.97
" " "	C.W. Allemong	30.53
" " "	Wainscotting lecture room	37.12
" " "	Cement (sub-cellar)	22.48
" " "	Scaffolding	21.62
" " "	E.W. Church, hymn books & grill work	22.00
" " "	J.W. Taylor, cleaning church & laying carpet	42.70
" " "	O.P. Grove, work on roof & ventilators	29.85
" " "	J.H. Snyder, repairs & part electric fixtures	117.49
" " "	H. Baetjer & Co., carpets	379.35
" " "	J.B. Russell & Bro., carpets & blinds	20.93
" " "	Miscellaneous articles [combined by editor]	193.73
Balance, cash on Hand		53.71

    Total $ 7888.00

Cost of Improvement

To cash paid as above itemized	$ 7834.29
" cost of lot	1100.00
Due Manitowoc Seating Works for pews	763.90
Due M.P. Möller, on Organ	55.00
	$ 9753.19

Deduct

Cash received for old material sold	$151.35	
" " from G.C. Miller for recording deed	95.20	

Due from City of Winchester for building line fence	5.00	253.80
		$ 9499.39
Indebtedness		
To W.V. Hodges, note dated Sept. 15, 1900 @ 5%		$ 1100.00
" cash borrowed from L.F. Cooper – 5%		3650.00
Unpaid bills		818.90
		$ 5568.90
Deduct		
Uncollected subscriptions	$1425.00	
Note of A.M.E. Church for old pews	67.70	
Due from Timber Ridge Church on pews	27.50	
" " City of Winchester on fence	5.00	
Cash on hand	53.71	1578.91
Total Indebtedness unprovided for		$ 3989.99

Material on Hand

Lot old frames & sash
Two chandeliers & other gas fixtures
Two chenille curtains & fixtures
Lot old brick
Glass partition
Lot old carpet, cocoa matting & old iron fence
One old furnace

      Respectfully submitted,
       J.L. Maphis
        Sec. & Treas.

Approved
 T.J. Cooper, chairman
 John K. Lewis
 Geo. H. Heist   Winchester, Virginia
 Henry Baetjer   June 10, 1901
 H.K. Green

After the services rededicating the church were held, *The Winchester Evening Star* of May 27, 1901, reported the occasion and described the church, as follows:

With the exception of recesses for dinner and supper, the services were almost continuous, and with the most impressive ceremony, the edifice was solemnly consecrated anew to the worship of the Triune God. The sweet songs and the profound services were inspiring, and the unusual spectacle of an entire congregation pledging themselves anew to the work of the Master, was affecting to a high degree.

The remodeled church was bright and animated. Relieved of any accusation of somberness by the mani-colored windows, the many and harmonious mural decorations and the general cheerful appearance of a well appointed House of God, it was further enhanced by the very large congregation, especially at the morning services. First there was the Young Peoples Prayer Meeting Service, conducted by Mr. John K. Lewis, while Mr. George Bushnell had charge of the singing. This occurred at 9:30 o'clock, and was followed at 11 o'clock by the dedication proper.

Rev. W.L. Seabrook, the pastor, had charge, and during the services paid a high compliment to the Building Committee for their untiring zeal and self-sacrifice. Rev. Taylor Yeakley read the scripture lessons bearing upon the consecration, and at the conclusion of the consecration, Rev. Dr. D.M. Gilbert, pastor of the Lutheran Church at Harrisburg, preached a very earnest dedicatory sermon from II Chronicles VI:18. Rev. J.E. Bushnell, D.D., offered up the prayer and after the congregation had sung the doxology, Rev. J.W. Strickler, pronounced the benediction.

At 2:30 o'clock in the afternoon, the Sunday School met in the school room, and at 3 o'clock proceeded to the auditorium, where they held special services. Rev. J.W. Strickler and Rev. Dr. Bushnell made special addresses. At night the services concluded with vespers and a sermon by Rev. Dr. Gilbert.

The remodeled church edifice in its altar and reredos was planned to conform with the historic Lutheran form of church buildings....

In the basement is the lecture room, remodeled by an inclined floor, giving an increased height of ceiling and in the rear of this is the council chamber and other retiring rooms.

The main auditorium is reached from West Water Street by a wide staircase of stone steps to the vestibule extending the width of the church. There are three aisles reaching to the chancel, the center one being five feet in width and side-aisles two and one-half feet each in width.

The approach to the pulpit platform of the altar is through the broken chancel rail and up three steps. The altar furnishings are of antique oak and the altar itself is thirty-three inches in height and five and one-half feet long. The reredos extends across the entire rear of the platform, about ten feet and is nine feet in height. The reredos is unlike any other in any church and was especially designed by Architect F.H. Jackson for Grace Church. The center pinnacle of the reredos is a sunburst with cross and the letters IHS in red with a cross of blue. On each side of the panels of the reredos are the letters Alpha and Omega, the first and the last. The pulpit is an octagon to the right of the center steps and on the left is the eagle lectern.

The general architectural style of the remodeled structure is Gothic combined with Romanesque in that a central arch spans the pulpit platform and on either side of this are arches of less width forming triple arches, spanned by an immense single arch stretching across the entire width of the edifice. To the arch at the left (west) is the large pipe organ and choir loft, and to the right (east) is the infant baptistery.

The frescoing is one of the most beautiful features of the remodeling, and its ornate and tasteful designs are unlike anything known in church mural decoration. The groundwork is olive green, and around the cove running into the ceiling the ecclesiastical symbol is carried out in the entire arrangement and in perfect taste. The Luther coat-of-arms in red, blue, white and gold is three times repeated, above and on either side of the center arch above the pulpit platform. The rose is carried around the cove alternating with panels, in one of which is a shell and palms and in the other a cross. Above the side arches in gold are the symbols of the Trinity, the triangle and three united circles.

The newspaper story went on to tell how the seating capacity was 500, how the pews were of the latest form and how the main floor was covered with red carpet, while the vestibule had green carpet. The steam plant, with direct and indirect radiation, was so constructed as always to insure fresh air. Brilliantly lighted by electricity, there were fifty incandescent lights on either side of the cove, ten more behind the center arch and still more against the walls in brass brackets. Both gas and electricity were used to light the Sunday School beneath. It was there that the congregation worshipped while the renovation was taking place.

Since the renovation of 1901, none but minor changes have been made to the building [1953]. The fire of 1902 necessitated repairing and repainting the damages. When the present organ [1953] was installed in 1914, it was placed on the east side of the chancel instead of on the west, where its predecessor had been. The installation of the Brevitt Chime led to the present gallery arrangement. And the new windows, provided by the Wall bequest, changed simply the appearance of things. So, too, the renovation of 1951, wherein the chancel was enlarged, and a dossal hung over the altar, and a needed, refurbished, new look given to the interior. Yet in all of this, nothing of the essential structure of the building has been changed from its reconstruction of more than fifty years ago [1953].

The Renovation of 1951.

The renovation of 1951, done at a cost of $13,726, included numerous items. New electric wiring was installed throughout. New light fixtures were placed in the narthex and church proper. Rock wool insulation was placed over the ceiling. The west choir loft and the chancel were enlarged by extending them forward, and the pulpit moved to the former east choir loft. The main floor was refinished and cork tile laid on the narthex floor. The narthex doors were upholstered in red plastic. Walls and ceiling were scraped and painted. New red carpet was laid in the chancel and aisles. And a red and gold dossal was hung above the altar.

This work was carried out by a committee composed of Frederick M. Ritter, chairman, Walter H. Bosserman, Jr., Dr. R. Fred Cline, Harry A. Schmidt and William E. Stine.

Sanctuary Building Upgrades.

Normally the repainting of property is a current expense operation and not a capital funds investment. The current expense treasury was in stringent circumstances in the spring of 1964, and the Council authorized the raising of funds before the work would be done. The Seaber Art and Decorating Company of Westernport, Maryland, had painted the sanctuary in 1951. On this occasion the company reduced its original bid from $2485, to $2,135, when it obtained a contract to paint the Market Street Methodist Church. In order to take advantage of an open period (August 1-15) and reduction in bid, the Council, at a called meeting July 19, 1964, authorized the work to go forward. Regular church services on August 9 and 16 were held in the fellowship hall of the Education Building. Re-gilding of the organ pipes was done at an additional cost of $90. Extra charges for repairs to the plaster and incidentals amounted to $89, making the total cost $2,314. Clarence Swisher was authorized to paint the outside window frames and doors at a cost of $75. The sanctuary was painted again in 1976. The narthex was painted in 1975 and carpeted in 1978 by The Floor Shop. The nave was carpeted in 1975. Art Leaded Glass Company covered the stained glass windows with Lexon in 1980 and along with the cost of the Luxlite coverings in the Education Building the cost was $9,300.

Responding to a general awareness of the need to make the facility handicap accessible, Church Council proposed that a 4 foot x 3 foot residential elevator be purchased, the cost not to exceed $28,000. This plan was soundly defeated on December 13, 1981. In the fall of 1985, Council again considered either a pair of chairlifts or a custom-built miniature elevator. The chairlift option was approved on December 15, 1985, at a cost of $7,595. Thanks to the leadership of Roger Milburn and contributions of many caring persons, this service became available in May 1986 to allow those who were previously unable to now join in worship and fellowship.

The steeple tower required extensive work to repair slate and paint the wood in 1971. The American Rigging Service of Edgewater, Maryland, completed the job in November at a cost of $1,955. Expenses were paid out of contributions to a special maintenance fund. Replacing broken slate, painting the flashing and adding bird repellant comprised the 1979 repairs to the steeple. Repair, painting and bird deterrent was done again in December 1996 by John Robinson. A new standing-seam metal roof was authorized in 1959 at $3,000. The roof was repaired in 1987 and currently is well maintained.

Howard Shockey and Sons sandblasted the peeling yellow paint from the exterior brick of the sanctuary building in 1974. John Robinson siliconized the brick in 1978 and was given a contract in 1996 to seal/waterproof the entire brick surface of the sanctuary building and portions of the Ad/Ed Building. His price of $36,650 included the 1996 steeple repairs.

The sidewalk bricks were dug up and re-laid as an Eagle Scout project by Chuck Swartz in 1977. Carroll Construction repaired the concrete sidewalk, rebuilt the steps to the Ad/Ed Building and repaired the decorative masonry to the Ad/Ed Building in 1996.

The South Loudoun Street Parsonage.

The purchase of the residence at the northeast corner of Loudoun and Cecil Streets for a parsonage has already been related under the pastorate of Charles Porterfield Krauth [1848-1855]. The property, a brick residence owned by George W. Seever, was bought for $3,000 in the spring of 1851. Messrs. William Miller, Jacob Baker, Thomas B. Campbell, Wm. B. Miller and Wm. B. Baker were appointed trustees on the part of the congregation, and the deed was ordered to be made out to them. Gaslights were installed in 1856.

As a parsonage it was occupied by the Krauths, Essicks, Baums, Doshes and Gilberts. After Virginia joined the Confederate States and the Baum family returned to Pennsylvania, the building was rented. Mrs. G.W. Ward was the tenant for one year beginning in April 1864, and it was rented to Dr. W.A. Bradford for one year, beginning May 1865.

Just when Pastor and Mrs. Dosh moved into the parsonage is not clear. The minutes say nothing further about renting the home. The building received a thoroughgoing renovation in 1870, and it is certain the Doshes were living there that year. Additional repairs were made in 1872 upon the expected arrival of the Gilbert family.

The trustees conveyed this property by deed to Charles B. Hancock, March 10, 1888. The home is still standing [at 320 S. Loudoun Street].

The North Cameron Street Parsonage.

This property, located on the east side of the street between those of A.H. Miller on the north, and F.W.M. Holliday on the south, originally extended through the block to Kent Street. The house, a brick residence, was owned by C.B. Hancock, and before that by a Mrs. Tuley. Mr. Hancock owed $3,000 on the property.

By a contract made January 16, 1888, between Trustee W.B. Baker and Mr. Hancock, it was agreed to exchange the above mentioned property for the South Loudoun Street Parsonage, the church to assume the $3,000 indebtedness. This transaction was approved by the Council February 8, and it was consummated March 10 with the exchange of deeds, Charles B. Hancock and wife conveying the Cameron Street property to the trustees of the church, and they in turn conveying the deed to the Loudoun Street property, and in addition, giving a deed of trust for $3,000.

This residence became the third parsonage owned by the congregation. Here the family of Dr. L.G.M. Miller lived, followed by the Seabrook family. Because of various and sundry needed repairs, the Seabrooks moved out and lived on West Piccadilly Street in the residence beside the Jack Hotel. The parsonage in turn was rented for about four years, the Misses Briggs being the occupants prior to Dr. Bowers' arrival in Winchester.

In order to raise funds with which to pay for needed extensive repairs, the Kent Street end of the property was sold to Fred A. Graichen and Carrie D. Graichen. This plot of ground, having a 56-foot frontage and a 110 foot depth, was deeded by the trustees to the buyers, February 10, 1902, for a consideration of $535. Further extensive repairs were made in 1911.

The Bowers, the Kelly and the Freed families likewise lived in the Cameron Street parsonage during their respective sojourns in Winchester. The Thomases also resided there until the Stewart Street parsonage was ready for occupancy.

Buildings and Properties

The parsonage at 126 N. Cameron Street.

The offer of Hansbrough and Carter of $20,000 for this property was reported to the Council by Capt. Lewis F. Cooper on April 28, 1930. The Council countered with a $25,000 proposition, which it later withdrew in order to recommend to the congregation that the first offer be accepted. At a congregational meeting, June 22, acceptance was authorized. Five days later the sale was made.

The Northern Virginia Power Company was the purchaser through the agency of Hansbrough and Carter. The residence was torn down and in its place the present [1953] line and service department building was erected.

In July 1971 the trustees of the church were asked to sign a quitclaim deed to the Potomac Edison Power Company (formerly the Northern Virginia Power Company) regarding the alley immediately in the rear of the power company property leading to Kent Street and north of the power company substation. At the time the North Cameron Street property was sold no one realized that the church still owned fee simple title to the strip of land used as an alley by both the church parsonage and the power company. The deed dated March 14, 1931, conveyed only the property from Cameron Street east to the rear of the power company lot. The congregation rejected an offer of $200 from the power company. The power company rejected a request of $1,000 by the congregation. The congregation later accepted the offer of $200.

The Sunday School Building.

Under the pastorate of A.A. Kelly the story of the building of the Sunday School has been delineated. Additional details may be given, however, concerning its dedication.

Dedicatory services were held March 29, 1925. At 9:40 a.m. a procession entered the new building singing "Onward Christian Soldiers," with Superintendents E.B. Cooper and Carl R. Ritter in the lead. The program that followed included representation from the Cradle Roll, motion exercises and song by the Beginners Department and exercises by the Primary Department. A song was sung by the Men's Bible Class. Then came two five-minute addresses, the first by the Rev. C. Brown Cox, D.D., President of the Lutheran Synod of Virginia. Dr. D. Burt Smith, Associate Editor of *Sunday School Literature*, was the second speaker. And so the day got off to a good start with 500 persons reported present at this service.

At the 11 o'clock service Rev. Luther B. Hafer, supply pastor, presided over the gathering of subscriptions and offerings, which seems to have been the chief point of emphasis. He and Capt. Lewis F. Cooper addressed the congregation on matters financial.

The service of dedication proper took place at 2:30 in the afternoon. Dr. Cox performed the act of dedication and delivered the address of the occasion. In the evening at 7:30 Editor

Smith brought the message, bringing to a conclusion the ceremonies of the day.

Members of the committee in charge were:	
W.H. Bosserman	Chairman
Rev. Norman E. Cooper	Secretary
Lewis F. Cooper	Chairman Building Committee
G. Casper Fries)	
Dr. J.A. Richard)	
H.A. Schmidt)	Members Building Committee
W.H. Bosserman)	
Eugene B. Cooper)	
Carl R. Ritter)	Superintendents
Lake J. Frazier, Esq.	Publicity
Howard K. Grove	Representing the Men's Class
Miss Kate Miller	Representing the Primary Department
Mrs. J.A. Richard	Representing the Home Department
Miss Grace Forney	Representing the Cradle Roll
Mrs. Harry C. Stouffer	Representing the Choir
Miss Jennie Green	Representing the Young Peoples' Society
Miss Grace Carpenter	Representing the Senior Luther League
Rev. Luther B. Hafer	Supply Pastor

The Sunday School Building Renovation 1961.

A growing need for more adequate facilities for the 200 and more baptized children of the parish led to a special meeting May 15, 1958, where the congregation voted unanimously to reconstruct the Sunday School Building established in 1924. After spirited debate an additional resolution proposed by Robert K. Woltz was also unanimously adopted: "That 35 percent of the estimated cost of renovation be obtained in cash and pledges and that not less than 25 percent of such cost shall be in cash before a construction contract shall be let." The original motion was given in the June 1958 issue of the new parish newsletter, *Tidings*:

That the congregation approve the reconstruction of the Sunday School

Building with the appointment of the following committees:

(1) A Building Committee of 5 members whose duty it shall be to employ an architect, employ a contractor, and supervise the general reconstruction of the building.

(2) A Ways and Means Committee of 5 members whose duty it shall be to plan an initial solicitation of all members of the congregation in an effort to raise $35,000 within a 12-month period, and to submit to the congregation a plan for financing the balance needed.

(3) A Steering Committee, composed of the Chairman of the Building Committee, the Chairman of the Ways and Means Committee and a third member to be Chairman of this Committee, which Committee shall have as its duty the coordination of the whole program.

W. Carlisle Fisher was appointed chairman of the Steering Committee, L. Marshall Castleman chairman of the Building Committee, and Robert K. Woltz chairman of the Ways and Means Committee. Several local churches had chosen to hire a professional fundraiser for such a project but this plan was rejected. An appeal to the congregation, separate from the annual budget appeal, based on pledges payable over a three-year period in twelve quarterly installments had a goal of $100,000.

Milton Grigg, who had designed the Parish House of Christ Episcopal Church and the Braddock Street Methodist Church, was employed as architect. Outstanding and dedicated leaders of twelve groups of were organized by M.K. Aulick to solicit funds. The gifts of four building lots near James Wood High School on Amherst Street donated by Branson P. Myers and two lots on the Shenandoah River donated by Mr. and Mrs. B.L. Megeath boosted the amount subscribed by members of the congregation. Upon his death in November 1960, Charles W. Fries left $33,000 to the congregation for the renovation. His father, G. Casper Fries, had contributed $25,000 to the construction of the first Sunday School Building in 1924.

Initial floor plans were adjusted and the ground floor of the church building was included in the renovation to allow for more classroom space. The cost estimate of $165,000 was accepted by the congregation on March 22, 1961. An entire new heating plant and furnishings were included but a suggestion for air conditioning was deemed too prohibitive in price. The Farmers and Merchants Bank was willing to lend the congregation $100,000 at the rate of five percent on unsecured notes.

The work of reconstructing the educational plant of Grace Church began Monday, May 8, by workmen from the contracting firm of Howard Shockey and Sons. During the preceding week all equipment in the building had been removed. Following the eleven o'clock church service on May 7 the congregation followed the choir in recessional from the church sanctuary into the bare Sunday School auditorium and members of the Building Committee each struck a blow with a sledge hammer, the counterpart of a groundbreaking ceremony.

During the months required for reconstruction, the Sunday School departments met in temporary quarters: Nursery, G&M Storeroom, first floor, 9 S. Braddock St.; Kindergarten, Bell Building, second floor, 27 W. Boscawen St.; Primary and Junior Departments, Rouss Fire Hall, second floor; Intermediate and Senior Young Peoples, Godfrey Miller Home, first floor, 28 S. Loudoun St.; Adult Department in church sanctuary. The church office was operated from the parsonage.

In May 1961 Richard Lucas headed an appeal to members of the congregation who had not yet made a subscription to the Sunday School Building Fund Drive. Contributions kept pace with the work of the renovation crews throughout the summer and fall. Winchester Electric Company received the electrical work contract. The firm of Miller and Anderson put in the new heating plant. Classes resumed in their new quarters in January 1962.

In addition to newly organized classrooms, office space, choir rehearsal room, kitchen and fellowship hall, a new parlor and library were created. By action of the Church Council at its July 1961 meeting, approval was given to the recommendation from the Building Committee that the new church parlor be known as the Christian Streit Room. The new room occupied the former nursery room facing Boscawen Street on the main floor of the Sunday School Building. The new church library occupied the former church office adjacent to this room. A description of the new parlor was given in the February 1962 issue of *Tidings*.

> The Christian Streit Room, the new church parlor and general meeting room for the Church Council and other groups up to twenty-five persons, is practically finished. Its pegged oak floor of boards of varying widths is interesting and lovely. Done in an Early American style, the room has a chair rail around the walls and a wooden mold on the edges of the ceiling. Draperies for the windows are being made by Mrs. J.A. Hott and Mrs. Ralph Boyce. Through the generosity of Mr. and Mrs. Ralph A. Cain, the entire room will be furnished with maple furnishings— tables, sofas and chairs. Mementos of the Streit family are being assembled, as well as those pertaining to the early years of the congregation's life, and will be used as decorations for the walls.

Three prominent ministers of the United Lutheran Church were invited for the dedication of the Parish School Building. Dr. Henry H. Bagger, Philadelphia, preached at the 11:00 a.m. service on March 4. Dr. Bagger had been president of the Philadelphia Seminary for the past ten years and was a former president of the Pittsburgh Synod. In the afternoon at 3:00 p.m. the act of dedication and the address of the occasion was brought by the president of the Lutheran Synod of Virginia, Dr. J. Luther Mauney. All who attended enjoyed an inspection of the new facilities and a reception in the fellowship hall. Mr. James Christian Streit, donor of the portrait of his great grandfather, which was hung in a place of honor in the Christian Streit Room, along with his wife and other guests, were in the receiving line.

On Monday evening, March 5, Dr. Theodore George Shuey was scheduled to speak. Those arriving to begin meal preparations were met with 43 cartons of new green-bordered dishes that needed to be unpacked and washed. About mid-morning the dish wipers reported that it had begun to snow and conditions worsened considerably during the afternoon. Preparations had gone too far and the meal was not cancelled. Since Dr. Shuey was snowbound at his home in Staunton, Virginia, Mrs. John Fosbrink, visiting from North Carolina, agreed to give the address. On the roughest night of the winter, 185 persons enjoyed the delicious baked ham and musical program which celebrated the execution of the entire reconstruction program.

Education Building Upgrades.

Reflecting greater outreach activities, the Sunday School Building became known as the Parish School Building in 1962. Before long the facility was called the Education Building, and today it is referred to as the Administrative/Education (Ad/Ed) Building.

With the coming of Pastor Moyer in 1968, new shelving and carpet were provided for the pastor's study and a new rug was put in the Christian Streit Room. The hiring of Assistant Pastor Morrill in 1972 required partitioning the kindergarten classroom to provide an office for the senior pastor. The Church Property Committee conducted surveys in 1969 and 1972 to prioritize needs for the upkeep of the Education Building. The entrance was painted in 1975. Paint and new drapes were furnished to the Christian Streit Room.

According to the October 1969 issue of *Tidings*, approval was given to air condition the church nave and the first and second floors of the Education Building by congregational vote on June 29, 1969. At this same meeting, the congregation instructed the Council to investigate the possibility

Buildings and Properties

of adding the two ground floors to the system. Bids from four firms were received, but the approach to the system, the capacity of the system and the costs involved were so varied that the Council did not feel competent to make a decision on this matter. Contacts with the Potomac Edison Power Company and Shenandoah Gas Company helped to clarify the situation somewhat, but serious questions were still unresolved about the proper design of the system.

The Church Council recommended that approval be given to employing an engineering firm as a consultant on the air conditioning of the church buildings in order that the design, capacity, installation and operation of the air conditioning system might be properly cared for. The services of Sowers, Rodes and Whitescarver of Roanoke, Virginia, were provided in two stages. The first step was the development of a preliminary scheme for air conditioning all parts of the church with cost estimates of the system included. This first stage cost approximately $1,500. The second step was the development of the working drawings, specifications, securing the bids and supervision of installation. The second stage cost $3,500.

Robert F. Zeigler Air Conditioning Specialists was awarded the contract in 1969, with an anticipated completion date of late spring 1970. Numerous delays were frustrating and had a detrimental effect on the efforts to secure financial gifts toward this project. A final payment was made in December 1970, and the total cost was $52,400. In June 1972 the air conditioning loan balance was carried by the Godfrey Miller Home loan.

A vigorous plan of remodeling began in January 1978 when the fellowship hall was renamed Eisenberg Hall to honor our former pastor during the 225th Anniversary year. Donald Dennis was contracted for paint, chair rail and vinyl wallpaper for $1,275. Melvin Aikens refurbished the tile floor for $3000. Also in 1978, Anderson Sheet Metal put on a new roof, and the plaster was repaired throughout the building.

More painting occurred on the first floor during 1979 and the stair area between the church library and the narthex was floored over to provide coatroom space. In 1980 all windows in the Education Building were given protective covers. Fluorescent lights were installed throughout and the hallways and offices on the first floor were carpeted. Solid sound barrier walls were added in the choir room. The masonry cross on the roof was deemed unstable and was repaired by John Robinson in 1982.

The Redesign and Remodeling Task Group initiated plans in 1993 for a renovation plan in three phases: Phase 1—CEC, Phase 2—Sanctuary, Phase 3—Ad/Ed Building. Phase 1 was completed in 1993 and Phase 2 in 1994. Concerns for funding and the subsequent purchase of the G&M Building in 1999 left the Ad/Ed Building remodeling on hold. In 1995 the Church Property Committee brought forward several major repairs that could not wait. Under the leadership of Chairman Hal Lehman, the projects came in under the budgeted amounts that were given congregational approval on June 25, 1995. The Board of Architectural Review allowed Wine-Stillwell to replace the deteriorating slate roof of the Ad/Ed Building with a standing-seam metal roof to match the sanctuary building. The cost was $18,875. R.F. Zeigler provided a new gas boiler for $16,200. At the end of 1996, the outside masonry work had been completed as part of the contract with John Robinson.

The South Stewart Street Parsonage.

The site of the present parsonage, as has been noted previously, was given to the congregation by Misses Margaretta and Marianna Miller. A note of appreciation, dated July 7, 1930, was sent to the donors. It reads:

> Dear Misses Miller:
> On behalf of Grace Evangelical Lutheran congregation we desire to extend to you our deep appreciation for the generous and magnificent gift of the lot on Stewart Street for the erection of the new parsonage. The value of this gift is magnified many times when we recall the lifelong love and devotion of your father and mother and sister Emma for Grace Lutheran Church and congregation, and the deep spiritual impress they left by their Christian lives, not only on our congregation and Sunday School, but upon our city.
>
> Very sincerely yours,
> Trustees – J. Geo. Baetjer, Lewis F. Cooper, Dr. A.D. Henkel
> Church Council – J. Few Brown, Geo. R. Theis, W.H. Bosserman, Fred Thwaite, C.K. Over, Lewis F. Cooper, Dr. J.A. Richard, Joseph Miller, H.A. Schmidt, J. George Baetjer, Chas. W. Fries, C.M. Smith, Elmer Lamp, Dr. Geo. H. Heist, O.C. Cassell, Curtis Bowers.
> Pastor – L.A. Thomas
> Grace Evangelical Lutheran Congregation.

Deed to the lot was presented to Dr. Thomas by Walter H. Bosserman in December, and after it had been read to the Council by the secretary, the pastor turned it over to the trustees. The deed was dated December 9, 1930, and was executed December 13. It gave to the congregation the right to dispose of the property at any time it might see fit. The trustees, in the name of the congregation, duly acknowledged receipt of the same.

Capt. Lewis F. Cooper reported on the construction of the new parsonage, April 27, 1931. He declared:

> As treasurer of the old parsonage fund I feel it proper that I should make a preliminary report on the new parsonage. The building is practically completed...I can give the cost of the same in so far as I have in hand the bills that have been presented. I regret to say that the money so far expended has run far ahead of any estimate.... I have now paid out $17,551.82, and there is in the bank to our credit $2,628.56. I can surmise that when all is paid it will run to, and likely over, $18,000, especially if we keep on adding expenses. I feel that in justice to an expecting congregation we should now at once set aside out of the original old parsonage fund the sum of $2,000...to be applied on the Sunday School debt. [Council adopted the proposal.]

The following minority report, however, was presented by those who disagreed.

> We are entirely in accord with Mr. Cooper and all those who hold that the new parsonage has cost more than it should have cost. And we sincerely regret that such is the case. But the Council will remember that there was a difference of opinion in our committee at the very outset with respect to the choice of the lot on which to build, that the Council was then appealed to, and that it directed the erection of the building where it now stands. It is our belief that no small part of the disappointingly large total cost had its origin in the difficult nature of the ground on which the committee was directed to build, and the expensive necessity of treating the site in such a manner as to secure pleasing results in outside appearances.
>
> And furthermore, additional expense was incurred in doing some things in better ways than were at first contemplated.

This Heritage

The parsonage at 605 S. Stewart Street.

A tile floor on the front porch, instead of wood, is an instance of this; another is the installation of a bath and toilet on the third floor to provide for a servant who might live in the house. And there were additional costs here and there such as are the experiences of almost every builder of a house. In many of these things the committee was unanimous in its decisions; in others its decisions were those of a substantial majority.

We think it would be better to finish the small part of the work remaining to be done and that is now in progress, before making any payment on the church debt. And then, after paying all outstanding bills, to pay over all that may remain. But while holding strongly to this view, we are quite willing to have the desired payment made if the Council will so authorize and direct the Trustees. In that case, however, we feel that our work is in the hands of the Council and we shall respectfully ask that the Committee be dismissed.

Respectfully submitted,
W.H. Bosserman
J.A. Richard
J. Fred Thwaite
Harry A. Schmidt

Pastor and Mrs. Thomas were the first to live in the new parsonage at 605 S. Stewart Street. Others to abide there were C. Worthington Lowe, Pastor and Mrs. Honeycutt and Dr. and Mrs. Eisenberg. The Property Committee studied the needs of the residence in 1967. According to the January 1968 issue of *Tidings,* a generous gift from Mrs. Ella Brown Bauserman, the Buncutter family and the Wade C. Emmart family made a new heating system a reality. Elwood McIntire was contracted to remodel the kitchen. Members of the congregation organized to paint the interior before Pastor and Mrs. Moyer took up residence in July 1968. The day-long painting effort featured a lunch provided by the Lutheran Church Women.

Members contributed to a Parsonage Fund, however, the costs associated with the repairs were beyond the financial resources of the congregation. In response to the congregation's appeal, the Board of Directors of the Godfrey Miller Home made available a $5,000 loan at four and one-half percent interest to cover the remaining costs.

In a little over a year Pastor Moyer informed the Council that he planned to purchase a lot and build a home in the community. A Parsonage Committee of Ralph Yount, Chairman, Wade Emmart and Richard Lucas was established to study the future use of the parsonage and to make recommendations to the Church Council for future action. Upon the advice of local realtors it was deemed advantageous to sell the property and invest the funds to generate money for a parsonage allowance for the pastor. Thus the parsonage was sold to Peter D. Shoemaker for $50,000 on April 13, 1970.

Children's Education Center 1992-1993.

Just as major decisions for the future of the entire physical plant began to take shape in 1992, the trustees were approached with an offer to purchase the property known as Noble's Travel World. Council approved the acquisition of the building and property at 16 N. Braddock Street (north and of back of the church) for $387,000. On Sundays, April 26 and May 3, forums were offered to hear questions and concerns regarding the recommendation. In the May 3, 1992, issue of *Tidings,* Pastors Utt and Fitzsimmons wrote:

> We greet the recommendation of the Congregation Council to purchase the Noble's Travel World building and property with a hearty enthusiasm. We do so knowing the kind of immediate solutions that this acquisition will bring to the problems of needed classroom spaces for our growing children's programs, especially our Sunday Church School. We're simply running out of space! This acquisition will also provide temporary office space during anticipated remodeling of the present office areas. It will also give us some control over our own "space needs" destiny.

A letter from the trustees to the congregation on May 3, 1992, set forth recommendations for financing:

> The trustees have met and decided to recommend to the Congregation Council that the financing for the purchase of the Noble's Travel World building and properties be composed of borrowing from the various funds held currently by the trustees to the maximum extent possible with the remaining needed amount borrowed externally at a negotiated interest rate.
>
> The decision to borrow rather than expend discretionary funds presently held by the trustees was based on the fact that additional time would be needed to properly liquidate current investments if the final decision is to use current trustee monies and, that by taking this approach in the short-term, additional financing opportunities might be available to carry out the recommendations of the Redesign and Remodeling Task Force as ultimately approved by the Congregation.
>
> It is the recommendation of the trustees that discretionary income (interest, designated specifically for this purchase, etc.) received by the trustees be used to pay the debt service on the short-term financing until such time as the congregation has approved the redesign and remodeling program cost and financing.

At a special congregational meeting held on May 10, 1992, the congregation voted unanimously to purchase for $387,000 the building and properties at 16 N. Braddock Street, with financing coming from $200,000 in short-term trustee investments, a $96,000 loan from the Godfrey Miller Home and a $91,000 gift from M.K. Aulick. By July, plans were being made to use the second floor to begin the 1992-1993 Sunday Church School in September. Repairs, adding partitions, plumbing, electrical, painting and carpeting were accomplished during the summer of 1993 as Phase 1 of the Redesign and Remodeling project. General Contractor Howard Shockey and Sons worked with the Construction Oversight Committee: Vera Crawford, Sharon Hetland, Teresa Lehman, Bill VanHorssen, Charles Woodruff and Lee Simpson, Chair. The preschool teachers made considerable effort in getting the classrooms ready for the September opening. Many volunteers gave generously of their time. A dedication ceremony and open house were held on Sunday, September 5, 1993. Final costs relative to the development of the CEC were:

$388,200	Children's Education Center property
107,267	Guaranteed maximum contract price
2,682	Architect fees
4,444	The Floor Shop for tile and carpeting
3,405	Omega Drywall for ceiling tile
8,000	Contingency: fire and smoke detection, roof repair, extra painting and removal of signs
9,820	Exterior wall painting, summer of 1995

The Children's Education Center provided space for expansion of Grace Church Preschool programs, the expansion of Sunday Church School and Vacation Bible School classes and space for more community-based groups such as Cub Scout Pack 1.

Redesign and Remodeling of Sanctuary 1994.

Under the visionary leadership of Pastor James H. Utt, membership growth and program development resulted in the adoption of a new mission statement in 1988. Council appointed a Long-Range Planning Committee charged to develop and recommend a comprehensive five- to ten-year mission and ministry plan with specific goals and objectives. From January 1989 to December 1990, the Long-Range Planning Committee conducted surveys of the congregation, identified values of the congregation and studied the need for expanding programs and facilities to meet membership growth.

In January 1991 the congregation approved the recommended long-range plan, *Heritage for the Future*, containing four goals and twenty-one objectives (See Chapter XII). To implement these goals, Council appointed various task groups. In May 1991 the Redesign and Remodeling (R&R) Task Group, chaired by Jim Diehl, was authorized to develop a plan of renovation to accomplish facility goals regarding worship, education, fellowship and administration.

After defining the scope of its charge from the Council and interviewing several architects, the firm of Clovis Heimsath Architects of Austin, Texas, was recommended by the R&R Task Group and approved by the congregation at the annual report meeting in January 1992. Funding to cover initial fees was also approved. A design workshop conducted by the architects in March 1992 identified these general principles:

> 1. Maintain and enhance the historical character of the facilities, especially the sanctuary.

2. Keep the center axis and up-front focus of the sanctuary, but provide greater room and flexibility in the chancel area.
3. Use the area between the existing buildings to provide better traffic flow and fellowship space.
4. Make better use of present facilities by redesigning interior space especially for classrooms, offices and fellowship areas.
5. Upgrade all facilities, giving attention to meeting latest codes and needs of handicapped individuals (access and bathrooms), adding light, evaluating mechanical systems and generally refurbishing all facility components—roofs, ceilings, walls, windows, doors, fixtures, etc.
6. Give attention to the needs for an expanded narthex, balcony and working sacristy close to the altar area.

As previously told, the property at 16 N. Braddock Street was acquired in 1992 to provide classroom space for children's programming. With the purchase of the new property, the R&R Task Group felt the need to appoint three sub-task groups: Children's Education Center (CEC), Organ and Sanctuary Furnishings and Capital Fund Raising and Stewardship Appeal.

By September 1992 work between the architects and the R&R Task Group, which included the addition of the new CEC, yielded a master floor plan. The congregation gave general approval to this plan with costs being projected at $1.2-1.5 million, not including the purchase cost of the CEC, a new organ, furnishings and fees. A recommendation to proceed with a "negotiated contractor" was approved. After interviews with three contractors, Howard Shockey and Sons was selected, and the Council approved a letter of intent. The congregation approved additional funds for the design and development documents.

In October Council authorized Risk Evaluation and Control to survey the facilities for asbestos. The general contractor began receiving sub-contractor bids and the architect provided initial design and development drawings and elevations. The trustees worked to have Church Alley conveyed to the church by the City of Winchester. The Organ and Sanctuary Furnishings sub-task group recommended three organ companies to do initial design work with the architect. The R&R Task Group appointed another sub-task group, Major Gifts and Recognition, and approved a recommendation from the Capital Fund Raising Campaign and Stewardship Appeal sub-task group to enter into contract with Resident Stewardship Services (RSS) of the ELCA.

November saw congregational approval of a contract with RSS to conduct the fund raising campaign and stewardship appeal and Council approval of the R&R Task Group request to set a congregational meeting date of January 17, 1993. The stained glass windows were surveyed by Shenandoah Stained Glass Windows and found to be in generally good condition, but needing structural attention. This cost and the costly containment and removal of asbestos increased the design cost to $2.2 million. Reduction options were considered, but the addition of the organ and purchase price of the CEC drove the total cost up to $2.7 million. The basic design was excellent, and the proposed remodeling would replace equipment and upgrade furnishings that had been delayed in anticipation of the renovation.

Once again members of the Redesign and Remodeling Task Group were available after services on three Sundays to answer questions about the proposed remodeling. The special called congregational meeting of January 17, 1993, provided information via slides and presentations on three considerations that were approved by voice vote:

1. That the congregation approve the revised redesign and remodeling plans developed by the R&R Task Group.
2. That the congregation accept the challenge of a $1,000,000 goal for the capital fund raising campaign to be conducted by RSS March 20-29.
3. That the congregation proceed with the terms of the architect's contract calling for the development of the construction documents and that the congregation authorize the trustees to use, at their discretion, unrestricted funds and income generated from accounts managed by the trustees, in the amount of $68,000 plus expenses.

Meanwhile, a final price for Church Alley was negotiated with the City of Winchester. Clifford and Associates developed a site plan with Heritage for the Future funds. The Organ and Furnishings sub-task group recommended the building of a Schantz organ. A Construction Oversight Committee was named and the architect and contractor meetings gave special attention to a sky bridge concept to connect the CEC with the Ad/Ed Building.

The RSS program began with three pre-program days: January 27-29, 1993. Our director Stan Rose met with the office staff, reviewed materials and trained the leaders: David Ray—Chair of the General Committee, and various sub-committee chairs: Marty and Gail Mayfield—Visitation, Ken Carr—Advanced Gifts, Anne Ashby and

Linda Milburn—Arrangements, Teresa Lehman—Publicity, Marilee VanHorssen—Bible Study, Anne Olinger and Barbara Black—Hosting, Evelyn Goode—Telephone. The success of the RSS campaign and appeal was dependent upon everyone becoming involved in this total congregational effort. The welcome to Stan Rose by the congregation at both services on March 21 was followed by a series of two Bible studies emphasizing stewardship, an Every Member Fellowship Dinner and Program on March 27 and an Every Member Stewardship Visitation on Sunday, March 28. While the total amount received in pledges was less than anticipated, the $600,000 in capital expense pledges and $210,000 pledged toward the annual budget was acknowledged to be the largest amount pledged in the congregation's history.

By May 1993 the short-term and long-term financial situation caused the renovation process to be divided into three phases: Phase 1—renovate the CEC building and perform site preparation for Phase 2; Phase 2—renovate the present sanctuary; Phase 3—renovate the Ad/Ed Building. A special congregational meeting was called for June 6, 1993. The three-phase concept was Recommendation #1, and it passed on a voice vote. Recommendation #2 established that each phase would have a negotiated guaranteed maximum contract price that would be approved by the congregation, and it was also approved.

Phase 1 began in the summer of 1993 with the remodeling of the building at 16 N. Braddock Street, which had become known as the Children's Education Center and asbestos removal in the boiler room of the Ad/Ed Building. By September the R&R Task Group was back at work planning Phase 2. The committee revised the initial cost estimates, revised the architectural design and development documents and gave approval to the construction documents prepared by Clovis Heimsath Architects. The guaranteed maximum contract price did not include the organ, the atrium feature or the sky bridge.

Council approved recommendations of the R&R Task Group on November 14, 1993, and structural studies began in January 1994. Questions were answered and costs finalized for the special congregational meeting on March 20, 1994. At long last, approval was given for the renovation of the present sanctuary.

Following the 11:00 a.m. service on Easter Day, April 3, 1994, members began removing items from the sanctuary. Shenandoah Stained Glass of Front Royal removed the "picture" stained glass windows. Pews and other valuable furnishings were transferred to other locations for refurbishment. Insulation Specialists of Fishersville removed asbestos in the undercroft. On May 8, 1994,

Buildings and Properties

The Sanctuary in 1994 (above) and in 2002.

word was received that the new organ would be delivered on November 14. The addition of 12 feet to the sanctuary was begun to house the organ pipes and the sacristy. Serving on the Construction Oversight Committee were: Lee Simpson, Chair, Charles Woodruff, Arlene Maul, Dot Tillotson, John Weissenberger, Martha Prusch, Pastor Utt and Pastor Fitzsimmons.

The congregation worked feverishly during the last days of December 1994 to clean the newly renovated sanctuary and to prepare for the Christmas season. They were rewarded with the sound of the new Schantz organ, the lovely candles, poinsettias and our Chrismon tree for the December 24 services. Formal dedication services were held January 8 and 22, 1995.

G&M Building 2002.

During March 2000 the Lenten Cottage Meetings provided a forum for members of the congregation to discuss the preliminary data gathered by the Long-Range Planning Task Group in the areas of membership, resources, programs and staff. There was a clear need expressed for more facilities. The trustees were authorized to explore options for obtaining additional property. On April 9, 2000, the Congregation Council recommended the purchase of the G&M Building at 38 W. Boscawen Street, adjacent to the west side of the Administration/Education Building.

Built in 1927 on a 40' x 100' lot, the two-story brick structure offered 7,520 square feet and rustic attic space. Although structurally sound, the electrical and plumbing systems were outdated and in need of replacement. An estimate of $11,000 to repair the roof reduced the initial price of $300,000 to $289,000. At a special called meeting on June 11, 2000, the congregation approved borrowing that amount from the line of credit held by the congregation at the F&M Bank for the purchase of the G&M building

The congregation also authorized the Congregation Council to plan and implement a one-time capital fund-raising plan to reduce the borrowed funds. One Great Night for G&M (Grace and Ministry) was held October 28, 2000, at the Braddock Street Methodist Church. Pledges received by April 15, 2003, exceeded $150,000 and reduced the amount that needed to be borrowed from the bank.

Three reasons were put forth in recommending the purchase: 1) to provide space for future development of ministry programs for congregation and outreach ministries to the community, 2) to allow for control of future development of church property on the western boundary and 3) to coordinate space with current classrooms, offices, fellowship space and future facility needs due to proximity.

Possible future uses for the G&M Building as discussed in the Long-Range Planning process were: 1) Family Life Center, 2) recreational facility, 3) fellowship space, 4) play space for preschool and after-school programs, 5) additional classrooms and space for Sunday School and Vacation Bible School, 6) space for outreach programs for children and youth, and 7) downtown location for a recreational and learning center for children and youth.

The Long-Range Planning Committee presented its plan, *Growing in Grace*, in December 2000. As future uses of the G&M Building were explored in depth it soon became apparent that the existing structure did not meet minimum building codes and could not be utilized with groups as a public rather than commercial structure. The Architectural Review Team (ART) was established to prioritize the uses of the building and identify specific improvements required for each use. A full report was planned for early 2003.

Endnotes – Chapter IX

[1] See D.M. Gilbert's *The Praises of the Lord in the Story of our Fathers: A Historical Discourse, Delivered in Grace Evangelical Church, Winchester, Virginia, on Sunday Morning, May 13, 1877*, New Market, Va.: Henkel & Co., 1877, 24.

[2] *The Winchester Evening Star*, October 29, 1938, 2.

[3] Ibid., November 1, 1938, 2.

[4] Ibid., October 31, 1938, 2.

Chapter X
Order, Officers, Organizations

It is the purpose of this chapter (1) to record the constitutions by which the congregation has been governed, together with their amendments; (2) to give a list in chronological order of the officers of the congregation, insofar as they are known; (3) to present brief sketches of the auxiliary organizations that have existed in connection with the congregation as gleaned from meager existing records.

THE FIRST CONSTITUTION: Effective 1813

This is the one and only document on record in the German language that has been preserved to the congregation. It appears at the beginning of Volume I of the Minutes of the Church Council. This volume was started by Abraham Reck with the year 1813. The translation of the *Kirchen Ordnung* here given follows the German original in the record book.

CHURCH RULES AND REGULATIONS of the Evangelical Lutheran Congregation of Winchester in Virginia. [Translated from the German.]
Because God is a God of order, and not of confusion; and because no civil nor religious society can long subsist without certain Principles and rules: therefore we the subscribers unite and obligate ourselves, by the subscription of our names to the observation of the following Church-rules, with all the articles and maxims therein comprised.
1. Only such persons, who profess and hold the Confession Augsburgh, and in general, all those who profess and hold the Evangelical Lutheran Religion, can be considered and received members of our Congregation.
2. The Clergyman shall at all times be such, who is lawfully called, and not one without permission, or without being a member of the Synod. – On Sabbath and common holy days he shall preach the Word of God unadulterated and pure, according to the principles of our holy Religion – Instruct the young of the congregation – Have the superintendence of the School – Frequently visit the sick of the Congregation, and edify them with the word of God and (if it be requested) comfort them with the Lord's Supper – And with a virtuous and pious life be exemplary to the Congregation. But if the Minister does not conduct agreeably to these Rules, or commits any material fault in one or her point, he shall then be treated in the following manner. – No accusation shall be brought or received against the Clergyman without two or three witnesses, except by a resolution of the Elders; and then the accusation shall be laid against the Minister, and several days given him, to vindicate or excuse himself – But if he be not able to justify himself, then shall the Elders admonish him in a paternal manner to reform from his crime, and, upon promise of amendment, let him continue his office. But if the crime be repeated and evidently proved, then the Elders have privilege and power to discharge him from service, except, upon due publication thereof, two thirds of the Members of the Congregation declare themselves against it, within four weeks. But he has privilege yet, to refer the circumstance to the investigation of two clergymen and two members of other congregations, of whom the Minister chooses one Clergymen and one member, the Elders the remaining persons; and the resolution of a majority decides. – After the above manner, shall also all other points of controversy (which might take place between the Clergyman & the Elders of the Congregation) be decided, if it cannot

420

be done between themselves. – The Clergyman is at all times *Praeses* or Chairman in the Consistory and is entitled to two votes – The Clergyman and Elders compose a consistory.

3. The number of Elders shall be four, and serve two years, so that there be always two old ones and two newly elected ones together, and that consequently there be an annual election held for two, by a majority of votes. The Elders may be re-elected; in this election there shall be a threefold proposition by the Consistory and church wardens, and herein particular regard shall be had to those who have been resident in the Congregation for a considerable time, and by age, have come to greater experience, among whom, such who conducted faithfully during their Church wardenship, shall always have the preference.

The duty of the Elders is, to assist the Clergyman (if there be any in the congregation) in making such regulations and appointments, as may be most conducive to the Spiritual and temporal welfare of the Congregation, to the making of which (regulations and appointments) at all times a majority must be agreed, to which they may avail themselves of the assistance of the Church wardens and particularly in matters of importance. Each resolution formed by the Consistory shall be published to the congregation three weeks before, and can within this time be disannulled by two-thirds of the congregation.

The Elders shall reprove all vices and offences in the congregation, at the best season; they shall discover to the Clergyman all such who intend coming to the Lords-table, and such who intend becoming Sponsors being disqualified – Contentious parties they shall admonish to unity, and if it cannot be done among themselves, excite them to have it settled before the Consistory, if possible, in order to avoid, as much as practicable, all Lawsuits, and processes at court.

The Elders shall lead an honest and pious life; but if they be addicted to any vice, or otherwise give offence, they shall after the third fruitless admonition, before the termination of the time of their service, be deposed or removed from office. The first admonition shall be by another Elder, the second by the Clergyman, and the third by the whole Consistory. But in case there be no Clergyman in the Congregation, then the remaining Elders together give the second admonition, and Elders and Church wardens the third. No accusation shall be brought against an Elder, except by two or three witnesses, neither shall there be a regular reprimand given, except by the assent of a majority of the Consistory.

4. The Church wardens shall be elected in the same manner as the Elders; they shall be four in number, & serve two years. Church wardens shall not be re-elected untill six years of their non-employment have expired – Their duty is to execute all resolutions, and perform all appointments of the Consistory – They shall keep good order at the time of divine service, and render all necessary assistance to the Clergyman at the Administration of the Sacraments – Collect the alms in the congregation, and give an annual account to the Congregation of all revenues and disbursements. They also must lead a virtuous and pious life, and in case they be guilty of any material crime, they shall be treated in like manner with the Elders –

The annual Election of Elders and Church wardens shall be held on the first Sabbath in August, when there shall first be a Sermon preached; after the Sermon the congregational accounts shall be read to the Congregation, and then the votes be handed in by ticket. The newly elected persons shall be consecrated at the next day of worship; when they step before the Altar, hear their duties read to them from these Church rules, they avow to observe them, being blessed to succeed by divine assistance; the congregation is exhorted to conduct themselves properly towards them. The old Consistory and Church wardens set sometime previous to the day of election and nominate such persons from among the subscribing and contributing members of the congregation, as they intend to propose for Elders and Church wardens at the election. No person elected Elder or Church warden may refuse serving without most important reasons, or else he shall be liable to pay a certain fine for the utility of the congregation, (viz) an Elder 3, and a Churchwarden 2 dollars.

5. Members of the congregation are all such, and only such, who subscribe these Church-rules, and according to their ability, make contributions toward the Stipend or Salary of the Minister, and whenever it is necessary, contribute toward building, repairing, & purchasing of such things as relate to the church, & shall be appointed by a resolution of the Consistory. – Their duty likewise is, to conduct [themselves] virtuously and piously, and then have right and claim to all spiritual and corporal prerogatives and possessions of the congregation; and that only such, who live in any prevailing vice, (especially those that transgress the Sixth commandment) shall so long be excluded from the Eucharist, and from becoming Sponsors, till they acknowledge their faults before the Consistory, & through the Clergyman or the Consistory, solicit the pardon of the Congregation.

All resolutions of the Consistory, with all accounts relative to the Congregation, shall be recorded, and any member of the Congregation, at any time, have the privilege to peruse the Church-rules and records.

All the above stated articles and rules shall continue in force, untill two thirds of the members of the Congregation unite for an Alteration or amendment on one or other point thereof, and then the Alteration or amendment shall be made by a resolution of the Consistory.

Save now, I beseech thee, O Lord: O Lord, I beseech thee, send now prosperity.
Save thy people, and bless thine inheritance: feed them also, and lift them up forever.

January 28, 1814

(The date here given refers simply to the day of entry into the record book of the foregoing translation.)

AMENDMENTS TO THE FIRST CONSTITUTION adopted January 1, 1813.

Resolved, that it is expedient to make the following alterations in the Rules and regulations adopted by the German Lutheran Congregation:

1st. The number of elders shall consist of six and serve during Good behaviour. Two of whom shall be appointed Trustees. All vacancies to be filled by the remaining Elders; all new appointments shall be published in the Church and if two thirds of the congregation disagree to the new appointment, within four weeks from the time of such publication, it shall be void.

2nd. No person shall be eligible to the Eldership who has not communed in this or some other Lutheran Congregation.

3rd. All persons who have contributed to the Building of the Church, or enclosing of the Burial Ground, shall be considered Members, and as such, be entitled the Burying Ground, for themselves and their Children.

4th. All persons who contribute to the support of the Church and Minister, and so long as they continue so to do, shall be considered Members, and as such, be entitled to the Burying Ground, for themselves and all white persons of their Family.

5th. Strangers, or persons who are not members, but wish the privilege of the Burying Ground for their dead, shall pay to the Treasurer, two dollars for each person over twelve years, and one dollar for all under that age, before such privilege shall be granted.

6th. In all Elections, every male member shall have one vote.

7th. The Original Rules and Regulations shall be in full force, excepting, so far as these amendments and alterations affect them, which is hereby repealed.

8th. All subscribers to the Bells shall have them tolled (if required) for their own and their children's funerals free, excepting the sexton's fee. And non-subscribers shall pay to the Treasurer one dollar for each funeral exclusive of the sexton's fee.

9th. The Minister's Salary or Stipend shall be laid on the pews of the Church, and for that purpose, to be let or rented on the following conditions, viz: Nos. 1, 10, 19 & 26 at $15 pr. annum; No 6, 14, 15 & 22 at 20 Dollars pr. annum, and the Residue at 10 Dollars pr. annum, to be paid half yearly. All who take a pew, or part thereof, will be chargeable for the same untill He or they give notice of His or their intention to withdraw, which may be done by giving any of the elders notice at least three months before the next payment becomes due of such an intention.

AMENDMENT – adopted November 10, 1818.

Objection being raised to the continuation in office of Elders during good behavior, an amendment was passed November 10, 1818, as follows:

Resolved, that it is expedient for the well ordering of the affairs of the congregation, that two of the Elders retire from office every year, by seniority, but previous to such vacation, the Board of Elders for the time being, shall nominate persons eligible to the office to fill such vacancy, which nomination shall be submitted to the congregation for their concurrence.

AMENDMENT – adopted February 7, 1821.

There shall hereafter be as prescribed in Article 3rd of the Constitution Four Elders, & as prescribed in Article 4th of said Constitution, there shall continue to be four Wardens in the Government of the Church, with this deviation from said Articles as to placing the said officers into office, That they shall, as heretofore practiced, be nominated by the consistory and published for the period (heretofore noted) to the Congregation, and if not objected to by Two Thirds of the Congregation, shall be regularly inaugurated.

THE SECOND CONSTITUTION: Effective 1829

This document, the work of Jacob Baker, was adopted by the congregation on Monday, December 8, 1828. "After the meeting was organized...the draft of the constitution prepared by the meeting on the 24th November was read – and then ordered to be read section by section for the deliberation of the Congregation, which being accordingly done, and the Sections and Articles approved of, on Motion it was Resolved: That the preamble and the Constitution in the words and figures following, to wit, be adopted as a System of rules for the Government of this congregation, which was unanimously agreed to."

CONSTITUTION OF THE LUTHERAN CHURCH IN WINCHESTER

When in the course of events, it becomes necessary for the members of any association, to repeal an old, and adopt a new system of government, a due regard to explicitness requires that they state the motives that induce them, and the principles within whose operation they intend to act.

Now, therefore, we the members of the Lutheran Congregation in Winchester, holding these truths to be self-evident: That every association, whether religious or civil, has the right and power within itself, to frame and adopt the rules of their own government: That when any system from the changes of time, or any other cause whatsoever, becomes defective, and exceptionable or inadequate to the accomplishment of the original purposes for which it was adopted, it is the privilege, it is the duty, of the members, to revise, correct, or repeal it, as in their wisdom shall seem most expedient. And seeing that in the progress of years many imperfections have crept into the present constitution of our church do, therefore, declare it to be repealed and of non effect. Yet convinced that nothing conduces so much to the promotion of the objects, as well as the best interests of any society, as a well digested system of rules and principles properly and prudently enforced, and persuaded that no period for its accomplishment more favourable than the present will be afforded, do therefore upon mature reflection and in

humble reliance on Divine Providence adopt the following constitution for the future government of our church.
THE OFFICERS OF THIS CONGREGATION SHALL BE PASTOR, ELDERS & WARDENS
ARTICLE 1ST   OF THE PASTOR

Section 1st. No minister shall be pastor of this congregation who has not been regularly licensed or ordained by the Lutheran Church, who is not a member of and in full connection with some Synod of the Lutheran Church in the United States of America, who does not receive the scriptures of the old and new Testament as set forth in the Augsburg Confession as the ground of his faith, duty and practice, and who, besides leading a pious, consistent and exemplary life, does not in general subscribe to the principles and rules of the Evangelical Lutheran Church.

Section 2nd. The duties of the Pastor shall be principally the following: To expound the Scriptures; To conduct the public worship of God; To administer the sacraments; To superintend and conduct all social meetings in the congregation; To admonish men of their duties; and by all proper means in his power, either in public or in private, edify the members, and advance the best interests of this congregation.

ARTICLE 2ND   OF ELDERS

Section 1st. The number of Elders in this Congregation shall not exceed six, nor be less than two; they shall continue in office eight years and may always be re-elected.

Section 2nd. The principle duties of Elders are, besides setting an example of piety: to aid in administering the government of the church; in preserving peace and harmony among its members; to render all necessary assistance to the Pastor at the administration of the Lord's Supper; to watch over the purity and faithfulness of its members; to visit the sick and afflicted of the congregation; and perform all other duties which the Church Council may determine to be within their proper jurisdiction.

Section 3rd. No person shall be eligible to the office of Elder, who is not a member in full communion in the Church; who is not devoted to its interests; whose life and conduct do not correspond with the true Christian character as laid down in the Holy Scriptures and continue to be such, as a faithful discharge of the duties of this office laid down in Section above may require.

Section 4th. The Pastor and Elders only shall decide upon all cases of discipline and upon the qualifications of candidates for admission into full membership of the Church.

ARTICLE 3RD   OF WARDENS

Section 1st. The number of Wardens shall not exceed six nor be less than four. They shall be selected for their moral demeanor and exemplary life from the most active, orderly, and correct members in full communion in the Church.

Section 2nd. They shall be elected to serve for a term of three years and no one shall be re-eligible for the space of one year after the expiration of his term of service.

Section 3rd. In order to secure a rotation in office two of this body shall be annually elected.

Section 4th. They shall attend to the temporal concerns of the Church and perform all other duties which the Church Council may determine to be within the sphere of their jurisdiction.

ARTICLE 4TH   OF THE CHURCH COUNCIL

Section 1st. The Pastor, Elders, and Wardens shall constitute the Church Council and be the representatives of the Congregation: They shall make such special regulations and rules as may be necessary to carry into effect all the provisions of the Constitution.

Section 2nd. A majority of the members of the council shall constitute a quorum for the transaction of all ordinary business. The Pastor when present shall be ex-officio chairman and in his absence one of the Elders shall be elected Chairman *pro tem.*

Section 3rd. The Church Council may at any time be convened by the Pastor, and it shall be his duty to call a meeting when requested by any two members of the Council or any six members of the Congregation.

Section 4th. It shall be the duty of the Council to fill all vacancies which may occur in their body; but no such appointment shall be made except by the concurrence of two thirds of all the members of the Council. The person thus elected shall serve untill the regular expiration of the term of the member in whose place he was elected.

Section 5th. The Council shall keep a record of their proceedings and a register of all who are and who from time to time by baptism, confirmation or communion may become members in the Church, together with such other records as they may deem necessary. It shall also be their duty to appoint one of their body to represent the congregation at the annual meeting of the synod.

Section 6th. Whenever an individual shall feel personally aggrieved by any decision in the Church the matter may be referred to five private members in full communion in the congregation, two of whom shall be chosen by the party appealing, two by the Council, and the remaining one by the four thus appointed, and their decision shall be conclusive.

ARTICLE 5TH   OF MEMBERS OF THE CONGREGATION

Section 1st. The members of this congregation are all such persons as have been received into visible membership in the Lutheran Church by baptism, confirmation or communion, and reside within the jurisdiction of the town of Winchester and its vicinity.

Those individuals who have been received into the Church by baptism alone are members in the third or lowest degree.

Members by confirmation are those who after baptism have taken upon themselves the fulfillment of the baptismal vows according to the rites and ceremonies of the Lutheran Church, and these are members in the second degree.

Members by communion are all such individuals as after baptisms and confirmation have communed in the Church and have not been divested of the privileges and immunities of the society under the Church discipline, and these are members in the first degree.

Section 2nd. The voters of this congregation shall be all male members of good moral character, together with such other male persons possessing these express qualifications: that their families or individuals of their families be members of this Church; that they be not attached to or connected with any other denomination of Christians; that they evidence a preference for the Lutheran Church by their attendance on divine service; that they be of good moral character and contribute annually to the support of the minister and church.

Section 3rd. Every member is amenable to the church and must yield to its government properly and prudently administered.

ARTICLE 6TH   OF ELECTIONS

Section 1st. The council may publish a congregational meeting for an election or any other purpose when they shall deem it necessary, and they shall do so when requested by ten male members of the Church.

Section 2nd. All congregational elections shall be published by the Church Council at least two weeks before the election, except in the first under the constitution, which shall take place immediately upon its adoption.

Section 3rd. Prior to elections for members of the Church Council the existing council shall nominate as many persons as are to be elected, and the voters of church may nominate as many more, from whom the officers shall be chosen.

Section 4th. When an election is held in the congregation for Pastor, two thirds of all the voters shall be necessary to an election, and if the voters are not unanimous, it is recommended that the minority be respectfully invited to concur in the decision.

Section 5th. Whenever the congregation shall believe that the best interests of the Church would be consulted and advanced by the removal of the Minister, it shall be their right through the agency of the Council to call a meeting of the congregation to take the matter into consideration, and the decision thus made by a majority of the electors shall be conclusive.

No order for removal shall however take effect until twelve months after its passage.

Section 6th. If at any time the Pastor shall feel disposed to relinquish his charge of this congregation he may be at liberty to do so by giving a reasonable notice of the same to the congregation.

Section 7th. The elections in this congregation shall always be by ballot.

Section 8th. This constitution shall not be altered or amended but by the concurrence of two thirds of the male members of this congregation.

And now to the Most High: The divine Author of Christian faith: The Great Head of the Church: The Rock of our Salvation: The anchor of our hopes: do we commit ourselves, and this, the work of our hands. Let Thy mercy, O Lord, be upon us. Peace be within thy walls, O Zion, and prosperity within thy palaces. Amen.

AMENDMENT ONE, adopted May 22, 1843; Article 4th, Section 1st changed to read as follows:
"The Elders and Wardens shall constitute the Church Council, etc."

AMENDMENT TWO, adopted December 28, 1887; Article 5th, Section 2nd amended by adding the following: [The voters of this congregation shall be all male members…]

"And all female members who are in full communion with this church, who submit to its government and discipline regularly administered, and who contribute according to their ability and engagements to the pastor's support and all other necessary expenditures."

AMENDMENT THREE, adopted December 4, 1921; Article 2nd, Section 1st changed to read as follows:
"The number of Elders in this congregation shall be six, who shall continue in office for six years and shall not be eligible for re-election until they shall have been out of office for one year. Three shall be elected every three years."

AMENDMENT FOUR, adopted November 21, 1926; Article 3rd, Section 1st changed to read as follows:
"The number of deacons shall be not less than eight. They shall be selected etc."

THE THIRD CONSTITUTION: Effective 1932

With this document, adopted December 20, 1931, the congregation took the name Grace Evangelical Lutheran Church, Winchester, Virginia, and became a member congregation of the Evangelical Lutheran Synod of Virginia of the United Lutheran Church in America (ULCA). Three trustees would now be elected for life to hold the congregation's property. The pastor and twelve deacons (vice Elders and Wardens), three elected per year for 4-year terms, would comprise the Church Council. This constitution included By-Laws covering congregational meetings, members, the Church Council, standing committees, the Sunday School, application of moneys received and amendments.

PREAMBLE

In the Name of the Father, and of the Son, and of the Holy Ghost. Amen.

We, Members of the body of Christ, desiring to manifest that inner unity which we have with one another in the common confession, defense and maintenance of our faith, and in joint efforts for the performance of our Christian stewardship in extending the Kingdom of our Lord Jesus Christ, unite in the adoption of the Constitution hereunto following.

ARTICLE ONE: Title and Trustees

1. The Name and Title of this congregation shall be "Grace Evangelical Lutheran Church, Winchester, Virginia."

2. There shall be three Trustees elected by ballot by the congregation and confirmed by the Court. They shall be elected for life unless removed for some good cause, and shall legally hold the congregation's property in the name of the congregation and care for it as directed by the congregation through its Council.

ARTICLE TWO: Doctrinal Basis

1. This congregation receives and holds the canonical Scriptures of the Old and New Testaments as the inspired Word of God, and as the only infallible rule and standard of faith and practice, according to which all doctrines and teachers are to be judged.

2. This congregation accepts the three ecumenical creeds – namely, the Apostles', the Nicene, and the Athanasian – as important testimonies drawn from the Holy Scriptures, and rejects all errors which they condemn.

3. This congregation receives and holds the Unaltered Augsburg Confession as a correct exhibition of the faith and doctrine of the Evangelical Lutheran Church, founded upon the Word of God; and acknowledges all churches that sincerely hold and faithfully confess the doctrines of the Unaltered Augsburg Confession to be entitled to the name of Evangelical Lutheran.

4. This congregation recognizes the Apology of the Augsburg Confession, the Smalkald Articles, the Large and Small Catechisms of Luther, and the Formula of Concord, as in the harmony of one and same Scriptural faith.

To this Doctrinal Basis all instruction in the Church, the School, and the family shall conform.

ARTICLE THREE: Synodical Connection

This congregation shall be maintained in organic connection with the Evangelical Lutheran Synod of Virginia of The United Lutheran Church in America, and shall labor in the Lord's Kingdom in common with all other congregations of said Synod and others constituting The United Lutheran Church in America.

ARTICLE FOUR: Membership

1. This congregation shall consist of the Pastor, and other members of the Church of Christ who shall be baptized and admitted to the Sacrament of the Lord's Supper, and who unite as one communion under the covenants and obligations of this Constitution, accepting the same and performing the duties it enjoins; also such baptized members of their households as have not reached the age of separate responsibility but are subject to their control as parents, guardians or sponsors.

2. It is the duty of all members of this congregation to be steadfast in their baptismal covenant. If they are parents or guardians it is their duty early to bring the children under their care within the same, presenting them for holy baptism; to bring such children up in the nurture and admonition of the Lord; to instruct or cause them to be instructed in Biblical knowledge and church consciousness in the home and school; to see to it that they are early brought unto attendance upon the catechetical instruction by the pastor, and in due time prepared for the rite of confirmation and the Sacrament of the Lord's Supper.

That all may grow in grace and the knowledge of God, members are to give diligence to the study of the Holy Scripture, the reading of devout literature which accords with the Scriptures; and faithful attendance upon the services of God's House and the preaching of the Word, always seeking the light and aid of the Holy Spirit and all other needful gifts by fervent prayer, by self-examination, by confession and absolution. Confirmed members shall regularly receive the Lord's Supper.

They shall strive to be temperate in all things, to love and aid each other, and especially the needy and distressed, in every relation, and, while they have regard to the household of faith above all, they shall care for the souls and bodies of men everywhere. They shall regularly and faithfully avail themselves of the public worship, and not become lax in the sincere practice of family and private devotion. They shall diligently seek to avoid all false teachers and strange doctrines; heartily love reverence, pray for and sustain faithful ministers; and in all things seek to be con-formed to the mind and example of our blessed Lord and Savior.

Every confirmed member, as a good steward of the manifold gifts of God, shall contribute regularly, as God has prospered him or her, an offering to be placed upon the altar of the Lord for the support and promotion of the work of the kingdom at home and abroad. Unconfirmed children shall be taught early to contribute likewise.

ARTICLE FIVE: Voters

Every communicant member of the congregation not under Church censure, who regularly receives the Lord's Supper, at least once per year, and systematically (weekly if possible) contributes in accordance with its plans for local support and general benevolence, as God has prospered him, or her, shall be entitled to participate actively in all congregational meetings and vote at all elections, except in voting on propositions involving large financial obligations for the congregation where the legal age shall apply.

ARTICLE SIX: Meetings

1. Congregational meetings shall be held regularly as the congregation may determine by its By-Laws. Special meetings may also be provided for.

2. At congregational meetings all matters concerning the welfare of the congregation may be determined, including the filling of various offices in the congregation; matters pertaining to good order and conformity of ceremony to the usages prevailing in The United Lutheran Church in America; the purchase and disposal of property, or alteration of property, of the congregation; and the like.

3. The congregation may have the power to appoint Special committees with definite or general instructions; and to authorize the organization of approved societies or special associations within itself, subjecting the same to the control of the Church Council.

ARTICLE SEVEN: The Pastor

1. The pastor of this congregation shall be regularly installed, and must have been obligated, at his ordination or investiture as a Lutheran minister, to the confessions of the Evangelical Lutheran Church, namely, the Apostles' Creed, the Nicene Creed, and the Athanasian Creed, the Unaltered Augsburg Confession, the Apology, the Smalkald Articles, the Catechisms of Luther, and the Formula of Concord. He shall solemnly promise to perform the duties of his office in conformity with these confessions as a correct exhibition of the faith and doctrines of the Evangelical

This Heritage

Lutheran Church, founded upon the Holy Scriptures. He shall be, or at its next regular convention become a member of the Synod with which the congregation is united. He shall faithfully carry out the provisions of this Constitution.

2. The pastor shall be the teacher and spiritual guide of the congregation and its members. To this end he shall preach the Word, administer the sacraments, conform the manner of conducting public worship to the accepted practice of The United Lutheran Church in America, using such books of worship and instruction as have been accepted and approved by The United Lutheran Church in America, and the Synod to which this congregation belongs. He shall care for all the people of the congregation as individuals and as a congregation in common faith and harmonious interest with all other members and congregations of the Synod and of the United Lutheran Church in America. He shall impart catechetical instruction regularly; with the advice and consent of the Church Council he shall confirm those who have been duly instructed and give satisfactory evidence that they are earnestly desirous of being faithful followers of Christ. He shall perform the marriage ceremony in accordance with the laws of God and of the State; visit and minister to the sick and infirm; bury the dead; install regularly elected members of the Church Council, and, with the Council, administer discipline. He shall supervise all schools and auxiliary organizations of the congregation, and promote the building up of the Kingdom of our Lord Jesus Christ in the community, in the homeland, and abroad. He shall cooperate with the agencies and officers of the Synod in every way to educate the people to increased liberality for the causes of benevolence recommended by Synod, or supported by The United Lutheran Church in America. He shall seek to impart all the information concerning the work and problems as they arise before the Church; and use his best endeavor to stimulate piety in the individual and family life of the people, as well as knowledge of the Church and her work by the circulation of the literature of the Church. He shall labor to prevent all indifferences and fanaticism, all schism, heresy, separation, and alienation in the congregation; and in private and public, set an example of unfeigned piety, sound judgment, and propriety. He shall maintain the pulpit in full harmony with the faith confessed by the Evangelical Lutheran Church.

3. The pastor shall keep an accurate record of his ministerial acts in the congregation, in a book provided by and to remain the property of the congregation; and he shall annually report these statistics to the Synod, or to an official of the Synod appointed for that purpose.

4. When members of this congregation remove into the bounds of another congregation of the same faith, the pastor shall advise such members to connect themselves with the congregation into whose territory they have moved. He shall immediately notify the pastor of the said other congregation of such removal; and upon application the Church Council shall furnish certificates of transfer to such as are entitled to the same.

5. It shall be the duty of the pastor to preside at all meetings of the congregation and the Church Council, unless he be voluntarily absent or is temporarily unwilling, for special and accepted reasons, to preside, in either of which cases, the Vice Chairman of the Council shall preside. No act of the Councilor of the congregation shall take effect without his knowledge and his having had opportunity to be heard.

6. When there is a vacancy in the pastorate the Church Council shall at once inform the President of Synod, or other such officer elected by Synod for this purpose, and solicit his advice. The Council shall provide for the supply of the pulpit ad interim; they shall nominate after prayerful examination, a candidate, who is eligible according to paragraph (1) of this article of the Constitution. One candidate only shall be nominated at one time to be voted for or against by the electors, specified in Article Five, and the election and its returns shall be under the care of judges appointed by the Church Council. The election shall be by ballot.

7. When a pastor has been elected by a two-thirds majority by the voters present, a written statement of this fact, signed by the officers of the congregation, shall be sent him, and this shall constitute his call, and must specify the support which the congregation will guarantee him.

8. If serious accusation be lodged against a pastor before the Church Council in writing over the signature of five voting members in the congregation, the Council shall confer with him, endeavor to obviate all just cause of complaint, and seek to reconcile the matter; nor shall any further steps be taken until all proper efforts to this end on the part of the Church Council have been exhausted. If, in the judgment of the Church Council, and upon a hearing of evidence, at which hearing the pastor shall have full right to present his cause by witnesses and by the examination of witnesses, a prima facie case has been made out against the pastor, it shall report its findings in writing to the President of Synod, specifying the charges founded on the subscribed testimony of at least two credible witnesses. If the Church Council shall ignore an accusation regularly brought by five voting members of the congregation, duly signed, said members may in like manner present their charges to the President of the Synod.

ARTICLE EIGHT: The Church Council

1. The Church Council, charged with the administration of the temporal and spiritual affairs of the congregation, shall consist of the pastor and twelve deacons.

2. Any male voting member of the congregation of legal age is eligible to the office of deacon, provided he is a regular communicant, a contributor, and of good character, wisdom and fidelity.

3. Deacons are primarily the executive aids of the pastor in the work belonging to the congregation for the promotion of the cause of the Kingdom of Christ and the salvation of souls, therefore, aside from such duties as are from time to time assigned to them by the congregation or by the pastor, their regular duties are defined as follows:

They shall see to it that the services of God's House be held at proper times, especially on the Lord's Day, and the Festival Days of the Church Year, and conducted in accordance with the order of the Church; that the pure Word of God is preached as the Church confesses it, and only by those duly authorized by this Constitution; that provision be made for the Christian instruction of the young and all requiring it; that strict discipline be maintained, the erring be admonished and impertinent offenders be excluded from the communion of the Church; that the property of the congregation be cared for, and all that relates to its worldly affairs be properly administered. They shall plan and provide proper means for the systematic and regular collection and disbursement of all moneys for the welfare of the congregation, the maintenance of the property, salaries, the relief of the poor, and all Christian beneficence, especially the apportionments required by the Synod and the Church at large for the conduct of its work. They shall assist the pastor in the care of the sick and the needy, in the cultivation of harmony among the members, and in the promotion of the general welfare of the congregation; and they shall see to it that the house of God is not diverted to any uses alien to its character.

They shall not be unmindful that, while holiness of life and conversation is required of all who name the Name of the Lord, it is especially incumbent upon those who have been called to be office-bearers in His Church to show themselves in all things, by word and example, a pattern of good works.

4. The Church Council shall meet at regular intervals (monthly if possible) as may be determined in the By-Laws. It shall each year, at its January meeting or as soon thereafter as possible, elect from its members a Vice Chairman and a Secretary.

(a) The Vice Chairman shall preside at all Council and congregational meetings when the congregation is without a regular pastor, in the absence of the pastor, or if he declines to serve. Should the Vice Chairman die, or be unable to serve, or decline to do so, the Council shall select one of its members to take his place.

(b) The Secretary shall perform such duties as pertain to the office of Secretary for both the congregation and the Council, keeping records of all proceedings in a book provided for the purpose.

5. All salaries not otherwise provided for by the congregation shall be fixed and payment be arranged for by the Church Council.

6. Should a member of the Church Council, other than the pastor, be charged with neglect of his official duties, and after proper investigation by the Council be found guilty, and after admonition does not amend, he shall be deposed from his office should a two-thirds majority of the Council so vote; and an election for the unexpired term shall be held by the Council. Should a vacancy occur by death or resignation, an election shall be held by the Council to fill the same for the unexpired term.

ARTICLE NINE: The Financial Secretary and Treasurer

1. The Church Council shall elect, from among the members of the congregation, a Financial Secretary and a Treasurer for a term of one year. The Financial Secretary shall receive all moneys belonging to the church, keep proper accounts, render monthly statements to the Council in writing, and send quarterly statements to all members in arrears of amounts pledged. The Financial Secretary shall turn over to the Treasurer all moneys collected and the Treasurer shall keep a proper record of all money received and render monthly statements to the Council.

2. Should either the Financial Secretary or Treasurer or both, fail to attend to, or grow remiss in the performance of their official duties, and not amend after admonition, either or all shall be deposed from the office to which he or they have been elected on the majority vote of the Church Council, and his or their successor for the unexpired term shall be elected by the Council.

3. The Treasurer shall make all payments for the congregation, upon order issued by the Church Council, and perform such other duties as may be assigned this office by the Council.

4. The Financial Secretary may become a salaried official, if and when in the opinion of the minority of the Council, the financial condition of the Church is such that they may safely incur the necessary expense. Such Financial Secretary and Treasurer shall be bonded in an amount to be designated by the Council.

ARTICLE TEN: Discipline

1. The congregation is not only to acknowledge the obligation of God's law as a guide of life, and a corrector of evil, but is faithfully to use it in discipline for these ends. The discipline of the Church must be purely moral and spiritual, and in no case can pass beyond the withholding of her recognition, fellowship, and communion from offenders.

2. Violation of the divine commands should be followed by instruction, warning and exhortation by a member to whom the wrong is known, or by the pastor, first privately, then before witnesses in accordance with the directions of Christ (Matt. 18). This failing of its proper effect, the case shall be laid before the Church, as represented in the Council; and if the offender persistently refuses to hear the Church, he shall be suspended from communion until there be credible evidence of true penitence and reformation. Acts of discipline and the publication of them, shall require the concurrence of the Pastor and the Council, who by the authority of the Church and in its name, shall examine charges brought by reliable witnesses against the conduct of members. The charges against a member shall be given in writing over the signature of the person or persons preferring them; the offending member shall be furnished a copy and is entitled to be present through the whole actual procedure against him, and has the right of being heard and producing testimony in his own defense. The exclusion and the restoration shall be publicly announced. Appeals from the decision in the discipline of the congregation shall be referred in accordance with the Constitution of the Synod with which it is connected.

ARTICLE ELEVEN: By-Laws and Amendments

1. By-Laws not in conflict with the letter or the spirit of this Constitution, may be made by the congregation, to provide an order of business, to fix the time and place for announcing and holding congregational meetings and elections, and the way of conducting both; to determine the proportion which shall constitute a quorum; to fix the term of service of the Church Council; to fix the details of procedure in the discipline of members; to regulate the making and changing of the By-Laws themselves; and in general to conduct all things, the principles and methods of which are defined in the Constitution, but the details of which are undetermined.

2. Article Two (subject, Doctrinal Basis) of this Constitution shall not be altered or amended by this congregation.

3. Articles of Constitution providing for Synodical relation shall not be amended unless said amendments have been first submitted to the President of the Synod with which the congregation is connected, and have received his approval.

4. This Constitution, except as provided in paragraphs 2 and 3 of this Article, may be amended by a two-thirds vote of the members present at a regular annual meeting of the congregation, provided that the proposed amendment be moved and presented in writing ata preceding annual congregational meeting by at least six members in good standing, and the same has been publicly announced to the congregation at its services on two or more Sundays (immediately preceding) to said meeting when the action is to be taken.

5. Everything in any By-Law, resolution, or enactment of the congregation, differing from, or in conflict with this Constitution, is hereby superceded and repealed.

SUMMARY OF AMENDMENTS TO THE THIRD CONSTITUTION

On December 27, 1936, an amendment was passed stating that the Council would nominate one candidate (vice two) for each Council vacancy. An amendment passed December 24, 1944, changed the annual congregational meeting from December to January. On January 14, 1953, a By-Law was adopted calling for the election of a Superintendent and an Assistant Superintendent of the Sunday School, each for a 1-year term with reelection permitted. Term length for the three trustees was changed from life to nine years. On January 31, 1954, an amendment was approved authorizing the Church Council to appoint Standing Committees. While an amendment approved January 10, 1957, added the words "male or female" following "any voting member" to the description of who was eligible to become a Council member (deacon), a subsequent amendment, approved January 9, 1958, deleted the added words and changed the wording to "Any voting member of the congregation of legal age...." A By-Law approved December 2, 1957, stated that no Church Council member elected to serve a 4-year term was eligible for reelection until the expiration of one year after his retirement, but a member elected to fill a vacancy was eligible to succeed himself.

THE FOURTH CONSTITUTION: Effective 1965

In September 1962, The United Lutheran Church in America merged with the Augustana Lutheran Church, the American Evangelical Lutheran Church, and the Finnish Evangelical Lutheran Church to form the Lutheran Church in America (LCA). A new model or suggested constitution for congregations was prepared to bring each into the pattern of the new church. This led to the approval of Grace's fourth Constitution on January 28, 1964, and it went into effect in 1965. This constitution stated that the pastor would be a man, and he would be ex officio president of the congregation and the Church Council. It called for three trustees to be elected for 9-year terms, without limit to the number of terms. It also called for twelve elected deacons, four to be elected per year for 3-year terms, and the pastor(s) to comprise the Church Council, and it authorized the Council to appoint standing committees. It specifically established committees on Christian Education, Church Property, Evangelism, Finance, Social Ministry, Stewardship, and Worship and Music. By-Laws were approved January 14, 1965.

SUMMARY OF AMENDMENTS TO THE FOURTH CONSTITUTION

At a special called meeting of the congregation on April 17, 1966, By-Laws Section V, which established a framework to govern the Sunday School, was presented and accepted, making this constitution a full and complete governing document. Amendments were approved January 20, 1969, that changed the schedule and order of business for Church Council meetings. At a special called meeting of the congregation on June 29, 1969, amendments were approved that called for the nomination of Church Council member (deacon) candidates—two per position to be filled—in September, their election in October (vice January) and their installation in January (vice February). Amendments approved January 18, 1970, allowed all confirmed active members to vote at congregational meetings, be elected deacons or serve as delegates to Synod conventions and district meetings, with the exception that persons under 21 years of age would not be eligible to vote on purchasing, selling or encumbering real estate. Amendments approved on January 16, 1977, reduced the voting age to 18 for purchasing, selling or encumbering real estate and declared that 50 confirmed members on the active roll who are eligible to vote in congregational meetings constitute a quorum. Amendments approved February 5, 1978, changed "confirmed members on the active roll" to "communing members"; clarified quorum requirements for congregational meetings; officially added a youth representative to the Church Council to serve a one-year term and to have all the rights, powers, privileges and responsibilities of a deacon; changed the Church Council meeting night from "first Monday" to "second Sunday"; and changed the number of nominees for each Church Council position from two to one.

THE FIFTH CONSTITUTION: Effective 1982

On January 31, 1982, the congregation adopted its fifth Constitution and By-laws. This document changed "deacons" to "Church Council members"; called for the Church Council to consist of the pastor or pastors and twelve elected members, together with a youth representive; no longer called for the pastor to be president of the congregation and the Church Council; and added the Youth Ministry Committee as the eighth standing committee. While several amendments to this document were recommended, studied and discussed, none ever came to the congregation for approval.

THE SIXTH CONSTITUTION: Effective 1992

In May 1987, delegates of three uniting Lutheran bodies (the Lutheran Church in America, the American Lutheran Church and the Association of Evangelical Lutheran Churches) met in convention to take the necessary steps to create the largest single body of Lutherans in the world - the Evangelical Lutheran Church in America

(ELCA) - effective January 1, 1988. The Church Council of Grace appointed a task group on January 8, 1989, to write a new constitution for the congregation, based on the new Model Constitution for the Congregations of the ELCA. The sixth Constitution and By-Laws were adopted by the congregation on December 1, 1991. Eighteen chapters comprised the Constitution and seven sections the By-Laws. The Constitution called for a Congregational Council (vice Church Council) to consist of the pastor(s) and twenty voting members, including two youth representatives - the former to serve 3-year terms and the latter 1-year terms; raised the age to 21 for voting members "to vote on purchasing, selling, making extensive repairs to, or encumbering real estate"; established an Executive Committee and provided for the appointment of a Nominating Committee, an Audit Committee, a Call Committee and other committees, "as the need arises, by decision of the Congregational Council." Included in the By-Laws were the newly adopted [1988] mission statement of the congregation; provision for two annual meetings of the congregation; enumeration of the duties of the congregation's officers; scheduling of Congregational Council meetings for the second Sunday of each month; enumeration of Congregational Council meeting agenda items; establishment and enumeration of duties assigned to the Executive Committee, the Nominating Committee, the Audit Committee, the Call Committee, the Mutual Ministry Committee(s), and nine standing committees (Worship and Music, Christian Education, Youth Ministry, Fellowship, Stewardship, Finance, Church Property, Evangelism, and Social Ministry).

SUMMARY OF AMENDMENTS TO THE SIXTH CONSTITUTION

Amendments to the Constitution and By-laws were approved by the congregation on December 22, 1996, that made editorial corrections; incorporated changes to the Model Constitution for Congregations of the ELCA from the 1991, 1993 and 1995 ELCA Churchwide Assemblies; and added a definition of "inactive members" that had been omitted from the earlier document. Amendments were also approved by the congregation on January 25, 1998, that incorporated changes to the Model Constitution for Congregations of the ELCA from the 1997 ELCA Churchwide Assembly and added the Parish Health Ministry Committee as the tenth standing committee. On December 19, 1999, the congregation approved amendments that incorporated changes to the Model Constitution for Congregations of the ELCA from the 1999 ELCA Churchwide Assembly and renamed and expanded the mission of the Fellowship Committee to make it the Fellowship and Shepherding Committee. More amendments were approved by the congregation on December 17, 2000, that established an Archives Committee and clarified the extent of the duties of the Audit Committee.

OFFICERS OF THE CONGREGATION

TRUSTEES
David Dieterick, under Fairfax Grant, 1753
Christopher Lambert, under Fairfax Grant, 1753
George Michael Laubinger, under Fairfax Grant, 1753
Jacob Siebert, under Fairfax Grant, 1753
Philip Hoover, 1813-1815
Peter Lauck, 1813-1819
Abraham Lauck, 1815
John Baker, 1819
John Slagle, 1819
John W. Miller, 1819
John W. Miller, 1840-1846
Jacob Baker, 1840-1874
Abraham Miller, 1840-1842
Joseph Slagle, 1840-1847
Thomas B. Campbell, 1840-1858
Peter Miller, 1842-1853
Robert B. Wolfe, 1846-1871
John Hoff, 1847-1851
William Miller, 1847-1863
William B. Baker, 1847-1888
John S. Heist, 1847-1859
Henry S. Baker, 1864-1889
Godfrey S. Miller, 1864-1877
Charles F. Eichelberger, 1873-1895
John G. Miller, 1878-1915
J. Edwin Cooper, 1889-1921
Jacob E. Baker, 1889-1909
Oscar Barr, 1895-1910
Henry Baetjer, 1910-1912
Edward M. Barr, 1910-1912
J. George Baetjer, 1912-1932
Oliver P. Grove, 1912
William A. Bell, 1915
Alfred D. Henkel, 1918-1932
Lewis F. Cooper, 1921-1932

J. George Baetjer, 1932-1942
Alfred D. Henkel, 1932-1947
Lewis F. Cooper, 1932-1938
Eugene B. Cooper, 1938-1957
Harry A. Schmidt, 1942-1952
Boyd H. Hamman, 1947-1957
Ralph P. Yount, 1952-1976
R. Edwin Buncutter, 1957-1960
Robert K. Woltz, 1957-1973
R. Frederick Cline, 1960-1987
Richard P. Lucas, 1973-1994
Jerry P. Kerr, 1976-Present
J. Kenly Carr, 1987-Present
Roger Milburn, 1994-Present

ELDERS, UNDER FIRST CONSTITUTION
Peter Helfenstein, 1771
Jacob Bucher, 1771
Thomas Schmidt, 1771
Christopher Heiskell, 1771
Lewis Hoff, 1771
George Laubinger, 1771
Lewis Hoff, 1785
George Linn, 1785
Philip Hoover, 1813-1815
Peter Lauck, 1813-1819
Abraham Lauck, 1813-1819
Thomas Heist, 1813-1820
Lewis Hoff, 1813-1820
John Slagle, 1813-1820
John Baker, 1815-1821
William H. Grove, 1819-1820
John W. Miller, 1819-1820
Abraham Lauck, 1820-1821
Isaac Baker, 1821-1824
John Miller, 1821-1824
Henry William Baker, 1821-1822
John Van Buskirk, 1821-1822
Abraham Lauck, 1822-1828
John Crockwell, 1824-1828
Thomas Heist, 1824-1828
Abraham Grove, 1826-1828

ELDERS, UNDER SECOND CONSTITUTION
Lewis Hoff, 1828-c.1830
Isaac Baker, 1828-1829
Abraham Lauck, 1828-c.1834
John Crockwell, 1828-1851
John Hoff, 1828-c.1833
John Baker, 1830-1841
Andrew Bush, 1832-1835
John Miller, 1838-1841
John Hoff, 1838-1841
William H. Grove, 1841-1863
William Miller, 1845-1863
Jacob Baker, 1845-1874
William Seemer, 1845-1853
Thomas B. Campbell, 1845-1858
Peter Miller, 1851-1853
Robert B. Wolfe, 1853-1871
Caspar Nott, 1853-1885
Edward Hoffman, 1859-1888
Henry S. Baker, 1863-1889
William B. Baker, 1863-1888
Godfrey S. Miller, 1871-1877
Charles F. Eichelberger, 1874-1895
John G. Miller, 1877-1915
George F. Glaize, 1885-1896
Henry Baetjer, 1888-1903
Oscar Barr, 1888-1907
Jacob E. Baker, 1889-1895
J. Edwin Cooper, 1895-1922
Hugh K. Green, 1895-1919
A. Harry Miller, 1896-1919
Thomas J. Cooper, 1903-1922
J. Few Brown, 1907-1922
Philip J. Williams, 1915-1922
Alfred L. Green, 1919-1922
Alfred D. Henkel, 1919-1925
Lewis F. Cooper, 1922-1928
G. Casper Fries, 1922-1928
Charles M. Lupton, 1922-1928
William S. Hiett, 1922-1925
Harry B. Keckley, 1922-1925
J. George Baetjer, 1925-1931

George H. Heist, 1925-1931
J. Few Brown, 1925-1931
George R. Theis, 1928-1932
Jacob A. Richard, 1928-1932
Harry A. Schmidt, 1928-1930
Lewis F. Cooper, 1930-1932
S. Porter House, 1931-1932
J. William Lupton, 1931-1932
Robert W. Schultz, 1931-1932
[Third Constitution abolished office of Elder.]

WARDENS: UNDER FIRST CONSTITUTION
George Kiger, 1785
Michael Altridge, 1785
Henry William Baker, 1785
Henry Baker, 1786
Jacob Kiger, 1786
Peter Lauck, 1787
Philip Hoover, 1787
Jacob Bucher, 1788
Simon Lauck, 1788
Peter Lauck, 1809
John Heist, 1809
John Reile, 1809
Abraham Lauck, 1809
Philip Hoover, 1809
John Linn, 1809
Jacob Baker, 1820-1823
Joseph Slagle, 1820-1823
William H. Grove, 1820-1822
John W. Miller, 1820-1822
Jacob Mesmer, 1822-1824
Samuel H. Lauck, 1822-1824
Henry F. Baker, 1823-1825
William H. Grove, 1823-1825
Andrew Bush, 1824-1828
Michael Copenhaver, 1824-1828
Peter Lauck, Jr., 1826-1826

WARDENS: UNDER SECOND CONSTITUTION
John W. Miller, 1828-1835
Jacob Baker, 1828-1831
William H. Grove, 1828-1835

Joseph Slagle, 1828-1831
Henry Baker, 1828-1831
William Seemer, 1830-1835
Theophilus F. Conradt, 1832-1836
Peter Bell, 1832-1836
Thomas B. Campbell, 1834-1845
Henry F. Baker, 1834-1838
Jacob Baker, 1836-1845
John W. Miller, 1836-1845
William Seemer, 1836-1845
Jacob Mesmer, 1836-1841
William H. Grove, 1838-1841
William Miller, 1841-1845
Robert B. Wolfe, 1841-1853
Edward Hoffman, 1845-1858
William B. Baker, 1845-1863
John S. Heist, 1845-1859
Peter Miller, 1845-1851
Caspar Nott, 1845-1853
Henry S. Baker, 1851-1860
Godfrey S. Miller, 1853-1860
Charles W. Price, 1853-1861
Benjamin Miller, 1858-1861
John S. Miller, 1859-1862
George F. Miller, 1860-1863
Solomon Horn, 1860-1862
Henry S. Baker, 1861-1863
David J. Slagle, 1861-1864
Benjamin Miller, 1862-1863
Charles W. Price, 1862-1864
Godfrey S. Miller, 1863-1868
Charles F. Eichelberger, 1863-1866
Oliver M. Brown, 1863-1867
George F. Miller, 1864-1866
William J. Slagle, 1864-1867
Josiah L. Baker, 1864-1868
Charles W. Price, 1866-1869
Andrew Bush, 1866-1869
Frederick W. Kohlhousen, 1867-1870
Enos Dinkle, 1867-1869
Reese B. Yeakley, 1868-1869
Stephen Harry, 1868-1871

Godfrey S. Miller, 1869-1871
V.H. Flinn, 1869-1872
William J. Slagle, 1869-1870
Charles W. Price, 1870-1870
Charles F. Eichelberger, 1870-1873
Josiah A. Richardson, 1870-1873

DEACONS
Albert P. Miller, 1871-1874
Samuel S. House, 1871-1874
William H. Baker, 1871-1871
Reese B. Yeakley, 1872-1875
Stephen Harry, 1872-1875
William H. Baker, 1873-1876
V.H. Flinn, 1873-1874
Charles F. Eichelberger, 1874-1874
Henry Baetjer, 1874-1877
Thomas J. Cooper, 1874-1877
Albert P. Miller, 1875-1878
Josiah A. Richardson, 1875-1876
Josiah L. Baker, 1875-1878
Thomas W. Miller, 1876-1878
J. Few Brown, 1876-1879
Frederick A. Ohrenschall, 1877-1880
Oscar Barr, 1877-1880
A. Harry Miller, 1878-1881
William H. Baker, 1878-1881
Albert P. Miller, 1878-1881
Henry Baetjer, 1879-1882
J. Edwin Cooper, 1880-1883
J. Few Brown, 1880-1883
Oscar Barr, 1881-1884
George F. Glaize, 1881-1884
Josiah L. Baker, 1881-1885
A. Harry Miller, 1882-1885
Henry Baetjer, 1883-1886
Mathias S. Henkel, 1883-1884
J. Edwin Cooper, 1884-1887
William H. Baker, 1884-1887
George F. Glaize, 1885-1885
G. Goodwin Baker, 1885-1888
J. Few Brown, 1885-1886

A. Harry Miller, 1885-1888
Oscar Barr, 1886-1888
Hugh K. Green, 1886-1889
F. August Graichen, 1887-1890
Henry Schneider, 1887-1890
Henry Baetjer, 1888-1888
J. Edwin Cooper, 1888-1891
John K. Lewis, 1888-1891
A. Harry Miller, 1889-1892
J. Few Brown, 1889-1892
William C. Graichen, 1890-1893
Alfred D. Henkel, 1890-1893
Thomas J. Cooper, 1891-1894
W.O. Towns, 1891-1894
J. Edwin Cooper, 1892-1895
Hugh K. Green, 1892-1895
G. Goodwin Baker, 1893-1896
A. Harry Miller, 1893-1896
J. Luther Maphis, 1894-1897
Julius C. Davis, 1894-1897
Henry Schneider, 1895-1898
G. Casper Fries, 1895-1898
J. George Baetjer, 1896-1899
George H. Heist, 1896-1899
William F. Hottel, 1897-1900
G. Goodwin Baker, 1897-1900
J. Few Brown, 1898-1901
Julius C. Davis, 1898-1901
Lewis B. Bloyer, 1899-1902
J. Luther Maphis, 1899-1902
John K. Lewis, 1900-1903
George H. Heist, 1900-1903
William C. Graichen, 1901-1904
Alfred L. Green, 1901-1904
J. Few Brown, 1902-1905
Henry Schneider, 1902-1905
J. Luther Maphis, 1903-1906
Camillus B. Grim, 1903-1906
G. Goodwin Baker, 1904-1907
William S. Hiett, 1904-1907
William C. Graichen, 1905-1908
Oliver T. Ritter, 1905-1908

Jacob Schneider, 1906-1909
S. Fred Grim, 1906-1907
Jacob A. Richard, 1907-1909
Alfred D. Henkel, 1907-1910
Camillus B. Grim, 1907-1910
William S. Hiett, 1908-1911
Philip J. Williams, 1908-1911
Harry B. Keckley, 1909-1912
Jacob A. Richard, 1909-1912
Clark M. Smith, 1910-1913
Hollie B. Dunlap, 1910-1913
Camillus B. Grim, 1911-1914
Oliver T. Ritter, 1911-1914
Alfred D. Henkel, 1912-1915
Taylor M. Rudolph, 1912-1915
William S. Hiett, 1913-1916
Robert W. Schultz, 1913-1916
Carl R. Ritter, 1914-1917
Henry W. Brown, 1914-1914
Alfred D. Henkel, 1915-1917
George H. Heist, 1915-1918
William A. Stultz, 1915-1918
Clark M. Smith, 1916-1919
C. Fred Barr, 1916-1919
Ben F. Davis, 1917-1920
Robert W. Schultz, 1917-1920
Alfred D. Henkel, 1918-1919
George R. Theis, 1918-1921
Jacob A. Richard, 1919-1922
William S. Hiett, 1919-1922
Walter H. Bosserman, 1919-1921
Carl R. Ritter, 1920-1923
Charles K. Over, 1920-1923
Walter H. Bosserman, 1921-1924
Edgar C. White, 1921-1924
Edgar R. Himelright, 1922-1923
Harry A. Schmidt, 1922-1925
Eugene B. Cooper, 1923-1926
Jacob A. Richard, 1923-1926
Ben F. Davis, 1924-1925
Lake J. Frazier, 1924-1927
Clark M. Smith, 1924-1927

Walter H. Bosserman, 1925-1928
Howard K. Grove, 1925-1928
Paul A. Beck, 1926-1929
Emery J. Snapp, 1926-1929
Oliver T. Ritter, 1927-1930
Carl R. Ritter, 1927-1930
Eugene B. Cooper, 1927-1930
Robert W. Schultz, 1927-1930
Osborn C. Cassell, 1928-1931
J. Fred Thwaite, 1928-1931
Charles W. Fries, 1928-1931
Charles K. Over, 1928-1931
Walter H. Bosserman, 1929-1932
Elmer C. Lamp, 1929-1932
Clark M. Smith, 1930-1932
Harry A. Schmidt, 1930-1932
Joseph P. Miller, 1930-1932
L. Curtis Bowers, 1930-1932
Samuel G. Miller, 1931-1932
Robert L. Jones, 1931-1932
Paul A. Beck, 1931-1932
Carl R. Ritter, 1931-1932

ALL DEACONS OR COUNCIL MEMBERS: UNDER THIRD, FOURTH, FIFTH & SIXTH CONSTITUTIONS
Ben F. Davis, 1932-1933
Clark M. Smith, 1932-1933
Joseph P. Miller, 1932-1933
Robert L. Jones, 1932-1934
Lewis F. Cooper, 1932-1934
Carl R. Ritter, 1932-1934
Charles W. Fries, 1932-1935
Charles K. Over, 1932-1935
J. Fred Thwaite, 1932-1935
J. George Baetjer, 1932-1936
Robert W. Schultz, 1932-1933
S. Porter House, 1932-1936
Samuel G. Miller, 1933-1937
Elmer C. Lamp, 1933-1937
Boyd H. Hamman, 1933-1937
James A. Miller, 1933-1936
Clark M. Smith, 1934-1938

Walter H. Bosserman, 1934-1938
Jacob A. Richard, 1934-1934
Harry A. Schmidt, 1934-1938
Robert S. Bell, 1935-1939
Eugene B. Cooper, 1935-1939
Joseph P. Miller, 1935-1939
Ben F. Davis, 1936-1940
James A. Miller, 1936-1940
Carl R. Ritter, 1936-1940
R. Edwin Buncutter, 1937-1941
Charles W. Fries, 1937-1941
Laurens P. Jones, 1937-1941
R. Fred Cline, 1938-1942
Samuel G. Miller, 1938-1942
Abram Zirkle, 1938-1942
Walter H. Bosserman, 1939-1943
Oscar S. Brown, 1939-1943
Boyd H. Hamman, 1939-1943
J. Clayton Cochran, 1940-1944
Eugene B. Cooper, 1940-1944
W. Jacob Hottel, 1940-1944
John H. Kern, 1941-1945
Harry A. Schmidt, 1941-1945
Joseph P. Miller, 1941-1945
William F. Brown, 1942-1946
William H. Hammond, 1942-1946
Elmer C. Lamp, 1942-1946
Samuel G. Miller, 1943-1947
R. Edwin Buncutter, 1943-1947
Carl R. Ritter, 1943-1947
Walter H. Bosserman, 1944-1948
Boyd H. Hamman, 1944-1948
Ralph P. Yount, 1944-1948
Eugene B. Cooper, 1945-1949
William E. Stine, 1945-1949
Gilbert R. Whitmire, 1945-1949
Walter H. Bosserman, Jr., 1946-1950
Claude T. Gore, 1946-1950
Harry A. Schmidt, 1946-1950
Elmer C. Lamp, 1947-1951
Julian Buncutter, 1947-1951
Frederick M. Ritter, 1947-1951

Joseph P. Miller, 1948-1952
Ernest W. Frye, 1948-1952
J. Clayton Cochran, 1948-1952
Boyd H. Hamman, 1949-1953
Clyde S. Campbell, 1949-1951
Carl R. Ritter, 1949-1953
William E. Stine, 1950-1953
Robert K. Woltz, 1950-1953
Ralph P. Yount, 1950-1953
Harry A. Schmidt, 1951-1952
R. Edwin Buncutter, 1951-1954
Ronald L. Itnyre, 1951-1952
L. Baker Soper, 1951-1953
R. Frederick Cline, 1952-1955
Elmer C. Lamp, 1952-1955
Howard H. Shockey, 1952-1955
Claude T. Gore, 1952-1954
Walter H. Bosserman, Sr., 1953-1956
William F. Brown, 1953-1956
Joseph P. Miller, 1953-1956
Oliver G. Cramer, Jr., 1954-1954
Boyd H. Hamman, 1954-1957
Frederick M. Ritter, 1954-1957
W. Carlisle Fisher, 1954-1957
Richard P. Lucas, 1955-1958
Robert K. Woltz, 1955-1958
Carl J. Fischer, 1955-1958
Peter N. Georges, 1956-1959
Oliver G. Cramer, Jr., 1956-1958
Claude T. Gore, 1956-1959
L. Marshall Castleman, 1957-1960
R. Frederick Cline, 1957-1960
E. Guenter Skole, 1957-1959
John T. Wolfe, 1958-1961
Alvin H. Crawford, 1958-1961
Vernon S. McClintock, 1958-1961
Ralph A. Cain, 1959-1962
Frederick M. Ritter, 1959-1962
William F. Brown, 1959-1962
Richard P. Lucas, 1960-1963
Oliver G. Cramer, Jr., 1960-1960
Fred D. Bentzel, 1960-1960

Robert K. Woltz, 1960-1963
W. Wayne Capper, 1961-1963
Carl R. Napps, 1961-1964
Richard H. Petonke, 1961-1964
Rex E. Simpson, 1961-1965
Mary Katherine Aulick, 1962-1965
Richard K. Goode, 1962-1965
L. Merhle Slifer, 1962-1965
W. Carlisle Fisher, 1963-1966
Paul H. Miller, 1963-1966
William L. Petersen, 1963-1966
Richard A. Cates, 1964-1966
Leonard O. Fears, Jr., 1964-1966
William H. Peffer, 1964-1967
James W. Brown, 1965-1966
Lenore H. Eavis, 1965-1967
Paul H. Smith, 1965-1965
John M. Ewing, 1966-1968
C. Kenneth Lamp, 1966-1967
Rosie R. Hott, 1966-1968
Carsten H. Schwartz, 1966-1968
W. Wayne Capper, 1967-1969
Wade C. Emmart, 1967-1969
Jack R. Kerr, 1967-1969
Mary Katherine Aulick, 1967-1967
Robert F. Whitehill, 1967-1967
Richard P. Lucas, 1967-1969
Clara Buncutter, 1968-1970
J. Kenly Carr, 1968-1970
James H. Diehl, 1968-1970
James V. Rife, 1968-1968
Richard H. Petonke, 1968-1968
C. Edward Manuel, 1969-1970
Donal A. Funkhouser, 1969-1971
Ralph E. Lamp, 1969-1971
Philip O. Olinger, 1969-1971
Ralph P. Yount, 1969-1971
Henry J. Eavis, 1970-1972
Lucy F. Lamp, 1970-1972
Paul H. Miller, 1970-1972
Ramon C. Riley, 1970-1972
James W. Brown, 1971-1973

Jerry P. Kerr, 1971-1973
Ronald E. Sonafelt, 1971-1973
J. Frederick Walk, 1971-1973
C. Lloyd Broadstreet, 1972-1974
Wayne E. Ennen, 1972-1973
Mary Whitehill, 1972-1974
Philip R. Yount, 1972-1974
William Lamp, 1972-1972-Y[a]
Anne Ashby, 1973-1975
Barbara Black, 1973-1975
Gene E. Fisher, 1973-1975
Cornelia Gray Revell, 1973-1974
Nancy Nixon, 1973-1973-Y
J. Kenly Carr, 1974-1976
Elaine Diehl, 1974-1976
William W. Everly, 1974-1976
R. Charles Hott, 1974-1976
Carsten H. Schwartz, 1974-1977
Tracy Carr, 1974-1974-Y
Julian Buncutter, 1975-1977
Philip Olinger, 1975-1977
Robert K. Woltz, 1975-1977
Carol Black, 1975-1975
Beth Ann Walk, 1975-1977-Y
Lyall Cates, 1976-1978
Charles Greeb, Jr., 1976-1978
Dale Hoffman, 1976-1978
Roger Milburn, 1976-1978
Anne Ashby, 1977-1979
Marian Carr, 1977-1979
James Longerbeam, 1977-1979
Polly Manuel, 1977-1979
George A. Bowman, 1978-1980
Michael Ferraro, 1978-1978
Steven Miller, 1978-1980
Elaine Walk, 1978-1980
Vera Crawford, 1978-1980
Betsy Fisher, 1979-1981
Evelyn B. Goode, 1979-1981

---

[a] First Youth Member appointed to a one year term. The letter "Y" indicates subsequent youth members.

Charles E. Rice, 1979-1981
Robert K. Woltz, 1979-1981
Tracy L. Cahill, 1979-1980-Y
Carol Black, 1980-1982
Lyall Cates, 1980-1982
Charles Greeb, Jr., 1980-1982
C. Edward Manuel, 1980-1982
Mark Broadstreet, 1981-1981-Y
Lenore Eavis, 1981-1983
Eloise Joppa, 1981-1983
Jerry P. Kerr, 1981-1983
Gregory Sorrell, 1981-1982
Donna Broadstreet, 1982-1984
Vera Crawford, 1982-1984
James F. Maddux, 1982-1984
David A. Ray, 1982-1984
Benjamin Swartz, 1982-1982-Y
Roger L. Milburn, 1983-1985
Eugene Edward Froehlich, Jr., 1983-1985
Shelda Longerbeam, 1983-1984
Charles E. Rice, 1983-1985
David Drayer, 1983-1985
Callie Emmart, 1983-1983-Y
Gene E. Burkhart, 1984-1986
Marian Carr, 1984-1986
John A. Weissenberger, 1984-1986
Dee Dee K. Lockhart, 1984-1984-Y
Mary Margaret Hollar, 1985-1985
C.B. Ashby, 1985-1986
Joette Cates, 1985-1986
Carol Kerr, 1985-1987
Jane Lucas, 1985-1987
Arlene L. Maul, 1985-1988
Chuck Ashby, 1985-1985-Y
John Westervelt, 1985-1988
Katherine Ashby, 1986-1987-Y
Susan E. Collins, 1986-1988
Hunter R. Hollar, 1986-1988
James W. Brown, 1986-1989
Dorothy Holt, 1987-1987
Paul Rago, 1987-1989
Dave Schroeder, 1987-1989

David Jeffcoat, 1987-1989
Elaine Diehl, 1987-1987
David Ray, 1988-1990
Lenore Eavis, 1988-1990
Gail Mayfield, 1988-1990
Ron Brown, 1988-1990
Tom Milburn, 1988-1988-Y
Anne Ashby, 1989-1991
Dana Froom, 1989-1991
Eloise Joppa, 1989-1991
Joanna Pecha, 1989-1991
Roger Milburn, 1989-1990
Joy Woodruff, 1989-1989-Y
Ken Riley, 1990-1992
Don Michaels, 1990-1991
Marilee VanHorssen, 1990-1992
Jonathan "J" Riley, 1990-1992-Y
Ashlee VanHorssen, 1990-1990-Y
Marian Carr, 1991-1993
William Collins, 1991-1992
Sheila Woodruff, 1991-1992
Jay Lucas, 1991-1993
Arlene Maul, 1991-1993
Sally Coates, 1992-1993
John Venskoske, 1992-1993
Peter Synowietz, 1992-1993
Charles Bailey, 1992-1993
Sharon Hetland, 1992-1994
Carol Westervelt, 1992-1992
Paul Rago, 1992-1992
Roger Kloos, 1992-1992
John Henry, 1992-1992
Polly Manuel, 1992-1994
Dirk Olinger, 1992-1994
Jim Diehl, 1992-1993
Elizabeth Thornton, 1992-1992-Y
Jeff Everly, 1993-1994
Nancy Braswell, 1993-1995
Wayne Carbaugh, 1993-1995
Mary Miller Froehlich, 1993-1995
Chris Jones, 1993-1994
Roger Milburn, 1993-1995

Lee Simpson, 1993-1995
Charles Woodruff, 1994-1994
Rebecca Froehlich, 1993-1993-Y
Tim Mayfield, 1993-1993-Y
Martha Prusch, 1994-1994
Mike Ashwood, 1994-1996
Frank Claywell, 1994-1995
Hartmut Doerwaldt, 1994-1996
Janet Frye, 1994-1994
Neal Riemenschneider, 1994-1996
Elizabeth Weissenberger, 1994-1996
Emily Utt, 1994-1994-Y
Trent Bauserman, 1994-1994-Y
Gary Hetland, 1995-1995
Hal Lehman, 1995-1996
Barbara Wilson, 1995-1996
Anne Ashby, 1995-1997
Perry Benshoof, 1995-1996
Wilson Gilbert, 1995-1997
Linda Humphrey, 1995-1997
Harold Mummert, 1995-1997
Joyce Ray, 1995-1997
Marcus Swaim, 1995-1995-Y
Valerie Weissenberger, 1995-1995-Y
Lori Elton, 1996-1997
Gene Fisher, 1996-1998
David Griffin, 1996-1998
Kathy Melby, 1996-1998
John Tilelli, 1996-1997
Carol Westervelt, 1996-1998
Jeffrey Bohnsack, 1996-1996-Y
Jessica Ray, 1996-1996-Y
Tyson Utt, 1996-1996-Y
Robert Garlitz, 1997-1997
Kathy Bohnsack, 1997-1998
Richard Helsley, 1998-1998
Amonda Ashwood, 1997-1999
Wayne Fleming, 1997-1999
Greg Kerr, 1997-1999
Jamie Mangels, 1997-1997
Polly Manuel, 1997-1999
Bob Wibberley, 1997-1998

Susan Short, 1997-1999
John Franklin, 1997-1997-Y
Caitlin McCabe, 1997-1997-Y
Deborah Bauserman, 1998-2000
Wayne Carbaugh, 1998-2000
Tom Milburn, 1998-2000
Jeffrey Nethers, 1998-2000
Cindy Swaim, 1998-2000
Barbara Wilson, 1998-2000
Matthew Humphrey, 1998-1998-Y
Olivia Schroeder, 1998-1998-Y
Susan Conway, 1999-1999
Tina Combs, 1999-2001
William Heidelberger, 1999-2001
Susan Helsley, 1999-2001
David Jeffcoat, 1999-2001
David Ray, 1999-2001
Mark Lynch, 1999-1999
Anna Lucas, 1999-1999-Y
Andrew Mayfield, 1999-1999-Y
Mimi Mayfield, 2000-2002
Barbara Morrell, 2000-2002
Mary Riley, 2000-2002
Gordon Thomas, 2000-2002
Wendy Venskoske, 2000-2002
David Zerull, 2000-2002
Michael Rohrbacher, 2000-2000
Harold Mummert, 2000-2001
Nathan May, 2000-2000-Y
Angelina Moseley, 2000-2000-Y
David Behr, 2001-2003
Dottie Farley, 2001-2003
Todd Heidelberger, 2001-2003
David Melton, 2001-2002
Tim Sadler, 2001-2003
Betty Viens, 2001-2003
Tim Garlitz, 2001-2001-Y
Johanna Ray, 2001-2001-Y
Eileen Caldwell, 2002-2003
Greg Crawford, 2002-2004
Mary Miller Froehlich, 2002-2004
Clay Hoxton, 2002-2004

Cheryl Robson, 2002-2004
Rhonda Smith, 2002-2004
David Stern, 2002-2004
Darin Ashwood, 2002-2002-Y
Matthew Venskoske, 2002-2002-Y

PRESIDENTS OF COUNCIL UNDER SIXTH CONSTITUTION
Nancy Braswell, 1994
Wayne Carbaugh, 1995
Anne Ashby, 1996-1997
Gene Fisher, 1998
Susan Short, 1999
Wayne Carbaugh, 2000
Susan Helsley, 2001
David Zerull, 2002

VICE-CHAIRMEN OF COUNCIL
[VICE-PRESIDENTS UNDER SIXTH CONSTITUTION]
Lewis F. Cooper, 1927-1927
Jacob A. Richard, 1928-1929
Lewis F. Cooper, 1930-1933
Jacob A. Richard, 1934-1934
J. George Baetjer, 1934-1935
Clark M. Smith, 1936-1937
Eugene B. Cooper, 1938-1938
Boyd H. Hamman, 1939-1942
Eugene B. Cooper, 1943-1943
Boyd H. Hamman, 1944-1947
Joseph P. Miller, 1948-1948
Boyd H. Hamman, 1949-1951
R. Frederick Cline, 1952-1955
Frederick M. Ritter, 1956-1958
R. Frederick Cline, 1958-1961
Frederick M. Ritter, 1961-1963
W. Carlisle Fisher, 1963-1966
Richard P. Lucas, 1967-1968
Wade C. Emmart, 1968-1970
Ralph P. Yount, 1970-1971
Ramon C. Riley, 1971-1973
J. Frederick Walk, 1973-1974
Carsten H. Schwartz, 1974-1975
Gene E. Fisher, 1975-1976
J. Kenly Carr, 1976-1977
Dale Hoffman, 1977-1979

Vera Crawford, 1979-1981
Charles Greeb, 1981-1984
Charles Rice, 1984-1985
Roger Milburn, 1985-1986
Hunter Hollar, 1986-1989
Gail Mayfield, 1989-1991
Ken Riley, 1991-1992
William Collins, 1992-1993
Polly Manuel, 1993-1994
Wayne Carbaugh, 1994-1994
Anne Ashby, 1995-1995
Gene E. Fisher, 1996-1997
Susan Short, 1998-1998
Wayne Carbaugh, 1999-1999
Susan Helsley, 2000-2000
David Ray, 2001-2001
David Behr, 2002-2002

SECRETARIES OF COUNCIL
Lewis Hoff, 1813-1820
Jacob Baker, 1820-1823
Henry F. Baker, 1823-1825
John Crockwell, 1825
Jacob Baker, 1828-1830
Theophilus F. Conradt, 1835-1836
Henry F. Baker, 1836-1838
John W. Miller, 1839-1842
Oliver M. Brown, 1842-1843
John W. Miller, 1843-1845
William B. Baker, 1845-1888
Charles F. Eichelberger, 1888-1895
J. Edwin Cooper, 1895-1918
Clark M. Smith (pro tem), 1918-1919
Walter H. Bosserman, 1919-1920
Carl R. Ritter, 1920-1921
Jacob A. Richard, 1921-1922
Charles K. Over, 1922-1923
Harry A. Schmidt, 1923-1925
Norman E. Cooper, 1925-1927
Paul A. Beck, 1927-1929
Charles K. Over, 1929-1931
L. Curtis Bowers, 1931-1932
Ben F. Davis, 1932-1933

This Heritage

Charles K. Over, 1933-1935
Harry A. Schmidt, 1935-1938
Laurens P. Jones, 1938-1941
John H. Kern, 1941-1945
William E. Stine, 1945-1946
Walter H. Bosserman, Jr., 1946-1950
Clyde S. Campbell, 1950-1951
L. Baker Soper, 1951-1953
Claude T. Gore, 1953-1955
Richard P. Lucas, 1955-1956
Oliver G. Cramer, Jr., 1956-1958
E. Guenter Skole, 1958-1960
Robert K. Woltz, 1960-1962
L. Merhle Slifer, 1962-1963
Richard H. Petonke, 1963-1964
Rex E. Simpson, 1964-1965
Mary Katherine Aulick, 1965-1966
John M. Ewing, 1966-1968
Clara Buncutter, 1968-1971
J. Frederick Walk, 1971-1973
Barbara Black, 1973-1976
Charles Hott, 1976-1977
Marian Carr, 1977-1978
Anne Ashby, 1978-1979
Betsy Fisher, 1979-1982
Eloise Joppa, 1982-1984
Marian Carr, 1984-1985
Carol Kerr, 1985-1987
David Schroeder, 1987-1989
Eloise Joppa, 1989-1991
Sheila Woodruff, 1991-1993
Marian Carr, 1993-1994
Mary Miller Froehlich, 1994-1995
Wilson Gilbert, 1996-1996
David Griffin, 1997-1997
Carol Black Westervelt, 1998-1998
Tom Milburn, 1999-1999
Mary Riley, 2000-2000
Betty Viens, 2001-2001
Mary Miller Froehlich, 2002-Present

TREASURERS
Philip Hoover, 1813-1815
Peter Lauck, 1815-1819
Lewis Hoff, 1819-1820
John Baker, 1820-1821
Isaac Baker, 1821-1824
Abraham Lauck, 1824-1829
John W. Miller, 1829-1835
Thomas B. Campbell, 1835-1856
Robert B. Wolfe, 1856-1870
Godfrey S. Miller, 1870-1877
Henry Baetjer, 1877-1902
J. Luther Maphis, 1902-1915
Clark M. Smith, 1915-1916
J. Luther Maphis, 1916-1923
Lake J. Frazier, 1923-1926
Carl R. Ritter, 1926-1968
John M. Ewing, 1968-1970
Evangeline Ebersole, 1970-1971
Clara Buncutter, 1971-1976
David Drayer, 1976-1978
Louis Noe, 1978-1978
Roger Milburn, 1978-1984
Elmer Nixon, 1984-1985
Hunter Hollar, 1985-1985
David Jeffcoat, 1986-1986
Roger Milburn, 1986-Present
Carol Kerr, 2000-Present (Assistant)

FINANCIAL SECRETARIES
Jacob A. Richard, 1915
Harry B. Keckley, 1915
Clark M. Smith, 1919-1921
Howard K. Grove, 1921-1934
William R. Miller, 1934-1937
Robert S. Bell, 1937-1956
Evva May Miller, 1956-1973
Charlotte Beauchamp, 1973-1982
Joyce Ray, 1982-1989
Carol Kerr, 1989-1999
Marilee VanHorssen, 1999-2002
Gerald Amt, 2002-Present

OTHER SECRETARIES
Rebecca Paris, Parish Helper, 1931
Grace Forney, Secretary of Congregation, 1933
Howard K. Grove, Secretary of the Congregation, 1937
Grace Forney, Office Secretary, 1924
Esther McDonald, Office Secretary, 1940
Evva May Miller, Office Secretary, 1947-1973
Kim DeHaven, Parish Secretary, 1973-1976
Joan Bly, Parish Secretary, 1976-1984
Pamela J. Henshaw, Parish Secretary, 1984-1989
Sherri Lee, Parish Secretary, 1990-2000
Joan Carroll, Parish Secretary, 2000-Present

PARISH ADMINISTRATIVE ASSISTANTS
Nancy Braswell, 1997-2001
Carolyn Hawks, 2001-Present

ORGANISTS & CHOIR LEADERS
William A. Baker, 1819
Catherine Baker, 1829
Joseph M. Baker, 1850
Miss Shepard, 1860
John I. Baker, 1862
Godfrey S. Miller, 1863
Miss Hardesty (soloist), 1878
Kate Wolfe, 1900
Agnes Bell (director), 1912
Mrs. W.E. Cooper, 1913
Mary B. Baker (soloist), 1915
Mr. Courson (director), 1920
Mrs. Harry C. Stouffer, 1922
H.E. Griffin, 1924
Philomena Larew (soloist), 1925
Mrs. Harry C. Stouffer, 1925
Mrs. F.L. Buckley (director), 1925
Mildred Jones, 1934
Helen Woore. 1935
Floyd Haines (director), 1936
Mrs. Wm. H. McIlwee, 1937
June A. Cline, 1938
Dorothy Larrick, 1940-1945

Order, Officers, Organizations

June A. Cline, 1946
Harmon C. McMurtry, 1946-1952
William Fraula (director), 1949-1950
Roy B. Wickes, Jr. (director), 1951-1953
Marian M. Pasquet (organist), 1952-1977
Marian M. Pasquet (director), 1953-1977
Alice Cussen (organist and director), 1978-1978
Carol Black Westervelt (organist and director), 1978-1979
Stephen Shaner (organist and director), 1979-1982
Dorothy L. Tillotson (organist and director), 1982-Present
Sharon Hetland (Children's Worship and Music Ministries Assistant), 2000-2001
Larry and Sue Correll (Worship Ministries Assistants), 2002-Present

CHRISTIAN EDUCATION STAFF
Martha Stine Cahill, Director of Christian Education, 1962-1982
Vicki Lemp-McDonald, Minister of Education and Youth Ministry, 1983-1984
Adair Fretwell, Christian Education Coordinator, 1989-1990
Teresa Lehman, Educational and Youth Ministries Assistant, 1996-Present

SEXTONS
Gilbert Nokes, 1815
Benjamin Matson, 1816
James Foster, 1820
William Divin, 1824
Abraham Grove, 1832
John Taylor, 1835
Joseph Stevens, 1864
Albert Franklin, 1868
William Lovett, 1870
Gabriel Festus (died), 1893
David Festus, 1896
William Washington, 1896
John Taylor, 1903
Robert Jeffries, 1904
George Johnson, 1907
Edward Washington, 1907
I.N. Comer, 1924
Joe Willis, 1926
Floyd Finley, 1938
George Monroe, 1945

Lewis Jackson, 1956
Philip Madagan's Cleaning
Service, 1969
Mrs. Rose Prather, Marie Foster & Frank Foreman, 1972
Randolph Brown, 1973
Trinh Huynh, 1983
Elwood Webber & Carlton Gardiner, 1985
Donnie Seal, Ed Reiginger & Doris Jones, 1987
Carl Funk & Carol Funk, 1992-1997
Paul Fisher, 1998-Present

ORGANIZATIONS
THE GERMAN SCHOOL

The first auxiliary enterprise of the congregation, if not strictly speaking an organization, was the school conducted for the children of the community whose parents wanted them to be instructed in the German language.

The date of the school's beginning goes back to the very start of the congregation itself. It must be remembered that C.F. Wildbahn, around whose leadership the organized congregation first centered, was a schoolmaster serving in the community before he was licensed to perform ministerial acts. The school's origin, therefore, antedates the year 1762.

It is the contention of the present writer that the German Reformed people concentrated their effort in building a log church on their grant of land from Lord Fairfax, while their Lutheran neighbors erected a school house on their adjoining lot. It is believed that this building was of log construction also. We know for certain that both groups used the log church for worship for many years. Since, therefore, the Reformed had no school of their own, the conclusion that the one school served both groups seems altogether likely, just as the one church building served both congregations.

Order, Officers, Organizations

Church Officers 1953: seated, left to right, R.F. Cline, W.E. Stine, W.F. Brown, R.P. Yount, R.K. Woltz, J.P. Miller, and C.R. Ritter; standing, B.H. Hamman, E.B. Cooper, H.H. Shockey, R.E. Buncutter, Pastor Eisenberg, Elmer Lamp, R.S. Bell, L.B. Soper, and C.T. Gore. (W.H. Bosserman, Jr. and H.K. Grove are not pictured.)

2002 Council: front row, left to right, Cheryl Robson, Barbara Morrell, Dottie Farley, Eileen Caldwell, Mary Riley, Wendy Venskoske, and Pastor Martha Sims; back row, left to right, Greg Crawford, Matthew Venskoske, Daren Ashwood, David Stern, David Behr, Tim Sadler, David Zerull, Rhonda Smith, Clay Hoxton, Mary Froehlich, Todd Heidelberger, and Pastor James H. Utt. (Mimi Mayfield and Betty Viens are not pictured.)

The names of but three schoolmasters have been preserved. C.F. Wildbahn remained on the job until the danger of attack from Indians in 1763 caused him to flee with his family back to Pennsylvania.

Next there was Schoolmaster Antony whose name was written on the cornerstone document of 1764. Unfortunately, we neither know how long he remained in his position nor how many successors he had before the year 1785. With Christian Streit's arrival on the scene, his brother, William Streit, became the third known schoolmaster serving in this capacity, but for no more than three years, since he died in 1788. There are indications that Christian Streit himself may have conducted the school following his brother's death, but by this time the transition to English had already set in and his school teaching in Winchester seems to have been primarily in the English language. By 1812 the school house had been converted into living quarters for the sexton.

SUNDAY SCHOOL

A Sunday School was started during the ministry of Abraham Reck, although the precise date of its beginning is unknown.

On July 7, 1824, action was taken, namely, "that this Council sanction the revival of a Sunday School in our Congregation." A revival, therefore, clearly indicates a formerly existing organization.

Pastor Reck and H.F. Baker, furthermore, were appointed to examine any resolutions that may have been passed "during the time that a Sunday School was held in the Church," but the record tells nothing more about what they found or did.

A second revival of the Sunday School took place under

Lewis Eichelberger. He gives the following information about it in his letter of resignation (April 1833): "The sabbath school of the congregation, instituted at the time of my coming among you [1828], and continued through various changes, is now in a most prosperous and pleasing condition – now being from 75 to 100 scholars and under the care of attentive teachers. It possesses a well selected library and books of every description necessary for its use."

In 1847 and in 1852 we read of a Sunday School debt. In each instance the congregation did not demand that the school maintain itself financially. Members came to the rescue and wiped out the obligations.

The school has maintained a substantial, if variable, growth through the years. In 1882 there was an enrollment of 273 pupils; in 1892 an enrollment of 349; in 1902, 302; in 1912, 279; in 1925, 470; in 1940, 326; in 1953, 412. With numerical strength there came an increasing financial strength which has been used largely in the support of foreign mission objectives. In addition to assisting in the salary support of the congregation's missionary to Japan, the Sunday School for more than twenty years supported its own native evangelist in that country. So too has the Sunday School assisted generously with the congregation's special offerings at Easter and at the Festival of Ingathering for benevolent and other special objectives in the way of improvements to the church property.

Since 1877 the Christmas program, or service, has been held in the church sanctuary. The change in time of weekly meeting from Sunday afternoon to Sunday morning was inaugurated in the summer of 1911.

Organization of the Sunday School before the present building was constructed consisted of an infant department and a main school. Mention is made of Miss Katie Miller, Miss Kate Wolfe and Miss Fannie Wolfe who gave decades of time to instructing the children of the parish, Miss Katie Miller teaching for fifty-six years. With the facilities of the new building, separate departments are now maintained for nursery, primary, junior-intermediate, and the senior-adult groups. The increased birth rate of recent years has changed the proportion favorably for the primary department over what had been a predominantly adult school.

The Men's Bible Class, organized in 1919 as part of the Sunday School, has made an important contribution to the life of the church for thirty-four years [1953]. When the Union Fire Hall was purchased, the Men's Bible Class renovated the hall as a place for its meetings. During the erection of the present Sunday School building [1924], the church sanctuary had to be used, but with the completion of the new building the former ground floor lecture room beneath the church was remodeled by the class for its use. The class's annual banquet has become a well-established tradition.

Other organized groups of the Sunday School are three classes for women: the Women's Bible Class, the Mary-Martha Class and the Lenoir-Rhyne Class; and a fourth, the C.P. Krauth Class for married couples.

These established classes elected officers and dispersed the Sunday Church School offerings from their class to various worthy activities. The Sunday School itself was led by a superintendent, assistant superintendent, secretary and treasurer. Leadership experiences fostered a strong lay commitment to the program of Christian Education. In the years since 1953, the Sunday School has continued to flourish.

Following a survey in 1967, a Couples Class for young adults was begun. Classes included Sunday Church School material, Bible study and social issues of the time. A nursery for small children was provided by the members. The group met once a month in social settings: progressive dinners, bowling, movies, visiting in members' homes, etc. They were called

Men's Bible Class, c. 1920

Honoring Dr. R. Frederick Cline in 1987 for his years of service as trustee are: (left to right) Pastor James H. Utt, Trustee J. Kenly Carr, Trustee Jerry P. Kerr, former Trustee R. Frederick Cline, Council Vice Chairman Hunter Hollar, Trustee Richard P. Lucas, and Pastor Paul Gunsten.

upon to support families in grief, to sponsor a softball team and to provide basic necessities for a native Korean family. This class provided leaders and workers for Grace Church in the following years even until today.

In 1984 the Couples Class was renamed the Martin Luther Class. Also at this time the Men's Bible Class joined with the C.P. Krauth Class and the Mary Martha Class to form the Adult Bible Class. Dr. Gregory Sorrell started the Adult Forum and served as its leader for many years. Other new adult groups were the Good News Class and the Christian Living Class. The purpose of the adult Sunday School is to meet the Christian educational needs of all adults through the study of the Bible, Lutheran theology and church history and through the study of contemporary issues, social concerns, developmental stages of life and faith journeys.

The school-age population grew by leaps and bounds after 1953 and the Sunday School rolls were large for each grade. The main purpose of the renovation of the Parish Education Building in 1961-1962 was to provide adequate classroom space. Teachers were recruited continuously and training classes were offered several times.

The Sunday School sponsored monthly activities for children in grades 3-6. These fellowship opportunities encouraged children to bring friends along.

The opening of Sunday School each fall was celebrated with Rally Day activities, awards and student promotions to the next grade. The tradition continues under the name "Super Sunday."

Since 1984 monthly openings have been designed as an intergenerational fellowship affair, taking place on the first Sunday of the month. Coffee, juice, hot chocolate and donuts are enjoyed. Blood pressure checks are available. Announcements are made and birthdays and anniversaries are given recognition by the Christian Education Committee. Coffee is available every Sunday.

The Sunday School also celebrates the end of the school year with recognition of student work and teacher dedication with a brunch hosted by the youth. For some years multi-age activities were held on Sunday mornings during the summer. Currently, only the Adult Bible Class meets during the summer months.

The congregation benefited greatly from the service of paid staff positions to coordinate the Christian Education ministry. Martha Cahill, Vicki Lemp-McDonald, Adair Fretwell and Teresa Lehman have worked with the pastors and the Christian Education Committee to select curriculum, to plan activities and to nurture educational opportunities for all ages: Nursery, Kindergarten-Grade 5 (including preparation for First Communion), Grades 6-8 (including catechetical instruction), Grades 9-12 (confirmed youth) and a variety of adult classes.

For several years the chair of the Christian Education Committee assumed leadership in planning Sunday Church School events. Among those who served were: Henrietta Brown, Bridget Diehl, Diane Fletcher, Amonda Ashwood, Ruth Riemenschnieder, John Tilelli, Tina Combs and Mary Riley.

In the beginning, leadership for the Sunday School was given to the superintendent. Persons filling this position were approved by the Council and frequently an assistant superintendent was selected. More recently the position of superintendent has been held by a volunteer willing to take attendance on Sunday morning and to make sure classes have the supplies they need.

Prior to 1888 when William B. Baker died, he had served for many years – nearly forty, it is said – as superintendent of the Sunday School. He was succeeded by J. Edwin Cooper, who was followed in turn by A.L.Green, until his death in 1922. Eugene B. Cooper, Carl R. Ritter, Charles K. Over, Oscar S. Brown and Carl R. Ritter again, served in this important capacity until 1944. Since then the superintendents have been:

Oscar S. Brown, 1944
Carl R. Ritter, 1945-1946
Claude T. Gore, 1947-1948
Clyde S. Campbell, 1949-1950
Claude T. Gore, 1951-1951
William G. Waters, 1952-1952
Oliver G. Cramer, Jr., 1953-1956
L. Marshall Castleman, 1956-1959
E. Guenter Skole, 1959-1959
S. Mason Carbaugh, 1960-1961
Paul H. Miller, 1961-1964
Lawrence P. Kroggel, 1964-1964
William H. Peffer, 1965-1965
Rex E. Simpson, 1965-1967

Richard H. Petonke, 1967-1968
Polly Manuel, 1968-1971
Philip Olinger, 1971-1972
Lee Rathman, 1972-1975
Polly Manuel, 1975-1976
Vera Crawford, 1976-1978
Charles Rice, 1978-1980
(None) 1980-1981
Linda Milburn, 1982-1987
Bridget Diehl, 1987-1989
Shirley Jeffcoat, 1989-1990
Peter Synowietz, 1990-1992
Linda Milburn, 1992-1993
Diane Fletcher, 1993-1995
Peter Synowietz, 1995-1996
Amonda Ashwood, 1996-1997
John Tilelli, 1997-1998
Wendy Venskoske, 1998-Present

MISSIONARY AND EDUCATION SOCIETY

Next to the Sunday School in age was a society within the congregation to promote the missionary and education causes within the church. By the missionary cause was meant primarily home missions, and the education cause meant chiefly the training of men for the ministry. As a matter of fact, this society with sister chapters in many congregations came to be the spearhead of the Church's developing program of organized benevolence. The Council authorized this group on May 19, 1824, and it was intended for both men and women. Pastor Reck and John Crockwell were appointed "to carry the above into effect on behalf of the males," and the pastor was empowered to solicit "two of the most influential female members" to interest the ladies. The record does not tell us, however, the names we would like to know. It would appear that this society flourished and served the needs of the congregation for about half a century.

SEWING SOCIETY

In the days of Pastor Joseph FewSmith [1843-1848], there came into existence among the women of the congregation a sewing society. Instead of making garments for the relief of the poor and needy, the purpose of the organization seems to have been to make articles for sale at an annual fair, or bazaar. In this way the ladies assisted in removing the church debt of the 1840s.

The society continued to flourish during the pastorate of Charles Porterfield Krauth. It made large contributions toward the cost of portico and cupola and new pipe organ of 1850, $835 to be explicit, in 1853 another gift of $335 was made on the parsonage debt, and two years later still another of $450.

In 1870 the following action of the Council is recorded: "That the thanks of this Council are due and are hereby accorded to the ladies of the Sewing Society of the Lutheran Congregation for the beautiful and appropriate Cushions and Reading Desk, which have recently been furnished by them for the pulpit & altar table."

Two years later when the ladies requested the use of the lecture room for a Festival & Fair in the month of May, the secretary of Council was requested to advise them "to secure, if possible, a room or hall on Main Street, as being in the opinion of the Council, a more desirable locality."

During Dr. Gilbert's ministry the energies of this group were directed along missionary lines. Several Hindu students were supported in India and several ministerial students at theological seminary.

During the 1940s the Sewing Society of a dozen or more became active on a regular basis creating lap robes for nursing homes and ditty bags for veterans' homes. At the present time, the small but active Sewing Group meets several times a month.

The Kneelers Guild began in 2002 to prepare 20 needlepoint kneelers for the communion rail in the sanctuary. Dorothy E. Libby generously donated the funds for the project in memory of her parents, William Edward Eisenberg and Dorothy Jones Eisenberg, and her husband, Robert Reed Libby. Over 30 women worked diligently to have the kneelers completed for dedication during the 250th Anniversary year. The project was coordinated by Martha Prusch.

MITE SOCIETY

This organization first appears on the scene in 1870 with an offer of money to repair the parsonage roof. It seems to have taken over the Sewing Society's Festival & Fair of 1872, referred to above, for when it was held, Council passed a resolution thanking the Mite Society for the excellent results obtained. Mrs. J. Flinn, Miss R. Hartman, and Miss V. Price are mentioned by name as leaders of the undertaking. This society fostered interest in the upkeep of the parsonage and rendered valued assistance for some forty years. In 1908 it presented a handsome pulpit Bible to the church.

MISSIONARY SOCIETY

First mention of the Women's Home and Foreign Missionary Society is made in the financial report for 1884. It is presumed, therefore, that it was organized sometime that year. Its service to the congregation has been primarily educational, planting the seeds of missionary inspiration and endeavor by means of study programs, books, tracts and other literature and special missionary services and speakers. This society continues its existence in the life of the congregation today [1954] as an integral part of the Women of the Church organization.

In turn, it has sponsored the Children's Missionary Society, the Junior Missionary Society, the Light Brigade and the Children of the Church. As a leader of the Light Brigade and the Children of the Church, Mrs. Charles W. Fries gave many years of faithful service. The Junior Missionary Society in 1921 presented offering plates to the church.

YOUNG PEOPLE'S SOCIETY

Organized in 1888 by Miss Portia Baker, the Young People's Society soon won for itself an important place in the life of the congregation. Originally a society for young women, from the beginning it inspired an imaginative, energetic, willing and consecrated devotion within its members. It created a loyalty to the best interests of the church, and a loyalty within itself. In 1925, for example, it was still called the Young People's Society with many of the original members still working valiantly.

Among its many accomplishments were these: a lectern was purchased for the lecture room in 1889; a petition was sent to the Council in 1892 asking for the stone in the cemetery fence for ultimate use in enlarging the church, which was readily granted; a donation of twelve hundred dollars in 1914 toward the purchase of the present pipe organ [1953]; a contribution of $4,000 in 1916 to construct a chapel in Hakata, Japan; a new piano was given to the Sunday School in 1918; a pair of brass altar vases in memory of Miss Portia Baker were donated in 1921; and a gift of $1,000 was made to the Orphans' Home in 1925. The society at last changed its name to the Women's Auxiliary and in 1945 gave up its individual identity by becoming a part of the Women of the Church organization.

LUTHER LEAGUE

Junior and Senior Luther Leagues were started during the ministry of Mr. Kelly [1917-1924]. The group for older young people has had a continuing existence to the present day.

Hayrides, picnics, pool parties, scavenger hunts—the high school age students had lots of fun in Luther League while building lasting friendships within the church family. In 1961, an Intermediate Luther League was formed separate from the Senior Luther League. Although not specifically a Luther League event, many youth stayed a week in the Douglass cabin at the Massanetta Lutheran Summer Assembly near Harrisonburg, Virginia. Others enjoyed outdoor camping and followed the first camper from Grace Church, Sally Crawford, to Caroline Furnace in the Fort Valley.

Officers elected by both groups developed valuable leadership skills. In addition to weekly meetings on Sunday evenings, there was strong participation in the Valley District Luther League. Barbara Eavis served as chairman of that group in 1962-1963. When serving as president of the Luther League at Grace, Barbara set such an example of leadership that her sister, Kathy, and her brother, John, each subsequently held that office. During the 1960s Grace Church sent delegates to the annual conventions of the Luther League of the Virginia Synod at Roanoke College with sessions that focused on leadership development. In 1972, Bill Lamp was the first representative from the Senior Youth Group to serve on Church Council.

YOUTH OF GRACE

The end of the national and Synod-supported Luther League following the 1968 Lutheran Church in America convention could have presented a problem, but Junior and Senior Youth Groups continued to flourish under the guidance of their parents, other adult sponsors and the pastors. Generally the assistant pastor, associate pastor or co-pastor took the lead, strengthened the programs for youth and worked closely with the Youth Ministry Committee. The fun continued—pizza parties, lock-ins, Easter breakfast preparation and Youth Sunday services.

Recent youth ministry activities focus around three major emphases important to the faith development of youth: service, learning and fellowship. Trained to serve as lay worship assistants through the Order of St. John (acolyte, crucifer, Bible bearer, banner bearer, torch bearer), youth also serve as lectors, choir members, ushers and communion assistants. They regularly tape worship services for homebound members and volunteer with enthusiasm during the week of Vacation Bible School. Synod-sponsored leadership events consisting of wonderful blends of worship and fun include: Seventh Day (Grades 5-6), Lost and Found (Grades 7-8) and Kairos and Winter Celebration for high school students.

Servant camp projects to southwest Virginia were undertaken in 1995 and 1996. In the summer of 2002 Grace Church sponsored Caroline Furnace camp staff positions for Matthew Humphrey and Johanna Ray. Summer trips have been taken to New York City, Hershey Park, Baltimore, Williamsburg, Nags Head and Kure Beach, North Carolina. Representatives were sent to the National Youth Event in Dallas (1991), New Orleans (1994) and to St. Louis (2000). Plans are underway to send a large group of youth to Atlanta in 2003.

Junior and Senior Youth Groups meet the first and third Sundays and continue to grow spiritually, to serve the church and to develop positive social relationships. An opportunity for fellowship and homework assistance is available at GELYROL on a mid-week evening. This clever name represents Grace Evangelical Lutheran Youth Room Open Lounge.

SCOUTS

Through the early abiding interest of Eugene B. Cooper in the Boy Scout movement, Troop 1 was given meeting quarters at the church in 1922. Cooper served as scoutmaster for many years. Later, Troop 1 came to be sponsored by the Men's Bible Class.

Mr. Cooper served twenty-five years as scoutmaster of Troop 1 (1922-1947). Twenty-one scouts received the Eagle Award under his leadership. He established a regular summer camp (White Rock at Capon Bridge, West Virginia), served as the first President of the Shenandoah Area Council, was the first recipient of the Silver Beaver Award in 1931 and was recognized in 1963 for 50 years of scouting excellence (1913-1963).

Subsequent scoutmasters have been: Harry A. Nelson, Clyde Campbell, Howard H. Shockey, Fred Neumann, Robert Wolfe, James H. Fleming, William Locke, Lewis H. Clewell, James Blackburn, George E. Troxel (1968-1978), Bernard Witsberger, James Swartz (1979-1993),

John Kucharski and Rob Humphrey (1994-Present). Scout Sunday has been celebrated each February at Grace since 1963. The annual Flea Market fundraiser began in 1970. Scouts have had a long history of participating in the Shenandoah Apple Blossom Festival by selling seats for the parade. Currently, 20 boys are enrolled in Troop 1.

Members of Grace Lutheran Church have served faithfully on the troop committee. Some of them have been: Asa K. Wingert, C. Kenneth Lamp, Lucy Lamp, Wayne Koehler, H. Nelson Orndoff, Paul H. Miller, Elmer Nixon, C. Edward Manuel, R. Bruce Rowland, Milton McInturff, Sr., Lyall Cates, Rex Simpson, Dorothy Holt, William Stern, Nancy Stern, Wilson Gilbert, Linda Humphrey, Jim Swartz and Mark Robson. Bill Wolfersberger served as Scout Executive of the Shenandoah Area Council (1969-1992).

Scouts of Troop 1 have performed many service projects at Grace Lutheran Church: relaid brick sidewalk (1980 - Chuck Swartz, project chairman), cleaned furnace room (1984 - Chuck Stern), compiled comprehensive church directory (1987 - David Stern), helped with emergency lighting and fire alarms (1989 - Tim Stern), created an Archives Room in northwest corner of basement under the sanctuary (1996-1997 - Mitch Dickey), cleaned and restored bell tower (2000 - Matthew Humphrey) and renovated classroom in Children's Education Center (2002 - Eric Robson).

Cub Pack 1 was chartered in 1959 with eleven boys under the leadership of Floyd Shanholtz and Frederick Ritch. Den mothers were Mrs. Ralph Boyce, Mrs. Frederick Ritch and Mrs. Mason Carbaugh. Subsequent cubmasters have been: Lewis H. Clewell, William Peffer, Ronald M. Laign, Bruce Rowland, Lloyd and Donna Broadstreet, William and Nancy Stern, Robert Lofton, Allen A. Wingfield, Pauline K. Powell, Lyall Cates, Dick Bray, Terry Golliday, Larry Baker, Beck Halstead and David Sweeney. Forty boys are enrolled in Cub Pack 1 for 2002-2003.

Many cub scouts have earned the religious training award by working with our pastor or an appointed member of the church. Some of the faithful parents assisting with Pack 1 have been: Loretta Swartz, Anne Ashby, Carol Kerr, Amonda Ashwood, Jay Lucas, Bob and Joanna Pecha, David Ray, Sally Coates, Dave Jeffcoat and Barbara Black.

Since 1994 Girl Scout Troops 304, 51, 705 and 323 have met at Grace Lutheran Church from time to time.

WOMEN OF THE CHURCH

Begun in 1945 as a single organization for the women of the parish, the Women of the Church was actually the result of a merger of the former Missionary Society and the former Women's Auxiliary.

Subdivided into eight circles, the program of the church's work was studied from month to month. Generous contributions of money enabled the society to carry out an extensive missionary program as well as numerous needful activities in the local congregation through the work of the following committees: education, visitation, youth, hospitality, altar, vestment and finance. Active participation on the part of 145 women [1946] was won, though all women of the congregation were considered members.

The constitution and by-laws were adopted September 13, 1945, having been drawn up by a committee composed of Mrs. C.M. Henkel, Mrs. Cora Massie, Mrs. F.M. Ritter, Mrs. A.B. Cadwallader, Mrs. Raoul Garrabrandt, and Misses M.K. Aulick and Virginia Jackson. Since then, the following persons have served as president:

> Mrs. William E. Eisenberg, 1945-1947
> Mrs. Frederick M. Ritter, 1947-1949
> Mrs. S. Vincent Miller, 1949-1950
> Mrs. Joseph A. Hott, 1950-1952
> Mrs. W. Wayne Capper, 1952-1954
> Mrs. Joseph W. McDaniel, 1954-1956
> Miss Evangeline Ebersole, 1956-1958
> Mrs. Henry J. Eavis, 1958-1959
> Mrs. C. Edward Manuel, 1959-1961
> Miss Betty Lou Bradfield, 1961-1962

LUTHERAN CHURCH WOMEN

The Women of the Church adopted the name Lutheran Church Women in 1963 along with a new constitution as required by the Lutheran Church in America. As more women began to seek employment outside of the home in the 1970s, participation fell steadily but annual dues continued to be paid to LCA by the treasurer, Dot Nixon. These women provided leadership to the Lutheran Church Women.

>Mrs. Frederick M. Ritter, 1963-1965
>Mrs. Laurens P. Jones, 1965-1967
>Mrs. Elmer O. Nixon, 1967-1968
>Mrs. H. Nelson Orndoff, 1968-1969
>Mrs. James W. Brown, 1970-1971
>Mrs. John K. Carr, 1971-1972
>Mrs. Philip S. Olinger, 1972-1973
>Mrs. Charles B. Ashby, 1974-1975
>Miss Fietta Rosenberger, 1975-1976
>Mrs. David Drayer, 1976-1978
>Mrs. Charles B. Ashby, 1979-1979

To celebrate the Bicentennial of the United States in 1976, several members of the LCW at Grace wrote about the role of women in the life of our church. These are the thoughts of Mrs. S. Vincent Miller, Mrs. William E. Eisenberg, Miss Evangeline Ebersole, Mrs. Frederick M. Ritter and Miss Clara Buncutter:

• Throughout the years, the ladies have prepared and served luncheons, suppers and refreshments for congregational meetings, visiting missionaries, speakers, college students, Luther Leagues, Brotherhood and Men's Class as well as their own activities. Transportation and housing was provided for the various college choirs which have given concerts in Grace Church.

• The organization tried to keep in touch with our local membership in many ways, by remembering the sick and shut-ins during the year with visits and small remembrances and by endeavoring to make new members welcome.

• Choir robes, altar linens and banners have been made by the women in the organization and the kitchen supplied with equipment and linens. Clothing and blankets have been made or purchased for the needy in our community, as well as around the world. Most of the beautiful Chrismons on our Christmas trees were made by the Women of the Church. The Mission fields of the church were supported and supplied by LCW as well as the Institutions and Homes of the Church.

• The work of the Church Women United in our local community has been supported regularly. Personal items have been given for servicemen, veterans and patients in Western State and veterans' hospitals. Materials and teachers to assist at the Migrant Workers' Camp were part of our program. Nursery schools have been given small gifts and our own Kindergarten has been supported. Filled stockings, dressed teddy bears and dolls were made for distribution by the Salvation Army at Christmas.

• Delegates were sent to Synodical Conventions and District Conferences. Many remember well the Virginia Synodical Convention hosted at Grace Church during 1953, our own Bicentennial year, when delegates were fed and housed by our ladies.

• In 1970, the 150th Anniversary of the Synod of Maryland and Virginia (first organized in Winchester in 1820) was celebrated and our church served as host. LCW handled arrangements for necessary housing, assisted with banquet plans and decorations. The banquet was held at Lee-Jackson Restaurant for over four hundred guests. Worthwhile and attractive historical displays were worked out and arranged by our women.

WOMEN OF GRACE

In 1984 an effort was made to revive Lutheran Church Women. The new name chosen was Women of Grace. The women responsible for this were Judy Drayer, Evelyn Goode, Helene Harder, Mary Margaret Hollar and Anne Olinger. Meetings are held monthly for fellowship and Bible study, using the resources provided in the periodical, *Lutheran Woman Today*. A new constitution was adopted in 1995 following the transition to the Evangelical Lutheran Church in America. After many years of faithful service, Dot Nixon retired as treasurer in 1997 and Clarene H. Wolfe accepted the position. Coordinators of Women of Grace have been:

Elaine Diehl, 1984-1986
Joyce Ray and Cinda Brand, 1987-1990
Evelyn Goode and Lenore Eavis, 1991-1993
Nancy Braswell and Lenore Eavis, 1994-Present

W.I.L.D. WOMEN OF GRACE

A new and exciting intergenerational group for women began in the fall of 2002. Serving on the steering committee were: Elaine Diehl, Karen Marsh, Rita Peters, Teresa Lehman, Joyce Ray, Dilly Rucker, Angie Haecker and Emily Thomas.

All women are welcome as **W**illing **I**nviting **L**oving **D**isciples to share a meal, enjoy fellowship and grow spiritually through Bible study and devotions.

WEEKDAY CHURCH SCHOOL

The first session of Weekday Church School was held in the spring of 1957 for the fifth and sixth graders. Mrs. W.E. Eisenberg and Mrs. J.G. Fosbrink were the teachers.

In 1958 began the first full session with 26 pupils in grades four, five and six. Work was integrated according to public school standards. Mrs. H.J. Eavis coordinated the planning and ordering of materials. Mrs. J.A. Madden taught fourth grade; Mrs. J.A. Hott taught fifth grade; Mrs. W.E. Eisenberg taught sixth grade. Beginning in October, classes for fifth and sixth grades were held in conjunction with rehearsals for the Junior and Youth Choirs. A junior catechetical class taught by Pastor Eisenberg was included for seventh graders. A class for third graders taught by Mrs. Marshall Stine was added. The total enrollment was 42.

In 1960-1961 the classes were temporarily stopped due to the reconstruction of the Parish Education Building. Classes for grades three through seven resumed in February 1962. In 1964 classes included grades three through six with catechetical instruction for grade seven taught by Mrs. Eavis and eighth grade taught by Pastor Eisenberg. This continued for a few years until attendance waned. Catechetical instruction continued on Sunday afternoons for several more years.

VACATION CHURCH SCHOOL/VACATION BIBLE SCHOOL

The best week of every summer at Grace Lutheran Church is the week of Vacation Bible School (VBS). Singing, crafts, Bible stories, games and snack are offered for all ages by caring adults and youth.

Called Vacation Church School (VCS) for many years, it was suspended only in 1961 during the remodeling of the Parish Education Building. Beginning in 1976, we joined with Christ Episcopal Church and made many new friends, young and old. VBS spread the gospel to

300 children in the summer of 2002. VBS is a growing outreach to the un-churched of the downtown Winchester area.

Although evening, afternoon and two-week formats were tried during various weeks, for many years the event has been held successfully the second week in July from 9:00 a.m. until 12:00 noon. Serving as director of VCS during the 1950s and 1960s were: Mrs. A.H. Crawford, Jr., Mrs. Merrick Shawe, Mrs. Howard H. Shockey, Mrs. Carl S. Napps, Mrs. Richard Petonke, Mrs. James V. Rife, Mrs. James H. Diehl, Mrs. C. Kenneth Lamp. Parish staff took charge during the 1970s and early 1980s. Mary Miller Froehlich served as director 1987-1992. Teresa Lehman has provided dynamic leadership since 1993.

KINDERGARTEN AND PRESCHOOL

Nineteen sixty-two marked the beginning of a new and exciting venture for Grace Church. After the dedication of the newly reconstructed Parish Education Building, it was determined that the additional available space should be used to the fullest. On September 13, 1962, Grace Church Kindergarten came into being under the direction of Martha Stine Cahill. The members of the first Kindergarten Board to support this bold decision were Richard H. Petonke, chairman; Mrs. Joseph W. McDaniel, secretary; Paul H. Miller, treasurer; Mrs. Henry J. Eavis and Mrs. C. Edward Manuel, curriculum; and John T. Wolfe. Tuition was $15 per month and the budget was supplemented by donations of materials and cash from parish members.

Mrs. Cahill was assisted for two years by Mrs. Marie Griffith. The first class of thirteen four- and five-year-olds assembled Monday to Friday from 9:00 a.m. until noon with activities to help the children from the congregation and the community grow physically stronger, emotionally more secure, mentally alert and spiritually more resolute. In 1966, Mrs. Vivian Kline joined the staff to teach the four-year-olds, and Mrs. Cahill taught the five-year-olds.

When public schools added kindergarten in 1974, the program became known as Grace Lutheran Preschool and two-day classes for three-year-olds were added. Among the dedicated teachers have been Betsy Fisher, Linda Humphrey, Kristi Riggleman, Lynn Riley, Marla Austin, Dana Fitzsimmons and Jill Kerr. After twenty years of serving the preschool and the church as Director of Christian Education, Martha Cahill resigned in 1982. Subsequent directors of the preschool have been Joette Cates (1983-1988), Christy Barbour (1989-1993), Kathy Melby (1994-1995) and Lisa Gilbert (1996 to the present).

The preschool operates under its own bylaws and is governed

First Grace Church Kindergarten Class, September 13, 1962, front row (left to right): Debra Mallory, Lisa Ewing, Carla Leight, Terry Marshall; second row, Kurt Roinestad, Cathy Dodson, Carl Braithwaite, Linda Kroggel, Susan Shafer; third row, Hartmut Doerwaldt, Bret Patterson, Alexander Simpson; absent Shannon Laign.

by a board of directors with its own operating budget. In 1992 the congregation purchased Noble's Travel World at 16 N. Braddock Street and, after remodeling in 1993, this building became known as the Children's Education Center (CEC). Housing eight classes of 94 children for the 40th year, 2002-2003, tuition is now $75 per month.

Funds were contributed in memory of Martha Cahill upon her death in 1987. Interest from these funds provides scholarships for children requiring financial assistance. Scholarship requests have grown along with the preschool and over $6,000 was distributed to children in 2002. The Martha Cahill Fund covers a portion of those scholarships. Fundraising endeavors include the annual Shrove Tuesday Pancake Supper and the sale of seats for the Apple Blossom Festival parades. The fraternal groups, Aid Association for Lutherans and Lutheran Brotherhood, have been most supportive with matching donations.

As an extension of the ministry of Grace, the preschool has a strong outreach and presence in the community. The staff and board of directors strive to continue the mission that was set forth forty years ago.

GODFREY MILLER FELLOWSHIP CENTER

Established in 1976, the Godfrey Miller Fellowship Center is dedicated to serving adults of the community by providing a special place for fellowship, programs and benevolent services. The evolution of the present center from its original opening as a residence for elderly ladies is told elsewhere in this volume [Chapter XI]. The goal of the center is to make participants happy and healthy. Health, fellowship and educational services currently serve Winchester and Frederick County residents from all walks of life.

The center is open Monday through Thursday from 10:00 a.m. until 3:00 p.m. with special programming events taking place throughout the week. An extension of the ministry of Grace Lutheran Church, it welcomes vital, active, imaginative and fun-loving adults to programs fostering Christian fellowship and social sharing.

PRIMETIMERS

A kick-off breakfast to meet and greet interested members of Grace who are of retirement age was held on October 11, 1994, at Manuel's and Wife Restaurant. Designed for monthly social activities on a weekday, usually involving a breakfast or lunch, short day trips in the spring and fall also were scheduled. An interest in fun and fellowship with Grace members and friends was the main criterion. According to the October 2, 1994, issue of *Tidings*, Carol and Hal Lehman agreed to coordinate the group.

Primetimers continues to meet the second Tuesday of each month at Carper's Valley Golf Club featuring guest speakers. The group takes spring and fall bus trips to nearby states. Beginning in 1999 summer activities were co-sponsored with the Godfrey Miller Fellowship Center. A summer covered dish picnic and a Christmas banquet are held jointly with the Adult Bible Class. Attendance in 2002 for the breakfast programs ranged from 60 to 85. Barbara Wilson serves as treasurer.

MEN OF THE BIBLE BREAKFAST

The first Men of the Bible Breakfast (MOBB) was held on January 8, 1998, at the Godfrey Miller Fellowship Center. All Christian men of the community were invited for food, Christian fellowship and discussion of men in the Bible. Hal Lehman and Howard Slothower served as founding co-chairmen of this group that meets on the second Thursday of each month. This ecumenical group has participants from about ten local churches.

This Heritage

PARISH NURSING AND HEALTH MINISTRY

Through 1996, Grace's health ministry outreach was primarily focused on homebound persons and members residing in long-term care. With the direction of the clergy, other parishioners experiencing loss, grief or crisis received prepared meals and were placed on the prayer list for healing. Other than additional spoken prayers during worship, no other formal health ministry activities were in place.

On July 14, 1996, the Congregation Council "approved in principle the congregation's participation in the parish nurse health ministry and accepted with appreciation Lisa Zerull's volunteer status to serve as our congregation's first parish nurse."

Zerull explained the concept in the "Dear Partners" column of *Tidings* for October 13, 1996: "A parish nurse is a registered nurse who has had additional education in holistic ministry (body, mind and spirit) and who provides special health promotion services to a faith community. Some of the different aspects of the parish nurse role include a health educator, a health counselor, a referral source of information and a listener. Parish nursing is not hands-on technical care, but rather a helpful and spiritual presence within the congregation."

The Parish Health Ministry Committee was established as the tenth standing committee in 1997. Its activities have included:

- Prayers for Healing services on the fifth Sunday of the month
- Blood Pressure Checks on the 1st and 3rd Sunday of the month or by request
- Holistic health information shared as the "The Health Corner" in the church newsletter—*Tidings*
- Annual flu shot clinic targeting persons in need throughout the greater Winchester community in collaboration with a physician member of Grace
- Holistic health information placed on a bulletin board display in the main hallway
- Health topic presentations given to the Primetimers group and at the Godfrey Miller Fellowship Center
- Annual "Body and Soul" health fair offered on St. Luke's Sunday in October in collaboration with Christ Episcopal Church for members from both congregations
- Active card ministry using special stationery called the "Random Acts of Kindness" cards
- Collaboration with the layperson home visitors to formalize visitation to "Members at Home" (homebound) and "Members in Special Care" (long-term care).

• Complementing clergy visitation to homes, hospitals and nursing homes.

On November 14, 1999, Mary Sonafelt, RN, was called as the second parish nurse with a primary role to visit members at home and in special care. In 2002 regular office hours were established in the administrative area on Tuesdays from noon to 2:00 p.m. for Grace parishioners and the surrounding community. It has been a blessing to see parishioners begin to understand the link between faith and health. With God's help, the clergy's continued support and the congregation's willingness to minister to one another's body, mind and spirit, so many more opportunities exist for growth and expansion of the health ministry outreach.

PRAYER CHAIN

Since 1998, prayer chain members have provided distinctively Christian care through prayer with personal confidentiality. Volunteers participate in the chain using the telephone or email. Currently the Grace Prayer Chain concentrates on the needs of individuals who are ill, bereaved, or in an emotional or spiritual crisis. It is grounded in Jesus' command to love and care for one another.

LITURGICAL ARTS AND MUSIC CAMP

Offered for the first time in the summer of 2001, this week of music and crafts provides enrichment experiences for about 30 children of upper elementary school age. Sharon Hetland serves as the coordinator.

That Grace Evangelical Lutheran Church has a growing commitment to the community is evidenced by the auxiliary organizations that have been presented here. The emphasis on a strong lay leadership for the standing committees of Church Council in the 1970s along with the emerging elected leadership of women in the congregation fostered rich opportunities for special ministries. The expansion of programs called for an expansion in facilities. As more groups used our facilities, ever more programs evolved. The new century saw Grace Church hosting the annual Spring Community Dinner with our friends at Community House and the Northwestern Workshop. Teams supported construction of a Habitat for Humanity house. Many years of scheduling space for adult education classes led to their inclusion in 2002 in the Lifelong Learning Center along with English as a Second Language classes. Future plans include a hand bell group and after school arts and music activities in a newly renovated G&M Building.

Grace Confirmation Class, May 17, 1964, front row (left to right): Diane Bush, Martha Miller, Virginia Hoke, Sharon Snarr, Sarah Pingley, Sandy Ritter, Barbara Mallory; second row, Becky Wolfe, Sally Crawford, Patricia Gochenour, Carol Carr, Vicki Tucker, Karen Lou Jennings; third row, Tommy Evans, Scott Douglas Keller, Floyd Shanholtz, Toby Boyce, David Barnett; back row, David Jeffcoat, Bruce Lucas, Pastor W.E. Eisenberg, Max Bayliss, and Nelson Orndoff.

Grace Confirmation Class, September 22, 2002, front row (left to right): Hope Savolainen, Lindsay Forse, Brittney Greene; second row, Joey Behr, Katharine Melby, Zachary Hockman, Pastor James H. Utt; third row, Pastor Martha Sims, Christina Weissenberger, Abby Manzano, Melinda Forsyth, and Hannah Doerwaldt.

The Men and Women of Grace

Henry Baetjer

J. George Baetjer

Catherine Streit Baker

Henry S. Baker

Jacob Baker

William B. Baker

J. Edwin Cooper

Lewis F. Cooper

Thomas J. Cooper

This Heritage

The Men and Women of Grace

G. Casper Fries

Hugh K. Green

Alfred D. Henkel

J. Luther Maphis

Miss Katie Miller

William R. Miller

Jacob A. Richard

Harry A. Schmidt

Clark M. Smith

Miss Kate O. Wolfe   Rufus Benton Peery   L.S.G. Miller

Miss Margaretta Miller (left) and Miss Portia B. Baker

J. Few Brown and A. Harry Miller (photo on near right) and Ben F. Davis

This Heritage

The Men and Women of Grace

Mary Katherine Aulick

Nancy Braswell

Martha Cahill

Vera Crawford

J. Kenly Carr

Paul H. Miller

Marian Pasquet

Dorothy Tillotson

Mary Whitehill

Chapter XI
The Larger Vision

In every congregation there are to be found choice souls who have not been afraid to venture along the path of faith. Above and beyond their general calling as Christians they have heard the overtones of their Master's voice, and they have heeded His promptings.

Throughout the past two hundred years Grace Church has had a goodly company of noble spirits of this kind. They had ears to hear, and they heard. They had eyes to see, and they caught the glimpse of glory. And what they heard, and what they saw were translated into deed and action. Nor were they disobedient to their heavenly visions.

First, we would think of the men of the congregation who have gone into the ministry of the Gospel.

Second, we would list those devoted hearts, which by bequest or special gift, have remembered the congregation and work of the Church.

Third, we would point with gratitude to the missionaries to Japan[a] whom the congregation has supported, and remark upon that enterprise.

Fourth, we would submit, for the sake of the record, something about the few Negro members of the congregation.

Fifth, we would mention the congregation's lengthened shadow of influence through her daughters who have become the wives of ministers.

Sixth, we would recount the start of the Godfrey Miller Home. And seventh, we would enter a concluding word.

---

[a] Currently missionaries are supported in Africa as well.

1. MEN IN THE MINISTRY

JOHN B. RECK. This young man was supported by the congregation in his study for the ministry at New Market under S.S. Schmucker, while his brother, Abraham Reck, was pastor. The fact that he was listed as coming from Winchester would seem to indicate that he resided in the town. The Maryland Synod appointed him its missionary to the West in 1835, and he remained in Ohio.

ISAAC BAKER. Licensed by the Synod of Virginia in 1838, and ordained in 1843, Isaac Baker, a member of the Winchester church, son of Mr. and Mrs. John Baker, served congregations at Wardensville and Harrisonburg. He died in 1876.

JOHN MILLER EICHELBERGER. This son of Pastor and Mrs. Lewis Eichelberger was born at Winchester and educated at Gettysburg College and Seminary. November 14, 1852, he delivered a sermon on the death of Daniel Webster in his home church. He soon took up law and became a member of the St. Louis, Missouri, bar, dying shortly thereafter in 1854.

ENOS DINKLE. October 3, 1859, Enos Dinkle, a son of the congregation confirmed June 27, 1858, was recommended by the Council to the Education Society of the Synod of Virginia as a person of proper moral character for the ministry. He became a ministerial candidate of the Synod. With the outbreak of the Civil War, however, he disappeared from the picture. He died in 1861, but whether as a war casualty we do not know.

DAVID H. BAUSLIN, D.D., LL.D. Born in Winchester in 1854 and baptized by Charles Porterfield Krauth, the family of David H. Bauslin moved away in 1861 because the father was a Union man. He grew up at Clearspring, Washington County, Maryland. He was educated at Wittenberg College and the Theological Seminary at Springfield, Ohio. Ordained to the ministry in 1878, he served parishes in Ohio until in 1896 he was elected to the faculty of the Theological Seminary at Springfield, where as professor and dean, he had a long and notable career.

WILLIAM MILLER BAUM, JR., D.D. Born while his father was pastor at Winchester and baptized October 16, 1858, by Dr. Krauth, W.M. Baum, Jr., was educated at the College and Seminary at Gettysburg. After ordination in 1880 he was pastor at Phoenixville, Pennsylvania, for three years, followed by a longtime ministry at Canajoharie, New York.

JOHN EICHELBERGER BUSHNELL. This son of the congregation, baptized July 18, 1857, confirmed March 28, 1869, and educated at Roanoke College and Yale University, served the Church in South Carolina, Virginia, Maryland, California and South Carolina again. His home mission work established First Lutheran Church, Oakland, California. In Virginia, he was pastor of St. Mark's, Roanoke (1885-1890), St. Paul's, Frederick County, and Lebanon Church, Shenandoah County (1899-1901) and the Blacksburg Parish (1903-1905). He died November 13, 1917, aboard a train at Augusta, Georgia.

L.G.M. MILLER, D.D. The story of this former pastor, who was also reared in the congregation, has been given elsewhere. While a student at Washington and Lee, his college nickname was "Latin, Greek and Mathematics" Miller.

GEORGE EDWARD KRAUTH. The son of Charles Porterfield and Mary Virginia Baker Krauth was born September 30, 1859. He was educated at the University of Pennsylvania. After engaging in teaching and business for some thirteen years, he prepared for the ministry at the Philadelphia Seminary and was ordained in 1897. He served congregations in Philadelphia, Pennsylvania; Cleveland, Ohio; and Harrisonburg, Virginia. He died in 1905. Following the death of his father, his mother returned to her native Winchester where she spent the rest of her days.

JOHN GEORGE GRAICHEN. The son of Mr. and Mrs. F.

August Graichen, he was born in Baltimore and moved with his family at an early age to Winchester. He was confirmed July 2, 1881. Educated at Roanoke College and Gettysburg Seminary, he served churches at Iowa City, Iowa; Hays City, Kansas; Lexington, South Carolina; Waynesboro, Virginia; and Morristown, Tennessee.

TAYLOR BABB YEAKLEY. Confirmed March 29, 1891, Taylor B. Yeakley also was educated at Roanoke College and Gettysburg Seminary. His ministry was mainly in the Pittsburgh Synod, where he served Temple Church and Mt. Zion Church in the steel city, followed by a long pastorate at First Lutheran Church, New Kensington, Pennsylvania.

LEWIS SAMUEL GODFREY MILLER. The son of Pastor and Mrs. L.G.M. Miller, he was confirmed April 2, 1893. As the second missionary of the congregation to Japan, he will be considered at another place in this chapter.

RALPH ROY RICHARD. A native of Frederick County, Virginia, Ralph R. Richard was confirmed in Grace Church, May 3, 1896. His family resided in Winchester during the years 1887-1899 when his father, the Rev. Asa Richard, was pastor of St. Paul's and Lebanon rural congregations. His mother, a brother and several sisters were members of Grace Church likewise.[b]

NORMAN ELMORE COOPER. The son of Mr. and Mrs. Lewis F. Cooper, Norman E. Cooper was educated at Roanoke College and Gettysburg Seminary and served the North River

---

[b] A graduate of Roanoke College and the Gettysburg Lutheran Theological Seminary, the Rev. Ralph Richard served Pennsylvania parishes in the Shippenville, Smicksburg, North Carrol and Shanksville charges as well as Second Lutheran Church of Chambersburg and St. Luke Lutheran Church after his ordination in 1915. He retired from active ministry in 1949 and died November 26, 1963, in Hagerstown, Maryland.

Parish of the Virginia Synod from 1918-1922. For reasons of health, he left the active work of the pastorate and became associated with his father's business firm. In 1946 he demitted the ministry and united with the Seventh Day Adventist congregation in Winchester.

ROBERT BAKER AND LUTHER YEAKLEY. *The History of the Lutheran Church in Virginia and East Tennessee*, edited by C.W. Cassell, W.J. Finck and E.O. Henkel, credits Grace Church with Robert Baker and Luther Yeakley as sons in the ministry. No facts indicating their membership in the congregation have been discovered.

CHARLES ALFRED STUART ROBERTSON. Confirmed December 26, 1954, Charles Robertson served in the U. S. Navy, graduated from George Washington University (1957) and from Philadelphia Theological Seminary (1960). He was ordained at Grace Lutheran Church June 12, 1960.

As a mission developer he established St. Matthew's in East Richmond and Nativity in Alexandria, Virginia. Deciding to enter a foreign mission field, he and his wife worked with slum dwellers in Lima, Peru. They began their work there in 1969 and aided victims of the 1970 earthquake before political unrest forced the family to flee leaving all their belongings behind. They then settled in Miami, Florida.

On August 25, 1956, Charles Robertson married Mary Martha Eisenberg, daughter of Pastor and Mrs. William E. Eisenberg. They are the parents of Miriam, Edward, Kevin, Philip and Stephen. Mrs. Robertson became ill following their experience in Peru and the couple divorced. Rev. Robertson married Leann Kronmann in 1979 and they have a daughter, Anna. He is pastor of St. Mark's Lutheran Church, Coral Gables, Florida.

FREDERICK MARSHALL RITTER, JR. Son of Frederick Marshall and Henrietta Cornwell Ritter, Frederick Ritter was born February 22, 1938, baptized in Grace Church April 16, 1939, and confirmed April 2, 1950. He received his education at Gettysburg College (1960) and Gettysburg Seminary (1963) and was called as pastor by Redeemer Lutheran Church, Pearisburg, Virginia.

Married to Sue Ella Sybert at Grace Church in 1960, they had a son, Frederick Marshall Ritter, III. The couple later divorced. As a result of a swimming accident in 1975, Pastor Ritter became a paraplegic. He married DeeDee White Tyree in 1979 and they lived in Norfolk, Virginia, where he worked as a mental health therapist and was a chaplain at Lake Taylor Hospital. He died February 3, 2002.

DUANE LESLIE STEELE. Duane Leslie Steele, his wife Janet Bauer, and their two daughters, Jennifer Leslie and Christine Elizabeth transferred from Nativity Lutheran Church in Alexandria, Virginia, to Grace Church on January 7, 1973. Totally blind, Duane graduated from Shenandoah Conservatory of Music and Gettysburg Seminary (1978). He was ordained June 25, 1978, in Grace Church and received a call to and serves the Gladesboro Lutheran Parish in Southwest Virginia.

JEFFREY RONALD SONAFELT. The son of Ronald and Mary Sickles Sonafelt, Jeffrey Sonafelt was confirmed May 27, 1973, at Grace Church. A graduate of James Madison University and Lutheran Southern Seminary, he was ordained June 1, 1984, and received a call from Redeemer and Lutheran Memorial Churches in Giles County, Virginia. He has also served Mt. Zion in the Quicksburg Parish, Virginia, and St. Paul's in Shenandoah, Virginia. He is now serving Trinity Lutheran in Newport News, Virginia. Jeff and Tracy Lastor were married in 1979.

KARL DAVID SKOLE. Son of Guenther and June Skole, David was baptized June 16, 1957, at Grace Church. He graduated from Cornell University (1979) and Gettysburg Seminary (1987) and was ordained at the Constituting Convention of the Virginia Synod at Roanoke College on May 29, 1987. He accepted a call as associate pastor of St. John's Lutheran Church, Springfield, Ohio, and later returned to the Salem Church, Mt. Sidney, Virginia. Married to Diane DeLoach (1987), they have a son and a daughter. He served at Mountain of Faith Church, Stansbury Park, Utah, until 2001. He is now pastor at Christ Church, Roanoke.

H. LEE BRUMBACK II. Son of Harvey Lee and Elizabeth Bywaters Brumback, Lee was baptized at Grace on March 25, 1945, and received a degree in agronomy from Virginia Tech (1963). He entered the Peace Corps and served in Jamaica and Fiji. With Lutheran World Relief, he served in Vietnam, Greece and Ethiopia helping to solve problems of increased populations with shrinking food supply. Brumback graduated from Gettysburg Seminary with a Master of Divinity (1991) and Master of Sacred Theology (1995). He received his Doctor of Ministry (2001) from the Lutheran Theological Seminary at Philadelphia. He was ordained at Grace Church on August 25, 1991, by Bishop Maurice G. Zumbrun of the Maryland-Delaware Synod. Since 1991 he has served as pastor of St. Mary Evangelical Lutheran Church, Silver Run, near Westminster, Maryland. Married to Ann Headley Keister (1970), they have two sons.

2. BEQUESTS AND SPECIAL GIFTS

By the will of John Lemley, who died in 1784, the residue of his estate was left to the trustees of the congregation "for use and assistance in finishing the Lutheran Church."

During the years when Peter Lauck and Philip Hoover were trustees of the congregation (1813-1815) a bequest was received which was invested in 7 shares of stock in the Farmers Bank of Virginia. This devise was to be devoted exclusively for repairs to the church. With the renovation of the church in the 1820s the above-mentioned stock was sold and the proceeds used to help pay the costs.

1851. Through the will of John Hoff the church received $750 for the South Loudoun Street parsonage, $200 for the cause of Foreign Missions, and the Sunday School received the income from an endowment of $250. This latter sum was invested in a land bond which had doubled in value after twenty years.

1878. A.H. Miller, on June 3, stated to the Council that he wished to pay over to the trustees of the church $250 to be invested for the benefit of the Sunday School, this being part of the inheritance he had received from Mrs. Rea, his mother-in-law, who had expressed her wish and intention, a short time before her death, to aid the Sunday School. The trustees were authorized to receive this sum and to invest it as they might deem best.

1887. By the will of Matthias Schultz the sum of $500 was left for the upkeep of the cemetery.

1888. William B. Baker devised the sum of $300 for the benefit of the Sunday School. This was invested by the trustees for additional endowment.

1889. Henry S. Baker left to the church certain undeveloped lots in the city of Keokuk, Iowa. After paying taxes on them for five years, they were sold and $450 was realized.

1900. J. Abraham Miller left a bequest of $200 for the use of the Sunday School.

1906. Miss Nora C. Nott devised to the trustees the sum of $700. This money became the nucleus of the fund for the pipe organ purchased in 1914.

1914. The written request of Miss Sarah Glaize that $500 be paid from her estate to the congregation for mission work in Japan was honored by her administrator, Fred L. Glaize, her nephew, and paid the following year.

1914. Mrs. Charlotte E. Lupton left land on National Avenue to the church to be sold and the proceeds used for mission work. The property brought $3,625. Half of this amount went to the Hakata church in Japan, and half to the Church Extension Fund of the United Synod of the South.

1915. Dr. John Godfrey Miller left to the trustees of the congregation the sum of $2,000. This was used in the purchase of the Union Fire Company property in 1919.

1915. The sum of $250 was received from Mrs. Jane Swisher.

1916. Five thousand dollars received from the will of Mrs. Elizabeth Baker Glaize was used to install the Brevitt Chime of ten bells in 1917. An additional sum of $4,527 from the same estate was received for maintaining and lighting the chime.

For thirty-six years now [1953] the bells have been played each week with a fair regularity. Their fine clear notes can be heard throughout the whole community. Their playing has become a local institution, anticipated and appreciated by many.

Maria Briscoe Croker penned the following lines some years ago after hearing the bells play:

> *I came at eve to Winchester, Virginia's ancient town;*
> *A place of martial memories, of valor and renown.*

Far in the distance, soaring the Alleghenies rose,
Sun-kissed, serenely beautiful in nature's calm repose.
There was no soul in Winchester to bid me welcome there,
But, oh, I heard the sunset chimes ring sweetly on the air!
They played the old-time hymns of faith – songs of uplifting power –
"Lead Kindly Light," and strong and clear, "I Need Thee Every Hour."
Then, as the sweet notes trembled in distance far away,
A hush of reverent silence o'er all the city lay.
I was no longer lonely, the bells made welcome there,
I knew that kindred spirits had joined with me in prayer.

Edward Washington, the sexton, became the first bell ringer. Others who have played them have been Prof. William H. McIlwee, Marshall Snapp, Ben Davis, Jr., Frank M. Dick and, since 1946, Wilbur Kern.

Mr. Kern's many years of service to the church were recognized on Sunday, January 20, 1984, when he was presented a plaque, a stereo system and a monetary gift for his dedication. Various members of the congregation played the bells following Mr. Kern's retirement.

To commemorate the seventieth anniversary of the installation and dedication of the Brevitt Chime, the descendants, relatives and friends of the David S. and Elizabeth B. Glaize family were invited to a ceremony on Sunday, October 25, 1987. Following a chime prelude a new memorial plaque near the entrance to the sanctuary was unveiled.

The structure of the bells was strengthened in 1969. "The Brevitt Chime was electrified in 1994 as a part of the renovation of the sanctuary," recollected Dorothy Tillotson in February 2002. "This means the bells can be played in a computerized system by using a keyboard in the recording room instead of playing in the Bell Tower by using levers to play the bells. However, the old system can still be used. They can be programmed to play at any hour and as many times as needed. At the time the new organ was installed in December 1994, the bells were computerized to be used on the organ Great Manual, which is a wonderful asset for celebrations, funerals and weddings. This project cost was $32,000. The money was provided through the Brevitt Chime Fund that had built up through interest over many years. Now, a high school student programs the bells, guided by the themes of the Liturgical Year." The Bell Tower housing the bells was refurbished by Matthew Humphrey as an Eagle Scout Project in 2000.

1917. From the estate of Mrs. Sarah Hoffman Wall the sum of $2,520 was received. This was used the following year to place new windows in the church in memory of Edward Hoffman, Mrs. Wall's father.

1917. Miss Portia B. Baker made a bequest of $50 "towards a chapel or lecture room for Grace Church."

1917. Miss Emily M. Miller left $500 "for our work in Japan."

1919. By the generosity of Miss Katie Miller a gift of $1,085 was made to the congregation, which amount, added to the bequest from Dr. John Godfrey Miller, was used in purchasing the Union Fire Company property.

1919. By the will of Hugh K. Green $3,000 was left for mission work in Japan.

1920. A sum of $1,000 was left to the trustees of the congregation to be administered for the poor by the will of Mrs. Susan Winkley.

1921. A brass altar cross was presented to the church by Mrs. Grover C. Rose and George B. Bushnell in memory of their sister, Marie (May) Louise Bushnell.

1922. George Casper Fries made the dream of a new Sunday School a reality by his gift of $25,000. This gift was not made in a lump sum, but paid over a period of years. During this time Mr. Fries paid interest on the unpaid portion of the principal. He died before the entire obligation had been met. His son, Charles W. Fries, with an equally fine generosity, completed the payments. A tablet to the memory of George Casper Fries was placed in the Sunday School in 1939.

1927. By the will of Miss Kate O. Wolfe, $300 was left for Home Mission work, $500 for Foreign Mission work, and $300 for the work of the Sunday School. This was to be known as the Robert B.

Wolfe Fund. By the will of Miss Fannie R. Wolfe, an additional $500 was added to the fund.

1930. The church received $200 from the estate of Charles A. Williams.

1930. From the estate of Mrs. Laura V. Graichen, $5,000 was received and used to reduce the indebtedness incurred in the erection of the Sunday School. Mrs. Graichen also left $1,500 to the Lutheran Orphan's Home at Salem.

1930. Misses Margaretta and Marianna Miller presented to the congregation the lot on which the present parsonage stands.[c]

1931. Record was made in the minutes on September 7, concerning the disposition of the following funds: The J. Abraham Miller, Mrs. Rea, Mrs. Jane Swisher, W.B. Baker and John Hoff Funds were by action of the council applied to the Sunday School Building debt. The Susan Winkley Fund was invested, the interest to be used for the poor of the church.

1934. $500 from the estate of Thomas J. Cooper was applied on the church debt.

1935. $25 from the estate of Mrs. Sarah E. McCann was used to start a fund for new hymn books.

1935. A gift of $1,000 was made to the church by Mr. and Mrs. David H. Patterson of California. Before marriage Mrs. Patterson was Miss Nannie M. Zirkle, a member of the congregation.

1936. A pair of brass candlesticks for the altar was given in memory of Charles K. Over by his family.

1938. Miss Margaretta Miller devised $5,000 to the trustees of the congregation: $5,000 for work in Kumamoto, Japan; $5,000 to the Lutheran Orphan's Home at Salem; $5,000

---

[c] In 1953, the parsonage was located at 605 S. Stewart Street. There is currently no parsonage.

to the work of home missions; $1,000 to the Women's Auxiliary of Grace Church; $300 to Salem Hebrew Mission; and $300 to the American Bible Society. In addition, she left her home with $5,000 endowment and a one-third interest in an undeveloped tract of land on South Stewart Street to the trustees of Grace Church for an old ladies' home to be known as "The Godfrey Miller Home."

1943. Five hundred dollars was received from the Lee W. Lamp estate.

1944. By the will of Miss Katie Miller a bequest of $1,000 was left to the trustees of the church, together with the residue of her estate, which amounted to $5,484.

1947. By the will of Oliver F. Snapp, who attended services of the church, though he was not a member, the congregation received $106.

1947. Audio-visual equipment for use of the congregation was made possible by a gift of $500 from Mr. and Mrs. N.E. Cooper.

1948. By the terms of the will of Miss Peggy Miller, a member of the Presbyterian Church, Grace Church received $1,000.

1949. Another $1,000 bequest to the church was made by Miss Jennie M. Green, who also left $2,000 for Japan mission work; $1,000 to the orphanage at Salem; and $500 for Lutheran Mountain Mission work in Southwest Virginia.

1952. The will of J. George Baetjer left $500 to the Lowman Home, White Rock, South Carolina, and $500 to the Lutheran Children's Home of the South, at Salem, Virginia.

1952. A handsome pair of brass floor candlebra was presented to the church by Mrs. Howard K. Grove, Mrs. J. Gordon Lindsay, J. Luther Maphis, Jr., and J. Alan Maphis in memory of their father, Mr. J. Luther Maphis.

1953. A set of white altar and pulpit paraments embroidered in gold was given in memory of Harry A. Schmidt by Mrs. Schmidt.

1953. Specially designed benches with music racks for the choir were presented in memory of Ben F. Davis by Mrs. Davis.

In the last 50 years many individuals have generously remembered Grace Church and the Godfrey Miller Home. Space does not allow us to share each item but the archives has a listing of each bequest. Thanks be to God!

---

3. MISSIONARIES TO JAPAN

In the story that has been recounted thus far, ample testimony has been submitted to show the congregation's positive concern for the wider reaches of Christ's Kingdom. While the home missionary cause has not been slighted, there has been a particular interest in and love for the foreign mission work of the Lutheran Church in Japan.

This concern for the foreign mission enterprise goes back more than a hundred years [1953], as witness the bequest of John Hoff [1851]. Good seed had been planted in good soil before the War of '61, and after the paralysis of that conflict had been overcome, Dr. Gilbert and Dr. Miller not only continued to plant and water, but to harvest as well. These two pastors were trusted leaders in the Lutheran Church in the South, and what the congregation at Winchester did in behalf of the foreign mission cause led the way for congregations in the entire area.

With the decision of the United Synod of the South to begin mission work in Japan, L.G.M. Miller felt an increased sense of responsibility. He provided the congregation with the leadership of the challenge, and his people caught the vision of his dream. They decided, therefore, to send their own missionary and to back him with their gifts. It is claimed that this particular action was the first of its kind taken by any congregation in what is now the United Lutheran Church in America [1953], and no evidence to the contrary has been found. If this claim be true, Grace Church is grateful to God and happy in it.

RUFUS BENTON PEERY. Rufus Benton Peery was the congregation's first missionary. He was a native of Burke's Garden, Virginia, where he was born April 9, 1868. He graduated at Roanoke College (1890) and at Gettysburg Seminary (1892). Going to Japan [in 1892], he was, with J.A.B. Scherer, one of the two original Lutheran missionaries sent from America. In this capacity he continued until 1904, and throughout the twelve years of his service received his salary support from Grace Church. In 1895 he married Ann Letitia Rich and they became the parents of six sons.

Returning to America in 1903, Mr. Peery remained in this country. He was pastor in Philadelphia (1904-1905), in Denver, Colorado (1905-1912), at Polo, Illinois (1919-1920), at Hickory, North Carolina (1920-1924), at Wooster, Ohio (1924-1931), and at Raleigh, North Carolina (1931-1933). He was president of Midland College, Fremont, Nebraska (1912-1919), and professor in Lenoir College (1920-1924). He was the author of various writings on Japan, and the translator of the Common Service and of Lutheran ministerial acts into Japanese. He died October 25, 1934, and was buried at Raleigh, North Carolina.

The support of the work in Japan continued. In the interim up to 1907, Missionary Charles L. Brown is referred to as "our missionary to Japan" at least once in the records. In the fall of 1907 the congregation sent out its second representative, who labored there abundantly until 1951. He was L.S.G. Miller, son of the congregation.

LEWIS SAMUEL GODFREY MILLER. Lewis Samuel Godfrey Miller was born at Salem, Virginia, August 23, 1881. After graduating from Roanoke College, Class 1901, he was employed for several years at Wheeling, West Virginia, before entering the theological seminary at Mt. Airy, Philadelphia, where he graduated in 1907. Being called to mission work in Japan, he was commissioned in Grace Church and sent to the Orient that fall, the congregation in Winchester assuming his support.

In 1909 he married Miss Daisy B. Sutton, a missionary of the Methodist Church to Japan and a native of Eastern Virginia. To them two children were born, a daughter, Mary, and a son, Lewis Godfrey Meineke. The boy died in early life.

For forty-four years L.S.G. Miller served the cause of Christ in Japan. Stationed first at Hakata, he was instrumental in building up a congregation and erecting a church in that city, the funds being supplied by interested friends in Winchester. Moving to Kumamoto, likewise a city on the island of Kyushu, he became head of a mission school for boys, Kyushu Gakuin, and here the major portion of his ministry was spent.

Mrs. Miller died in 1933. In 1935 Dr. Miller married Miss Martha Harder, Lutheran missionary to Japan. With the outbreak of war (1939), they were forced to return to America. During this interval Dr. Miller served home mission congregations at Elberton, Georgia, and at Laurel, Mississippi.

At the end of the war the Millers returned to Japan. Dr. Miller not only was the first Lutheran missionary from America to return, he was the first Protestant missionary to be re-admitted into the country. They remained in the field until 1951, when Dr. Miller's age and Mrs. Miller's health conspired to bring about their retirement and return home. Many farewell honors were heaped upon them by church, city and state. The Japanese emperor made note of the occasion and presented Dr. Miller with an award in recognition of his long and conspicuous service to the nation.

Dr. and Mrs. Miller came to Winchester in 1952 and resided here for a year. In March 1953, they moved to Los Angeles, where they [lived and worked] among the Japanese of Southern California, under the auspices of the Board of American Missions, ULCA.

The third and most recent missionary supported by Grace church in Japan is [1953] the Reverend James Arnold Scherer, stationed in Tokyo. Upon recommendation of Dr. L.S.G. Miller and the Board of Foreign Missions, the congregation by official action, June 28, 1953, voted to assume his partial support to the amount of $600 per year. A native of Indiana, Missionary Scherer stands at the entrance of his career.

RECENT MISSIONARY ACTIVITY

Lewis Samuel Godfrey Miller. Dr. and Mrs. L.S.G. Miller entered full retirement in 1957 with a final move to 107 Lee Street, Winchester. For the next 20 years, Dr. Miller led a quiet, happy life doing a good bit of supply work at various churches and serving as vice-pastor of Grace Church 1967-1968. L.S.G. Miller died August 29, 1977. On December 30, 1985, Mrs. Miller entered the National Lutheran Home in Rockville, Maryland. She died March 4, 1993. They are buried in Mount Hebron Cemetery, Winchester, Virginia.

James Arnold and Frances Scherer. James and Frances Shildesser Scherer served as missionaries in Japan 1952-1957 (1953-1957 with Grace Church support). Reverend Scherer prepared an English section for the *Japan Lutheran Theological Quarterly*, in cooperation with the president of the Japan Lutheran Theological Seminary in Tokyo. Later he was elected to finish the unexpired term of the Associate Editor of the *Japan Christian Quarterly*, the organ of the Fellowship of Christian Missionaries that has been recognized as the representative chronicle of the Japanese Protestant Christian movement. While he was still a Japanese language student, he conducted worship services, preached and administered Holy

Communion in Japanese. After completing language study, he was assigned pastoral duties in Kyushu. Reverend Scherer is now retired and lives in Oak Park, Illinois.

Sedoris and Hazel McCartney. Sedoris and Hazel McCartney served in Japan in student evangelism with Grace Church support 1958-1963. (They had previously served as missionaries in Japan in 1948 and 1952—prior to his ordination in 1958.) Reverend McCartney taught English classes at a growing Japanese university and led English Bible classes at Kagoshima Lutheran Church, a young mission church near the university. Mrs. McCartney wrote for church magazines and authored several books. She also taught Bible lessons to Japanese children and, together with her husband, did some personal counseling. Declining health led to the McCartneys' retirement in 1963 to California. Reverend McCartney died February 19, 1995.

Helene Harder. Helene Harder received Grace Church support 1963-1965. The daughter of Pastor Christopher H. and Dorothea Paulson Harder, Helene attended the University of Nebraska and graduated from Midland College, Fremont, Nebraska. Primarily engaged in kindergarten work among Japanese children after her arrival in Japan in 1927, she was stationed at Fukuoka until her retirement in 1965. She was the sister of Martha Harder Miller and, after living in Winchester 1965-1985, resided with her at the National Lutheran Home until her death on February 23, 1993.

William and Doris Billow. William and Doris Pretorius Billow served 1954-1977 in Japan (1966-1977 with Grace Church support). Born in Indiana, Reverend Billow was a graduate of Wittenberg University (1950) and the Chicago Theological Seminary (1954). Reverend Billow did evangelistic work in the Yokohama area and served as Promotional Secretary for the Lutheran Literature Society, as an evangelistic social worker at Tokyo Bethany Home, as a consultant in the Tokyo Area Social Welfare Institutions (one home for the aged, three homes for widows and their children, and four day nurseries) and as business manager for the Joint Lutheran Missionary Office of the LCA and ALC Mission Groups. He resigned in 1977 to accept a position on the faculty of Concordia College in Seward, Nebraska. He is no longer on the ELCA Clergy Roster.

Luther and Dorothy Kistler. Luther and Dorothy Stevenback Kistler served as missionaries in Japan under Grace Church sponsorship 1977-1986. After graduating from Muhlenberg College and the Lutheran Theological Seminary in Philadelphia, Reverend Kistler served as pastor of St. John Lutheran Church in Winter Park, Florida (1956-1964). He began his missionary work in Japan in 1964 as assistant pastor of Musashino Lutheran Church in Tokyo, specializing in parish programming, public school and community work and evangelism. The

Kistlers returned to the United States in 1986 for him to become the pastor/developer for a new congregation in Palm City, Florida. He is now retired and lives in Celebration, Florida.

C. Thomas and Martha Snapp. In June 1981, Thomas and Martha Saverbrey Snapp were busy in parish ministry and microbiology in southern Florida before moving to Japan to learn Japanese and become missionaries. They worked with the Tokuyama Lutheran Church and area churches in Yamaguchi in pastoral ministry and evangelism through English teaching and other special projects. Grace Church supported their missionary work 1987-1989. They left Japan in July 1988 and returned to the United States for graduate study in Columbus, Ohio. They never returned to Japan and resigned as missionaries effective August 1, 1989. Reverend Snapp returned to parish ministry and pastoral counseling in the Columbus, Ohio, area. He is no longer on the ELCA Clergy Roster.

Jerry and Janice Livingston. Reverend Jerry and Janice Koon Livingston served as missionaries to Japan 1958-1998 (1990-1998 with Grace Church support). While a missionary, Reverend Livingston served as a parish pastor, a parish pastor developer (beginning a congregation), a prison chaplain and as president of the Japan Evangelical Lutheran Church. The Livingstons are now retired and live in West Columbia, South Carolina.

James and Carol Sack. James and Carol Sack met while teaching English in Japan in the 1970s and married in 1979. Since his ordination in 1982, they have served as missionaries in Japan; they were assigned to serve two congregations in Kyushu as pastor and missionary for four years. After returning to the United States for further study in pastoral counseling and earning his doctorate, they were assigned to work at the Japan Lutheran College and Theological Seminary in Tokyo, where Dr. Sack served as director of the Personal Growth and Counseling Center, taught pastoral care and counseling, trained people to work in the field of social welfare and was involved with grief support groups. Mrs. Sack taught English at a Christian junior and senior high school called Joshi Gakuin. Grace Church began their support of the Sacks in 1999. In 2000 the Sacks returned to the United States for a 2-year study leave for Mrs. Sack to enter the "Chalice of Repose Project," a unique end-of-life patient care program and graduate-level school of music-thanatology. They look forward to using these newly developed ministry skills in their future counseling work in Japan. In 2002 the Sack family returned to Tokyo.

OTHER MISSIONARY ACTIVITY

Frederick and Dolores Wehrenberg, Jr. Frederick and Dolores Busse Wehrenberg served as missionaries in Liberia 1978-1985. In 1979 Grace

Church embarked on another mission support project by sending a donation to the Curran Lutheran Hospital in Zor Zor, Liberia, where Mr. Wehrenberg was assigned to serve as a missionary administrator in 1978. The Wehrenbergs stayed connected with Grace Church through frequent correspondence (copies available in the Grace Church Archives) and through visits by Grace members to Liberia and by the Wehrenbergs to Winchester while on home leave.

Dennis and Meredith Murnyak. Dennis and Meredith Murnyak are fisheries biologists who began an aquaculture (fish farming) project for the Evangelical Lutheran Church in Tanzania in the Arusha Region of northern Tanzania in 1983 to combat hunger and improve nutrition for the people of Tanzania. Grace Church broadened its missionary support effort in 1987 by adding the Murnyaks as global mission partners. Mr. Murnyak helped local populations in villages build their own fish ponds and raise fish that are healthy sources of protein. He has also been involved in dairy cattle and goat projects, the Integrated Agriculture Training Center and an alcohol abuse recovery program. Mrs. Murnyak has worked as a community organizer for women's work and health-related issues, taught after-school classes and served as Sunday School superintendent at the Arusha Community Church. After returning to Tanzania from home leave in 2000, the Murnyaks became involved with the Heifer Project International.

J. David and Eunice Simonson. David and Eunice Nordby Simonson served as missionaries to Tanzania 1956-1978 and 1981-1996. In 1988 and 1989 Grace Church made financial contributions to the Massai Health Services Project, including the building of a children's hospital in the Arusha region of Tanzania, where Reverend and Mrs. Simonson served. They are now retired and live in Madison, Wisconsin.

Tanzania Visit 2000. In September 2002 Pastor and Susan Utt visited the pastors and people of the Northern Diocese-Evangelical Lutheran Church in Tanzania, East Africa. The Congregation Council gave approval to support the financial needs of this trip by a free will offering of gifts from members. The Utts took educational and medical supplies, toys and gifts with them to share on this mission related trip. During recent Christmas seasons members were given an opportunity to support our mission in Tanzania through the Alternative Gifts Catalog.

4. NEGRO MEMBERS

Throughout the years the congregation has maintained an attitude of official benevolence toward members of the

Negro race. Christian Streit records a number of pastoral acts performed among them. A gallery in the old church was set apart for their use. The gallery of the present building [1953] has been frequently used by them. Family servants were always welcome to attend services, as were members of the sexton's family. In this way a few came to be connected with the congregation. But there seems to have been no serious effort exerted to win colored members for the sake of their souls, and no more than one or two have been members at a given time.

The family of Gabriel Festus offers the best illustration at hand. Gabriel, long-time church sexton who died in 1893, was married to Ellen Barnett, October 27, 1859, by Pastor W.M. Baum. The record states that both T.W. Dosh and D.M. Gilbert were present on this particular occasion, though the circumstances under which those two future pastors were in attendance are not known. In due time D.M. Gilbert baptized on June 9, 1873, Mary Emma, Mildred Ann, and David Festus, their children. David succeeded his father as sexton, and Ellen Festus, his daughter, was confirmed in January 1897, and became a faithful communicant of the church. Another faithful communing member was Mollie Toliver (Mary Taliaferro) who was received by adult baptism, April 9, 1876. So, too, was Charles L. Miller, confirmed in December 1899. Several other pastoral acts are recorded of Negroes – infant baptisms, weddings and funerals – but there is no evidence that there was other connection with the congregation.

In recent decades men, women and children from many ethnic groups have been accepted for membership. All persons are welcome and wanted at Grace Evangelical Lutheran Church.

5. INTO PARSONAGES

Here is given a list, culled from incomplete records, of daughters of the parish who have married minister husbands.

Mary Catherine Baker married the Rev. Benjamin Kurtz.

Mary Ann Miller married Pastor Lewis Eichelberger.

Mary Virginia Baker became the second wife of Charles Porterfield Krauth.

Kate Brown became the wife of Pastor T.W. Dosh.

Virginia Brown married the Rev. Luther L. Smith and was the mother of two well-known Lutheran college presidents, Charles J. Smith of Roanoke and G. Morris Smith of Susquehanna University.

Laura Campbell married L.G.M. Miller and was the mother of Missionary L.S.G. Miller.

Emily C. Baker was united in marriage to the Rev. Lemuel Sibole.

Ella Baker married an Episcopal clergyman, the Rev. C.R. Page.

Mrs. Charlotte Sperry Eichelberger, widow of Charles F. Eichelberger, took for her second husband a minister of the Presbyterian Church, the Rev. Jonah W. Lupton.

Mary Dosh became the wife of the Rev. Clarence E. Krumbholz.

Catherine Baetjer married the Rev. Daniel C. Buchanan, for many years missionary of the Presbyterian Church, U.S.A., to Japan.

Grace Cooper married the Rev. Lloyd Warren Walter.

Edith Brown became the bride of the Rev. Thomas A. Painter, a Presbyterian minister.

June Cline married the Rev. Robert E. Hook.

On August 25, 1956, Mary Martha Eisenberg, a daughter of the Reverend William E. and Dorothy Jones Eisenberg, married Charles

Alfred Stuart Robertson, a Lutheran pastor and missionary, and served with him in Peru.

Susan Jane Gore, a daughter of Claude T. and Eva Lamp Gore, was united in marriage on August 13, 1960, to Bruce Andrew Macbeth, a Presbyterian minister.

6. THE GODFREY MILLER HOME

Margaretta Miller, daughter of Mr. and Mrs. Godfrey Sperry Miller had lived all her life in the large old stone and brick residence at 28 South Loudoun Street. It had been the home of her branch of the Miller family since 1812. The exact date of its construction has not been determined. It seems to have been built between the years 1785 and 1800. Miss Miller's parents and two sisters had preceded her in death. She was the last of her immediate family. She died November 12, 1938.

A member of the congregation for 88 years, the church and its wider work had been her interest, her joy and her life. In planning the ultimate disposition of her sizable estate she kept the church in the foreground of her thinking. She made her will March 1, 1929, including within it the following provision:

"The old home with adjoining lot is to be given to the trustees of Grace Lutheran Church, for an old ladies' home, to be known as The Godfrey Miller Home, with $5,000 endowment." The will further provided that "the lots on Stewart Street that are not sold or given away are to be left to Wm. C. Miller; he is to give one-third of them, when and in the way he thinks best, to the trustees of Grace Lutheran Church for the endowment of the Godfrey Miller Home."

Under date of November 4, 1936, Miss Miller added a codicil to her will, a paragraph of which reads as follows:

"I have willed to the Lutheran Church of Winchester, Virginia, my home property on the east side of South Loudoun Street, with lot adjoining and a money bequest, to be used as a home for old ladies. In event that the church does not accept said bequest, I devise said property to my friend, Wm. C. Miller, to do with as he pleases."

From the time of the probating of the will, complications of one kind or another arose. First to be reckoned with was the pathetic internal condition of the congregation. Morale was at low ebb on account of the demoralizing fiasco of the preceding two years.[d] Miss Gettie, by her bequest, confronted the congregation with one of the finest challenging opportunities of its long lifetime, but on account of the existing sad state of affairs, there was no courage to act and no will to do.

Then there was the question of authority. Whose prerogative was it to accept or decline the trust? Did it belong to the trustees of the congregation? Or to the Church Council? Or where? The three trustees at the time were J. George Baetjer, Dr. Alfred D. Henkel and Eugene B. Cooper. They themselves were emphatically divided in their opinions. Mr. Baetjer believed that the proposition should be declined because the congregation would never be able to carry out the implied terms of the trust. And what Mr. Baetjer believed, he believed. Dr. Henkel, on the other hand, believed just the opposite with equal ardor. While he had no plan for the operation of the home, he could not be reconciled to sacrificing the opportunity without tackling the undertaking. He vowed that as a trustee he would never be a party to signing off the congregation's rights in the case. Between these two most amicable enemies stood Mr. Cooper with a neutral point of view.

And so, nothing was done. Neither a "no" answer nor a "yes" answer was made for more than eight years.

Meanwhile, Mr. William Cross Miller, eccentric bachelor

---

[d] This occurred during the pastorate of C.W. Lowe.

cousin of Miss Gettie and executor of her estate, had moved into the property and made it his residence. With the continued passage of time and no action on the congregation's part, he proceeded to admit a man and several women as co-occupants with him. He had a cast-iron plate made entitled "Godfrey Miller Home" which he placed upon the front door. "When are you Lutherans going to take over the property?" he asked continually of members of the congregation.

There were laymen in the church who were giving the matter serious thought. Ben F. Davis was one of them. He looked at the situation realistically and saw that, if the congregation should decide to assume the trust, money would be needed to renovate the property, which was being allowed deliberately to deteriorate at an accelerated pace with each passing year. He came forward, therefore, with the first concrete proposal for action – the offer of one thousand dollars toward the needed renovation. In this he was soon seconded by Joseph P. Miller, who matched his offer.

Here, then, was a new talking point, which the Council had to recognize. A committee of three was appointed in May 1946 to make a study of the matter and to bring in a report. Ben Davis, Ralph P. Yount and William E. Eisenberg were the committee. After considerable investigation and study the report was submitted September 15. It recommended (1) that the property be accepted according to the terms of the will; and (2) that a special group of trustees be appointed to develop and manage the home. This report was received by the Council without action.

Further meetings of this special committee followed first with the church trustees (H.A. Schmidt had replaced J. George Baetjer as a trustee, meanwhile) and then with the trustees and Church Council. On September 30, Harry K. Benham, local attorney, met with the combined groups to discuss legal phases for the property. Following this discussion, Mr. Davis came forward with a new offer: he and Mrs. Davis would give $10,000 toward the expenses of the home, should the congregation accept it, $1,000 when the property should be accepted, and $1,000 annually for nine years. Here was the essential help that was needed.

The special committee, with the addition of Councilman Boyd H. Hamman and Trustee Schmidt, also formulated a plan of operation, should the trust be accepted. This plan proposed, in order to keep within the modest income available, that lodging only be provided residents of the home, and "that, as income should justify, board and medical care be provided at a later time. In other words, the idea was propounded that the home need not be an outright and complete charity in the sense that everything be provided gratis to the occupants; over and beyond the power of the limited income to provide, residents would be required to pay at non-profit rates on a monthly schedule. It was argued that to operate on a non-profit, pay-as-you-go basis not only was feasible, but in keeping with the latest modern trend in financing institutions of the kind, and entirely legitimate within the terms of the trust.

The point of view, as described, came to prevail. It was determined, therefore, to present the whole question to the congregation at the next annual meeting for final decision.

January 15, 1947, arrived, the meeting was held, and by a ratio of 13 to 1 the verdict was rendered in favor of accepting the trust and the gifts from Mr. and Mrs. Davis and Mr. Miller. And so the die was cast.

No sooner had the decision been made than the tune of William Cross Miller, the executor of the estate, changed its note perceptibly. "You Lutherans waited too long." "The property is mine." "It's my residence and I am operating a home for old ladies." Such were his words, and he refused to turn over the property to the church trustees.

This attitude on the part of W.C. Miller was quite in keeping with his record. Over a period of some twenty-five years he had been made executor of several other wills and had never settled any of them. Nor was he required to make final settlement by the court, because no one would bring action against him.

Here was the point where a decision of a new kind was needed. Should the matter be taken to law? A chancery suit would be required and it would cost money. Messrs. Davis and J.P. Miller were willing to let their gifts be used for the same.

The trustees decided to enter a chancery suit. Harry K. Benham was engaged to represent the congregation's interests. The case went on during the summer and fall of 1947. By verdict issued by Judge Elliot Marshall of the Corporation Court of the City of Winchester the property was turned over to the trustees of Grace Church to operate as a home for women according to the terms of the trust. The congregation's claim to the one-third interest in the Stewart Street lots was likewise strengthened. Judge Marshall's decision was rendered April 27, 1948.

The trustees of the church proceeded to have the Godfrey Miller Home incorporated. This was done by the State Corporation Commission, September 23. The trustees in turn elected a board of directors from the membership of the congregation and turned over the Home to it for renovation and development, as well as for operation and management. The personnel of this nine-member board was as follows: Miss Mary Katherine Aulick, Mrs. W.H. Bosserman, Sr., Dr. R. Fred Cline, Mr. and Mrs. B.F. Davis, W.E. Eisenberg, J.P. Miller, Robert K. Woltz and Ralph P. Yount.

By-laws prepared by Messrs. Yount, Woltz and Eisenberg were adopted and officers elected; Pastor Eisenberg, president; B.F. Davis, vice-president; Robert K. Woltz, secretary; J.P. Miller, treasurer; and Miss M.K. Aulick, member of the executive committee.

Then followed, in 1949, the beginning of the renovation of the property. This major undertaking was placed in charge of Ben Davis, who with ability and devotion personally supervised it.

Work on the grounds and exterior of the building was started first. A log barn, a stable, a carriage shed, a corn crib and several other outbuildings had to be razed. A new fence was erected on the north, east and south sides of the property. The east end of the lawn had to be graded, grass and shrubbery planted, and cement walks laid.

Exterior alterations to the house itself included the removal of an ell-shaped, two-story, side porch and the rebuilding of a smaller two-story porch from salvaged materials, together with the changing of several doors into windows, and the removal of a box-like frame room at the east end of the brick addition. Repairs were made to the roof, all window frames and door frames were caulked, new screens and screen doors obtained and all wood work scraped and painted.

Lest there be those who may ponder the existence of a cannon ball in the east wall of the original stone dwelling let the story be set straight here and now. It was not fired from any Rebel or Yankee battery during those tempestuous years of 1861-1865. Nothing so dramatic as that, it must be confessed. Rather, it was just a little prosaic item of the recent renovation. A hole in the wall, caused by the removal of outmoded plumbing, had to be filled. The writer inquired of Bismark S. Preffitt, stonemason on the job, what to do about it. Mr. Preffitt, an artist in his own way, answered with imagination: "If I just had a cannon ball." With jubilation the reply was made, "Mr. Preffitt, you're a man after my own heart. I have already found the cannon ball in the basement."

And so the deed was done.

Renovation of the interior followed next in order. Four new bathrooms were installed, the old parlor divided into two bedrooms, and partitions were removed and the ceiling raised in the bedroom at the east end of the house. Five closets were built. New electric wiring and fixtures were installed throughout. All floors were sanded and refinished. In the old outkitchen, converted into a laundry, a cement floor was laid, as was the case in the basement also, where a new oil furnace was installed. All rooms and hallways had to be papered and all woodwork painted.

Besides all this, furnishings had to be obtained. Many pieces of furniture left in the home were found to be usable, after being repaired and refinished. Other items, notably, beds, mattresses, floor lamps, carpet and rugs had to be purchased. From 1947, when the first $600 had to be expended on the chancery case, to 1953, when operation of the home began, the total cost of the entire project had been less than $15,000.

Where did the money come from? And how was it possible, in a time of excessively high prices, to get so much accomplished at such a reasonable figure?

In addition to the initial gifts from Mr. and Mrs. Davis

and J.P. Miller and the annual gift of $1,000 from the Davises, another thousand dollars came from the estate of Mrs. C.E. Aulick as a gift from her children, while numerous smaller gifts ranging from $1.00 to $250 were received from other individual members of the congregation and interested friends. In a number of instances these gifts were made repeatedly.

A combined yard party and sale of discarded pieces of furniture and other articles left in the house was held in the summer of 1949, and the following summer a second yard party was held. These two adventures netted about $2,000.

A third source of financial assistance came from organizations within the congregation, especially in the matter of furnishing the home. The Women of the Church made the kitchen their particular project and supplied the needed furnishings. The Mary Martha Class provided shades for all the windows. So, too, were curtains and electric fixtures supplied by the Women of the Church assisted by the C.P. Krauth Class. The congregation as a congregation has given a special Christmas offering to the Home for the past several years [1953].

A fourth source of revenue has come from the Home's invested endowment. The bequest of $5,000 from Miss Gettie Miller was received when the property was awarded to the church trustees. By the terms of the same will $17,700 additional has been received for endowment, this being the one-third interest in the Stewart Street lots. March 12, 1949, Mr. W.C. Miller died after being struck by an automobile several days earlier. His jumbled affairs were finally untangled by devious legal procedures and his holdings sold. In 1951 the trustees received their portion of the proceeds, which was invested promptly that it might start work for the Home.

Through the will of Mrs. Helen Dean Herrell, who died

in 1951, the Home eventually will receive [1953] a part of her estate, appraised at $38,000 at the time of her death. Mrs. Herrell, a Winchester resident for many years, was a member of Trinity Lutheran Church, Stephens City.

The second question to be answered is how it was possible to accomplish so much for so little in a day of notoriously high building costs. The answers are three. The project was singularly fortunate in having Ben F. Davis personally supervise the renovation. He knew what had to be done and how to do it. He knew what had to be bought and how to buy it at best advantage. In spite of a heart condition, he was on the job from morning till night superintending every move that was made. He was a man who was continually at work. January 20, 1951, his work was over. But the cause for which he prayed and labored with generosity and untiring zeal was well on its way to reality.

With the death of Mr. Davis, Miss Mary Katherine Aulick assumed responsibility for supervising the remaining work of renovation. Under her direction the house was papered and painted throughout, in keeping with the best traditions of its colonial past. From the outset of the endeavor Miss Aulick's interest in the undertaking, her willingness to assist in anything that had to be done, her keen sense of values, her sound judgment and her uncommonly good common sense made her an invaluable assistant in carrying the endeavor forward to completion. And under her able guidance devalued dollars came to take on a new elasticity. This is answer number two.

The third answer is to be found in the many-sided generosity that the whole undertaking called forth. Men and women and young people from the congregation willingly contributed hours upon hours of work, from the initial inventory of every nook and corner to oft-repeated cleanings and dustings and mowing of the lawn and hauling away of rubbish. Merchants gave their best discounts on purchases made; contractors made their bids at special rates; painters, carpenters, floor finishers, plumbers, paper hangers, all contributed something of their services, and so did furniture repair men, and plasterers and stonemasons and workers in cement. Everybody had the willing spirit to do something extra for the sake of advancing the work. And the city fathers wrote the property off the tax records.

Should there be those who think that the Home was unusually slow in opening up its doors, let them be reminded of the two factors of income and management.

It was altogether essential for the Board of Directors to learn what the endowment, not obtained until 1951, would produce. Since the backing of the Home was confined to one congregation – a fact, which is unique among the 134 Lutheran homes for the aged scattered throughout the country – every step had to be taken with deliberate caution lest the whole enterprise be jeopardized. At the same time the interests of the congregation had to be given prior consideration to safeguard them and to keep from hanging a millstone around the church's neck. The task of putting the property in shape, therefore, had to be done piece by piece as the money in hand permitted. The result is that the Home has been kept virtually free of debt.

When the possibility of opening the Home for its intended purpose drew near, the immediate question was, who will run it? Here again the undertaking has been singularly blest. Mrs. J. George Baetjer offered her services to the board in November 1952, and she was duly elected to superintend and man-

Godfrey Miller Home and Yard

Godfrey Miller Home Living Room

age its operation in the official capacity of Director of the Home. A trained nurse by profession, Mrs. Baetjer [was] admirably fitted for the position. A granddaughter of Oliver M. Brown, a great-granddaughter of Jacob Baker, and a great-great granddaughter of Christian Streit, she [embodied] in her background a heritage steeped in the traditions of the congregation. By offering her services at no cost to the Home, she made it possible for the Home to be opened June 1, 1953.

After six months in operation the Home had six residents. It has also cared for a number of temporary guests.

Thus was the Godfrey Miller Home begun. Its work has just started [1953]. What has been done has been accomplished because God's benediction has been upon it. With His continued blessing, its usefulness has limitless possibilities.

On January 1, 1956, Mrs. Robert L. (Arvella) Fisher of Keyser, West Virginia, took the helm as resident director, a position she faithfully held for fourteen years. During this time, the facility functioned at full capacity with six permanent residents, the director and a live-in cook. A parking lot was created behind the residence in 1962. Two years later, Miss Virginia Henkel's home at 29 S. Cameron Street was sold and a portion of the proceeds benefited the Godfrey Miller Home.

Mrs. Vernon S. (Goldie) McClintock, a member of Grace Church, served as the director from 1970 until 1973. The Shenandoah Fellowship Foundation approached the Board of Directors in 1972 about the possible sale, lease or gift of property extending from the back of the home to 27 S. Cameron Street. After much consideration it was revealed that selling the property was most advisable and the Executive Committee voted to do so on November 16, 1975. The 80 apartments in Winchester House built on that lot provided affordable housing for the elderly.

Staffing became a difficult task. With the introduction of more advanced state fire codes and other regulations, the home struggled to remain open. Finally, in June 1973, it was closed. During the twenty-year period of time that the home was in operation, over fifty ladies lived there paying only a nominal fee for room and board.

For a brief time, Pastor Robert Koons and his wife Grace lived in the home while the Board of Directors petitioned the court to allow the board to operate a daytime center for adults. "We had to notify several hundred of the Millers' known descendants of the court proceedings to substitute a new purpose," recollected Judge Robert K. Woltz in an article that was published in *The Winchester Star* on February 23, 1998.

Approval for the change finally came in 1976 and the Godfrey Miller Fellowship Center opened in October as an adult fellowship center. One of the first "senior centers" in the area, the GMFC has always been self-sustaining, using no public funds. Early programming gave adults over age 60 the opportunity to talk, eat and participate in activities. Recently, with the relocation of more people to Winchester from metropolitan areas for their retirement years, the program's scope has broadened. It now caters to an active over 55 population by offering more intensive programming in the areas of recreation, education, and day and overnight trips.

The Godfrey Miller Fellowship Center is supported by a staff consisting of a full-time director, an assistant director and many volunteers. Larry Crawley-Woods was hired as the first director. Barbara Porterfield succeeded him in 1977. In 1978 Susan Rathman agreed to be director on a temporary basis and stayed for seven years. During this time the daily routine of the center became firmly established and outreach to the Winchester community grew each year. Other directors have been Linda Stern (1986-1993), Judith Ann Williams (1993-1996), Nancy A. Lewis (1996-1997) and Lynn V. Miller (1998-1999). Currently Shelley Williams is the director and Lisa Carey is the assistant director.

A Board of Directors is responsible for the management of the home and the employment of a director to carry out the day-to-day operation of the Fellowship Center. Members of the 2002 Board included William Black, Robert Calamari, Tina Combs, Betty Demuth, Lenore Eavis, Marie Everly, Philip Farley, Kristen Goff, Harold Lehman, Shelda Longerbeam, Jane Lucas, Polly Manuel, Donald Nesselrodt, Tom Nichols, Philip Olinger, Richard Pell, Anne Simpson, Judge Robert K. Woltz and Rev. Dr. James H. Utt.

Strong and conscientious leaders have carried the mission of the Godfrey Miller Home through the decades. Among those serving as president of the Board of Directors have been: Rev. Dr. William Edward Eisenberg, Mary Katherine Aulick, Rev. V.A. Moyer, Jr., J. Frederick Walk, Karen Shipp, Philip Olinger, Shelda Longerbeam, William Black, B.J. Dove and Hal Lehman. Judge Robert K. Woltz served as secretary of the board for the first twenty-five years and still continues as vice-president.

For many years a Participant's Association, consisting of individuals who attended the center, planned activities and sponsored the annual Christmas bazaar. Proceeds from the bazaar were used to refurbish areas of the home. Currently a Friends of Godfrey Miller group includes participants and other individuals desiring to support the program.

Activities at the center include:
- programs of music and sing-alongs
- board games, bridge, and other card games
- weekly blood pressure clinics and programs on healthy living
- access to the Senior Navigator website of Winchester Medical Center
- computer classes
- day trips to a variety of interesting places
- knowledgeable guest speakers on many educational subjects
- Bible study by representatives of various denominations
- home safety helps
- fellowship through brunch, picnics, and theme parties
- occasional monthly dinner club
- art classes, crafts, quilting, etc.
- service projects and activities

Because of an expanding and evolving program, the Board held a planning retreat in 1998. The leadership began a "forward look" for providing more effective services to our community while still preserving the home's wonderful historic heritage. The addition of a multi-purpose pavilion, named in honor of Judge Robert K. Woltz and dedicated on September 27, 2002, represented a key step in this exciting vision for assisting the participants and others in their pursuit of health and wellness of body, mind and spirit. From June 2000 to June 2001 over $200,000 was raised for the "Vision 2000" campaign. Reader and Swartz, P.C., served as the architect and Dave Holliday Construction was the builder of the addition. Renovation and redecoration of the home itself will be done in the near future to enhance the historical heritage as well as continue and expand the Fellowship Center's programs.

It is well over two centuries since the old home was built and over half a century since the corporation was formed to carry out the beneficent provision of Margaretta Miller's will. Even so, the spirit of the Godfrey Miller Center in the year 2003 is young and looks forward to the future.

7. CONCLUSION

And what shall I say more? For time would fail me to tell of John Kerr, who left to the City of Winchester money for a public school, or Frederick Henry Baetjer, renowned roentgenologist of Johns Hopkins University, or Joseph Edwin Cooper, who was thwarted in his purpose to enter the ministry because of ill health, and who came to be content as a layman to serve his Lord and Church with marvelous devotion and generosity.

All these, and many, many more whose names, if unrecorded here, are written where it matters most, walked by faith and not by sight. Under the shadow of the Church's influence they lived and labored. Theirs has been a goodly heritage. It is a heritage more precious than anything else, passed on to us by an unbroken chain of witnesses. It is a worthy heritage, handed down to us who make up this latest generation. But it belongs especially to them who keep the faith.

Grace Evangelical Lutheran Parish Staff, 2002 - seated (left to right) are Joan Carroll, Pastor Martha Sims, Pastor James H. Utt, Dorothy Tillotson; standing (left to right): Carol Kerr, Carolyn Hawks, Gerald Amt, Paul Fisher, Roger Milburn and Teresa Lehman

Chapter XII
A Heritage for the Future

When dictionaries define the word "heritage," they invariably include references to such things as property that can be inherited, things that are passed down from previous generations and status that is acquired through birth. All this and more are part and parcel of Grace Evangelical Church's heritage that began with the land grant dated 1753 to the German Lutherans by Thomas, Lord Fairfax.

The primary duty of the earliest Christians was spelled out clearly by God's son, Jesus, shortly after His crucifixion and resurrection: "All authority in heaven and on earth has been given to me. Go, therefore and make disciples of all nations, baptizing them in the name of the Father and of the Son and of the Holy Spirit, teaching them to observe all that I have commanded you; and, lo, I am with you always, to the close of the age."

The Great Commission was first given to the disciples of Jesus, a fact confirmed by Matthew 28:18-20. They could not, after His death and resurrection, doubt that Jesus was the divine Son of God, but they may well have doubted their own ability to "make disciples of all nations." But on the day of Pentecost, the apostles were filled with the Holy Ghost, and Jews dwelling in Jerusalem who heard Peter speak and "gladly received (God's) word were baptized; and the same day there were added unto them about three thousand souls." The miracles of that fateful day and earlier days surely served to convince the apostles that making disciples of all nations was an achievable goal.[1]

From its beginnings in the wilderness of the new world, the congregation at Winchester was guided by the Holy Spirit, experienced growth and responded to the needs of its members without written goals. In 1967 a Core Committee chaired by Jim Diehl was established to give support to standing committees. The Parish Life Ministry Development program was instituted in 1975 to encourage the Council and standing committees to consider what the congregation hoped to become. Our first Mission and Purpose Statement was developed by a committee during the Koons' pastorate and adopted by the congregation on June 22, 1975. Under the leadership of Pastor James Utt and Pastor Paul Gunsten the Council approved and the congregation adopted a new statement in May 1988.

MISSION STATEMENT 1988

Grace Evangelical Lutheran Church, as a part of the body of Christ,

- ***Lives*** to celebrate and proclaim the gospel through word and sacrament;
- ***Gathers*** to provide for the needs of people through worship, education, fellowship and support;
- ***Goes*** to extend the gospel to the broader community through personal involvement and financial support;
- ***Grows*** in the stewardship of all God's gifts through care of creation and use of resources for ministry.

The Mission Statement of 1988 guided advocates of a long-range plan that ultimately led to the *Heritage For The Future* document (HFTF), which was approved by Grace's congregation in 1991. The archives of Grace Church disclose that the first step in this direction was taken during the August 1987 meeting of the Church Council. At that time Pastor Utt spoke about long-range planning and presented a paper documenting the needs he saw for the coming years. The congregation's annual reports reflect the attention devoutly accorded the planning process by Council members and clergy leaders. For example, the 1988 annual report includes a forceful declaration by Pastor Utt: "We must have the foresight that our predecessors at Grace had!"[2]

Jerry P. Kerr, one of the church's three trustees, was selected to chair the Long-Range Planning Committee. The original committee was comprised of Mr. Kerr and the following:

George Bowman, Jr.	Cinda Brand	G. Ronald Brown
James Diehl	Dorothy Farley	Evelyn Goode
Rev. Paul G. Gunsten	Lewis Lamp	Arlene Maul
Gail Mayfield	Robert Pence	Paul Rago
Rev. James H. Utt	William VanHorssen	Carol Westervelt

The committee was established in November 1988 for the purposes of studying, developing, writing and submitting for approval a long-range plan for our congregation for the next five to ten years. It was agreed that the Word of God, the Lutheran Confessions, the Mission Statement, the long-held values of the congregation, survey results, currrent growth trends and the creative vision for the future would be the principal factors guiding the development of the long-range plan. After surveying the standing committees, auxiliaries and members of the congregation, the results were summarized, analyzed and studied for over two years. The work of the Long-Range Planning Committee culminated on January 20, 1991, with the approval of the plan by the congregation.[3]

Heritage For The Future, a long-range plan to celebrate the past, empower the present and envision the future of mission and ministry had four goals:

1. To recognize the history and heritage of Grace Evangelical Lutheran Church and celebrate its contributions to the community, the church at large and the world.
2. To broaden the worship experiences of the congregation and to emphasize and enlarge the congregation's musical opportunities in order to meet the needs of members of Grace Evangelical Lutheran Church and the people of the community.
3. To expand the educational and fellowship ministry programs of the congregation in order to enhance the spiritual, physical, emotional and intellectual growth of members of Grace Evangelical Lutheran Church and the people of the Winchester community.
4. To expand the stewardship and evangelism ministry programs of the congregation and enhance opportunities for members to live out daily their baptismal faith through the outreach ministry of the congregation and their personal commitment to local, state, national and global issues of environment, justice and peace.[4]

The common need that was embodied in the objectives for all four goals was the need for additional and redesigned facilities. To fulfill this need, the Redesign and Remodeling Task Group was appointed and held its initial meeting on May 14, 1991. That committee under the capable leadership of Jim Diehl [and after his death, Charles Woodruff] worked diligently to gather input from the congregation, select an architect, [and] give feedback to the congregation.[5]

At a special called meeting on September 16, 1992, the congregation was asked to approve the floor plan and authorize additional expenditures in order that the task group might proceed toward accomplishing additional objectives included in our long-range plan. In a letter to the congregation dated September 1, 1992, Jerry Kerr asked the question, "Why do we want to do the redesign and remodeling that is being proposed?" His answer was to:

> allow us to achieve the objectives that support the goals of our long-range plan; that our long-range plan fulfills the Mission Statement of Grace Evangelical Lutheran Church; and our Mission Statement fulfills the Gospel of our Lord and Saviour. Since early in 1988...there has been a concerted effort to involve and obtain input from *all* the members of Grace,

give feedback to *all* the members of Grace and give the opportunity for *all* the members to discuss, debate and to make recommendations regarding the decisions that have been made. There has not always been unanimous agreement, but in all cases a consensus has been reached. This has been a healthy process and one that has strengthened the congregation to enable us to better fulfill our mission.[6]

To provide money for the renovations, the Heritage for the Future Fund was established in 1991 with a $10,000 gift from an anonymous donor. Contributions of $51,500 were made in 1992. With a target of one million dollars, a capital campaign aimed to raise money for the redesign and remodeling of the church. The congregation hired ELCA Resident Stewardship Services to lead the campaign program that also included Bible studies and every-member response visitations. About 350 persons attended the Fellowship Dinner held at the cafeteria of James Wood High School on March 27, 1993. About $600,000 was committed to the Heritage for the Future Fund through one-time gifts and a three-year pledge opportunity. Through 2002 a total of $1,154,794 had been contributed.

The goal-centered plan energized the various standing committees and created special committees, task groups and teams to tackle new assignments. The congregation's achievements during the life of the *Heritage For The Future* document included:

Goal 1: History and Heritage
- Established the Heritage and History Task Group.
- Preserved the remaining wall of the original house of worship at Mount Hebron Cemetery and the adjoining Lutheran Cemetery.
- Established an Archives Room and created an Editorial Committee dedicated to publishing in 2003 an updated version of Dr. Eisenberg's 1954 history of the congregation, *This Heritage*.
- Scheduled worship services and special events for 2003 to mark the congregation's 250th anniversary.
- Developed a plan to make needlepoint kneelers for our communion rail.

Goal 2: Worship and Music
- Established Redesign and Remodeling Task Group to enlarge and extensively renovate the sanctuary, narthex and balcony in 1994 from Easter to Advent.
- Installed the new $240,000 Schantz pipe organ in December 1994.

A Heritage for the Future

- Used *Now the Feast* and *With One Voice* hymnal supplements and Holden Evening Prayer service.

Goal 3: Education and Fellowship
- Purchased and remodeled 16 N. Braddock Street (former Noble's Travel World building) to create the Children's Education Center in the summer of 1993.
- Established Primetimers group for "senior" members and friends.
- Continued ecumenical efforts with the downtown churches (annual pulpit exchange, Palm Sunday celebration on the Old Town Mall) and strengthened ties with Christ Episcopal Church (shared Vacation Bible School, Epiphany service and fall Health Fair).
- Established Future Parish Staffing Task Group to study parish needs resulting from expanding programs.
- Established the parish nurse program and hired a full-time sexton.
- Developed recommendations regarding space for administrative offices, parish health office, kitchen area and equipment storage.

Goal 4: Stewardship and Evangelism
- Established Shepherding Zones.
- Broadcast worship services on Cable Channel 6 one month a year (and 11:00 p.m. Christmas Eve service.)
- Increased our benevolence contribution by 1 percent.
- Developed guidelines for use of our facilities by community groups.[7]

The congregation has supported the trustees, Jerry Kerr, J. Kenly Carr and Roger Milburn, in their action to service the congregation's indebtedness and also provide insurance coverage for all of its facilities. To maintain its line of credit, the congregation is making minimum annual payments of $26,000 on its $400,000 loan from the Godfrey Miller Home and $16,640 on its $256,000 loan from the BB&T Bank (formerly F&M). The rates of interest are 6.5 percent on the Miller Home loan and 5.5 percent on the bank loan.

The foregoing accomplishments certainly suggest that the Holy Spirit is exerting a strong influence on the clergy, lay leaders and members of Grace Evangelical Lutheran Church. All clearly were willing to help plan the numerous improvements now evident and also help contribute generously toward the cost of these improvements.[8]

A unique opportunity presented itself to the congregation in 2000 when the building owned by the G&M Music store at 38 W. Boscawen

Street became available for purchase. Recognizing the close proximity to our administration building and the continuing demands on existing space to meet the needs of outreach programs, the congregation voted to purchase the site for $289,000.

On October 28, 2000, the family of Grace Church assembled in the Reception Hall of Braddock Street United Methodist Church to dine together, be entertained and be inspired to offer gifts for the purchase of the G&M Music building. Following piano entertainment by Pastor Duane Steele (former member now at Gladesboro Lutheran Church), gifts and pledges were announced.

On Sunday, December 17, 2000, a new long-range plan for mission and ministry in a new century was presented at the annual business meeting. The congregation enthusiastically approved the *Growing in Grace* document. An excerpt from its introduction describes the evolution of our most recent long-range plan:

> The *Heritage for the Future* document served the congregation well in the 1990s and provided the impetus for the development of a new long-range plan. Cottage meetings conducted during the season of Lent 2000 provided the opportunity for all members of Grace to study and provide input into a new vision.
>
> During the past two years, the Congregation Council, the standing committees and auxiliaries of the congregation met to review the work of the 1991 Long-Range Planning Committee as well as determine future program and space needs.
>
> The Long-Range Planning Task Group hopes you will notice this plan embraces the concept of a church turned upside down and represents initiatives strongly rooted in lay ministry. These bold initiatives are intended to empower the laity and seek to enhance the responsibility and integrity of lay ministry. The success of this plan is dependent upon each member's individual response, support and involvement.
>
> Our long-range planning journey has taken all of us beyond the scope of the original *Heritage for the Future* toward a new vision, one of *Growing in Grace*. This document represents a journey in progress and embraces the spirit of the congregation and Long-Range Planning Task Group.
>
> *Growing in Grace* has truly been a work of the entire congregation. For historical purposes, the following were members of the Long-Range Planning Task Group:[9]

Gerry Amt	Nancy Braswell	Wayne Carbaugh
J. Kenly Carr	Scott Crumpler	Matthew Humphrey
Bill Heidelberger	Leigh Ann Lynch	Polly Manuel
Pastor Jeffrey May	Barbara Morrell, Chair	Clara Orndoff
Susan Short	Lee Simpson	Pastor James Utt
Carol Westervelt		

The new long-range plan was developed to fulfill the mission and ministry of Grace Evangelical Lutheran Church as expressed in the Mission Statement of 1988. As a result of the intense study of this document the italicized words were added to the Mission Statement which appeared in the *Growing in Grace* 2000 document:

Mission Statement 2000
Grace Evangelical Lutheran Church, as part of the body of Christ,
- *Lives* to celebrate and proclaim the Gospel through Word and Sacrament;
- *Gathers* to provide for the needs of people, *nurturing wholeness* through worship, education, fellowship, and support;
- *Goes* to extend the Gospel to the broader community, *reaching out to all with the Good News* through personal involvement and financial support;
- *Grows* in the stewardship of all God's gifts through care of creation and use of resources for ministry.[10]

A set of goals was defined for each major segment of the Mission Statement 2000. Each goal, in turn, was followed by a list of objectives, or specific actions, that were intended to reach the goal. A time frame was indicated for the initiation or completion of each objective.

The intention of the goals under each segment was:
- *Lives* to increase lay leadership; expand worship opportunities and broaden the musical ministry and liturgical experiences.
- *Gathers* to equip members for a life of discipleship; enhance educational ministries; give greater attention to the needs of youth and foster greater fellowship and support.
- *Goes* to develop plans for witnessing to the un-churched; increase social ministry involvement; strengthen mission partnerships locally and abroad and strengthen and develop specialized ministries.
- *Grows* to expand stewardship opportunities; expand, maintain and protect facilities; study organizational structure; celebrate our history and heritage and provide and support the parish staff.

At the conclusion of the *Growing in Grace* long-range plan, the committee noted the relationship between the call for increased lay leadership and the initiatives related to the expansion of staff and facilities. Task group members urged Congregation Council to provide for an annual review to assess accomplishments and revise timelines as necessary. It was also their recommendation that a successor task group should be appointed in 2005.

We close the final chapter of *This Heritage* with words from the *Growing in Grace* document, which was presented at the annual business meeting of the congregation on Sunday, December 17, 2000:

> The congregation of believers now known as Grace Evangelical Lutheran Church has been privileged to carry on this work of faith and has endeavored to provide the programs, facilities, leadership, and support necessary to further extend this sacred heritage.[11]

Endnotes – Chapter XII

[1] Charles Bailey, "Heritage for the Future Chapter." November 2001.
[2] Ibid.
[3] Jerry P. Kerr, "Background and History of Long-Range Planning Process." Letter to congregation. September 1, 1992.
[4] *Heritage for the Future*. Winchester, Virginia: Grace Evangelical Lutheran Church. 1991.
[5] "Background and History."
[6] Ibid.
[7] "Heritage for the Future Status Report: Congregation Council Retreat." March 1999.
[8] "Heritage for the Future Chapter."
[9] *Growing in Grace*. Winchester, Virginia: Grace Evangelical Lutheran Church. December 2000.
[10] Ibid.
[11] Ibid.

Appendix A
Baptisms performed in the Shenandoah Valley by the Rev. John Casper Stoever, Jr., 1734-1742[a]

Taken from the *Records of Rev. John Casper Stoever, Baptismal and Marriage, 1730-1779*, Harrisburg, Pa.: Harrisburg Publishing Co., 1896
Translated by Rev. F.J.F. Schantz, D.D., Myerstown, Pennsylvania[b]

Date of Baptism	Locality	Child's Name	Date of Birth	Father's Name	Sponsors
1734 Apr. 28	Moesenutten	John Ludwig	Feb. 23, 1734	Mattheis Seltzer	Ludwig Stein & wife
Jun. 5	Opequon	Theobaldt		Carl Ehrhardt	Theobaldt Gerlach
1735 Mar. 31	Shenandoah	John Frederick	Feb. 17, 1735	Nicolaus Brintzler	John Frederick Strubel
May 16	Opequon	Zacharias	Oct. 8, 1734	Jacob Sikles	Jost Heydt & wife & Abraham Weissman
" "	"	John Heinrich	Apr. 8, 1734	Peter Stephan	Heinrich Krauss
" "	"	Anna Christiana	Apr. 15, 1735	Abraham Weissman	John Heydt & Anna Christiana Stephan
" "	"	Abraham	Oct. 15, ___	Jacob Christman	John Heydt
" "	"	Sara	Sept. 23, 1734	Jacob Christman	Maria Baumann
" "	"	John George	Apr. 27, 1732	George Baumann	Jost Heydt

[a] Roy Lutz Winters, *John Caspar Stoever, Colonial Pastor and Founder of Churches*, Norristown, PA: Pennsylvania German Society, 1948. Winters summarizes Stoever's ministrations in Virginia as follows: Conojohela (18 baptisms, 2 weddings); Opequon (48 baptisms, 4 weddings); Shenandoah (25 baptisms, 1 triple wedding); and Moesenutten [Massanutten] (7 baptisms), 39.
[b] F.J.F. Schantz, translator, and Elizabeth P. Bentley, indexer, *Early Lutheran Baptisms and Marriages in Southeastern Pennsylvania: The Records of Rev. John Casper Stoever from 1730 to 1779*, Reprint, Baltimore, Md.: Genealogical Publishing Co., 1988 and 1998. Since this material is well-known and readily available elsewhere, this appendix has not been included in the index.

This Heritage

Date of Baptism	Locality	Child's Name	Date of Birth	Father's Name	Sponsors
1735 May 16	Opequon	John Jacob	Dec. 2, 1733	George Baumann	Jacob Christman
" "	"	Sarah	Nov. 16, 1732	Paul Fromman	Susanna Weissman
" "	"	John Paul	Oct. 16, 1734	Paul Fromman	Ludtwig Stephan
" "	"	Rebecca	Nov. 16, 1733	John Colvert	Maria Baumann
" "	"	Anna Catharina	Sept. 28, 1734	Johannes Schnepf	Anna Maria Kleesz
" "	"	Maria Barbara	Apr. 4, 1735	John Philipp Kleesz	Elizabetha Hartzenbuehler
" "	"	Rosina	Feb. 9, 1735	John Ulrich Buger	Jost Heydt, Susanna Weissman & Barbara Schnepf
Nov. 5	"	Maria	May __ 1734	John George Dieter	Christoph Schlegel[1] & Wife[c]
1736 May 2	"	Anna Maria	Sept. 29, 1735	Jacob Christman	The mother
" "	"	Maria Christina	Mar. 1, 1736	Paul Fromman	Peter Stephan & his wife Maria Christina
" "	"	Elizabetha	Nov. 1, 1735	Rudi Maag	Carl Ehrhardt & Susanna Barbara Buger

[c] There is an interesting letter in the archives of Grace Evangelical Church from Abdel Ross Wentz of the Lutheran Theological Seminary in Gettysburg to Reverend Eisenberg dated May 17, 1954. Wentz writes: "At one place ...you find Stoever in error with reference to his record of the baptism of one of the residents at Opequon. I believe you make a mistake in ascribing this error to Stoever's record. I once had occasion to go over the original manuscript of that record. It is deposited in the manuscript division of the Pennsylvania Historical Society in Philadelphia. I found that there were two kinds of writing in connection with many (perhaps most) of his entries. It seemed clear to me that originally Stoever did not assign any place or locality to the ministerial act, but that long afterwards he went over his records and with different ink and a slightly different hand set down alongside of the entry the place where the party concerned was located at the time he made the additions to the entries. If you keep this in mind, and if you will remember that Dr. Schantz did not always transcribe correctly and did not distinguish between the place where the ministerial act was performed and the place where the parties concerned were later resident, it may help you to correct a number of the facts pertaining to the early settlements there on the Opequon and in the Shenandoah Valley." Obviously Eisenberg saved the letter with the intention of including the information in any future edition.

Date of Baptism	Locality	Child's Name	Date of Birth	Father's Name	Sponsors
1736 May 2	Opequon	Sarah	Jul. 2, 1728	William Crisp	Paul Fromman & Wife Elizabetha
3	"	6 boys, 2 girls	————	Jacob Delinger	————
1737 Mar. 18[2]	"	Elizabetha	Jan. 5, 1735	George Baumann	Paul Fromman & wife Elizabetha
May 2[3]	"	Emma Maria	Nov. 9, 1735	George Baumann	John Leenviel & his spouse Anna Christina Stephan
June 5	"	Isaac	Nov. 9, 1736	Jacob Christman	John Jost Heydt, Isaac Heydt, Anna Maria Heydt
" "	"	John George	Dec. 15, 1735	John Philipp Kleesz	Johannes Schnepf
" "	"	John	Nov. __ 1736	John Ulrich Buger	Jost Heydt & wife Anna Maria & John Schnepp
" "	"	Susanna	Sep. __ 1736	John George Dieter	Jacob Christman & wife Magdalena
" "	"	A daughter	————	Christian Blanck	Carl Ehrhardt, Theobaldt Gerlach & wives
" 6	"	Henry	Jun. 5, 1737	James McKnees	"Evidences"[d]– his grandfather & grandmother
" 7	Shenandoah	Lewis	Feb., 20, 1737	John Leenwil (Leenviel)	Lewis Stephan
" 8	"	Rebecca	Jul. 6, 1732	Andrew Bird	"Evidences" – James Gill & Sarah Moor
" "	"	James	Oct. __ 1733	William Breedyes	"Testes"[e]– the parents
" "	"	Hanna	Aug. __ 1734	William Breedyes	"Testes" – the parents
" 8	"	Terkis	Feb. 15, 1732	Rilie Moor	"Testis" – Catharine Gerlach
" "	"	Thomas	Oct. __ 1732	Rilie Moor	"Testes" – Theobaldt Gerlach & wife
" "	"	Jacob	Dec. __ 1734	Rilie Moor	"Testis" – Andrew Bird
" "	"	John	Nov. __ 1736	Rilie Moor	"Testes" – Charles Ehrhardt & his wife Clara
" "	"	Thomas	Sept. 15, 1728	James Guill	"Testis" – John Dawbin

[d] "Evidences" means witnesses.

[e] "Testes" means witnesses or sponsors and "testis" indicates a witness or sponsor.

This Heritage

Date of Baptism	Locality	Child's Name	Date of Birth	Father's Name	Sponsors
1737 June 8	Shenandoah	James	Aug. __ 1732	James Guill	"Testis" – Elizabeth Dawbin
" "	"	Mary	Jan. 15, 1735	James Guill	The father
" "	"	John	May 11, 1737	James Guill	The father
" "	"	Thomas	Nov. 8, 1735	John Dawbin	"Testis" – James Guill
" "	"	David	Aug. 2, 1733	John Hodge	"Testes" – Mr. & Mrs. James Guill & the parents
" "	"	Elizabeth	Apr. 7. 1735	John Hodge	"Testes" – Mr. & Mrs. James Guill & the parents
" "	"	Ruth	Feb. 28, 1732	William White	The parents
" "	"	Charity	Mar. 6, 1734	William White	The parents
" "	"	Benjamin	Jan 11, 1736	William White	The parents
" 15	Opequon	Christian	May 15, 1737	Johannes Schnepf	Philip Schless & Barbara Burger[4]
1738 Mar. 23	Moesenutten	Anna Maria	Mar. 16, 1738	George Adam Heyl	Peter Schmidt & Elizabetha Barbara Heyl
Apr. 9	Shenandoah	Maria Elizabetha	Jan. 23, 1738	Nicolaus Brintzler	John Frederick Strubel
May 28	Moesenutten	John Heinrich	Sept. 12, 1737	Mattheis Seltzer	John Heinrich Schneid & Christoph Zimmerman
1738 June 2	Opequon	Mary Catharina	Nov. 22, 1737	Jacob Delinger	Maria Baumann
" 4	"	Elizabeth	May 8, 1738	Paul Fromma	George Baumann & wife Maria
" 4	"	Johannes	Mar. 28, 1737	Christian Blanck	Johannes Heydt & wife
" "	"	Paulus	May 13, 1738	John Phillipp Kleez	Paul Fromman & wife
" "	Shenandoah	John George	Nov. 22, 1737	Theobaldt Gerlach	John George Baumann & wife Maria
_____	"	Rohamy	May 8, 1738	John Hodge	"Testes" – Mr. & Mrs. James Guill & the parents
_____	"	Rebecca	_____	Daniel Hoolman	"Testes" – James Guill & the mother
_____	"	Isaac	_____	Daniel Hoolman	"Testes" – James Guill & the mother
1739 Apr. 19	Opequon	Johannes	Aug. 12, 1738	Lorentz Schnepf	Thomas Schnepp & wife
" 27	"	Anna Elizabeth	Aug. 15, 1738	Valentin Wendel	Anna Elizabeth Stoeckle
" 29	"	Anna	Apr. 9, 1735	Henry Jones	Jacob Neuschwanger & Susan Weissmann
" "	"	David	Jan. 16, 1737	Henry Jones	Abraham Weissmann & Maria Neuschwanger
" "	"	Anna Maria	Dec. 25, 1738	John Heydt	Jost Heydt & wife
" "	"	William	Aug. 11, 1736	John Dyart	"Testis" – Lorentz Schnepf

Date of Baptism	Locality	Child's Name	Date of Birth	Father's Name	Sponsors
1739 Apr. 29	Opequon	John[f]	Mar. 26, 1739	John Cuntz	Caspar Stoever, Jacob Neuschwanger & Maria Baumann
" "	"	Johannes	Mar. 9, 1739	Jacob Christman	John Heydt & Sara
" "	"	Johannes	Dec. 19, 1738	George Baumann	John Heydt & wife Sara
" "	"	Jacob	Apr 29, 1739	John Ulrich Buger	Jost Heydt & Barbara Schnepf
" "	"	John George	Mar. 9, 1739	John George Dieter	George Baumann & wife Maria
1739 May 1	Shenandoah	Emma Christina	Jan. 26, 1739	Michael Rheinhardt	Anna Christina Seltzer
" "	"	Catarina	Dec. 20, 1734	Adam Mueller	"Testes" – Pater, Mater & Anna Christina Seltzer
" "	"	Adam	July 16, 1736	Adam Mueller	"Testes" – Pater, Mater & Anna Christina Seltzer
" "	"	Anna Christina	Oct. 18, 1738	Adam Mueller	"Testes" – Pater, Mater & Anna Christina Seltzer
July 8	Moesennutten	John Adam	July 7, 1739	George Adam Heyl	John Stephan Traenckel & John Adam Hambrecht & wife
1740 Apr. 29	Opequon	Lorentz	Feb. 29, 1740	Lorentz Schnepf	Ulrich Buger & Barbara Schnepf
" "	"	John	Mar. 1, 1740	Johann Broband	John Cuntz & wife Anna Elizabetha Catharina
" "	"	Johannes	Nov. 23, 1739	Peter Maag	Abraham Weissmann
1741 Nov. 22	"	John	Oct. 22, 1741	Frederick Ohnselt	John Herr & Maria Elizabetha Haussahn
1742 May 27	Moesennutten	Anna Christina	____ 1741	Mattheis Seltzer	Elizabetha Heyl

MARRIAGES PERFORMED BY J.C. STOEVER, JR.

May 3, 1736   "Married two English couples at Opecken, in the presence of Lord Fairfax, in the County of Orange and in the colony of Virginia."

June 8, 1737   "John Hodge and Elizabeth Windseeth
Jacob Thigh and Mary White
Daniel Hoolman and Elizabeth Cartlay, North River, Shenandoah, vulgo[g] Cockel Town in Orange County, in the colony of Virginia."

June 5, 1738   "John Jacob Neuschwanger and Maria Gertraudt Brumback, Opaken."
April 30, 1739   "Peter Maag and Juliana Rheinhart, Opekan in Orange County, Virginia."

---

[f] This child is the nephew of Reverend Stoever. His only sister, Anna Elisabetha Catharina Stoever, married Johannes Koontz/Kumtz/Countz/Cuntze/Cuntz in Earltown (now New Holland), Lancaster County, Pennsylvania, June 25, 1738. They later settled in the Opequon area.

[g] "Vulgo" signifies commonly known as.

Endnotes – Appendix A

[1] The date of baptism and name of sponsors of this entry are undoubtedly in error. Christoph Schlegel is listed as living at Conewago and there, on Nov. 5, 1735, his own child was baptized. Probably June 5, 1737.

[2] Probably May 16, 1735.

[3] Probably May 2, 1736.

[4] Possibly Philip Kleesz and Barbara Buger.

Appendix B
Diary of Christian Streit[a]
July 19, 1785 to November 28, 1788

First transcribed as to its English parts by R.E. Griffith of Winchester, Virginia; then transcribed again with all foreign words and expressions translated, all abbreviations expanded, and all Scriptural references verified, by the Rev. William J. Finck, D.D., New Market, Virginia
1937
(Used by permission)
With the addition of
Introductory Notes and the
Family Record of Christian Streit.

Introductory Notes

1. *Battletown*: the present Berryville, county seat of Clarke County, twelve miles east of Winchester.
2. *Cape Capon (Cacapon)*: On or near the Cacapon River between Capon Bridge and Yellow Springs, West Virginia, twenty to twenty-five miles west by south from Winchester. George Horn and Mr. Millschlagel lived in this area.
3. *Carpenter, Mr.*: The Rev. William Carpenter, a son of Old Hebron Church, Madison County, and pastor there from 1787 to 1813.
4. *Cornstown*: Possibly Kernstown, two miles south of Winchester.

---

[a] The diary is in the collection of the Lutheran Theological Seminary at Philadelphia, Pennsylvania. Consisting of 83 pages and measuring 4 by 5 inches, the leather cover shows signs of wear and is apparently stained with oil. The majority of the entries are written in English. A copy is available at the Handley Regional Library, Winchester, Virginia.

5. *Culpeper*: Hebron Church, oldest Lutheran congregation in Virginia, located in Madison County, east of the Blue Ridge mountains, about sixty-five miles southeast of Winchester. Until 1793, Madison County was a part of Culpeper; hence the name.
6. *de Mauz* (probably more correctly du Mas): Lived near Gerrardstown, Berkeley County, West Virginia,[b] some twelve miles north of Winchester.
7. *Dowdal, Col.*: James Gambell Dowdall, Winchester merchant and a justice of the peace.
8. *Fredericktown*: The present Frederick, Maryland.
9. *Funkstown*: About four miles southeast of Hagerstown, Maryland.
10. *German College*: The present Franklin and Marshall College, Lancaster, Pennsylvania.
11. *Harr, Mr.*: Simon Harr, schoolmaster and lay leader of the congregation at Strasburg.
12. *Heard, James*: This is Maj. James Heard, whose wife, Elizabeth Morgan, was a daughter of Gen. Daniel Morgan
13. *Hill Church*: An outparish of New Hanover Church in Pennsylvania served by Streit before coming to Winchester.
14. *Hinckel, Mr.*: The Rev. Paul Henkel, noted Lutheran home missionary and organizer of congregations and synods, whose base of operations for many years centered in Shenandoah County and New Market.
15. *Massie, Maj.*: Thomas Massie, officer in the Revolution and a justice of the peace.
16. *Millerstown (Muellerstadt)*: Woodstock, county seat of Shenandoah County, thirty miles southwest of Winchester.
17. *New Hanover*: The oldest Lutheran Congregation of German origin in the country, located in Montgomery County, Pennsylvania, about twenty miles southeast of Reading. Streit came from this parish to Winchester.
18. *New Holland*: In Lancaster County, Pennsylvania, about twelve miles northeast of the city of Lancaster.
19. *New Store*: Now called Amityville, an outparish of New Hanover Church in Pennsylvania served by Streit before coming to Winchester.
20. *Newtown*: Later called Stephensburg, now Stephens City, eight miles south of Winchester, and named for Peter Stephan, the original settler.
21. *Old Furnace*: Still called by the name; now the site of St. John's Lutheran Church, Frederick County;[c] about fifteen miles west of Winchester.

---

[b] During Streit's lifetime, Berkeley was a Virginia county.
[c] Formerly known as the Old Furnace Church, the Taylor Furnace Church and the Valley Taylor Furnace Church.

Appendix B

22. *Philadelphia, The New Church*: Zion Church, dedicated in 1769.
23. *Philadelphia, The Old Church*: St. Michael's Church, built by H.M. Muhlenberg in 1748.
24. *Picket Mountain (Peaked Mountain)*: A union Lutheran and Reformed congregation near the southern end of the Massanutten range at McGaheysville, Rockingham County.
25. *Pine Church*: (a).When first so called in the diary as being six miles from Newtown, it is synonymous to Pine Hills. (b).When mentioned as being "where Mr. Hinckel lives" it refers to the present St. Mary's Church, Shenandoah County, three miles west of Mt. Jackson, some forty-five miles southwest of Winchester. Rev. Paul Henkel lived there at the time.
26. *Pine Hills*: Called St. Joseph in the Pines, a church in which Lutherans had an interest, located some six miles east by south of Stephens City, not far from Nineveh, Warren County. Rev. Paul Henkel ministered here for a time. It is no longer in existence.
27. *Roder's (Raders)*: On the outskirts of Timberville, Rockingham County, approximately sixty miles southwest of Winchester.
28. *Slater's, Capt.*: Thought to have been in Western Frederick, as the county is now constituted.
29. *Stein's (Stone's)*: Now known as Stone's Chapel, located in northwest corner of Clarke County, about twelve miles northeast from Winchester. Now a Presbyterian Church.
30. *Stovertown*: Also called Staufferstadt, now Strasburg, eighteen miles south of Winchester.
31. *Swedesboro*: In Gloucester County, New Jersey, southeast of Philadelphia.
32. *Thruston, Col.*: Charles Mynn Thruston, member of Virginia House of Delegates.
33. *Trap Hill*: Northern suburbs of Battletown, now Berryville, Clarke County, about twelve miles east of Winchester.
34. *Trappe*: Augustus Lutheran Church, Trappe, Montgomery County, Pennsylvania, built in 1743 by the Rev. H.M. Muhlenberg. Near Valley Forge.
35. *Warm Springs*: Undoubtedly the original settlement of the currently existing Old Stone (Evangelical United Brethren) Church and schoolhouse at Greenspring, Frederick County, near White Hall, ten to twelve miles north of Winchester.
36. *Winchester*: During the period covered by the diary, Lutheran services were conducted in the log church owned by the Reformed congregation, as well as in the nearby schoolhouse owned by the Lutherans.
37. *Young, Mr.*: The Rev. John George Young, Lutheran pastor, Hagerstown, Maryland, and vicinity.

FROM THE INSIDE OF THE FRONT COVER
Picket Mountain
May 4th:
Baptized 11 children
Communicants 83
Confirmed 20

Memorandum for Philadelphia. Enquire for a butler servant for Mr. Lauck. Mr. Gilbraith, merchant in Chestnut near 2d street is to advance the money, if I get one; if not he is to try...

        John
              Jacob
                    January

Feb. 14 Sold to Mr. Baker thirteen pounds Indigo @ 6/6
     do   Col. Dowdel 16 ½ lb.

1785

July 19th. Arrived with my family at Winchester.

25th. Preached in the morning German on the Gospel for the day, being the Parable of the unjust steward; subject, The wise concern for the future condition. In the afternoon in English on Matt.22:16. Subject 1. The way of God which Christ taught; 2. That he taught it in truth.

27th. Married Michael Sommers, widower, and Catharine Braun, widow, in Winchester.

28th. Married John Askew to Mary Dougherty by license in Winchester.

August 1st. Preached at Newtown in the morning on the word of the Gospel, Luke 19:42, and in the afternoon in Winchester on the latter part of verse 44 of the same, both in German. After service in Winchester had a short conference in church with some of the heads of the Germans about choosing deacons and concerning my brother's keeping the German school. [See introductory notes 20 and 36.]

August 7th. Preached at Steins in the morning German on Luke 8:13,14, part of the Gospel for the day being the 11th Sunday after Trinity. In the afternoon in Winchester on the Gospel. Enlarged on the character of the Pharisees and Publicans. [See introductory note 29.]

August 13th. Baptized George West and wife Mary Elizabeth their child in my house, named Catharine, born April 5, 1784. Parents Sponsors, Lutherans.

Appendix B

14th. Preached in Winchester in the morning German on part of the Gospel Mark 7, last verse; subject, Jesus Who doeth all things well; in the afternoon at Battletown English the same subject. [See note 1.]

21st. Baptized Jesse Anderson and his wife Rachel their child Thomas born Sept. 2, 1784. Sponsors John Gerst and Charlotte Hofman, in Winchester.

21st. Preached in Winchester in the morning German on the Gospel, being the 13th Sunday after Trinity. Subject, Jesus the merciful Samaritan. In the afternoon in Newtown, the same subject.

Same day, previous notice having been given, there was an election held in the Lutheran school house in Winchester for deacons, the number 4, the 2 highest in votes to serve the next year for elders, which elders to continue three years and then either reelected or others chosen. The two lowest to serve two years as deacons and then others to be chosen in their stead. Accordingly were elected:

Louis Hoff   }
          highest in votes
George Len   }
George Geiger
Michael Altrit
Next to these in votes were Baker, Wetzel, Lantz and Jacob Geiger.

August 25, 1785. Buried in the English Churchyard in Winchester John Braun, a native of Copenhagen aged about 26 years.

28th. Preached in the morning in Trap Hill meeting house in English on Matt.22:42, What think ye of Christ? In the afternoon at Steins in German on the Gospel; subject, Spiritual leprosy healed through Christianity, and the gratitude due Him. – Publish first time, Daniel Hoch, son of Rudolph, and Christina Hunsicker, daughter of Daniel, both in Frederick County. [See introductory note 33.]

September 1st. Married Amos Laughlin and Elizabeth Teall, by license.

4th. Preached in Winchester in the morning German on part of the Gospel Matt.6:33; in the afternoon English on the same. — Baptized Jacob Anderson and wife Christina their twins, Catharine and Margaret, born August 8th. Sponsors Henrich and Barbara Weiso. — baptized also Stephen Bolen and wife Maria Elizabeth their child Sarah, born May 1784. Sponsor Eva Rubsamen.

7th. Began Latin school with three.

11th. Preached in Newtown forenoon, and afternoon Winchester German on the Gospel in the morning on verse 10, in the afternoon on verse 14. Morning, Christ the Prophet; afternoon Spiritual Resurrection.

14th. Had a conference with the deacons, &c., about finishing the church; concluded that a lottery should be made, but as no money could be raised by the lottery till next spring, it was agreed that window shutters and doors should be made by private persons, two or three joining together to make one door or window, etc., to be done this fall that we might keep service in it.

19th. Baptized John George Lamp and wife Elizabeth their child John born March 13th. Sponsors John Lamb [Lamp?] and wife Anna.

September 18, 1785. Preached at Stones German and English, both on the last verse of the Gospel, being the 17th Sunday after Trinity. Subject, The nature and motives of humility. [See introductory note 29.]

20th. Married Daniel Hoch to Christina Hunsacker at Steins by license.

23rd. Buried in Winchester John Hatsabieler 18 years and ____ months old. Text Job 14:1.

25th. Preached in Winchester in the morning German and in the afternoon English; on the Gospel in German The Nature and Motives of the love of God. In English on Luke 21:33, The Truth and principal parts of the words of Christ.

25th. Baptized Jacob Bentler and his wife Barbara their child Maria Catharine, born September 21, 1785. Sponsors Conrad Schuler and wife Maria Catharine.

28th. Mr. Mays son came to the Latin school.

25th. Married in the evening by license John Bartlett and Susanna Laubinger.

October 2nd. Preached in Stovertown in the morning German on part of the Gospel for the 19th Sunday after Trinity verse 4: Jesus a searcher of the heart. In the afternoon in Newtown on part of the Epistle, verse 24, Putting on the new man. [See note 30.]

5th. Married by license William Low and Mary Peterson.

9th. 20th Sunday after Trinity. Preached in the morning in Winchester on the Gospel; subject, The Loss of the Heavenly Kingdom. In the afternoon at Steins on the same subject.

12th. Buried Mr. Haymaker's child in Winchester.

16th. 21st Sunday after Trinity. Preached in the morning German and in the afternoon English in Winchester on part of the Gospel verse 53. Also 16th. Baptized Abraham Sovein and his wife Lydia their child Abraham, born October 4, 1785. Sponsors Parents.

17th. Baptized George Helm and wife Catharine their child Catharine, born April 12, 1785, sponsors Jacob Anderson and wife

Appendix B

Christina; at the same time married Frederick August Bernard and Dorothea Helm, and also in the evening James Heard and Betsey Morgan. [See note 12.]

October 18, 1785. Married a couple at Newtown.

22nd. Preparation for Sacrament at Winchester.

23rd. Being the 22nd Sunday after Trinity, held Sacrament at Winchester and preached on the Gospel, namely Forgiveness of sin and forgiveness of injury done by our neighbor. Preached in the afternoon at Newtown on the same subject.

26th. Married in Winchester John Palmer and Anne Bonham.

29th. Preparation for Lord's Supper at Steins.

30th. Held Sacrament at Steins in the morning, preached on part of the Gospel, 12 communicants, being 23rd Sunday after Trinity, on verse 21, Our duty to Government and our duty to God. Was to have preached in English in Winchester in the afternoon but bad weather prevented public worship.

November 6th. 24th Sunday after Trinity. Held Sacrament at Newtown, 15 communicants; preached on the Gospel, Christ the God Who helps us in the time of death. In the afternoon preached in Winchester on the same subject. Baptized in the evening the following children:

Philip Scharer	Elizabeth	Conrad Cramer
Wife Rosina	born October 8	Wife Catharine
John Sload	Jacob	Jacob Grim
Wife Barbara	born October 26	Wife Maria Magdalena
John Poh	John	John Sload
Wife Anna Margaret	born October 30	Mrs. Lauck

7th. Baptized in the evening Peter Lauck's child.

8th. Married John Rinedel and Margaret Anderson by license.

10th. Married William Sharp and Deborah Allen.

11th. Rode up to Stovertown in the forenoon and put up at Leonard Baltis's; in the afternoon went with Mr. Harr to the school house and heard him catechise the young people who were to be confirmed to the number of 22; examined them also myself. [See note 11.]

12th. Again heard the young people in the forenoon. In the afternoon I confirmed them; they appeared greatly affected. And held preparation for the Sacrament. In the evening baptized 3 children, one of which belonged to English parents who were then on their way moving to Carolina.

November 13, 1785. Being 25th Sunday after Trinity. Baptized two children in Mr. Harr's house before service and administered the Communion in an adjoining small house to two very aged widows who were not able to go to church. Went to church, baptized a child before service, preached on John 1:29. The audience was much moved. Administered the Sacrament to 29, besides the young people who went the first time. After the service baptized a child in church, and one also at Mr. Baltis's. Rode then to Newtown ten miles and preached on Matt. 11:28, 29, 30, with effect. In the evening came home eight miles. — The whole time of my absence indisposed.

20th. Preached in Winchester in the morning German on part of the Gospel, being the 26th Sunday after Trinity. Subject, 1) Proof of the Last Judgment. 2) The Blessedness of those invited. 3) The Attributes of the same persons.

26th. Married in the evening James Lawrence to Margaret Cummins by license in my house.

27th. Being the first Sunday in Advent. Preached in the morning in Winchester in German on verse 5 of the Gospel: 1) The King, 2) He comes, 3) To You, 4) Accept, Say, Behold, Thine. In the afternoon preached at Steins on the same.

28th. Married Charles Bryan and Sarah Walters.

29th. John Cox and Sarah Parks.

December 3rd. Married Edward Wells and Rebecca Powel, as also John Bailey and Elizabeth Long.

1st. Preached at Warm Springs German and English both on the Gospel of the proceeding Sunday; baptized 5 children. [See note 35.]

2nd. On my way home baptized a sick child. Had a fever on the journey.

3rd. Had appointed to keep preparation for Sacrament in Pine Church 6 miles from Newtown, being one of Mr. Hinckel's congregations, but being indisposed and Mr. Hinckel being in town he went and did it himself. I took medicine. [See notes 25a, 26 and 14.]

December 4, 1785. Rode to the aforesaid church, held confession and absolution with the communicants, preached on the Gospel, being 2nd Sunday in Advent, verse 36: 1) The worthiness, 2) The blessedness, 3) The means of obtaining worthiness; namely, watchfulness and prayer. And administered the Sacrament to 18.

5th. Rode to Stovertown, preached on the 1st verse of the Epistle for the preceding day, The proper use of the Scriptures. Baptized 4 adults and 3 infants.

6th. Buried in Winchester Anna Margaret Holtzel, between 57 and 58 years of age. Text, Rev. 14:13.

N.B. On the 19th of November I administered the Sacrament to Michael Altrit's mother-in-law, being very old, blind and decrepit, in Albert's house and at the same time baptized Michael Altrit and his wife their child Catharine, born October 15, of this year. As also Nicholas Mismer and wife child Henry, born May 27th of this year. For the former sponsors Nicholas Mismer and wife Anna Maria, for the latter Michael Altrit and wife Ann Margaret.

December 9th. Baptized at Mr. Len's the following children of Andrew Heyl and his wife Catharine:

Children	Sponsors
George Michael born May 22, 1778	George Len
John Jacob born Dec. 27, 1780	Jacob Michael
John William born Sept. 20, 1782	Abraham Sobine and wife Lydia
Mary Catharine born October 11, 1784	George Len's wife Anna Maria

11th. Preached in Winchester in the morning in English on Psalm 73:24; in the afternoon in German on the last words of verse 5 of the Gospel, being the 3rd Sunday in Advent. Subject, The Preaching of the Gospel: 1) The Gospel; 2) The Preaching of the same. And buried after service Christian Lehrug out of Mr. Frey's house.

12th. Buried Catharine wife of Henry Altrit, aged 27 years and 10 months. Text, Psalm 103:15, 16, 17.

December 18, 1785. Preached in the morning at Steins, being the 4th Sunday in Advent, on verse 26 of the chapter of the Gospel. Subject, The Christ unknown in the midst of the people: 1) He mingled among the people; 2) Proof that he was there generally unknown. In the afternoon preached in Winchester German on the same subject.

21st. Baptized a child a mile out of town for one Howe, English.

13th. married Thomas Edwards and Martha Kesner.

25th. Baptized Peter and Elizabeth Baer their child Mary Sarah, born Sept. 23, 1785. Sponsors George Linn[d] and wife Anna Mary. Being Christmas preached in the morning in German on the last verse of the Gospel in Winchester, and in the afternoon at Newtown on the same subject.

26th. Preached at Stovertown on the first two verses of the Epistle of the previous day; had an election for two new deacons.

1786

January 1, 1786. Baptized Martin Zuber and wife Catharine their child Martin born November 8, 1784. Sponsors John Barnhart Ehrhart and wife.

---

[d] "Linn" also appears as "Len," "Lind" and "Lens."

5th. Preached at Steins on Psalm 90:12, The Spiritual Arithmetic.

6th and 7th. Rode to Pine Church where Mr. Hinckel lives. [See note 25b.]

8th. Preached at Pine Church and administered the Communion to about 30 communicants. Text, out of the Gospel, being the first Sunday after Epiphany: Know ye not that I must be about my Father's Business? In the afternoon went 3 miles and administered the Communion to an old decrepit man, where was also his son-in-law, who fell from a horse a few days before and shattered his brains, so that tho' he yet lived he was deprived of the use of reason and speech. Mr. Hinckel prayed with the people who were collected, at least 20 or 30, and I admonished them suitable to the occasion.

9th. Rode to Rader's Church about 9 miles farther and kept Sacrament there with about 10[e], text Matt. 11:27, 28, etc. Came that evening to Millerstown. [See notes 27 and 16.]

10th. Having lodged at Mr. Savage's at Millerstown, I baptized his child early in the morning, and came home that day.

11th. Married Perez Drew and Mary Richardson in the evening.

12th. Married Robert Oglesby to Honor Holding.

January 15, 1786. Preached at Newtown in the morning, it being the 2nd Sunday after Epiphany. Preached on part of the Gospel, namely, verse 5 Obedience to Christ, and in the afternoon at Stovertown on the same subject, and came home.

17th. Married Jacob Marcker and Mary Klein and buried Ann Margaret Mismer, aged 79 years and 6 months; text Psalm 90:10.

19th. Married George Madden and Phebe Parmer.

Omission.

January 1st. Preached in Winchester in the morning German on the name Jesus and the right use thereof; and in the afternoon English on "Redeeming the time seeing the days are evil."

22nd. Preached in the morning at Winchester in German and in the afternoon English both on part of the Gospel, namely, Speak but a word and my servant shall be healed. Matt. 8. The Power of Christ. Baptized the following children:

John Clerck	John	Henrich Spengel
Wife Margaret	born Dec. 18, 1785	
Michael Harger	Anna Maria	Christopher Brith
Wife Maria Dorothea	born Oct. 7, 1785	and wife Elizabeth
Fred. Aug. Bernard	Maria Magdalena	Wolfgang Lackmiller
Wife Dorothea	born January 16th	Dorothea Glasser

---

[e] There is no extant communicant list.

25th. Preached at one Horns at Cape Capon German and English. In the evening married Hugh Molley and Margaret Davis in Winchester. [See note 2.]

27th. Baptized Robert Wood and his wife Comfort their child William, born January 5th. Parents sponsors; — and also buried John Hoff's child Mary, aged 4 years and 9 months.

28th. Buried Smith's Mr. Bush's son-in-law's child Nathaniel, aged about 5 years.

29th. Preached at Steins in the Morning and Winchester in the afternoon on the last part of the Gospel, What manner of man is this, etc., Matt. 8, subject, The true obedience to Jesus.

After service in Winchester made a defense against some blame thrown upon me about my brother's school being very poorly kept. In the evening baptized Adam Young and wife Catharine their child John, born July 11, 1785. Sponsors John Lentz and wife Susanna Catharine.

February 1, 1786. Buried Col. Dowdal's little son aged about 5 years. [See note 7.]

3rd. Buried Peter Lauck's child Jacob aged 2 years, 11 months and some days.

5th. 5th Sunday after Epiphany. Preached in the morning at Stovertown and in the afternoon at Newtown on the words of the Gospel, The kingdom of heaven is like unto a man sowing seed in his field. Subject, The excellence of the Divine Word; to prove that the Word of God is good seed.

7th. Married Thomas Murgrave to Mary Newton.

12th. Preached in Winchester in the morning German and in the afternoon English, the Gospel being for Septuagesima Sunday. Subject, the great and gracious reward of the labourers in the vineyard of Christ. Baptized Philip Huber and wife Elizabeth their child Catharine Elizabeth born October 1, 1785. Sponsors Michael Sommer and wife Ann Catharine.

7th. Buried John Bucher's child near Newtown, named Henry, aged 2 years, 2 months and 6 days. Text, Job 30:23.

18th. Buried George Hinckel aged 78 years, 9 months, 6 miles out of town.

19th. Preached in the morning in Winchester and in the afternoon at Steins on the last verse of the Gospel Sexagesima. Subject, The proper use and the wholesome fruit of the Divine Word.

20th. Instructed the catechumens for confirmation first time in Winchester. Number 33.

23rd. Sick.

26th. Sunday *Esto Mihi* (*Quinquagesima* Sunday). Being still sick did not go out.

27th. Catechised, received 3 more.

March 1st. Was to have preached at Warm Springs, but not being right well yet it was not proper for me to go so I staid at home.

3rd. Catechised.

5th. Preached at Winchester German and English, being the Sunday *Invocavit* on the words, Thou shalt worship, etc.

7th. Catechised.

March 9, 1786. Married Garrison White and Elizabeth Reisser; also Michael Copinhufer and Margaret Price.

12th. Preached at Steins in the morning and at Winchester in the afternoon on the words of the Gospel, O woman, great is thy faith, etc., being the Sunday *Reminiscere*.

14th. Catechised.

15th. Buried Henry Forst, aged 70 years and 7 months. Text, Heb. 9:27.

16th. Married Thomas Edmondson and Ann Campbell.

17th. Baptized Godfried Miller's and wife Anna Maria child Godfried born March 3rd. Reverend Paul Hinckel and wife sponsors.

19th. Preached at Newtown in the morning and in the afternoon at Stovertown on part of the Epistle for the day Sunday *Oculi* verses 1 and 2, The true following of God.

20th. Baptized Philip Bauer and wife Sarah child John Adam, born February 1st. Sponsor, Adam Young's wife Catharine.

22nd. Buried Mrs. De la Marque. Exhorted in English on Rev. 14:13.

26th. Preached Winchester German. Fourth Sunday in Lent Christ the Prophet promised of God. English, Titus 2:11, 12, The Grace of God.

27th. Married Jasper Cather and Sarah Moore.

28th. Buried Frederick Maack aged 27 years, 7 months.
    Married John Park and Mary Millschlagel
    William McChesney and Rebecca Schadacre
    George Weiser and Mary Luckleiter
    William Carper and Margaret Ritter

30th. Married Nathan Clark and Elizabeth Matson.

[April 2nd. Preached at Culpeper and administered the sacrament.]f

Married April 4th:
    Adam Klein and Catharine Magdalena Poker
    Jacob Hite and Catharine Shoner
    John Sullivan and Margaret Hare.

---

f For no apparent reason, Streit records the list of those who communicated on this occasion later in his diary. The information follows his entry for August 27, 1786.

Appendix B

4th. Baptized John Lentz and wife Susanna Catharine child John, born February 28th. Sponsors the parents.

5th. Baptized John Duffield and wife Mary child John, born April 3rd, parents sponsors.

April 9, 1786. Preached in the morning in Stovertown and in the afternoon in Newtown on the Gospel; subject, The proper honor due Jesus as our King. Baptized 2 children.

13th. Married Samuel Davis and Phebe Connel.

14th. Preached in the morning on the words, It is finished, being Good Friday, and in the afternoon in Winchester and confirmed the young people in number 36, and held preparation for Sacrament with the old ones, preached on the words, Behold the Man!

16th. Being Easter. Preached in Winchester on The significance and the use of the Resurrection of Jesus, based on the Gospel. Administered the Sacrament to old and young in the forenoon and in the afternoon preached on the same subject in English.

Easter Monday. Preached at Newtown in the morning and in the afternoon at Stovertown both German and after the German service an English discourse in Stovertown; baptized 4 children.

23rd. Preached in Winchester in the morning upon The fruits of the Resurrection of Jesus; namely, joy, peace, and the Holy Spirit. Was to have gone to Steins but it having rained very much the Opeckon was too high to cross.

24th. Buried Mr. Peter Lauck's child John aged 8 months and 8 days; Text, Psalm 16:6. And also Daniel Klipstein's child about 9 months of age.

Persons who announced themselves during Holy Week as intending on Easter to come to the Lord's Supper in Winchester:

Margaret Garst	Philip Huber
Maria Elizabeth Poh	Maria Ritter
Ernest Eltz	Elizabeth Grim, Jo Grim's wife
Andrew Baker	Elizabeth Forst
Louis Frederick Maxholt and wife Anna Elizabeth	Peter Bar, wife Elizabeth Daughter Elizabeth
Catharine Busch	Catharine Zuber
	Henry Bruhl

April 16, 1786. Easter. Baptized

Henry Altrit Mother deceased	John born Nov. 2, 1782 [?]	John Raindel Elizabeth Hitel

This Heritage

John Kortehel Wife Anna Elizabeth	Elizabeth born July 13, 1785	Maria Elizabeth Ley
John Hoff Wife Elizabeth	Elizabeth born Jan. 29, 1785	George Oberacker and wife Margaret

Easter Monday preached at Newtown in the morning and in the afternoon in Stovertown first German then in English, baptized 4 children.[g]

18th. Married Isaac Wemmer and Catharine Bastion.

Turn back two leaves for some that ought to come in here.

25th. Married 3 couples here in town.

26th. Baptized Conrad Kremer and wife Catharine child Catharine, born April 14th. Sponsors Peter Lauck and wife Amelia.

30th. Preached in Stovertown in the morning and married a couple, and in the afternoon preached in Newtown, both places on The Excellence of Christ as a Shepherd and the duties of his sheep.

May 1st. Buried Charles Grim's child aged 1 year, 10 months, and 2 weeks.

2nd. Buried Catharine Trinkel aged 76 years, and rode up to Cape Capon.

3rd. Preached in the morning German and baptized 2 children, in the afternoon English at George Horn's, married a couple and came part way home.

4th. Came home indisposed. Major Massie came for his tickets. [See note 15.]

5th. Married a couple in the morning. Sent Col. Thruston his tickets. [See note 32.]

7th. Preached in the morning German in Winchester on part of Gospel being 3rd Sunday after Easter. The beneficial sorrow of the pious, from verses 20 and 22. Baptized an English child from the country. In the afternoon preached English on Luke 14: 18, 1) The offers of the Gospel; 2) That men reject them; 3) Their vain excuses.

10th. Preached at Culpeper German in the morning on [subject not given], and administered the Sacrament to 80 communicants.[h] In the afternoon preached in English on [subject not given]. Baptized this day 22 children German and English. [See note 5.]

May 14, 1786. Sunday *Cantate*. Preached at Stein's in the forenoon and Winchester in the afternoon on the Gospel, The operations of the Holy Spirit among men; namely, to punish, lead, comfort, proclaim Christ.

---

[g] Streit repeats himself. The same entry appears at the top of the page.

[h] There is no extant list of communicants in the Hebron records for 1786.

21st. Preached at Newtown in the morning and Stovertown in the afternoon, German and English on the first two verses of the Gospel; 1) The object. 2) The manner. 3) The motives of Prayer. Baptized this day 2 children.

22nd. Baptized Adam Albert and wife Elizabeth child Elizabeth, born May 6th. Sponsors Jacob Michael and Catharine Elizabeth Albert.

23rd. Rode to Warm Springs.

24th. Catechised.

25th. Confirmed 17 persons who had been instructed during the winter partly by a schoolmaster and partly by their parents. Amongst them were a father and his daughter and a mother and her 2 daughters. Preached on Matt. 11:28, 29; kept the Sacrament with 54 communicants, including those confirmed. Baptized 12 children.

26th. Came home from the Warm Springs. Had to swim two creeks, it having rained for several days.

28th. Being the Sunday before Whitsunday, I was to have preached in Winchester in the morning English, but there being a great rain no people gathered together; preached German in the afternoon on part of the Gospel. Subject, The double testimony of the Holy Spirit and the disciples of Jesus.

June 2nd. Married William Alexander and Sarah Cafford.

4th. Being Whitsunday. Preached in the forenoon in Winchester German on the first 4 verses of the Epistle and in the afternoon preached at Steins on the same. Baptized 4 children.

5th. Preached at Stovertown in the morning and in the afternoon at Newtown on part of Gospel; namely John 3:16.

6th. Great noise on account of a letter I wrote to the Trustees of the Grammar School in Winchester, wherein I made a proposal and some took it for a high affront, and I was not a little exposed by my enemies, but "The hand (of effort) increases under a load, and burdened strength triumphs!" [Latin quotation.]

June 11,1786. Trinity Sunday. Preached at Winchester forenoon and in the afternoon at Steins on the last verse of the Gospel.

12th. Buried Mrs. Elizabeth McDonald aged 29 years and 5 months.

14th. Married Conrad Fungonie [?] and Rebecca Scott

16th. Buried one Adolph an old man.

Young people who announced themselves for instruction on Whitsunday 1786 at Steins:

Henry	17	His father Caspar Sieber
Mathias Frey	17	With Mr. Henry Krum

Michael Schall	18	His father Nicolas
Catharine	16	Her father John Mauser
George	16}	Their father George
Elizabeth	15}	Seidelmayer
John	16}	Their father Jacob Dorflinger
Elizabeth	17}	
Eva Margaret	15}	
Sibella	16}	Their father David Hawman
Peter	18}	
Jacob Schwemlin	15	His stepfather Jacob Boltz
Abraham	}	Their father Jacob Krebs
Henry	}	
Catharine	}	
Michael	16}	Their father Michael Trinkel
Margaret	17}	
Catharine	14}	
Christina Benner		Her mother Anna Maria
John Smith		Married
Eva Liebestein		Her father Adam
Elizabeth Boltz	13 1/2	Her father Michael

June 18, 1786. Preached in Winchester in the morning in English on Luke 8:15, and in the afternoon in German on the Gospel for 1st Sunday after Trinity.

22nd. Married Henry Altrit and Elizabeth Whipple.

25th. Preached in the morning at Newtown and in the afternoon at Stovertown, both on the words of the Gospel, "Come for all things are now ready!" Second Sunday after Trinity.

July 2nd. Preached in the morning at Steins and in the afternoon in Winchester on the Gospel for 3rd Sunday after Trinity. Subject, The Excellence of the human soul. Baptized 2 children at Steins.

About this time buried Conrad Kreb's child Jacob, aged 10 months and 2 weeks.

3rd. Baptized Michael Damly and Elizabeth his wife their child Mary born September 30, 1785. Parents sponsors.

9th. Preached in Winchester in the morning German, in the afternoon English on the words of the Gospel "Be ye therefore merciful as your Father also is merciful." Luke 6:36.

16th. Preached at Stovertown in the morning, and in the afternoon at Newtown on the words of the Gospel, "Henceforth thou shalt catch men!" Baptized 5 children.

Appendix B

Children who announced themselves today for instruction, 5th Sunday after Trinity. In Newtown.

Antony Klein's children:		Caspar 19, Maria Barbara 18
Sarah	16	Her father George Gantz
Maria	14	Her father Michael Gartner
Barbara	16}	Their father
Susanna	14}	Adam Klein
Elizabeth	}	Their father Anthony Bilman
Rosina	}	
Maria Barbara	19	Her father Henry Zoll

17th. Married James Cleavinger and Martha McGrew.

Buried Abraham Sovein's child Abraham aged 9 months and 12 days. Text, Phil. 4:5, last sentence.

July 18, 1786. Baptized Christian Singhaus and wife Barbara their child Elizabeth, born June 3, 1785. Sponsor Elizabeth Bar.

20th. Buried Michael Harger's child Anna Maria aged 9 months and 12 days. Text, John 6:68, last sentence.

21st. Buried Andrew Kiger's child Mary, aged 3 years, 10 months. Text, 1 Cor. 15:19.

Same day Mr. Carpenter came to live with me. [See note 3.]

23rd. Preached in the morning in Winchester on the first verse of the Gospel for the 6th Sunday after Trinity; in the afternoon at Steins on Rom. 2:4. Baptized a child at Steins and in the evening Mr. Dromgold's child Betsy.

24th. Married Jesse Pugh and Elizabeth Gray.

24th or 25th. Buried Adam Sell aged 31 years. Text, Job 14:14.

28th. Preached at one De Mauz's 12 miles from town, who lay very low with consumption; baptized 5 of his children and 5 others. [See note 6.]

30th. Preached in the morning German on the Gospel for the 7th Sunday after Trinity, The Excellence of Christ and duties flowing therefrom. In the afternoon English on the same, both in Winchester. Baptized in the evening John Grim's child.

This day also an election was held for deacons, Moses H. Baker and Jacob Kyger [?].

August 1st. Married William Mercer and Anne Webb.

6th. Preached in the morning at Newtown on part of the Gospel. Subject, The lamentable end of fruitless lives. And in the afternoon at Stovertown first in German on the Epistle. Subject, The advantages of the gifts of the Holy Spirit; and then in English on Psalm 73: 25, 26.

13th. Baptized Peter born November 7, 1783; Parents, Nicolas

This Heritage

and wife Anne Elizabeth Parcells; sponsors, Conrad Schuler and wife Catharine. Having preached in the morning at Steins and in the afternoon in Winchester on part of the Gospel for the 9th Sunday after Trinity. Subject, Spiritual Wisdom. Baptized a child at Steins.

14th. Married Thomas Lindsay and Mary Reagan.

18th. Buried a child at the church at Steins; namely, Daniel Hukedorn's named Daniel, aged 6 years, 7 months, 2 weeks and 2 days.

August 20, 1786. Preached in the morning German in Winchester, on the things that belong to our peace, the subject taken from the Gospel for the day, being the 10th Sunday after Trinity. In the afternoon English on Rom. 8:18. — This day new deacons were consecrated.

22nd. Married Jonas Likens and Mary Eckstine.

About this time buried Mr. Mesmer's child.

24th. Married James Dunn and Rachel Prinz.

27th. Preached in the morning at Stovertown on the Gospel for the day. Subject, The characters of the Pharisees and Publicans. Baptized two children. In the afternoon preached on the last verses of the Gospel at Newtown; namely, Justification and the way of obtaining it in the example of the Publican. Baptized 3 children.

Names of persons who communed a few weeks before Easter [April 2, 1786] in Culpeper:

Andrew Carpenter
His wife Barbara
Elizabeth Schweiger
Nicolas Grickler (now Crigler)
His wife Margaret
George Rieser
His wife Margaret
Henry Lepp
His wife Elizabeth
Julia Maria
Adam Gaar
Christopher Mayer
Cornelius Carpenter
His wife Maria
Barbara Ehler
Michael Blankenbiger
His wife Elizabeth
John Fleischmann
His wife Elizabeth
Jacob Rieser
His wife Susanna
George Rausch and Mother Elizabeth Rausch
Michael Lutz
Wife Susanna
John Lehman
John Schmitt
Martin Hirsch
Christian Leps
Wife Maria
Nicolas Schmitt
Wife Susanna
John Blankenbiger
Wife Barbara
Ephraim Rausch
Daniel Lutz
Wife Maria
Christopher Thallert
Wife Elizabeth
Nicolas Schmitt
Wife Maria
William Carpenter
Wife Maria
Three daughters, Elizabeth, Maria & Ann
Zacharias Fleischmann
Frederick Danner [Tanner]
Wife Maria

Appendix B

Margaret Danner widow	Samuel Carpenter
Zacharias Blankenbiger	Wife Dina
Wife Elizabeth	Samuel Blakenbiger
Daniel Bohmen	Conrad Delp
Wife Nancy	Wife Magdalena
Mother Catharine	Dorothea Carpenter
Daniel Koch	Eberhard Reiter
William Carpenter Jr.	Michael Gaar
Adam Jager	Wife Elizabeth
	[Sum Total 68]

September 3, 1786. Was to have preached in Winchester in the morning but Mr. Kunkle preached. In the afternoon preached at Steins on part of Epistle 2 Cor. 3:9, The superior glory of the Gospel above the law.

10th. Preached in the morning German in Winchester on the Gospel for the 13th Sunday after Trinity. Subject, The love of God. Baptized Lewis Wolfe's and Brother Will's children.

25 Sept. baptized William Ball and wife Elizabeth child Mary born July 16. Sponsors Peter Lauck and wife.

12th. Buried on the way to Warm Springs 9 miles from town Maria Agnes, wife of George Schweier, born in Hohenstadt in Germany, married 36 years, died in the evening of the 10th. Age 76 years and about 2 months.

15th. Preached at Steins on Micah 6:8.

17th. Preached in the morning at Newtown; as it rained very hard I could not go to Stovertown as was appointed.

22nd. Baptized Lewis Will and Catharine his wife their child Maria Barbara, born July 13, 1786. Sponsors John Rein and wife Anna Margaret.

24th. Preached at Steins in the morning on the words of the Gospel "Seek ye first the kingdom of God," etc., and in the afternoon in Winchester on verses 26 and 28 of the chapter of the Gospel, subject, Taught by the irrational creatures of God. Matt. 6:26, 28.

26th. Set off for Philadelphia with my wife and child in stage wagon.

October 8th. Being 17th Sunday after Trinity preached at New Store on Micah 6:8, "He hath showed thee, O man!" [See note 19.]

15th. Preached in New Hanover from the Gospel on the Love of God and in the afternoon in the Hill Church on the words of the Epistle "Who hath called you to the fellowship of his Son!" [See notes 17 and 13.]

29th. Preached in the morning at Stovertown on The loss of the

Heavenly Kingdom from the Gospel, being the 20th Sunday after Trinity. Baptized 2 children. In the afternoon at Newtown on Wedding Garments. Baptized two children.

31st. Buried Martin Reily's child Jacob aged 2 years and 8 months. Text, "The time is short!"

November 5th. Preached at Steins in the morning from the Gospel, The Exemplary faith of the nobleman. Baptized 3 children and in the afternoon in Winchester from the Epistle The helmet of salvation and the sword of the Spirit.

November 7, 1786. Baptized one Hard's child from Culpeper in my house.

11th. Buried at John Poker's near Newtown Michael Bland's child born June 25, 1786 [should be 1785]. A little more than 7 weeks ago, she lost her mother and a few days later she took sick, and day before yesterday in the evening at 8 o'clock she died. Age 1 year, 4 months, 2 weeks and 1 day. [Sponsors David Pfeifer and wife Barbara,] named Sarah.

12th. 22nd Sunday after Trinity. Preached in the morning German and in the afternoon English, both on part of the Gospel. Subject, The great debt of Sin.

18th. Held preparation for Sacrament and confirmed 10 young people at Newtown.

19th. Preached on the words of the Gospel "Render unto Caesar, etc." and held the Sacrament with about 36 including the young people confirmed the day before. Baptized 1 infant. In the afternoon preached at Stovertown upon the same subject and baptized 1 infant.

26th. Preached in the morning German at Winchester and in the afternoon English at Steins, both on part of the Epistle; namely, on the words "Who hath made us meet for etc." Baptized at Steins 2 children.

William Carpenter	Anna Maria
A man at Mr. Wack's	Elizabeth Reily
Henry Holtzel	Anna Maria Heinle widow,
John Geier at Krebs	Christopher Frey
George Linn	and wife
Gotfried Miller and wife	Eva Heiskel

All these persons announced themselves during the preceding week for the Communion, and attended, on the 1st Sunday in Advent, being the 3rd day of December, at which time I preached in German in Winchester on the Gospel; subject, Christ's Office of King. This service was held in the morning; in the afternoon; preached in English on the words, "And they that were ready went in with him to the marriage, and the door was shut." Matt. 25:10.

December 10, 1786. Being the 2nd Sunday in Advent. Was to

have been in Stovertown but bad weather prevented.

11th. Went out to preach at Newtown, but it being very cold, and the roof of the church not done, no people came.

13th. Buried at midnight [?] George Paul Mercker, born in Alsace...in 1727. Reared in a Christian manner according to the Lutheran doctrine. Joined in wedlock on the ship on the voyage hither in the year 1752. Three children survive, all living and married. Sick for two weeks. Died Monday the 11th of this month. Age 59.

17th. 3rd Sunday in Advent. Preached in the morning at Steins on the words of the Gospel, "The Gospel is preached to the poor." Did not preach in the afternoon in Winchester on account of the badness of the road and the shortness of the day. Confirmed at Steins the preceding day 22, and preached a preparation for the Sacrament that was held the next day, about 20 communicants besides those confirmed the day before. Baptized 2.

24th. 4th Sunday in Advent. Preached at Winchester German in the morning on the words of the Gospel, "Make straight the way of the Lord!" Was to have preached English in the afternoon but on account of the extreme cold it was omitted.

25th. Being Christmas preached in Winchester only, German on the Gospel. Subject, The first Christmas celebration as a pattern for us.

26th. Preached at Steins on the Epistle for the preceding day. Subject, The reasons why God sent his Son into the world.

About this time buried Ernst Ander's child, scalded to death, called Abraham, aged 2 years, 5 months, 1 week.

	Baptized 25th December	
Jacob Ritter	Catharine	Adam Ancese [?]
Wife Maria	born December 9, 1785	and wife Sabilla
Mathias Ritter	Lydia	Lydia Pierce
Wife Maria	born September 29, 1785	
George Post	Hannah	John Kneister
Wife Catharine	born June 15, 1785	and Wife Hannah

December 31, 1786. Preached at Stovertown on Psalm 90:12. Subject, The Spiritual Arithmetic. Baptized 3 children.

1787

January 1st. Preached at Newtown on the Gospel. Subject, How to begin the New Year in the Name of Jesus. Baptized 2 children.

7th. Preached in the morning at Steins on the question of the Gospel: "Know ye not that I must be about my Father's business?" In the afternoon in Winchester on the same subject.

21st. Preached in the morning at Newtown and in the afternoon in Winchester, both on the Gospel, particularly the words: "I will; be thou clean!" Subject, The great willingness of Christ to help us in our spiritual needs.

21st. Baptized Jacob Herman and wife Margaret their child Samuel, born October 28, 1786. Sponsors Adam Albert and his wife Elizabeth Albert; also Smith Hansbrough and wife Susannah their child Daniel, born February 28, 1786. Sponsors John Hansbrough and Mary Kirk; also Michael Miller and wife Magdalena their child Rachel, born November 25, 1784. Sponsors Jacob Kiger and Anna Maria Linn.

27th. Preached at Steins on the Gospel for the 4th Sunday after Epiphany. Subject, The benefits of the fellowship and guidance of Christ.

28th. Baptized the following children:

Parents		
John Rudi Wife Catharine	Anna Catharine born May 27, 1786	Henry Winkel Wife Anna Maria
Christian Kamerer Wife Barbara	John born April 23, 1786	John Rudi Wife Catharine
Henry Winkel Wife Anna Maria	Anna Maria born October 16, 1786	Christian Kamerer and wife Barbara

Preached in Winchester in the morning German on the Gospel, being the 4th Sunday after Epiphany. Subject, The benefits of the fellowship and guidance of Christ in bodily and spiritual matters. And in the afternoon English on the words, "And the men marveled, saying What manner of man is this?"

February 4, 1787. Preached in Winchester in the morning German on part of the Epistle, being *Septuagesima* Sunday, on the words, "So run that you may obtain." In the afternoon English on the words, "What think ye of Christ?"

10th. Preached in the afternoon at Newtown an Ecclesiastes, last verse, namely, "Let us hear the conclusion of the whole matter."

11th. Preached German in Stovertown on the last verse of the Gospel, being *Sexagesima* Sunday, "That on the good ground, etc."

18th. Preached in the morning at Steins on the Gospel, being *Esto Mihi* (*Quinquagesima*), The helpful consideration of the Sufferings of Jesus: 1) The right consideration; 2) The helpful fruits. Baptized 2 children. In the afternoon preached in Winchester on same subject.

25th. Preached in the morning in Winchester in German on the words of the Gospel, "Thou shalt worship, etc." and in the afternoon English on the same: 1) Idolatry, gross and subtile; 2) True worship principally insisted on the honorableness and sublimity of the duty.

March 4th. Preached at Newtown in the morning and in the afternoon at Winchester on last part of Epistle, "Ye are not called to uncleanness but unto holiness."

Baptized Michael Copenhafer and wife Mary child John, born December 12th. Sponsors Andrew Kiger and wife Hannah.

8th. Baptized Lewis Miller and wife Catharine their child John, born April 11, 1775. Sponsor Mother.

10th. Buried at Newtown Maria Magdalena Klein, aged 87 years, 10 ½ months. Text Genesis 47:9.

11th. Preached in the morning in Winchester on first part of Epistle, being 3rd Sunday in Lent; namely, The true following of God and of Christ. In the afternoon at Steins (where I baptized 2 children) on the same.

Baptized on the same day in Winchester George Heil [?] and wife Eva child Eva Margaret, born January 22,1787 [1786]; sponsors Martin Friess [?] and wife Catharine.

18th. Preached in the morning German on the words of the Epistle, "But the Jerusalem which is from above is free, etc.," being the 4th Sunday in Lent. In the afternoon in English on the words of the Gospel, "This is of a truth that Prophet, etc."

March 25, 1787. Preached in the morning in Newtown from the Epistle on The High priestly Office of Jesus. In the afternoon at Pine Hills on the last part of the Epistle The Mediatorial Office of Jesus, in German and English. Baptized at Newtown and at Pine Hills 3 children.

28th. Preached at Old Furnace German on Micah 6:8, and in English on the last verses of Ecclesiastes. Baptized 3 children. [See note 21.]

April 1st. Preached in the morning at Steins on the Gospel; subject, The proper conduct toward the Sovereignty of Christ. In the afternoon in Winchester on the Epistle, The two Natures of Christ and our duties resulting therefrom.

6th. Preached in the morning at Newtown on Phil. 2:8, and in the afternoon at Pine Hills on "It is finished," as it was Good Friday. Baptized 2 white and 1 black child.

8th. Being Easter, preached in the morning German and in the afternoon English in Winchester on 2 Tim. 2:8.

9th. Buried at Steins Eva Rosina wife of George Somer, born November 14, 1760; the parents were Jacob Schuh and Catharine; married 15 months and 4 days; leaves one son; age 26 years, 4 months, 3 weeks, and 3 days; text, Job 19:25. In the afternoon preached in Winchester on the same.

10th. Baptized Henry Ritter's child John, born September 27,

1785; sponsors John Highland and wife Sarah.

14th. Held preparation at Culpeper for Sacrament.

15th. Preached German on the Gospel. Verifying the truth and conveying the fruits of the Resurrection. Administered the Sacrament to 120. In the afternoon preached English on Ecclesiastes, the last verses. Baptized this day 7 German and 11 English children.

A list of over 120 communicants of the first Sunday after Easter [April 15, 1787] is recorded in the Hebron Register. This list appears on page 22 of the microfilmed version of the Hebron Register that is available through interlibrary loan from the Library of Virginia: Madison County, Virginia, reel 28.

Those who were in attendance who were communicants included:

Andreas Carpenter
Elizabeth Weber
Barbara Carpenter, Widow
Maria Carpenter, Wilhelm's Wife
  & Daughters Elisabeth & Maria
Johannes Jäger & Wife Maria
  & [Peter?]
Adam Jäger
Jacob Blankenbücher
Johannes Weiland, Wife Rosina
Michael Haus
Margretha Haus
Nicolaus Smith, Wife Maria
Adam Gar
Johannes Carpenter
Nicholas Krigler
Zacharias Blankenbücher, Wife Elis
Michael Carpenter, Wife Maria
Georg Koch
Michael Blankenbücher, Wife
  Elisabeth & Daughter Rosina
Peter Smith, Wife Margreth
Josua Jäger, Wife Maria
Georg Utz, Wife Margaretha
Samuel Blankenbücher [#1]
Ludwig Krigler, Wife Anna
Ephraim Utz, Wife Christina
Johannes Utz
Jacob Blankenbücher,
  Wife Elisabeth
Martin Hirsch [#1]

Maria Wilheit
Joseph Carpenter, Wife Catharina
Georg Christler,
  Wife Anna Magdalena
  & Son Julius & Daughter Elisabeth
Thomas Blankenbücher
Abraham Danner
Peter Weber
Johann Bungart, Wife Eva
Georg Risser, Wife Margaretha
Martin Hirsch [#2], Wife Anna
  Maria & Daughter Barbara
Jacob Bungart & Sister Margreth
Daniel Reiner, Wife Elisabeth
  & Sisters Maria Reiner
  & Sarah Reiner
Henrich Christler, Wife Elisabeth
Michael Fleischman, Wife Maria
Samuel Blankenbücher [#2]
Adam Christler, Wife Elisabeth
Johannes Koch
Ephraim Fleischman, Wife
  Susannah & His Mother
  Elisabeth Fleischman
Johannes Rausch, Wife Maria
Elias Christler, Wife Eleonora
Zacharias Fleischman
  & Sister Maria
Andreas Hirsch, Wife Susannah
Michael Delp, Wife Margaretha
Christopher Zimmerman,
  Wife Maria & Daughter Susannah

556

Appendix B

Ephraim Rausch	Maria Elisabeth Schmith
Mathias Haus	Wilhelm Carpenter
Christoph Krigler, Wife Catharina	Catharina Isom
Henrich Weiland	Peter Räser, Wife Phronica
Rosina Zimmerman	Johannes Zimmerman, Wife
Margareth Carpenter	Ursula
Susanna Carpenter	Henrich Lepp
Christina Blankenbücher	Children Daniel Lepp
Barbara Koch [#1]	& Elis[abeth] Lepp
Margareth Schneider	Christoph Meyers, Wife Catharina
Cath[arina] Hirsch	Magdalena Hofman
Margareth Koch	Susanna Holtzklau
Dorothea Koch	Jemima Holtzklau
Barbara Koch [#2]	Susanna Schmith
Susanna Berri	Maria Lepp

[Sum Total 122]

22nd. Preached in the morning in Winchester and in the afternoon at Steins on the Gospel on The excellence of the Shepherd and the duties of the sheep. Baptized 2 children at Steins.

Baptized same day in Winchester:

Christopher Buddi	John Carl	Carl Grim
Wife Elizabeth	born February 16th	Wife Magdalena
Maria Wendel	Maria Margaret born October 2d	The same

April 28, 1787. Preached English at Capt. Slater's on Eccle. last verses. Baptized 2 children. [See note 28.]

[2]9th. Preached in the morning German and in the afternoon English in Winchester on part of the Gospel. Subject, The joy felt for the Holy Jesus.

May 4th. [Inserted from inside front cover.] Picket Mountain Baptized 11 children; communicants 83; confirmed 20. [See note 24.][i]

The Peaked Mountain Church Register records that the Reverend Christian Streit baptized the following nine children on May 4, 1788:

Charles Schmidt	Anna Maria	John Risch
and Anna Maria	born September 13, 1787	and Anna Maria

---

[i] This entry should be 1788 not 1787.

Henry Miller and Anna Maria	Elizabeth born February 22, 1788	Grandmother Miller
Peter Nicholas and Juliana	Jacob born September 9, 1787	Jacob Nicholas
Peter Miller and Barbara [Nicholas]	Elizabeth born January 30, 1788	Elizabeth Nicholas
Henry Nicholas and Magdalena	Anna Barbara born February 27, 1788	Grandmother Barbara Nicholas
William Gaul and Anna Barbara	Christian born December 22, 1787	Parents
Christopher Rau and Elizabeth	Anna Catharine born October 10, 1787	George Mallo, Junior and Anna Catharine
Adam Pens and Margaret	George born January 15, 1788	George Pens, Junior (single)
Augustin Prisch and Margaret	Juliana born December 11, 1787	Peter Nicholas and Juliana

There is unfortunately no extant list of communicants in the Peaked Mountain Register for either 1787 or 1788. In addition, the Peaked Mountain Register gives no indication that Streit ever visited the church 1787.

May 5th. Preparation for Lord's Supper at Stovertown; baptized 1 child; text 1 John 1:9.

6th. In the morning confirmed a middle aged woman, married. Preached on the Gospel, The Acts of the Holy Spirit among men. Administered the Sacrament to 45. Baptized 12 children at Stovertown. Was to have preached afterwards at Newtown but a stranger preached.

12th. Catechised in the forenoon at Steins those who had been confirmed last fall. Afternoon preparation for Sacrament, Text, Rom. 2:4, "Not knowing that the goodness of God leadeth thee to repentance."

13th. Sacrament at Steins. 45 communed. Text, two first verses of Gospel for the 5th Sunday after Easter. Baptized 3. In the afternoon preached at Winchester on same text.

16th. Preparation for Sacrament at Old Furnace.

17th. Being Ascension preached on the Gospel: 1) Ascension of

Christ; 2) His Session at the right hand of God. Administered communion to 35; Baptized 6, and preached English on the same subject.

20th. Preached in Winchester, in the morning German and in the afternoon English, both on the words of the Gospel, "And this will they do because they have not known the Father, etc." Subject, The true knowledge of God and Christ, and motives thereto.

23rd. Baptized an infant in Winchester.

24th. Baptized an infant in Winchester.

26th. Preached preparation for Sacrament. Confirmed 15.

27th. Being Whitsunday preached in the morning in Winchester on the Gospel; subject, The three gifts of the Kingdom of God: Righteousness, peace and joy in the Holy Ghost; Administered the Sacrament to 62, including the newly confirmed; Baptized 2. In the afternoon preached at Steins on Rom. 14:17. Baptized 5.

April 28, 1787. Preached in the morning at Newtown on Rom. 14:17. Baptized 2. In the afternoon at Pine Hills on Rom. 8:1. Baptized 3.

29th. Baptized Peter Lauck's child

June 3rd. Conference at Lancaster where I attended.

6th. Dedication of the German College. [See note 10.]

10th. Preached in Winchester in the morning in German and in the afternoon in English on the words of the Gospel, "And the poor man died also and was carried by the angels into Abraham's bosom!" Baptized 2 children.

15th. Buried Peter Anderson, aged 74 years and nearly 6 months. Text, Luke 2:29, 30.

17th. Preached in the morning at Newtown and in the afternoon at Pine Hills, both on the words of the Gospel verse 23, being the 2nd Sunday after Trinity. Subject, The invitation of the heathen to the Kingdom of God. Baptized 1 child; in the evening married a couple.

24th. 3rd Sunday after Trinity. Preached at Steins in the morning and in the afternoon in Winchester on the words of the Gospel, "This man receiveth sinners!" Baptized at Steins 3 children.

July 1st. Preached in the morning German and in the afternoon English in Winchester on part of Epistle for the Day; namely, Rom. 8:21, The intended beneficial effects of the Gospel on the Gentiles.

8th. Preached in the morning at Pine Hills, The true following of Christ. Baptized 3. In the afternoon at Newtown, first part of the Gospel, The people pressed upon Jesus to hear the word of God. Baptized 1 white and 2 black children.

15th. Mr. Young preached in Winchester, I at Steins. 1) The Heavenly Kingdom; 2) Vain Righteousness; 3) The Saving Righteousness. [See note 37.]

16th. Set off for Philadelphia.

23rd. Arrived in Philadelphia.

27th. In the evening preached in the old Church in Philadelphia, Rom. 2:4. [See note 23.]

29th. Preached forenoon in the new church on the words of the Gospel being 8th Sunday after Trinity, verse 21, "Not all that say," and in the evening in same place on Psalm 73:24. [See note 22.]

July 30, 1787. Left Philadelphia to come home.

August 5th. Preached in the morning in Winchester on the Gospel. Subject, In what particulars we must imitate the unjust steward. In the afternoon at Steins; on the same day chose deacons at Steins.

9th. At Warm Springs, catechised young people, whom I had previously confirmed, and 3 new ones for confirmation.

10th. Preached on Rev. 3:20, confirmed the 3 fore mentioned young persons, and held sacrament with, in all, 41 communicants. In the evening administered the Sacrament to an aged woman 9 miles from the Springs. On this journey baptized 10 children.

12th. Preached in Winchester German in the morning and in the afternoon English, the former on the Gospel; subject, The reasons of God's Judgments. The latter on Matt. 7:21.

19th. Preached in the morning at Newtown and in the afternoon at Pine Hills on the Gospel, The right manner of public worship, what it is not and what it really is. Baptized this day 6 infants.

20th. Baptized George Kaufman and wife Mary their children Margaret and Elizabeth: the former born January 6, 1784, and the latter August 2, 1785. Parents sponsors.

22nd. Preached at the Methodist meeting in the neighborhood of Harts; first in German on Eccles. last verses and then in English on Matt. 7:21. Baptized 3 infants.

26th. Preached at Steins in the morning and in the afternoon in Winchester on the last verse of the Gospel, being the 12th Sunday after Trinity.

September 2nd. Preached in the morning in German on part of Gospel Luke 10:25, 26. In the afternoon English on Eccles. last verses. This day chose Peter Lauck and Philip Huber for deacons in Winchester.

6th. Buried Mrs. Wetzel's mother Ann Maria Kiefer at the North Mountain. Text Psalm 73:24. Age 76 years, 3 months.

9th. Was to have preached at Newtown this morning but a stranger preached. In the afternoon preached at Pine Hills on part of Epistle verse 24. Baptized this day 3 children.

14th. Baptized a Baker child.

16th. Preached in the morning in Winchester, ordained deacons.

Appendix B

In the afternoon at Steins; both on the words of the Gospel. "Are ye not much more than they?" 1) The advantage of human beings; 2) The consequent divine teachings of God's Providence and the duties.

September 22nd, 1787. Preached at Cape Capon on Matt. 7:21; baptized 7 children.

23rd. Preached in the morning at Pine Hills on part of the Epistle verse 18, being the 16th Sunday after Trinity. Baptized 3 infants and at Mr. Helfensteins 2 adults. In the afternoon preached at Winchester on the whole Epistle. Baptized after the sermon 1 white and 1 black infant; the white one was Mr. Reiley's son's child.

29th. Preached at Old Furnace on the last 2 verses of the Gospel, being St. Michael's, namely verses 10, 12. Baptized 4.

30th. Preached in the morning in Winchester on the last verse of the Gospel, The nature of self-exaltation and reasons against it. In the afternoon the same at Newtown.

October 4th. Baptized 4 children for one man.

7th. Preached in the morning at Steins on The Love of our neighbor from the Gospel for the 18th Sunday after Trinity; was to have preached in Winchester in the afternoon but Mrs. Norton's funeral being then and occupying the church I was prevented.^{j}

13th. Preached at Pine Hills on the Gospel for the ensuing day, the 19th Sunday after Trinity, The power of Christ to forgive sins and to save. Baptized 1.

14th. Preached in Winchester in the morning on part of the Gospel; namely verse 4. Baptized 1. In the afternoon preached at the Old Furnace on the same. Baptized 2.

16th. Baptized 1 at Henry Brill's.

19th. Baptized 1 at Mordecai Bean's.

21st. Preached at Newtown on the Epistle, The wise foresight in Christian conduct. Baptized 2. In the afternoon in Winchester from a verse of the Epistle, The Proper use of time.

28th. Preached in the morning in Winchester a discourse in memory of Dr. Muhlenberg on Psalm 73:24. [H.M. Muhlenberg had died October 7, 1787]. In the afternoon at Steins on the Gospel. Subject, The union of faith and obedience. 21st Sunday after Trinity.

November 1, 1787. Buried Adam Albert's wife.

---

^{j} Mrs. Norton was Sarah (Thurston) Norton the wife of George Flowerdew Norton, a prominent citizen of Winchester known to have transacted business regularly with Warner Washington, a first cousin of George Washington. Her parents were Charles Minn and Ann (Alexander) Thurston, members of Streit's congregation.

2nd. Went to Horn's at Capon to preach and administer the Sacrament, according to a previous appointment, but they had mistaken the day.

3rd. Preached at Old Furnace German and English on the Gospel for the next day, being the 22nd Sunday after Trinity. The way of discharging our spiritual debt.

4th. Preached the same both at Pine Hills and Winchester.

10th. Preached at Newtown on the Epistle for next day, the 23rd Sunday after Trinity. Subject, The disastrous conduct of the godless and the beneficial conduct of the pious.

11th. Preached in the morning German on the gospel verse 21. In the afternoon English on Ephesians 4:3, both in Winchester.

12th. Baptized John Koch and wife Rosina Dorothea child Salome, born September 7th; parents sponsors.

18th. Preached in the morning at Steins and in the afternoon in Winchester on verse 13 of the Epistle; namely, "Who saves us, etc." Baptized at Steins a child.

25th. Was to have preached in the morning in Winchester but Mr. Weiner kept Sacrament. In the afternoon preached at Old Furnace on part of the Gospel, being 25th Sunday after Trinity. Verse 16, The speedy salvation of our souls.

December 2nd. Preached in the morning at Newtown on the Epistle: 1) The duties; 2) The motives. Baptized 8 child[ren]. In the afternoon in Winchester on the same subject, being 1st Sunday in Advent.

9th. In the morning in Winchester on the last 2 verses of the Gospel. In the afternoon at Pine Hills on the same. Baptized 2 children.

15th. Preached at Old Furnace on the words of the Gospel for next day: "Behold, I send my messenger, etc."

Had election for deacons and there were elected: Lutherans, Henry Brill and John Kiefer; Reformed, Ellis Keckley and Jacob Weiss.

16th. Being 3rd Sunday in Advent, preached in Winchester a funeral sermon in English on Eccles. 12:1, for Joseph Pierce, who was buried the preceding Sunday; aged 21 years and some weeks. In the afternoon preached at Steins on the last words of the Gospel. Baptized 2 children.

December 19, 1787. Baptized Wetzel's child 8 days old named George; sponsor George Linn.

22nd. Baptized George Kaufman and wife Mary their child George, born October 25th; sponsor George Baker.

23rd. Preached in the morning in Winchester on part of the Gospel; namely, verse 23. In the afternoon at Newtown on the Epistle.

25th. Preached in Winchester and at Newtown on "Without controversy great is the mystery of godliness: God was manifest in the flesh."

Appendix B

26th. Preached at Pine Hills on the Gospel Luke 2:15-20. The right application of the announcement of the birth of Christ.

30th. Preached in Winchester in the morning on the Gospel, being the Sunday after Christmas, verses 34, 35.

1788

January 1st. Was to have preached at Steins in the morning and Winchester in the afternoon, but the dangerous illness of my wife hindered.

6th. Was to have preached at Old Furnace and Winchester but my wife being at the point of death I was prevented.

13th. My insuperable distress for the death of my wife hindered my preaching today, which was appointed to have been at Newtown and Winchester.

Memorandum.

December 16, 1787, my wife Salome was delivered of a daughter who died the 27th, and the mother followed the 6th day of January 1788 and was buried the 8th.

The day before her death, being overcome with grief as her recovery was now entirely despaired of and having the most painful feelings for her groanings and ravings, and being much weakened from want of appetite and rest from distress of mind and having taken incautiously too much brandy and water, and having gone out of doors a little, and came in and sat down by the fire with my head hanging down, as I was rising up I fell into a swoon, and after lying a little while in bed the dinner of salt pork which I had eaten being too strong for the weak state of my stomach, I puked it up. This was ascribed to intoxication. — The Lord have mercy upon my poor soul.

January 14, 1788. Baptized Conrad and Elizabeth Ling's child Susanna born January 6th. Sponsors Conrad Kramer and wife.

20th. Preached in the morning in Winchester on the words of the Epistle, "And that Rock was Christ!"

24th. Rode to Hagerstown.

27th. Preached for Mr. Young at Funkstown on Psalm 73:24, "Thou shalt guide me, etc."k [See note 9.]

February 1st. Returned to Winchester .

3rd. Preached in the morning at Winchester and in the afternoon at Newtown on the last verses of the Gospel for *Esto Mihi* Sunday, The cure for spiritual blindness. In the evening baptized Jacob Bucher's child.

---

k After the death of Henry Melchoir Muhlenberg, October 7, 1787, Streit had used the same text for his memorial sermon at Winchester.

10th. Preached in the morning at Steins and in the afternoon in Winchester, on the Gospel: 1) Explanation of the three temptations of Christ; 2) Comments for our use.

17th. Preached in the morning in Winchester on the Gospel, The prayer that is heard, and the reasons why the Lord nevertheless withholds his help. In the afternoon at Pine Hills on the last verse of the Epistle.

18th. Buried at Old Furnace Jacob Keckley aged 86 years from Stammein, Wurtemberg. Text, Rev. 14:13.

21st. Baptized John and Mary Poh's child Andrew, born October 21, 1787. Sponsor, Andrew Baker.

24th. Preached in the morning at Newtown. In the afternoon in Winchester. Both on the last verse of the Gospel for 3rd Sunday in Lent.

March 1st. Preached in the morning in Winchester and in the afternoon at Steins: at Winchester on 1 Cor.1:30; at Steins on the Gospel. The Excellence of Christ as a Prophet.

8th. Preached at Pine Hills and on the 9th at Old Furnace and Winchester, all on the Gospel for Sunday *Judica*, The excellence of Christ as a Teacher.

9th. Baptized Isaac Weimer and wife Catharine child John born February 21, 1787. Sponsors, John Bastion and wife Christina. And also John Adam Bastion and wife Juliana child Anna Maria born October 14th. Sponsors, the Parents. Also at Adam Kiger's his own child and another.

March 10, 1788. Buried old McCord aged 82.

16th. Palm Sunday. Preached in the morning in Winchester on verse 9 of the Gospel-chapter, The proper conduct in view of the Sovereignty of Christ. In the afternoon at Newtown on 1st verse of Epistle, The mind of Jesus and why we should be of the same mind. Baptized 2.

21st. Preached in the morning in Winchester on John 1:29, and in the afternoon at Pine Hills on the same. Baptized March 21st John Erhart and wife Magdalena their child Susanna Margaret, born the 10th of August of previous year. John Gerat and his wife Margaret.

23rd. Being Easter, preached in the morning at Steins on 2 Tim. 2:8, "Remember that Christ, etc." In the afternoon in Winchester on Rev. 1:17, 18.

23rd. Baptized William Albert and wife Catharine child Maria Salome, born December 1, 1787. Sponsors Adam Albert and wife. Also, John Williams child Jenny illegitimate, born November 26th. Sponsors Jacob Friess and wife.

24th. Preached in the morning at the Old Furnace on 2 Tim.2:8. Baptized 2. In the afternoon at Newtown on Rev. 1:17, 18.

29th. Preached at Pine Hills on the Gospel for next day, Religious peace and way of obtaining it.

30th. Baptized Isaac Wemmer an adult born October 12, 1765. Preached in the morning at Winchester on the first 2 verses of the Gospel, True Christians the greatest Heroes. In the afternoon at Old Furnace on the Gospel, Righteousness, peace and joy in the Holy Ghost.

31st. Baptized George Caghill and Catharine his wife their child Nancy born January 6th. Parents sponsors. Also, Peter Gordon and wife Mary child Elizabeth, born August 15th. Mother sponsor.

April 6th. Preached at Newtown in the morning and in the afternoon in Winchester, both on the last verse of the Gospel, being the 2nd. Sunday after Easter.

13th. Preached in the morning at Winchester and in the afternoon at Steins, both on part of Gospel; namely, John 16:18; subject, Human ignorance in spiritual matters.

April 19, 1788. Preached at Old Furnace on part of the Epistle verse 21 for Sunday *Cantate*.

20th. Administered the Sacrament at Pine Hills. Text Rev. 3:20. Number communed 21. In the afternoon preached at Winchester on the last verse of the Epistle, being Sunday *Cantate*.

12th. Buried an old woman who died at Hofman's. Text. Ps. 42:1, 2.

20th. Baptized Philip Banes child Anna Maria born March 22nd Sponsors Godfrey and wife.

26th. Preached at Steins on the Epistle for next day, being Sunday Rogate. Baptized 1.

19th. Young people for instruction at Old Furnace:

John	age 20	)	Their father John Kiefer
George	18	)	
Martin	15	)	
Jacob	21		His father Jacob Siebert
Magdalena	15		Her father Henry Bruhl
Anna Margaret	15		Her father Joseph Wiesend, deceased
Catharine	18		Her father Adam Schreiber
Benjamin Frey			

27th. Baptized John Clark and wife Margaret child James born January 14, 1788. Sponsors James Clark and wife.

Preached in the morning at Winchester on part of Gospel; namely, John 16:26, last part: "And I say unto you, etc." In the afternoon at Newtown on the same.

May 1st. Preached at Peaked Mountain on the Epistle, it being Ascension Day.

3rd. Preparation for Sacrament same place on 1 John 1:9.

4th. Preached at Peaked Mountain on Matt.11:28, 29. Confirmed 20. Administered the Sacrament to 104. Baptized 12.[1]

8th. Baptized 4 children for the widow Pierce, two grown up, and one child for Matthias Ritter.

May 10, 1788. Preached at Pine Hills on Psalm 143:10, latter part of verse. In the afternoon preparation in Winchester; baptized 1 child for Young.

11th. Preached on part of Gospel, being Whitsunday, verse 26. Administered Sacrament to 15 communicants, one of whom was William Banes who was confirmed the evening before. In the afternoon preached at Steins on Psalm 143:10, latter part, "Lead me into the land of uprightness." Baptized 1.

12th. Preached in the morning at Old Furnace on the preceding text and in the afternoon the same at Newtown. Baptized this day 8 children.

13th. Set off for Reading.

18th. In the afternoon came to Reading.

19th & 20th. Attended Conference.

21st. Came to New Hanover.

22nd. The Trappe. [See note 34.]

24th. To Philadelphia.

25th. Preached in the evening in Philadelphia on the words "We love him because he first loved us," being part of the Epistle for the day.

June 1st. Preached in Swedesboro on the words of the Gospel, "Come for all things are now ready!" [See note 31.]

2nd. Left Philadelphia.

7th. Came home.

8th. Preached in the morning in Winchester on the whole Epistle, being the 3rd. Sunday after Trinity. In the afternoon at Pine Hills on the words of the Gospel, "Jesus receiveth sinners." And in the evening at Newtown on the whole Epistle. Baptized at Pine Hills 2, at Newtown also 2.

12th. Baptized at Winchester Carl Aulich and wife Mary their child Catharine Elizabeth born 9th of May. Sponsors Henry Briel and wife Catharine.

June 14, 1788. Preached in the morning at Old Furnace.

15th. Preached in the morning at Newtown on part of the Gospel,

---

[1] See previous insert for May 4, 1787.

Appendix B

being 4th Sunday after Trinity, from the beginning to the words, "so it shall be given, etc." Baptized at Cornstown 4 children. Preached in the afternoon in Winchester on the same words as before. [See note 4.]

22nd. Preached in the morning at Winchester on the last words of the Epistle, being the 5th Sunday after Trinity, "But sanctify the Lord God in your hearts." In the afternoon preached at Steins on the same.

28th. Preached at Pine Hills on the first verse of the Gospel for the next day, the 6th Sunday after Trinity.

29th. Preached in the morning at Old Furnace on the same subject as before mentioned; baptized 3 children. In the afternoon at Winchester on the Epistle, The Obligation of Baptism to Holiness.

July 6th. Preached in the morning at Winchester on the Gospel, The loving provision of Jesus for body and soul. In the afternoon at Newtown on the last words of the Epistle, it being the 7th Sunday after Trinity. Baptized Cramer's child at Winchester and also a child at Newtown.

13th. Preached in the morning at Steins on the 19th verse of the Gospel. Matt. 7. Baptized 1. In the afternoon Winchester on the same and baptized Adam Anderson and wife Sabilla's child Adam born May 3rd. Sponsors David Osborn and Wife Margaret. Also Jacob Ritter and wife Ann Mary's child Adam born December 15th, 1787. Sponsors Adam Anderson and wife Sabilla.

20th. Preached in the morning at Winchester on part of the Gospel verse 2 of Luke 16. In the afternoon at Pine Hills on part of the Epistle; namely, 1 Cor. 10:12. Baptized 2.

23rd. Baptized a child from the country at Kniester's.

27th. Preached in the morning at Newtown on part of the Gospel verse 1, The Tears of Jesus. In the afternoon at Winchester the same subject. Baptized Andrew Kiger's child Magdalena. Sponsor Widow Copenhafer.

August 3rd. Preached in the afternoon at Steins. As a stranger preached in Winchester in the morning I did not.

5th. Baptized Christian Reif and wife Magdalena child John born June 8, 1787. Parents sponsors.

August 6, 1788. Preached at Stovertown on the Transfiguration of Christ. Baptized 5.

10th. Preached at Old Furnace in the morning and in the afternoon in Winchester on the use and abuse of the ears and tongue, from the Gospel, being 12th Sunday after Trinity.

16th. Preached at Pine Hills on the Gospel for the next day, Our spiritual wounds and cure.

17th. Preached at Winchester in the morning and in the afternoon at Old Furnace, all on the Gospel, How to obtain Eternal Life. Baptized at Old Furnace one infant.

23rd. Preparation for Sacrament at Steins.

24th. In the morning sermon from the Gospel on Giving God the Glory, Sacrament, 18 communed; baptized 4 at Steins. In the afternoon at Winchester on the same subject. In the evening baptized M. Altrit's and Mesmore's children and Kurtz's.

31st. Preached at Winchester on the Gospel, being 15th Sunday after Trinity, Divine Providence and our relation to it.

September 3rd. William died and buried the 5th. [Christian Streit's brother].

7th. Preached at Pine Hills in the morning and in the afternoon in Winchester from the Gospel, The Voice of the Son of God.

8th. Baptized Spencer Cooper and wife Anne their child William born the 10th of February. Parents sponsors.

14th. Preached in the morning in Winchester and in the afternoon at Old Furnace on first 3 verses of Epistle, being 17th Sunday after Trinity. Baptized at Old Furnace 3.

16th. Baptized John Grim and wife Elizabeth child Susanna born 7th September. Sponsors Charles Grim and wife.

22nd. Preached at Fredericktown, Maryland. [See note 8.]

28th. Preached at New Holland. [See note 18.]

Was dreadfully melancholy for several weeks on the road to, at and from Philadelphia, and at home.

October 24th. Buried one Schwartz's child aged 9 weeks and 4 days; and baptized 1 child.

October 25, 1788. Baptized a child in my house.

26th. Preached in the morning in Winchester on the words of the Gospel, "Thou teachest the way of God in truth," being the 23rd Sunday after Trinity; subject, The excellence of the teaching of Jesus. And in the afternoon preached, at Pine Hills on the words of the Gospel, "Render unto Caesar, etc." Baptized 2 children at Pine Hills and in the evening 2 for Mr. Haas.

28th. Baptized David Pates and Elizabeth his wife their child Sarah born 22nd of same month. Parents sponsors.

November 1st. Being 24th Sunday after Trinity. Confirmed 16 at Old Furnace, 9 of whom were married. Preached on part of the Epistle verse 12, "Giving thanks unto the Father, etc." Preached English on the same. Held Sacrament, about 36 communicants, including those confirmed. Baptized 1 child.

9th. Preached at Old Furnace in the morning on the Gospel, being the 25th Sunday after Trinity: 1) Judgments in time; 2) The concern

Appendix B

of Jesus for the pious in the same; 3) If the punishment in time is great, how great must be the eternal punishment! 4) The necessary, speedy salvation of our souls. Baptized 1 child. In the afternoon preached on the last verse of the Gospel in Winchester. Election for deacons: Jacob Bucher and Simon Lauck were chosen. Baptized Mrs. Dromgold's child Catharine born November 9, 1786. Also Rosina Streit's William[m] born October 2, 1788. Mothers sponsors.

13th. Preached German at Millschlagel's near Cape Capon on Matt. 28:19, 20. Baptized 5 children.

15th. Preached at Pine Hills on the Epistle for the next day, the 26th Sunday after Trinity. Baptized 3.

16th. Preached in the morning at Winchester on part of the Gospel; namely, verse 24. In the afternoon at Steins on the Epistle.

17th. Baptized Peter Grim's and wife Eleonora children Anne Robeson born February 7, 1786; parents sponsors; and Eleonora born 20th August, 1788; sponsor Margaret Bailey.

19th. William Rust and Mary his wife child Frederick Robert born 10th March. Sponsors Frederick Hofman and wife Charlotte.

22nd. Preparation for Lord's Supper at Culpeper. Matt. 5:6.

23rd. Preached in the morning in German on the words of the Gospel, being the 27th Sunday after Trinity, "And they that were ready went in...and the door was shut." Administered the Sacrament to 116.

A list of 113 of the possible 116 communicants on the 27th Sunday after Trinity [November 23, 1788] is recorded in the Hebron Register. While the register is largely without pagination, the list appears on pages 23 and 24 of the microfilmed version of the Hebron Register that is available at several major Virginia repositories and is also available through Interlibrary Loan: Library of Virginia Microfilm, Madison County, Virginia, reel 28.

Those in attendance who were communicants included:

William Carpenter Jun[n]	Daniel Böhme, Wife Nancy
William Carpenter, Wife Maria	Catharina Böhmein
Daughters Elisabeth & Maria	Johann Blankenbiker, Wife Barbara
Andreas Carpenter, Wife Barbara	Peter Koch, Wife Maria
Elisabeth Weberin	Joseph Carpenter, Wife Catharina
Barbara Carpenterin	Christoph Zimmermann,
Christoph Crikler, Wife Catharina	Wife Maria
Nicolaus Schmidt, Wife Maria	Susannah Zimmermann
Michael Blankenbicher,	Johann Blankenbicher,
Wife Elisabeth	Wife Marcretha
Zacharias Blankenbicher, Wife Els[a]	

---

[m] Possibly a nephew of Christian Streit.
[n] He was pastor at Hebron from 1787-1813.

Philip Schneider
Johann Wäyland, Wife Rosina
Rebecca Carpenterin
Samuel Carpenter, Wife Dinah
Adam Jäger
Johann Jäger, Wife Maria
Conrad Delph, Wife Magdalena
Ephraim Fleischmann, Wife
   Susanna
Maria Jägerin - Maria Wilheitin*
Elisabeth Fleischmannin
   - Elisabeth Reinerin*
Elisabeth Schmidt [#1]
   - Margretha Schmidt*
Elisabeth Schmidt [#2]
   - Maria Schneiderin*
Anna Prat
Nicolaus Crikler,
   Wife Maria Marcreth
Martin Rausch - Adam Gaar*
Mathias Hauss,
   Wife Maria Margreth
Sons Michael & Mathias
Daughter Margreth
George Raser, Wife Margretha
Georg Koch
Moses Breil, Wife Barbara
Josua Jäger, Wife Maria
Heinrich Wäyland
Catharina Wäylandin
Daniel Reiner, Wife Elisabeth
Johannes Koch [Utz?]
   *These names may have been
   added to the list.

Nicholas Schmidt, Wife Susanna
Andreas Hirsch, Wife Susanna
[page break]
Jacob Blankenbiker, Wife Elisabeth
Eberhardt Reiner
Ludwich Koch
Michael Schneider, Wife Maria
Friedrich Tanna, Wife Maria
Martin Hirsch
Michael Jäger, Wife Elisabeth
George Wilheit, Wife Elisabeth
Catharina Mäyer
Maria Lepsin
Margretha Tanna
Dorothea Gaarin
Margretha Schneiderin
Maria Schmidt
Elisabeth Holsklauin
Magdelena Holsklauin
Susanna Perrey
Susanna Rückstuhlin
Jemima Holsklauin
Margretha Baedlin [Birdlin?]
Susanna Holsklauin
Susanna Fleischmannin
Margaretha Fleischmannin
Christina [?] Weberin
Maria Reinerin
Barbara Hirschin
Peter Penniger, Wife Magdalena
Magdalena Holsklauin
Julius Christler
Sum Total 116 [113]

In the afternoon preached English on the same text. Baptized...at Culpeper. November 24, 1788. Baptized one child at Mrs. Leps's, and in the evening gave the Sacrament to an aged sick woman at Culpeper.
28th Preached at Old Furnace on the words of the Gospel:
"Tell ye the Daughter of Zion, Behold Thy King cometh unto Thee! Meek, etc."

Appendix B

Marriages from October 4, 1785 the time of being authorized by Court.

1785

October 5th. William Low and Mary Peterson
    18th. Jeremiah Eberly and Christina Baker by license from Shenandoah.
    17th. Frederick August Bernard and Dorothea Helm
    21st. William Streit and Rosannah Smith°
    26th. John Palmer and Anne Bonham
November 1st. William Berkel and Mary Sherndorfer
    2nd. Ezekiel Carter and Anne Brookover
    7th. William Collins and Anne Jones
    " Samuel Park and Anne McKeever
November 8th. John Rinedel and Margaret Anderson
    9th. William Sharp and Deborah Allen
    26th. James Lawrence to Margaret Cummins
    28th. Charles Bryan and Mary Walters
    29th. John Cox and Sarah Park
December 3rd. Edward Wells and Rebecca Powel
    " John Baily and Elizabeth Long
    13th. Thomas Edwards and Martha Kesner

1786

January 11th. Perez Drew and Mary Richardson
    12th. Robert Oglesby to Honor Holding
    17th. Jacob Marker and Mary Klyne
    19th. George Madders and Phebe Parmer
    25th. Hugh Moloy and Margaret Davis
February 7th. Thomas Murgrave and Mary Newton
    22nd. John Williams and Sarah Ashby
March 9th. Garrison White and Elizabeth Reiser
    " Michael Copinhaver and Margaret Price
    16th. Thomas Edmondson and Ann Cambell
    27th. Jasper Cather and Sarah Moore
    28th. William Carper and Mary Ritter
    " John Park and Margaret Millschlagel
    " William McChesney and Rebecca Shadacre
    " George Weiser and Mary Luckleiter
    30th. Nathan Clarke and Elizabeth Matson
April 4th. Jacob Hite and Catharine Shener
    " Adam Klyne and Catharine Magdalena Poker
    " John Sullivan and Margaret Hare
    13th. Samuel Davis and Phebe Connel
    18th. Isaac Wemmer and Catharine Bastion

° Christian Streit's brother and sister-in-law. Her name was likely rendered as "Rosina" when her son William was baptized on 9 November 1788.

This Heritage

    25th. Christopher Ellis and Elizabeth Carver
April 25th. Cornelius Huff and Elizabeth Ronimus
    "   Henry Ronimus and Catharine Anderson
May 4th. George Miles and Hannah Parker
April 30th. Christopher Shultz and Elizabeth Feltner by license from Shenandoah
May 3rd. William Aldereton and Margaret Edward by license from Hampshire
June 2nd. William Alexander and Sarah Cafford
    14th. Conrad Fungonies and Rebecca Scott
    29th. Michael Regan and Jenny Craig
    22nd. Henry Aldred and Elizabeth Whipple
    29th. Thomas Dawkins and Patty Langland
July 3rd. George Marriele and Elizabeth Kearns
    17th. James Cleavinger and Martha McGrew
    24th. Jesse Pugh and Elizabeth Gray
August 1st. William Mercer and Anne Webb
    14th. Thomas Lindsay and Mary Reagan
    22nd. Jonas Likens and Mary Eckstine
    24th. James Dunn and Rachel Prinz
    26th. Henry Lewis and Susanna Hoge
    31st. George Black and Rody Anderson
September 5th. John Pickering and Sarah Likens
    "   Samuel Trinary and Sarah Grimes
    11th. Robert Fulton and Mary Ann Rauter
    14th. Michael Myers and Jane Peterson
    20th. Benjamin Shipman and Margaret Shepe
    24th. John Wetzel and Barbara Shaver
    24th. Michael Everhart and Barbara Smith
November 9th. John Black and Catharine Weaver
    Adam Harter and Margaret McDonald
December 12th. Buried Henry Altrit's wife: not paid for
    11th. Abraham Mason and Elizabeth Grove
    14th. George Shener and Elizabeth More, widow
    19th. George Lathan and Lucy Drake
    27th. In Hampshire George Horn, Jun. and Hannah Pugh

1787

January 21st. William Noland and Rosina Biton
    30th. John Carn and Elizabeth Light
February 2nd. William Hance and Margaret Northent
    8th. George Benegar and Mary Bennet
    6th. William Vance and Rebecca Hinton
    12th. John Ash and Elizabeth Carpenter
    13th. John Hansbury and Margaret Kirk
    20th. Peter Romine and Peggy Northern
March 7th. William Reading and Amy Jacobs
April 10th. George Price and Catharine Grapes

Appendix B

      Also Seth Stratten and Mary Greenway
      11th. Christopher Doush and Elizabeth Bo____
      9th. John Mouser and Catharine Hunsecker
      3rd. William Jacobs and Litty Suttle
      5th. William Miller and Rebecca Powel
      21st. John Luke and Susanna Johnston
May 1st. Conrad Link and Elizabeth Helphenstine
      2nd. Eli Webb and Christina Upp
      23rd. Hanson Corbeth and Susanna Miller
      Also Joseph Edwards and Elizabeth Vance
      28th. Charles Breedlove and Theodosia Clevenger
      29th. Samuel Bond and Mary Longacre
      24th. Frederick Schultz and Mary Loy
June 17th. Eliot Rutherford and Ruth Wilkins
      25th. Philip Koons and Abigail Baker in Shenandoah County
      ____ Thomas Neill and Abigail Dunn
      ____ ____l Emmonds and Sarah Grubb
August 18th. William Davis and Nancy Wright
      22nd. John Conner and Elizabeth Barnes
      30th. Reuben Elbon and Margaret Niswanger
October 4th. Casper Seidelmeier and Amy Willcox
      9th. Casper Miller and Barbara Weaver
      ___ William Collins and Hephzebeth Mason
      13th. George Keiser and Mary Clunk
      16th. Michael Brill and Eve Foss
      18th. Thomas Pollock and Elizabeth Disponet
      24th. Patrick Alexander and Elizabeth Eckstine
      30th. John Dick and Catharine Rominus
      Also John Rogers and Mary Olleman
November 7th. Joseph Swarm and Christiana Lindy
      8th. Robert True and Anne Payne Jon(es)
      9th. Jonathan Barrett and Rachel George
      14th. Robert Branson and Bulah Painter
      15th. Thomas Cassaday and Barbara Fulk
      27th. Frederick Reecer and Calia Cooper
      29th. Philip Graham and Nelly Beasly
      Also Thomas Sommersett and Mary Sholeberger
December 6th. Richard Price and Sarah Starks
      8th. From Berkley, Michael Kerson Biton (and) Catharine Boyles
      11th. Christian Carmer and Mary Ehrhart
      Also Christopher Schlosser and Christina Gold
      12th. David Jennings and Polly Parker
      13th. Daniel Snider and Catharine Bowman
December 20th. Solomon Hinton and Nancy Audle
      27th. Henry Cooe and Sarah Anderson
      Also Michael Lay and Thesby Anderson

1788

January 1st. Frederick Carper and Mary Shener
    Also John Frank and Anne Taylor
    And John Copenhaver and Margaret Hofman
    Also Daniel Brown and Sarah Southward
    13th. Benjamin Hopewell and Sarah Wilson
February 12th. Charles Helgel [?] and Kitty Hoover
    15th. Joshua Antrim and Ann Collins
    20th. William Anson and Elizabeth Lucas
    26th. William Bennet and Sarah Oglesby
    27th. Edward Burnes and Mary Moore
March 2nd. Frederick Ersman and Mary Seidelmeier
    ____ J____ Flemming and Jean Short
    ____ ____ale and Elizabeth Sell
    ____ ____brey Shopper and Elizabeth Darflinger
    ____ Ephraim [?] Garn and Nancy Helt
    24th. Thomas Butterfield and Ann Newberry
June 10th. Amos Gordon and Elizabeth Carter
    28th. George Miller and Eve Gilbert
July 22nd. Michael Sommers and Barbara Myers
    " William Hobson and Sarah Milburn
August 9th. Edward Williams and Mary Green
    19th. Ezekiel Stanbury and Esther Kremer
September 2nd. Jesse McPherson and Anne Ashe
    4th. Lewis Barnes and Mary Iles
    9th. Aaron Oglesby and Susannah Ammens
November 9th. George Bower and Catharine Albert

FAMILY RECORD OF CHRISTIAN STREIT

Christian Streit[p]

Born June 7, 1749, near Bedminster, Somerset County, New Jersey. Died March 10, 1812, at Winchester, Virginia, aged 62 years, 9 months, 3 days.

Married (1) Anna Margaret Christina Elizabeth Hoff, Charleston,
    South Carolina, July 20, 1778. She died and
    was buried at New Hanover Church, Pennsylvania, August
    20, 1782, aged 22 years, 6 months and 2 weeks.

---

[p] A grandson of the immigrant, Christian Streit, he was the son of Johann Leonhardt Streit, born July 28, 1720, and Catharine Riemer. Leonhardt and Catherine married July 29, 1748, in New Jersey. The ancestral home of the Streit family in Germany was Kirberg.

(2) Salome Graef, Philadelphia, Pennsylvania, February 19, 1783.[q] She died at Winchester, Virginia., January 6, 1788, aged 23 years, 4 months and 3 weeks.

(3) Susannah Barr,[r] Winchester, Virginia, October 15, 1789.[s] She was born May 9, 1769. She died April 2, 1836.[t] aged 66 years, 10 months and 24 days.

Children:
1st. John Melchior — July 9, 1779 to 1782.
2nd. Catharine – April 7, 1784 to April 13, 1784.
3rd. Jacob[u] – April 17, 1785 to ____.
4th. Margaret – December 16, 1787 to December 27, 1787.
5th. Maria Elizabeth – August 17, 1790 to June 30, 1853. Married a Mr. Wilson.
6th. Frederick Augustus – August 31,1791 to November 23, 1815.

---

[q] They married at St. Michael's and Zion Church in Philadelphia.
[r] She was a daughter of John Barr who was born January 23, 1723.
[s] They were married by the Reverend Alexander Balmain in Winchester.
[t] Her husband's will provides that she receive "...all the residue of my Estate both real and personal, during her life – then [to be] equally divided amongst her children." The will was probated April 5, 1812. City of Winchester, Will Book 1, 1794-1823, 122-125. The "Inventory and Appraisement of the Slaves and Personal Estate of Christian Streit decd taken April 17th 1812" indicates his estate was valued at $1,037.25 and included the following: "Negro Anna, $25; Negro Esther, $300; one silver watch, $10; six table spoons, twelve teaspoons, pair sugar tongs and silver cream jug, $30." City of Winchester, Will Book 1, 1794-1823, 126-128.
[u] Jacob is mentioned in his father's will written the 4th day of April 1808. "To Jacob – the sum of three hundred dollars which I lately lent him – and also surrender to my said son, any claim I might have for any money I might have given him before as also his horse." City of Winchester, Will Book 1, 1794-1823, 122.

This Heritage

7th. John – March 4, 1793 to October 3, 1794.
8th. Catharine Bush – November 2, 1794 to November 5, 1860. Married Jacob Baker.[v]
9th. Mary Bush – October 28, 1796 to January 18, 1871. Married a Mr. Mansfield.[w]
10th. Evelina Norton – August 19, 1798 to April 19, 1875. Unmarried.
11th. Edward S. – November 11, 1800 to June 28, 1817.
12th. Henry Bush – July 14, 1802 to December 30, 1863.
13th. Philip Bush – September 3, 1804 to November 9, 1860. Married Ann McAllister Glass.
14th. William Hill – October 23, 1806 to August 6, 1882. Married Nancy Bell.
15th. Emily Susan – June 16, 1809 to January 18, 1842. Married George W. Baker.
16th. Frances Ann – March 18, 1811 to November 12, 1866. Married John B. White,[x] Romney.

---

[v] The son of Henry W. Baker and Catherine Miller, Jacob Baker was born November 7, 1789 and died March 10, 1874. The marriage occurred on January 6, 1814.

[w] John George Mansfield.

[x] John Baker White was born August 4, 1794 and died, in Richmond, October 9, 1862. Frances Streit was his second wife.

Appendix C
Membership Lists
COMMUNICANTS - JULY 20, 1856

Afflick, Jane
Anderson, Elizabeth
Baker, Alcinda C.
Baker Chris. F.
Baker, Elizabeth
Baker, Fannie E.
Baker, Mrs. George
Baker, Geo. P.
Baker, H.S.
Baker, Mrs. J.
Baker, Jacob
Baker, Josiah L.
Baker, Julia E.
Baker, Sarah
Baker, Sidney
Baker, Susan
Baker, Wm. B.
Barley, Betty
Barnhart, Jas. H.
Barnhart, Mary
Beck, Elizabeth
Bowers, Harriet E.
Bowles, Elizabeth
Bush, Chas. H.
Bush, John A.
Bush, Mary Ann
Bushnell, Margaretta
Brown, O.M.
Brown, Susan
Campbell, A.A.
Campbell, J.W.
Campbell, Mary A.
Campbell, Rachael
Campbell, Thomas B.
Carpenter, Ann
Chandler, E.H.
Copenhaver, Elizabeth
Dinkle, Abagail
Dinkle, Enos
Dinkle, John

Dinkle, Rebecca
Dunn, Mary E.
Fletcher, Rebecca
Funk, E.S.
Gaenslen, Mrs.
Gay, Anna
Gelwicks, Chas. F.
Grove, Mary
Grove, W.H.
Hampton, Catharine E.
Hardy, John
Harman, Elizabeth
Hartman, Rebecca J.
Hartman, Mrs. Sarah
Hays, Mrs.
Heist, Mrs. Caroline
Heist, John S.
Heist, R.A.
Heist, W.H.
Heist, William
Hoff, Elizabeth
Hoff, John
Hoff, Maria
Hoffman, Edward
Hoffman, Mary A.
Horn, Hannah
Horn, Solomon
Jenkins, Mary
Kemp, Maria M.
Kemp, Mary A.F.
Kern, Eliza
Kolhousen, Eliza
Kolhousen, F.W.
Kremer, Mary Ann
Kremer, Virginia C.
Mantz, Eliza F.
March, L.M.
March, R.M.
Marsh, John N.

May, R.C.
McEndree, Mrs.
McKeever, Frances
Messmore, Emily C.
Messmore, Margaret
Miller, Benjamin
Miller, Emma M.
Miller, George G.
Miller, Mrs. Godfrey
Miller, John S.
Miller, Lila S.
Miller, Marianna
Miller, Martha
Miller, Sidney O.
Milton, Emma M.
Myers, Mary Jane
Nott, Mrs. C.
Nott, Caspar
Pritchard, Emma V.
Pritchard, Margaret F.
Quantz, Henry
Quantz, Louisa
Rea, Rebecca E.
Rea, William J.
Renner, Isaac N.
Renner, Josiah
Richards, Henry W.
Schultz, Matthias
Senseny, Catharine
Singhass, Samuel
Slagle, Margaret
Slagle, Wm. J.
Smith, Ann
Snyder, E.A.
Sower, Lydia
Streit, Evelina
Taylor, John T.
Willis, Polly
Young, Julia

This Heritage

CONFIRMED MEMBERSHIP – DECEMBER 31, 1953

Mrs. W.E. Adams
Eugene Adams
Gordon W. Aikin
Mrs. Gordon W. Aikin
Patricia L. Aikin
Conrad H. Akers
Mrs. Conrad H. Akers
M. D. Albin
Mrs. M.D. Albin
Mary Katherine Aulick
Mrs. J. George Baetjer
Beverley A. Bailey
Mrs. Beverley A. Bailey
Gibson G. Baker
Mrs. Gibson G. Baker
Julia Baker
Laura Baker
Margaret Baker
Portia G. Baker
Raymond W. Baker
Mrs. Raymond W. Baker
Mrs. Walter E. Barr
M. D. Bauserman
Mrs. M. D. Bauserman
Diana W. Bauserman
Mrs. W. Marion Bayliss
Rebecca Bell
Robert S. Bell
Mrs. Peter M. Benben
Newton W. Borden
Mrs. Newton W. Borden
Walter H. Bosserman
Mrs. Walter H. Bosserman
Grace E. Bosserman
Walter H. Bosserman, Jr.
Mrs. Walter H. Bosserman, Jr.
Ann C. Bosserman
William T. Bosserman
Mrs. Fred Boulineau
G. Richard Bowers

Mrs. G. Richard Bowers
Mrs. Hattie C. Bowman
James C. Boyce
Mrs. James C. Boyce
Mrs. Ralph R. Boyce
Roy R. Boyce
Mrs. Roy R. Boyce
Arthur F. Braithwaite
Mrs. Arthur F. Braithwaite
Mrs. W.S. Bromley
Mrs. Frank Brown
William F. Brown
Mrs. William F. Brown
James W. Brown
R. Thornton Bryarly
Mrs. R. Thorton Bryarly
Mrs. J.R. Bucher
Mrs. Robert F. Bumgardner
Robert L. Bumgardner
R. Edwin Buncutter
Mrs. R. Edwin Buncutter
Clara Buncutter
Julian Buncutter
Richard Buncutter
Mrs. Richard Buncutter
Mrs. W.M. Burner
Mrs. Charles W. Bush
R. Dovel Bush
Mrs. R. Dovel Bush
Alfred W. Bushong
Mrs. Alfred W. Bushong
Clarence L. Butler
Mamie Butler
Oscar S. Bywaters
Mrs. Oscar S. Bywaters
August H. Cahill
Mrs. August H. Cahill
Mrs. Howard J. Cahill
Leroy F. Cahill
Mrs. Leroy F. Cahill

M. Eileen Cahill
Patricia A. Cahill
Ralph A. Cain
Mrs. Ralph A. Cain
Anna Belle Capper
J. Wilda Capper
W. Wayne Capper
Mrs. W. Wayne Capper
John H. Carpenter
Mrs. John H. Carpenter
Richard Carpenter
Mrs. Harry F. Carper
Merenes Castleman
Mrs. Merenes Castleman
JoAnn V. Castleman
Louise Castleman
L. Marshall Castleman
Mrs. L. Marshall Castleman
Mrs. Herbert Cather
Mrs. Harry C. Clark
Roy Clark
Mrs. Roy Clark
Walter P. Claus
R. Fred Cline
Mrs. R. Fred Cline
Mrs. Mifflin B. Clowe, Sr.
Lewis C. Clowser
Mrs. Stanley Clowser
James Edgar Clowser
J. Clayton Cochran
Mrs. J. Clayton Cochran
Donald M. Cochran
Douglas E. Cochran
J. Clayton Cochran, Jr.
Walter S. Cochran
Mrs. Walter S. Cochran
W. Raymond Cochran
Charles A. Coe, Jr.
Mrs. Charles A. Coe, Jr.
Elizabeth Combs

578

R. Genevieve Combs
Mrs. Samuel Conard
Mrs. Helen S. Conner
Eugene B. Cooper
Mrs. Eugene B. Cooper
Dorothy M. Cooper
Douglas Cooper
E. Bestor Cooper, Jr.
Mrs. Norman E. Cooper
Mrs. O.H. Cornwell
L. Mae Crabill
Oliver G. Cramer, Jr.
Mrs. Oliver G. Cramer, Jr.
Alvin H. Crawford, Jr.
Mrs. Alvin H. Crawford, Jr.
Mrs. Granville M. Creel
Richard D. Crenshaw
Mrs. Richard D. Crenshaw
Mrs. Helen Z. Crisman
Mrs. Jacob L. Crisman
Richard Z. Crisman
Mrs. Wesley O. Crisman
Richard Cromer
Mrs. Richard Cromer
Kenneth W. Curl
Mrs. Kenneth W. Curl
Mrs. Robert Dailey
Mrs. Ben F. Davis
Mrs. Edith F. Dellinger
Mrs. Wallace Derry, Jr.
Frank M. Dick
Mrs. Frank M. Dick
Mrs. Frank T. Dick
Dorothy K. Dick
Raymond B. Dick
H. William Dolan
Mrs. Nacie S. Dorsey
Russell H. Druschel
Mrs. Russell H. Druschel
Hollie B. Dunlap
Mrs. Lohr E. Dunlap
Mrs. Henry J. Eavis

Evangeline Ebersole
Paul K. Ebersole
Mrs. Paul K. Ebersole
W. Ray Ebersole
Mrs. W. Ray Ebersole
Mrs. Douglas Ebert
William E. Eisenberg
Mrs. William E. Eisenberg
Dorothy D. Eisenberg
Mary Martha Eisenberg
Mrs. Wade C. Emmart
Edwin B. Estes
Mrs. Edwin B. Estes
Kelly Estes
Melvin A. Estes
Mrs. Eugenia Evans
Mrs. Mary B. Fahrney
Samuel H. Fenton
Mrs. Samuel H. Fenton
Carl J. Fischer
Mrs. Carl J. Fischer
W. Carlisle Fisher
Mrs. W. Carlisle Fisher
Carl E. Fix
Mrs. Carl E. Fix
Mrs. William L. Fletcher
Grace V. Forney
John G. Fosbrink
Mrs. John G. Fosbrink
Charles W. Fries
Mrs. Charles W. Fries
Martin G. Fries
Ernest W. Frye
Mrs. Ernest W. Frye
Brooke G. Funk
Mrs. Brooke G. Funk
Gibson Funk
Mrs. Rebecca Funk
John L. Funk
Ellen M. Funkhouser
Gloria Jean Garber
Mrs. Raoul Garrabrandt

Mrs. Norman W. Garrison
Peter Georges
Mrs. Peter Georges
Eric Giese
Mrs. Eric Giese
Erna M. Giese
M. Freda Giese
Richard K. Goode
Mrs. Richard K. Goode
Harriet A. Goode
Richard B. Goode
Claude T. Gore
Mrs. Claude T. Gore
Susan J. Gore
O.O. Grandstaff
Mrs. O.O. Grandstaff
Barbara A. Grandstaff
Donald L. Grandstaff
Mrs. O.L. Greathouse
Mrs. Robert D. Grim
William A. Grim
Clifton H. Grimm
Louis H. Grimm
Anna Grove
Howard K. Grove
Mrs. Howard K. Grove
Chris R. Grubb
Mrs. Florence S. Hagan
Ruth Haines
Betty Jo Halterman
Richard L. Hamm
Mrs. Richard L. Hamm
Mrs. P. J. Hammack
Boyd H. Hamman
Boyd J. Hamman
E. Homer Harloe
Mrs. E. Homer Harloe
Mrs. Burr P. Harrison
Donald W. Hayes
Mrs. Donald W. Hayes
Donald F. Hayes
Mrs. John Helsley

CONFIRMED MEMBERSHIP – DECEMBER 31, 1953 (Cont'd)

Alfred S. Henkel
Virginia Henkel
Mrs. C. M. Henkel
Mrs. Kenneth E. Henry
Robert M. Henry
James A. Hepner
Mrs. James A. Hepner
Mrs. Lillian R. Hickerson
Fred Hiett
Mrs. Sue Himelright
Mrs. Charles Hirth
Charles E. Hitt
Garland H. Hitt
Mrs. Garland H. Hitt
Mrs. Herbert Holliday
Mrs. Luella Hook
Mrs. Harry D. Hoover
Mary June Hoover
Joseph A. Hott
Mrs. Joseph A. Hott
Mrs. Eva H. Hottel
W. Jacob Hottel
Mrs. W. Jacob Hottel
Mrs. Ida T. Huff
Richard E. Huff
Joseph T. Huffman
Mrs. Joseph T. Huffman
Russell T. Hupp
Mrs. Russell T. Hupp
Mrs. Thurinda Isaacson
Hubert E. Jackson
Mrs. Hubert E. Jackson
David W. Jackson
R.W. Jackson
Mrs. R.W. Jackson
Patricia A. Jackson
Mrs. T.E. Jackson
Mrs. Virginia Jackson
Virginia Jackson
J. Wilbur Jeffcoat
Mrs. J. Wilbur Jeffcoat

Jackson K. Jenkins
Mrs. Jackson K. Jenkins
Jackson K. Jenkins, Jr.
Abner I. Johnson
Mrs. Abner I. Johnson
Walter B. Johnson
Mrs. Walter B. Johnson
Virginia A. Johnson
Bennie H. Jones, Sr.
Mrs. Bennie H. Jones, Sr.
Jack Jones
William. F. Jones
Bennie H. Jones, Jr.
Mrs. Bennie H. Jones, Jr.
Donald H. Jones
Clara Jones
Mary Jones
George W. Jones
Mrs. George W. Jones
Ann E. Jones
Douglas B. Jones
J. Harry Jones
Mrs. J. Harry Jones
Ruth Jones
J. Luther Jones
Mrs. J. Luther Jones
Joel C. Jones
Mrs. Joel C. Jones
Laurens P. Jones
Mrs. Laurens P. Jones
Robert L. Jones, Sr.
Mrs. Robert L. Jones, Sr.
Robert L. Jones, Jr.
Mrs. Robert L. Jones, Jr.
W. Edward Jones
Mrs. W. Edward Jones
John W. Jones
Mildred Jones
Virginia L. Jones
Frank Keckley
Mrs. Margaret A. Keffer

J. Warren Keller
Mrs. J. Warren Keller
Lester Keller
Mrs. Lester Keller
Mrs. James W. Kenney
Harry C. Kern
Mrs. Harry C. Kern
Richard D. Kern
Mrs. Richard D. Kern
Mrs. Samuel Kerr
Jack R. Kerr
Daniel S. Kinter
Mrs. Daniel S. Kinter
David L. Kinter
Mrs. David L. Kinter
David L. Kinter, Jr.
John F. Kinter
Arthur P. Kissner
Mrs. Arthur P. Kissner
Mrs. Charles Kline
Mrs. Louis Knieling
J. Richard Kremer
Donald B. Kremer
J. Richard Kremer, Jr.
Lillian Kremer
Ruth Kremer
Mrs. Merton W. Kremer
Carl W. Lamp
C. Kenneth Lamp
Mrs. C. Kenneth Lamp
Clarence Lamp
Mrs. Clarence Lamp
Elmer C. Lamp
Harold G. Lamp
Mrs. James H. Lamp
Lewis A. Lamp, Sr.
Lewis A. Lamp, Jr.
Mrs. Lewis A. Lamp, Jr.
Ralph Lamp
Mrs. Ralph Lamp
Russell H. Lamp

Appendix C

Mrs. Russell H. Lamp
William F. Lampmann
Mrs. William F. Lampmann
Clarence P. Lane
Mrs. Clarence P. Lane
Victor J. Lankenau
Mrs. Victor J. Lankenau
Mrs. Charlotte Larrick
Susan Larrick
Floyd O. Leighton
Mrs. Floyd O. Leighton
Mrs. Rodney Levi
Mrs. Maria Levitsky
Oscar H. Lewis
Oscar H. Lewis, Jr.
Albin L. Lindall
Mary Lindamood
Mrs. P. A. Lindamood
Dorothy Lindamood
Robert M. Lindsay
Mrs. Robert M. Lindsay
Richard Lineburg
Mrs. Richard Lineburg
Sandra L. Lineburg
John W. Lloyd
Mrs. John W. Lloyd
Lawrence T. Long
Mrs. Lawrence T. Long
Shirley C. Long
Mrs. Evelyn Lowery
Betty N. Lowery
Elizabeth A. Lowery
James Loy
Mrs. James Loy
James A. Loy
J. Frank Loy
Richard P. Lucas
Mrs. Richard P. Lucas
Mrs. Edward L. Lupton
Mrs. John Lupton
Burrell C. Luttrell
George V. Lutz
Mrs. George V. Lutz
G. Vernon Lutz, Jr.
James E. Madden
Mrs. James E. Madden
Sally A. Madden
Mrs. Ray O. Mahaney
Mrs. William Mallory
Mrs. James B. Marco
Mrs. Frank Marple
Patricia A. Marple
Mrs. J. Lee Massey
Margaret L. Massey
Mrs. Cora Massie
Mrs. C. H. Maxfield
Mrs. Beulah McAdoo
Charles R. McCann
V.S. McClintock
Mrs. V.S. McClintock
Vernon C. McClintock
Mrs. Vernon C. McClintock
Mrs. Minnie McDaniel
Mrs. Joseph W. McDaniel
Mrs. Robert M. McDaniel
J. Newton McDonald
Mrs. M. H. McDonald
A.H. McFarland
James S. McGuire
Mrs. James S. McGuire
Delmar P. McIlwee
Mrs. Delmar P. McIlwee
Mrs. George R. Mellon
James Merriner
Mrs. James Merriner
Bernie A. Miller
Mrs. Bernie A. Miller
Ellen S. Miller
Jennie Miller
Rebecca Miller
Joseph P. Miller
Mrs. Joseph P. Miller
Joe R. Miller
Leonard I. Miller
Paul H. Miller
Mrs. Paul H. Miller
Mrs. Samuel G. Miller
Sidney G. Miller
Mrs. Sidney G. Miller
S. Vincent Miller
Mrs. S. Vincent Miller
William A. Miller
Mrs. William A. Miller
Frederick Moesta
Mrs. Glen B. Morrison
Branson P. Myers
William D. Nash
Mrs. William D. Nash
Mrs. David S. Neff
Fred P. Nelson
Mrs. Fred P. Nelson
Fred P. Nelson, Jr.
Linda P. Nelson
Mary A. Nelson
Mrs. H.A. Neumann
Fred H. Neumann
W. Glen Nichols
Mrs. W. Glen Nichols
Susan Z. Nichols
Mrs. Donald Nixdorff
Elmer O. Nixon
Mrs. Elmer O. Nixon
Charles E. O'Connor
B. Irene Olinger
Mrs. Anna B. Orndorff
Colleen E. Orndorff
Caroline Painter
Elizabeth Parlett
Mrs. Thomas S. Parlett
Alfred A. Parlett
Mrs. William Peffer
Virginia Pifer
Mrs. W. Ralph Pifer
Mrs. Edna C. Pingley
David B. Pingley
Frances M. Pingley

581

CONFIRMED MEMBERSHIP – DECEMBER 31, 1953 (Cont'd)

Harry Pingley
William E. Pitcock
Leslie G. Polhamus
Bismark S. Preffitt
Mrs. Bismark S. Preffitt
Mrs. Luther W. Price
Mrs. Helene Rau
William T. Reuter
Mrs. William T. Reuter
Janet M. Rhodes
Jeanette L. Rhodes
Evelyn Richard
Mrs. Jacob A. Richard
Mrs. Wyatt H. Richard
Mrs. William J. Rickard
Carl R. Ritter
Mrs. Carl R. Ritter
Davis Ritter
Mrs. Davis Ritter
Frederick M. Ritter
Mrs. Frederick M. Ritter
Frederick M. Ritter, Jr.
Joseph C. Ritter
Mrs. Joseph C. Ritter
Marcus O. Ritter
Mrs. Oliver T. Ritter
O. Thomas Ritter, Jr.
Mrs. O. Thomas Ritter, Jr.
Randolph Ritter
Mrs. Randolph Ritter
Mrs. Robert O. Ritter
Samuel B. Ritter
Mrs. Samuel B. Ritter
Lewis C. Robertson
Grover C. Rose
Mrs. Grover C. Rose
William Rosenberger
Mrs. William Rosenberger
Joanne G. Rosenberger
Mrs. Frank J. Ross, Jr.
Mrs. Grace Rosser

Juanita E. Ruleman
Richard E. Rush
Courtney Sager
Mrs. Courtney Sager
Mrs. Herman R. Sandy
Mrs. Harry A. Schmidt
Gertrude Schneider
Paul Schneider
Mrs. Paul Schneider
Katherine Schultz
Mrs. Ralph T. Scott
James A. Seabright
Mrs. James A. Seabright
Mrs. Albert Seal
Mrs. Alvin W. Shade
Floyd L. Shanholtz
Mrs. Floyd L. Shanholtz
Clara V. Shank
L.C. Shaw
Mrs. L.C. Shaw
George D. Shaw
Paul Shearer
Mrs. Paul Shearer
Mrs. Harry Shendow
Champe D. Shepherd
Mrs. Champe D. Shepherd
Howard H. Shockey
Mrs. Howard H. Shockey
Howard H. Shockey, Jr.
William V. Shubert
Mrs. William V. Shubert
Edgar P. Slifer
J. Gordon Slonaker
Sarah J. Slonaker
Mrs. Wesley L. Slonaker
Burette B. Sloop
Mrs. Burette B. Sloop
Alman C. Smedley
Mrs. Clark M. Smith
Mrs. G. Oliver Snapp
Newton Snapp

Mrs. Edwin T. Snider
Edwin T. Snder, Jr.
Mrs. Edwin T. Snider, Jr.
George H. Snyder
Mrs. George H. Snyder
L. Baker Soper
Mrs. L. Baker Soper
Edward L. Soper
Mrs. Ralph S. Speaks
Howard Stine
Marshall Stine
Mrs. Marshall Stine
Mary Katherine Stine
Mrs. Walter B. Stine
William E. Stine
Mrs. Amon Strosnider
William A. Stultz
Philomena Stultz
Mrs. William E. Sumner
Ross M. Swimley
Mrs. Arthur L. Swisher
Mrs. Albert L. Taylor
Albert L. Taylor, Jr.
J. Howard Taylor
Mrs. J. Howard Taylor
J. Howard Taylor, Jr.
Mrs. John Taylor
Mrs. Gordon Teeple
Paul Terretta
Mrs. Paul Terretta
Carolyn M. Terretta
Eston H. Tevalt
Mrs. Eston H. Tevalt
Mrs. Marion Tevalt
Mrs. John Russell Thompson
James C. Tisinger
Mrs. James C. Tisinger
Ward Thresh
Mrs. Ward Thresh
Bessie Trenary
Charles M. Trenary

Appendix C

CONFIRMED MEMBERSHIP – DECEMBER 31, 1953 (Cont'd)

Mrs. Charles M. Trenary
Elmer S. Trenary
Mrs. Elmer S. Trenary
Robert N. Trenary
Emmett M. Tucker
Mrs. Emmett M. Tucker
Mrs. McKinley Turner
Mrs. Max Tyson
Richard Voitel
Mrs. Richard Voitel
Raymond F. Ward
Mrs. Raymond F. Ward
William G. Waters
Mrs. William G. Waters
Julian G. Watson
Mrs. Julian G. Watson
Douglas A. Ways
Archie E. Weatherholtz
Mrs. Archie E. Weatherholtz
Ann Weatherholtz
Jack M. Weatherholtz
Mrs. Guy Webber
Vernon M. Wentz
Mrs. Vernon M. Wentz
Virginia Wentz
Mrs. Edgar C. White
Edgar C. White, Jr.
Natalie White
Mrs. W.R. Whitlock
Gilbert Whitmire
Mrs. Roy B. Wickes, Jr.
A.K. Wingert
Mrs. Eleanor Wingfield
Dennis B. Wingfield
John T. Wolfe
Mrs. John T. Wolfe
Mrs. P.H. Wolfe
Margaret Wolfe
Robert K. Woltz
Mrs. Franklin Woore
Perry B. Wright
Mrs. Perry B. Wright
Ralph P. Yount
Mrs. Ralph P. Yount
Earl J. Zimmerman
Mrs. Earl J. Zimmerman
Abram Zirkle
Mrs. Abram Zirkle
Nan L. Zirkle
William S. Zirkle
Mrs. Frank B. Zydelis

BAPTIZED MEMBERSHIP – December 31, 2002

Abrell, Mandy
Abrell, Barbara
Abrell, Larry
Adams, Colleen
Albanus, Jennifer
Albanus, Julie
Altemose, Ed
Altemose, Jill
Altemose, Jenny
Altemose, Kathleen
Amt, Barbra
Amt, Gerry
Andrews, Brenna
Andrews, Zachary
Arnold, Lenore
Ashby, Anne
Ashwood, Amonda
Ashwood, Daniel
Ashwood, Darin
Ashwood, Melissa
Ashwood, Mike
Athey, Jo Ann
Auer, Jim
Auer, Patrick
Auer, Susan
Bailey, Charles
Bailey, Jason
Bailey, Jerry
Bailey, Pattie
Bancroft, Ruth
Barker, Erin
Barker, John
Barker, Ryan
Barker, Tyler
Barnes, Alexander
Barnes, Ashleigh
Barnes, Austin
Barnes, Dixie
Barnes, Paul
Barnett, Alisa
Barnett, Brian
Barnett, David
Barnett, Ruth
Barnett, Susan
Bartko, Janice
Bartko, Norma
Bauserman, Deb
Bauserman, Alec
Bauserman, Steve
Bauserman, Trent
Behr, David
Behr, Joseph
Behr, Lisa
Behr, Melissa
Behr, Nathan
Bellingham, Claire
Beneke, Evan
Beneke, Haley
Beneke, Rose
Beneke, Terry
Beneke, Vicki
Berry, Lorraine
Berry, Vance

BAPTIZED MEMBERSHIP – December 31, 2002 (Cont'd)

Besselievre, Donn
Besselievre, Lorene
Betterman, Amy
Black, Barbara
Black, William
Bloomfield, Jody
Bloomfield, Sherrie
Bloomfield, Trey
Bodnaruk, Suzette
Boggess, Ingeborg
Boggess, Jack
Bohnsack, Bruce
Bohnsack, Jeff
Bohnsack, Kathy
Bohnsack, Robby
Borgel, Pam
Bouck, Dane
Bouck, Derek
Bowers, Edie
Bowers, Ray
Bowman, Elise
Bowman, George
Boyce, Julie
Boyce, Laurie
Boyce, Toby
Braden, Audrey
Braden, Skip
Braswell, Gary
Braswell, Nancy
Bresnahan, Ginny
Brown, Allen
Brown, Jim
Brown, Linda
Brown, Paul
Brown, Shannon
Bryarly, Mary
Buncutter, Clara
Buncutter, Julian
Burger, Carrie Ellen
Burgess, Nora
Burgess, Phebe
Burkhart, Ben
Burkhart, Gene
Burkhart, Lois
Burkhart, Lucille
Bush, Josephine
Bush, Olin
Byrnes, Patricia
Cabaniss, Pat
Cain, Carol
Cain, Mack
Cain, Annie
Cain, Jackson
Cain, Jacob
Cain, John
Calamari, Jan
Caldwell, Ed
Caldwell, Eileen
Cameron, Lyle
Carbaugh, Arlene
Carbaugh, Wayne
Cardella, John
Carlisle, Loretta
Carmichael, Glen
Carmichael, Jack
Carmichael, Maribeth
Carpenter, Bettie
Carper, Anita
Carper, Stuart
Carr, Ken
Cartier, Nancy
Carver, Jimmy
Cates, Nancy
Cates, Richard
Cather, Yula
Cerrone, Benjamin
Cerrone, Patricia
Cerrone, Ryan
Coates, Jennifer
Coates, Sally
Cochran, Clayton
Coffman, Joan
Combs, Bryan
Combs, Ross
Combs, Justin
Combs, Tina
Cornwell, Christine
Correll, Larry
Correll, Sue
Cowherd, Polly
Cowherd, Bill
Cowley, Anna
Cowley, Ellen
Cowley, Mitzi
Cowley, Rodney
Crawford, Bambi
Crawford, Greg
Crawford, Ryan
Crim, Shawn
Crisman, Frances
Cromer, Dick
Cromer, Virginia
Crumpler, Matthew
Crumpler, Christine
Crumpler, Robert
Crumpler, Scott
Cunningham, Betty
Curtin, Roxanne
Cyr, Gini
Dailey, Princess
Dailey, Bob
Damron, Joe
Damron, Joseph
Damron, Kathy
de Azagra, Sandra
Dempsey, Maddison
Dempsey, Michele
Dempsey, Nicholas
DeVere, Danielle
Dickerson, Betty Jo

Dickey, Debbie
Dickey, Mike
Dickey, Mitch
Diehl, Elaine
Dishart, Hedwig
Dittmer, Kent
Dittmer, Lee
Dittmer, Nancy
Dockeney, Clay
Dockeney, Kiersten
Dockeney, Miranda
Dockeney, Vicki
Dodson, Betty
Doerwaldt, Celeste
Doerwaldt, Christa
Doerwaldt, Christel
Doerwaldt, Hannah
Doerwaldt, Hartmut
Doerwaldt, Ian
Doerwaldt, Jennifer
Doerwaldt, Max
Doerwaldt, Skylar
Doerwaldt, Werner
Dove, B.J.
Eavis, Lenore
Eberly, Jean
Ebersole, Ada
Ebersole, Evangeline
Elliott, Don
Elliott, Ann
Elson, Jody
Elson, Nathan
Elson, Rob
Elson, Sarah
Emmart, Callie
Emmart, Cameron
Emmart, Elizabeth
Emmart, Jim
Emmart, Peggy
Emmart, Susan
Erickson, Joyce
Erickson, Ray

Evans, Eugenia
Everly, Mandy
Everly, Jeff
Everly, Katie
Everly, Marie
Everly, Mitzi
Everly, Bill
Falls, Donn
Falls, Patricia
Farley, Dottie
Farley, Heather
Farley, Nathan
Farley, Philip
Farley, Phil
Fears, Muriel
Fellman, Anna
Fellman, Karl
Fellman, Laureen
Fellman, Mary Kate
Fellman, Natalie
Fickes, Betty
Fisher, Barbara
Fisher, Betsy
Fisher, Gene
Fisher, Paul
Flagg, Mary
Flagg, Michael
Flagg, Michael
Flagg, Natalie
Fleming, Amber
Fleming, Brittany
Fleming, Denise
Fleming, Wayne
Fleming-Sole, Tamara
Fletcher, Crystal
Fletcher, Diane
Fletcher, Juanita
Fogle, China
Foreman, Trisha
Forse, Brian
Forse, Cindy
Forse, Rick

Forse, Lindsay
Forse, Shelby
Forsyth, Melinda
Fournier, Kristen
Fournier, Ryan
Foust, Linda
Foust, Bob
Franklin, John
Froehlich, Ed
Froehlich, Mary
Froehlich, Rebecca
Fromme, Kyle
Frye, Ben
Frye, Janet
Frye, Roni
Frye, Terry
Frye, Tim
Funk, Carl
Funk, Jane
Funk, Zachary
Funkhouser, Chrystal
Funkhouser, Donal
Gallagher, Donna
Gallagher, John
Galloway, Ashton
Galloway, Debbie
Galloway, Elliott
Garlitz, Barbara
Garlitz, Danny
Garlitz, Bob
Garlitz, Tim
Garrison, Norman
Gause, Dan
Gause, Danielle
Gause/Wilcox, David
Gause/Wilcox, Kyle
Geary, Brandon
Geary, Diane
Geary, Justin
Geary, Randy
Gilbert, Kelsey
Gilbert, Kristin

BAPTIZED MEMBERSHIP – December 31, 2002 (Cont'd)

Gilbert, Lisa
Gilbert, Wilson
Girardi, Cheryl
Girardi, Garrett
Girardi, Joe
Girardi, Maggie
Girardi, Michael
Glawe, Frank
Glawe, Marie
Gluch, Katrina
Gluch, Sharon
Goode, Carol
Goode, David
Goode, Evelyn
Goode, Jessica
Goode, Kathy
Goode, Matt
Goodrich, John
Goss, Duane
Gray, Peggy
Greene, Brittney
Greene, Terry
Griffin, Anna
Griffin, David
Griffin, Kathleen
Griffin, Laurel
Griffin, Peter
Grove, Ben
Grove, Elizabeth
Grove, Kim
Grove, Morgan
Grove, Renee
Grove, Tim
Haddock, Andre
Haecker, Aaron
Haecker, Angie
Haecker, Catherine
Haecker, Paul
Hagman, Niki
Haines, Jack
Haines, Lucas
Haines, Marjorie
Halsted, Beck
Halsted, Ben
Halsted, Dale
Halsted, Gaye
Hammack, Cee Ann
Hanlon, Dave
Hanlon, Greg
Hanlon, Joel
Hanlon, Sue
Hartman, Sally
Hartman, Talen
Hartzell, Howard
Hawks, Carolyn
Hawks, Madeleine
Hawks, Millicent
Hawks, Olivia
Headley, Joe
Headley, Regina
Heidelberger, Bennett
Heidelberger, Dana
Heidelberger, Ingrid
Heidelberger, Livia
Heidelberger, Max
Heidelberger, Nina
Heidelberger, Todd
Heidelberger, Bill
Heishman, Jim
Heishman, Robert
Heishman, Wilda
Heishman, Zachary
Helsley, Amanda
Helsley, Catherine
Helsley, Dick
Helsley, Ricky
Helsley, Susan
Henry, Edith
Henry, John
Henry, Vivian
Henschen, Irv
Henschen, Marian
Herb, Jill
Hetland, Catherann
Hetland, Christopher
Hetland, Gary
Hetland, Sharon
Hildebran, Adler
Hildum, Sylvia
Hillyard, Mary
Himelright, Alexandra
Himelright, Marsha
Hockman, Ciara
Hockman, Donald
Hockman, Doug
Hockman, Michael
Hockman, Nicholas
Hockman, Patricia
Hockman, Robin
Hockman, Robin
Hockman, Steven
Hockman, Zachary
Hoenig, George
Hoenig, Linda
Hoke, Mary
Holle, Amber
Holle, Destiny
Holle, Terry
Holliday, Margaret
Holzer, Cody
Holzer, Austin
Hoover, Carole
Hott, Carolyn
Hott, Charles
Hott, Jackie
Hott, John
Hott, Jay
Hott, Kay
Hott, Nicholas
Hoxton, Alexandra
Hoxton, Caroline
Hoxton, Clay
Hoxton, Kim

Appendix C

Hufnagle, Max
Hufnagle, Samuel
Hufnagle, Shane
Hufnagle, Susan
Hulver, Ruby
Humphrey, Rob
Humphrey, Linda
Humphrey, Matthew
Hupp, Ann
Hupp, Cliff
Hupp, Stuart
Jacobs, LaRita
Jacobs, Laura
Jacobson, Jade
Jacobson, Lynette
Jacobson, Rozella
Jarl, David
Jarl, Emily
Jarl, Kay
Jarl, Keith
Jeffcoat, David
Jeffcoat, Vicky
Jenkins, Edith
John, Mary
Johnson, Doris
Johnson, Jennifer
Johnson, Walter
Jones, Alice
Jones, Catrina
Keeler, Ashley
Kerr, Ann Bailey
Kerr, Carol
Kerr, David
Kerr, Greg
Kerr, Gunner
Kerr, Jerry
Kerr, Jill
Kerr, John
Kerr, Tanner
Keyl, Barbara
Keyl, Rudy
Kidwell, Linda

Kidwell, Paul
Kinter, Flossie
Kirkpatrick, George
Kitchin, Harold
Kitchin, Theresa
Kline, Viola
Knazik, Kylee
Knazik, Cheryl
Knazik, Ray
Koehler, Wayne
Krause, Dinah
Lamp, Lucy
Lawrence, Savannah
Lehman, Alan
Lehman, Anna
Lehman, Carol
Lehman, Hal
Lehman, Sara
Lehman, Teresa
Lepore, Lou
Lepore, Nancy
Levy, Claudia
Levy, Kim
Levy, Bill
Lewis, Lillian
Linck, Bill
Lineburg, Connie
Lineburg, Michael
Lippy, Christine
Lippy, Jeff
Lippy, Matthew
Lippy, Mitchell
Long, Geneva
Long, Lawrence
Longerbeam, Jim
Longerbeam, Shelda
Lucas, Anna
Lucas, Gail
Lucas, Helen
Lucas, Jacob
Lucas, Jane
Lucas, Jay

Lucas, Dick
Lynch, Abigail
Lynch, Caroline
Lynch, Leigh Ann
Lynch, Mark
Maddox, Libby
Maddux-Anderson, Susan
Malone, Brenda
Malone, Chase
Malone, Keely
Malone, Kelly
Manuel, Amanda
Manuel, Polly
Manuel, Scott
Manuel, Terri
Manuel, Tyler
Manzano, Abby
Marco, Flora
Marco, Jim
Marcus, Blakeley
Marcus, Sandra
Markley, Ruby
Marsh, Graham
Marsh, Karen
Marshall, Liza
Marshall, Nicholas
Marshall, Tim
Martin, Nick
Martin, Rebecca
Martin, Renaye
Mason, Brooke
Mason, Cathy
Mason, Olivia
Massonneau, Andrew
Massonneau, Brenda
Massonneau, Chris
Massonneau, Ryan
Matko, Aidan
Matthews, Carolyn
Matthews, Gary
Matthews, Gary Holder
Matthews, Josiah

This Heritage

BAPTIZED MEMBERSHIP – December 31, 2002 (Cont'd)

Matthews, Kaitlyn
Matthews, Tamara
Matticks, John
Matticks, Linda
Maul, Edna
Mayfield, Andrew
Mayfield, Marty
Mayfield, Mimi
Mayfield, Tim
McCabe, Caitlin
McCabe, Jackie
McCabe, William
McCann, Micaela
McCann, Mike
McDonnell, Jo Ann
McDonnell, Bill
McDowell, Becky
McGoff, Edie
McInturff, Elsie
McKee, Danny
McMinn, Bunny
McMinn, Sharon
McMinn, Stephen
McMinn, Steve
McTague, Carolyn
McTague, Reed
Meehan, Catie
Meehan, Beth
Meehan, Tom
Megeath, Colleen
Melby, Katie
Melby, Kathy
Melby, Richard
Melby, Justin
Mellon, Wilda
Melton, David
Mendel, Ken
Mendel, Peggy
Merkel, Tim
Milburn, Clare
Milburn, Daniel

Milburn, Diane
Milburn, Linda
Milburn, Roger
Milburn, Tom
Miller, Cynthia
Miller, Debbie
Miller, Esther
Miller, Evva May
Miller, Gordon
Miller, Joan
Miller, John
Miller, Josh
Miller, Mary
Miller, Megan
Miller, Nicky
Miller, Ruth
Miller, Sally
Miller, Sam
Miller, Sarah
Miller, Stephanie
Miller, Stephanie
Miller, Steve
Miller, William
Mitchell, Diana
Mitchell, Jeffrey H.
Moore, Beatrice
Morrell, Barbara
Morris, Leigh Ann
Moseley, Angelina
Moseley, Laura
Mummert, Carolyn
Mummert, Harold
Myers, Michael
Nail, Ashleigh
Nail, Corey
Nail, Greg
Nail, Ginger
Nail, Madison
Nail, Sean
Nesselrodt, Don
Nesselrodt, Nancy

Nethers, Chase
Nethers, Chelsea
Nethers, Jeff
Nethers, Stacey
Nichols, Janie
Nixon, David
Nixon, Dot
Noe, Louis
Norton, Elia
Norton, Katie
O'Leary, Carol
O'Leary, Sarah
Oates, David
Oates, Kaitlyn
Olinger, Dirk
Olinger, Jennifer
Olinger, Lauren
Olinger, Anne
Olinger, Phil
Orndoff, Clara
Orndoff, Trey
Padgett, Curtis
Padgett, Joan
Padgett, Justin
Padgett, Katie
Pearce, Christine
Pearce, Ellen
Pearce, Laura
Pearce, Michelle
Pepper, Ann
Pepper, Ruth
Perrone, John
Perrone, Michelle
Perrone, Nathan
Perrone, Nicole
Perrone, Ronald
Peters, Kendra
Peters, Mikaela
Peters, Rita
Pierce, Joy
Pierce, Mary

Appendix C

Pifer, Court
Pifer, Diane
Pifer, Richie
Pinkley, Robert
Pinkley, Shelia
Place, Hallie
Poole, Lia
Poole, Linda
Prebble, Bobby
Presgraves, Candice
Presgraves, Sydney
Prusch, Catharine
Prusch, Elizabeth
Prusch, Martha
Pryde, Courtney
Pryde, Gail
Pryde, Kyle
Pullen, Betsy
Pullen, Michelle
Pullen, Tom
Rabe, Jerry
Rajaratnam, Lawrance
Rajaratnam, Shanthi
Ray, Brian
Ray, David
Ray, Jessica
Ray, Johanna
Ray, Jonathan
Ray, Joyce
Rayburn, Katherine
Reed, Dakota
Reed, Duane
Reed, Ford
Reed, Kathy
Reed, Noah
Reed, Tyler
Reier, George
Reier, Ruth
Renner, Barbara
Renner, Kara
Renner, Larry
Renner, Zachary

Rhodes, Janet
Rhodes, Jeanette
Rice, Daniel
Rice, Dillon
Rice, Gay
Rice, John
Rice, Kelly
Rice, Pat
Rice, Tim
Riemenschneider, Gina
Riemenschneider, Neal
Riemenschneider, Ruth
Riemenschneider, Shea
Riley, Jonathan
Riley, Mary
Riley, Rob
Riley, Tracy
Ritenour, Barbara
Ritenour, Kay
Rittenhouse, Ed
Rittenhouse, Karen
Ritter, Emilee
Ritter, Helen
Ritter, Melissa
Ritter, Thelma
Ritter, Tyler
Robertson, Beulah
Robinson, Abigail
Robinson, Dawn
Robinson, Elfriede
Robinson, Jacob
Robinson, Mark
Robson, Cheryl
Robson, Elizabeth
Robson, Eric
Robson, Mark
Rohrbacher, Charles
Rohrbacher, Judy
Rohrbacher, Marie
Rohrbacher, Michael
Rohrbacher, Steven
Rohrbacher, Suzanne

Rucker, Dilly
Runion, James
Ruos, Mary
Rush, Gail
Rush, Robert
Sabanosh, Grace
Sabanosh, John
Sabol, Krista
Sabol, Michael
Sadler, Timothy
Sadowski, Connor
Sadowski, Evan
Sadowski, Grant
Sadowski, Hannah
Sadowski, Lori
Sadowski, Vincent
Sager, Kim
Sager, Scott
Saunders, Drew
Saunders, Wayne
Saunders, Gretchen
Savolainen, Hope
Savolainen, Tia
Savolainen, Toby
Schettler, Alex
Schettler, Ashley
Schreiner, John
Schroeder, Jordan
Schroeder, Matt
Schroeder, Olivia
Schulz, John
Schulz, Mazie
Schuster, Adam
Schuster, Chris
Schuster, Ed
Schuster, Leslie
Schuster, Linda
Scott, Barbara
Scott, Kevin
Shaffer, Brittany
Sheetz, Carter
Sheetz, Olivia

BAPTIZED MEMBERSHIP – December 31, 2002 (Cont'd)

Shewbart, George
Shickle, Terry
Shidel, Hilda
Shidel, Megan
Shidel, Rachel
Shook, Linda
Shook, Madison
Short, Forrest
Short, Susan
Shrader, Peggy
Shultz, Gay
Simpson, Alex
Simpson, Anne
Simpson, Blair
Simpson, Caleb
Simpson, Kate
Simpson, Lee
Simpson, Martin
Simpson, Wilda
Sims, George
Sims, Martha
Slaughter, Debbie
Slaughter, Stacey
Slaughter, Steve
Slothower, Howard
Slothower, Sharlene
Smith, Danny
Smith, Debbie
Smith, Jane
Smith, Nancy
Smith, Rhonda
Snarr, Doris
Snarr, James
Snyder, Brittany
Sole, Andrew
Sonafelt, Mary
Sonnabend, Cheryl
Sonnabend, James
Sorrell, Gregory
Sorrell, Jeanne
Spore, Amanda
Spore, Mary Jane
Spore, Tim
Spore, Timothy
Starks, Wyatt
Stein, Kitty
Stein, Harris
Stern, Chuck
Stern, David
Stern, Nancy
Stern, Tim
Stern, Bill
Stine, Michael
Swaim, Cindy
Swaim, Lindsey
Swaim, Marcus
Swaim, Mark
Swanson, Jennifer
Swanson, Rebecca
Swartz, Jim
Swartz, Loretta
Thatcher, Seth
Thomas, Bob
Thomas, Emily
Thomas, Gordon
Thompson-Valentine, Jane
Thornton, Matthew
Thornton, Michael
Thornton, Sharon
Tillotson, Dot
Timbrook, Kelly
Timbrook, Ricky II
Torkelson, Kathy
Torkelson, Mallory
Torkelson, Mike
Tri, Chelsea
Tri, Lenny
Tri, Johnny
Tri, Lisa
Turner, Ruth
Ulsh, Jonathan
Ulsh, Larry
Ulsh, Susan
Utt, Jim
Utt, Susan
Utt, Tyson
VanHorssen, Marilee
VanHorssen, Bill
Vannorsdall, Joan
Venskoske, Jeremy
Venskoske, John
Venskoske, Matt
Venskoske, Wendy
Viens, Betty
Walker, Greg
Wann, Abigail
Wann, Kate
Wann, Trey
Waters, Jean
Waters, Loring
Watkins, Earl
Watkins, Kevin
Watkins, Lois
Watkins, Margaret
Watkins, Meghan
Watkins, Owen
Watkins, Russell
Waymouth, Pam
Waymouth, Sam
Weissenberger, Christina
Weissenberger, David
Weissenberger, John
Weissenberger, Sheila
Weissenberger, Valerie
Westervelt, Carol
Westervelt, John
Wheeler, June
Wibberley, Barbara
Wibberley, Bob
Wilcox, Addrianne
Wilson, Barbara
Wilson, Camilla
Wilson, Jim

Appendix C

Wilson, Michael
Wilson, Parker
Wilson, Payne
Wolfe, Clarene
Wolfe, Mary
Wolfersberger, Lois
Wolfersberger, Bill
Woltz, Robert
Woodruff, Charles
Wynn, Whitney
Wynn, Jane
Wynn, Kirstine
Wynn, Tim
Yaider, Ashley
Yaider, Lauren
Yaider, Rusty
Yaider, Seth
Yaider, Vicki
Zerull, Anne
Zerull, Dave
Zerull, Lisa
Zerull, Scott

This Heritage

Every Name Index

Not included in this index are church officers, Council members and some church staff in Chapter X, names in Appendix A (Stoever Record) and Appendix C (Membership lists).

A

Adam, George M. 370
Adam, Ludwig 39, 42
Adolph 547
Aikens, Melvin 407
Albert, Adam 547, 554, 561, 564
Albert, Catharine Elizabeth 547, 564, 574
Albert, Elizabeth 547, 554
Albert, Jacob Michael 547
Albert, Maria Salome 564
Albert, William 564
Aldereton, William 572
Aldred, Henry 572
Alexander, Patrick 573
Alexander, William 547, 572
Allemong, C.W. 393
Allen, Deborah 539, 571
Altefoi, John 106
Altrit, Ann Margaret 541
Altrit, Catharine 541
Altrit, Henry 541, 545, 548
Altrit, John 545
Altrit/Altridge, Michael 101, 537, 540, 541, 568
Altrit, Mrs. Henry 572
Altrith/Aldrich/Eldridge, Christoph 39, 44
Amherst, General Jeffrey 51
Ammens, Susannah 574
Amt, Gerry 518, 525
Ancese, Adam 553
Ancese, Sabilla 553
Ander, Abraham 553

Ander, Ernst 553
Anderson, Adam 567
Anderson, Catharine 537, 572
Anderson, Christina 537, 539
Anderson, D.M. 393
Anderson, Jacob 537, 538
Anderson, Jesse 537
Anderson, John 371
Anderson, Margaret 537, 539, 571
Anderson, Peter 559
Anderson, R. Homer 248, 249
Anderson, Rachel 537
Anderson, Rody 572
Anderson, Sabilla 567
Anderson, Sarah 573
Anderson, Thesby 573
Anderson, Thomas 537
Anne, Queen of England 3
Anson, William 574
Antony, Master 37, 39, 42, 43, 373, 456
Antrim, Joshua 574
Arm, Philip 101
Arnold, General Benedict 67
Ash, John 572
Ashby, Anne 415, 468
Ashby, Sarah 571
Ashby, General Turner 363
Ashe, Anne 574
Ashwood, Amonda 461, 468
Ashwood, Daren 455
Askew, John 536
Audle, Nancy 573

593

Aulich, Carl Christopher Edman 69, 566
Aulich, Catharine Elizabeth 566
Aulich, Mary 566
Aulick, Charles 101
Aulick, Frederick 117
Aulick, George 130, 371
Aulick, Mary Katherine xi, xiii, 404, 412, 469, 482, 509, 512, 516
Aulick, Mrs. C.E. 511
Austin, Claire Kay (Mrs. John Chamberlain Bellingham) 301
Austin, Marla 473

B

Baart, Madam 83
Bachman, J. 158, 159
Baedlin, Margretha 570
Baer, Elizabeth 541
Baer, Mary Sarah 541
Baer, Peter 541
Baetjer, Catherine 503
Baetjer, Frederick Henry 518
Baetjer, Henry 193, 204, 205, 209, 214, 216, 392, 393, 394, 479
Baetjer, J. George 204, 244, 245, 408, 479, 494, 505, 506
Baetjer, Susan Brown (Mrs. J. George Baetjer) xi, xii, xiii, 246, 249, 513
Bagger, Henry H. xiii, 406
Bagger, Mrs. Henry H. xii
Bailey, Charles W. vii, viii
Bailey/Baily, John 540, 571
Bailey, Margaret 569
Baker, Elizabeth 130
Baker, Alcinda 364
Baker, Abigail 573

Baker, Abraham 130
Baker, Andrew 101, 564
Baker, Camillus S. 217
Baker, Catherine Streit 479
Baker, Christina 571
Baker, Ella 503
Baker, Emily C. 503
Baker, Emily Susan 142, 384
Baker, Emma 144
Baker, G. Gibson 209, 225, 392
Baker, George W. 100, 130, 142, 384, 385, 562, 576
Baker, H.S. 187, 359, 367
Baker, H.W. 95, 101, 125
Baker, Halford (Red) viii
Baker, Henry 44, 69, 96, 97, 100, 130, 132
Baker, Henry F. 130, 134, 456
Baker, Henry Streit 222, 479, 489
Baker, Henry William 69, 123, 130, 131
Baker, Isaac 130, 484
Baker, Jacob 100, 117, 121, 123, 124, 126, 127, 130, 132, 137, 138, 139, 142, 146, 147, 152, 155, 157, 158, 162, 165, 175, 187, 244, 369, 378, 379, 384, 388, 389, 399, 422, 479, 515, 576
Baker, Jacob E. 211, 387
Baker, John 118, 124, 130, 132, 134, 136, 137, 378, 484
Baker, John I. 181
Baker, Joseph 130
Baker, Julia xii
Baker, Larry 468
Baker, Laura xii
Baker, Margaret xii
Baker, Mary Catherine 128, 131, 503

594

Baker, Mary Virginia (Mrs. Charles Porterfield Krauth) 165, 503
Baker, Moses H. 549
Baker, Mr. 536, 537, 560
Baker, Mrs. John 484
Baker, Mrs. S. 134
Baker, Nathan C. 130
Baker, Portia B. xii, 465, 481, 492
Baker, R.M. 182
Baker, Robert 487
Baker, Samuel C. 371
Baker, William Alexander 122, 130
Baker, William B. 152, 158, 159, 168, 171, 173, 177, 187, 189, 193, 201, 358, 360, 385, 392, 399, 400, 461, 479, 489, 493
Baldwin, A.S. 370
Baldwin, Robert T. 371
Ball, Elizabeth 551
Ball, Mary 551
Ball, Miss 134
Ball, William 551
Balmain, Alexander 93, 575
Baltis, Leonard 539, 540
Banes, Anna Maria 565
Banes, Philip 565
Banes, William 566
Bangle, James H. 323
Banks, General Nathaniel P. 343
Bansemer, Richard F. 332, 339
Bar, Elizabeth 545
Barbour, Christy 473
Barnes, Elizabeth 573
Barnes, Lewis 574
Barnett, David 478
Barnett, Ellen 502
Barnhart, George 371
Barr, E.M. 214
Barr, John 575
Barr, Oscar 201, 206, 216

Barr, Susannah (Mrs. Christian Streit) 93, 575
Barre, Mary Elizabeth (Mrs. Carl Adams Honeycutt) 252
Barrett, Jonathan 573
Bartgis, Matthias 97
Bartlett, Chuck 285
Bartlett, John 538
Bastion, Anna Maria 564
Bastion, Catharine 546, 571
Bastion, Christina 564
Bastion, John Adam 564
Bastion, Juliana 564
Bauer, Janet (Mrs. Duane Leslie Steele) 488
Bauer, John Adam 544
Bauer, Philip 544
Bauer, Sarah 544
Baughman, Harry F. 252, 253
Baum, Fred L. 236
Baum, Frederick John 177, 236
Baum, John C. 177
Baum, Mrs. William Miller 177
Baum, William Miller 171, 172, 174, 175, 176, 177, 178, 181, 200, 236, 502
Baum, William Miller, Jr. 177, 485
Bauserman, Ella Brown 410
Bauslin, David H. 484
Bayliss, John 29
Bayliss, Max 478
Bean, Mordecai 561
Beasly, Nelly 573
Beck, Frank F. 225
Beck, Walter E. 225
Becker, Henrick 39, 44
Behr, David 455
Behr, Joey 478
Bell, Lancelot 130
Bell, Mrs. W.A. 223
Bell, Nancy 576

Bell, Peter 136, 370
Bell, R. 134
Bell, Robert S. xii, xiii, 455
Bellingham, Claire Kay Austin 300
Bellingham, John Chamberlain 295, 300, 301, 302
Bellingham, John David 301
Bellingham, Jonathan 301
Bellingham, Kristin 301
Bellingham, Mae Fors 301
Bellingham, Rebecca 301
Bellingham, Virginia 301
Benegar, George 572
Benham, Harry K. 507, 508
Benner, Anna Maria 548
Benner, Christina 548
Bennet, Mary 572
Bennet, William 574
Bentler, Barbara 538
Bentler, Jacob 538
Bentler, Maria Catharine 538
Berkel, William 571
Bernard, Dorothea 542
Bernard, Frederick August 539, 542, 571
Berri, Susanna 557
Beutel, Mr. 207
Bile, S. 134
Billow, Doris Pretorius 499
Billow, William 499
Bilman, Anthony 549
Bilman, Elizabeth 549
Bilman, Rosina 549
Birdlin, Margretha 570
Bishop, Jacob 118
Biton, Michael Kerson 573
Biton, Rosina 572
Bittle, David F. 120, 187
Black, Barbara 416, 468
Black, George 572
Black, John 572
Black, William 516
Blackburn, James 467
Blanck, Christian 20
Bland, Michael 552
Bland, Sarah 552
Blankenbicher/Blankenbaker, Elisabeth 569
Blankenbicher/Blankenbaker, Els[a] 569
Blankenbicher/Blankenbaker, Johann 569
Blankenbicher/Blankenbaker, Marcretha 569
Blankenbicher/Blankenbaker, Michael 569
Blankenbicher/Blankenbaker, Zacharias 569
Blankenbiger/Blankenbaker, Barbara 550
Blankenbiger/Blankenbaker, Elizabeth 550, 551
Blankenbiger/Blankenbaker, John 550
Blankenbiger/Blankenbaker, Michael 550
Blankenbiger/Blankenbaker, Samuel 551
Blankenbiger/Blankenbaker, Zacharias 551
Blankenbiker/Blankenbaker, Barbara 569
Blankenbiker/Blankenbaker, Elisabeth 570
Blankenbiker/Blankenbaker, Jacob 570
Blankenbiker/Blankenbaker, Johann 569
Blankenbücher/Blankenbaker, Christina 557
Blankenbücher/Blankenbaker, Elis 556

Index

Blankenbücher/Blankenbaker, Elisabeth 556
Blankenbücher/Blankenbaker, Jacob 556
Blankenbücher/Blankenbaker, Michael 556
Blankenbücher/Blankenbaker, Rosina 556
Blankenbücher/Blankenbaker, Samuel 556
Blankenbücher/Blankenbaker, Thomas 556
Blankenbücher/Blankenbaker, Zacharias 556
Bly, Joan 302
Bo____, Elizabeth 573
Böhme, Daniel 569
Böhme, Nancy 569
Böhmein/Bohmen, Catharine 551, 569
Bohmen, Daniel 551
Bohmen, Nancy 551
Bolen, Maria Elizabeth 537
Bolen, Sarah 537
Bolen, Stephen 537
Boltz, Elizabeth 548
Boltz, Jacob 548
Boltz, Michael 548
Bond, Samuel 573
Bonham, Anne 539, 571
Bosek family 291
Bosserman, Mrs. Walter H. xiii, 509
Bosserman, Walter H. 231, 235, 241, 243, 403, 408, 410
Bosserman, Walter H., Jr. 250, 397, 455
Bott, James H., Jr. 250
Bower, George 574
Bower, P. 101
Bowers, Curtis 408
Bowers, G. Hubert 225
Bowers, George Spener 216, 218, 219, 220, 223, 224, 225, 226, 227, 228, 234, 249, 362, 400
Bowers, Melville D. 225
Bowers, H. 134
Bowers, S.A. 134
Bowers, Mrs. George Spener 228
Bowman, Abraham 68
Bowman, Catharine 573
Bowman, Elizabeth 19
Bowman, George 19
Bowman, George, Jr. 520
Bowman, Grace (Mrs. Robert Warren Koons) 281
Bowman, John 101
Bowman, John George 19
Bowman, John Jacob 19
Bowman, Mary Hite 19
Boyce, Mrs. Ralph 405, 468
Boyce, Toby 478
Boyd-Rush, Dorothy A. v, viii
Boyles, Catharine 573
Braddock, Edward 27
Bradford, W.A. 181, 399
Braithwaite, Carl 474
Brand, Cinda 520
Brannon, Robert 371
Branson, Robert 573
Braswell, Gary 337
Braswell, Nancy S. vii, 313, 330, 482, 525
Braun, Catharine 536
Braun, Jacob 39, 44
Braun, Johannes 107
Braun, John 537
Bray, Dick 468
Breedlove, Charles 573
Breil, Barbara 570
Brent, Henry M. 370
Briel, Catharine 566

Briel, Henry 566
Briggs, Misses 216
Brill, Henry 561, 562
Brill, Michael 573
Brinker, Catherine 101
Brith, Christopher 542
Brith, Elizabeth 542
Broadstreet, Donna 468
Broadstreet, Lloyd 468
Brookover, Anne 571
Brown, Charles L. 221, 496
Brown, Daniel 371, 574
Brown, Edith 503
Brown, G. Ronald 520
Brown, Henrietta 461
Brown, J. Few 209, 217, 408, 481
Brown, Jacob 44
Brown, James Allen 168
Brown, Jim 287, 383
Brown, John 107, 342, 371
Brown, Kate Baker (Mrs. Thomas William Dosh) 181, 503
Brown, Martin 371
Brown, Oliver M. 181, 515
Brown, Oscar S. 246, 461
Brown, Virginia 503
Brown, W.F. 455
Brown, William H. 225
Bruhl, Henry 565
Bruhl, Magdalena 565
Brumback, H. Lee, II 488
Brumback, Harvey Lee 488
Brumback, Mary Gertrude 20
Brumback, Philip Lee 329
Brumback, Sherry Morrison 313, 329, 330, 331
Brun, John 370
Bryan, Charles 540, 571
Bryarly, R. Thornton xiii
Buchanan, Daniel C. 503
Bucher, John Ulrich 19

Bucher, Henry 543
Bucher, Imanuel 44
Bucher, Jacob 64, 563, 569
Bucher, John 543
Bucher, Rosina 19
Buddi, Christopher 557
Buddi, Elizabeth 557
Buddi, John Carl 557
Buger, Imanuel 39, 44
Buncutter, Clara 470
Buncutter, Julian H. 250
Buncutter, R.E. 455
Buncutter, Richard A. 250
Bungart, Eva 556
Bungart, Jacob 556
Bungart, Johann 556
Bungart, Margreth 556
Burgoyne, General John 82
Burnes, Edward 574
Busch, Catharine 545
Bush, Andrew 117
Bush, Diane 478
Bush, Mr. 543
Bush, Philip 92, 96, 101
Bushman, Mary C. (Mrs. Austin Augustus Kelly) 235
Bushnell, George 205, 395
Bushnell, George B. 492
Bushnell, John Eichelberger 214, 395, 485
Bushnell, Marie (May) Louise 492
Bushong, Alfred W. 250
Butterfield, Thomas 574
Byars, Michael 134
Byrd, Harry Flood, Jr. 255
Byrd, William, III 64, 66

C

Cadwallader, Mrs. A.B. 469
Cafford, Sarah 547, 572
Caghill, Catharine 565

Index

Caghill, George 565
Caghill, Nancy 565
Cahill, Leroy F. 250
Cahill, Martha Stine 271, 284, 295, 460, 473, 474, 482
Cain, Mrs. Ralph A. 405
Cain, Ralph A. 250, 405
Calamari, Robert 516
Caldwell, Eileen 455
Campbell, Ann 544, 571
Campbell, Carl 250
Campbell, Clyde 467
Campbell, John B. 134, 370
Campbell, Laura M. (Mrs. L.G.M. Miller) 201, 503
Campbell, Thomas B. 130, 134, 139, 142, 146, 147, 152, 155, 158, 162, 201, 384, 385, 388, 389, 399
Carbaugh, Mrs. Mason 468
Carbaugh, Wayne 312, 525
Carey, Lisa 516
Carmer, Christian 573
Carn, John 572
Carpenter, Andreas 550, 556, 569
Carpenter, Anna Maria 550, 552
Carpenter/Carpenterin, Barbara 550, 556, 569
Carpenter, Catharina 556, 569
Carpenter, Cornelius 550
Carpenter, Dinah 551, 570
Carpenter, Dorothea 551
Carpenter, Elisabeth 550, 556, 569, 572
Carpenter, Grace 403
Carpenter, Johannes 556
Carpenter, John W. 250
Carpenter, Joseph 556, 569
Carpenter, Margareth 557
Carpenter, Maria 550, 556, 569
Carpenter, Michael 556
Carpenter, Mr. 549
Carpenter/Carpenterin, Rebecca 570
Carpenter, Richard M. 250
Carpenter, Samuel 551, 570
Carpenter, Susanna 557
Carpenter, William 92, 102, 103, 104, 533, 549, 550, 552, 556, 557, 569
Carpenter, William, Jr. 551, 569
Carper, Frederick 574
Carper, William 544, 571
Carr, Carol 478
Carr, J. Kenly vii, 373, 383, 415, 459, 482, 523, 525
Carroll, Joan 518
Carson, J.S. 162
Carter, Elizabeth 574
Carter, Ezekiel 571
Carver, Elizabeth 572
Cassaday, Thomas 573
Cassell, C.W. 487
Cassell, O.C. 408
Castleman, L. Marshall 250, 404
Cates, Joette 473
Cates, Lyall 468
Cather, Jasper 544, 571
Charles I, King of England 22
Charles II, King of England 22, 23
Chief Pontiac 27
Christianson, Conrad 295
Christler, Adam 556
Christler, Anna Magdalena 556
Christler, Eleonora 556
Christler, Elias 556
Christler, Elisabeth 556
Christler, Georg 556
Christler, Henrich 556
Christler, Julius 556, 570
Christler, Maria 556
Christman, Abraham 19

Christman, Jacob 19
Christman, Magdalena Hite 19
Christman, Sara 19
Church, E.W. 393
Clark, Charles H. 385
Clark, James 565
Clark, John 565
Clark, Margaret 565
Clark, Nathan 544, 571
Cleavinger, James 549, 572
Clerck, John 542
Clerck, Margaret 542
Clevenger, Theodosia 573
Clewell, Lewis H. 467, 468
Cline, June 503
Cline, R. Frederick 246, 250, 397, 455, 459, 509
Clunk, Mary 573
Coates, Sally vii, viii, 373, 468
Cochran, Charles A. 250
Cochran, E. Clinton 250
Cochran, John C., Jr. 250
Coe, Charles A., Jr. 250
Collins, Ann 574
Collins, William 571, 573
Colvert, John 19
Colvert, Rebecca 19
Combs, Tina 461, 516
Comes, Joseph 371
Connel, Phebe 545, 571
Conner, John 101, 573
Conrad, Frederick William 146, 147, 192
Conrad, Henry 106
Conradt, Mrs. 134
Conradt, Theophilus F. 130, 136
Cooe, Henry 573
Cooke, John 66, 101
Cooper, Alison D. 380
Cooper, Anne 568
Cooper, Calia 573

Cooper, Eugene B. xi, xiii, 225, 402, 403, 455, 461, 467, 505
Cooper, Grace 503
Cooper, J. Edwin 206, 209, 213, 216, 461, 479
Cooper, Jacob 130
Cooper, Joseph Edwin 518
Cooper, Lewis F. 214, 225, 231, 235, 241, 243, 244, 245, 392, 394, 401, 402, 403, 408, 409, 479, 486
Cooper, Mrs. E.B. xiii
Cooper, Mrs. Lewis F. 486
Cooper, Mrs. Norman Elmore 494
Cooper, Nannie O. xiii
Cooper, Norman Elmore 403, 486, 494
Cooper, Norman Elmore, Jr. 250
Cooper, Spencer 568
Cooper, Thomas J. 206, 213, 222, 228, 394, 479, 493
Cooper, V. Wayne 225
Cooper, W. Douglas 250
Cooper, William 568
Copenhafer, John 555
Copenhafer, Mary 555
Copenhafer, Michael 555
Copenhafer, Mrs. 567
Copenhaver, Jacob 45, 370
Copenhaver, John 101, 370, 574
Copenhaver/Copinhufer, Michael 101, 117, 544
Corbeth, Hanson 573
Cox, C. Brown 402
Cox, John 540, 571
Cox, Marcia 306
Craig, Jenny 572
Cramer, Catharine 539
Cramer, Conrad 539
Cramer, Mr. 567
Crawford, Greg 455

Crawford, Sally 466, 478
Crawford, Vera K. (Mrs. A.H. Crawford, Jr.) 306, 412, 473, 482
Crawley-Woods, Larry 516
Crikler/Crigler, Catharina 569
Crikler/Crigler, Christoph 569
Crikler/Crigler, Maria Marcreth 570
Crikler/Crigler, Nicolaus 550, 570
Crisman, Frederick A. 250
Crisman, Richard Z. 250
Crisp, William 20
Cristler, Elisabeth 556
Crockwell, John N. 130, 134, 136, 142, 152, 462
Croker, Maria Briscoe 490
Croll, Maria Louisa (Mrs. William Miller Baum) 175
Cromwell, Oliver 22
Crook, General George 344
Crumpler, Scott 525
Culpeper, Lady Catherine 23
Culpeper, Lady Margaret 23
Cummins, Margaret 540, 571
Cussen, Alice 289

D

Damly, Elizabeth 548
Damly, Mary 548
Damly, Michael 548
Danner, Abraham 556
Danner, Frederick 550
Danner, Margaret 551
Danner, Maria 550
Darflinger, Elizabeth 574
Dary, Jacob 106
Daser, Mr. 85
Davis, Ben F. 244, 481, 495, 506, 507, 508, 509, 510, 512

Davis, Ben F., Jr. 250, 491
Davis, John B. 169
Davis, Mrs. Ben F. xiii, 495, 507, 509, 510, 543, 571
Davis, Samuel 545, 571
Davis, William 573
Dawkins, Thomas 572
de la Marque, Mrs. 544
de Mauz/du Mas 534
Dearing, Eberhard 44
Dederick, David 28, 29
DeHaven, Kim 286
Dellinger, George 106
Dellinger, Jacob 20
DeLoach, Diane 488
Delp, Margaretha 556
Delp, Michael 556
Delph, Conrad 551, 570
Delph, Magdalena 551, 570
Demuth, Betty 516
Dennis, Donald 407
Detrick, David 43
Dick, Frank M. 250, 491
Dick, John 573
Dickey, Mitch 468
Diehl, Bridget 461
Diehl, Elaine (Mrs. James H. Diehl) 472, 473
Diehl, George 142, 169
Diehl, James H. 287, 310, 413, 519, 520, 521
Dieter, John George 11, 20
Dieterick, David 39, 43
Dinkle, Enos 484
Dinwiddie, Robert 26
Disponet, Elizabeth 573
Doberstein, John W. xii
Dodd, Solomon 134
Dodson, Cathy 474
Doerwaldt, Hannah 478
Doerwaldt, Hartmut 474

Dorey, Frances Annette (Mrs. George Spener Bowers) 228
Dorflinger, Elizabeth 548
Dorflinger, Eva Margaret 548
Dorflinger, Jacob 548
Doring, Eberhard 39, 44
Dorsey, Edwin 171
Dosh, Mary 503
Dosh, Mrs. Thomas William 187, 399
Dosh, Thomas William Luther 178, 179, 181, 182, 183, 185, 186, 187, 188, 345, 399, 502, 503
Dougherty, Mary 536
Doush, Christopher 573
Dove, B.J. 516
Dowdal/Dowdall, James Gambell/Gamul 96, 534, 536, 543
Drake, Lucy 572
Drayer, David 287
Drayer, Judy 471
Drew, Perez 542, 571
Dromgold, Betsy 549
Dromgold, Catharine 569
Dromgold, Mr. 549
Dromgold, Mrs. 569
du Mas 534
DuBois, Anna Maria 9
Duchee, Jacob 56, 59
Duff, William 14
Duffield, John 545
Duffield, Mary 545
Dulany, William H. 105
Dunn, Abigail 573
Dunn, James 550, 572

E

Early, General Jubal 344
Eavis, Barbara 466
Eavis, John 466
Eavis, Kathy 466
Eavis, Lenore (Mrs. Henry J. Eavis) vii, viii, 373, 472, 473, 516
Eberly, Jeremiah 571
Ebersole, Evangeline 470
Eckstine, Elizabeth 573
Eckstine, Mary 550, 572
Eddy, C. Vernon xii
Edmondson, Thomas 544, 571
Edward, Margaret 572
Edwards, Joseph 573
Edwards, Thomas 541, 571
Eger, Albrecht 101
Ehler, Barbara 550
Ehrhart, Carl 20
Ehrhart, John Barnhart 541
Ehrhart, Mary 573
Eichelberger, Mrs. Lewis 484
Eichelberger, Charles F. 187, 189, 193, 201, 209, 359, 372, 392, 503
Eichelberger, Charlotte Sperry 503
Eichelberger, John Miller 165, 484
Eichelberger, Lewis 126, 128, 129, 132, 134, 135, 136, 138, 138, 142, 147, 148, 150, 169, 374, 457, 484, 503
Eichelberger, Mrs. Charles F. 197
Eisenberg, Dorothy Darlington 253
Eisenberg, Mary Martha 253, 487, 503
Eisenberg, Mrs. William Edward ix, 372, 410, 464, 470, 472, 487, 503
Eisenberg, William Edward v, vi, viii, xiii, 252, 268, 279, 291, 372, 410, 455, 464, 472, 478, 487, 503, 506, 509, 516, 522
Elbon, Reuben 573

Eldridge, Christoph 44
Ellis, Christopher 572
Eltz, Ernest 101, 545
Emel, Chas. 393
Emmart, Wade C. 411
Emmonds, ____l 573
Erhart, John 564
Erhart, Magdalena 564
Erhart, Susanna Margaret 564
Ersman, Frederick 574
Essick, Abraham 168, 169, 170, 171
Estes, Edwin B., Jr. 250
Estes, Melvin A. 250
Estes, R. Kelly 250
Evans, Tommy 478
Everhart, Michael 572
Everly, Jacob 370
Everly, Marie 516
Ewing, Lisa 474

F

Fairfax, George William, Esq. 64
Fairfax, Thomas, Lord 18, 21, 22, 23, 24, 25, 26, 28, 30, 39, 41, 52, 366, 454, 519
Falckner, Daniel 10, 76
Falckner, Justus 76
Falligant, Mary Rutledge (Mrs. David McConaughy Gilbert) 190
Farley, Dorothy 455, 520
Farley, Philip 516
Fauquier, Francis 39
Feck/Feg, Anna Eva 4
Feg, Johann Peter 4
Feltner, Elizabeth 572
Festus, David 502
Festus, Ellen 502
Festus, Gabriel 207, 502
Festus, Mary Emma 502
Festus, Mildred Ann 502

FewSmith, Joseph, Jr. 147, 148, 149, 151, 152, 153, 463
Finck, Theodore K. xii
Finck, William J. xii, 249, 487, 533
Fisher, Arvella (Mrs. Robert L. Fisher) 515
Fisher, Betsy 473
Fisher, Gene 286, 383
Fisher, Paul 518
Fisher, W. Carlisle 404
Fithian, Philip V. 51, 65, 98, 377
Fitzhugh, Susanna Stuart 377
Fitzsimmons, Dana Gail Weaver 322, 325, 473
Fitzsimmons, Elmer 323
Fitzsimmons, Evan Weaver 325
Fitzsimmons, Kyle Weaver 325
Fitzsimmons, Margaret Staehli 323
Fitzsimmons, Mark Elmer vii, 312, 322, 323, 324, 325, 326, 327, 411, 418
Fleischmann/Fleischman/ Fleischmannin, Elizabeth 550, 556, 570
Fleischmann/Fleischman, Ephraim 556, 570
Fleischmann/Fleischman, John 550
Fleischmann/Fleischman/ Fleischmannin, Margaretha 570
Fleischmann/Fleischman, Maria 556
Fleischmann/Fleischman, Michael 556
Fleischmann/Fleischman/ Fleischmannin, Susannah 556, 570
Fleischmann/Fleischman, Zacharias 550, 556

Fleming, James H. 467
Flemming, J____ 574
Fletcher, Diane 461
Fletcher, John 370
Flickinger, S.L 249
Flinn, Mrs. J. 464
Flinn, V.H. 187, 189
Forney, Grace 403
Forse, Lindsay 478
Forst, Henry 544
Forsyth, Melinda 478
Fosbrink, Mrs. John G. xiii, 406, 472
Foss, Eve 573
Foster, James 374
Foster, Jane 200
Fraenckel, Stephen 44
Framman, Sara 19
Franck, Jacob 53, 82
Frank, John 574
Frazier, Lake J., Esq. 403
Freed, Charles Abram 235, 236, 237, 238, 240, 241
Freed, Conrad 241
Freed, Elizabeth 241
Freed, Janet 241
Freed, Joe 241
Fretwell, Adair 321, 460
Frey, Benjamin 565
Frey, Christopher 552
Frey, Mathias 547
Frey, Mr. 541
Fridley, Andreas 39, 44, 66
Fridley, Henry 101
Fries, Charles W. xiii, 238, 244, 404, 408, 492
Fries, George Casper 231, 403, 404, 480, 492
Fries, Mrs. Charles W. 465
Friess, Catharine 555
Friess, Jacob 564
Friess, Martin 555
Froehlich, Mary Miller vii, viii, 455, 473
Fromman, Elizabeth Hite 19
Fromman, John Paul 19
Fromman, Lizzie 19
Fromman, Paul 19
Fry, Christopher 66, 101
Fry, Franklin Clark 254
Fry, Samuel 370
Fulk, Barbara 573
Fulton, Robert 572
Fultz, Linwood 250
Fungonie/Fungonies, Conrad 547, 572

G

Gaar, Adam 550, 570
Gaar, Elizabeth 551
Gaar, Michael 551
Gaarin, Dorothea 570
Gantz, George 549
Gantz, Sarah 549
Gar/Gaar, Adam 556
Gardner, Dedrick 101
Garfield, James A. 140
Garn, Ephraim 574
Garrabrandt, Mrs. Raoul 469
Garst, Margaret 545
Gartner, Maria 549
Gartner, Michael 549
Gates, Horatio 66
Gaul, Anna Barbara 558
Gaul, Christian 558
Gaul, William 558
Geary, General John White 344
Geier, John 552
Geiger, George 537
Geiger, Jacob 537
Gelwick, Charles F. 130
George II, King of Great Britain 29

George III, King of Great Britain 39
George, Rachel 573
Gerat, John 564
Gerat, Margaret 564
Gerlach, Theobold 20
Gerst, John 537
Gilbert, David McConaughy 34, 42, 44, 45, 50, 52, 56, 64, 69, 90, 98, 102, 140, 188, 189, 190, 192, 194, 195, 196, 197, 198, 199, 200, 201, 204, 214, 218, 375, 395, 463, 495, 502
Gilbert, Eve 574
Gilbert, Jane E. Brown 189
Gilbert, Lisa 473
Gilbert, W. Kent 274
Gilbert, Wilson 468
Gilbraith, Mr. 536
Gillo, Commodore 86
Glaize, Anna Maria 19
Glaize, David Brevitt 222
Glaize, David S. 222, 491
Glaize, Elizabeth Baker 222, 490, 491
Glaize, Fred L. 490
Glaize, George F. 201, 206
Glaize, John Philip 19
Glaize, Mary Barbara 19
Glaize, Mrs. David S. 222
Glaize, Sarah 490
Glass, Ann McAllister 576
Glass, W.W. xi, xii, 131
Glasser, Dorothea 542
Glick/Glueck, Michael 39, 45
Gochenour, Patricia 478
Godfrey, Mr. 565
Goertner, Mrs. Nicholas Westermann 137
Goertner, Nicholas Westermann 137, 138, 139, 375, 380
Goff, Kristen 516
Gold, Christina 573
Golliday, Terry 468
Gooch, William 8
Goode, Evelyn 416, 471, 520
Goode, Richard K. 250
Gordon, Amos 574
Gordon, Elizabeth 565
Gordon, Mary 565
Gordon, Patrick 10
Gordon, Peter 565
Gore, Claude T. 455, 504
Gore, Eva Lamp 504
Gore, Susan Jane 504
Goss, John 101
Graef, Salome (Mrs. Christian Streit) 87, 575
Graham, Philip 573
Graichen, Carrie D. 216, 400
Graichen, F. August 216, 400, 485
Graichen, John George 485
Graichen, Laura V. 493
Graichen, Mrs. F. August 485
Grant, Stewart 117, 130, 370
Grapes, Catharine 572
Graves, George B. 371
Gray, Elizabeth 549, 572
Greeb, Charles, Jr. 287, 294, 304
Green, Alfred L. 461
Green, Hugh K. 201, 206, 209, 214, 228, 234, 250, 394, 480, 492
Green, Jennie M. 403, 494
Green, Mary 574
Green, Robert 14
Greene, Brittney 478
Greene, John W. 250
Greenleaf, R.K. 305
Greenway, Mary 573

Grickler, Margaret 550
Grickler, Nicolas 550
Griffith, Marie 473
Griffith, R.E., Sr. 376, 533
Grigg, Milton 404
Grim, Carl 557
Grim, Charles 67, 101, 546, 568
Grim, Eleonora 569
Grim, Elizabeth 545, 568
Grim, George W. 130
Grim, Jacob 539
Grim, Jo 545
Grim, John 66, 69, 71, 101, 568
Grim, Maria Magdalena 539, 557
Grim, Peter 569
Grim, Susanna 568
Grim, Winston C. 250
Grimes, Sarah 572
Grob, John 117
Grove, Abraham 130, 134, 374
Grove, Ada (Mrs. Charles Abram Freed) 241
Grove, Elizabeth 572
Grove, Howard K. xiii, 232, 241, 403, 455
Grove, Howard K., Jr. 250
Grove, Michael 101
Grove, Mrs. Howard K. xiii, 494
Grove, Mrs. M. 134
Grove, O.P. 393
Grove, William H. 126, 130, 134, 136, 152
Grubb, Sarah 573
Gunsten, Anna Kristin 319, 321
Gunsten, Kristin Ruth Hanson 318, 319, 321
Gunsten, Lucretia Colleen Post 319
Gunsten, Paul Gerhard vii, 306, 311, 317, 318, 319, 320, 321, 322, 459, 519, 520
Gunsten, Paul H. 319

Gunsten, Sarah Colleen 318, 319, 321

H

Haas, Mr. 568
Haecker, Angie 472
Haenli, John Sigmond 39, 45, 64, 65
Hafer, Luther Bowers 236, 267, 402, 403
Halstead, Beck 468
Hamman, Boyd H. 455, 507
Hamman, Boyd J. 250
Hampton, S. 134
Hampton, Mrs. 134
Hance, William 572
Hancock, Charles B. 399, 400
Handschue, John Frederick 32
Hansbrough, Daniel 554
Hansbrough, John 554
Hansbrough, Smith 554
Hansbury, John 572
Hanson, Kristin Ruth (Mrs. Paul Gerhard Gunsten) 319
Hard/Hart, Mr. 552, 560
Harder, Christopher H. 499
Harder, Dorothea Paulson 499
Harder, Helene 471, 499
Harder, Martha 497
Hardesty, Miss 197
Hare, Margaret 544, 571
Harger, Anna Maria 549
Harger, Maria Dorothea 542
Harger, Michael 542, 549
Harloe, Curtis G. 225
Harloe, William E. 225
Harmer, Jacob 371
Harr, Simon 90, 534, 539
Harter, Adam 572
Hartman, Daniel 370
Hartman, R. 464

Index

Hartwick/Hartweg, John Christopher 32, 48, 50, 51, 52
Hartzenbuehler, Elizabeth 19
Hass, Frederick 96
Hatanaka, Mr. 221
Hatsabieler, John 538
Haus/Hauss, Margreth 570
Haus/Hauss, Margretha 556
Haus/Hauss, Maria Margreth 570
Haus/Hauss, Mathias 557, 570
Haus/Hauss, Michael 556, 570
Haverstick, Henry 138
Hawkins, Ephraim 370
Hawks, Carolyn 518
Hawman, David 548
Hawman, Peter 548
Hawman, Sibella 548
Hay, Charles A. 158
Hay, Penelope A. (Mrs. Lewis Eichelberger) 136
Haymaker, Mr. 538
Heard, James 534, 539
Heidelberger, Bill 525
Heidelberger, Todd 455
Heil, Eva Margaret 555
Heil, George 555
Heinle, Anna Maria 552
Heintz, Christoph 39, 44
Heiskel/Heiskell, Adam 67, 70, 71, 96, 101
Heiskel/Heiskell, Catharine Susan 154
Heiskel/Heiskell, Christopher 43, 64, 101
Heiskel/Heiskell, Eva 552
Heiskel/Heiskell, George 67
Heiskel/Heiskell, John 130, 370
Heiskel/Heiskell, Peter 69
Heist, Charles F. 101
Heist, George H. 214, 241, 370, 394, 408
Heist, John S. 152
Heist, Thomas 107, 116, 121
Helfenstein, Mr. 561
Helfenstein, P. 101
Helfenstein, Peter 39, 43, 64, 66, 68, 81
Helfenstein, Philip 69
Helgel, Charles 574
Heller, C.A. 205
Helm, Catharine 538
Helm, Dorothea 539, 571
Helm, George 538
Helfenstein, Roy C. xii
Helphenstine, Elizabeth 573
Helt, Nancy 574
Helvestine/Helfenenstein, Peter 43
Henkel, Alfred D. xi, 228, 245, 249, 372, 408, 480, 505
Henkel, Alfred S. 225
Henkel, Anthony 11
Henkel, Claude M., Jr. 250
Henkel, E.O. 487
Henkel, Emerson D. 250
Henkel, Gerhardt 11
Henkel, Mrs. C.M. 469
Henkel, Mrs. Solomon 130
Henkel, Paul 11, 92, 102, 104, 534, 535
Henkel, Solomon 363
Henkel, Virginia xii, xiii, 515
Henley, John Sigmond 45
Henry, E.L. 217
Henschen, Irv 383
Hepner, C.W. 221
Herman, Jacob 554
Herman, Margaret 554
Herman, Samuel 554
Herrell, Helen Dean 511
Hesser, Samuel L. 370
Hetland, Sharon 334, 412, 477
Hetzell, Charles 101

Heusckel, Christoph 39, 43
Heydt/Heyt/Hite, Abraham 18
Heydt/Heyt/Hite, Anna Magdalena 9, 10, 19
Heydt/Heyt/Hite, Anna Maria 9, 10, 19, 20
Heydt/Heyt/Hite, Anna Maria Dubois 11, 20
Heydt/Heyt/Hite, Elizabeth 10, 19
Heydt/Heyt/Hite, Isaac 18
Heydt/Heyt/Hite, Jacob 18, 544, 571
Heydt/Heyt/Hite, Johannes/John 9. 15, 18, 19, 20
Heydt/Heyt/Hite, Hans Joist/Jost/Justus 2, 3, 5, 9, 10, 14, 15, 18, 19, 20, 21, 24, 37, 68
Heydt/Heyt/Hite, Joseph 18
Heydt/Heyt/Hite, Sara 19
Heydt/Heyt/Hite, Susanna 19
Heyl, Andrew 541
Heyl, Catharine 541
Heyl, George Michael 541
Heyl, John Jacob 541
Heyl, John William 541
Heyl, Mary Catharine 541
Hiegel, Dewald 39, 45
Highland, John 556
Highland, Sarah 556
Hill, William 92, 109, 127, 131
Himelright, E.R. 232
Hinckel, George 543
Hinckel, Paul 534, 535, 540, 542, 544
Hinton, Rebecca 572
Hinton, Solomon 573
Hirsch, Andreas 556, 570
Hirsch, Anna Maria 556
Hirsch/Hirschin, Barbara 556, 570
Hirsch, Catharina 557
Hirsch, Martin 550, 556, 570
Hirsch, Susanna/Susannah 556, 570
Hitel, Elizabeth 545
Hoch, Daniel 537, 538
Hoch, Rudolph 537
Hockman, Zachary 478
Hodges, W.V. 211, 217, 386, 394
Hoff, Anna Margaret Christina Elizabeth (Mrs. Christian Streit) 87, 574
Hoff, Charles 100
Hoff, Elizabeth 546
Hoff, Isaac 370
Hoff, Jacob 100
Hoff, John 101, 134, 136, 157, 385, 489, 493, 495, 543, 546
Hoff, Lewis 64, 96, 97, 100, 116, 122, 125, 126, 127, 370, 537
Hoff, Mary 543
Hoff, P. 134
Hoff, Mrs. 134
Hoffman, Ann 286
Hoffman, Edward 152, 158, 187, 193, 358, 360, 392, 492
Hoffman, F. 101
Hoffman, Sally 364
Hoffmeier, Barbara Anne (Mrs. Rudolf Joseph Stephanus Keyl) 328
Hoffmeyer, William 290
Hofman, Charlotte 537, 569
Hofman, Frederick 565, 569
Hofman, Magdalena 557
Hofman, Margaret 574
Hoge, Susanna 572
Hoke, Virginia 478
Holding, Honor 542, 571
Hollar, Hunter 308, 459
Hollar, Mary Margaret 471
Holliday, F.W.M. 162, 400

Index

Holliday, Robert B. 162
Holliday, William 120, 374
Holmes, Joseph 96
Holsklauin, Elisabeth 570
Holsklauin/Holtzklau, Jemima 557, 570
Holsklauin, Magdalena 570
Holsklauin/Holtzklau, Susanna 557, 570
Holt, Dorothy 468
Holtzel, Anna Margaret 540
Holtzel, Henry 552
Honeycutt, Carl Adams 248, 249, 250, 251, 252, 255, 291, 410
Honeycutt, Mary Carolyn 252
Honeycutt, Mrs. Carl Adams 252, 410
Hook, Robert E. 503
Hoover, Harvey D. 249, 252
Hoover, Kitty 574
Hoover, Philip 101, 116, 489
Hopewell, Benjamin 574
Horn, George 533, 546
Horn, George, Jr. 572
Horn, Mr. 91, 562
Hornell, Mr. 49
Hort, Margaret J. xii
Hott, Mrs. J.A. 405, 472
House, S. Porter 244
House, S.S. 187
Houser, Donald L. 274
Howe, Mr. 541
Hoxton, Clay 455
Huber, Catharine Elizabeth 543
Huber, Elizabeth 543
Huber, Philip 543, 560
Huff, Cornelius 572
Hukedorn, Daniel 550
Humphrey, Linda 468, 473
Humphrey, Matthew 467, 468, 491, 525

Humphrey, Rob 468
Hunsacker/Hunsicker, Christina 537, 538
Hunsecker, Catharine 573
Hunsicker, Daniel 537
Huynh family 291

I

Iles, Mary 574
Isom, Catharina 557

J

Jackson, F.H. 393, 396
Jackson, L. 232
Jackson, General Thomas "Stonewall" 343, 344, 360
Jackson, Virginia 469
Jacobs, Amy 572
Jacobs, William 573
Jäger, Adam 551, 556, 570
Jäger, Elisabeth 570
Jäger, Johann 570
Jäger, Johannes 556
Jäger, Josua 556, 570
Jäger, Maria 556, 570
Jäger, Michael 570
Jäger, Peter 556
Jägerin/Jäger, Maria 570
Jeffcoat, David 468, 478
Jeffcoat family 307
Jenkens, Stephen 372
Jenkins, Jack 287
Jenkins, Jane 287
Jenkins, Stephen 117, 130, 371
Jenkins, Wilbur H. 250
Jennings, David 573
Jennings, Karen Lou 478
Johnston, General Joseph E. 343, 358
Johnston, Susanna 573

Jones, Anne Payne 571, 573
Jones, Benny H., Jr. 250
Jones, Dorothy Darlington (Mrs. William Edward Eisenberg) 253
Jones, Forrest E. 250
Jones, Henry 20
Jones, Jack E. 250
Jones, Jacqueline Mildred (Mrs. Virgil Albert Moyer, Jr.) 269
Jones, John W. xiii, 250
Jones, Mrs. J. Luther xiii
Jones, Robert H. 340
Jones, Robert L. 244
Jones, Robert L., Jr. 250
Jones, William 370
Joppa, Eloise S. 304

K

Kaltheisen, Mr. 83, 86
Kamerer, Barbara 554
Kamerer, Christian 554
Kamerer, John 554
Kaufman, Elizabeth 560
Kaufman, George 560, 562
Kaufman, Margaret 560
Kaufman, Mary 560, 562
Kearns, Elizabeth 572
Keckley, Ellis 562
Keckley, Jacob 564
Keffer, James E., Jr. 250
Kehler, John 118
Keiser, George 573
Keiser, James Robertson 145, 146, 147
Keister, Ann Headley 488
Keller, Ezra 120
Keller, Scott Douglas 478
Kelly, Austin Augustus 228, 229, 230, 233, 234, 235, 402, 466

Kelly, George Benner 235
Kemmerer, Mr. 165
Kendziorra family 258
Kern, Harry C. 250
Kern, Raymond W. 250
Kern, Wilbur 307, 491
Kerr, Carol 322, 468, 518
Kerr, Jerry P. 286, 308, 309, 373, 459, 520, 521, 523
Kerr, Jill 473
Kerr, John 518
Kesner, Martha 541, 571
Keyl, Barbara Hoffmeier 327, 328
Keyl, Deborah 328
Keyl, Ida Christina Emelia Dickhart 328
Keyl, Rudolf Joseph Stephanus, Jr. 313, 326, 327, 328, 330, 373
Keyl, Rudolf Joseph Stephanus, Sr. 328
Keyl, Stephen 328
Keyl, Timothy 328
Kiefer, Ann Maria 560
Kiefer, Frederick 118
Kiefer, George 565
Kiefer, John 562, 565
Kiefer, Martin 565
Kiger, Adam 101, 564
Kiger, Andrew 101, 371, 549, 555, 567
Kiger, Augustus 371
Kiger, George 96, 97, 101
Kiger, Hannah 555
Kiger, Isaac 370
Kiger, Jacob 101, 130, 554
Kiger, John 66, 69
Kiger, Magdalena 567
Kiger, Mrs. 134
Kimmel, Mr. 86
Kirchner, Johann Caspar 38, 39, 41, 42

Index

Kirk, Margaret 572
Kirk, Mary 554
Kistler, Dorothy Stevenback 499
Kistler, Luther 499
Klein, Adam 544
Klein, Antony 549
Klein, Maria Barbara 549
Klein, Maria Magdalena 555
Klein, Mary 542
Klein, Susanna 549
Kline, Vivian 473
Klipstein, Daniel 545
Klipstine, P. 101
Klug, George Samuel 54, 55
Klyne, Mary 571
Kneister, Hannah 553
Kneister, John 553, 567
Knipp, J.C. 393
Knox, Susanna 377
Koch, Barbara 557
Koch, Daniel 551
Koch, Dorothea 557
Koch, Georg 556, 570
Koch, Johannes 556, 562, 570
Koch, Ludwich 570
Koch, Margareth 557
Koch, Maria 569
Koch, Peter 569
Koch, Rosina Dorothea 562
Koch, Salome 562
Koehler, Wayne 468
Kohlhousen, Roy 225
Koons, Ann 281
Koons, Grace (Mrs. Robert Warren Koons) 281, 293, 294
Koons, John Raymond 281
Koons, Kathryn Annabelle Herr 281
Koons, Philip 281, 573
Koons, Robert Warren 281, 282, 283, 284, 288, 289, 290, 291, 292, 293, 294, 295, 296, 297, 300, 302, 317, 515, 519
Koons, Stephen 281
Koontz, Johannes 18, 531
Koppenhaber, Jacob 39, 45
Kortehel, Anna Elizabeth 546
Kortehel, Elizabeth 546
Kortehel, John 546
Kramer, Conrad 563
Krauss, Henry 19
Krauth, Charles Philip 118, 119, 154, 169
Krauth, Charles Porterfield 34, 43, 46, 64, 65, 98, 99, 111, 119, 154, 155, 157, 159, 161, 162, 163, 164, 165, 166, 167, 168, 169, 203, 382, 399, 463, 484, 485, 503
Krauth, George Edward 485
Krauth, Mary Virginia Baker 485
Krauth, Mrs. Charles Porterfield 157
Kreb/Krebs, Conrad 548
Kreb/Krebs, Jacob 548
Krebs, Abraham 548
Krebs, Catharine 548
Krebs, Henry 548
Krebs, Mr. 552
Kremer, Carl P. 225
Kremer, Catharine 546
Kremer, Conrad 66, 69, 97, 101, 125, 130, 546
Kremer, Esther 574
Kremer/Kreemer, George 371
Kremer, J. Richardson 225
Kremer, Paul 225
Krigler/Crigler, Anna 556
Krigler/Crigler, Catharina 557
Krigler/Crigler, Christoph 557
Krigler/Crigler, Ludwig 556

Krigler/Crigler, Nicholas 556
Kroggel, Linda 474
Kronmann, Lean Ann 487
Krum, Henry 547
Krumbholz, Clarence E. 255, 503
Krumbholz, Mrs. Clarence E. xii
Kucharski, John 468
Kuhn, Daniel 77, 78
Kunkle, Mr. 551
Kurtz, Abraham 362
Kurtz, Adam 67, 101
Kurtz, Benjamin 118, 119, 131, 132, 133, 503
Kurtz, Daniel 117, 118
Kurtz, Frederick 67, 70
Kurtz, Mary Catherine 132, 362
Kurtz, Mary E. 362
Kurtz, J. 134
Kurtz, Mr. 568
Kyger, Jacob 549

L

Lackmiller, Wolfgang 542
Lacy, B. Tucker 360
Laemly, Johannes 39, 45
Laign, Ronald M. 468
Laign, Shannon 474
Lake, Douglas A. 250
Lamb, John 538
Lambert, Christopher 28, 29, 39, 45
Lamp, Anna 538
Lamp, Bill 466
Lamp, C. Kenneth 468
Lamp, Carl W. 250
Lamp, Elizabeth 538
Lamp, Elmer 408, 455
Lamp, John 538
Lamp, John George 538
Lamp, Lee W. 494
Lamp, Lewis 520
Lamp, Lucy (Mrs. C. Kenneth Lamp) 468, 473
Lamp, Ralph E. 250
Lamp, Robert H. 250
Lang, Sue 290, 294, 295
Langland, Patty 572
Lantz, Johannes 45
Lantz, Mr. 537
Lastor, Tracy 488
Lathan, George 572
Laubinger, Georg/George Michael 39, 44, 64, 201
Laubinger, Susanna 538
Lauck, Abraham 101, 116, 121, 125, 127, 130
Lauck, Amelia 546
Lauck, Jacob 543
Lauck, John 545
Lauck, M. 134
Lauck, Mr. 536
Lauck, Peter 66, 67, 70, 71, 96, 97, 101, 116, 130, 373, 489, 539, 543, 545, 546, 551, 559, 560
Lauck, Simon 67, 101, 569
Laughlin, Amos 537
Lavinder, Barbara 101
Lawrence, James 540, 571
Lay, Michael 573
Lee, Captain 360
Lee, Charles 66, 80
Lee, Daniel 105
Lee, Sherri 326, 327, 328, 330
Lehman, Alan vii
Lehman, Carol 475
Lehman, Harold 408, 475, 516
Lehman, John 550
Lehman, Teresa 330, 335, 336, 412, 416, 460, 472, 473, 518
Lehrug, Christian 541

Index

Leight, Carla 474
Lemley, Johannes 45
Lemley, John 489
Lemp-McDonald, Vicki 460
Len, Anna Maria 541
Len, George 537, 541
Len, Mr. 541
Lentz, Johannes 39, 45
Lentz, John 543, 545
Lentz, Susanna Catharine 543, 545
Lepp, Daniel 557
Lepp, Elizabeth 550, 557
Lepp, Henrich 550, 557
Leps/Lepp, Christian 550
Leps/Lepp/Lepsin, Maria 550, 557, 570
Leps/Lepp, Mrs. 570
Lewis, Andrew 66
Lewis, Henry 572
Lewis, Hugh M. 225
Lewis, John K. 214, 393, 394, 395
Lewis, Nancy A. 516
Ley, Maria Elizabeth 546
Libby, Dorothy Eisenberg 464
Libby, Robert Reed 464
Lidenius, John Abraham 112
Liebestein, Adam 548
Liebestein, Eva 548
Light, Elizabeth 572
Likens, Jonas 550, 572
Likens, Sarah 572
Lincoln, Abraham 361
Lincoln, General Benjamin 86
Lind, Anna Mary 541
Lind, George 541
Lindsay, Mrs. J. Gordon 494
Lindsay, Thomas 550, 572
Lindy, Christiana 573
Ling, Conrad 563
Ling, Elizabeth 563

Ling, Susanna 563
Link, Conrad 573
Linn, Anna Maria 554
Linn, Daniel 121, 126, 128, 134, 370, 374
Linn, George 95, 96, 101, 552, 562
Linn, E. 134
Linville, John 20
Livingston, Elizabeth R. (Mrs. Abraham Essick) 171
Livingston, Emma C. (Mrs. Joseph FewSmith, Jr.,) 153
Livingston, Janice Koon 500
Livingston, Jerry 500
Locke, James D. 250
Locke, William 467
Loehr, Frederick 118
Lofton, Robert 468
Lonas, E. Romie 225
Long, Conrad 101
Long, Elizabeth 540, 571
Longacre, Mary 573
Longerbeam, Shelda 516
Lord Baltimore 23
Louis Philippe, King of the French 71
Louis XIV, King of France 2
Lovinger, Georg/George Michael 28, 29, 44
Low, William 538, 571
Lowe, Charles Worthington vii, 247, 410
Loy, Mary 573
Lucas, Bruce 478
Lucas, Elizabeth 574
Lucas, Jane 516
Lucas, Jay 468
Lucas, Richard P. 405, 411, 459
Luckleiter, Mary 544, 571
Ludi, Antony 42

Luke, John 573
Lupton, Charlotte E. 490
Lupton, John S. 181
Lupton, Jonah W. 503
Lutz, Daniel 550
Lutz, Maria 550
Lutz, Michael 550
Lutz, Susanna 550
Lynch, Leigh Ann 525
Lynch, Mary Jane (Mrs. Theophilus F. Stork) 140

M

Maack, Frederick 544
MacArthur, General Arthur, Jr. 250
Macbeth, Bruce Andrew 504
Madden, George 542
Madden, Mrs. J.A. 472
Madders, George 571
Maddox, Elizabeth Bywaters Brumback 488
Mallo, Anna Catharine 558
Mallory, Barbara 478
Mallory, Debra 474
Mangum, Linda Carol (Mrs. William Collins Wood, II) 296
Mansfield, John George 576
Manuel, C. Edward 468
Manuel, Polly (Mrs. C. Edward Manuel) 383, 473, 516, 525
Manzano, Abby 478
Maphis, J. Alan 225, 494
Maphis, J. Luther 213, 392, 394, 480, 494
Maphis, J. Luther, Jr. 225, 494
Marcker/Marker, Jacob 542, 571
Marlborough, Duke of 2

Marriele, George 572
Marsh, Karen 472
Marshall, Elliot 508
Marshall, Peyton J. xii
Marshall, Robert J. 274
Marshall, Terry 474
Marshall, Thomas 371
Martin, J.D. 158
Martin, Thomas S. 364
Martin, W. Thomas B. 29
Martins, Dr. 38
Mason, Abraham 572
Mason, Hephzebeth 573
Massie, Cora 469
Massie, Major James W. 97, 534, 546
Massie, Josiah 371
Massie, Thomas 96, 534
Masters, Charles 105
Mathias, Jacob 370
Matson, Benjamin 374
Matson, Elizabeth 544, 571
Mauck, Peter 20
Mauck, Rudolph 20
Maul, Arlene 418, 520
Mauney, J. Luther 268, 271, 274, 278, 279, 297, 406
Mauney, James F. 328, 337
Mauser, Catharine 548
Mauser, John 548
Maxholt, Anna Elizabeth 545
Maxholt, Louis Frederick 545
May, Dennis Grant 333
May, Jeffrey Dennis vii, 313, 314, 328, 332, 333, 334, 335, 336, 337, 338, 339, 383, 525
May, Karla Kay Rosenow 336
May, Mary Jane Turner 333
May, Melissa Lynn 333, 336
May, Mr. 92, 538

May, Nathan Blaine 333, 336
May, Rosina 101
Mäyer, Catharina 570
Mayer, Christopher 550
Mayfield, Gail 415, 520
Mayfield, Marty 415
Mayfield, Mimi 455
McCann, Sarah E. 493
McCartney, Hazel 499
McCartney, Sedoris 499
McChesney, William 544
McClintock, Goldie (Mrs. Vernon S. McClintock) 515
McClintock, Vernon C. 250
McCord, Mr. 564
McCormick, F. 370
McCormick, Province 371
McCron, John N. 363
McDaniel, Mrs. Joseph W. 473
McDonald, Elizabeth 547
McDonald, Margaret 572
McGrew, Martha 549, 572
McIlwee, William H. 491
McIntire, Elwood 411
McInturff, Milton, Sr. 468
McKay, Robert 14, 15
McKeever, Anne 571
McKnees, James 20
McKnight, Harvey Washington 188
McPherson, Jesse 574
McReynolds, Colonel Andrew T. 180
Medtard, Jacob 126
Megeath, B.L. 404
Megeath, Mrs. B.L. 404
Melby, Katharine 478
Melby, Kathy 473
Melsheimer, F.V. 115
Melton, Ebon 370
Mercer, Hugh 59, 60

Mercer, William 549, 572
Merckel, Christian 13
Merckel, Maria Catharina 13
Mercker, George Paul 553
Merckle, Abraham 9
Merckle, Anna Maria 9, 20
Mesmer, H.J. 162
Mesmer, Jacob 117, 130, 134
Mesmer/Mesmore, Mr. 550, 568
Mesmer, Nicholas 101
Meyerheffer/Meyerhoeffer, Michael 118
Meyers, Catharina 557
Meyers, Christoph 557
Michael, Jacob 541
Michler, P.S. 158
Mierzwa, Louise 290
Milburn, Linda 416
Milburn, Roger 302, 373, 398, 518, 523
Milburn, Sarah 574
Miles, George 572
Miller, A. Harry 400, 481, 489
Miller, Abraham 121, 130, 131, 132, 142, 146, 384
Miller, Adam 6, 130
Miller, Albert P. 187, 193, 392
Miller, Anna 364
Miller, Anna Maria 130, 544, 558
Miller, Barbara 558
Miller, Benjamin 358
Miller, Carl 339
Miller, Casper 573
Miller, Catharine 555, 576
Miller, Charles L. 502
Miller, David 130
Miller, Elizabeth 558
Miller, Emily M. 492
Miller, Emma 345, 408
Miller, Evva May (Mrs. S. Vincent Miller) iii, v, viii, xiii, 271, 313, 470

Miller, George 574
Miller, George Clarence 386, 392, 393
Miller, Godfrey/Godfried 121, 128, 130, 372, 374, 544, 552
Miller, Godfrey Sperry 187, 344, 367, 504
Miller, Henry 558
Miller, J. Abraham 246, 250, 490, 493
Miller, J.I. 184
Miller, J.W. 125, 134, 136, 142, 388
Miller, John 121, 123, 129, 130, 132, 134, 200, 374, 380, 555
Miller, John Godfrey 206, 490, 492
Miller, John Samuel 200
Miller, John W. 117, 126, 130, 134, 146, 147, 374, 378, 384
Miller, Joseph P. 244, 408, 455, 506, 508, 509, 511
Miller, Katie xi, 403, 458, 480, 492, 494
Miller, Lewis 555
Miller, Lewis Godfrey Meineke 200, 201, 202, 203, 204, 205, 207, 208, 209, 217, 218, 221, 400, 485, 486, 495, 497, 503
Miller, Lewis Samuel Godfrey 221, 238, 271, 481, 486, 496, 497, 498, 503
Miller, Lynn V. 516
Miller, Magdalena 554
Miller, Margaretta vi, 197, 223, 243, 255, 344, 358, 359, 360, 364, 408, 481, 493, 504, 505, 506, 511, 517
Miller, Marianna 223, 243, 345, 408, 493
Miller, Marilee 339
Miller Martha 478
Miller, Martha Harder (Mrs. L.S.G. Miller) 498, 499
Miller, Mary 497
Miller, Mary Ann (Mrs. Lewis Eichelberger) 129, 132, 503
Miller, Michael 554
Miller, Mrs. 134, 558
Miller, Mrs. Godfrey Sperry 344, 360, 363, 364, 504
Miller, Mrs. L.S.G. 271
Miller, Mrs. Lewis Godfrey Meineke 486
Miller, Paul H. 250, 291, 468, 473, 482
Miller, Peggy 494
Miller, Peter 130, 134, 146, 152, 558
Miller, Rachel 554
Miller, Rebecca 130, 134
Miller, S. Vincent 250
Miller, S.G. 246
Miller, Samuel 130
Miller, Susanna 573
Miller, Thomas 130
Miller, William 130, 147, 152, 155, 158, 162, 168, 171, 173, 358, 367, 385, 389, 399, 573
Miller, William B. 399
Miller, William Cross 504, 505, 508, 511
Miller, William H. 250
Miller, William R. 480
Miller, William S. 372
Millschlagel, Margaret 571
Millschlagel, Mary 544
Millschlagel, Mr. 91, 533, 569
Milroy, General Robert H. 343, 344, 359

Mischler, Johann Peter 52, 53, 54
Mismer, Ann Margaret 542
Mismer, Anna Maria 541
Mismer, Henry 541
Mismer, Nicholas 541
Moeller, Henry 48, 52
Moll, Edwin 249
Möller, M.P. 393
Molley/Moloy, Hugh 543, 571
Montgomery, General Richard 67
Moore, Mary 574
Moore, Sarah 544, 571
More, Elizabeth 572
Morgan, Daniel 66, 67, 70, 92, 104, 534
Morgan, Elizabeth 534, 539
Morrell, Barbara 455, 525
Morrill, Jason Alan 281
Morrill, Alma Smolin 280
Morrill, Christopher Ryan 281
Morrill, John Charles, II 277, 278, 279, 280, 281, 291, 406
Morris, William 371
Morrison, Barbara Morrison 329
Morrison, Stanley 329
Mort, Charles F. 250
Mouser, John 573
Moyer, Keith 270
Moyer, Jacqueline Jones (Mrs. Virgil Albert Moyer, Jr.) 272, 411
Moyer, Ruth McCune 268
Moyer, Virgil Albert, Jr. 268, 269, 270, 271, 272, 273, 274, 275, 276, 277, 278, 279, 280, 281, 291, 300, 302, 303, 305, 318, 406, 411, 516
Moyer, Virgil Albert, Sr. 268
Mueller, Gottfried 200
Muhlenberg, Frederick 68, 75, 84
Muhlenberg, Frederick Augustus 61, 78
Muhlenberg, Hannah 79, 83, 84
Muhlenberg, Henry Ernest 61, 75, 78, 106
Muhlenberg, Henry Melchior viii, xii, 4, 10, 28, 29, 31, 33, 34, 37, 38, 42, 55, 56, 58, 59, 75, 76, 78, 79, 83, 87, 88, 112, 535, 561
Muhlenberg, John Peter Gabriel viii, 5, 44, 48, 56, 57, 58, 59, 60, 61, 62, 63, 64, 66, 68, 75, 77, 78, 79, 80, 81, 82, 83, 84, 86, 87, 88, 89
Muhlenberg, Maria 79
Muhlenberg, Mrs. Peter 86
Muhlenberg, Sally 86
Mullen, Mrs. S.M. 364
Mullen, Philip Hiram Ribold 236
Mullen, S.M. 182, 183
Müller, Adam 17
Mummert, Carolyn 302
Murgrave, Thomas 543, 571
Murnyak, Dennis 501
Murnyak, Meredith 501
Murphy, Eliza (Mrs. James Robertson Keiser) 147
Myers, Barbara 574
Myers, Branson P. 404
Myers, Jacob 105
Myers, Jesse 371
Myers, Michael 572

N

Naomaru, Yamanouchi 210, 221
Napps, Mrs. Carl S. 473
Neill, Thomas 573
Nelson, Fred P., Jr. 250
Nelson, Harry A. 467
Nelson, William 64
Nesselrodt, Donald 516

Neuberger, Christian 39, 45
Neumann, Fred 467
Newberger, Christian 45
Newberry, Ann 574
Newborough, J. 370
Newton, Mary 543, 571
Neyschwanger, Christian 10, 20
Neyschwanger, Maria 20
Neyschwanger, Maria Magdalena 20
Nicewanger, John Jacob 20
Nicewanger, Maria 20
Nicewanger/Niswanger, Margaret 573
Nicholas, Anna Barbara 558
Nicholas, Barbara 558
Nicholas, Elizabeth 558
Nicholas, Henry 558
Nicholas, Jacob 558
Nicholas, Juliana 558
Nicholas, Magdalena 558
Nicholas, Peter 558
Nichols, Tom 516
Nielsen, Gail Frances (Mrs. John Charles Morrill, II) 280, 281
Niswanger/Nicewanger Margaret 573
Nixon, Dot 470, 471
Nixon, Elmer 468
Nokes, Gilbert 373, 374
Noland, William 572
Nolen, Andrew 370
Northent, Margaret 572
Northern, Peggy 572
Norton, Sarah Thurston 561
Nott, Caspar 152, 158, 187
Nott, Nora C. 222, 490
Nulton, Abraham 130

O

Oberacker, George 546
Oberacker, Margaret 546
O'Connor, Charles 250
Oglesby, Aaron 574
Oglesby, Robert 542, 571
Oglesby, Sarah 574
Ohrenschall, F.A. 191, 193, 392
Olinger, Anne vii, viii, 416, 471
Olinger, Philip 516
Olleman, Mary 573
Orndoff, Clara 525
Orndoff, H. Nelson 468
Orndoff, Nelson 478
Orrick, Davenport 371
Orso, Paul M. 274, 275
Osborn, David 567
Osborn, Margaret 567
Ott, Jacob 106, 118
Otto, Tobias 39, 44
Over, Charles K. 244, 408, 461, 493
Overaker, Daniel 101
Owen, Mary Susan (Mrs. James Howard Utt) 303

P

Page, C.R. 503
Painter, Bulah 573
Painter, Thomas A. 503
Palmer, John 539, 571
Parcells, Anne Elizabeth 550
Parcells, Nicolas 549
Parcells, Peter 549
Park, John 544
Park/Parks, Sarah 540, 571
Parker, Hannah 572
Parker, Polly 573
Parlett, Alfred A. 250

Parmer, Phebe 542, 571
Pasquet, Marian 271, 289, 482
Paten, James 370
Pates, David 568
Pates, Elizabeth 568
Pates, Sarah 568
Patterson, Bret 474
Patterson, David H. 493
Patterson, Mrs. David H. 493
Payne, Tom 377
Pecha, Bob 468
Pecha, Joanna 468
Peck, Mrs. 134
Peery, Mrs. Rufus Benton 219
Peery, Rufus Benton 205, 218, 481, 496
Peffer, William 468
Pell, Richard 516
Pelter, George 371
Pence, Robert 520
Pendleton, E.H. 370
Penn, William 23
Penniger, Magdalena 570
Penniger, Peter 570
Pennypacker, Samuel 10
Pens, Adam 558
Pens, Margaret 558
Perrey, Susanna 570
Peters, Richard 56, 59, 60, 77
Peters, Rita 472
Peterson, Jane 572
Peterson, Mary 538, 571
Petonke, Mrs. Richard H. 473
Petonke, Richard H. 473
Peyton, John 96
Pfeifer, Barbara 552
Pfeifer, David 552
Philips, Philip 101
Pickering, John 572
Pierce, Amos 173
Pierce, Joseph 562

Pierce, Lydia 553
Pierce, Mrs. 566
Pifer, Clark S. 225
Pingley, Sarah 478
Poh, Andrew 564
Poh, Anna Margaret 539
Poh/Po, Balthasar 39, 45
Poh, John 539, 564
Poh, Maria Elizabeth 545
Poh, Mary 564
Pohlmann, August 217
Poker, Catharine Magdalena 544, 571
Poker, John 552
Polhamus, L.G., Jr. 250
Pollock, Alexander 106
Pollock, Thomas 573
Porterfield, Barbara 516
Porterfield, Charles 67
Post, Catharine 553
Post, George 553
Post, Hannah 553
Powel, Rebecca 540, 571, 573
Powell, Pauline K. 468
Powers, Mary 385
Prat, Anna 570
Preffitt, Bismark S. 510
Price, Charles W. 359, 364
Price, George 572
Price, Margaret 544, 571
Price, Richard 573
Price, V. 464
Prinz, Rachel 550, 572
Prisch, Augustin 558
Prisch, Juliana 558
Prisch, Margaret 558
Prusch, Martha Miller 418, 464
Pugh, Hannah 572
Pugh, Jesse 549, 572
Pugh, Wilson 250

Q

Quarles, Garland R. xii
Quaynant 4

R

Rabenhorst, Mrs. Christian 85
Raindel, John 545
Raser, George 570
Raser, Margretha 570
Räser, Peter 557
Räser, Phronica 557
Rathman, Susan 516
Rau, Christopher 558
Rau, Elizabeth 558
Rausch, Elizabeth 550
Rausch, Ephraim 550, 557
Rausch, George 550
Rausch, Johannes 556
Rausch, Maria 556
Rausch, Martin 570
Rausch, Mrs. 550
Rauter, Mary Ann 572
Ray, David 373, 383, 415, 468
Ray, Johanna 467
Ray, Joyce 472
Rea, Mrs. 489, 493
Reading, William 572
Reagan, Mary 550, 572
Reck, Abraham 115, 118, 119, 120, 121, 122, 123, 124, 125, 126, 128, 141, 154, 374, 420, 456, 462, 484
Reck, John B. 119, 484
Reecer, Frederick 573
Regan, Michael 572
Reif, Christian 567
Reif, John 567
Reif, Magdalena 567
Reily/Reiley, Mr. 561
Reily, Elizabeth 552

Reily/Riely, J.P. 381
Reily, Jacob 552
Reily, Martin 552
Reimer, Catharine 574
Rein, Anna Margaret 551
Rein, John 551
Reiner, Daniel 556, 570
Reiner, Eberhardt 570
Reiner/Reinerin, Elisabeth 556, 570
Reiner/Reinerin, Maria 556, 570
Reiner, Sarah 556
Reiser, Elizabeth 571
Reisser/Reiser, Elizabeth 544
Reiter, Eberhard 551
Repass, Stephen Albion 188
Reynolds, Susan (Mrs. C.P. Krauth) 154
Rhinehart, Juliana 20
Rhodes, George H. 235
Rich, Ann Letitia 496
Richard, Asa 486
Richard, Jacob A. 187, 231, 235, 241, 243, 403, 408, 410, 480
Richard, Mrs. Jacob A. xiii, 403
Richard, Ralph Roy 486
Richards, M.B. 370
Richardson, John 130
Richardson, Mary 542, 571
Richter, A.A. 231
Rider, Jacob 101
Riemenschnieder, Ruth 461
Rieser, George 550
Rieser, Jacob 550
Rieser, Margaret 550
Rieser, Susanna 550
Rife, Mrs. James V. 473
Riggleman, Kristi 473
Riley, Corinne B. xii
Riley, George M. 101
Riley, John 101

Riley, Lynn 473
Riley, Martin 101
Riley, Mary 455, 461
Riley, Mrs. John W. xii
Rinedel, John 539, 571
Rinker, Catherine 101
Risch, Anna Maria 4, 557
Risch, John 557
Risser, Margaretha 556
Risser, Georg 556
Ritch, Frederick 468
Ritch, Mrs. Frederick 468
Ritchie, William J. 250
Ritter, Adam 567
Ritter, Ann Mary 567
Ritter, Carl R. 241, 244, 402, 403, 455, 461
Ritter, Catharine 553
Ritter, Frederick Marshall 397, 487
Ritter, Frederick Marshall, III 487
Ritter, Frederick Marshall, Jr. 291, 487, 488
Ritter, Henrietta Cornwell (Mrs. Frederick Marshall Ritter) 287, 469, 470, 487
Ritter, Henry 555
Ritter, Jacob 553, 567
Ritter, John 555
Ritter, Joseph C. 250
Ritter, Lydia 553
Ritter, Margaret 544
Ritter, Maria 553
Ritter, Matthias 553, 566
Ritter, Oliver T. 250
Ritter, Randolph Brown 250
Ritter, Sandy 478
Roberts, William 371
Robertson, Anna 487
Robertson, Charles Alfred Stuart 487, 503
Robertson, Edward 487

Robertson, Kevin 487
Robertson, Miriam 487
Robertson, Philip 487
Robertson, Stephen 487
Robeson, Anne 569
Robinson, John 384, 398, 407, 408
Robinson, Jonathan 385
Robson, Cheryl 455
Robson, Eric 468
Robson, Mark 468
Roe, Joseph H. 225
Roger, Michael 39, 45
Rogers, John 573
Roinestad, Kurt 474
Romine, Peter 572
Rominus, Catharine 573
Ronda, D. 221
Ronimus, Elizabeth 572
Rose, Mrs. Grover C. 492
Rose, Stan 415, 416
Rosemiller, Lewis A. 134
Rosenow, Karla Kay (Mrs. Jeffrey Dennis May) 333
Rouss, Charles B. 367
Rowland, R. Bruce 468
Rubsamen, Eva 537
Rucker, Dilly 472
Rückstuhlin, Susanna 570
Rudi, Anna Catharine 554
Rudi, Catharine 554
Rudi, John 554
Rush, Richard E. xiii
Rusmiselle, William 172
Russell, J.B. 393
Rust, Frederick Robert 569
Rust, Mary 569
Rust, William 569
Rutherford, Eliot 573
Ruthrauff, W.P. 188
Ryan, Claude H. 225

Ryan, Glenn W. 225
Ryan, Patricia (Mrs. John Charles Morrill, II) 281
Ryland, W.S. 173

S

Sack, Carol 500
Sack, James 500
Sackman, Martin 118
Sadler, Tim 455
Savage, Mr. 542
Savolainen, Hope 478
Schadacre, Rebecca 544
Schaeffer, David F. 118, 119, 124
Schall, Michael 548
Schall, Nicolas 548
Scharer, Philip 539
Scharer, Rosina 539
Scherer, Frances Shildesser 498
Scherer, James A.B. 217, 496
Scherer, James Arnold 498, 499
Schlosser, Christopher 573
Schmidt, Anna Maria 557
Schmidt, Carl F. 225
Schmidt, Charles 557
Schmidt, Elisabeth 570
Schmidt, Friedrich 112
Schmidt, Harry A. 231, 241, 243, 244, 397, 403, 408, 410, 480, 495, 506, 507
Schmidt, Margretha 570
Schmidt/Schmitt, Maria 550, 569, 570
Schmidt, Mrs. Harry A. xii, 495
Schmidt/Schmitt, Nicholas 550, 569, 570
Schmidt/Schmitt/Schmith, Susanna 550, 557, 570
Schmidt, Thomas 39, 43, 64
Schmith, Maria Elisabeth 557
Schmitt, John 550
Schmucker, Nicholas 118
Schmucker, S.S. 118, 119, 158, 484
Schneider, Henry 217
Schneider/Schneiderin, Margareth 557, 570
Schneider/Schneiderin, Maria 570
Schneider, Michael 570
Schneider, Paul 250
Schneider, Philip 570
Schock, James L. 168
Schrack, Nicolaus 38, 39, 43
Schreiber, Adam 565
Schreiber, Catharine 565
Schuh, Catharine 555
Schuh, Jacob 555
Schuler, Catharine 550
Schuler, Conrad 538, 550
Schuler, Maria Catharine 538
Schultz, Frederick 371, 573
Schultz, George 371
Schultz, John 66, 67, 70, 130
Schultz, John Billy 364
Schultz, Matthias 370, 372, 489
Schultz, Mr. 169
Schultz, Robert W. 241, 244
Schulz, John Christian 12
Schumacher, Christian 45
Schumacher, Georg 39, 45
Schwarbach, John 54, 55
Schwartz, Mr. 568
Schweier, George 551
Schweier, Maria Agnes 551
Schweiger, Elizabeth 550
Schwemlin, Jacob 548
Scott, Rebecca 547, 572
Seabright, J.W. 392
Seabrook, Mrs. William Levin 210
Seabrook, William Levin 209, 210, 211, 214, 215, 216, 218, 236, 395
Seals, Reuben 375

Index

Seemer, Mrs. William 134
Seemer, William 134, 136, 152, 371
Seever, Casper 91
Seever/Seevers, George William 157, 371, 399
Seevers/Seever, Nathaniel 371
Seibert, Jacob 44
Seidelmayer, Elizabeth 548
Seidelmayer, George 548
Seidelmeier, Casper 573
Seidelmeier, Mary 574
Seiss, Joseph Augustus 168
Sell, Adam 549
Sell, Elizabeth 574
Senseny, Jacob 130
Shadacre, Rebecca 571
Shafer, Susan 474
Shaner, Steven 295
Shanholtz, Floyd 468, 478
Sharp, William 539, 571
Shaver, Barbara 572
Shawe, Mrs. Merrick 473
Shearer, Jacob 371
Shener, Catharine 571
Shener, George 572
Shener, Mary 574
Shepe, Margaret 572
Shephard, Miss 174
Sherer, Philip 371
Sheridan, General Philip H. 344, 360
Sherndorfer, Mary 571
Sherrard, Joseph 371
Shipman, Benjamin 572
Shipp, Karen 516
Shockey, Howard H. 455, 467
Shockey, Mrs. Howard H. 473
Shoemaker, Peter D., Jr. 272, 411
Sholeberger, Mary 573
Shoner, Catharine 544

Shopper, Mr. 574
Short, Jean 574
Short, Susan 383, 525
Shryock, George 118
Shuey, Theodore George 406
Shultz, Christopher 572
Shultz, John 101
Shumaker, Georg 45
Sibert, Jacob 28, 29
Sibole, Lemuel 503
Sickles, Jacob 19
Sickles, Zacharias 19
Sieber, Caspar 547
Sieber, Henry 547
Siebert, Jacob 39, 44, 565
Simon, J.S. 224
Simonson, Eunice 501
Simonson, J. David 501
Simpson, Alexander 474
Simpson, Anne 516
Simpson, Lee 412, 418, 525
Simpson, Rex 468
Sims, David 339
Sims, George L. 339, 340
Sims, Kristen 339
Sims, Martha Miller vii, 314, 337, 338, 339, 340, 341, 455, 478, 518
Singhaus, Barbara 549
Singhaus, Christian 549
Singhaus, Elizabeth 549
Singleton, Judith 370
Sitler, Isaac 101
Skole, Guenther 488
Skole, June 488
Skole, Karl David 358, 359, 488
Slagle, John 116, 373
Slagle, Joseph 126, 130, 131, 134, 142, 146, 374, 384, 385, 388
Slagle, Mrs. Joseph 134

623

Slagle, W.J. 360
Slater, Captain 91, 535, 557
Sload, Barbara 539
Sload/Sloat/Slote, Jacob 371, 539
Sload/Sloat/Slote, John 101, 117, 130, 371, 539
Sloots, Margaret, 69
Slote, Henry 371
Slothower, Howard 475
Smeltzer, J.P. 172
Smith, Barbara 572
Smith, Charles J. xii, 249, 503
Smith, Clark M. 235, 245, 246, 408, 480
Smith, D. Burt 402
Smith, Dr. 59
Smith, Edward 96, 370
Smith, G. Morris 503
Smith, John 548
Smith, Luther L. 503
Smith, Margreth 556
Smith, Maria 556
Smith, Mr. 543
Smith, Mrs. Clark M. xii
Smith, Nathaniel 543
Smith, Nicolaus 556
Smith, Peter 556
Smith, Rhonda 455
Smith, Rosannah 91, 571
Smith, Sallie R. (Mrs. Abraham Essick) 171
Smith, Thomas 43
Smith, William 56, 77
Snapp, Anna Catharine 19
Snapp, Barbara 19
Snapp, C. Thomas 500
Snapp, Ethel xii
Snapp, F.R. 393
Snapp, John 19
Snapp, Lawrence 20
Snapp, Leslie M. 225

Snapp, Louis E. 225
Snapp, Marshall 491
Snapp, Martha Saverbrey 500
Snapp, Oliver F. 494
Snapp, Thomas 20
Snarr, Sharon 478
Snider, Daniel 573
Snider, Edwin T., Jr. 250
Snyder, G.C. 393
Snyder, George H. 250
Snyder, J.H. 393
Sobine, Abraham 541
Sobine, Lydia 541
Solenberger, J.S. 392
Somer, Eva Rosina 555
Somer, George 555
Sommer, Ann Catharine 543
Sommer/Sommers, Michael 536, 543, 574
Sommersett, Thomas 573
Sonafelt, Jeffrey Ronald 488
Sonafelt, Mary Sickles 336, 477, 488
Sonafelt, Ronald 488
Soper, L.B. 455
Sorrell, Gregory 460
Southward, Sarah 574
Souvannasoth family 307
Sovein, Abraham 538, 549
Sovein, Lydia 538
Spangler, Philip 105
Spangler, Solomon P. 370
Spengel, Henrich 542
Sperry, J. Evans 211, 212
Sperry, Jacob 67, 70, 371
Sperry, Peter E. 130, 141, 371
Sperry, Regina 376
Sperry, William M. 141, 371
Spickert, Julius 39, 45
Spirey, Jacob 67
Spong, Mrs. Bernard 274

Index

Spotswood, Alexander 7
Spritz, C. Thomas, Jr. 274
Staling, Mr. 206
Stanbury, Ezekiel 574
Starks, Sarah 573
Steele, Christine Elizabeth 488
Steele, Duane Leslie 291, 488, 524
Steele, Jennifer Leslie 488
Steimle, Edmund 274
Stephen, Adam 66
Stephens, Anna Christina 19, 20
Stephens, John Henry 19
Stephens, Lewis 19
Stephens, Mary Christina 19
Stephens/Stephan, Peter 19, 534
Stephenson, J. 392
Stern, Chuck 468
Stern, David 455, 468
Stern, Linda 516
Stern, Nancy 468
Stern, Tim 468
Stern, William 468
Stickley, Anna Elizabeth 20
Stief, Charles 286
Stine, Howard F. 250
Stine, Isaac 343
Stine, Mrs. Marshall 472
Stine, William E. 397, 455
Stirewalt, A.J. 221
Stoever, Anna Elisabetha Catharina 18, 531
Stoever, John Casper, Jr. 11, 12, 14, 17, 18, 19, 20, 21
Stoever, John Casper, Sr. 11, 13, 54
Stoever, Maria Magdalena 11
Stork, Charles Augustus 140, 144
Stork, Theophilus B. 144
Stork, Theophilus F. 140, 142, 144, 145, 171, 172, 384
Stork, William L. 144
Stouffer, Harry C. 403
Stratten, Seth 573
Streit, Anna Margaret 87, 574
Streit, Anna Maria 5
Streit, Anna Ursula 76
Streit, Catharine 575
Streit, Catharine Riemer 574
Streit, Catharine Bush 576
Streit/Stright/Strite/Streight, Christian 2, 5, 33, 45, 65, 68, 71, 75, 76, 77, 78, 79, 81, 82, 83, 84, 86, 87, 88, 89, 90, 91, 92, 93, 95, 96, 98, 99, 100, 101, 102, 103, 104, 105, 106, 107, 108, 109, 111, 112, 115, 373, 374, 377, 379, 456, 502, 515, 533, 534, 557, 558, 568, 569, 574, 575
Streit, Edward S. 576
Streit, Emily Susan 576
Streit, Evelina Norton 92, 128, 141, 576
Streit, Frances Ann 576
Streit, Frederick Augustus 117, 575
Streit, Henry Bush 576
Streit, Jacob 93, 575
Streit, James Christian 406
Streit, Johann Christian 75
Streit, Johann Leonhardt/John Leonard 5, 76, 574
Streit, John 576
Streit, John Melchior 87, 575
Streit, Kristiaan 3
Streit, Leonard 5, 76
Streit, Margaret 575
Streit, Maria Elizabeth 575
Streit, Maria Ursula 5
Streit, Mary Bush 576
Streit, Philip Bush 130, 576
Streit, Rosannah 91

Streit, Rosina 569
Streit, Salome 93, 563, 575
Streit, Susan Barr 105, 106, 575
Streit, William 91, 117, 456, 551, 568, 569, 571
Streit, William Hill 576
Strickler, J.W. 395
Sullivan, John 544
Suttle, Litty 573
Sutton, Daisy B. 497
Swaine, Francis 79
Swaine, Maria 79
Swaine, Maria Muhlenberg 87
Swarm, Joseph 573
Swartz, Chuck 399, 468
Swartz, James 467, 468
Swartz, Loretta 468
Sweeney, David 468
Swisher, Clarence 398
Swisher, Jane 490, 493
Sybert, Sue Ella 487

T

Taggert, Daniel 371
Taliaferro, Mary 502
Tammaru, Philip Alexander 254
Tanna/Tanner, Friedrich 570
Tanna/Tanner, Margretha 570
Tanna/Tanner, Maria 570
Tanner, Frederick 550
Tappert, Theodore G. xii, 42
Taylor, Anne 574
Taylor, J.W. 393
Taylor, John T. 375
Taylor, Mr. 361
Teall, Elizabeth 537
Tevalt, Eston H. 250
Thallert, Christopher 550
Thallert, Elizabeth 550
Theis, Geo. R. 408

Thomas, Carl E. 274
Thomas, Emily 472
Thomas, Grace 245
Thomas, Karl 245
Thomas, Luther A., Jr. 245
Thomas, Luther Alexander 241, 242, 244, 245, 246, 249, 408, 410
Thomas, Mrs. Luther Alexander 245, 410
Thompson, Colonel William 80
Thresh, Mrs. Ward xiii
Thrift, James W. 250
Thurston, Colonel Charles Mynn 96, 97, 535, 546, 561
Thwaite, J. Fred 241, 243, 244, 408, 410
Tidball, A.S. 371
Tidball, John 162
Tidball, T.A. 162
Tilelli, John 461
Tillotson, Dorothy L. 295, 302, 306, 314, 321, 323, 326, 334, 418, 482, 491, 518
Toliver, Mollie 502
Traenckel, Stephen 39, 44
Trautwein/Troutwine, George Jacob 39, 45, 69
Treutlen, John Adam 83, 84, 85
Triebner, Christoph Friedrich 85
Trinkel, Catharine 546, 548
Trinkel, Margaret 548
Trinkel, Michael 548
Trinkle, Stephen 44
Troxel, George E. 467
True, Robert 573
Tucker, Henry St. George 104, 105, 108
Tucker, J.R. 162
Tucker, Vicki 478
Tuley, Mrs. 400

Turenne, Marshall 2
Tyree, DeeDee White 488

U

Uebele, Anna Magdalena 4
Upp, Christina 573
Utt, Eldon W. 303
Utt, Emily Reeve 303, 304
Utt, James Howard vi, vii, viii,
　　300, 302, 303, 304, 305,
　　306, 310, 313, 314, 315,
　　316, 317, 320, 321, 323,
　　324, 325, 326, 327, 328,
　　329, 330, 331, 332, 333,
　　336, 337, 340, 341, 367,
　　373, 383, 411, 413, 418,
　　455, 459, 478, 501, 516,
　　518, 519, 520, 525
Utt, Mary Susan Owen
　　303, 304, 315, 501
Utt, Maxine Lyon 303
Utt, Tyson James 303, 304
Utz, Christina 556
Utz, Ephraim 556
Utz, Georg 556
Utz, Johannes 556, 570
Utz, Margaretha 556

V

Valentine, Milton 157, 158
Van Fossen, Captain John
　　Crawford 205
Van Meter, Isaac 8, 14
Van Meter, John 8, 14
Van Meteren/Van Meter, Jan 9
Van Welden, John 101
Vance, Elizabeth 573
Vance, William 412, 572
VanHorssen, William 520
VanHorssen, Marilee 416

Vanorden, John 58
Venskoske, Matthew 455
Venskoske, Wendy 455
Viens, Betty 455
Villars, Marshall 2
Voigt, A.G. 241
Von Riesen, Julia 371

W

Wachter, Michael 118
Wack, Mr. 552
Waite, Obed 128
Walters, Sarah 540
Walk, J. Frederick 516
Wall, Mrs. T.T. 223
Wall, Sarah Hoffman 492
Wallace, Paul A.W. xii
Walls, John 371
Waltemyer, William C. 252
Walter, Lloyd Warren 503
Walters, Mary 571
Walters, Sarah 540
Ward, George W. 173
Ward, Mrs. George W. 181, 399
Ware, Joseph W. 370
Warnig, Michael 39, 45
Washabaugh, William 130
Washington, Edward 491
Washington, George 26, 27, 44,
　　66, 67, 81, 82, 343, 362
Wäyland, Heinrich 570
Wäyland, Johann 570
Wäyland, Rosina 570
Wäylandin/Wäyland, Catharina
　　570
Weaver, Barbara 573
Weaver, Catharine 572
Weaver, Dana Gail (Mrs. Mark
　　Elmer Fitzsimmons) 323
Webb, Anne 549, 572
Webb, Eli 573

Webber, Miss 134
Weber/Weberin, Christina 570
Weber/Weberin, Elizabeth 556, 569
Weber, Mr. 191
Weber, Peter 556
Webster, Daniel 165, 484
Weddell, A.J. 182, 188
Wehrenberg, Dolores Busse 291, 500
Wehrenberg, Frederick, Jr. 291, 500
Weiland, Henrich 557
Weiland, Johannes 556
Weiland, Rosina 556
Weimer, Catharine 564
Weimer, Isaac 564
Weimer, John 564
Weiner, Mr. 562
Weiser, Anna Maria 5
Weiser, Conrad 4, 60
Weiser, George 544
Weiser, Johann/John Conrad/ Koenraet 2, 3, 4, 5
Weiso, Barbara 537
Weiso, Henrich 537
Weiss, Jacob 562
Weissenberger, Christina 478
Weissenberger, John 418
Weller, Henrich 45
Wells, Edward 540, 571
Wemmer, Isaac 546, 565, 571
Wendel, Maria Margaret 557
Wendel, Samuel 39, 45
Wentz, Abdel Ross xii, 50
Werly, Mr. 86
Werly, Mrs. 86
West, Catharine 536
West, George 536
West, Mary Elizabeth 536
Westermann, Dwayne J. 318, 319

Westervelt, Carol Black 289, 520, 525
Westervelt, John P. vii
Wetzel, Christoph 39, 43, 101
Wetzel, George 64, 65, 562
Wetzel, John 572
Wetzel, Mr. 537, 562
Wetzel, Mrs. 560
Wetzel, Nancy 43
Weyl, E.C. 382
Whetzel, Christoph 43, 64
Whetzel, Nancy 64
Whipple, Elizabeth 548, 572
Whitacre, Lee N. xii
White, Garrison 544, 571
White, John Baker 576
White, General Julius 344
Whitehill, Mary 287, 482
Wiesend, Anna Margaret 565
Wiesend, Joseph 565
Wildbahn, Carl Friedrich 28, 31, 32, 33, 34, 36, 37, 48, 49, 50, 373, 454, 456
Wilheit, Elisabeth 570
Wilheit, George 570
Wilheit/Wilheitin, Maria 556, 570
Wilkins, Ruth 573
Will, Catharine 551
Will, Lewis 551
Will, Maria Barbara, 551
Willcox, Amy 573
William 371
Williams, Charles A. 493
Williams, Edward 574
Williams, Jenny 564
Williams, John 564, 571
Williams, Judith Ann 516
Williams, Philip 249
Williams, Shelley 516
Wilson, Barbara 475
Wilson, J.G. 393

Index

Wilson, Mr. 575
Wilson, Sarah 574
Windle, Samuel 45
Windle, Valentine 20
Wingert, Asa K. 468
Wingfield, Allen A. 468
Winkel, Anna Maria 554
Winkel, Henry 554
Winkley, Susan 492, 493
Wiseman, Abraham 19
Wiseman, Anna Christina 19
Wiseman, Sue 19
Witsberger, Bernard 467
Wolfe, Becky 478
Wolfe, Clarene H. 471
Wolfe, Fannie R. 458, 493
Wolfe, George 371
Wolfe, John T. 473
Wolfe, Kate 134, 215, 458, 481, 492
Wolfe, Lewis 130, 551
Wolfe, C. 134
Wolfe, S. 134
Wolfe, Miss 134
Wolfe, Misses 219
Wolfe, Mrs. George 130
Wolfe, Robert B. 147, 152, 168, 171, 173, 358, 360, 385, 467, 492
Wolfersberger, Bill 468
Woltz, Robert K. v, viii, xiii, 383, 403, 404, 455, 509, 516, 517
Wood, Comfort 543
Wood, James 15, 25, 58, 60, 385
Wood, James, Jr. 57
Wood, Laura Kathryn 299
Wood, Linda Carol Magum 296, 297, 299
Wood, Margaret Lois Howell 296
Wood, Patricia Ann 299
Wood, Robert 543
Wood, William 543
Wood, William Collins, II 289, 290, 295, 296, 297, 298, 299, 300, 317
Wood, William Collins, Jr. 296
Woodruff, Charles 310, 412, 418, 521
Wrangel, Charles Mangus 32, 61, 77, 87
Wright, Nancy 573
Wust, Klaus xii

Y

Yeakley, Luther 487
Yeakley, Taylor Babb 214, 395, 486
Young, Adam 101, 543, 544
Young, Catharine 543, 544
Young, John 543
Young, John David 100, 101, 102, 103, 104
Young, John George 78, 100, 535, 559, 563
Young, Mr. 566
Young, Philip 381
Yount, Ralph P. 411, 455, 506, 509

Z

Zehring, Matthias 88
Zeigler, Robert F. 408
Zerull, David 455
Zerull, Lisa 336, 476
Ziegenhagen, Frederick Michael 56
Zimmerman/Zimmermann, Christopher/Christoph

556, 569
Zimmerman, Johannes 557
Zimmerman/Zimmermann,
    Maria 556, 569
Zimmerman, Rosina 557
Zimmerman/Zimmermann,
    Susannah 556, 569
Zimmerman, Ursula 557
Zirkle, Nannie M. 493
Zirkle, W. Godfrey 250
Zoll, Henry 549
Zoll, Maria Barbara 549
Zuber, Catharine 541
Zuber, Martin 541
Zubly, David 83
Zumbrun, Maurice G. 488

Not included in this index are church officers, Council members and some church staff in Chapter X, names in Appendix A (Stoever Record) and Appendix C (Membership lists).